Cases in
STRATEGIC MANAGEMENT

Ninth Edition

Paul W. Beamish

Richard Ivey School of Business
The University of Western Ontario

**McGraw-Hill
Ryerson**

Toronto Montréal Boston Burr Ridge IL Dubuque IA Madison WI New York San Francisco
St Louis Bangkok Bogatá Caracas Kuala Lumpur Lisbon London Madrid Mexico City
Milan New Delhi Santiago Seoul Singapore Sydney Taipei

Cases in Strategic Management
Ninth Edition

ISBN-13: 978-0-07-097981-9
ISBN-10: 0-07-097981-2

1 2 3 4 5 6 7 8 9 10 TCG 0 9

Printed and bound in Canada.

Care has been taken to trace ownership of copyright material contained in this text; however, the publisher will welcome any information that enables them to rectify any reference or credit for subsequent editions.

Vice-President and Editor-in-Chief: Joanna Cotton
Senior Sponsoring Editor: Kim Brewster
Senior Marketing Manager: Joy Armitage Taylor
Developmental Editor: Arlene Bautista
Senior Editorial Associate: Christine Lomas
Manager, Editorial Services: Margaret Henderson
Copy Editor: Evan Turner
Production Coordinator: Sheryl MacAdam
Cover Design: Michelle Losier/Finelines Design
Cover Image: © Eric Jacobson/Getty Images
Interior Design: Liz Harasymczuk
Page Layout: Lynda Powell
Printer: Transcontinental Gagne

Library and Archives Canada Cataloguing in Publication

Beamish, Paul W., 1953-
    Cases in strategic management / Paul W. Beamish. — 9th ed.

5th ed. published under title: Strategic management : text, readings and cases.
Includes bibliographical references.
ISBN 978-0-07-097981-9

    1. Strategic planning—Canada—Case studies. 2. Industrial management—Canada—Case studies. I. Beamish, Paul W., 1953- . Strategic management.
II. Title.

HD30.28.B3322 2009   658.4'0120971   C2008-906658-8

To the memory of two splendid teachers:

John and Catherine Beamish

About the Author

Paul W. Beamish is Professor of International Strategy at the Richard Ivey School of Business, University of Western Ontario. He is the author or co-author of 46 books, over 100 articles or contributed chapters, and over 100 case studies. His articles have appeared in *Strategic Management Journal*, *Journal of International Business Studies*, *Academy of Management Journal*, *Academy of Management Review*, and elsewhere. His consulting and management training activities have been in both the public and the private sector for such organizations as Boeing, Labatt/Interbrew, The World Bank, the Canadian Foreign Service Institute, and the Harvard Institute for International Development. He has received case writing awards from the European Foundation for Management Development, The Management Development Centre of Hong Kong, The Academy of International Business, and the Administrative Sciences Association of Canada. He worked for the Procter & Gamble Company of Canada and Wilfrid Laurier University before joining Ivey's faculty in 1987. He is the founding Director of Ivey's Asian Management Institute, and is the Director of Ivey Publishing.

Contents

In early January 2008, David Yach, Chief Technology Officer for Software at Research In Motion (RIM), had just come back from Christmas break. Returning to his desk in Waterloo, Ontario, relaxed and refreshed, he noted that his Executive Assistant had placed the preliminary holiday sales figures for BlackBerry on top of his in-box with a note that read "Meeting with Mike tomorrow." Knowing 2007 had been an extraordinarily good year, with the number of BlackBerry units sold doubling, Dave was curious: Why did Mike Lazaridis, RIM's visionary founder and co-CEO want a meeting? A sticky note on page 3 flagged the issue. Mike wanted to discuss Dave's research and development (R&D) plans—even though R&D spending was up $124M from the prior year, it had dropped significantly as a percentage of sales. In an industry driven by engineering innovations and evaluated on technological advances, this was an issue.

PlentyofFish.com is the world's most profitable website on a per capita basis, the 96th most popular website in terms of page views, and the most popular online dating site in existence. Remarkably, it is managed by its owner and founder and only one other employee. It is a free dating site that generates $10 million in ad revenues per year, and a profit to the owner in excess of $9 million. PlentyofFish.com has achieved stellar growth in the face of stringent competition. Is it sustainable? A number of possible alternatives are offered for analysis.

In September 2007, the senior managers at MacTara Limited were participating in a strategic planning retreat. As the largest wood products company in Nova Scotia, there were some very good opportunities for the company in sectors like wood pellets for fuel (high demand for inexpensively priced renewable energy sources). However, the Canadian lumber industry as a whole is not attractive at this time (distortionary effects of the Canadian–U.S. softwood lumber dispute, low price of lumber, sales denominated in the free-falling U.S. dollar, inflexible cost structure, etc.). The fact that MacTara is a somewhat vertically integrated company—from construction lumber, to chips for paper mills, to fuel pellets made out of wood waste—makes planning very difficult because the health of each sector impacts on the prospects for the others. Company executives need to find a way to make all the various pieces of the business fit together into a profitable whole while they still have money and time. The Canadian lumber industry is in crisis and the eastern Canadian industry is ripe for consolidation.

Case 4 Loblaw Companies Limited   44

The president of Loblaw Companies Limited must decide what to do in response to the rumoured introduction of Wal-Mart's SuperCenters (combining grocery and non-food items) in Canada. The potential launch of SuperCenters in Canada was seen by observers as a threat to Loblaw, the market leader in Canadian grocery. Wal-Mart is a vigorous competitor, and the Every Day Low Prices strategy of Wal-Mart's SuperCenters could wean away traffic from Loblaw's various banners.

Case 5 TVOntario   63

TVOntario is a non-profit television station owned by the Ontario government that provides educational programming commercial-free. TVOntario is recognized as a world leader in quality educational programming for all ages as well as providing programming on important issues within the province. However, the television broadcasting industry is very competitive, and larger networks have greater cash flows to produce programs that encourage advertising and increase revenues. TVOntario's Sales and Licensing Department revenues continue to decline, and the managing director of revenue and development is faced with determining the future of the department. The station's board of directors has put pressure on him to make a decision and he needs to come up with a plan before they decide to shut the department down.

Part 3 Assessing the Internal Environment of the Firm

Case 6 IKEA (Canada) Ltd.—1986 (Condensed)   80

The new Sears catalogue contained a 20-page section called Elements. This section bore a striking resemblance to the format of an IKEA catalogue, and the furniture being offered was similar to IKEA's knocked-down self-assembly line. The head of IKEA's North American operations wondered how serious Sears was about its new initiative and what, if anything, IKEA should do in response.

Case 7 Carrefour China, Building a Greener Store   91

Carrefour, the second-largest retailer in the world, had just announced that it would open its first "Green Store" in Beijing before the 2008 Olympic Games. David Monaco, asset and construction director of Carrefour China, had little experience with green building, and was struggling with how to translate that announcement into specifications for store design and operations. Monaco has to evaluate the situation carefully both from ecological and economic perspectives. In addition, he must take the regulatory and infrastructure situation in China into account, where no official green building standard exists and only few suppliers of energy saving equipment operate. He had already collected energy and cost data from several suppliers, and wondered how this could be used to decide among environmental technology options. Given that at least 150 additional company stores were scheduled for opening or renovation during the next three years in China, the project would have long-term implications for Carrefour.

Case 8 The Prince Edward Island Preserve Company: Turnaround   110

In April 2008, Bruce MacNaughton, president of The Prince Edward Island Preserve Co. Ltd. (P.E.I. Preserves), was focused on turnaround. The company he had founded in 1985 had gone into receivership in May 2007. Although this had resulted in losses for various mortgage holders and unsecured creditors, MacNaughton had been able to buy back his New Glasgow shop/café, the adjacent garden property and inventory, and restart the business. He now needed a viable product–market strategy.

Part 4 Recognizing a Firm's Intellectual Assets: Moving Beyond a Firm's Tangible Resources

Optical Recording Corporation (ORC) of Toronto secured the rights to a technology known as digital optical audio recording. During the time it took to negotiate the final transfer of the technology ownership, it was rumoured that some major electronics manufacturers were developing compact disc (CD) players that recorded digital optical audio signals. A patent lawyer advised ORC that the compact disc players and compact discs recently released by these companies might be infringing the claims of ORC's newly acquired patents. Based on this information, the company negotiated licensing agreements with the two largest CD manufacturers. The third-largest manufacturer, WEA Manufacturing, a subsidiary of Time Warner Inc., maintained a position of non-infringement and invalid patents. With the U.S. patent expiry date looming, ORC decided to sue Time Warner for patent infringement. When the defense counsel presented testimony that questioned the integrity of the licensing agreement, ORC's president realized that the entire licensing program was in jeopardy and must decide whether he should accept a settlement or proceed with the lawsuit.

Majestica Hotels Inc., a leading European operator of luxury hotels, was trying to reach an agreement with Commercial Properties of Shanghai regarding the management contract for a new hotel in Shanghai. A series of issues require resolution for the deal to proceed, including length of contract term, name, staffing and many other control issues. Majestica was reluctant to make further concessions for fear that doing so might jeopardize its service culture, arguably the key success factor in this industry. At issue was whether Majestica should adopt a contingency approach and relax its operating philosophy, or stick to its principles, even if it meant not entering a lucrative market.

Part 5 Business-Level Strategy: Creating and Sustaining Competitive Advantages

The founder of Kids Market Consulting, a market research firm dedicated to the kids, tweens and teens segments, is faced with increasing competition and slowing revenue, and was exploring a variety of possibilities for the future strategic direction of the business. In particular, she must formulate the best plan for protecting the niche market and decide how aggressively to pursue expansion. In addition, there was the existing relationship with her business partner and Kids Market Consulting was part of his group of marketing firms. Any changes the founder chose had to respect his relationship and she was therefore restricted to a limited number of options. The over-arching corporate objective for the company was to defend the market from larger businesses who were trying to increase their share of the market research industry.

Eli Lilly and Company is a leading U.S. pharmaceutical company. The new president of intercontinental operations is re-evaluating all of the company's divisions, including the joint venture with Ranbaxy Laboratories Limited, one of India's largest pharmaceutical companies. This joint venture has run smoothly for a number of years despite their difference in focus, but recently Ranbaxy was experiencing cash flow difficulties due to its network of international sales. In addition, the Indian government was changing regulations for businesses in India, and joining the World Trade Organization would have an effect on India's chemical and drug regulations. The president must determine if this international joint venture still fits Eli Lilly's strategic objectives.

Part 6 Corporate-Level Strategy: Creating Value Through Diversification

Vincor International Inc. was Canada's largest wine company and North America's fourth largest in 2002. The company had decided to internationalize and as the first step had entered the United States through two acquisitions. The company's chief executive officer felt that to be among the top 10 wineries in the world, Vincor needed to look beyond the region. To that end, he was considering the acquisition of an Australian company, Goundrey Wines. He must analyze the strategic rationale for the acquisition of Goundrey as well as to probe questions of strategic fit and value.

At the end of 2001, the Canadian Imperial Bank of Commerce (CIBC) and Barclays Bank PLC were in advanced negotiations regarding the potential merger of their respective retail, corporate and offshore banking operations in the Caribbean. Some members of each board wondered whether this was the best direction to take. Would the combined company be able to deliver superior returns? Would it be possible to integrate, within budget, companies that had competed with each other in the region for decades? Would either firm be better off divesting regional operations instead? Should the two firms just continue to go-it-alone with emphasis on continual improvement? A decision needed to be made with the coming week.

Part 7 International Strategy: Creating Value in Global Markets

On July 30, 2007 the senior executive team of Mattel under the leadership of Bob Eckert, chief executive officer, received reports that the surface paint on the Sarge Cars, made in China, contained lead in excess of U.S. federal regulations. It was certainly not good news for Mattel, which was about to recall 967,000 other Chinese-made children's character toys because of excess lead in the paint. Not surprisingly, the decision ahead was not only about whether to recall the Sarge Cars and other toys that might be unsafe, but also how to deal with the recall situation. The (A) case details the events leading up to the recall and highlights the difficulties a multinational enterprise faces in managing global operations.

The chief executive officer of Calgary-based Guest-Tek Interactive Entertainment Ltd., a leading provider of high-speed Internet access to the hotel industry, must consider whether and how his company should grow its business overseas. Ninety-seven per cent of Guest-Tek's fiscal year 2003 revenue was derived from North American hotels—a market he knew would eventually become saturated. Guest-Tek had listed publicly in January 2004. Both internal and external investors now demanded results. Other geographic markets held the promise of new growth and competitors were already pursuing those opportunities.

Activplant is a software firm specializing in monitoring, measuring and analyzing the performance of factory automation systems in London, Ontario, Canada. It is a pioneer of the industry, and has installations in most of the largest automobile manufacturing firms in North America as well as some clients in consumer goods. Activplant is considering the opportunity of expanding their business to include a much more aggressive sales and service approach in Europe. An entrance into Europe involves how both sales and service will be delivered to clients, which could be done through a number of different channels including: consulting partners, value-added resellers, a joint venture or full-time Activplant staff. The case allows students to evaluate both the dollar costs and benefits of each choice as well as qualitative concerns like product quality and maintaining contact with customers.

Part 8 Competitive Dynamics and Entrepreneurial Strategies

Part 9 Strategic Control and Corporate Governance

Part 10 Creating Effective Organizational Designs

Case 31 ING Insurance Asia/Pacific   415

The new chief executive officer (CEO) of ING Insurance Asia/Pacific wants to improve the regional operation of the company. ING Group was a global financial services company of Dutch origin with more than 150 years of experience. As part of ING International, ING Insurance Asia/Pacific was responsible for life insurance and asset/wealth management activities throughout the region. The company was doing well, but the new CEO believed that there were still important strategic and operational improvements possible. This case can be used to discuss the "local versus regional or global" management issue and will yield best results if the class has already been introduced to different strategic and organizational alternatives in the international business context.

Case 32 Victoria Heavy Equipment Limited   428

Victoria Heavy Equipment (Victoria) was a family owned and managed firm that had been led by an ambitious, entrepreneurial chief executive officer who now wanted to take a less active role in the business. His son and daughter were not yet ready to succeed him so he wondered what kind of person he should hire to become president. Victoria had been through two reorganizations in recent years, which contributed to organizational and strategic issues which would need to be addressed by a new president. Among these was the need to align the organization design (staffing, structure, systems) to fit the desired strategy.

Case 33 Bombardier Transportation and the Adtranz Acquisition   438

Bombardier Transportation, one of the world's largest manufacturers of passenger rail cars, has successfully negotiated the purchase of Adtranz, a large European manufacturer of rail equipment. The newly appointed chief executive officer has been brought in to manage the acquisition. The new CEO faces many challenges including decisions about the pace of integration, location of headquarters, organization structure, personnel retention and personal management style.

Part 11 Strategic Leadership: Creating a Learning Organization and an Ethical Organization

Case 34 Leading Change at SJHC and LHSC   456

The transfer of perinatal services at St. Joseph's Health Care Centre (SJHC) to the Women's and Children's Services at London Health Sciences Centre (LHSC), included the relocation of clinical programs, 500 staff and about 40 physicians. The hospital's comprehensive care for newborns included providing care for very sick infants and extremely premature babies. The move to LHSC was a source of much concern to key stakeholders, scientists and specialists with much negative impact on recruitment, retention and staff morale. The vice-president, acute and ambulatory care at SJHC and the vice-president, women and children's clinical business unit at LHSC were appointed to help prepare leaders throughout all stages of the restructuring. On their agenda were the following issues: culture, safety procedures, team conflict, excessive turnover, structure, leadership orientation, among others. Where should they start; and how could they get physicians, patient care leaders and staff to think past six months, given that there are numerous issues that keep them busy on a daily, weekly and monthly basis?

Preface and Acknowledgements

This book was made possible with the academic and intellectual support from colleagues at the Ivey Business School at the University of Western Ontario (UWO), and others across the country. The primary stimulus for this book was the ongoing need for new, high-quality Canadian material.

Having decided to produce a book of cases in strategic management, a number of other decisions were made: (1) to bring together primarily Canadian cases written not only at Ivey, but by faculty across North America, Europe, and Asia; (2) to include only decision-oriented cases, which arguably provide the best training for future managers; and (3) to include cases dealing with international business, high-technology industries, service industries, not-for-profit industries, and business ethics.

Much useful feedback was solicited and received on the eighth edition from colleagues at dozens of institutions across Canada. This included detailed reviews from the following individuals:

Ian Anderson, Algonquin College
Jonathan Calof, University of Ottawa
Brooke Dobni, University of Saskatchewan
Dwight Dyson, Centennial College
Peter F. Johnson, McMaster University
Anthony Mallette, Southern Alberta Institute of Technology
Terry Power, Royal Roads University
Mark Simpson, George Brown College
Ron D. Smith, Ryerson University
Francis Tapon, University of Guelph

This edition contains three updated cases.

- Coral Divers Resort (Revised)
- Victoria Heavy Equipment Limited
- Phil Chan

There are also 12 new cases.

- Research in Motion: Managing Explosive Growth
- Swimming in the Virtual Community Pool with PlentyofFish
- MacTara Limited and the Wood Products Industry in Nova Scotia
- Carrefour China, Building a Greener Store
- The Prince Edward Island Preserve Company: Turnaround
- Yunnan Baiyao: Traditional Medicine Meets Product/Market Diversification
- Mattel and the Toy Recalls
- Guest-Tek Interactive Entertainment: International Sales
- Activplant: The European Opportunity
- West Lake Home Furnishings Ltd.

- ING Insurance Asia/Pacific
- Leading Change at SJHC and LHSC

New cases were written or selected not only for their ability to achieve the desired pedagogical objectives, but with an eye to retaining student interest. Some of the new cases deal with such topical issues as product recalls, growth, turnarounds, and diversification, and are set in industries ranging from toys to healthcare to on-line dating to banking.

Professors wishing to delve deeply into certain industries have the option of reorganizing the available material. The book contains multiple cases in each of the following industry groups:

- Recreation
- Furniture
- Consumer Products
- Financial Services
- Children's market
- Internet services
- Health
- Retailers

The cases themselves have been organized into the 12 subject areas that follow. These subject areas follow closely the current, mainstream approach to the teaching of strategic management.

1. Strategic Management: Creating Competitive Advantages
2. Analyzing the External Environment of the Firm
3. Assessing the Internal Environment of the Firm
4. Recognizing a Firm's Intellectual Assets: Moving Beyond a Firm's Tangible Resources
5. Business-Level Strategy: Creating and Sustaining Competitive Advantages
6. Corporate-Level Strategy: Creating Value through Diversification
7. International Strategy: Creating Value in Global Markets
8. Competitive Dynamics and Entrepreneurial Strategies
9. Strategic Control and Corporate Governance
10. Creating Effective Organizational Designs
11. Strategic Leadership: Creating a Learning Organization and an Ethical Organization
12. Managing Innovation and Fostering Corporate Entrepreneurship

A comprehensive Case Teaching Notes package is available at www.mcgrawhill.ca/olc/beamish to text adopters. This Case Teaching Notes manual contains detailed teaching notes for each of the cases. It also includes an overview of the cases, possible industry groupings, case sequencing and possible course outlines, follow-up cases, and Web addresses.

I am indebted to several groups of people for assisting in the preparation of this book. First, I am grateful to the case contributors from Ivey, and wish to thank Nick Fry, Rob Klassen, Eric Morse, Jean-Louis Schaan, Gerard Seijts, Larry Tapp, Stewart Thornhill, Rod White, and Charlene Zietsma, in addition to the following doctoral and research assistants: D. Barrett, Kevin Boeh, J. Bubel, W. Cheung, C. Ellison, N. Goodwin, S. Hill, P. Kumar, J. Kyle, Nathan Lupton, Ken

Mark, Daina Mazutis, M. McCune, S. Morrison, George Peng, Gail Robertson, J. Royce, Andreas Schotter, Vanessa Strike, and S. Taylor.

Cases were also contributed by colleagues from other institutions:

John Adamson, Optical Recording Corporation
Hari Bapuji, University of Manitoba
Julian Birkinshaw, London Business School
Nikhil Celly, Loyola University, New Orleans
Charles Dhanaraj, Indiana University
Anthony Goerzen, University of Victoria
Amy Hillman, Arizona State University
Trevor Hunter, King's College, University of Western Ontario
Jane Lu, National University of Singapore
Laurie Milton, University of Calgary
Allen Morrison, IMD, Switzerland
Kent Neupert, Boise State University
Michael Parent, Simon Fraser University
Thomas Poynter, St. John's, Newfoundland
Julia Sagebien, Dalhousie University
F. C. Schultz, Michigan State University
Marilyn Seymann, Arizona State University
Rick Shaver, MacTara Limited, Nova Scotia
Jing'an Tang, Sacred Heart University, Connecticutt
O. Vynogradov, International Management Institute, Kiev
Don Wood, University of West Indies, Barbados

In addition, I wish to thank the various executives who provided the required access to complete the cases in this book, and to recognize those students on whom the cases were tested for classroom use.

I look forward to your feedback.

Paul W. Beamish

Superior Service

Service takes on a whole new meaning with McGraw-Hill Ryerson and *Cases in Strategic Management*, Ninth Edition. More than just bringing you the textbook, we have consistently raised the bar in terms of innovation and educational research—both in management and in education in general. These investments in learning and the education community have helped us to understand the needs of students and educators across the country, and allowed us to foster the growth of truly innovative, integrated learning.

Integrated Learning

Your Integrated Learning Sales Specialist is a McGraw-Hill Ryerson representative who has the experience, product knowledge, training, and support to help you assess and integrate any of our products, technology, and services into your course for optimum teaching and learning performance. Whether it's helping your students improve their grades, or putting your entire course online, your *i*Learning Sales Specialist is there to help you do it. Contact your local *i*Learning Sales Specialist today to learn how to maximize all of McGraw-Hill Ryerson's resources!

*i*Learning Services Program

McGraw-Hill Ryerson offers a unique *i*Learning Services package designed for Canadian faculty. Our mission is to equip providers of higher education with superior tools and resources required for excellence in teaching. For additional information, visit www.mcgrawhill.ca/highereducation/iservices.

Teaching, Technology & Learning Conference Series

The educational environment has changed tremendously in recent years, and McGraw-Hill Ryerson continues to be committed to helping you acquire the skills you need to succeed in this new milieu. Our innovative Teaching, Technology & Learning Conference Series brings faculty together from across Canada with 3M Teaching Excellence award winners to share teaching and learning best practices in a collaborative and stimulating environment. Pre-conference workshops on general topics, such as teaching large classes and technology integration, will also be offered. We will also work with you at your own institution to customize workshops that best suit the needs of your faculty.

Primis Online

Primis Online gives you access to our resources in the best medium for your students: printed textbooks or electronic e-books. There are over 350,000 pages of content available from which you can create customized learning tools from our online database at www.mhhe.com/primis.

Coursesmart

CourseSmart brings together thousands of textbooks across hundreds of courses in an eTextbook format providing unique benefits to students and faculty. By purchasing an eTextbook, students can save up to 50 percent off the cost of a print textbook; reduce their impact on the environment; and gain access to powerful Web tools for learning, including full text search, notes and highlighting, and e-mail tools for sharing notes between classmates. For faculty, CourseSmart provides instant access to review and compare textbooks and course materials in their discipline area without the time, cost, and environmental impact of mailing print examination copies. For further details contact your *i*Learning Sales Specialist or go to www.coursesmart.com.

Research in Motion: Managing Explosive Growth

In early January 2008, David Yach, chief technology officer for software at Research In Motion (RIM), had just come back from Christmas break. Returning to his desk in Waterloo, Ontario, relaxed and refreshed, he noted that his executive assistant had placed the preliminary holiday sales figures for BlackBerry on top of his in-box with a note that read "Meeting with Mike tomorrow." Knowing 2007 had been an extraordinarily good year, with the number of BlackBerry units sold doubling, Dave was curious: Why did Mike Lazaridis, RIM's visionary founder and co-chief executive officer, want a meeting? A sticky note on page three flagged the issue. Mike wanted to discuss Dave's research and development (R&D) plans—even though R&D spending was up $124 million from the prior year, it had dropped significantly as a percentage of sales. In an industry driven by engineering innovations and evaluated on technological advances, this was an issue.

R&D was the core of the BlackBerry's success—but success, Dave knew, could be a double-edged sword. Although RIM's engineers were continually delivering award-winning products, explosive growth and increased competition were creating pressures on his team to develop new solutions to keep up with changes in the global smartphone marketplace. With 2007 revenue up 98 per cent from the previous year, his team of approximately 1,400 software engineers should also have doubled—but both talent and space were getting increasingly scarce. The current model of "organic" growth was not keeping pace and his engineers were feeling the strain. As the day progressed, Dave considered how he should manage this expansion on top of meeting existing commitments, thinking "How do you change the engine, while you're speeding along at 200 kilometres per hour?" As his BlackBerry notified him of dozens of other urgent messages, he wondered how to present his growth and implementation plan to Mike the next morning.

Daina Mazutis wrote this case under the supervision of Professors Rod White and Paul W. Beamish solely to provide material for class discussion. The authors do not intend to illustrate either effective or ineffective handling of a managerial situation. The authors may have disguised certain names and other identifying information to protect confidentiality.

IVEY

Richard Ivey School of Business
The University of Western Ontario

RIM: RESEARCH IN MOTION LTD.

RIM was a world leader in the mobile communications market. Founded in 1984 by 23-year-old University of Waterloo student Mike Lazaridis, RIM designed, manufactured and marketed the very popular line of BlackBerry products that had recently reached 14 million subscribers worldwide and had just over $6 billion in revenue (see Exhibits 1 and 2). In early 2008, RIM was one of Canada's largest companies with a market capitalization of $69.4 billion.[1]

The BlackBerry wireless platform and line of handhelds could integrate e-mail, phone, Instant Messaging (IM), Short Message Service (SMS), internet, music, camera, video, radio, organizer, Global Positioning System (GPS) and a variety of other applications in one wireless solution that was dubbed "always on, always connected." These features, especially the immediate pushed message delivery, in addition to the BlackBerry's small size, long battery life, and ease of use, made the product extremely popular with busy executives who valued the safe and secure delivery of corporate mail and seamless extension of other enterprise and internet services.

In particular, organizations that relied on sensitive information, such as the U.S. government and large financial institutions, were early and loyal adopters of Black-Berry and RIM's largest customers. RIM's enterprise e-mail servers, which were attached to the customer's e-mail and IM servers behind company firewalls, encrypted and redirected e-mail and other data before forwarding the information to end consumers through wireless service providers (see Exhibit 3). Having been the first to market with a "push" e-mail architecture and a value proposition built on security, RIM had more than 100,000 enterprise customers and an estimated 42 per cent market share of converged devices, and significantly higher market share of data-only devices, in North America.[2]

RIM generated revenue through the "complete BlackBerry wireless solution" which included wireless devices, software and services. Revenues, however, were heavily skewed to handheld sales (73 per cent), followed by service (18 per cent), software (6 per cent) and other revenues (3 per cent). In handhelds, RIM had recently introduced the award-winning BlackBerry Pearl and BlackBerry Curve, which were a significant design departure from previous models and for the first time targeted both consumer and business professionals (see Exhibit 4). RIM had accumulated a wide range of product design and innovation awards, including recognition from Computerworld as one of the Top 10 Products of the Past 40 Years.[3] Analysts and technophiles eagerly awaited the next-generation BlackBerry series expected for release in 2008.

Although originally built for busy professionals, BlackBerry had made considerable headway in the consumer market and had become something of a social phenomenon. Celebrity sightings put the BlackBerry in the hands of Madonna and Paris Hilton among others. The term "crackberry," used to describe the addictive or obsessive use of the BlackBerry, was added to Webster's New Millennium dictionary. Just six months after launching Facebook for BlackBerry, downloads of the popular social networking software application had topped one million, indicating that younger

---

[1] D. George-Cosh, "Analysts cheer RIM results, hike targets," *Financial Post*, April 4, 2008, http://www.nationalpost.com/scripts/story.html?id=420318; accessed April 22, 2008.

[2] Of converged device shipments (smartphones and wireless handhelds). Canalys Smart Mobile Device Analysis service, Press Release, February 5, 2008, http://www.canalys.com/pr/2008/r2008021.htm, accessed April 2, 2008.

[3] http://www.rim.com/newsroom/news/awards/index.shtml

consumers were gravitating towards the popular handhelds.[4] RIM also actively sought partnerships with software developers to bring popular games such as Guitar Hero III to the BlackBerry mobile platform,[5] suggesting a more aggressive move to the consumer, or at least prosumer,[6] smartphone space.

Wireless carriers, such as Rogers in Canada and Verizon in the United States, were RIM's primary direct customers. These carriers bundled BlackBerry handhelds and software with airtime and sold the complete solution to end users. In 2007, RIM had over 270 carrier partnerships in more than 110 countries around the world. Through the BlackBerry Connect licensing program other leading device manufacturers such as Motorola, Nokia, Samsung and Sony Ericsson could also equip their handsets with BlackBerry functionality, including push technology to automatically deliver e-mail and other data. Expanding the global reach of BlackBerry solutions was therefore a fundamental part of RIM's strategy. In 2007, 57.9 per cent of RIM's revenues were derived from the United States, 7.3 per cent from Canada and the remaining 34.8 per cent from other countries. To date, RIM had offices in North America, Europe and Asia Pacific, however, it had only three wholly owned subsidiaries—two in Delaware and one in England.

THE WIRELESS COMMUNICATIONS MARKET AND SMARTPHONES

Mobile wireless communication involved the transmission of signals using radio frequencies between wireless networks and mobile access devices. Although RIM was one of the first to market with two-way messaging, recent technological developments had encouraged numerous handheld and handset vendors to go beyond traditional "telephony" and release new "converged"[7] devices including smartphones, Personal Digital Assistants (PDA), phone/PDA hybrids, converged voice and data devices and other end-to-end integrated wireless solutions. A shift in the telecommunication industry was moving demand beyond just cellphones to smartphones—complete communications tools that marry all the functions of mobile phones with fully integrated e-mail, browser and organizer applications. In 2007, key competitors to RIM's BlackBerry line-up included the Palm Treo 700 and 750, Sony Ericsson P900 Series, the Nokia E62, Motorola Q and the Apple iPhone.

The number of wireless subscriber connections worldwide had reached three billion by the end of 2007. China led with over 524 million subscribers, followed by the United States at 254 million and India with 237 million (see Exhibit 5). Year over year growth in the United States, however, was only 9.5 per cent, with an already high market penetration rate (87 per cent). In contrast, China's growth was 18.3 per cent with only 39 per cent penetration. In sheer numbers, India was experiencing the fastest growth rate with a 60 per cent increase and room to grow with 21 per cent market penetration.

---

[4] AFX International Focus, "RIM: Facebook for BlackBerry downloads top 1M," April 1, 2008, http://global.factiva.com, accessed April 1, 2008.

[5] Business Wire, "Guitar Hero III Mobile will rock your BlackBerry Smartphone," April 1, 2008, http://global.factiva.com, accessed April 1, 2008.

[6] Prosumer refers to "professional consumers," customers that use their mobile devices for both business and personal communications.

[7] "Converged" refers to the convergence of the digital wireless communication industry (cellular telephony) and information technology industries, signaled by the arrival of 2G networks which merged voice and data transmissions.

To put that into context, in late 2007 there were almost 300,000 new wireless network subscribers in India every day.[8]

Since the launch of Apple's iPhone in June 2007, competition in the smartphone segment of the mobile telecommunications industry had intensified. The iPhone "set a new standard for usability."[9] In 2007, smartphones represented only 10 per cent of the global mobile phone market in units. However, this segment was projected to reach over 30 per cent market share within five years.[10] In the U.S. the number of smartphone users had doubled in 2007 to about 14.6 million[11] while global shipments of smartphones rose by 53 per cent worldwide hitting 118 million in 2007.[12] Some analysts saw the opportunity for smart phones as "immense," predicting that during 2008 and 2009, 500 million smart devices would be sold globally and cumulative global shipments would pass the one billion mark by 2012.[13]

Worldwide demand for wireless handhelds had been fueled by several global trends, including the commercial availability of high-speed wireless networks, the emergence of mobile access to corporate intranets, and the broad acceptance of e-mail and text messaging as reliable, secure and indispensable means of communication. Coupled with the growth of instant messaging as both a business and personal communications tool, the demand for wireless handhelds and smartphones was robust.

COMPETING PLATFORMS

Symbian, a proprietary Operating System (OS) designed for mobile devices and jointly owned by Nokia, Ericsson, Sony Ericsson, Panasonic, Siemens AG and Samsung, held an estimated 65 per cent worldwide share of the converged devices, shipping 77.3 million smartphones in 2007 (up 50 per cent from 2006).[14] This was significantly ahead of Microsoft's Windows Mobile OS (12 per cent) and RIM's BlackBerry OS (11 per cent). However, in North America, RIM led with 42 per cent of shipments, ahead of Apple (27 per cent), Microsoft (21 per cent) and Palm (less than nine per cent and shrinking).[15]

However, RIM could not afford to rest on its laurels. In the North American market place, Apple had recently announced that it would be actively pursuing the business segment. Conceding that push-email and calendar integration were key to securing enterprise users, Apple licensed ActiveSync Direct Push, a Microsoft technology. Apple hoped to entice corporate users to adopt the iPhone as their converged device of choice.[16] Similarly, Microsoft, which had struggled to gain widespread acceptance for its Windows Mobile OS, had recently revamped its marketing efforts and announced

---

[8] GSMA 20 year factsheet, http://www.gsmworld.com/documents/20_year_factsheet.pdf, accessed April 5, 2008.

[9] P. Svensson, "Microsoft Upgrades Windows Mobile," Associated Press Newswire, April 1, 2008, http://global.factiva.com, accessed April 1, 2008.

[10] Esmerk Finish News, "Global: Survey: Nokia has best innovation strategy," March 25, 2008, http://global.factiva.com, accessed April 1, 2008.

[11] N. Gohring, "Smartphones on the rise? Thank the iPone panel says," *Washington Post*, March 31, 2008, http://washingtonpost.com/wp-dyn/content/article/2008/03/31/AR2008033102392.html, accessed online April 1, 2008.

[12] Canalys Smart Mobile Device Analysis service, Press Release, February 5, 2008, http://www.canalys.com/pr/2008/r2008021.htm, accessed April 2, 2008.

[13] Chris Ambrosio, Strategy Analytics, January 2008 and Pete Cunningham, Canalys, as quoted on www.symbian.com, accessed April 3, 2008.

[14] www.symbian.com, accessed April 3, 2008.

[15] Canalys Smart Mobile Device Analysis service, Press Release, February 5, 2008, http://www.canalys.com/pr/2008/r2008021.htm, accessed April 2, 2008.

[16] A. Hesseldahl, "How the iPhone is suiting up for work," *BusinessWeek*, March 6, 2008, www.businessweek.com, accessed March 21, 2008.

an end-to-end solution for enterprise customers as well as desktop-grade web browsing for Windows Mobile enabled phones.[17] Even Google had entered the fray with Android, an open and free mobile platform which included an OS, middleware and key applications. Rivalry, it seemed, was intensifying.

In early 2008, an analyst commented about the increasing competition in the converged device (smartphone and wireless handheld) segment:

> Apple's innovation in its mobile phone user interface has prompted a lot of design activity among competitors. We saw the beginnings of that in 2007, but we will see a lot more in 2008 as other smart phone vendors try to catch up and then get back in front. Experience shows that a vendor with only one smart phone design, no matter how good that design is, will soon struggle. A broad, continually refreshed portfolio is needed to retain and grow share in this dynamic market. This race is a marathon, but you pretty much have to sprint every lap.[18]

Another analyst observed:

> The good news for RIM? There still aren't many trusted alternatives for business-class mobile e-mail. This company could be one of the world's biggest handset manufacturers one day. It's hard for me to believe there won't be e-mail on every phone in the world. RIM is going to be a major force in this market.[19]

Given the rapid advances in the mobile communications industry, no technological platform had become the industry standard. In light of the dynamic market situation, RIM needed to ensure that its investment in R&D kept up with the pace of change in the industry.

R&D AT RIM

R&D and engineering were the heart and soul of RIM. In March 2007, RIM employed just over 2,100 people with different R&D areas of expertise: radio frequency engineering, hardware and software design, audio and display improvement, antenna design, circuit board design, power management, industrial design, and manufacturing engineering, among others. R&D efforts focused on improving the functionality, security and performance of the BlackBerry solution, as well as developing new devices for current and emerging network technologies and market segments. The ratio of software to hardware developers was approximately 2:1 and about 40 per cent of the software engineers were involved in core design work while another 40 per cent were engaged in testing and documentation (the remaining 20 per cent were in management, and support functions like documentation and project management).

R&D had increased significantly both in terms of the total number of employees as well as the geographic scope of its operations. Since 2000, the R&D group had grown more than tenfold, from 200 to 2,100 people and expanded to two more locations in Canada (Ottawa and Mississauga), several in the United States (Dallas, Chicago, Atlanta, Seattle and Palo Alto) and one in England. Waterloo was still the principal location—home to a vibrant and collaborative culture of young and talented engineers.

---

[17]"Microsoft unveils smartphone advancements to improve ability to work and play with one phone," April 1, 2008, Press Release; and "Microsoft announces enterprise-class mobile solution," April 1, 2008, Press Release, www.microsoft.com/prespass/press/2008/apr08

[18]Canalys Smart Mobile Device Analysis service, Press Release, February 5, 2008, http://www.canalys.com/pr/2008/r2008021.htm, accessed April 2, 2008.

[19]Ken Dulaney of Gartner, as quoted in A. Hesseldahl, "RIM: Growth rules the day," February 22, 2008, www.businessweek.com

RIM's cryptographic and software source code played a key role in the success of the company, delivering the safe and secure voice and data transmission on which the BlackBerry reputation was built. Chris Wormald, vice-president of strategic alliances, who was responsible for acquisitions, licensing and partnerships described the challenge as follows:

> At the end of the day, our source code is really among our few enduring technical assets. We have gone through extraordinary measures to protect it. Extraordinary is probably still too shallow of a word. We don't give anyone any access under any circumstances. RIM was founded on a principle of "we can do it better ourselves"—it is a philosophy that is embedded in our DNA. This vertical integration of technology makes geographic expansion and outsourcing of software development very difficult.

Intellectual property rights were thus diligently guarded through a combination of patent, copyright and contractual agreements. It was also strategically managed through a geography strategy that divided core platform development from product and technology development, with most of the core work (on the chip sets, software source code, product design) still occurring in Waterloo. However, the exponential growth in sales, competition and industry changes was placing tremendous pressures on the R&D teams at the Canadian headquarters.

Similar to other players in the telecommunications industry (see Exhibit 6), it was RIM's policy to maintain its R&D spending as a consistent percentage of total sales. Investment analysts often looked to this number to gauge the sustainability of revenue growth. R&D expenses were seen as a proxy for new product or service development and therefore used as a key indicator of future revenue potential. Human capital represented the bulk of R&D dollars and the organizational development team in charge of hiring at RIM was working overtime to try and keep up with the growing demand for the qualified engineers needed to deliver on both customer and investor expectations.

ORGANIZATIONAL DEVELOPMENT FOR R&D AT RIM

The 2,100 R&D employees made up about 35 per cent of RIM's 6,254 employees.[20] Total headcount had also been growing in double digits over the last five years (see Exhibit 7). However, if investment analysts were correct and sales grew by almost 70 per cent again in 2008,[21] the large numbers involved could hinder RIM's ability to rely on its historic growth strategy: sourcing from the local talent pool, through employee referrals and new graduate recruitment, and making selective acquisitions of small technology companies. It needed to find upwards of 1,400 new software developers just to maintain the status quo in R&D. And not only did they have to find large numbers of talented individuals, they also had to figure out where they would be located and how to integrate them into RIM's culture.

The culture at RIM headquarters was seen as one of its differentiators and was a key factor in RIM's low employee turnover rate. In fact, the company had recently

---

[20]The remaining groups included 836 in sales, marketing and business development; 1,098 in customer care and technical support; 1,158 in manufacturing; and 1,002 in administration, which included information technology, BlackBerry network operations and service development, finance, legal, facilities and corporate administration.

[21]http://finance.yahoo.com/q/ae?s=RIMM

been recognized as one of "Canada's 10 Most Admired Corporate Cultures."[22] In describing the way things worked in the software development group at RIM, Dayna Perry, director of organizational development for R&D, commented:

> What we have here is flexibility, adaptability and the ability to work collaboratively and collegially. We haven't had a lot of process or the kind of bureaucracy that you may see in other larger organizations....It is what has allowed us to be very responsive to market opportunities. It is sort of the "magic" or the "secret sauce" of how things just work and we get things done.

A software developer leading a team working on BlackBerry's many multi-lingual devices agreed, saying:

> RIM, in comparison to some of its competitors, is a nice and dynamic environment ... RIM is a place engineers like to work. Some of our competitors treat their engineers as something unimportant. They don't participate in decisions. They are interchangeable. There is a very very strong bureaucracy... it's crazy. RIM is very different.

Maintaining its unique culture was a priority for RIM. Remaining centered in Waterloo nurtured this ability. But it was becoming clear that growing mostly in Waterloo was going to become increasingly difficult. Not only did RIM already employ most of the best developers in the area, it already attracted the best and brightest of the nearby University of Waterloo's engineering and computer science graduates. About 300 students came on board every semester through the company's coveted co-op program and many were asked to remain with RIM after graduation. In fact, the talent at the University of Waterloo was so widely recognized that even Bill Gates made frequent visits to the university to court the best students[23] and Google had recently opened facilities there, acknowledging that "Waterloo is an incredible pool of talent"[24] and that it was ready to start hiring the best and the brightest "as quickly as possible."[25]

Attracting outside talent to Waterloo was difficult given the competitive nature of the global software development industry. Most of the big players in the smartphone space were also ramping up. For example, Sony Ericsson had posted 230 design and engineering jobs in Sweden, China and the United States. Nokia was looking for 375 R&D employees in Finland, the United States, India and Germany, among other development sites. In California's Silicon Valley, Apple and Google had scooped up many of the top mobile browser developers in a technology cluster famous for its exaggerated employee benefits and unbeatable climate. Motorola could be the exception to the rule, having announced layoffs of engineers. Although Waterloo, Ontario had recently been named ICF's "Intelligent Community of the Year," the city of 115,000 people[26] might not be perceived by some candidates to be as attractive as other high tech centers which were more cosmopolitan, for example: Silicon Valley, or previous winners of the ICF, Taipei (2006), Mitaka (2005) or Glasgow (2004).[27]

---

[22] Canada's 10 Most Admired Corporate Cultures for 2006, www.waterstonehc.com, accessed on April 5, 2008.
[23] D. Friend, "Microsoft hunting IT grads," *London Free Press*, March 22, 2008.
[24] "Google expands Waterloo base," http://atuw.ca/feature-google-expands-waterloo-base/, accessed April 11, 2008.
[25] A. Petroff, "A Recruiter's Waterloo?" http://www.financialpost.com/trading_desk/technology/story.html?id=389305, accessed April 11, 2008.
[26] The greater Kitchener-Waterloo area had approximately 450,000 inhabitants.
[27] Intelligent Community Forum, 2007 Intelligent Community of the Year Awards, Press release May 18, 2007, http://www.intelligentcommunity.org/displaycommon.cfm?an=1&subarticlenbr=221, accessed April 5, 2008.

Compounding the problem was a shortage of physical space at RIM's Waterloo campus that was a running joke around headquarters. Even company founder Mike Lazaridis had to laugh about it—responding to a reporter's question about his most embarrassing moment, Lazaridis replied: "Scraping my Aston Martin in RIM's driveway. I was leaving a space and a car came from nowhere. The scratches have been fixed, but not the too-busy parking lot. It's a hazard of a growing company."[28]

On top of it all, RIM was looking to hire a very particular mix of engineers. Although new graduates were essential, to be ahead of the game a good proportion of the incoming employees was going to have to be senior hires. RIM needed people who could fit with the culture and hit the ground running. Dayna noted: "We just don't have the luxury of time to grow all our own talent. We do that in parallel and do a lot of internal promotion, but that is an investment you make in the future, it is not going to help you solve your problem today." And it wasn't just a question of the number of engineers. In software, breakthrough innovations often came from small teams led by a visionary. Many at RIM believed that "software is as much about art as it is about engineering." And in the dynamic wireless communications market, exceptional software developers were scarce.

MANAGING EXPLOSIVE GROWTH

The approach to growth used by RIM in the past would not deliver the scale and scope of R&D resources required to maintain its technical superiority. RIM had several options.

Do What We Do Now, Only More of It

RIM had been very successful in its local recruiting strategy as well as nation-wide campus recruitment drives. It relied heavily on the personal and professional networks of existing employees as an ear-on-the-ground approach to finding new talent. One option was to expand co-op programs to other universities as well as increase the frequency and intensity of its new graduate recruitment efforts. Microsoft's intern program, for example, included subsidized housing and transportation (car rental or bike purchase plan), paid travel to Redmond, health club memberships and even subsidized housecleaning![29]

Likewise, RIM could follow Microsoft's lead and form a global scouting group dedicated to finding the best talent worldwide and bringing them into RIM. Canada ranked as one of the best countries in the world to live in terms of life expectancy, literacy, education and other standards of living.[30] These and other benefits could attract young developers particularly from emerging markets. As well, the stronger dollar made Canada more attractive.

Similar to other players in the industry (e.g. Apple, Motorola, Sony Ericson, Nokia), RIM posted many of its job openings online and potential employees searched and applied for the positions best suited for their skills and interests. However, with over 800 worldwide job postings, finding the right job was often a daunting task. RIM also had no formal way to manage qualified candidates that may have simply applied to the wrong team and hence good leads were potentially lost. Some competitors allowed

---

[28] J. Shillingford, "A life run by BlackBerry," *Financial Times*, March 19, 2008, http://global.factiva.com, accessed on April 1, 2008.
[29] http://www.microsoft.com/college/ip_overview.mspx
[30] United Nations Human Development Index 2007/2008.

candidates to build an open application (similar to Monster or Workopolis) that could then be viewed by anyone in the organization looking for talent. Revamping the careers website and being more creative in the way in which they structured recruiting was being considered.

Some competitors had also formalized hiring and the onboarding processes of computer scientists by hiring in "waves." Rather than posting individual job openings, Symbian, for example, solicited resumes once a year, which were then reviewed, and successful candidates invited to the London, U.K.-based head office to attend one of nine Assessment Days. If the attendees passed a series of tests and interviews, they were then inducted into the company during a formal "bootcamp" training session that lasted five weeks.[31] Symbian had also set up extensive collaborations with 44 universities in 17 countries including China, Russia and India as well as Ethiopia, Kuwait, Lebanon, Thailand and the United States. Dubbed The Symbian Academy, this network allowed partners and licensees to post jobs for Symbian Academy students and for professors to collaborate on the research and development of innovative applications such as pollution monitors on GPS-enabled Symbian smartphones.[32] Although RIM enjoyed an excellent relationship with the University of Waterloo, it did not currently have a recruiting strategy of this scope.

Grow and Expand Existing Geographies

RIM had established R&D operations beyond Waterloo, in Ottawa, Mississauga, Dallas and Chicago over the last five years. It was also expanding the number of product and technology development facilities in locations such as Fort Lauderdale by recruiting through general job fairs. This strategy, however, had to be balanced with a number of trade-offs. First, RIM wanted to ensure that its geographic expansion was not haphazard, but rather strategically executed. Second, the cost of talent in various locations had to be considered. Software engineers in Palo Alto, for example, commanded much higher wages than in Waterloo and the competition there was even more intense, with high turnover costs incurred when employees were wooed away by the many other high tech companies in the area.

There was also some internal resistance to expanding R&D to locations outside of Waterloo. Although there was a growing realization that RIM could no longer continue to grow locally, one senior executive commented:

> There are people here, even leaders and senior people, who have said: "What? Products being built elsewhere? No! We can't do that! Then we won't have any control!" So some of it is a cultural shift and a mind shift for the people that have been here and it is hard for them to let go and to be part of a really big company. And RIM is getting to be a big company now. And for some people, from an organizational culture perspective, it just doesn't resonate well with them.

This sentiment was not uncommon among software-centric organizations. Despite some geographic expansion, Microsoft, for example, had recently recommitted to its Redmond, Washington campus, spending over $1 billion on new and upgraded facilities there with room to house an additional 12,000 employees.[33] Google was also

---

[31] http://www.symbian.com/about/careers/graduate%20program/index.html, accessed April 3, 2008.
[32] www.symbian.com, accessed April 3, 2008.
[33] B. Romano, "Microsoft campus expands, transforms, inside out," *The Seattle Times*, November 23, 2007, http://seattletimes.nwsource.com/cgi-bin/PrintStory.pl?document_id=2004007121&zsection_id=20 03750725&slug=microsoft11&date=20071111, accessed April 22, 2008.

strongly committed to maintaining its Mountain View, California headquarters, with only a few satellite offices. Its unique company culture, built on attracting and keeping the best talent in a young and fun environment was part of Google's incredible success story, and helped it achieve the status of the number one company to work for according to Fortune Magazine.[34] Other large software companies such as Oracle and Apple also kept their software developers in one location to foster innovation. In some ways, RIM was already more geographically distributed than many larger software organizations.

Although establishing a geographic expansion plan posed difficulties, RIM had nevertheless laid out several criteria for selecting new locations for product and technology development sites. First, the area had to already have a pool of talent that housed a mature skill set; the city or region had be home to an existing base of software or hardware companies, thus ensuring that a critical mass of highly skilled employees was available. RIM's strategic expansion into Ottawa, for example, was influenced by the availability of talented software engineers in the area in the wake of Nortel's massive layoffs.[35] Lastly, the city or region had to have universities with strong technical programs. This allowed RIM to expand on its successful co-op programs and graduate recruitment initiatives. Once a satellite development site was set up, however, there was still the issue of how to transfer RIM's young and dynamic corporate culture to these locations.

Increase Acquisitions

RIM had success in bringing people on board through acquisition. Several years earlier, RIM had acquired Slangsoft, a high tech start-up in Israel that was developing code which allowed for the ability to display and input Chinese characters—key to tailoring BlackBerry for Asian and other foreign markets. As part of the acquisition, RIM worked with Immigration Canada to relocate 11 of the engineers to Waterloo, 10 of whom were still with RIM more than six years later.

Growth by acquisition was a common practice in the high tech and telecommunications sectors. Google had made its initial move to Waterloo in 2006, for example, through the acquisition of a small wireless software company, subsequently discontinuing the company's web browser product, making it a purchase of talent and intellectual property.[36] Other companies had also made strategic acquisitions of technology. In 2002, Apple, for example, purchased EMagic, a small German company whose software was then used in the development of the popular Mac program Garage Band.[37] In larger and more public acquisitions, Nokia and Motorola had both recently acquired software companies in the hopes of gaining faster access to the growing smartphone market. In 2006, Nokia purchased Intellisync Corporation, a wireless messaging and mobile-software developer for $430 million, creating Nokia's "business mobility solutions" group.[38] Also in 2006, Motorola purchased Good Technology for a rumored

---

[34] http://money.cnn.com/magazines/fortune/bestcompanies/2007/snapshots/1.html, accessed April 22, 2008.

[35] Estimated at over 15,000 total jobs in the last eight years; B. Hill, "Nortel to keep Ottawa as main R&D centre," April 4, 2008, *The Montreal Gazette*, http://www.canada.com/montrealgazette/news/business/story.html?id=24aa8d53-154a-4d88-aa9d-593ce9794e10, accessed April 11, 2008.

[36] M. Evans, "Waterloo gets Googled," January 6, 2006, http://www.financialpost.com/story.html?id=c4f6f084-d72f-43ea-8a82-affe38df3830&k=58579, accessed April 11, 2008.

[37] A. Hesseldahl, "What to do with Apple's cash," *BusinessWeek*, March 1, 2007, http://www.businessweek.com/technology/content/mar2007/tc20070301_402290.htm, accessed April 11, 2008.

[38] TelecomWeb News Digest, "Nokia completes Intellisync purchase," February 10, 2006, http://global.factiva.com, accessed April 11, 2008.

$500 million and released Good 5.0, allowing for secure access to corporate intranets so enterprise users could download, edit and send documents remotely.[39]

Given the depressed economic climate in the United States in early 2008, many smaller firms and technology start-ups were struggling financially as were some larger competitors. There were persistent rumors that Palm, for example, was in severe financial trouble.[40] Further, growth by acquisition could also allow for the tactical expansion in other strategic markets.

The European mobile telecommunications market, in particular, was highly "nationalistic," with end users favoring home grown companies over foreign solutions. Establishing a presence there through acquisition could buy RIM goodwill and serve as a portal to this lucrative market. The economic downturn in the United States and recent competitor plant closures in Europe presented RIM with the potential for opportunistic acquisitions, either of technology or of software engineering talent.

Go Global

In early 2008, most of the R&D was still done in Waterloo, with some core work also being done in Ottawa and product and technology sites throughout the United States and in the United Kingdom. RIM was exploring a broader global expansion. It already had customer service operations in Singapore and sales & marketing representative offices in France, Germany, Italy, Spain, China, Australia, Hong Kong and Japan. Yet it had stopped short of establishing core research and development sites outside of Canada. Nonetheless, despite a strong desire to keep R&D close to home, RIM estimated that of all the new hires in 2008, likely half would have to be outside of Canada. In addition to the United States, it was looking to Europe, the Middle East and Africa (EMEA) and Eastern Europe. The same selection criteria of a mature skill set and strong technological universities applied to choosing R&D sites outside North America.

Some of RIM's key competitors had a long history of global expansion of their R&D activities. Symbian, for example, opened an R&D center in Beijing in August 2007, already having three others in the United Kingdom and India.[41] Motorola, had been present in China since 1993 when it established its first R&D center there as part of its Global Software Group (GSG). It had since set up R&D activities in Beijing, Tianjin, Shanghai, Nanjing, Chengdu and Hangzhou, investing an estimated US$800 million and employing more than 3,000 R&D staff in China. In 2007, Motorola added R&D sites in Vietnam and South Korea[42] and announced it would open an additional R&D complex in Wangjing, China, with another 3,000 employees.[43]

China in particular was beginning to gain worldwide recognition as a center for innovation. The number of patent applications was doubling every two years and the R&D to GDP ratio had also doubled in the last decade. In addition to Motorola, Nokia had set up a number of research bases in China.[44] In 2005, Nokia had five R&D units there, employing more than 600 people; an estimated 40 per cent of its global Mobile

---

[39]RCR Wireless News, "Motorola set to leverage Good in competitive e-mail market," June 25, 2007, http://global.factiva.com, accessed April 11, 2008.

[40]S. Weinberg, "Palm acquisition not considered threat to RIM," Dow Jones Newswire, http://global factiva.com, accessed April 11, 2008.

[41]Business Monitor International, *Asia Pacific Telecommunications Insight*, April 2008, Issue 24.

[42]Business Monitor International, *Asia Pacific Telecommunications Insight*, January 2008, Issue 21.

[43]Press Release, "Twenty years' commitment ensures a more successful future," November 8, 2007, http://www.motorola.com/mediacenter/news/detail.jsp?globalObjectId=8923_8852_23&page=archive

[44]Business Monitor International, Asia Pacific Telecommunications Insight, November 2007, Issue 19.

Phones Business Group handsets were designed and developed in the Beijing Product Creation Center.[45] The company had also recently announced a long-term joint research program with Tsinghua University in Beijing that would see 20 Nokia researchers working alongside 30 professors and associates and up to 50 students.[46] Globally, Nokia Research Centers (NRC) described its R&D strategy as:

> NRC has a two-fold approach to achieving its mandate of leading Nokia into the future. The work for core technology breakthroughs supporting Nokia's existing businesses takes place in the Core Technology Centers, the CTCs. More visionary, exploratory systems research that goes well beyond any current business model is conducted at the many System Research Centers, the SRCs.[47]

Nokia's core technology centers were in Finland, with the SRCs in China, Germany, the United Kingdom, United States, Finland and Japan. The company employed 112,262 people of which 30,415, or 27 per cent, were in R&D.[48]

The Motorola Global Software Group (GSG) was more decentralized. In addition to China it had R&D centers in Australia, Singapore, Mexico, Argentina, the United Kingdom, Poland, Russia, Italy, Canada and India, among others and employed approximately 27,000 R&D employees worldwide. The Motorola GSG in India had nearly 3,500 engineers and was responsible for designing 40 per cent of the software used in Motorola phones worldwide, including the MOTORAZR and MOTO Q. However, Motorola was not noted for having world-class smartphone software. The GSG structure was speculated to have contributed to Motorola's inability to deliver a successful follow-up product to the RAZR as well as to have precipitated the company's recent financial downturn.[49]

Nonetheless, partnering with major research institutes to source top talent appeared to be a fairly common strategy. Motorola India collaborated with six of the seven Indian Institutes of Technology (IIT), as well as the Indian Institute of Science (IISC) and the Indian Institute of Information Technology (IIIT).[50] Other technology firms were also partnering with emerging market governmental and educational institutions to secure a foothold in future markets. Cisco Systems, for example, a leading manufacturer of network equipment, had recently announced a US$16 billion expansion plan into China, including investments in manufacturing, venture capital and education. Working with China's Ministry of Education, Cisco had established 200 "Networking Academies" in 70 cities in China and had trained more than 90,000 students.[51]

These types of collaborations and international research consortiums, however, raised not only logistical but also legal issues. Source code loss, software piracy and product imitations were more common in developing countries where IP protection laws (or enforcement) lagged the United States or Canada, leading to both explicit and tacit knowledge "leakage." For example, despite its strong commitment to China, Nokia was recently forced to file suit against two Beijing firms for manufacturing and selling mobile phones that were a direct copy of its proprietary and legally protected

---

[45] Press Release, May 21, 2004, "Nokia Expands R&D in China," http://press.nokia.com/PR/200405/946603_5.html

[46] Press Release, May 28, 2007, "Nokia and Tsinghua University announce new research framework," http://www.nokia.com/A4136001?newsid=1129236

[47] http://research.nokia.com/centers/index.html

[48] Nokia annual report 2007.

[49] "What's on Motorola's agenda?" *BusinessWeek*, January 9, 2008, http://www.businessweek.com/innovate/content/jan2008/id2008014_304911_page_2.htm, accessed April 16, 2008.

[50] Motorola 2007 10-K and http://www.motorola.com/mot/doc/6/6294_MotDoc.pdf

[51] Business Monitor International, Asia Pacific Telecommunications Insight, January 2008, Issue 21.

industrial designs.[52] Other large high tech companies such as Cisco and Microsoft had also suffered source code breaches. In late 2006, China Unicom, the state-run telecommunications company, had launched its own wireless e-mail service which it boldly named the Redberry, announcing that their Redberry brand not only continued the already familiar "BlackBerry" image and name, it also fully reflected the symbolic meaning of China Unicom's new red corporate logo.[53] For much of East Asia, reverse engineering and copying foreign products were important sources of learning, helping to transition these markets from imitators of technology to innovators and competitive threats.[54]

Wormald described the difficulties with emerging market dynamics as follows:

> I was just talking to a Fortune 500 CEO the other day who is closing up shop in India. This company had a 45 per cent employee turnover rate. They just walk down the street and go work for his competitor and he was tired of his source code just walking out the door.

For RIM, going global was therefore problematic on a number of fronts, most notably because the BlackBerry source code had to be protected. In addition, expanding to emerging markets was also complicated by restrictions regarding cryptographic software. Most governments, including those of Canada and the United States, along with Russia and China, regulated the import and export of encryption products due to national security issues. Encryption was seen as a "dual-use technology" which could have both commercial and military value and was thus carefully monitored. The U.S. government would not purchase any product that had not passed the "Federal Information Processing Standard" (FIPS) certification tests. This would preclude any product that had encrypted data in China because "if you encrypt data in China, you have to provide the Chinese government with the ability to access the keys."[55] India had also recently notified RIM that it planned to eavesdrop on BlackBerry users, claiming that terrorists may be hiding behind the encrypted messages to avoid detection.[56]

Even if these hurdles could be overcome, going global also brought with it additional challenges of organizational design, communication and integration between head office and other geographically dispersed locations. Some competitors had chosen to expand globally by product line, while others had outsourced less sensitive functions such as testing and documentation. Eastern European countries such as Poland and Hungary, for example, were emerging as strong contenders for quality assurance testing. The lower cost of labor in developing and transitional economies, however, was showing signs of inflationary pressures in some locales and any planned savings might be somewhat offset by the increased monitoring, coordination and integration costs. Furthermore, RIM was not set up to manage a multi-country

---

[52] Shanghai Daily, "Nokia files suit over alleged copy of model," June 29, 2006, http://global.factiva.com, accessed April 16, 2008.

[53] Hesseldahl, A. "BlackBerry vs. Redberry in China," September 25, 2006, *BusinessWeek* http://www.businessweek.com/technology/content/apr2006/tc20060413_266291.htm?chan=search, accessed April 16, 2008.

[54] United Nations World Investment Report 2005, Transnational Corporations and the Internationalization of R&D, New York and Geneva, 2005, p. 165.

[55] E. Messmer, "Encryption Restrictions" and "Federal encryption purchasing requirements," *Network World*, March 15, 2004, http://www.networkworld.com/careers/2004/0315man.html?page=1; accessed April 22, 2008.

[56] N. Lakshman, "India wants to eavesdrop on BlackBerrys," *BusinessWeek*, April 1, 2008, http://global.factiva.com, accessed April 7, 2008.

research consortium and the mindset in Waterloo was still very much such that core engineers needed to be seen to be perceived as valuable. On the other hand, the potential could not be ignored. In China, where the penetration rate was only 38 per cent, the Symbian OS system used in Nokia, Samsung, Sony Ericsson and LG smartphones enjoyed a 68.7 per cent share, and iPhone sales had reached 400,000 "unlocked" units.[57] In India, where the penetration rate stood at 21 per cent, Virgin Mobile had recently struck a brand franchise agreement with Tata Teleservices, announcing plans to gain at least 50 million young subscribers to its mobile services, generating estimated revenues of US$350 billion.[58] The sheer number of potential new users was overwhelming.

CONCLUSION

Looking at the holiday sales numbers and the projected growth for 2008, Yach took a minute to think about the path he was on. He knew that first quarter revenue projections alone were estimated at $2.2 billion to $2.3 billion and that RIM was expecting to add another 2.2 million BlackBerry subscribers by the end of May 2008.[59] At that rate, analysts projected that 2008 would bring at least another 70 per cent growth in sales.[60] Furthermore, Mike Lazaridis had recently said in an interview:

> If you really want to build something sustainable and innovative you have to invest in R&D. If you build the right culture and invest in the right facilities and you encourage and motivate and inspire both young and seasoned people and put them all in the right environment—then it really performs for you. It's what I call sustainable innovation. And it's very different from the idea that you come up with something and then maximize value by reducing its costs. But building a sustainable innovation cycle requires an enormous investment in R&D. You have to understand all the technologies involved.[61]

Yach knew that his software developers were key to RIM's continued success; he was committed to delivering on the expectations for continued and sustainable growth in 2008 and beyond. Although he wanted to keep growing organically, sourcing talent locally and bringing his engineers into the cultural fold of RIM in Waterloo, he suspected this era was ending. In light of the unprecedented and exponential growth of the last year, coupled with the increasing competition and untapped global opportunities, he needed a plan.

Leaving the office after a hectic and frenetic first day back, Yach thought to himself—"How can I plan for this growth when it is just one of 10 burning issues on my agenda? We can't take a time-out to decide how to execute the growth." Grabbing the sales numbers to prepare for tomorrow's meeting, Yach knew he had the evening to consider the way ahead. The vacation was definitely over.

---

[57] Business Monitor International, Asia Pacific Telecommunications Insight, April 2008, Issue 24.
[58] Business Monitor International, Asia Pacific Telecommunications Insight, April 2008, Issue 24.
[59] Press Release, April 2, 2008: http://www.rim.com/news/press/2008/pr-02_04_2008-01.shtml
[60] http://finance.yahoo.com/q/ae?s=RIMM
[61] A. Hesseldahl, "BlackBerry: Innovation Behind the Icon," *BusinessWeek*, April 4, 2008, http://www.businessweek.com/innovate/content/apr2008/id2008044_416784.htm?chan=search, accessed April 6, 2008.

Exhibit 1

BlackBerry Subscriber Account Base (In Millions)

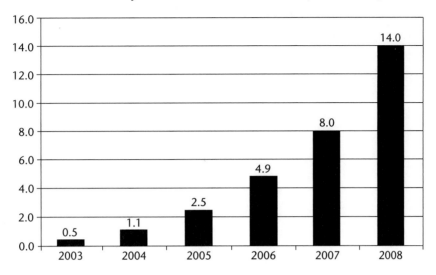

RIM Annual Revenue (In Millions of U.S. dollars)

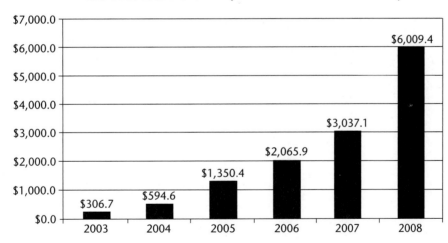

Note: RIM Fiscal year ends in March (Fiscal 2008 is the year ending March 31, 2008).
Source: RIM Fiscal 2007 Annual Report and Fiscal 2008 Press Release (April 2, 2008).

Exhibit 2   Consolidated Statement of Operations

Research In Motion Limited Incorporated under the Laws of Ontario (United States dollars, in thousands except per share data)					
	For the year ended				
	Mar. 1, 2008 (Projected)	Mar. 3, 2007	Mar. 4, 2006	Feb. 26, 2005	Feb. 28, 2004
Revenue	$6,009,395	$3,037,103	$2,065,845	$1,350,447	$594,616
Cost of sales	2,928,814	1,379,301	925,598	636,310	323,365
Gross margin	3,080,581	1,657,802	1,140,247	714,137	271,251
Gross margin %	51.30%	54.60%	55.20%	52.88%	45.62%
Expenses					
Research and development	359,828	236,173	158,887	102,665	62,638
Selling, marketing & admin.	881,482	537,922	314,317	193,838	108,492
Amortization	108,112	76,879	49,951	35,941	27,911
Litigation			201,791	352,628	35,187
	1,349,422	850,974	724,946	685,072	234,228
Income from operations	1,731,159	806,828	415,301	29,065	37,023
Investment income	79,361	52,117	66,218	37,107	10,606
Income before income taxes	1,810,520	858,945	481,519	66,172	47,629
Provision for income taxes					
Current	587,845	123,553	14,515	1,425	
Deferred	−71,192	103,820	92,348	(140,865)	
	516,653	227,373	106,863	(139,440)	−4,200
Net Income	$1,293,867	$631,572	$374,656	$205,612	51,829
Earnings per share					
Basic	$2.31	$1.14	$1.98	$1.10	$0.33
Diluted	$2.26	$1.10	$1.91	$1.04	$0.31

Source: Company Annual Reports; Fiscal 2008 form; Press Release, April 2, 2008, Research in Motion reports Fourth Quarter and Year-End Results for Fiscal 2008, http://www.rim.com/news/press/2008/pr-02_04_2008-01.shtml

Exhibit 3   BlackBerry Enterprise Solution Architecture

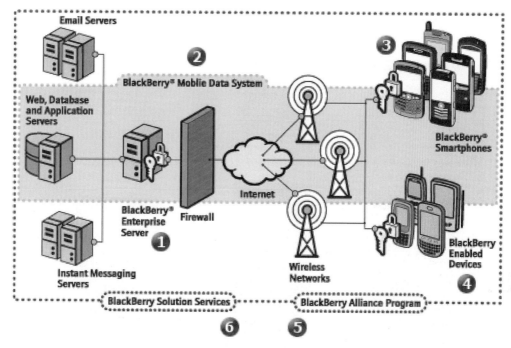

1. **BlackBerry® Enterprise Server:** Robust software that acts as the centralized link between wireless devices, wireless networks and enterprise applications. The server integrates with enterprise messaging and collaboration systems to provide mobile users with access to email, enterprise instant messaging and personal information management tools. All data between applications and BlackBerry® smartphones flows centrally through the server.

2. **BlackBerry® Mobile Data System (BlackBerry MDS):** An optimized framework for creating, deploying and managing applications for the BlackBerry Enterprise Solution. It provides essential components that enable applications beyond email to be deployed to mobile users, including developer tools, administrative services and BlackBerry® Device Software. It also uses the same proven BlackBerry push delivery model and advanced security features used for BlackBerry email.

3. **BlackBerry Smartphones:** Integrated wireless voice and data devices that are optimized to work with the BlackBerry Enterprise Solution. They provide push-based access to email and data from enterprise applications and systems in addition to web, MMS, SMS and organizer applications.

4. **BlackBerry® Connect™ Devices:** Devices available from leading manufacturers that feature BlackBerry push delivery technology and connect to the BlackBerry Enterprise Server.

5. **BlackBerry® Alliance Program:** A large community of independent software vendors, system integrators and solution providers that offer applications, services and solutions for the BlackBerry Enterprise Solution. It is designed to help organizations make the most of the BlackBerry Enterprise Solution when mobilizing their enterprises.

6. **BlackBerry Solution Services:** A group of services that include: BlackBerry® Technical Support Services, BlackBerry® Training, RIM® Professional Services and the Corporate Development Program. These tools and programs are designed to help organizations deploy, manage and extend their wireless solution.

Source: http://na.blackberry.com/eng/ataglance/solutions/architecture.jsp

Exhibit 4   The Evolution of the BlackBerry Product Line (Select Models)

RIM Inter@ctive Pager 850   RIM 957   BlackBerry 6200

BlackBerry 8820   BlackBerry Pearl 8110   BlackBerry Curve 8330

Source: http://www.rim.com/newsroom/media/gallery/index.shtml and Fortune, "BlackBerry: Evolution of an icon," Jon Fortt, Sept 21, 2007, accessed April 7, 2008: http://bigtech.blogs.fortune.cnn.com/blackberry-evolution-of-an-icon-photos-610/

Exhibit 5   Mobile Telephone Users Worldwide (In Millions)

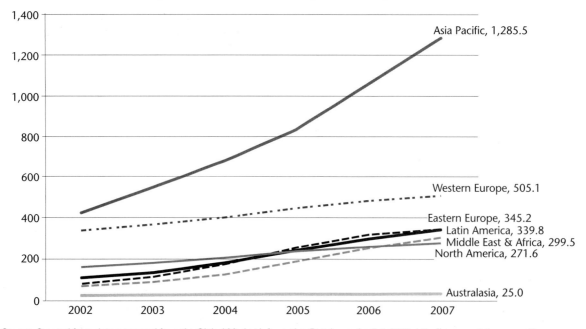

Source: Created from data accessed from the Global Market Information Database, April 4, 2008, http://www.portal.euromonitor.com. proxy1.lib.uwo.ca:2048/portal/server.pt?control=SetCommunity&CommunityID=207&PageID=720&cached=false&space=CommunityPage

Exhibit 6 Competitive R&D Spend (Select Competitors)

In Millions (US$)

Nokia		Dec. 31/04	Dec. 31/05	Dec. 31/06	Dec. 31/07
Revenue		$46,606	$54,022	$64,971	$80,672
R&D		$5,784	$6,020	$6,157	$8,229
		12.41%	11.14%	9.48%	10.20%
Microsoft	June 30/03	June 30/04	June 30/05	June 30/06	June 30/07
Revenue	$32,187	$36,835	$39,788	$44,282	$51,122
R&D	$6,595	$7,735	$6,097	$6,584	$7,121
	20.49%	21.00%	15.32%	14.87%	13.93%
Motorola	Dec. 31/03	Dec. 31/04	Dec. 31/05	Dec. 31/06	Dec. 31/07
Revenue	$23,155	$29,663	$35,310	$42,847	$36,622
R&D	$2,979	$3,316	$3,600	$4,106	$4,429
	12.87%	11.18%	10.20%	9.58%	12.09%
Apple	Sept. 27/03	Sept. 25/04	Sept. 24/05	Sept. 30/06	Sept. 29/07
Revenue	$6,207	$8,279	$13,931	$19,315	$24,006
R&D	$471	$491	$535	$712	$782
	7.59%	5.93%	3.84%	3.69%	3.26%
RIM	Feb. 28/04	Feb. 26/05	Mar. 4/06	Mar. 3/07	Proj. Mar./08
Revenue	$595	$1,350	$2,066	$3,037	$6,009
R&D	$63	$103	$159	$236	$360
	10.59%	7.63%	7.70%	7.77%	5.99%
Palm	May 31/03	May 31/04	May 31/05	May 31/06	May 31/07
Revenue	$838	$950	$1,270	$1,578	$1,561
R&D	$70	$69	$90	$136	$191
	8.35%	7.26%	7.09%	8.62%	12.24%

Note: Nokia 2007 includes Nokia Siemens.
Source: Company Annual Reports.

Exhibit 7   Employee Growth at RIM

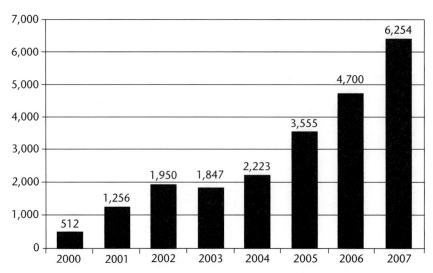

Source: RIM Annual Reports.

Swimming in the Virtual Community Pool with Plentyoffish

On a Monday morning in January of 2008, Markus Frind, chief executive officer (CEO) and founder of PlentyofFish.com, was undoubtedly the topic of many conversations as people grabbed their morning coffees from a local vendor. The *New York Times* had just published an article about the Vancouverite's free, online dating site, PlentyofFish (PoF). Now that the world was watching and salivating at the $10 million per year that the site was generating, one had to question whether its business model could be sustained. Could Frind maintain his strong foothold in the virtual world of social networking sites? Could PlentyofFish continue to maintain its financial success with advertising as its only source of revenue?

If the concept of offering a free, online dating site was so fatally flawed, PoF would not have experienced the success that it had. Frind did not spend the $10 million a month on marketing that some of his competitors like Match.com, eHarmony and Lavalife did. What he was doing was working just fine—for now, and continued to generate a substantial annual profit.

Frind had proudly announced, on many occasions, that his company consisted of just one employee—himself. While he had hired another employee in late 2007, it was only to assist in providing customer service. As the sole operator of the site, Frind had been able to handle massive amounts of traffic. In fact, for the week of April 28, 2007, PlentyofFish was ranked by HitWise as the 96th-busiest website in the United States. To put this into perspective, PoF outranked Apple.com in terms of traffic! How then, was he able to do all of this alone? Did his success lie in his web design philosophy that allowed users to take part in running the site? Was it the automation of the processing? Could he chalk it all up to efficiency? Other concerns included whether this

Wilfred Cheung, Chris Ellison, Prarthana Kumar, Jeremy Kyle and Stacey Morrison wrote this case under the supervision of Professor Michael Parent solely to provide material for class discussion. The authors do not intend to illustrate either effective or ineffective handling of a managerial situation. The authors may have disguised certain names and other identifying information to protect confidentiality.

Version: (A) 2008-03-06

Richard Ivey School of Business
The University of Western Ontario

model could be easily replicated, and should PlentyofFish be concerned about others entering the market with better technology and fancier sites?

As people milled around the corner, some on bikes, and others on rollerblades, several couples casually walked along the street, holding hands. With millions having surfed websites looking for that special someone, one had to wonder how many of these people met through PlentyofFish and how much longer others would continue to do so.

THE CONCEPT

Social Networking

The term "social network" was coined by J.A. Barnes who defined it as a group of 100 to 150 people drawn together by family, work or a hobby. In 2008, thanks mainly to the Internet, social networking had expanded to hundreds of millions of people around the world, creating a virtual community for people to interact with one another about anything and everything. Members created their own online "profiles" with biographical data, pictures, likes, dislikes and any other information they chose to post and share. They communicated with each other by voice, instant messaging, videoconference and blogs. In many cases, these sites also served as a vehicle for meeting in person. One could find dating sites, friendship sites, and sites with a business networking purpose or hybrids that offered a combination of these applications.

Looking for Mr. or Ms. Right or looking at your neighbour's pictures from vacation while checking your e-mail at the same time seemed to define the growing industry of social networking websites. The genius of these sites lay in their ability to capture the essence of informal exchanges while expanding the matrix of searchable, linked pages. Social networking on the Internet was a growing phenomenon which could be broadly categorized into three segments—virtual communities like Facebook; classified listing sites such as Craigslist; and the growing plethora of dating sites like PlentyofFish.

As participants in a social network started to become more entrenched in the social aspect of their network they often became members of that particular virtual community. A virtual community described "People who use computers to communicate, form friendships that sometimes form the basis of communities, but you have to be careful to not mistake the tool for the task and think that just writing words on a screen is the same thing as real community."[1] Much like a real community, a virtual social networking community was based on the idea that once one joined, they needed to actively participate. There was a reciprocal nature to being part of a virtual community; they depended upon social interaction and exchange among users. A person in a virtual community was motivated to contribute valuable information to the group, starting with a valid profile or an honest response with the expectation that they would receive the same in return.

The lifecycle of a membership in a virtual community went through the same stages as that of any other community. Members of virtual communities began their lifecycle first as visitors, clicking through and around a site to determine whether they could connect with other users and fit into the group. After deciding to break into the community and set up a profile or username, they began participating in the virtual

---

[1] Howard Rheingold, *The Virtual Community*, http://www.rheingold.com/vc/book/intro.html, access January 27, 2008.

community. Those who contributed for a sustained period of time became regulars. If they took the initiative to recruit others to join the community, they became leaders.

Another category of social networking sites were ones that focused on classified listings and operated as a hub aggregating buyers and sellers. Buyers listed a variety of goods ranging from private planes to services such as housekeeping. Craigslist was one of the most popular sites of this kind.

Dating websites allowed individuals to post their profile, view others' and perhaps develop a romantic or intimate relationship. The market was dominated by several large commercial websites such as Lavalife, eHarmony, and Match.com as well as the newer PlentyofFish. These sites targeted teens to retirees, with a number of new sites targeting niche markets based on religion, race, and occupation. They were based on a shift in thinking about web applications, built on interactivity between developer and users called Web 2.0.

Web 2.0

Web 2.0 was a term first coined in 2004 at a Web conference whose theme was "The Web has become a platform, a foundation upon which thousands of new forms of business would emerge."[2] According to Tim O'Reilly, one of the conference's moderators,

> Web 2.0 is the business revolution in the computer industry caused by the move to the Internet as platform, and an attempt to understand the rules for success on that new platform. Chief among those rules is this: Build applications that harness network effects to get better the more people use them. (This is what I've elsewhere called "harnessing collective intelligence.")
>
> Tim O'Reilly[3]

Web 2.0 systems were theoretically unconstrained as they would harness "the power of user contribution, collective intelligence, and network effects."[4] PlentyofFish was able to take advantage of this new business model by encouraging user contributions and their collective intelligence, while also capitalizing on the network effects it had built with these very users.

PLENTYOFFISH.COM
Business Model

Founded in 2003, PlentyofFish was free to users, a feature that differentiated it from other online dating sites. This was reinforced in the site's slogan: "100% Free. Put away your credit card." However, this came at a cost to users. While other online dating sites provided customer support as part of their service, PlentyofFish did not have that same support structure. It only responded to fraudulent identity notifications and subpoena requests. For example, instead of providing customer service,

---

[2] Web 2.0 SUMMIT, *About Web Summit 2.0*, http://conferences.oreillynet.com/pub/w/62/about.html, accessed January 27, 2008.
[3] Tim O'Reilly, "Web 2.0. Compact Definition: Trying Again," O'Reilly *Radar: O'Reilly Media Inc.*, December 10, 2006, http://radar.oreilly.com/archives/2006/12/web_20_compact.html, accessed January 27, 2008.
[4] Ibid

"…users rely on fellow members, whose advice is found in online forums. The Dating & Advice category listed more than 320,000 posts, making up in sheer quantity what it lacked in a soothing live presence available by phone."[5] However, this also meant that users had to be willing to comb through the wide array of content before finding the information they needed. Therefore, while the growth of Web 2.0 aided Frind in achieving his goal of allowing users to drive the website, this setup raised questions about the quality of content being provided.

Despite it, the site had proven popular, with more than three million members in January 2008—double the membership in the past year, and despite an attrition rate of 30 per cent of members per month who were purged from the site for inactivity. These members generated traffic volume of more than 600,000 unique logins per day, and more than 1.5 billion page views per month (an average of roughly 50 million page views per day!). PlentyofFish had managed to grow its membership not only in number, but in terms of active members, despite the growing number of alternative online dating services. This was especially appealing to advertisers.

With the overwhelming supply of online dating sites in the market, one had to marvel at what set PlentyofFish apart: PlentyofFish had built an engaged, passionate community of users who felt emotionally attached to the site. This created high switching costs for users as well as allowing PlentyofFish to benefit from network effects.

PlentyofFish was sustained by revenue from companies advertising on the site. The advertising mix currently returned an estimated $10 million per year through banner ads, Google ads (AdSense), and affiliated dating sites. Ads sent users to other sites, even other dating sites, which in turn generated revenue for PlentyofFish. For example, when a user clicked on a banner ad for a dating and relationship book, PlentyofFish might receive the full revenue from the sale of the book as the advertiser gained another customer who might become profitable. In this way, the other site cheaply outsourced customer acquisition to PlentyofFish.

The Technology Behind PlentyofFish—ASP.NET

While Frind originally created the site to learn the ASP.NET web application framework, it was still being used for PlentyofFish in 2008. Frind claimed that he had stuck with using ASP.NET "because it's trivial and easy and gets the job done."[6] Additionally, Frind believed that he had "gotten really, really good at it" pointing out that, "(what he had) done is about 10 to 20 times more efficient than what anybody else has done with ASP.NET."[7] In fact, PlentyofFish had grown to the scale where "nothing can be brought off the shelf and everything must be built from the ground up."[8] Therefore, while there was no one software package that could accommodate PlentyofFish's needs, Frind believed that he could adapt ASP.NET to meet its needs

---

[5]Randall Stross, "From 10 hours a Week, $10 million a Year," *NY Times [US]*, January 13, 2008, http://www.nytimes.com/2008/01/13/business/13digi.html?_r=2&scp=1&sq=plenty+of+fish&st=nyt&oref=slogin&oref=slogin, accessed January 22, 2008.

[6]Plentyoffish.com, "Changing the Online Dating Industry," *Plentyoffish Media Inc.* http://www.PlentyofFish.com/about_team.aspx, accessed January 27, 2008.

[7]Ibid

[8]Markus Frind, "The Paradigm Shift—Adapt or Die," *Plentyoffish Media Inc.* http://PlentyofFish.wordpress.com/2007/08/08/looking-for-3-senior-software-developers, accessed January 27, 2008.

In June 2006, when PlentyofFish was receiving approximately "500 million page views a month," Frind believed that he would have "no problem running it by (himself) even if it gets to three times its current size."[9] This stemmed from his belief that he could be successful in automating more and more as the site grew. In early 2008, PlentyofFish was serving 1.2 billion page views.

ASP.NET coding enabled the site to maintain itself through automated recognition of spam on its forums and the allowance of user-screening for the thousands of photos uploaded daily. This combination of site automation and user engagement made it possible for only one person to operate the site. For example, the "Love and Dating" forum had 320,000+ posts in January, 2008, all of which had to be monitored for unwanted postings and spam. Frind had been able to effectively rid his site of spam by refining "a formula for analysing customer feedback and arriving at a determination of whether a given forum post is spam and should automatically be deleted."[10] Posted photos were checked by users to ensure they did not contain nudity and were of a person. In fact, some 120 "member volunteers"—unpaid members dedicated to monitoring photographs posted to the site—reportedly checked 100,000 photos each year. The founder explained this behaviour as a means of giving back to the free site: "Lots of people feel they want to give back to the site because it is free."[11] Frind likened this automation to putting his website on autopilot, with users supporting themselves through online forums, while receiving minimal support from the site administrator.

Servers

PoF was able to minimize the amount of servers it employed by being more efficient. Frind stated that he used "one web server, one mail server, two database servers now and a couple of little web servers to run the Userplane instant messenger. So under 10 but I've started to scale up."[12] To bring this into perspective, similar social networking sites such as Friendster and AmericanSingles.com (with less traffic) used 200 servers each. Having fewer servers meant that there was less or in Frind's case, no need to employ technicians to ensure that the servers were kept up and running. This translated to significantly lower operating costs.

PoF's servers ran on SQL Server 2005. The growth of the website meant that they would need to add new servers. In February 27, 2008, Microsoft released a number of upgrades—Windows Server 2008, Visual Studio 2008, and SQL Server 2008. Frind's need to add additional servers in the near future meant that he would likely have to make a decision on which servers—SQL server 2005 or 2008—to employ. With Frind's heavy reliance on creating efficiencies for his website, could he afford to wait to employ SQL Server 2008? Conversely, if he did switch to SQL

---

[9] Richard Macmanus, "Plenty of Cash for one-man band," ReadWriteWeb.com, June 10, 2006 http://www.readwriteweb.com/archives/plenty_of_cash.php, accessed January 27, 2008.

[10] Randall Stross, "From 10 hours a Week, $10 million a Year," *NY Times [US]*, January 13, 2008, http://www.nytimes.com/2008/01/13/business/13digi.html?_r=2&scp=1&sq=plenty+of+fish&st=nyt&oref=slogin&oref=slogin, accessed January 22, 2008.

[11] Randall Stross, "From 10 hours a Week, $10 million a Year," *NY Times [US]*, January 13, 2008, http://www.nytimes.com/2008/01/13/business/13digi.html?_r=2&scp=1&sq=plenty+of+fish&st=nyt&oref=slogin&oref=slogin, accessed January 22, 2008.

[12] Plentyoffish.com, "Changing the Online Dating Industry," Plentyoffish Media Inc. http://www.PlentyofFish.com/about_team.aspx, accessed January 27, 2008.

Server 2008, could he afford to work out the kinks which might ultimately cause problems for the site?

Scalability

At the heart of most database applications was a database management system (DBMS). For most mid-to-large scale databases this was either Oracle or Microsoft SQL Server. Understanding the nuanced differences between the two products could be difficult for even the most seasoned database professional. One very important difference between the two was that SQL Server ran only on the Windows platform, while Oracle ran on a variety of platforms like UNIX or Linux.

Frind's choice for a DBMS was SQL Server 2005, but other popular sites, such as Craigslist, had chosen Oracle to manage their databases. Craigslist received over nine billion page views per month. This was six times the number of page views that PoF received.

On the issue of scalability, there were two basic concepts—scaling up and scaling out. Scaling up meant adding additional expensive hardware to handle higher loads, while scaling out meant distributing the load using low cost multiple servers. Frind needed to consider what route he wanted to take if he continued to grow. Would he be able to achieve the scale that Oracle allowed for Craigslist, with SQL Server 2005 as PlentyofFish's DBMS?

The PlentyofFish User Experience

From the moment that you entered the website, until the moment you left, you were bombarded by pictures of users of the site. Intrigued by the fuzzy and distorted photos, one click and you were viewing a user's profile page. Simplistic in design, the profile page offered information such as height, age, body type and ethnicity. You read the brief description and curiously continued to scroll down the page. More pictures of your "fish" appeared and as you ran your cursor over each one, they expanded to give a much larger, clearer view. Hooked, you might have thought "How can I meet this attractive and witty individual?"

In order to contact any of the 600,000 "fish," a user first had to become a member. This was easily done by moving through the registration screens—two very simple and user-friendly pages. The entire process took only a couple of minutes to complete and the majority of information requested (aside from secure information such as a password) was presented on a profile page. By accurately representing themselves with respect to age, location and preferences, the user was instantly given the opportunity to connect with potential matches in the immediate area that were similar. The prospect of meeting new people immediately was one of the most important driving factors for the website's popularity.

This ability to connect with others so readily had been leveraged by PlentyofFish to create the company's successful online dating community. The longer the user was active, the greater the chance of building a network and finding the "right" match. This idea was reinforced by PlentyofFish's design, which matched users that would be most interested in each other based on their past messaging and searches. Moreover, new users were constantly adding themselves to the website's profile database, creating a new source of people to meet. Thus, how deep a "fish" chose to swim in the virtual community pool was user-determined.

Catching a Fish

Once the user had initiated contact or been contacted, the process of communication was quite simple. Assuming that the parties involved fulfilled the requirements outlined by the other individual such as age range or more specifically, "must not be looking for an intimate encounter," the user could openly send and receive messages. These messages were placed directly in the inbox and easily accessible as the system was similar in design to many other email platforms. Frind had also recently added a VoIP (voice-over-Internet protocol) which allowed users to send voice messages to other members as well.[13] This ease of use allowed members to immediately "jump into the pool," establishing online conversations with whomever they chose. The type of message sent—voice, email or instant message—was entirely up to the user.

However, not every match that a user made was going to be positive. Even the most optimistic user might have run into individuals that were rude, creepy or downright shocking. Thus, the user had to wade through the pools looking for "fish" that met their needs. If the user did establish contact with a disreputable individual they could block that other user. However, if someone was bent on creating havoc, a new user profile could always be created. There were no user services available to help deal with these types of issues, which made it difficult to fix any problems that did occur. In this sense, PlentyofFish could be thought of as the Wild West of online dating, whereby users policed themselves.

What was Lurking in the Sea?

There were several forces that posed serious threats to PlentyofFish. A significant force that PlentyofFish had to contend with was the threat of new entry. The capital, or rather lack of capital, required to start a dating site similar to that of PlentyofFish was minimal. All that one needed was the purchase of a domain name and servers to hold information. This meant that there were numerous potential competitors, ranging from major corporations such as Google to minor ones such as freelance web designers. Also, despite the scale that PlentyofFish had been able to achieve, there were no cost disadvantages for any new competitors. A second threat to PlentyofFish was from other, unrelated sites. While sites such as Craigslist and Facebook were not seen as dating sites, they had each branched into that area to attract more users. Craigslist had a personals section while Facebook added dating applications to its site. Dating sites, such as PlentyofFish, also had to contend with fierce rivalry from its current competitors. Whether they were first movers such as Lavalife or niche players such as HonestyOnline, the market for dating sites was becoming increasingly saturated. With spectacular success stories such as PlentyofFish, one could only expect firm rivalries to become more intense.

OTHER VIRTUAL COMMUNITIES

Friendster

With more than 58 million members worldwide, Friendster was the pioneer in the field of social networking. Driven by simplicity, Friendster prided itself on delivering

---

[13] Matt Harley, "Money and relationships: It's Love 3.0," *The Globe and Mail*, February 14, 2008, pp. B1 & B6.

a clean, user-friendly and interactive environment where users could easily connect with anyone around the world. Friendster targeted the 25-and-under market with no professional or group affiliation. Friendster set itself apart by being the first at introducing innovative features such as a network graph server, as well as launching a choice of languages to navigate the site, thus expanding its ability to tap non-English markets. Friendster continued to innovate and recently expanded its targeted demographic to include older adults.

LinkedIn

LinkedIn was an online network of more than 17 million professionals from around the world, representing over 150 industries. LinkedIn prided itself on claiming that it was not networking—it was what networking should be. The mission of the website was to help the user be more effective in their work and open doors to opportunities using the professional relationships they already had.

The registration process for LinkedIn closely resembled completing a professional resume. LinkedIn focused on information such as current or most recent job position, job industry, past experience, and professional overview. Firms used this site to keep internal and remote employees connected with each other, search out potential employees and as a knowledge management site where they could compare their job postings to their competitors'.

Members could join LinkedIn through invitations or by starting a network of their own. LinkedIn was not purely a free service, but rather offered levels of service ranging from free membership to premium accounts that charged users anywhere from $19.95 to $200 a month. In 2007, LinkedIn was the fourth most popular networking website, behind Yahoo 360, MySpace and Facebook.

Facebook

Facebook was a social utility that connected people through its website, requiring only a valid email address to register. To connect with coworkers or classmates, members used their school or work email addresses to join a network. Since its launch in February 2004, Facebook enrolled over 63 million users worldwide.

Facebook was completely free, and like PoF supported by ads. In August 2006 Facebook signed a three-year deal with Microsoft to provide and sell ads on their site in return for a revenue split. The deal followed an announcement from Facebook's direct competitor, MySpace who signed a similar deal with Google. The youthful demographic that both services attracted was highly prized amongst advertisers and a number of companies were eager to jump on the bandwagon. In July of 2006, Apple signed an agreement with Facebook to give away 10 million free iTunes samplers to Facebook members. There was even rumor of a Facebook credit card.

MySpace

MySpace was an online community that encouraged its members to create their "own" space online reflecting their personality in music, movies, photos, journal entries and interests that they might share with their growing network of friends. MySpace was for everyone—from friends to family, from singles to colleagues and from classmates to those looking for long lost friends. Although MySpace called itself a private community it gained great popularity through the increasing number of bands using this site to get their music heard and to connect with fans. Even Presidential candidates, such as Hillary Clinton, used MySpace as a means to journal their days on the campaign trail. MySpace was constantly expanding rapidly all over the world with the latest addition being China in 2007.

LISTING SITES

Craigslist

Craigslist was much like other social networking sites in its structure and revenue generation, operating as a hub that aggregated buyers and sellers. One of the top 10 busiest English language sites in the world, Craigslist was a free website which offered very little customer support. Since it only employed 25 staff, they only fixed problems sporadically, requiring users to serve themselves or request other members' assistance. Craigslist served buyers and sellers in 50 countries and 450 localities. Their sites generated 10 billion total page views and six million unique visitors a month, more than any other site of its kind. Craigslist, like other listing sites, charged fees for a few of its listings but did not contain commercial listings other than postings.

DATING SITES

Match.com

Launched in 1995, Match.com was an online dating site that charged for its service. It brought people together by creating the opportunity for them to post their profiles and pictures for others to view. With more than 15 million members worldwide, members of the site had the ability to interact with an enormous group of potential matches. Match.com was available on six different continents, in 30 different countries, and 18 different languages. This large scale approach increased members' chances of finding the person and relationship they were searching for. Match.com estimated 200,000 people entered into relationships because of the site. If, however, a member was finding it hard to find a match then he or she could browse through Match.com's free online magazine, Happen. This magazine contained helpful articles about romance, sex and relationships. Although communication between members required a fee, Match.com allowed visitors to browse the extensive library of profiles and pictures. This gave prospective users a sneak peak at the types of matches available to them if they joined. The site provided secure and anonymous interactions between members whether they communicated via email, instant messaging or audio and video. In addition to the traditional online communications, the company also offered a wireless dating experience whereby members could match via their cellular phones.

Sink or Swim?

There were several challenges that PlentyofFish might have to face, the most obvious of which was competition. The PlentyofFish website was also replete with unfinished patches and quirks that made the site visually unappealing.

Should Frind expand PlentyofFish globally? Should he follow the likes of Friendster and MySpace and develop sites in Korean, Japanese, Chinese and other languages? Should he increase the number of applications available on the site? If he did so, should he imitate Facebook and invite third-party developers to provide applications suited to his target market?

To increase or protect revenues, Frind could change the membership structure of the site to have members pay for basic access and optional services. If he chose to add these functions or features would ASP.NET be sufficient? If PlentyofFish continued to grow at its current rate would SQL Server 2005 or 2008 handle the load? To what extent did the business need to invest in new technology?

As commuters scrambled to get to work during the Monday morning rush hour, some of them might have thought of what it was like to be Markus Frind—not having to work 9 to 5. Frind had nicely summed up the situation he had created for himself, stating: "Most of the time I don't have to do anything."[14] Would this continue to be the case, or did he need to invest substantial time, money and effort in protecting his business? After five successful years of operation, had PlentyofFish run its course?

---

[14] Randall Stross, "From 10 hours a Week, $10 million a Year," *NY Times [US]*, January 13, 2008, http://www.nytimes.com/2008/01/13/business/13digi.html?_r=2&scp=1&sq=plenty+of+fish&st=nyt&oref=slogin&oref=slogin, accessed January 22, 2008.

MacTara Limited and the Wood Products Industry in Nova Scotia

On a sunny mid-September morning in 2007, Rick Shaver was driving from his home in Pictou County to his job as comptroller of MacTara Limited (MacTara) in Upper Musquodoboit, Nova Scotia, Canada. During the long drive to work, Shaver was preparing himself for the second day of the strategic planning retreat that he and other senior managers were holding. Shaver kept thinking about the best way to facilitate the session he was going to lead that morning. He felt that while there were some very good opportunities for MacTara in some sectors like wood pellets, the Canadian lumber industry as a whole was being squeezed on all sides. The fact that MacTara was a somewhat vertically integrated company—from construction lumber, to chips for use by pulp and paper mills, and fuel pellets made out of wood waste—meant that the health of each sector impacted on the prospects for the others. Shaver kept thinking to himself, "How can we make all the pieces of the puzzle fit together while we still have money and time?"

MACTARA'S ORIGINS

Hugh Layton Erskine, an experienced Nova Scotian timberland contractor, founded MacTara Limited in 1968. The company quickly became Nova Scotia's largest sawmill. Through the 1970s, '80s and early '90s, the company enjoyed considerable success and followed a course of sustained growth. Buoyed by a favourable exchange rate on the U.S. dollar and by strong, stable lumber prices, the 1990s witnessed a period of considerable prosperity and exponential growth for the company. In the mid-1990s, a new stud mill and planer mill were built, adding in excess of 30 million board feet to the plant's capacity thus creating a total production capacity of

Version: (A) 2007-12-12

Richard Ivey School of Business
The University of Western Ontario

180 million board feet of lumber. MacTara also acquired 41,000 hectares of timber-lands as a raw material source.

In 1997, MacTara was producing lumber at a level that by-produced 200,000 tonnes of waste bark a year. Disposal of that waste represented a significant problem for MacTara since, at that time, it had no practical use or market for the waste and it had to be disposed of somehow. Since one of the company's primary goals was to produce marketable products from 100 per cent of the logs it processed in an economically and environmentally friendly manner, the company was open to considering projects that could make usable products out of the waste. That same year, U.S.-based Fulghum Industries sold MacTara a crane and serendipitously gave the mill an environmentally friendly and financially attractive method of disposing of its bark waste. Affiliates of Fulghum Industries had secured funding for the construction of a pellet mill in the state of Georgia and were looking for about 200,000 tonnes of bark to turn into pellets. Overseas pellet transportation required the kind of deep-water port that Halifax could provide. Given the complementary interests of the two companies, and the strategic location of Halifax's port, MacTara and Fulghum entered into an agreement whereby MacTara would build and operate a wood pellet mill in Nova Scotia, and Fulghum would act as an export sales agent. MacTara would produce the pellets from the waste of its sawmill operations and Fulghum Fiber Fuels would act as the sales agent for European sales. In order to reduce risk, before the mill construction even began, a contract was obtained to export the bulk of the pellet mill's anticipated production to a European customer. In 1998 a pellet mill, the second of its kind in the world, was built across the street from MacTara's sawmill at a cost in excess of $10 million.

For a small rural Nova Scotia company in the lumber industry, MacTara had a sophisticated corporate social responsibility (CSR) agenda. In the 1990s, MacTara and several other local forests product companies developed a Forest Stewardship Agreement whereby woodlots were to be managed through sound "silviculture"[1] as a way to help build a strong, sustainable forest industry in Nova Scotia along with a stable high quality supply of raw material. In September 1997, MacTara launched an Excellence Refinement and Accountability (ERA) program that audited, monitored and documented all aspects of MacTara's forest operations, from planning and harvesting to trucking. The goals of the program were to: protect the environment, protect the people living and working in the environment, promote sustainable forest management, monitor and manage results, document all aspects of forest operation, be compliant, promote an organized and consistent approach for forest operations, and promote constant enhancement of the ERA system. In addition to maintaining an eco-efficient approach to lumber production and the sustainable treatment of forests, MacTara strived to contribute directly to the well-being of its local community by supporting community activities through philanthropic contributions.

Hugh Erskine had managed to design a company that was able to grow and harvest a portion of its own raw material in a sustainable manner, efficiently process logs into lumber for export to the United States, sell chips to Nova Scotian paper mills, and convert the waste into wood pellets destined for the European fuel market. In 1999, Mr. Erskine was awarded the title "Master Entrepreneur of the Year" in Atlantic Canada.

---

[1] Silviculture is the art and science of growing a forest.

PRODUCTION PROCESS—FROM SUSTAINABLE FORESTS TO LUMBER TO PELLETS

Logs

Most of MacTara's logs came from northern and eastern Nova Scotia. Some logs came from government-owned Crown land, and some were acquired from private owners. MacTara also bought logs through a Fibre Agreement with local pulp mills whereby MacTara purchased logs for a price significantly lower than the private-purchase market and, in return, sold the pulp mill the equivalent volume (tonne for tonne) in wood chips for paper making, at a below-market price. Many of these timberlands were managed under the silviculture principles outlined by the Forest Stewardship Agreement.

For some time, MacTara's own woodlots supplied a portion of the logs used by the mill. Though the purchase of the initial 44,000 hectares was meant to first be the cornerstone of a much larger woodlot ownership plan, the company was never able to assemble enough land to make this strategy viable. The land was sold in 2004.

Milling

Once received at the mill, logs were put through technologically advanced computerized sawmill equipment designed to get the highest yield from every log. After the bark was stripped from the logs in the wood-room, logs were transported on conveyor belts to the sawmill or the stud-mill. The sawmill produced random-length boards and the stud-mill produced stud-length boards. The lumber was then conveyed to the kilns where it was dried, and subsequently sent on to one of two planer-mills where it was dressed. Only the higher-grade lumber was then wrapped. MacTara produced mostly two-inch random- and stud-length lumber. Additionally, the mill produced one-inch lumber with any "sawable" material that could not be made into two-inch boards.

In 2006, the mill produced 130 million board feet of finished, kiln-dried lumber, about two-thirds of the lumber mill's maximum production capacity. For many years the local eastern Canadian market had been of insufficient size to absorb all of MacTara's production. In response, the company had to develop export markets for its lumber. By 1997, 98 per cent of MacTara's lumber production went via rail and truck to the United States, mainly to the mid-Atlantic states. The cost of shipping made expansion into more distant markets unattractive because lumber was traditionally sold on a delivered basis (the shipping cost being netted against the mill's eventual proceeds of sale).

Wood By-products—Chips, Shavings, Sawdust Wood Pellets

The company was committed to finding uses for 100 per cent of its raw material's biomass. Exhibit 1 shows a listing of product lines and Exhibit 2 shows log/product ratios. Chips were sold to paper mills, shavings and sawdust were used to kiln-dry its own wood, and bark and sawdust were used to make wood pellets. Since 2000, however, the mill was producing at less than capacity and therefore residues were not being produced in the volumes originally expected. As a result, the company found that it had to purchase additional material to make into pellets. Typically, this supplementary material was purchased from other sawmills and then trucked to the pellet mill in Upper Musquodoboit for processing.

In order to make pellets, the bark was dried, ground into a powder and then compressed into a pellet held together by about six per cent residual moisture; nothing else was added. By comparison, the raw material consisted of about 40 per cent moisture. As a result, it was more cost-effective to transport finished pellets since the water content of the raw material was not being transported. Wood pellets were trucked to the port of Halifax where they were put in grain elevators to await ocean shipment to industrial clients in Europe. Rising shipping rates were beginning to present a challenge, thanks to new competition for ocean freight capacity from the emerging economies of China and India. In 2006, 85,000 metric tonnes of wood pellets were produced, representing the pellet mill's effective production capacity as currently configured. Historically, the two major three-year U.S.-denominated contracts with the mill were from the Netherlands and Sweden. Sweden's contract matured in November 2006 and the Netherlands' contract would mature in September 2007. For a variety of reasons, when Sweden's contract matured, MacTara chose to sell most of its production to the Netherlands. MacTara extended its contract with the Netherlands when it matured.

After showing remarkably little movement for most of the time since the pellet mill was built, beginning in late 2004 and 2005 pellet prices began to become increasingly volatile, rising in response to environmental concerns, high fossil fuel prices and Kyoto Agreement-inspired government policy in Europe. Having sold for less than US$100 in the late '90s, prices rose to above US$100 by 2003 and the market price continued to rise thereafter. Although locked into multi-year contracts, MacTara was able to obtain pricing of US$145 from its Swedish customer for shipments beyond contract. Similarly, prices for the Dutch customer, while still under contract, rose from US$103 to US$115 in 2006 and to US$130 for the period ended August 2007. All prices were freight on board (FOB) destination and, therefore, inclusive of freight, which was the responsibility of MacTara. In 2007, a contract was negotiated with a new German customer for a price of US$145 FOB, with Halifax thereby passing the ocean freight burden on to the customer. While contracts like this were attractive, there was little doubt that customers would seek to offset rising ocean freight costs by reducing the price paid to MacTara for pellets. Furthermore, despite rising prices, contracts would likely continue to be denominated in U.S. dollars, the value of which has been falling drastically against the Canadian dollar. All of MacTara's costs, naturally, would continue to be in Canadian dollars. The net result would be an undermining of the net gain.

Challenges in the 21st Century

The early years of the 21st century were very rough for MacTara, as well as for the Canadian lumber industry as a whole. Like all commodities, lumber has fluctuating prices. The decline in lumber prices, which began in 2000 and accelerated following the terrorist attacks of September 2001, hurt the income stream of lumber producers in the early 2000s. Lumber prices did improve in 2004, given strong demand in the United States for lumber destined for reconstruction of the areas devastated by the major hurricanes of 2004 and 2005. However, demand dropped in 2006 and early 2007, and prices declined once again (see Exhibit 3).

Both MacTara's lumber and pellet export sales were denominated in U.S. dollars. While lumber prices fluctuated, wood pellet prices were fixed through three- to five-year supply contracts. A steady decline in the value of the U.S. dollar against the Canadian dollar from nearly Cdn$1.60 in 2001/2002 to less than Cdn$1.17 in February 2007 further reduced financial returns for the company by reducing the income stream in Canadian dollars derived from product sales denominated in U.S. dollars. The value of the U.S. dollar was expected to continue to drop and the two currencies were forecasted to reach par by late 2007. Starting in 2006, the sub-prime mortgage financial crisis in the United States caused a wave of property foreclosures, creating a glut in the housing market. This further reduced the need for new home construction and, in turn, the demand for construction lumber. Despite falling demand, lumber production in Canada was not proportionately reduced. In fact, shipments into the United States increased as British Columbia mills attempted to harvest, process and ship timber being destroyed by a pine beetle infestation.

Fortunately, the price of pellets was expected to continue rising because of increased demand resulting from factors such as the Kyoto Agreement, increases in oil prices, the new emphasis on the search for alternative fuels in the United States, Canada and Europe, changes in energy regulatory environments and tax structures in the European Union (EU) favoring wood pellet use, etc. Though the increased demand for wood pellets put upward pressure on prices, for MacTara, increasing the production volume of pellets to meet that demand had the perverse effect of putting downward pressure on margins. At MacTara, wood pellet margins depended on internally sourced bark, which was subject to an internal transfer price of less than $10 dollars per tonne. The effective cost of this material rose to closer to $12 per tonne by 2007. Furthermore, additional capacity reduction at MacTara in response to low lumber prices and a rising Canadian dollar had further reduced the supply of internally produced material available to the pellet mill. Any additional pellet production would require externally sourced bark.

In the early years of wood pellet production, bark was considered a waste product and bark from outside suppliers was comparable to the internal cost plus the cost of transportation, which was about as much as the cost of the bark itself. As the cost of energy escalated in the 1990s, wood mills and other industrial producers started using bark to produce heat and electricity. Once their own internal power needs were met, they sold the extra electricity to the Nova Scotia Power grid in co-production agreements. Bark, once a waste product sold at cost, was rapidly becoming an escalating commodity and by 2006, the cost of the external bark supplies had increased to about Cdn$15 per tonne and the transportation cost had increased to about Cdn$18 to $22 per tonne. The combined cost of external bark and transportation of the bark to MacTara's facilities fluctuated around Cdn$30 to $40 per tonne. By 2007, the net effect of larger volumes of higher priced, externally sourced bark (bought in Canadian dollars) and fixed-priced wood pellets contract sales (denominated in U.S. dollars) was to reduce wood pellets margins significantly.

A substantial increase in worldwide demand for wood pellets could also bring additional risks. Though pellets were a value-added product for MacTara, they were fundamentally undifferentiated, and with high levels of worldwide demand, new suppliers would enter the market, turning pellets into a commodity subject to the same risks of commodity pricing as lumber.

The long-standing Canada–U.S. softwood lumber dispute erupted once again in 2002 (see Exhibit 4). The United States imposed an eight per cent duty on Canadian lumber exports to the United States affecting nearly all of MacTara's lumber sales.

These duties cost the company over Cdn$9 million. In 2006, MacTara was able to recuperate more than Cdn$5 million of held-back duties as part of the dispute settlement terms. However, MacTara was not the only mill to recover held-back duties. This sudden cash injection saved from bankruptcy many inefficient mills in Atlantic Canada and British Columbia (B.C.) that would otherwise have exited the industry. The oversupply of B.C. lumber resulting from the pine beetle infestation exacerbated the supply/demand imbalance in the industry even further. In addition to the immediate damaging effect on prices of this imbalance, the results would almost certainly lead to a revival of the Canada–U.S. softwood lumber dispute and potentially a return of the duties.

The wood chip business also faced challenges. The local pulp mills that provided MacTara with logs at below-market prices in exchange for chips (Fibre Agreement) were beginning to feel the effects of new sources of competition. Brazilian pulp mills had lower cost structures and cheaper paper prices because they used eucalyptus trees grown in only seven years in a tropical climate, as opposed to the 70 years or so that it took to grow a softwood tree in Canada. A severe downturn in the production volumes of Nova Scotian pulp mills would mean that MacTara would have to find alternative uses for the wood chips it sold to these mills. Although these chips could be used to make pellets, the raw material cost would be considerably higher than current sources, perhaps even prohibitively expensive.

MacTara also suffered a number of misfortunes specific to the company. In 2002, the company's lumber broker went bankrupt, which cost the company several million dollars. That same year, severe flooding destroyed all five bridges leading to the company, affecting the movement of all material in and out of the mill for several weeks. In 2003 and 2004, pellet production was suspended for several weeks as a result of separate incidents that affected the storage and shipping facilities at the Port of Halifax. Hurricane Juan in September of 2003 disrupted operations in the province's woodlands, compromising MacTara's future raw material supply. Winter storms and severely cold weather frequently disrupted MacTara operations.

As a result of challenges in the industry and those specific to MacTara, by February of 2003 the company's financial condition had deteriorated to its lowest point ever. To address these challenges, the company took a number of actions to restructure the operation, including the sale of its timberlands, renegotiation of a number of loans, and a cash injection by a new equity partner. The recovery process was assisted by several months of higher lumber prices during the second quarter of 2004 and by MacTara's sale of 44,000 acres of land in the same year.

In May 2004 the company completely re-engineered its management and operations with the objective of increasing strategic responsiveness and competitive advantage, as well as enhancing profitability. Ongoing operations were placed under the guidance of Gordon Shuppe, president and chief executive officer, and a team of seven senior managers. Hugh Layton Erskine remained on the board of directors and was often called upon to provide expert advice. A feature of the new management style at MacTara was the creation of internal committees with specific but flexible mandates. Though company executives were now committed to proactive planning, they would have to overcome the legacy of managing a commodity product—being a reactive price taker at the mercy of market conditions beyond their control. By late 2004, the restructuring of ownership and the overhaul of the management processes improved the financial position of the company, providing the company a chance to stay in business.

ADDITIONAL PRODUCT-MARKET CONSIDERATIONS FOR THE STRATEGIC PLAN

Lumber

In 2007, the Atlantic Canadian lumber industry was in crisis. Mills like MacTara could neither increase the lumber prices nor reverse the decline of the U.S. dollar. Only a natural disaster like Hurricane Katrina was likely to create a surge in demand in the U.S. construction market and even that would unlikely be large enough or prolonged enough to correct the market imbalance.

Given the vagaries of exchange rates, commodity prices and, to a lesser extent, the rising cost of external bark supplies, the only financial parameter that the company could control directly was the cost of production. MacTara's production costs (overhead, electricity, repairs and maintenance, labour) were primarily "stepped fixed costs"—costs that remained constant until a certain new level of production was reached. Therefore, the cost structure could only be affected by dramatic reductions in production volume.

Many lumberyards had reduced lumber production dramatically or even shut down temporarily as a way to stave off the problems in the lumber industry. Some will never reopen. However, for MacTara, this was not an option. A drastic reduction in lumber production volumes would hurt the pellet business because pellet margins depended on the internal supply of bark. In late 2006, the company did reduce its volume from 140 million board feet to 80 million board feet and went from two shifts to only one shift.

Value-added lumber products could provide a way to maintain volume and increase margins. In addition, should there be another softwood lumber dispute with the United States, value-added products would avoid softwood lumber duties. MacTara had explored a number of options (see Exhibit 5). Whichever market they chose to enter would require a large capital expenditure in order to retool, and the hiring of a sales and marketing team.

The liquidation of Shaw Lumber in 2006, a Nova Scotian wood products company, gave MacTara a window through which to enter the value-added products market. MacTara bought a specialized molder from Shaw for approximately Cdn$100,000 installed. The molder could produce lumber products with the different profiles (shapes) that a number of the value-added products under consideration would require. Also, MacTara's existing lumber production facilities could be easily and inexpensively adjusted to produce dimensional lumber measured in the metric system for the British market. The market dynamics of the British market were somewhat different from that of the United States. Though lumber was sold as an undifferentiated commodity in the United States, lumberyards in the United Kingdom preferred branded products that they could rely on. Entrance requirements for the British market would include the development of the MacTara brand of products and the design of a quality-conscious distribution system that could build long-term relationships with British lumber merchants. Since MacTara lacked marketing expertise, one possibility would be to enlist MacTara's European lumber broker, Weyerhaeuser, as a representative and distributor.

Though the return of the softwood lumber dispute duties was certainly welcomed by a cash-starved industry, it could not stave off for long the impending bankruptcy of many weaker mills. Like many fractured mature industries, the Atlantic Canadian lumber industry was ripe for consolidation. A large mill like MacTara could lead this effort. The main obstacle was going to be to find either private or public investors willing to risk their capital in an industry in dire straits. The industry did provide many rural jobs; therefore, an appeal to the Nova Scotia government might have some success.

Wood Pellets

The future of the wood pellet market in Europe and in North America would depend to a great extent on the intensity of the search for alternative fuels from renewable sources for heat and electricity production. The price of oil and gas, as well as political pressure arising from environmental considerations, would be a key determinant in the Canadian government's willingness to support alternative fuel research and development investments, as well as tax credit and subsidy supports. Energy costs would also be a key determinant in the willingness of industrial, commercial, municipal and residential consumers to change their heating source consumption patterns. For eastern Canadian markets, besides being a sustainable and renewable clean fuel, MacTara pellets would have the added advantage of being locally produced and a good alternative to the current widespread use of coal in electricity generation.

Pellet fuel would have to compete with alternatives such as wind and solar power. Wind power was easy to generate in eastern Canada and was a truly renewable resource. Common complaints about wind power, however, were that the turbines were unsightly, created noise, disrupted bird migration patterns, were expensive to build and consumed a lot of energy to manufacture and install. In addition, for every unit of electricity generated by wind mills, utilities were mandated to have a parallel capacity able to produce the same number of units by means other than wind in order to ensure steady levels of electricity production should there not be enough wind to turn the windmills and electricity-generating turbines. Despite all of these drawbacks, major wind power projects were being developed in many parts of the world, including the Maritimes. Solar power was also a plentiful renewable resource. In 2007, however, solar power was expensive and required much maintenance and had not been used on a grand scale. The technology for pellet fuel, in contrast, was much more mature than that for wind and solar power, and furnace conversion was quite easy. The selling point for pellet fuel was its usefulness as an alternative, green, renewable energy source. All alternative technologies had some environmental drawbacks. A caveat to the "greenness" of pellet fuel was the need for the proper care of the forests that supplied the logs for pellet production. Nonetheless, the use of pellets as a fuel source in the domestic market was very new. The technology was not in widespread use, or available, and the concept did not enjoy widespread public recognition.

Further penetration of European pellet markets continued to be an alternative. The political environment in Europe promoted the use of alternative, green energy sources, especially those generated from renewable resources such as wood. European governments also allowed tax credits for companies, municipalities and individuals who used pellet fuel. In addition, the technology and logistics system for utilizing pellets as a heating source was much more advanced in Europe than in North America. In places like Sweden and the Netherlands, pellets were burned at large municipal heating plants and the heat was then piped to other buildings in the municipality. Many Europeans also heated their homes with pellet furnaces. The pellets were delivered to their homes with a similar distribution chain to that of home heating oil in North America.

Inexpensive, although often lower quality, Russian and Baltic wood products, including pellets, were likely to enter the European market soon and it behooved the company to diversify its client base.

If the Canadian federal or provincial governments were to issue tax credits for green fuels, as European governments did, a wood pellet fuel market could be developed quickly. A widespread change to pellet heating, however, would require, in addition to public acceptance, installation of pellet furnaces in residential, commercial and industrial markets and the creation of an efficient and reliable pellet-delivery channel.

The eastern Canadian wood pellet consumer market was small and was already served by bagged, white wood pellets. White wood pellets, made locally from sawdust, had an advantage over bark pellets—they left less residue than bark pellets. MacTara used most of its sawdust to fuel the kiln and it would be difficult to completely re-engineer this process in order to use the sawdust for white pellets. To compete in either the white or bark pellet residential market the company would also have to invest in a packaging process or partner with an existing company that had that capacity.

The eastern Canadian industrial market would be more attractive than the consumer market because of its size and structure. As in Europe, local municipal heating plants could burn pellets if adapted. The easiest systems to morph into a pellet burning system were those that used "Bunker C," heavy oil and coal. Pellets could also be used effectively to replace or complement coal-burning systems. There were some possible upcoming showcase opportunities for new local institutions that could be heated by a pellet furnace burning MacTara pellets. For example, Halifax was considering building a new sports stadium, central library and art college. MacTara could capitalize on these local showcase opportunities if it managed to garner marketing and research and development know-how.

No matter which market it chose to pursue, MacTara would have to resolve its bark supply constraints. Since MacTara owned the only pellet mill in the region, one option open to the company was to convince other lumber mills to provide the company with bark at more favorable prices in return for participation in the growth of the wood pellet industry. If MacTara were to lead an industry consolidation process it would be able to source larger volumes of internally produced bark. This lower cost structure would allow it sufficient margin with which to take advantage of the growth of the pellet market. Management was considering expanding capacity to meet the rising demand and was reviewing preliminary plans for a series of pellet mills of varying sizes, closer to the source of the bark than MacTara's large mill. The company would have to move quickly since many mills were reducing production volumes or simply shutting down for good.

The recent reduction in wood pellet margins had forced MacTara executives to consider alternative uses for the bark and other wood waste. The company could perhaps sell some of its bark to customers that use bark for their electricity production and co-production. This option was not attractive because, as a value-added product, pellet sales delivered a better margin than bark sales. MacTara could also turn the pellet mill into an electricity co-generation plant that burned bark or powder. The pellet operation could conceivably function alone in conjunction with a custom-chipping program for the pulp mills. All of these options required careful timing since they would require that the company end its European sales contracts and there were stiff non-performance penalties for doing so. Moreover, shutting down the pellet mill was not a realistic option since the mill represented a sunken multi-million dollar investment.

STRATEGIC PLANNING MEETING— JANUARY 2007

In early 2007, the Strategic Planning Committee decided to have a major review of the company's operations and strategic options in order to chart a path that could lead MacTara towards meeting its "Corporate Vision and Mission" as well as its CSR statement (see Exhibit 6).

Shaver arrived at the mill at 7:30 a.m. and quickly began preparing himself for the day's session. He laid out on his desk copious notes and a series of reports on operations and market opportunities as a way to help him set a course for the planning meeting that was about to begin. There were many angles to consider. Could the company combat the simultaneous decrease in the price of lumber and the increase in the value of the Canadian dollar against the U.S. dollar? Would lumber prices go up again? What would be the long-term impact of the end of the Canadian–U.S. softwood lumber dispute on MacTara and its competitors? Would another round of the dispute erupt again? How would the rise in the price of oil and the growth of the alternative fuel sectors (wood, wind, solar, ethanol, etc.) affect the wood pellet market? How should MacTara position itself profitably in sectors as disparate as wood pellet heating, chips for pulp mills, value-added wood products and construction lumber? Where would the money needed to grow the most promising sectors and survive the crisis in the lumber sector come from? Could MacTara lead an industry consolidation?

The financial assistance of the Centre for International Business Studies, Dalhousie University and of the Atlantic Canada Opportunities Agency in preparation of the case is gratefully acknowledged.

Exhibit 1   Product Lines

Lumber	Used mainly for residential construction in the United States
Chips	By-product of lumber sold to local pulp mills for making paper
Shavings	Mainly used to create heat to kiln dry MacTara's lumber
Bark	Used to make wood pellets
Sawdust	Used to make wood pellets and to kiln dry lumber
Pellets	Value added product sold to Europeans for use in industrial heating systems

Exhibit 2   Logs/Lumber/Bark/Chips/Pellet Ratios

3.5 tonnes of logs produce 1,000 board feet of green lumber (sawn, but not dried or planed)

1,000 board feet of undried, unplaned lumber results in 0.9 tonnes of bark

2.5 tonnes of bark are needed to produce 1 tonne of pellets

Exhibit 3   Random Lengths Framing Lumber Composite Price

December	US$ per 1,000 board feet
1996	434
1997	375
1998	356
1999	390
2000	278
2001	284
2002	276
2003	327
2004	376
2005	365
2006	285*

*Average composite last 2 quarters

Source: Random Lengths Publications, Inc. www.randomlengths.com.

Exhibit 4   Note on the Softwood Lumber Dispute

Background of the Dispute

"Disputes on softwood lumber have simmered for more than 20 years, but the most recent conflict boiled over in May 2002, when the United States imposed duties of 27 per cent on Canadian softwood lumber, arguing that Canada unfairly subsidized producers of spruce, pine and fir lumber.

The dispute centred on stumpage fees—set amounts charged to companies that harvest timber on public land. Many in the United States see Canadian stumpage fees as being too low, making them de facto subsidies. A U.S. coalition of lumber producers wants the provincial governments to follow the American system and auction off timber rights at market prices. The United States responded by levying tariffs on incoming Canadian lumber in May 2002.

An agreement in principle to end the dispute was reached in December 2003, but it collapsed two days later. The issue went before North American Free Trade Agreement panels and the World Trade Organization several times. Rulings have usually gone Canada's way.

Canada's protracted dispute with the United States over softwood lumber finally ended in April 2006 with an agreement that would require the United States to return about 80 per cent of the more than $5 billion in duties it had collected on lumber imports. The deal was signed in July 2006, but lumber industry groups in three provinces and the B.C. government said they would not support the final draft agreement. However, after the federal government made some adjustments, provincial governments agreed to support the deal. B.C. came on board first, with Ontario and Quebec following suit.

The deal removes tariffs on lumber, but includes export taxes that kick in if the price of lumber drops. Producers would have to pay an export tax between five per cent and 15 per cent depending on the price reduction. The agreement remains in effect for seven years, with the possibility of renewal."

Source: Adapted from "Indepth: Softwood Lumber Dispute," *CBC News Online*, August 23, 2006, retrieved on December 6, 2007, http://www.cbc.ca/news/background/softwood_lumber/.

The Dispute and the Maritime Provinces

In much of Canada, sawmills do obtain most of their raw material (logs) through payment of stumpage fees for the right to cut from Crown lands. In the Maritime provinces, the opposite is the case: most logs are obtained from private landowners who receive market price for their wood. As a result, the cost to obtain logs is considerably higher in the Maritimes than elsewhere in Canada.

Prior to 2001, under the softwood lumber agreement of the time, Canadian imports into the United States were limited by a combination of quotas and import taxes. The Maritimes were exempt from both. In 2002, however, the United States imposed two new duties: a very high, punitive countervailing duty on lumber produced in provinces that enjoyed the alleged subsidy provided by very low stumpage rates and a smaller anti-dumping duty imposed on all Canadian imports, including those from the Maritimes. All duties had to be paid by the producing mills prior to exportation of lumber to the United States. Despite being exempt from the harsher countervailing duty, the anti-dumping duty imposed a considerable financial hardship on this Maritimes industry, which was already struggling with high raw material costs. In the rest of Canada, notably British Columbia, mills were able to remain profitable, even in the face of combined countervailing and anti-dumping duties, thanks to low raw material costs for logs.

Because of their higher costs, Maritime mills cannot be as price-competitive as Western Canadian mills. The lack of a duty or quota, or both, on non-Maritime lumber imports hurt the Maritime lumber industry since unrestricted markets had the effect of lowering lumber prices.

Source: Rick Shaver

Exhibit 5   Possible Value-Added Products for the North American Market

Fencing sections in Atlantic Canada were made with poor quality lumber and were poorly constructed.

Softwood flooring was used in Europe but the market was non-existent in North America. In the United States, softwood flooring would have to compete with well-established products such as hardwood, laminate and ceramic.

Pre-fabricated homes in the United States are often customized though they are constructed in plants and delivered in parts. MacTara could develop specialized products for these builders or partner with selected operations to achieve volume sales.

The wood siding market in eastern Canada was already well served.

Decking for the Canadian and British markets offered good prospects.

Exhibit 6   Proposed Vision, Mission and CSR Statement

Vision
We wisely use what our forests offer to make life better.

Mission Statement
By utilizing our forest resources efficiently and prudently, we will provide our customers with superior products for better living, our people with rewarding employment, our partners with continuing prosperity, our owners with superior returns and our children with the permanent legacy of a rich natural resource.

Commitment to Corporate Social Responsibility
The company has on-going commitment to: 1) becoming the most efficient, environmentally friendly lumber manufacturer in Atlantic Canada; 2) moving beyond current standards for workplace safety by attempting to eliminate accidents and injuries; 3) being a leader on safety within the manufacturing industry; 4) educating the general public on the forest industry and creating healthy and sustainable woodlands for all; 5) continuing to provide strong full-time employment opportunities for the rural population in central Nova Scotia.

Case 4

Loblaw Companies Limited[1]

It was 8 a.m. on Wednesday October 1, 2003, when John A. Lederer, president of Loblaw Companies Limited, saw the following news item.[2]

Wal-Mart Canada Corp. is accelerating the pace of its expansion with plans for an undetermined number of Sam's Club wholesale mega-outlets. Some industry insiders have speculated that the company will launch as many as 10 to 15 Sam's Clubs next year to add to the first four it will open in Canada this fall. Many observers believe that setting up the grocery distribution network for Sam's Club will be the first step to U.S.-based Wal-Mart Stores Inc eventually bringing its giant Supercenters, carrying a complete supermarket assortment, to Canada.

Although Wal-Mart had entered Canada in 1994, it had been uncharacteristically cautious. Even a decade later, it had not expanded fully into groceries despite its own global experience that the addition of a grocery line in a store pushed the sales of the more profitable general merchandise upwards by over 30 per cent.[3] Canada was Wal-Mart's only overseas market in which it had not deployed its powerful Supercenter concept. The launch of its wholesale brand, Sam's Club, suggested that the arrival of Supercenters in Canada was imminent.

Richard Ivey School of Business
The University of Western Ontario

Ramasastry Chandrasekhar prepared this case under the supervision of Professor Charlene Zietsma solely to provide material for class discussion. The authors do not intend to illustrate either effective or ineffective handling of a managerial situation. The authors may have disguised certain names and other identifying information to protect confidentiality.

---

[1] This case has been written on the basis of published sources only. Consequently, the interpretation and perspectives presented in this case are not necessarily those of Loblaw Companies Limited or any of its employees.

[2] www.globeandmail.com/reportonbusiness/retail, accessed October 9, 2003.

[3] Kevin Libin, "The Last Retailer in Canada," *Canadian Business*, March 18, 2002, p.38.

TIME-TESTED STRATEGY

It was time for Loblaw to take a fresh look at its own strategy. The strategy had worked so far: Loblaw was the market leader in Canadian grocery, with a market share in excess of the combined market shares of its four nearest competitors, and it was the 24th largest grocery retailer in the world (see Exhibits 1 and 2).

The Loblaw strategy was both consistent and transparent, listing the following elements in the company's annual reports:[4]

- Use the cash flow generated in the business to invest in the future.
- Own real estate to maximize flexibility for future business opportunities.
- Use a multi-format approach to maximize market share over the longer term.
- Focus on food but serve the customer's everyday needs.
- Create customer loyalty and enhance price competitiveness through a superior control label program.
- Implement and execute plans and programs flawlessly.
- Constantly strive to improve the value proposition.

The strategy was driven by two objectives: driving down costs through size and operational efficiencies, and differentiating both its products (by pioneering its President's Choice brand and other private label brands) and its stores (by following a multi-banner, multi-format approach).

INDUSTRY OVERVIEW

Growing at an average rate of four per cent, food retailing was a $66.8 billion business in 2002 (see Exhibit 3). The rate of growth was impressive in light of two factors: Canadians paid the lowest prices for food in the world, and food inflation was less than two per cent per annum.[5] Grocery retailers also occupied four of the top 10 retailer rankings in Canada in 2002.

A broad spectrum of competitors prevailed in the Canadian grocery sector — from stand-alones with limited market presence to integrated firms involved in manufacturing, importing, wholesaling and retailing. They also operated at various levels: local, regional and national. The presence of high levels of discount stores and private labels and the high degree of market concentration had made Canadian grocery rank among "the most advanced grocery markets in the world."[6]

Canadian grocery stores often co-operated on the supply side even as they competed on the demand side. Smaller stores pooled up with large buying groups to negotiate volume discounts from suppliers. Integrated firms sold to independents. Retailers owned wholesalers and vice versa.[7] Such interactions made Canadian grocery a fertile area for mergers and acquisitions. By contrast, Loblaw's approach was characterized by an equal focus on organic growth.

---

[4]Loblaw Companies Limited, 2002 Annual Report, p.3.

[5]Ibid, p.7.

[6]Perry Caicco, "Loblaw Companies Ltd: A Company in Transition," *CIBC World Markets Equity Research Report*, February 18, 2004.

[7]"The Abuse of Dominance Provisions as Applied to Canadian Grocery Sector," *Competition Bureau November 2002 Bulletin, www.cb-bc.gc.ca*, accessed October 5, 2003.

CONSUMERS

Grocery shoppers were creatures of habit. They went to the same store to buy the same goods and services at almost the same time and day of a shopping period, making the business amenable to relationship building. The advent of supermarkets in the 1930s and the focus on self-service that gathered momentum in later decades had made shopping impersonal. Re-establishing that link with the customers, through the use of technology, was now being seen by mega-grocers as a means of gaining leverage over competitors. Most grocers offered a frequent-shopper loyalty card. The data gathered through it was also used to secure better terms with manufacturers and distributors.

There were three generic ways in which grocers built their revenues: penetration (increasing the number of households shopping in their stores), frequency (increasing the number of shopping trips the shoppers made) and basket size building (getting shoppers to spend more on each shopping trip). Low price, quality service, quality products and breadth of product assortment were important.

The increasing incidence of double income families fuelled the demand for ready-to-heat and ready-to-eat convenience foods. Fast-food chains, take-outs and restaurants were growing in response. This, in turn, reduced the share of unprocessed cooking ingredients in the overall food bill of a household, estimated at $6,438 per annum in 2002, or 11.12 per cent of annual household expenditure. However, 70 per cent of Canadian meals were consumed at home, even though most were not cooked from scratch.[8] Grocers developed new categories like home meals replacement (HMR) and offered on-site cooking demonstrations. Some had franchised restaurants in their premises both to lure traffic into the stores and to provide a value-added facility.

SUPPLIERS

Retailer–supplier relationships were characterized by power plays. The scale would tilt in favor of the one wielding the most clout at a point in time.

A supermarket was like a landlord letting out shelf space for rent. The rent was a combination of different allowances that a manufacturer paid to the retailer to get secure shelf and warehouse position of its products, to encourage advertising, and to reward high volume purchases.[9] They included, for example, listing fees, slotting fees, over and above allowances, vendor allowances for merchandise returns, quantity discounts and merchandising allowances. There was no standard basis on which the amount of each allowance was determined. The category manager[10] usually had the last word in deciding how the shelves were stocked.

Smaller suppliers often were at the mercy of their grocery customers since a large percentage of their business was in the hands of just a few buyers. Producers of category-leading products were in a better position: grocers had to carry their products (often as loss leaders) to attract and retain their customers. The higher a supplier's market share relative to a grocer's, the more power it commanded and vice versa. Consolidation among either suppliers or grocers would shift the balance of power temporarily, and consolidation was increasing on both sides.

---

[8] "Canadian Grocer," 2001-2002 Executive Report, p.15.

[9] Anne Kingston, *The Edible Man*, Macfarlane Walter and Ross, 1994, Chapter 2.

[10] A category was a group of products that were inter-related. A manager with profit center responsibility headed each category. Examples of categories were produce, meat, housewares, dairy and grocery.

Mega-grocers took a long-term view of the relationships with suppliers as part of ensuring cost-efficiencies and seamlessness in operations. They involved suppliers in merchandising, category management and supply chain management, using enterprise resource planning (ERP) technologies. Suppliers used their industry associations to push for standardization in the ERP programs of the mega-grocers to avoid having overlapping systems, one for each customer.

COMPETITORS

According to the National Market Survey 2002 conducted by *Canadian Grocer*, there were 1,791 supermarkets, 8,342 convenience stores, 3,906 affiliated independents and 10,109 unaffiliated independents in the Canadian grocery business (see Exhibit 4). The independent sector accounted for 39.3 per cent of the grocery market sales in 2002.[11] The unaffiliated independents (usually smaller stores) were facing tough times: 418 of them went out of business during 2002.

Grocery Chains

In 2003, there were 44 grocery chains in Canada (see Exhibit 5). Loblaw faced competition from four leading chains: Sobeys, Metro, A&P and Canada Safeway. Each had a distinctive profile.

Sobeys Inc.

In 1907, Sobeys Inc. set up in Nova Scotia, had over 1,500 stores in 10 provinces. It was the second-largest national distributor with an estimated 15 per cent share of the Canadian food market. Employing 33,000 people, Sobeys had sales of $10.41 billion in 2002. Its retail banners included IGA and PriceChopper.

Metro Inc.

Metro Inc., another home-grown enterprise of over 50 years standing, was the leading supermarket chain in Quebec. It had sales of $5.15 billion in 2002, and employed 10,733 people in its 833 stores. Metro had several banners, including the discounter Super C, and three private labels: The Irresistible, Econochoix and Super C.

Atlantic and Pacific (A&P)

Established in 1927, A&P had 240 stores in prime locations in Ontario generating sales of $3.99 billion in 2002 under three banners: discount grocer Food Basics; Dominion, mainly in Toronto; and A&P in the rest of Ontario. A&P Canada was the best performing division of the U.S.-based The Great Atlantic and Pacific Tea Co. Inc., which was in serious financial trouble. Having recently gone through major capital rejuvenation and a change in marketing strategy emphasizing freshness, A&P Canada was in a growth mode.

Canada Safeway

Canada Safeway was started in 1929 as a subsidiary of Safeway Inc., the third-largest supermarket operator in the United States. Canada Safeway had 214 stores located primarily in Western Canada, capturing a 28 per cent share there. Employing 28,000

---

[11] Jerry Tutunjian, "What's Up and What's Down," *Canadian Grocer*, February 2003, p.26.

people, it had sales of $3.48 billion in 2002. Canada Safeway served its own stores and independents through its three distribution centers.

Wholesale Clubs

Wholesale clubs charged an annual fee (ranging between $30 and $50), and offered a broad range of products and services at low prices for bulk purchases. They lured away high volume "stock-up shoppers" from the grocery chains. Stores were functional, sans frills. The wholesale club was a profitable format in Canada.

Costco Wholesale Canada was the leading wholesale club in Canada. It had 61 outlets and about four million members, which included small businesses and many individual consumers. The launch of Sam's Clubs in Canada by Wal-Mart posed a direct threat to Costco, which had enjoyed a first mover advantage in Canada since 1985. In the United States, Costco had dealt with competition from Wal-Mart through differentiation. Unlike Sam's Club, which went after bargain-hunting Wal-Mart customers, Costco U.S. had positioned itself towards small-business owners. The focus on a slightly higher-end customer had not only led to a significantly higher average sale per customer but also limited its competition with Sam's Clubs in the United States, which was generally perceived as downscale.

Specialty Chains

Specialty chains operated smaller stores in niche segments, such as ethnic groceries and organic foods. The ethnic foods market, estimated to be of the order of $6 billion,[12] was likely to grow due to immigration patterns. Its customers comprised the five major ethnic communities in Canada—Chinese, South Asian, Middle Eastern, Central and South American and Caribbean. The $1.8 billion organic foods market was growing at 20 per cent per annum.[13] The world's largest natural and organic foods chain, based in the United States, had opened its first overseas store in Toronto in May 2002. Whole Foods Inc. products competed directly with Loblaw's PC Organics natural food products.

Convenience Stores

Convenience stores complemented supermarkets by allowing consumers to fill up between shopping trips. The convenience store segment had grown faster than grocery supermarkets, increasing in number from 6,629 in 1997 to 8,342 in 2002.

Online Shopping

Online grocery shopping accounted for only $100 million in sales in Canada. Grocery Gateway, a Toronto-based e-grocer, dominated the market, growing its customer base from 7,000 in 1999 to 14,200 by mid-2002.[14]

---

[12]John Schofield, "The Ethnic Market in Canada," *Food in Canada Magazine*, November/December 2002, p.28.
[13]Lisa Rostoks, "Romancing the Organic Crowd," *Canadian Grocer*, August 2002.
[14]Lynne Davidson, "The Milkman Returneth," *pwcglobal.com/RealEstateTrendsSummer 2002*, accessed October 7, 2003.

AC Nielsen studies indicated that 57 per cent of Canadians were Internet users in 2000, up from 31 per cent in 1997. A survey in 2000 showed that grocery orders through the Internet numbered between 800 to 1,000 per day, and the average size of an order was $120. New families and young singles were driving contemporary online grocery sales in Canada, but electronic security was a major barrier to shopping online for some consumers.[15]

Competitive Outlook

Small entrants in the independent category entered the market frequently. Two of the most recent large entrants to the Canadian grocery were Whole Foods, which had entered a niche market of organics, and Wal-Mart, which had entered Canadian retail by acquiring 122 Woolco stores. Grocers in the mid-sized category were potential acquisitions for global firms pursuing expansion. European grocers were known to be on the prowl for acquisitions since their home markets had reached saturation levels and the rate of growth was slowing down.[16] However, the limited market size in Canada and lower margins were major disincentives. Each of the four leading grocers in Canada—including Loblaw—had been the subject of regular media speculation as a take-over target of various global firms.

GROCERY OPERATIONS

Supply Chain and Logistics

An average Canadian grocery store carried 25,000 to 40,000 stock keeping units (SKUs). Strong supply chain and logistics functions were thus crucial. Demand forecasts were, in large part, judgment-driven, despite the use of computers. Poor forecasting or logistics led to expired or obsolete products, which drained profitability, or conversely, to out-of-stocks, which reduced sales and customer satisfaction.

Technology

Canadian retail was leading the revolution in technology, ahead of U.S. retail, with its ECCnet. Put into place in mid-2003, ECCnet was a national, online, standardized product registry for synchronized data exchange. It provided the foundation on which subsequent technology platforms, like Radio Frequency Identification, could be deployed without delay. Potential savings for grocers were estimated at one per cent of sales.[17]

Scale

The average size of a Canadian supermarket was 28,000 square feet, generating average weekly sales of about $300,000. Goliath stores averaging 110,000 square feet could generate a million dollars in sales a week.[18] Scale advantages included lower costs of handling incoming materials and lower procurement costs, but backroom support was crucial, and the store had to run at full capacity.

---

[15]"Canadian Grocer," *2001-2002 Executive Report*, p.30.
[16]Peter Diekmeyer, "Are Canada's Retailers Ripe for the Picking?" *www.cdngrocer.com*, accessed October 7, 2003.
[17]"Canadian Grocer," *2001-2002 Executive Report*, August 2003, p.32.
[18]George H. Condon, "Taming a Goliath," *Canadian Grocer*, March 2002.

Profitability

The margins of a supermarket chain were among the lowest of all industries. Post-tax profits averaged between 0.5 per cent and two per cent. Independents had higher margins of up to five per cent but on lower sales (see Exhibit 6). Since store profitability was linked to space, costs were calculated per square foot (see Exhibit 7). The data on product profitability or even on category profitability was not always reliable due to the number of variables in cost allocation and cost apportionment.[19]

LOBLAW

Company Background

Loblaw Companies Limited was a part of George Weston Limited, a broadly based Canadian company operating in two distinct business segments: food processing and food distribution. Founded in 1919 by Theodore Pringle Loblaw and J. Milton Crok, Loblaw Grocetarias, as it was then known, was a prosperous chain of 113 stores spread in Ontario with sales of $50 million in 1947, when Garfield Weston, a young baker in Toronto, acquired a small stake in the company.[20] Now controlled by a third generation member of the Weston family and spearheaded by a professional team led by John Lederer, Loblaw was Canada's largest food distributor with sales of $23.1 billion in 2002 (see financial statements in Exhibits 8-10), and 122,300 employees. The Weston family held majority ownership.

Strategy Execution

The company's overall strategy, as reiterated regularly in its annual reports, was evident at the level of execution in the following ways.[21]

Real Estate

As opposed to its competitors who leased stores, Loblaw owned 63 per cent of its corporate stores in Canada, many of which were in very favorable locations.[22] Ownership provided flexibility at the operational level. Loblaw upgraded its stores every five years in contrast to the industry norm of seven years, and redesigned its formats to meet changing customer needs.

Control Label Program

Grocery stores were compelled to carry very popular branded products and sell them as loss leaders in order to keep their customers happy. Through its very successful control label program, Loblaw was able to take significant market share away from the big brands, competing with them strongly on prices yet ensuring margins due to lower costs. The popularity of its control label products also produced customer loyalty.

---

[19] *www.georgemorris.org/HMRupdate*, accessed October 12, 2003
[20] Charles Davies, *Bread Men*, Key Porter Books, 1987, p.92.
[21] Ann Leamon, Ray A. Goldberg and David E. Bell, "Loblaw Companies Ltd: The Road Ahead," *Harvard Business School Case 9-901-015*, p.9.
[22] Loblaw Companies 2002 Annual Report, p.34.

A Multi-Format Approach

A multi-banner, multi-format approach had enabled Loblaw to cover all price points in the grocery market and cater to all segments ranging from discount to bulk and gourmet. Each store had a local appeal.

Meeting Everyday Needs

Groceries were the core of Loblaw business, but a rich fare of non-food items was offered to meet the daily needs of every household. The control label initiative had also been extended to general merchandise by the company. Loblaw also operated over 100 gas stations in Canada.

Increasing Market Share per Store

Instead of pursuing national market share, Loblaw focused on increasing the market share of each individual store.

Organizational Structure and Human Resources

The organization structure of Loblaw is shown in Exhibit 11. Line managers reported to both regional heads and banner heads. Regional vice-presidents oversaw profitability in the Ontario, Quebec, Atlantic and Western regions. Senior banner managers held profit centre responsibility across regions. Corporate support departments included real estate, information technology (IT) and supply chain, legal, control label, finance and treasury, and labor relations.

The tenure of Loblaw's senior operating team averaged 18 years.[23] Stock options were a major performance driver for senior managers. One of the largest private sector employers in Canada, Loblaw offered top wages and benefits. The United Food and Commercial Workers represented Loblaw's employees.

Marketing

Loblaw stores advertised 35 to 50 sale items in a weekly flyer. Non-sale items earned higher margins. Beyond store marketing, Loblaw's three broad marketing initiatives were Stores-as-a-Brand, Control Label and Customer Loyalty.

Stores-As-A-Brand

Loblaw had acquired strong regional stores like *Fortinos* in Hamilton, *Zehrs* in Kitchener and *Provigo* in Quebec without changing their names or diluting their community character.

The Real Canadian Superstore, reigning in Western Canada; The Real Canadian Superstore was the first major Canadian attempt at establishing megastores. Averaging 125,000 square feet, the stores sold a variety of food and non-food merchandise including clothing, housewares, electronics, etc.; 60 per cent of the sales in Superstores came from higher margin non-food merchandise.[24]

---

[23] Loblaw Companies 2000 Annual Report, p.23.
[24] Susan Thorne, "Loblaws 84 years old Still Biggest Grocer by Far," www.icsc.org/srch/set/current/page24.html, accessed March 19, 2004.

The Real Canadian Wholesale Club was positioned against Costco/Price Club, with good prices on bulk purchases of mostly branded products (including President's Choice). *Extra Foods* focused on bulk purchases of inexpensive products, with a higher concentration of no-name products in the store. *SuperValue* and *Shop Easy Foods* were smaller stores that operated in downtown areas offering smaller package sizes and semi-processed foods. *Lucky Dollar* featured Asian ethnic foods. *No frills* provided low-cost, mostly no-name products in bulk and a limited range of produce and perishables. *Your Independent Grocer* and *ValuMart* were smaller stores, affiliates and independents, often located in small towns where the personal relationship between the store owner and the community was important. In the Maritimes, *Atlantic SaveEasy* was similar in concept to *No frills*. *Atlantic Superstore* was positioned similarly to Western Canada's *Real Canadian Superstore*, though the stores were smaller. *Dominion* (in Newfoundland) had a profile similar to *Loblaw* in Ontario.

Control Label Products

In 1984, Loblaw introduced its President's Choice (PC) private label program. High quality products were sourced, labelled as PC, and marketed through the "Insider's Report," a personal communiqué from Dave Nichol, the then-president of Loblaw Supermarkets. At one time, the Insider's Report attracted more readership than the mainstream newspapers in Canada. Other European and North American retailers also sold private label products, but Loblaw was the first to build a brand for its private label that could compete with national brands. In pioneering PC products, Loblaw paved the way for every major grocery chain in Canada to develop a private label program unique to its customer base. Private labels comprised about 25 per cent of grocery sales in Canada and their growth rate (seven per cent) outpaced that of national brands (six per cent), according to a study by AC Nielsen.[25]

Customer Loyalty Programs

Loblaw had developed, in 1997, a loyalty program that worked across its store banners. Launched as an extension of the *President's Choice* brand and offered under the aegis of *President's Choice Financial*, the benefits were two-fold. Customers could earn points redeemable for free groceries based on their purchases at any store in the chain. They could also obtain low-cost financial services such as everyday banking, loans, investments and mortgages through electronic banking and pavilions at select Loblaw family stores. The *PC MasterCard*, launched in 2001, reinforced the program. Planned expansions for PC Financial Services included more stores and more products, such as home and auto insurance.

Distribution

Loblaw had four types of stores as part of its distribution network: corporate stores; franchised stores; associated stores and independent accounts. The corporate stores were managed directly by the chain while the others were business affiliations aimed at enlarging the reach of the chain. The company had a total of 632 corporate stores, 406 franchised stores, 659 associated stores and 7,069 affiliated independents. They were all serviced by 34 warehouses across Canada.[26]

New supermarkets being opened in Canada by existing grocers were getting progressively larger in size. This was accompanied by a gradual decline in sales per square

[25]Lisa Rostoks, "Mastering Private Label," *Canadian Grocer*, February 2002.
[26]Loblaw Companies 2002 Annual Report, p.18.

foot. But Loblaw was different. Its annual average sales per square foot of corporate stores grew from $502 in 1994 to $575 in 2002, even as the average store size went up from 37,700 square feet to 48,900 square feet during the period. Future extensions of the large-format *Real Canadian Superstore* into other Canadian markets were planned, and five of them were under various stages of execution in 2003.

THE WAL-MART THREAT

Wal-Mart was the world's largest retailer with $245 billion in revenues in 2002[27] (see financial statements in Exhibits 12 and 13), and 1,383,000 employees. Wal-Mart had 516 million square feet of retail space with an average store size of 116,795 square feet. It was three times the size of the world's second largest retailer, France's Carrefour. Its "Every Day Low Prices" (EDLP) strategy was an extremely popular alternative to the weekly sale items advertised by other retailers. The company was wringing billions of dollars in cost efficiencies out of the retail supply chain and passing them on to shoppers as bargain prices. According to an estimate by New England Consulting, the company saved its U.S. customers $100 billion in 2002 alone, both through lowering its own prices and forcing competitors to do so. The "Wal-Mart effect" has helped suppress inflation and distribute productivity gains through the U.S. economy year after year. The company was known to derive cost advantages amounting to 22 per cent over U.S. competitors, based on the way it managed its "ecosystem" of business partners.[28] Wal-Mart earned US$403 per square foot in its domestic stores, with gross margins of 21.2 per cent.[29] Wal-Mart established close relationships with its suppliers, and although it drove a hard bargain on price, the company shared information and systems with its suppliers that made each company more efficient. A fierce competitor, Wal-Mart was widely touted as the cause of Kmart's bankruptcy, as that chain had tried to compete directly with Wal-Mart. Target, Wal-Mart's other major U.S. competitor, operated slightly up-market from Wal-Mart to avoid head on competition with the retail dynamo.

The company had internationalized with the opening of a Sam's Club in Mexico in 1991 (see Exhibit 14). Its international experience was mixed. While credited with "helping to hold down inflation in Mexico, improving Britain's cost of living and revolutionizing the distribution system in China,"[30] Wal-Mart did less well in Germany and Japan. Only four of its 10 overseas ventures were profitable.

When asked about Wal-Mart's plans for the future, Chief Executive Officer H. Lee Scott, Jr. indicated the company wanted "to be where we're not."[31] More than two-thirds of the value implicit in Wal-Mart's stock price was based on growth possibilities rather than on current operations.[32] Scott foresaw decades of growth in the core business, including more stores in smaller geographic centres than had previously been thought possible. Growth plans included significant expansion of their Supercenter format, with over 200 set to open during 2003, and 1,000 expected to

---

[27] Anthony Bianco and Wendy Zellner, "Is Wal-Mart Too Powerful?" *BusinessWeek*, October 6, 2003.

[28] Marco Iansiti and Roy Levien, "Strategy as Ecology," *Harvard Business Review*, March 2004.

[29] Pankaj Ghemawat, Ken A. Mark and Stephen P. Bradley, "Wal-Mart Stores in 2003," *Harvard Business School Case Study*, 9-704-430, p. 5.

[30] Robert Slater, "The Wal-Mart Decade," *Penguin USA 2003*, p. 133.

[31] Bill Saporito, "Can Wal-Mart Get Any Bigger?" *Time*, January 5, 2003.

[32] Luciano Catoni, Nora F. Larssen, James Naylor and Andrea Zocchi, "Travel Tips for Retailers," *The McKinsey Quarterly*, 2002. No. 3.

open in the U.S. alone in the next five years. Wal-Mart's Supercenter concept was a larger format store that added a full line of groceries and specialty services to its discount store. Food made up approximately 35 per cent of sales, and, though margins were slimmer (6.6 per cent for Supercenters versus nine per cent to 10 per cent for discount stores), inventory turned faster than in discount stores, and so return on assets was higher. A population base of 76,000 people was needed to support a Supercenter.[33] Sam's Club stores, which competed directly with Costco, did not perform as well as Supercenters and thus were scheduled for more limited growth.

The company also expected to grow geographically: it had targeted a third of its sales and profit growth to come from its international operations by 2005, doubling from 16 per cent in 2002.[34] Wal-Mart also announced the introduction of financial services for its customers in 2003.

Wal-Mart in Canada

Wal-Mart had entered Canada in 1994 by taking over 122 Woolco stores. It had raced past established retailers like Eaton's, Hudson's Bay Co. and Sears Canada to be ranked, by 2002, as No. 1 retailer in Canada. Wal-Mart Canada had become profitable by the second year of operations, providing a measure of confidence about the company's international operations in general.

Even as its Every Day Low Prices strategy had become popular with Canadian consumers, Wal-Mart had acceptance problems of a different kind. The UFCW Canada had filed charges of unfair labor practices against the company.[35] The first signs of discord had surfaced when Wal-Mart refused to buy any of the nine Woolworth stores where workers were enjoying UFCW Canada union contracts and benefits. The parent company, Wal-Mart Inc, had been a particular target for UFCW, even in the United States where it had successfully prevented unionization at all its stores. The largest private sector employer in the United States was widely blamed for the sorry state of retail wages in America.[36] Raids on U.S. Wal-Mart stores in 2003 found illegal immigrants working as sub-contracted cleaning staff for low wages, with no overtime or benefits pay and no taxes withheld.[37]

Traditionally, supermarkets like Loblaw used size and scale to achieve cost leadership. But Wal-Mart, already the world's largest retailer, was using technology to cut costs further. A centralized information system in Arkansas linked the operations of its 4,750 stores and 30,000 suppliers around the world, in real time. Wal-Mart also developed in-house, retail technology solutions to drive costs continuously down.[38]

According to an industry analyst,[39] Wal-Mart had quickly dominated most markets outside the United States within years of entry because the grocery markets in those countries lacked depth. The Canadian grocery market, in contrast, was characterized by several discount formats and many private labels. Wal-Mart also had

---

[33] This paragraph draws on information in Pankaj Ghemawat, Ken A. Mark and Stephen P. Bradley, "Wal-Mart Stores in 2003," *Harvard Business School Case Study, 9-704-430.*

[34] Chester Dawson, "Will Wal-Mart Conquer Japan?" *BusinessWeek US Edition*, April 1, 2002.

[35] "Threat of Wal-Mart expansion," *www.ufcw.ca*, press release dated November 25, 2002, accessed October 12, 2003.

[36] www.businessweek.com, accessed October 3, 2003.

[37] "Illegal immigrants arrested in raids sue Wal-Mart," *Associated Press, November 9, 2003, www.cnn.com,* accessed January 23, 2004.

[38] "The IT Inside the World's Biggest Company," *CIO Magazine*, July 2002.

[39] Interview with Perry Caicco of CIBC World Markets.

limited expertise in perishables (which comprised 67 per cent of total grocery sales in 2001).[40] The launch of Sam's Club wholesale megastores suggested that Wal-Mart was feeling confident about its ability to compete in Canada. Would Wal-Mart Super-centers be next?

THE RESPONSE

What should Lederer do, given the expected entry of Wal-Mart into the grocery business? Was it time to shake up the company's stable strategy?

Exhibit 1   Canadian Grocers' Market Shares—2002

	Sales (in million $)	Market Share (%)
Statistics Canada Supermarket Sales	58,191	78.0
Grocery Products in Other Channels	16,409	22.0
Total	74,600	100.0
Loblaw	**23,894**	**32.0**
Sobeys	10,960	14.7
Safeway	5,492	7.4
Metro	5,201	7.0
A&P	4,400	5.9
Costco Food	3,550	4.8
Convenience Stores	3,250	4.4
Wal-Mart	**2,758**	**3.7**
Co-Op	2,667	3.6
Drug Stores	2,659	3.6
Overwaitea	2,380	3.2
Commisso Wholesale	757	1.0
Hy Louie	595	0.8
Other Mass merchandisers	494	0.6
Commisso Food Markets	466	0.7
Thrifty Foods	374	0.5
North West Co	333	0.4
T&T Foods	170	0.2
Other Independents	4,200	5.6

Source: Canadian Grocer Executive Report 2003-2004.

---

[40] Jerry Tutunjian, "The Numbers are In," *Canadian Grocer*, November 2002, p.31.

Exhibit 2   World's Top Grocery Retailers 2001

Ranking	Company	Country	Stores Owned	Sales (in US$ million)
1	Carrefour	France	8,926	61,398
2	Ahold	The Netherlands	8,062	58,842
3	Metro	Germany	2,169	43,758
4	Kroger Co	USA	2,354	37,900
5	Albertson's	USA	2,533	37,900
6	**Wal-Mart (Food sales)**	**USA**	**4,190**	**36,865**
7	Safeway	USA	1,688	34,300
8	Tesco	UK	907	32,380
9	Rewe Zentrale	Germany	11,788	31,880
10	Aldi	Germany	4,388	26,480
11	Edeka/AVA	France	12,000	26,450
12	ITM Enterprises	France	8,545	26,140
13	J.Sainsbury	UK	626	26,130
14	It-Yokado	Japan	35,600	25,850
15	Group Casino	France	6,650	24,940
16	Daiei	Japan	7,800	23,740
17	Tengelmann	Germany	6,689	23,120
18	Supervalu	USA	1,194	21,300
19	Jusco	Japan	1,780	21,020
20	Auchan	France	243	20,130
21	E. Leclerc	France	555	17,940
22	Fleming Cos	USA	250	15,600
23	Delhaize "Le Lion" Group	Belgium	2,310	15,550
24	**Loblaw**	**Canada**	**606**	**15,100**
25	Winn-Dixie Stores	USA	1,079	13,000

Source: Canadian Grocer Executive Report 2003-2004.

Exhibit 3   Volume of Food Retail Trade in Canada

$ in million	2002	2001	2000	1999	1998
A. Supermarkets & Stores	62,049	58,858	56,592	54,500	53,346
B. All other Food Stores	4,778	4,793	4,498	4,389	4,318
C. Total Food Sales (A+B)	**66,827**	63,652	61,090	58,889	57,664
D. Total Retail Trade Sales	306,578	289,130	277,033	260,779	246,675
E. % of Food in Retail Sales	21.8	22.0	22.1	20.2	23.38

Source: www.statcan.ca.

Exhibit 4   Number of Grocery Stores in Canada

Year	Supermarkets	Convenience Stores	Affiliated Independents	Unaffiliated Independents	Total
2001	1,538	7,295	4,782	10,517	24,132
2000	1,581	6,812	5,269	11,850	25,512
1999	1,611	6,290	5,212	13,217	26,330
1998	1,687	6,401	5,078	12,926	26,092
1997	1,656	6,629	5,091	12,371	25,747

Source: Canadian Grocer February 2003 – Annual National Market Surveys.

Exhibit 5   Grocery Chains in Canada With More Than 20 Stores

Name of the Chain	Banners	Year Est.	No. of Stores	Ownership	Private Labels
A&P Canada	A&P	1927	81	Corporate	Body Basics, Master
	Dominion	1919	56	Corporate	Choice, Basics for Less
	Food Basics	1995	88	Corporate	Equality
Bulk Barn Foods	Bulk Barn	1982	63	Franchise	
Canada Safeway	Safeway	1929	213	Corporate	
Coop Atlantic	Coop Atlantic	1927	181	Cooperative	
The Grocers People	Bigway	1960	102	Family	West Best
Loblaw Companies	Atlantic Save Easy	–	56	Corp/Franch	Club Pack
	Atlantic Superstore	1986	50	Corporate	Exact
	Cash & Carry	1980	10	Corporate	Green
	Dominion in NFL	–	15	Corporate	President's Choice
	Extra Foods	1980	90	Corp/Franch	Today's Choice
	Fortino's	1961	18	Franchise	Too Good To Be True
	Loblaw	1920	98	Corporate	no name
	Lucky Dollar		102	JV/Franch	
	Maxi	1984	85	Corporate	
	Provigo	1969	138	Corp/Franch	
	Real Canadian SS	1980	57	Corporate	
	RealCanadianWSC	1991	32	Corporate	
	Shop Easy	1912	56	Franchise	
	Super Value	1903	29	Corp/Franch	
	Valu-Mart	1925	71	Franch/JV	
	Your Independent	1987	54	Franch/AD	
	Zehr's Markets	1950	58	Corporate	
	No Frills	1978	110	Franchise	
Metro Inc	Metro	1947	251	Family/Fran	The Irresistible
	Ami	1962	95	Family	Econochoix
	Gem	1960	268	Family	Super C
	Loeb	1912	43	Family/Fran	
	Marche	1952	142	Family	
	Super C	–	49	Corporate	
Overwaitea	Overwaitea Foods	1915	34	Corporate	Value-Priced
	Save-on-Foods	1982	50	Corporate	Western Classics, Western Family
Rabba's Fine Foods	Rabba's	–	26	Corporate	Our Compliments
Sobeys Inc	Boni Choix	1982	104	Franchise	
	Food Town	–	104	Corp/Franch	
	Food Land	–	94	Franchise	
	GardenMarket IGA	–	94	Corp/Franch	
	IGA	1951	433	Corp/Franch	
	IGA Extra	–	31	Corp/Franch	
	Knechtel	1930	46	Corp/Franch	
	Omni	1982	117	AD	
	Price Chopper	1992	88	Corp/Franch	
	Sobeys	1907	119	Corporate	
H Y Louie	IGA	1914	43	Corp/Franc	Our Compliments Smart Choice

Source: 2003 Directory of Retail Chains in Canada.

Exhibit 6   Operating Expenses of Canadian Grocetarias as % of Sales

Item of Expenditure	Conventional Stores	Supermarkets
Store Labor	10.0	9.9
Benefits	1.7	2.7
Occupancy	2.4	2.6
Utilities	1.2	1.0
Advertising	1.3	1.6
Maintenance	0.7	0.8
Stores Supplies	1.1	1.0
Interest	0.4	0.6
Others	3.1	4.0
Total	**21.9**	**24.2**

Source: Canadian Grocer Executive Report 2000-2001.

Exhibit 7   Productivity of Canadian Supermarkets

Productivity Measure	Conventional Stores	Supermarkets
Total Store Area (Sq Ft)	17,400	42,000
% of Selling Area to Total Area	73.90	74
Weekly Sales per Sq Ft of Selling Area ($)	9.10	11.06
Weekly PBT per Sq Ft of Selling Area ($)	0.20	0.26
Average Weekly Sales per Store ($)	102,574	310,567
Sales per Labor Hour ($)	82.33	107.17
Payroll Cost per Labor Hour ($)	7.76	10.44
Occupancy Cost per Sq Ft ($)	10.47	15.84
% of Occupancy Cost to Total Expenditure	15.40	13.40
Overall Store Inventory Turns (No of Times)	15.70	17.40
Average Number of Checkouts	6	10
Average Transaction Size ($)	14.60	21.34
Weekly Transactions/Checkouts (Nos)	1,356	1,269
Total Gross Margin as % of Sales	24.3	27.1
Total Store Labor Expenses as % of Sales	11.7	12.6
Profit Before Tax as % of Sales	2.2	3.0

Source: Canadian Grocer Executive Report 2000-2001.

Exhibit 8

LOBLAW COMPANIES LIMITED **Consolidated Balance Sheet**							
	2002	**2001**	**2000**	**1999**	**1998**	**1997**	**1996**
Assets							
Cash & S/Term Investments	1,127	1,001	1,050	726	672	562	720
Accounts Receivables	605	472	381	417	352	364	157
Inventories	1,702	1,512	1,310	1,222	1,141	707	659
Others	92	101	175	50	84	48	16
Total Current Assets	3,526	3,086	2,916	2,415	2,249	1,681	1,552
Fixed Assets	5,587	4,931	4,174	3,549	3,194	2,093	1,738
Investments & Advances	–	–	189	160	134	113	112
Intangible Assets	1,599	1,599	1,641	1,685	1,363	38	40
Other Assets	398	409	105	170	165	88	88
Total Assets	**11,110**	**10,025**	**9,025**	**7,979**	**7,105**	**4,013**	**3,530**
Liabilities							
Short Term Borrowings	639	367	889	746	1,150	374	421
Accounts Payables	2,336	2,291	2,240	2,066	1,806	1,084	931
Other Current Liabilities	179	138	78	0	0	21	47
Total Current Liabilities	3,154	2,796	3,207	2,812	2,956	1,479	1,399
Provisions	68	49	78	113	122	77	57
Long-term Debt	3,420	3,333	2,377	1,979	1,364	915	733
Other Liabilities	344	278	239	171	68	47	30
Total Liabilities	6,986	6,456	5,901	5,075	4,510	2,518	2,220
Retained Earnings	2,929	2,375	1,930	1,721	1,429	1,221	1,046
Common Share Capital	1,195	1,194	1,194	1,183	1,166	274	265
Total Shareholders' Equity	4,124	3,569	3,124	2,904	2,595	1,495	1,310
Total Liabilities & **Shareholders' Equity**	**11,110**	**10,025**	**9,025**	**7,979**	**7,105**	**4,013**	**3,530**

Exhibit 9

$ in million	2002	2001	2000	1999	1998	1997	1996
LOBLAW COMPANIES **Statement of Earnings**							
Sales	23,082	21,486	20,121	18,783	12,497	11,008	9,848
Cost of Sales	21,425	20,035	18,862	17,706	11,785	10,435	9,367
Depreciation	354	315	283	266	185	147	122
Oper. Income	1,303	1,136	976	811	527	426	359
Interest	161	158	143	112	68	44	46
Income Taxes	414	372	317	280	198	169	139
Goodwill	–	43	43	43	–	–	–
Net Earnings	728	563	473	376	261	213	174

Exhibit 10

$ in million	2002	2001	2000	1999	1998	1997	1996
LOBLAW COMPANIES **Retained Earnings**							
Year Beginning	2,375	1,930	1,721	1,429	1,221	1,046	902
Less: Misc. Charges	25	–	152	–	2	–	–
Add Net Earnings	728	563	473	376	261	213	174
Less Dividend Paid	149	118	112	84	51	38	30
Year End	2,929	2,375	1,930	1,721	1.429	1,221	1,046

Exhibit 11 Loblaw Companies Ltd. Organization Chart (Figures in brackets indicate age and tenure of service)

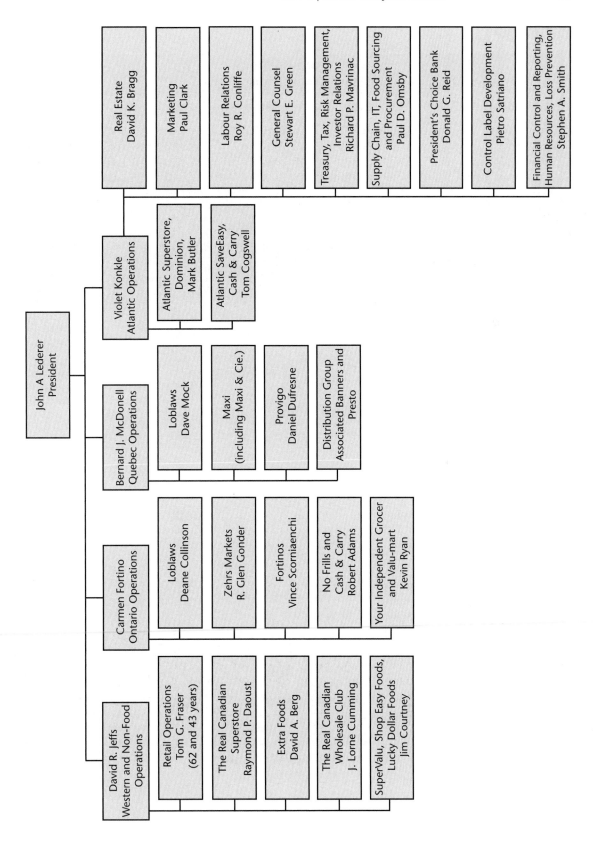

Exhibit 12

WAL-MART INC. Consolidated Balance Sheet					
$ in million	**2002**	**2001**	**2000**	**1999**	**1998**
Current Assets	28,170	26,555	24,356	21,132	19,352
Total Assets	83,375	78,130	70,349	49,996	45,384
Current Liabilities	27,173	28,949	25,803	16,762	14,460
Shareholders' Equity	35,102	31,343	25,834	21,112	18,503

Exhibit 13

WAL-MART INC. Consolidated Balance Sheet					
$ in million	**2002**	**2001**	**2000**	**1999**	**1998**
Net Sales	217,800	191,329	165,013	137,634	117,958
Other Income	2,013	1,966	1,796	1,574	1,341
Cost of Sales	171,562	150,255	129,664	108,725	93,438
Operating & Admin Costs	36,173	31,550	27,040	22,363	19,358
Operating Income	11,937	11,311	10,105	8,061	6,503
Interest	1,186	1,195	841	614	733
Taxes	3,897	3,692	3,338	2,740	2,115
Net Income	6,671	6,295	5,576	4,430	3,526

Exhibit 14 Wal-Mart Outside USA

Year of Entry	Country	Mode of Entry	Initial No. of Stores	No. of Stores in 2002	No of Employees in 2002	Sales in 2002 ($ mn)	Op. Income in 2002 ($ mn)
1991	Mexico	JV	1	595	92,708	10,980	656
1992	Puerto Rico	Expansion	1	55	7,500	2,000	104
1994	Canada	Acquisition	122	213	52,000	5,643	485
1995	Brazil	Expansion	5	22	6,000	421	−3
1995	Argentina	Expansion	3	11	4,000	100	−3
1996	China	JV	2	26	15,000	517	−8
1996	Indonesia	JV	–	–	–	–	–
1997	Germany	Acquisition	95	94	15,500	2,408	108
1998	South Korea	Acquisition	4	15	3,000	741	−18
1999	Britain	Acquisition	229	259	125,000	17,430	941
2002	Japan	Stakeholder	400	400	30,000	NA	NA

Source: Pankaj Ghemawat, Ken A Mark and Stephen P Bradley, "Wal-Mart Stores in 2003", *Harvard Business Review* case 9-704-430.

TVOntario

INTRODUCTION

In the fall of 2000, Bob Baker was appointed managing director of revenue and development at TVOntario (TVO), a Crown corporation of the province of Ontario. He was responsible for development (i.e., fundraising and membership services) and for the Sales and Licensing Department. During Baker's first few months on the job, it had become clear that the Sales and Licensing Department was continuing to experience rapidly declining revenues. Questions as to the true profitability of the department had been raised with management and with the board of directors.

Some members of TVO management and some members of the board of directors believed that the Sales and Licensing Department had outlived its usefulness and should be shut down. However, they wanted Baker to analyse the situation and propose any viable alternatives before they made a final decision.

It was spring of 2001, and Baker had been given only a few months to determine the future, if indeed there was to be one, for the TVOntario Sales and Licensing Department. He was under pressure from the board of directors and from the Sales and Licensing Department (where morale was at an all-time low) to make a decision as soon as possible. While Baker understood the need to act quickly, he wanted to be sure the decision would be in the best long-term interests of TVO, and had targeted late June for making his recommendations.

Richard Ivey School of Business
The University of Western Ontario

THE NORTH AMERICAN BROADCAST INDUSTRY[1,2]

The television broadcast industry was changing rapidly worldwide. The current industry configuration was dramatically different from what it had been 10 years ago and was likely to look completely different again a few years from now. It was a major challenge for any network and for TVO to thrive in this changing environment.

In 2000, the television market in the United States continued to be the largest in the world and was served by three key distribution channels: the national commercial television networks, the independent local commercial television stations and cable television services (including pay cable). Commercial broadcast television (TV) stations in the United States could be affiliated with one of the four national commercial television networks (ABC, CBS, NBC or Fox), with one of the two new networks (WB or UPN), or these stations could have no network affiliation at all. Commercial TV stations were required to broadcast at least 28 hours per week and at least two hours per day of educational programming to maintain a network license under Federal Communications Commission (FCC) regulations.

All the U.S. networks were divisions of larger corporations. ABC was owned by Walt Disney Co., CBS Corp. by Viacom Inc., Fox by News Corp. and NBC by General Electric Co. WB was 75 per cent owned by Time Warner Inc. and 25 per cent owned by Tribune Co. UPN was a 50-50 joint venture between Chris-Craft Industries Inc. and Viacom Inc. The U.S.-based Public Broadcasting System (PBS) was the station most closely aligned with the mandate of Canada's TVOntario. As of 1999, there were 1,616 full-power television stations in the United States. Of these, 1,243 were commercial stations and 373 were educational stations. In addition, 2,194 low-power television stations were licensed to operate.

The Canadian television market was dominated by Canada's major, government-funded network, Canadian Broadcasting Corporation (CBC), and by CanWest Global Broadcasting Corporation and CTV. In addition, there were numerous cable television specialty networks in Canada, as was the case in the United States. One difference between the Canadian and U.S. television markets was that while low-powered television stations in the United States served community channels and college markets, in Canada the networks used low-powered television stations as "repeaters" to carry programming signals to rural parts of the country.

CBC was made up largely of radio and television properties and its mandate was to:

- Tell Canadians stories reflecting the reality and the diversity of the country;
- Inform Canadians about news and issues of relevance and interest;
- Support Canadian arts and culture; and
- Build bridges among Canadians, between regions and two linguistic communities.[3]

In keeping with this mandate, CBC services were available to the vast majority of Canadians. However, with recent government cutbacks, CBC had some challenges

---

[1] Year 2000 Outlook Upbeat for Cable, Radio, and TV. Broadcasting & Cable Industry Survey, January 27, 2000. Broadcasting & Cable Magazine. pp. 1-23.
[2] Broadcasting & Cable Industry Survey, January 27, 2000.
[3] www.cbc.ca, June 1, 2001.

ahead. An organization called Friends of CBC had been lobbying actively to preserve the CBC for Canadians.

Global Television, a private corporation, had expanded its broadcast reach to include 94 per cent of English-speaking Canada by 2000. CanWest Global also boasted a leading film and TV production and distribution operation (CanWest Entertainment), a growing new media business (CanWest Interactive) and significant international broadcasting presence in New Zealand, Australia and Ireland, as well as being Canada's largest newspaper publisher, with many major papers under the CanWest umbrella.[4]

CTV was owned by Bell Globemedia, a premier multimedia company, which was in turn 70 per cent owned by BCE Inc., 20 per cent owned by Thomson Corporation and 10 per cent owned by The Woodbridge Company Ltd. CTV's conventional broadcast signals were able to reach 99 per cent of English-speaking Canadians. CTV offered a wide range of programming, and it owned a number of network stations: an independent station in Vancouver, six CBC affiliate stations along with ASN, and a satellite television service in the Maritimes. CTV had a strong showing in the specialty and pay TV arena. Included in its offerings were TSN, The Comedy Network and the award-winning Discovery Channel. CTV also owned a 50–per-cent interest in Landscape Entertainment Corp., a new Canadian production and content venture, which was expected to become a premier producer of worldwide content for film, television and the Internet, and which complemented CTV's ownership in production houses and music publishers. Included under the Bell Globemedia umbrella were also *The Globe and Mail* newspaper, and the Sympatico/Lycos Internet portal.[5]

Viewing trends showed that many Canadians preferred American content in programming. Thus, Canadian broadcasters regularly paid to rebroadcast syndicated American programs. As a result, polls repeatedly showed that as many as 19 of the top 20 television programs in Canada originated from the United States. To enable continued production of Canadian-made programs, Canadian networks were mandated by the CRTC to purchase and air domestic content.

Cable Television Systems

Cable system operators received signals from program providers through special antennas, microwave relay systems, earth stations and fibre-optic cables. The system amplified the signals, combined them with locally originated programs and ancillary services, and distributed them to subscribers. David Spencer, an associate professor of film and media studies at The University of Western Ontario, stated, "Cable providers have retransmitted network broadcasts for years without having a contract or having to pay them any royalties. This is because the networks realized that the cable providers were extending their audience reach for them."[6]

By May of 1999, the top 25 cable operators in the United States served approximately 91 per cent of that market's subscribers, up from 85 per cent in 1998. The 10 largest operators had signed up 71 per cent of the 68 million cable subscribers in the United States, up from 45 per cent in 1994. In Canada, Rogers Cablesystems was the major player, with similar cable penetration into the marketplace.

---

[4]www.canwestglobal.com, June 1, 2001.
[5]www.ctv.ca, June 1, 2001.
[6]David Spencer – Interview, September 28, 2000.

Cable revenues were primarily obtained from subscriber fees, as well as from installation charges, pay-per-view sales, set-top converter rentals, remote control sales and rentals, advertising, carriage fees from home shopping channels and fees from infomercial presenters. Other sources of revenue in the recent past had come from digital video services, high-speed Internet access, local and long-distance telephone services, commercial competitive local exchange carrier operation, high-definition television (HDTV), video on demand and e-commerce. Total revenues in the cable industry were increasing by 15 per cent annually, increases which were projected to continue through 2004.

The growth of cable had both helped (by increasing the audience reach) and hurt (in the battle for advertising dollars) the networks.

Broadcast Industry Regulation

In the United States, the broadcast industry was regulated primarily through the Federal Communications Commission (FCC). In Canada, the Canadian Radio-television and Telecommunications Commission (CRTC) had evolved from a series of commissions and hearings into an agency responsible for regulating broadcasting and telecommunications in Canada. The CRTC operated as an independent public authority, serving the public interest and governed by the Broadcasting Act of 1991 and the Telecommunications Act of 1993. The Broadcasting Act had been put in place to ensure that all Canadians would have access to a wide variety of high-quality, Canadian programming.

Fifty-five per cent of prime-time radio and television content was required to be Canadian. This content requirement was calculated on a rolling average basis so that the quotas were typically not difficult to meet. The CRTC regulated over 5,900 broadcasters in television, cable distribution, AM and FM radio, pay and specialty television, direct-to-home satellite systems, multipoint distribution systems, subscription television and pay audio. As was the case in the United States, the Canadian broadcast industry was becoming saturated and highly competitive.

Revenue Generation in the Broadcast Industry

The North American broadcast industry revenues came primarily from three sources: national spot advertising sold to national and regional advertisers, advertising time sold to local advertisers and network compensation payments (payments to affiliates for broadcast network commercials and programming). Thus, television stations had traditionally relied largely on advertising revenues to fund operations. Cable system operators were less dependent on advertising, obtaining 65 per cent to 70 per cent of revenues from subscriber fees paid by consumers. TVO and the U.S.-based networks like PBS received no traditional advertising funding, but instead received money from government grants and public donations in the form of membership and/or sponsorship. Fifteen per cent of the PBS budget came from government funding, while TVO received 70 per cent of its funding from government sources. Many TVO viewers also had access to PBS through their signal providers, and PBS had a high membership penetration in southern Ontario. PBS was thus a key competitor to TVO, especially in the children's program arena, where they often aired the same programs, and in the area of membership solicitation.

In North America, there were tens of thousands of individual broadcast and cable companies, but the larger networks commanded the lion's share of the advertising business. In the United States, ABC, CBS and NBC accounted for more than 40 per cent of total industry advertising revenues, and even more in Olympic years. Because of this revenue base, these networks were able to purchase and provide first-run programming for prime-time hours (8 p.m. to 11 p.m. Eastern and Pacific time) and thus attract a larger share of the television audience.

Part of the negotiation process that ensued upon sale of a program to a station or network was the determination of who would obtain and/or keep the advertising revenues.

Program Syndication

Content producers were free to sell and syndicate their programs to competing and international stations.

Regardless of their network affiliation, all broadcast stations obtained some programs from independent sources, mainly syndicated TV shows or syndicated feature films which were either made for TV or had been previously shown in theatres and on cable television.

Broadcast stations (both local stations and network affiliates) could purchase a license to air a syndicated program, which gave them the ability to sell the advertising slots and keep the revenues to offset the cost of the program. The cash price for a program varied, based on its desirability and the number of times it was to be aired. The competitive environment for a particular type of programming also influenced the going rate for that program.

Thus, networks could also earn revenues through the sale of in-house productions. TVO had additionally done this through its Sales and Licensing Department. However, due to the increasingly competitive nature of the industry, TVO was unable to command higher prices for its products, prices that had been commonplace only a decade ago.

HISTORY OF TVONTARIO

TVOntario was established in 1970 as the Ontario Educational Communications Authority (OECA) by William (Bill) Davis, who was the minister of education for Ontario at that time. The mandate of OECA was to provide commercial-free television programming and interactive media resources that would educate, inform and entertain. The educational properties of OECA were to be closely linked to the province's education curriculum as well as to the skill and learning needs of the people of Ontario, from birth until long after retirement. The name of the English-language network was later changed to TVOntario (TVO). TVOntario was the corporate body which encompassed both the English-language network, TVO, and the French-language t/o network, which had been established in 1987.

To date, TVO had remained true to its original mandate and had been responsive to changes in education and technology. Over three million viewers watched TVO/t/o each week, with TVO available in 98.5 per cent of Ontario households and t/o to 77 per cent of all Ontario households. Outside Ontario, t/o was also available to over 400,000 French-speaking households in Atlantic Canada and Quebec through cable distribution, multimicrowave distribution systems and direct-to-home services. Throughout TVO's tenure, no other broadcaster had been linked as closely as TVO to the provincial education curriculum or to the lifelong learning needs of the people of Ontario.

TVO's children's programming had always been and continued to be non-violent, unbiased and uninterrupted by commercials. Research had shown a growing demand for quality programming for children under 12 years of age, and TVO had not only met that need, but had been recognized as a world leader in educational broadcasting for all ages, with more than 850 international awards to its credit. The children's shows *Polka Dot Door* and *Polka Dot Shorts*, both produced at TVO, had been widely acclaimed for their educational and entertainment value. TVO had been well recognized in the area of children's program broadcasting over the past few years. Of particular note was the success of its live, hosted children's programming, made available seven days a week. Through *TVO Kids*, it met preschooler needs in the morning and those of school-aged children in the afternoon and on weekends, with *TVO Kids Crawlspace* and *The Nook*. For French viewers, tfo's acclaimed *Mega* program met those same needs. While most networks in the business of broadcasting children's programming had some kind of hosted concept, not all were as successful as the TVO offerings.

TVO's adult programming had always explored important issues in the province of Ontario through debate, discussion and documentaries. TVO's *Studio 2* and tfo's *Panorama* focused on reflecting Ontario ideas and issues back to Ontario citizens. *Saturday Night at the Movies*, hosted for years by Elwy Yost, not only broadcast movies but set the artistic and historic context for viewers through artist, actor and behind-the-scenes interviews. A tribute to the quality of this programming was that *Saturday Night at the Movies* was often a required or recommended component of film studies courses. The Elwy Yost interviews were placed in the permanent archives of the Academy of Motion Picture Arts and Sciences in Los Angeles.

TVO had prided itself in meeting the needs of all of its consumer groups by offering a wide range of programming for all ages. Some of this programming was produced in-house, some was purchased for rebroadcast and some was co-produced.

TVO had recently created a new media division to implement a strategy of linking on-air educational broadcasting and Internet programming in the delivery of formal, curriculum-based education and lifelong learning skills development training. The direction and impact of this department had yet to be determined, though there was some optimism among those at TVO that revenue generation would be a part of the mix.

REVENUE GENERATION AND REVENUE SOURCES AT TVONTARIO

Revenues in the broadcast industry traditionally came largely from advertising. From its inception, TVO had chosen to rely on sources of revenue other than advertising.

In 2000–01, TVO's total operating budget was $63.2 million. Government funding accounted for $51.5 million in revenues, with $3.5 million coming from project and federal grants, and $48 million coming from the Ontario government. Earned revenues and development were $8.4 million, and other earned revenue was $3.3 million for that year.

There were six key sources of earned revenue for TVO:

Membership and Fundraising

TVO had approximately 79,000 members in 2001. Donations from memberships were becoming more important to the success of TVO over time. One could become a TVO member with any donation and receive *Signal* magazine with a donation of $40 or more. *Signal* was TVO's membership magazine, which included a program schedule and 'behind the scenes' stories on TVO/*tfo*. TVO membership campaigns had raised $5.1 million in 2000–01, down from previous years. TVO had traditionally accomplished its goals with the help of staff and a large contingent of volunteers. With this in mind, Baker had been working to rebuild this department to position it for future success.

Sponsorships

Corporate sponsorship for TVO programming had raised approximately $600,000 in 2000–01, with five major sponsors contributing to major initiatives:

- Dairy Farmers of Ontario—*TVO's Open House* and *TVO Kids "Bod Squad"*
- Alcan Aluminum Ltd—*TVO Teachers' Awards*
- Kodak Professional Motion Imaging—*TVO Telefest*
- Via Rail—*Saturday Night at the Movies* and *Cinema*
- The Globe and Mail—*Gregg and Company* and *Allan Gregg in Conversation with....*

Sponsorship revenues were down considerably from previous years, and the first half of the year found the department without staff. Baker had recently rebuilt this department and was confident that the new team would do great things in sponsorship in the future.

Sales and Licensing

The Sales and Licensing Department sold TVO programs primarily to other public broadcasters, educational networks, commercial cable and satellite networks and directly to educators for negotiated license fees. These license fees were generally based on usage rights and the volume of viewers in the geographical area. Thus, one broadcaster could pay $500 for a program while another broadcaster would pay $50,000 for the same program. Sales were primarily to other parts of Canada and the United States, but there had been sales to Europe, China and Latin America as well (close to 150 countries in total). At one time, revenues from this department had been in excess of $5 million, but there had been steady declines over the past few years, and net revenues of only $2.8 million were expected for the upcoming fiscal year end.

Through International Telefilm of Canada, TVO's Sales and Licensing Department sold video cassettes of curriculum resources to schools and school boards throughout Canada. Other distributors had been retained to handle international sales.

The Sales and Licensing Department had contracted Viewer Services, a private company, to handle all merchandise sales arising from the broadcast schedule, as well as offering TVO merchandise for sale at open houses and *TVO Kids* external events and live public broadcasts. Historically, merchandise sales had been low. At one time, TVO had attempted a partnership with Irwin Toys to sell the *Polka Dot Door* toy products, but it had not been profitable for either party, and the partnership was dissolved. Since 1994, there had been in excess of $2 million in retail sales of trademark licensing for *Polka Dot Door*. However, in light of declining sales, consumer product sales were terminated in March 2001.

New Business Ventures

TVO was developing partnerships with private sector businesses, earning over $600,000 in 1998–99 for contracts to maintain transmitters for OnTV, Global and Rogers in Ontario. Bell Sympatico carried *tfo* co-produced educational multimedia projects with major Canadian firms such as Enzyme and Micro-Intel (Quebecor) and their online games.

All of these revenue sources were considered important to TVO, and initiatives were in place to develop strategies for all areas. However, Baker's major concern at this time was with the future of the Sales and Licensing Department.

SALES AND LICENSING AT TVONTARIO

The Sales and Licensing Department at TVO had grown, as many departments of this type do, out of unsolicited consumer demand. As TVO developed its educational programs, broadcasters, educators and others began to approach TVO with requests to purchase programs, broadcast rights, video cassettes, etc. The demand continued to grow, and TVO management, recognizing a potentially important source of revenue, appointed one person to manage the sale of TVO products in the early 1970s. Over time, the Sales and Licensing Department was formed.

The Sales and Licensing Department had sold TVO products in 148 countries around the world; *Inquiring Minds* had been sold in 46 countries and *Polka Dot Shorts* in 43 countries, including the sale for broadcast through the BBC in England. TVO was the largest foreign supplier of curriculum materials to the U.S. Instructional television (ITV) market, and TVO materials had been sold into all 50 states.

The two most successful products for the Sales and Licensing Department had been the children's educational programs, *Concepts in Science* and *Concepts in Math*. However, with the decline of in-house production over the past 10 years, and most noticeably, the past five years, revenues from the Sales and Licensing Department had dropped dramatically, even for these programs. As well, the prices that the department could command for sale of programs had diminished over time. Prices in the United States, however, were not diminishing as drastically as prices in Canada and other parts of the world.

Cindy Galbraith, the manager of the Sales and Licensing Department, believed that things could be turned around for Sales and Licensing if TVO's Programming Department would produce some salable products. A salable product was that which had no marketing restrictions, i.e., no rights, content or technical restrictions; there could still be some geographical set-ups required, but they were typically manageable.

In 1996, TVO had produced 44.9 hours of new, salable product. That year, sales and licensing had earned $5.2 million in revenues. By 2000–01, TVO was producing only 8.1 hours of salable product with year-end revenues projected at $2.8 million. Galbraith felt strongly that with an 81 per cent decline in salable product, the Sales and Licensing Department staff should be commended for experiencing only a 46 per cent reduction in revenues. (See Exhibit 1 on the next page for an Analysis of Salable Product Decline.)

DECLINING REVENUES AT TVONTARIO

Other changes in the marketplace had contributed to the declining revenues in the Sales and Licensing Department and were of concern for the future.

Sixty per cent of sales and licensing revenues had typically come from the U.S. education market, these sales being totally dependent on curriculum correlations. The sales decline in this area over the past five years had been 20 per cent. *Third-party distribution rights* were responsible for minimizing the sales decline. However, an analysis of third-party distribution costs was not conclusive in determining whether or not it

Exhibit 1 Declining Product Analysis
            Ontario Educational Communications Authority Sales and Licensing Department

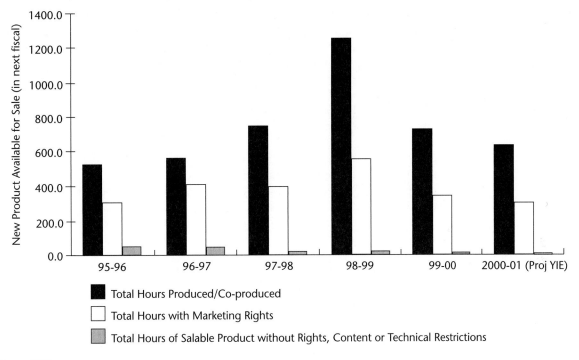

Legend:
■ Total Hours Produced/Co-produced
□ Total Hours with Marketing Rights
▨ Total Hours of Salable Product without Rights, Content or Technical Restrictions

Source: TVO

would be cost-effective to continue with these sales. As of November 2000, third-party product had generated $374,000 in gross revenues. After hard costs were applied (i.e., repurposing of tape, direct sales fulfilment, guide development, producer royalties), the net revenue was $92,000. Once the cost of labor and promotion, as well as the cost of the manager of product development (whose full-time job had been sourcing the product) was added, it was questionable whether the venture would be profitable over time. Thus, U.S. sales would be dependent on program inventory. The production year that was best in terms of production of TVO's top-10 U.S. sellers was 1988. No top-10 sellers had been produced in the last three years.

Programming had provided sales and licensing with interstitial material or mini clips that would fit within the confines of a full-length program in lieu of commercials, etc. (the shows *Video Clips*, *The Bod Squad*, *What's My Sign*, etc.). The curriculum was not sold for some of the interstitials produced so far. Sales and Licensing had tried to fit these mini-programs into the curriculum requirements of educational clients, but the short segments were ahead of their time and problematic for 99 per cent of the market which did not have access to computer delivery methods. While boards of education were asking for more Internet–based programming, the majority of teachers delivering the programs did not yet have the necessary computer access to utilize this type of programming.

Broadcast license fees were on the decline with the advent of new cable, satellite, and digital channels worldwide. While pricing rates could be as low as $400 per hour, they could still go as high as $10,000 to $15,000 per hour. At the lower rates, fees were at times insufficient to cover the cost of tape conversion for interstitial materials. It was becoming more and more difficult to find customers who would make it possible for TVO to sell programs at a profit.

The Programming Department at TVO had been developing more two-minute *interstitial segments* to replace 15-minute segments. Given that educational license fees were charged on a per-minute basis, significant potential revenue had been lost.

Programming at TVO, with the assistance of the Business Development Group, had over the past few years engaged in *pre-selling properties* that were to be produced in-house. These sales were not managed through the Sales and Licensing Department, and thus, 100 per cent of the resulting revenues were credited directly to the Programming Department. The Sales and Licensing Department had not traditionally devoted a great deal of energy to pre-sales, given the system that was in place for crediting revenue.

Copyright fees had always been an issue, and had become a more significant one. The step-up fees (i.e., the additional fees payable once a program was to be aired outside of the originally intended market area) to talent collectives upon sale of a program often made it unprofitable and, thus, impossible to make the sale where there were low license fees. Some one-off exception agreements had been struck with the talent collectives to make sales, but these were time-consuming to negotiate and hardly worth the effort.

Programming was no longer renewing Ontario broadcast rights, so Sales and Licensing now had to cover that cost, as well as the cost of step-ups for inventory. The renewal cost was typically 50 per cent of the original fee paid to the talent collectives.

Management and the board of directors at TVO did not want programming sold to their key competitor, CBC, in the interest of preserving the TVO brand. At one time, Galbraith had been confident she could sell *Polka Dot Shorts* and a number of other programs to CBC, given discussions she had had with CBC staff. *Polka Dot Shorts* would have been sold to CBC at a fee of $15,000 an hour. This window of opportunity appeared to have passed TVO by, and without the CBC sale, Galbraith was faced with her only market in Canada being British Columbia's Knowledge Network, where the fee paid would be $2,000 an hour.

Galbraith had made recommendations for the revitalization and growth of the TVO Sales and Licensing Department. She had recommended that each of the proposed steps be taken annually for the next five years to return Sales and Licensing to the $4-million-plus revenue level.

Galbraith's suggestions were:

- Produce, at TVO, a broadcast television series modelled after *Inquiring Minds* (13 × 30-minute segments), with two or three stand-alone segments that could be cut for curriculum use. Produce with on-screen hosts in link segments, so that international customers could replace hosts with their own; make music and effects, scripts and cue sheets standard deliverables.

- Produce, at TVO, a broadcast television series for children aged six to nine years of age, either 13 × 30-minute segments or 26 × 15-minute segments. The series could be either animated or live action with high production values.

- Produce, at TVO, three 60-minute documentaries similar to the former *Vista* documentaries.

- Produce, at TVO, a minimum of 15 hours of core curriculum programming in math, science or language arts for kindergarten to Grade 12 as a video series. Each series would be a minimum of 100 minutes with 10 × 15 minutes series being optimal.

- Produce, at TVO, English as a Second Language (ESL) programs, a high-demand product with limited worldwide supply.

- Produce, at TVO, an updated core curriculum series by doing some minor reshooting of current material.

- Set a more realistic contribution margin target for the Sales and Licensing Department. Anecdotal evidence indicated a realistic margin was 20 per cent to 35 per cent; TVO's target had been 50 per cent.

- Build meaningful communication between Programming and Sales and Licensing—given that Programming did not directly benefit from the Sales and Licensing revenues, communication and co-operation has been minimal.

The Sales and Licensing Department had devoted considerable energy over the past few years to securing distribution rights to third-party product and selling that product in Canada and internationally. Their greatest third-party success had come from the distribution of the *Pingu* series, which had been produced by a Dutch independent. However, the venture was not without problems. TVO's management and board of directors objected to selling the product to CBC, whom they believed to be TVO's key competitor in Ontario. CBC refused to purchase product for broadcast outside of Ontario only, as Ontario was its largest market and it was not reasonable or cost-effective to offer separate programming for the Ontario market. Without the CBC sale, Sales and Licensing was not able to forecast sufficient sales to interest the producers of the program. It remained to be seen whether third-party product distribution could still work in some form for TVO.

Galbraith recognized that it was virtually impossible to recoup total production costs through outside sale of product, but she believed that partial cost recovery had been and should continue to be the goal for in-house production. Galbraith believed that more than 70 per cent of the in-house production costs could be recovered through the efforts of Sales and Licensing with a well-researched and targeted program, but noted that any new programming would first have to meet the needs and mandate of the Programming Department. She had suggested to the senior administration that a portion of the Sales and Licensing revenue be funnelled into Programming to produce salable product, but the proposal had been declined repeatedly.

Sales and Licensing had also been fighting to have in-house product produced with a music and effects (M & E) version complete at the time of production. An M & E version of a program would allow international customers to dub in their own voice in their language of choice. Seldom was programming produced with an M & E version. The cost of adding M & E's post-production was three times the cost of doing it at the time of production and often made the sale impossible. Programming had not typically produced programs with M & E's at the time of production, as it was an added cost for programming with no guarantee that product would be sold by Sales and Licensing and with no return of the Sales and Licensing revenues directly to Programming. Senior management had issued a directive to Programming to produce with M & E's, but had not enforced the directive as of yet.

Distribution Alternatives

Galbraith had spent considerable time investigating the possibility of changing the method of distributing product under the umbrella of Sales and Licensing.

Currently Sales and Licensing had on staff, in addition to Galbraith, a sales executive in Canada, one international sales executive and three support staff, along with two sales executives based in the U.S. office in North Carolina (see Exhibit 2). In addition to the TVO staff, Sales and Licensing used the services of one educational non-broadcast distributor in Canada, five educational non-broadcast distributors in the United States and 10 to 12 international broadcast distributors on average. The non-broadcast distributors took 70 per cent to 75 per cent commission on sales, and the international broadcast distributors took 25 per cent to 30 per cent commission on sales.

A number of years ago, TVO had tried to sell products directly in the United States to save on distributor commissions, but between the cost of catalogues and the cost of managing sales from TVO, it had lost money over a five-year period.

Galbraith had looked closely at three alternative distribution models for Sales and Licensing:

- Contracting Canadian and international sales to an outside distributor;
- Contracting Canadian, international and U.S. sales to an outside distributor; and
- Contracting Canadian, and international sales to an outside distributor and handling U.S. sales out of Toronto.

Galbraith had concluded that net revenues would either decrease or would be minimal, making it impossible to justify the change (see Exhibit 3 on the next page for budget estimates for distribution alternatives).

Everyone in the Sales and Licensing department was fiercely loyal to TVO and wanted to do what was best for the organization as a whole. Galbraith summed up the feelings of those in the department when she said, "The painful death we're going through is so demoralizing . . ." Staff were at the point where they just wanted a decision made, regardless of which way it went. Meanwhile, they continued to work their hardest to bring in what revenues they could and to look for new solutions.

Exhibit 2   Sales and Licensing Staff (April 2000)

Manager
Sales & Licensing
Cindy Galbraith

Sales Executive Canada
Debra Bennett

Sales Executive International
Smilika Baiiozovic

Sales Executive U.S. ITV
Beth Stafford

Supervisor U.S. Sales
Vicky Etheridae

Sales Assistant
Kathy Marchese

Sales Fulfilment Co-ordinator
Carmela Nunes

Sales Analyst
Mari Cromb

Source: TVO

Exhibit 3 Distribution Alternatives – Financial Summary Sales and Licensing (all amounts in CDN$000)

	2000-01 Year End Forecast	Prop. Budget	2001-02 Alt A	2001-02 Alt B	2001-02 Alt C
Gross Revenue	2,785.5	2,569.9	2,569.9	2,569.9	2,569.9
Full-time salaries	444.9	448.7	346.7	202.0	302.0
Benefits	73.5	74.0	57.2	33.3	35.0
Overtime	8.0	8.0	8.0	8.0	8.0
Freelance	7.0	10.0	10.0	10.0	10.0
Sub-total Labor	533.4	540.7	421.9	253.3	355.0
Travel	34.0	48.0	37.0	17.0	37.0
Consulting		10.0	10.0	10.0	10.0
Telephone	18.0	18.0	18.0		
Office Supplies	6.0	9.0	9.0	5.0	5.0
Memberships	1.5	1.5	0.6	0.6	0.6
Periodicals	1.0	1.0	1.0	1.0	1.0
Translations		2.0	2.0	2.0	2.0
Subtotal Dept Oper'ns	60.5	89.5	77.6	35.6	55.6
Advertising	12.0	15.0	5.0	5.0	5.0
Promotion	80.0	120.0	70.0	30.0	70.0
Bldg. rental	17.0	23.0	23.0		
Equip. rental	5.0	6.0	6.0		
Mailing	10.0	12.0	12.0		
Tape	68.3	54.4	45.1	38.1	45.1
Publications	26.0	30.0	30.0	30.0	30.0
Dev't. fund	17.0	20.0	20.0	10.0	20.0
Cost of Sales	31.0	30.0	30.0	30.0	30.0
Bad Deb/WHolding Tax	174.8	22.4	22.4	162.4	162.4
Commission	250.0	212.4	375.0	1,075.1	375.1
Copyright	385.0	329.6	329.6	329.6	329.6
Subtotal Dep't. Specific	1,076.1	874.8	968.1	1,710.2	1,067.2
Project/Program costs	10.0				
Total Expenditures	1,680.0	1,505.0	1,467.6	1,999.1	1,477.8
Net Revenue	1,105.5	1,064.9	1,102.3	570.8	1,092.2
Contribution Margin	40%	41%	43%	22%	42%

Source: TVO

PROGRAMMING CHALLENGES

The programming departments at TVO were charged with filling their broadcast hours with programming that met the mandate of TVO, while staying within a modest budget. Programs for TVO came from three sources: in-house production, co-production and acquisition.

In-house production at TVO had become very costly over the past few years. On the surface, outsourcing production had seemed to be the most economical method of producing programming. TVO's production budget was $20 million per year; t*f*o's production budget was $10 million per year. Production costs ranged anywhere from $30,000 to $200,000 per hour for in-house production versus TVO's $2,000 to $5,000 per hour contribution for co-production. Outside producers had access to Telefilm funding, which was not available to TVO, though there were rumors in the industry that a change in funding criteria may be forthcoming. If TVO were to have access to this funding, it could change the programming decisions dramatically.

Given the current climate, TVO, which had in the past produced more properties in-house, was now producing only one-third of its programming in-house. Most of the in-house production money was going to the hosting shows for children's programming such as *The Crawlspace*, *The Nook* and *Mega* and for Ontario-based interview programs like *Studio 2* and *Panorama*.

TVO broadcasted an average of 8,647 hours per year, with a minimum of 70 per cent Canadian content. T*f*o broadcasted an average of 7,530 hours per year with a minimum of 60 per cent Canadian content.

In 1997–98, TVO delivered 255 hours of Canadian co-produced and independently produced programming, 604 hours of foreign co-productions and acquisitions and 719 hours of in-house production for airing. TVO, when co-producing a program, would negotiate for TVO's usage, based on the percentage of budget that TVO was putting up for the production. For a small percentage of the production cost, TVO was likely to have usage rights for Ontario only; for a larger share of the total cost, TVO could gain some exclusivity across Canada. The outside producer could ultimately sell the program to any and all broadcasters except where TVO had obtained exclusivity. Typically, TVO's creative head would make a pre-buy (usually more expensive than a standard license fee) in order to get a credit, and to get a first window or first airing for the productions. TVO would also look for sole broadcasting rights in Ontario, and the independent producer would have the right to sell the product anywhere else in the world. This arrangement made it economical for TVO to produce programs, but impossible for Sales and Licensing to resell the properties. Alternatively, TVO could purchase programming for rebroadcast, which they did for many of their children's programs, such as *Arthur* and *Magic School Bus*.

The programming managers did not typically communicate their plans to the Sales and Licensing Department, and were somewhat frustrated by the inability of Sales and Licensing to continue to sell their programs. Programming managers had suggested selling the formats of the interstitial programs, but had been told by Sales and Licensing staff that this was not as easy as it sounded, given that customers could easily develop their own formats without paying for them. Programming managers had also wondered whether there was a market for product spin-off sales from TVO properties. The characters associated with *TVO Kids Crawlspac*e and *The Nook* were very popular in Ontario. Children lined up for hours for an autograph whenever the show hosts went out into the Ontario community, and the TVO membership was always receptive to *TVO Kids* memorabilia. However, Cindy Galbraith had pointed out that while interest seemed high, not much TVO product had actually been purchased by these potential customers.

The programming managers were open to seeing the development of a business model for internal production of children's programs in particular, versus the current move to outsourcing. They also felt there might be some money to be made from cable flow-through and possibly from advertising, though advertising had not previously been considered at TVO. They wondered why *Polka Dot Shorts*, which had sold in 64 countries, was not selling in the United States, as it seemed to be a natural spin-off market. Sales and Licensing had said they could sell the program to CBC, but programming did not want to dilute their brand by selling to the competition. However, the United States was a totally different matter.

Programming managers stated they would be more than happy to have Sales and Licensing sell as much of their product as possible, given that their objective was exposure, both inside and outside of Ontario. With their current budgets, programming managers did not see how they could increase production of salable product. They wondered whether a more economical distribution system might be the answer.

FINANCIAL IMPLICATIONS

Sales and Licensing had been reasonably profitable throughout its existence at TVO, but not as profitable as membership or sponsorship activities. On the Sales and Licensing profit and loss statements, the department appeared to be earning 50 per cent margins. In reality, it was earning considerably less than that amount. Approximately 12 per cent of the Sales and Licensing revenues were required for administrative support. The Accounting Department argued that another 15 per cent to 20 per cent of the sales revenues was used for tape dubbing/reformatting, phone, mail, office space, warehousing, etc., making the actual profit margins much lower than they first appeared (see Exhibit 4 for Sales and Licensing financial statements).

Looking at the cost of other revenue-generating activities, Baker noted that the Membership Department spent 44 cents for every one dollar raised. However, he wasn't certain that Membership could make up for the revenue shortfall should Sales and Licensing shut down; nor did he believe TVO could make up the shortfall through sponsorships, at least not in the short term.

Baker had an expense budget of $5.5 million, which he was expected to use to generate $12 million in revenues. At present, there were 23 staff in his departments, including the Sales and Licensing staff. This was half of the staffing level prior to his arrival at TVO, and they were producing the same revenue.

Galbraith's wish list for salable programming was going to require considerable seed funding, and there were no guarantees that the programming would be picked up by broadcasters outside Ontario. Galbraith maintained that while Sales and Licensing would never recover total cost of production, new salable programming with solid production values would not only be an asset to the Programming Department, but would allow Sales and Licensing to make sales that would offset some of the costs of in-house production. No production cost estimates or sales estimates had been developed to date, though Baker wanted to see some solid projections before backing this option. However, there wasn't much time in which to develop them.

THE PROBLEM

Baker believed that the Sales and Licensing Department could be resuscitated, but not in its present form. He needed to come up with a plan before the board of directors decided to shut the department down. He saw early June as his deadline for development of a proposal for the board. One major concern was that Baker wasn't certain he would be able to implement anything substantial in time to salvage what was left of Sales and Licensing, even if he did come up with a viable proposal.

Exhibit 4   Sales and Licensing Revenue History (all amounts in CDN$000)

Manager of Sales: Revenues by Market Segment

Year	Licensing	Consumer Sales	Co-revenue
2001-02 Budget	5.0	25.0	300.0
2000-01 Proj.	10.0	30.0	300.0
1999-00 Actual	43.1	39.3	347.5
1998-99 Actual	39.8	34.1	266.8
1997-98 Actual	61.2	70.1	402.5

Licensing: U.K. license continuing for Polkaroo; no active Canadian licensees.
Consumer Sales: New partner Viewer Plus.
Co-Revenue: Targets set by past practice; all receivables from co-producing partners and royalty payments from copyright collectives.

Canadian Sales:

Year	Revenue
2001-02 Budget	242.3
2000-01 Projected	280.9
1999-00 Actual	360.1
1998-99 Actual	838.4
1997-98 Actual	1,001.9

International Sales:

Year	Revenue
2001-02 Budget	300.0
2000-01 Projected	200.0
1999-00 Actual	558.2
1998-99 Actual	1,075.8
1997-98 Actual	722.7

U.S. Sales by Segment:

Year	ITV	Cassettes	Publications
2001-02 Budget	1,409.0	360.2	28.0
2000-01 Projected	1,427.0	396.9	35.0
1999-00 Actual	1,340.6	563.7	26.0
1998-99 Actual	1,547.1	626.7	37.5
1997-98 Actual	1,496.4	729.5	37.2

Source: TVO

OPTIONS

Baker had been exploring his options and had come up with the following alternatives:

- Spin off an arm's-length production company from TVO. This production company would have access to the Telefilm grants and TVO would have first rights to the programs, which could also be sold through Sales and Licensing. Baker was in the early stages of looking at the feasibility of this option.

- Find a donor who would contribute the funds to produce a special program series, which would be of interest to the TVO audience, but would also be a salable commodity for Sales and Licensing.

- Find a more economical distribution system for Sales and Licensing.

- Develop a plan to gradually phase out the Sales and Licensing Department at TVO; put the Sales and Licensing budget dollars into Membership or Sponsorship activities to generate additional income from these activities.

Case 6

Ikea (Canada) Ltd. 1986 (Condensed)

Founded as a mail order business in rural Sweden in 1943, IKEA had grown to more than US$1 billion in sales and 70 retail outlets by 1985, and was considered by many to be one of the best-run furniture operations in the world. Although only 14 per cent of IKEA's sales were outside Europe, the company's fastest growth was occurring in North America.

Success, however, brought imitators. In mid–1986, Bjorn Bayley and Anders Berglund, the senior managers of IKEA's North American operations, were examining a just-published Sears Canada catalogue, which contained a new 20-page section called "Elements." This section bore a striking resemblance to the format of an IKEA Canada catalogue (see Exhibits 1 and 2 for sample pages), and the furniture being offered was similar to IKEA's knock-down, self-assembled line in which different "Elements" could be ordered by the customer to create particular designs. Bayley and Berglund wondered how serious Sears was about its new initiative, and what, if anything, IKEA should do in response.

THE CANADIAN FURNITURE MARKET

Canadian consumption of furniture totalled more than $2 billion in 1985, an average of well over $600 per household. Imports accounted for approximately 18 per cent of this total, half of which originated in the United States. The duties on furniture imported into Canada were approximately 15 per cent.

Furniture was sold to Canadian consumers through three types of stores: independents, specialty chains and department stores. Although the independents held a 70 per cent market share, this figure was declining due to their inability to compete with the

Richard Ivey School of Business
The University of Western Ontario

Professor Paul W. Beamish prepared this case solely to provide material for class discussion. The author does not intend to illustrate either effective or ineffective handling of a managerial situation. The author may have disguised certain names and other identifying information to protect confidentiality.

chains in terms of advertising, purchasing power, management sophistication and sales support. The average sales per square metre in 1985 for furniture stores of all three types was $1,666 (the figure was $2,606 for stores which also sold appliances) and the average cost of goods sold was 64.5 per cent.

While the major department stores such as Eaton's and Sears tended to carry traditional furniture lines close to the middle of the price/quality range, chains and independents operated from one end of the spectrum to the other. At the upper end of the market, specialty stores attempted to differentiate themselves by offering unique product lines, superior service and a specialized shopping atmosphere. The lower end of the market, on the other hand, was dominated by furniture warehouses which spent heavily on advertising, and offered lower price, less service, and less emphasis on a fancy image. The warehouses usually kept a larger inventory of furniture on hand than the department stores, but expected customers to pick up their purchases. Over half the warehouse sales involved promotional financing arrangements, including delayed payments, extended terms, and so on.

The major firms in this group—both of whom sold furniture and appliances—were The Brick and Leon's. The Brick had annual sales of $240 million from 15 Canadian stores, and was rapidly expanding from its western Canada base. With 30 additional stores in California under the Furnishings 2000 name, The Brick intended to become the largest furniture retailing company in the world. Leon's had annual sales of $160 million from 14 stores, and was growing rapidly from its Ontario base. These 14 stores were operated under a variety of names. Leon's also franchised its name in smaller cities in Canada. For part of their merchandise requirements, The Brick and Leon's often negotiated with manufacturers for exclusive products, styles and fabrics and imported from the U.S., Europe and the Far East. Although both firms had had problems earlier with entry to the U.S. market, each intended to expand there.

Most furniture retailers in Canada purchased their products from Canadian manufacturers after examining new designs and models at trade shows. There were approximately 1,400 Canadian furniture manufacturers, most of whom were located in Ontario and Quebec. Typically, these firms were small (78 per cent of Canadian furniture plants employed fewer than 50 people), undercapitalized and minimally automated. One industry executive quipped that one of the most significant technological developments for the industry had been the advent of the staple gun.

Canadian-produced furniture typically followed American and European styling, and was generally of adequate to excellent quality but was often more costly to produce. The reason for high Canadian costs was attributed to a combination of short manufacturing runs and high raw material, labor and distribution costs. In an attempt to reduce costs, a few of the larger manufacturers such as Kroehler had vertically integrated—purchasing sawmills, fabric warehouses, fiberboard and wood frame plants—but such practices were very much the exception in the industry.

THE IKEA FORMULA

IKEA's approach to business was fundamentally different from that of the traditional Canadian retailers. The company focused exclusively on what it called "quick assembly" furniture, which consumers carried from the store in flat packages and assembled at home. This furniture was primarily pine, had a clean European-designed look to it,

Exhibit 1   Sample Page from IKEA Catalogue

GUTE. EIGHTEEN DIFFERENT CHESTS OF DRAWERS TO FIT IN ALMOST ANYWHERE.

GUTE chests of drawers ●möbelfakta White lacquered or pine veneered particleboard, natural or nutbrown stained. W80 cm, D40 cm. QA.
49/2. 2 drawers. H49 cm. White **$94**. Natural or nutbrown **$98**.
49/6. 6 drawers. H49 cm. White **$115**. Natural or nutbrown **$125**.
87/4. 4 drawers. H87 cm. White **$130**. Natural or nutbrown **$145**.

87/8. 8 drawers. H87 cm. White **$170**. Natural or nutbrown **$185**.
126/6. 6 drawers. H126 cm. White **$175**. Natural or nutbrown **$195**.
126/10. 10 drawers. H126 cm. White **$215**. Natural or nutbrown **$225**.

and was priced at 15 per cent below the lowest prices for traditional furniture. Its major appeal appeared to be to young families, singles and frequent movers, who were looking for well-designed items that were economically priced and created instant impact.

According to company executives, IKEA was successful because of its revolutionary approach to the most important aspects of the business: product design, procurement, store operations, marketing and management philosophy, which stressed flexibility and market orientation rather than long-range strategy. Each of these items is discussed in turn.

Exhibit 2   Sample Page from Elements Section of Sears Catalogue

Dressers and chests whose quality and practicality are inherent— in the colors and sizes you want. Assemble them yourself with ease. Your choice of clear knot-free pine veneer over non-warp platewood core or White baked-on European-quality low gloss enamel on a platewood core.

3 Drawer Units. 38 cm deep, 54 cm high (15 x 21¼").
Wide. 75 cm wide (29½").
012 065 012 DLT – *Pine* Each.139.98
012 065 002 DLT – *White* Each.139.98
Narrow. 50 cm wide (19½").
012 065 015 DLT – *Pine* Each.119.98
012 065 005 DLT – *White* Each.119.98

4 Drawer Units. 38 cm deep, 69 cm high (15 x 27¼").
Wide. 75 cm wide (29½").
012 065 011 DLT – *Pine* Each.159.98
012 065 001 DLT – *White* Each.159.98
Narrow. 50 cm wide (19½").
012 065 014 DLT – *Pine* Each.139.98
012 065 004 DLT – *White* Each.139.98

6 Drawer Units. 38 cm deep, 99 cm high (15 x 39")
Wide. 75 cm wide (29½").
012 065 010 DLTJ – *Pine* Each.219.98
012 065 000 DLTJ – *White* Each.219.98
Narrow. 50 cm wide (19½").
012 065 013 DLT – *Pine* Each.189.98
012 065 003 DLT – *White* Each.189.98

Product Design

IKEA's European designers, not the company's suppliers, were responsible for the design of most of the furniture and accessories in IKEA's product line, which totalled 15,000 items. The heart of the company's design capability was a 50-person Swedish workshop which produced prototypes of new items of furniture and smaller components such as "an ingenious little snap lock for table legs which makes a table stronger and cheaper at the same time" and a "clever little screw attachment which allows for the assembly of a pin back chair in five minutes." IKEA's designers were very cost conscious, and were constantly working to lower costs in ways that were not critical to the consumer. "The quality of a work top," for example, would be superior to that of the back of a bookshelf which would never be seen. "Low price with a meaning" was the theme.

Although it was not impossible to copyright a particular design or process, IKEA's philosophy was "if somebody steals a model from us we do not bring a lawsuit, because a lawsuit is always negative. We solve the problem by making a new model that is even better."

Procurement

IKEA's early success in Sweden had so threatened traditional European furniture retailers that they had promised to boycott any major supplier that shipped products to the upstart firm. As a result, IKEA had no choice but to go to the smaller suppliers. Since these suppliers had limited resources, IKEA began assuming responsibility for the purchase of raw materials, packaging materials, storage, specialized equipment and machinery, and engineering. What began as a necessity soon became a cornerstone of IKEA's competitive strategy, and by 1986 the firm had nearly 100 production engineers working as purchasers. Together with IKEA's designers, these engineers assisted suppliers in every way they could to help them lower costs, dealing with everything from the introduction of new technology to the alteration of the dimensions of a shipping carton.

Although IKEA sometimes leased equipment and made loans to its suppliers, the firm was adamant that it would not enter the furniture manufacturing business itself. In fact, to avoid control over—and responsibility for—its suppliers, the company had a policy of limiting its purchases to 50 per cent of a supplier's capacity. Many products were obtained from multiple suppliers, and frequently suppliers produced only a single standardized component or input to the final product. Unfinished pine shelves, for example, were obtained directly from saw mills, cabinet doors were purchased from door factories, and cushions came from textile mills.

In total, IKEA purchased goods from 1,500 suppliers located in 40 countries. About 52 per cent of the company's purchases were from Scandinavia, 21 per cent from other countries of western Europe, 20 per cent from eastern Europe and seven per cent elsewhere.

Store Operations

IKEA stores were usually large one or two-storey buildings situated in relatively inexpensive stand-alone locations, neither in prime downtown sites nor as part of a shopping mall. Most stores were surrounded by a large parking lot, adorned with billboards explaining IKEA's delivery policy, product guarantee, and the existence of a coffee shop and/or restaurant.

On entering a store, the customer was immediately aware of the children's play area (a room filled with hollow multi-colored balls), a video room for older children, and a receptionist with copies of IKEA catalogues, a metric conversion guide, index cards for detailing purchases, and a store guide. The latter, supplemented by prominent signs, indicated that the store contained lockers and benches for shoppers, a first-aid area, restrooms, strollers and a baby-care area, an "As-Is" department (no returns permitted), numerous check-outs, suggestion boxes and, in many cases, a restaurant. All major credit cards were accepted.

Traffic flow in most IKEA stores was guided in order to pass by almost all of the merchandise in the store, which was displayed as it would look in the home, complete with all accessories. Throughout the store, employees could be identified by their bright red IKEA shirts. Part-time employees wore yellow shirts which read "Temporary Help—Please Don't Ask Me Any Hard Questions." The use of sales floor staff was minimal. The IKEA view was that "salesmen are expensive, and can also be irritating. IKEA leaves you to shop in peace."

While IKEA stores were all characterized by their self-serve, self-wrapping, self-transport, and self-assembly operations, the company's philosophy was that each new store would incorporate the latest ideas in use in any of its existing stores. The most recent trend in some countries was an IKEA Contract Sales section, which provided a delivery, invoicing and assembly service for commercial customers.

Marketing

IKEA's promotional activities were intended to educate the consumer public on the benefits of the IKEA concept and to build traffic by attracting new buyers and encouraging repeat visits from existing customers. The primary promotional vehicle was the annual IKEA catalogue which was selectively mailed out to prime target customers who, in the Toronto area for instance, had the following characteristics:

Income $35,000+	Primary Age Group 35–44
Owner Condominium or Townhouse	Secondary Age Group 25–34
University Degree	Husband/Wife both work
White Collar	Two Children
	Movers

With minor variations, this "upscale" profile was typical of IKEA's target customers in Europe and North America. In Canada, IKEA management acknowledged the target market, but felt that, in fact, the IKEA concept appealed to a much wider group of consumers.

IKEA also spent heavily on magazine advertisements, which were noted for their humorous, slightly off-beat approach. In Canada, IKEA spent $2.5 million to print 3.6 million catalogues, $2 million on magazine advertising, and $1.5 million on other forms of promotion in 1984.

Management Philosophy

The philosophy of Ingvar Kamprad, the founder of IKEA, was "to create a better everyday life for the majority of people." In practice, this creed meant that IKEA was dedicated to offering, and continuing to offer, the lowest prices possible on good quality furniture, so that IKEA products were available to as many people as possible. Fred Andersson, the head of IKEA's product range for the world, stated: "Unlike other companies, we are not fascinated with what we produce—we make what our customers want." Generally, IKEA management felt that no other company could match IKEA's combination of quality and price across the full width of the product line.

IKEA also made a concerted effort to stay "close to its customers," and it was not unusual for the general manager of IKEA Canada, for instance, to personally telephone customers who had made complaints or suggestions. Each week an employee newsletter detailed all customer comments, and indicated how management felt they should be dealt with.

Another guiding philosophy of the firm was that growth would be in "small bites." The growth objective in Canada, for instance, had been to increase sales and profits by 20 per cent per year, but care was given to sequence store openings so that managerial and financial resources would not be strained.

Internally, the company's philosophy was stated as "freedom, with responsibility," which meant that IKEA's managers typically operated with a good deal of autonomy. The Canadian operation, for instance, received little in the way of explicit suggestions from head office, even in the one year when the budget was not met. The Canadian management team travelled to head office as a group only once every several years. As Bjorn Bayley explained:

> We are a very informal management team, and try to have everyone who works for us believe that they have the freedom to do their job in the best way possible. It's almost impossible to push the philosophy down to the cashier level, but we try.

IKEA IN CANADA

IKEA's formula had worked well in Canada. Under the direction of a four-man management team, which included two Swedes, the company had grown from a single store in 1976 to nine stores totalling 800,000 square feet and, as shown in Exhibit 3, predicted 1986 sales of more than $140 million. The sales of IKEA Canada had exceeded budget in all but one of the past five years, and usually by a wide margin. Net profits were approximately five per cent of sales. Profit and loss statements for 1983 and 1984, the only financial statements available, are presented in Exhibit 4 (on the next page).

IKEA Canada carried just less than half of the company's total product line. Individual items were chosen on the basis of what management thought would sell in Canada, and if IKEA could not beat a competitor's price by 10 to 15 per cent on a particular item, it was dropped. Most of the goods sold in the Canadian stores were supplied from central warehouses in Sweden. To coordinate this process a five-person stock supply department in Vancouver provided Sweden with a three-year forecast of Canada's needs, and placed major orders twice a year. Actual volumes were expected to be within 10 per cent of the forecast level. As Bayley noted, "you needed a gambler in the stock supply job."

Exhibit 3   IKEA Canada Sales by Store (including mail order; Cdn. $000s)

	1981	1982	1983 (Actual)	1984	1985	1986 (Forecasted)	Mail[1] Order (%)
Vancouver	$12,122	$11,824	$12,885	$19,636	$19,240	$25,500	6.8
Calgary	7,379	8,550	7,420	7,848	9,220	11,500	8.6
Ottawa	5,730	6,914	8,352	9,015	10,119	12,500	1.8
Montreal			8,617	12,623	15,109	22,000[2]	2.2
Halifax	3,634	4,257	4,474	6,504	7,351	9,000	22.9
Toronto	11,231	13,191	16,249	18,318	22,673	30,500	1.8
Edmonton	6,506	7,474	8,075	8,743	9,986	16,000	15.4
Quebec City		5,057	8,284	9,027	10,037	12,000	6.1
Victoria					2,808	3,500	
Total	**$46,602**	**$57,267**	**$74,356**	**$91,714**	**$106,543**	**$142,500**	**6.7**

[1]1984 most recent data available

[2]Projected growth due to store size expansion

Exhibit 4   Statement of Earnings and Retained Earnings, Year Ended August 31, 1984 (with comparative figures for 1983)

	1984	1983
Sales	$92,185,188	$74,185,691
Cost of merchandise sold	49,836,889	38,085,173
Gross Profit	42,348,299	36,100,518
General, administrative and selling expenses	28,016,473	23,626,727
Operating profit before the undernoted	14,331,826	12,473,791
Depreciation and amortization	1,113,879	1,066,285
Franchise amortization	257,490	257,490
Franchise fee	2,765,558	2,225,571
	4,136,927	3,549,347
Earnings from operations	10,194,899	8,924,444
Rental income	769,719	815,683
Less: rental expense	245,803	258,296
	523,916	557,387
Interest expense	2,453,116	3,042,471
Less: other income	438,683	65,757
	2,014,433	2,976,714
Earnings before income taxes	8,704,382	6,505,117
Income Taxes:		
Current	3,789,773	2,716,645
Deferred	(70,400)	175,500
	3,719,373	2,892,145
Net earnings for the year	4,985,009	3,612,972
Retained earnings beginning of year	5,501,612	1,888,640
Retained earnings, end of year	$10,486,621	$ 5,501,612

Source: Consumer and Corporate Affairs, Canada

Individual stores were expected to maintain 13.5 weeks of inventory on hand (10.5 weeks in the store and three weeks in transit), and could order from the central warehouse in Montreal or, if a product was not in stock in Montreal, direct from Sweden. Shipments from Sweden took six to eight weeks to arrive, shipments from Montreal two to three weeks. In practice, about 50 per cent of the product arriving at a store came via each route.

IKEA's success in Canada meant that the firm was often hard pressed to keep the best selling items in stock. (Twenty per cent of the firm's present line constituted 80 per cent of sales volume.) At any given time in Canada IKEA stores might have 300 items out of stock, either because actual sales deviated significantly from forecasts or because suppliers could not meet their delivery promises. While management estimated that 75 per cent of customers were willing to wait for IKEA products in a stock-out situation, the company, nevertheless, began a deliberate policy of developing Canadian suppliers for high demand items, even if this meant paying a slight premium. In 1984, the stock control group purchased $57 million worth of goods on IKEA's behalf, $12 million of which was from 30 Canadian suppliers, up from $7 million the previous year.

As indicated in Exhibit 3, IKEA Canada sold products, rather reluctantly, by mail order to customers who preferred not to visit the stores. A senior manager explained:

> To date we have engaged in defensive mail order—only when the customer really wants it and the order is large enough. The separate handling, breaking down of orders and repackaging required for mail orders would be too expensive and go against the economies-through-volume approach of IKEA. Profit margins of mail order business tend to be half that of a store operation. There are more sales returns, particularly, because of damages— maybe four per cent—incurred in shipping. It is difficult to know where to draw the market boundaries for a mail order business. We don't want to be substituting mail order customers for store visitors.

In 1986, the management team which had brought success to IKEA's Canadian operations was breaking up. Bjorn Bayley, who had come to Canada in 1978, was slotted to move to Philadelphia to spearhead IKEA's entry into the U.S. market, which had begun in June 1985 with a single store. With early sales running at a level twice as high as the company had predicted, Bayley expected to be busy, and was taking Mike McDonald, the controller, and Mike McMullen, the personnel director, with him. Anders Berglund who, like Bayley, was a long-time IKEA employee and had been in Canada since 1979, was scheduled to take over the Canadian operation. Berglund would report through Bayley to IKEA's North American Sales Director, who was located in Europe.

NEW COMPETITION

IKEA's success in Canada had not gone unnoticed. IDOMO was a well-established Toronto-based competitor, and Sears Canada was a new entrant.

IDOMO

Like IKEA, IDOMO sold knocked-down furniture which customers were required to assemble at home. IDOMO offered a somewhat narrower selection than IKEA but emphasized teak furniture to a much greater extent. With stores in Hamilton, Mississauga (across from IKEA), Toronto and Montreal, IDOMO appeared to have capitalized on the excess demand that IKEA had developed but was not able to service.

The products and prices offered in both the 96-page IDOMO and 144-page IKEA catalogues were similar, with IKEA's prices slightly lower. Prices in the IKEA catalogues were in effect for a year. IDOMO reserved the right to make adjustments to prices and specifications. A mail order telephone number in Toronto was provided in the IDOMO catalogue. Of late, IDOMO had begun to employ an increased amount of television advertising. IDOMO purchased goods from around the world and operated a number of their own Canadian factories. Their primary source of goods was Denmark.

Sears

The newest entrant in the Canadian knocked-down furniture segment was Sears Canada, a wholly owned subsidiary of Sears Roebuck of Chicago and, with $3.8 billion in annual revenues, one of Canada's largest merchandising operations. Sears operated 75 department stores in Canada, selling a wide range (700 merchandise lines comprising 100,000 stock keeping units) of medium price and quality goods. Sears Canada also ran a major catalogue operation which distributed 12 annual catalogues to approximately four million Canadian families. Customers could place catalogue orders by mail, by telephone, or in person through one of the company's 1,500 catalogue sales units, which were spread throughout the country.

A quick check by Bayley and Berglund revealed that Sears' Elements line was being sold only in Canada and only through the major Sears catalogues. Elements products were not for sale, nor could they be viewed, in Sears' stores. In the fall/winter catalogue that they examined, which was over 700 pages in length, the Elements line was given 20 pages. Although Sears appeared to offer the same "type" of products as IKEA, there was a narrower selection within each category. Prices for Elements' products seemed almost identical to IKEA prices. One distinct difference between the catalogues was the much greater emphasis that IKEA placed on presenting a large number of coordinated settings and room designs.

Further checking indicated that at least some of the suppliers of the Elements line were Swedish, although it did not appear that IKEA and Sears had any suppliers in common.

The IKEA executives knew that Sears was generally able to exert a great deal of influence over its suppliers, usually obtaining prices at least equal to and often below those of its competitors, because of the huge volumes purchased. Sears also worked closely with its suppliers in marketing, research, design and development, production standards and production planning. Many lines of merchandise were manufactured with features exclusive to Sears and were sold under its private brand names. There was a 75 per cent buying overlap for the catalogue and store and about a 90 per cent overlap between regions on store purchases.

Like any Sears' product, Elements furniture could be charged to a Sears charge card. Delivery of catalogue items generally took about two weeks and, for a small extra charge, catalogue orders would be delivered right to the consumer's home in a Sears truck. If a catalogue item was out of stock, Sears policy was either to tell the customer if and when the product would be available, or to substitute an item of equal or greater value. If goods proved defective (10 per cent of Sears Roebuck mail-order furniture purchasers had received damaged or broken furniture), Sears provided home pick-up and replacement and was willing, for a fee, to install goods, provide parts, and do repairs as products aged. Sears emphasized that it serviced what it sold, and guaranteed everything that it sold—"satisfaction guaranteed or money refunded." In its advertising, which included all forms of media, Sears stressed its "hassle-free returns" and asked customers to "take a look at the services we offered . . . they'll bring you peace of mind, long after the bill is paid."

In their assessment of Sears Canada, Bayley and Berglund recognized that the company seemed to be going through something of a revival. Using the rallying cry that a "new" Sears was being created, Sears executives (the Canadian firm had 10 vice presidents) had experimented with new store layouts, pruned the product line, and improved customer service for catalogue orders. Richard Sharpe, the chairman of Sears Canada, personally addressed as many as 12,000 employees per year, and the company received 3,000 suggestions from employees annually. Perhaps as a result of these initiatives, and a cut in workforce from 65,000 to 50,000 over several years, Sears Canada posted its best-ever results in 1985.

CONCLUSION

With the limited data they had on Sears, IKEA management recognized that their comparison of the two companies would be incomplete. Nonetheless, a decision regarding the Sears competitive threat was required. Any solution would have to reflect Kamprad's philosophy:

> Expensive solutions to problems are often signs of mediocrity. We have no interest in a solution until we know what it costs.

Carrefour China, Building a Greener Store

"There is no turning back now!" said David Monaco, asset and construction director of Carrefour China. It was early on June 1, 2006, and Monaco had just finished reading the latest media statement from Luc Vandevelde, chairman of the supervisory board of Carrefour, the second largest retailer in the world. Vandevelde had just announced that the company would open its first "Green Store" in Beijing, before the 2008 Olympic Games. The Green Store was a new concept that would be built and operated with the most advanced environmental technologies available to reduce the consumption of nonrenewable resources. The site for the store was a brown field redevelopment[1] in an area with high population density and excellent public transportation. Almost everything in the store would be environmentally-friendly.

Monaco was excited about the project. For him, the focus was on store design and operations, not on retail products. Since discussions about the project had started a few months ago, several important questions had emerged. How should he define the scope of the project, and whom could he ask for support? Considering the complexity of this project, how would he be able to manage this project in addition to the other? Could the 150 Carrefour stores in China that were scheduled for opening or renovation during the next three years benefit from the experience gained in this project, or would it be a one-off? In about five weeks, Monaco had to present a final concept at a meeting in Paris, so time was precious now.

Richard Ivey School of Business
The University of Western Ontario

---

[1] A brown field was land that previously was used for industrial purposes like a factory. Many times, these developments had to be cleaned up first before they could be used for non-industrial developments.

CARREFOUR CHINA

Carrefour entered China in 1995, with its first store opening in Beijing, followed by a rapid expansion throughout the country. At that time, supermarkets and large shopping centers were an entirely new concept to Beijing residents. In China, most grocery shopping happened in traditional, so-called wet markets or street markets, with very limited choices and low hygiene standards. Supermarkets existed only in and around the few luxury hotels and executive apartment buildings that catered to the rapidly growing expatriate community.

From the beginning, Carrefour stores in China were a mixture of East and West (see Exhibits 1 and 2). A wide selection of live fish, frogs, turtles and freshly cut fish heads was presented in modern display cases next to dried pork snouts and whole poultry, while frozen pizza and other more Western-style food items were presented nearby. The non-food section included everything one could imagine important for daily life, including clothing, toys, household products, electronics and bicycles. The checkout area included more than 70 individual counters. The stores were all very brightly lit, colorful and clean. Carrefour's main aim was to mix its modern Western store concept with the local preference for freshness.

Most stores were organized on two floors, with a small mall for private vendors and a food court on the ground floor close to the checkout area. The upper level, with the main entrance, could be reached by travelator (a moving walkway), and usually accommodated the fresh food and consumable departments. The customers were guided through the store by a strategically planned layout that ensured no department would be bypassed before reaching the checkout area on the ground floor behind the non-food departments. Because Chinese consumers shopped frequently, due to limited space in their apartments and their preference for very fresh produce, most stores opened 365 days per year. Typically, 45,000 visitors would visit one of the larger stores each day, making 20,000 to 25,000 sales transactions.

By June 2006, the company operated 73 hypermarkets in 29 Chinese cities, with an average sales area of 95,000 square feet per store. The network stretched from Urumqi in Mongolia to Harbin in the far northeast, to Kunming and Shenzhen in the south. Carrefour was the number-one foreign retailer in China, growing faster than any of its foreign rivals, including Wal-Mart, German Metro, French Auchan and U.K.-based Tesco. Carrefour's 2005 turnover in China was US$2 billion making China, its fifth largest market. (Exhibit 3 shows the market share by the number of stores in the retail industry in China as of the end of 2005.) Carrefour China also operated smaller store formats of up to 11,000 square feet, branded as CHAMPION supermarkets, and DIA convenience stores, similar to their counterparts in France. These smaller stores were not as successful, however, as the larger hypermarkets under the flagship Carrefour banner.

The secret behind the success of the Carrefour hypermarkets was twofold: the company's previous experience in Taiwan, a market where consumer taste and shopping behavior were very similar to those in China, and the company's strong local strategy. A good example was the way the company approached the operating licensing issue, an obstacle with which other international retailers, including Wal-Mart and the Metro Group, had struggled. Officially, foreign firms were required to gain a nationwide license to operate retail stores, as local authorities could grant local licenses only to local operators. Instead, Carrefour applied for licenses under the name of its local partners to avoid being treated as a foreign company. This practice not only guaranteed a quicker processing of the retail licenses but also much smoother access to building permits and other required approvals.

Carrefour worked with a variety of partners, identifying one local, well-connected individual or property investor for each new city or region. As a result, Carrefour's expansion very rarely included ownership of the land and the building; Carrefour usually designed the entire shopping mall and the local partner typically held the ownership of the building. Although location is important for a retail store, the company did not regard brick-and-mortar assets as core to its business. However, the remaining infrastructure crucial for running the business without interruption was owned by Carrefour, including the display equipment, lighting, refrigeration equipment and usually the air-conditioning system.

In keeping with the conditions for its membership in the World Trade Organization (WTO), on December 11, 2005, China lifted most restrictions on foreign retailers. These restrictions included limits on the number of stores, rules confining foreign-operated retail stores to large cities only and regulations capping the foreigners' stake at 65 per cent. Aggressive expansion was crucial to the Carrefour China strategy; in 2006-07, Carrefour planned to open 100 new stores. Because the competition had recently stepped up its efforts significantly, it was important to minimize the time for store construction to maintain Carrefour's advantage in the race for top locations across the country. Management expected sales in China to grow by 30 per cent annually over the next couple of years.

STORE DEVELOPMENT IN CHINA DURING THE EARLY YEARS

In the early years, during the mid-1990s, Carrefour's typical approach in China was to identify an experienced store manager for each new project, usually a French national, to supervise everything from start to finish. Although a corporate guideline set the overall store design, the store managers had their own ideas, creative ambitions and previous experiences to lead them in creating a special shopping experience based on their experience with other openings in European countries or Asia. Individual managers also had their own relationships with equipment suppliers, which usually were carried over into China. Store managers were very particular about the store's appearance, with everything having a personal touch. However, very few had a sense of the technical aspects behind a commercial retail building, as Monaco revealed:

> In one of our first stores in Shanghai, the store manager who was responsible for the opening forced the supplier for the display cases to install a giant frying pan, which had to be custom-made in Europe. The reason was that he wanted to sell Paella, a traditional Spanish rice and seafood dish. He firmly believed that his local Chinese customers would love Paella, since it was a rice dish, a staple of the Chinese diet. The equipment cost was three times more than a regular display case. Unfortunately, no one in the store could actually cook Paella, nor were there customers who wanted to buy it. The equipment was replaced with a standard display case after only two months. On another occasion, a store manager ordered tiles from Italy because the local tiles were slightly smaller than the ones he wanted for the store. The additional cost was in the tens of thousands of dollars—and the scheduled store opening was put in serious jeopardy.

There was an internal competition among the store managers as to who would first try to expand their construction budgets up by negotiating with the country manager, and then later try to finish the project as far below budget as possible. The managers with the greatest savings compared to budget earned bragging rights. A common practice of store managers was to recover any additional costs by shifting money between budget categories, often with cuts to capital investment in areas that the store managers perceived to be of secondary importance. Unfortunately, the store managers' perceptions often did not match reality. In fact, most items that were cut by those investment adjustments were crucial for the trouble-free operation of the stores. For example, air-conditioning and refrigeration systems were among the most expensive components of a new store, accounting for 15 to 20 per cent of the total budget (and later, 30 per cent of the total energy consumption). Not surprisingly, these systems then became frequent targets of capital cost reductions. It was not uncommon for a store to have an undersized air-conditioning system because a store manager assumed that the store could handle slightly higher than normal store temperatures during some very hot days. However, the problems tended to cascade, with an undersized air-conditioning system creating trouble in the fresh-food area: the refrigerated display cases had to work much harder, and their energy consumption increased dramatically, along with the need for additional repairs. However, with the focus on rapid expansion, with four to eight new store openings per year in China at that time, these trade-offs were largely ignored by senior management. In addition, because all of the stores were quite new, the medium- and long-term impacts of the shortened lifespan of the equipment were not immediately felt.

To simplify and speed up store openings elsewhere in the world, Carrefour preferred to work with its network of trusted suppliers. This approach proved difficult in China, as most of these international companies had not yet entered the Chinese market, or were taking a cautious approach that employed local agents, who in turn, were not familiar with what Carrefour expected. Working with local, unfamiliar suppliers, or importing complex or custom equipment further delayed openings and escalated costs. Managing equipment suppliers was a growing challenge, as the rate of expansion continued to grow

MONACO'S CHANGES

By 1998, when David Monaco was hired by Carrefour, senior management was moving away from the decentralized approach to store development. Monaco had been with Wal-Mart for more than 10 years, and was known for working long hours, for detailed planning and for very close personal monitoring of the on-site construction progress. He was very particular when it came to quality and to deadlines. His extensive project experience in developing countries had also enabled him to develop a sixth sense for critical situations in ongoing projects. Monaco received a clear mandate to centralize and standardize all asset expansions and construction activities, to reduce costs, to improve construction and operating quality, and to significantly speed up store construction time. He had the full support of Jean-Luc Chéreau, the president of Carrefour China at the time.

Armed with a secretary and only a handful of local project managers, Monaco had his department up and running in less than six months. By then, all asset management and construction activities had been centralized. Not only did Monaco reduce the average store development costs by 25 per cent, he also worked to aggressively shorten the average construction time by 20 per cent, and reduce maintenance and operating costs by 12 per cent. Besides these early successes, he placed an emphasis on developing his local engineering team. The asset and construction department very quickly earned the respect of both the local store maintenance departments and the initially skeptical, mostly expatriate, store managers.

A crucial factor for his success was that Monaco standardized almost all equipment, so that every year he could invite all potential equipment suppliers to bid for a reference store, with all equipment priced per running meter or per unit. He then chose two suppliers for each piece of equipment or construction item, and split the orders for the next year between them. The standardization included refrigerated display cases, air-conditioning system, transformers, lighting, floor tiles, checkout counters, shopping trolleys, elevators, and many more items. This approach not only made the ordering process more transparent, but also gave Monaco the flexibility to move equipment between different stores if needed.

Monaco became known among suppliers as a hard but fair negotiator who liked to establish long-term relationships with reliable equipment manufacturers and contractors. Delays due to long delivery times or problems with the importing process of overseas equipment were not acceptable, and almost every international supplier was either forced to set up a local operation or face the danger of not getting any more orders from Carrefour. As one supplier for refrigeration equipment recalled:

> David makes his expectations very clear. You know that if you have caused problems to a project, you usually have no chance of coming back. Most suppliers know this by now.

Unfortunately, by 2005, many of the current stores that had opened prior to Monaco's arrival in China had started to show serious maintenance problems. Air-conditioning systems started to fail; refrigeration units broke down frequently, roofs leaked and electrical installations stopped working. A high profile green project would only take away scarce resources from pressing ongoing problems.

At this point, Monaco's priority list was simple: Firstly, make sure the store openings happen as scheduled or earlier; secondly, make sure the quality of the workmanship is, at minimum, as agreed upon in the contracts; thirdly, make each new store better, and more attractive for customers, while less expensive to develop than the previous store.

RETAIL OPERATIONS

Although *building* hypermarkets in China was challenging, *operating* a modern retail store proved even more difficult. Carrefour stores were always crowded, and both customers and staff did not really take care of the equipment. Both customers and staff were frequently seen climbing up inside display cases to reach the upper shelves or handling items without putting them back properly. Shopping trolleys smashed into glass cases, shelves were bent, pipes in display cases were ripped out, and cool room doors frequently were damaged, causing system failures.

It concerned Monaco that much of the technical equipment was imported and the suppliers did not have either local maintenance operations or spare parts available. Another problem was the Chinese climate: the hot and humid summers and the cold and dry winters were wearing hard on the equipment. In addition, frequent power shortages in the Chinese power grid caused regular equipment breakdowns.

Carrefour was wholly unprepared for the higher operating costs that resulted. Neither headquarters nor the store manager had budgeted for repairs or for costs incurred by additional skilled maintenance personnel. The resulting strategy was to blame the equipment suppliers and to pressure them to repair the equipment if they wanted to get another project in the future. This tactic resulted in many suppliers operating strictly by their supply agreements, only doing what was explicitly specified and refusing to coordinate with any party concerned on the construction site except for the store manager.

When Monaco started to address the problem, he initially had a hard time convincing the store managers to follow his recommendations and spend more on preventive maintenance. Officially, Monaco was only responsible for construction budgets and not operating budgets, which were in the hands of the store manager. Additional construction costs affected the store managers' individual performance appraisals directly; but they did not care about long-term implications because their tenure at each store was usually only one to two years.

Monaco was determined to work on this problem proactively. He assigned one of his engineers to audit the situation in all the stores and to start working with the individual store maintenance managers on a schedule for low-cost preventive maintenance. This schedule included the regular cleaning of the condensers on the rooftop, temperature monitoring throughout the store and a checklist for all vital operating parameters, which had to be recorded and submitted to Monaco on a regular basis.

He believed that his next challenge was to improve the operating efficiency of individual stores. Although energy was inexpensive, at US$0.05 per kilowatt-hour, and any energy savings usually did not justify the purchase of better equipment, Monaco tried to push for this whenever possible because future increases in energy costs could potentially harm the company's gross margins. Even the use of additional wall insulation could not be pushed because, in the opinion of the financial controllers, these items belonged to the building owner and were not under Carrefour's control to install. Moreover, because the consumer market in China had just started to develop, the firm was not sure that a store would remain open for the long term. Instead, a store might operate for several years and then be closed or relocated depending on other surrounding developments and its own success. So, first steps involved simple improvements, such as using waste heat from a refrigeration system to heat water within the stores.

THE ENVIRONMENTALLY-FRIENDLY INITIATIVE AT CARREFOUR

Carrefour published its first annual report on sustainability in 2001, which had been driven more by compliance with French law than by environmental concerns initiated by the company. However, by late 2003, Carrefour's headquarters in France was working with energy providers and equipment manufacturers on new innovative solutions to reduce energy consumption in its retail stores. These experimental trials were generally in-store pilot projects, which, when successful, would be then implemented in the construction of upcoming stores.

By 2005, big retailers in Europe and North America were facing increasing pressure from consumer and environmental groups to improve the environmental friendliness of the products they sold and the operations of their stores. Companies such as Wal-Mart and Carrefour were high-profile targets for anti-globalization campaigns and groups lobbying for improved health and environmental practices. Protests against genetically modified food products and the environmental impact of big-box stores became more frequent. These protests were by no means limited to North America or Europe; nongovernmental organizations and consumer interest groups became much more global in their approaches. For example, Greenpeace announced that it had found genetically engineered rice not approved for human consumption on sale at a Carrefour hypermarket in central China. With great fanfare, Greenpeace demanded that this rice be immediately withdrawn. On other occasions, local residents rallied against noise and air pollution created by large hypermarkets because of their enormous size or their proximity to residential units.

Energy conservation had not been on the high-priority list of Carrefour because energy costs equaled only about one per cent of the retailer's gross sales; however, recent worldwide price increases combined with the low-margin characteristic of the food retail business had brought energy consumption to the attention of the top management. A study by the U.S. government estimated that a 10 per cent reduction in energy costs for the average grocery chain could boost profits by almost six per cent.[2] Retailers such as Carrefour and Wal-Mart suddenly recognized the potential for real bottom-line effects.

So in late 2005, Carrefour signed a contract with Schneider Electric to improve energy performance in France. This contract, a first of its type in France, was aimed at reducing energy consumption per store by 10 to 15 per cent, an ambitious goal equivalent to the annual energy consumption of 150 households. Schneider Electric helped Carrefour identify and implement innovative solutions to reduce energy consumption while Carrefour provided the necessary investment and operational support.

Elsewhere, Carrefour was testing solar panels at six hypermarkets in Spain. In Italy, Carrefour had received the 2004 Greenlight Award from the European Commission for the use of T5 lights, which achieved a 15 per cent reduction in energy consumption. In Brazil, where Carrefour already recycled and processed its own waste cooking oil, the company organized the collection of used mineral oil from its customers in two pilot stores. A total of 3,500 liters of oil was collected and processed by the University of Sao Paulo to produce 1,000 liters of bio-diesel for the electricity generators used by the stores.

In France, Carrefour tested different in-store refrigeration systems that had reduced global warming potential. In Southeast Asia, Carrefour deployed new refrigeration units, which used the HCFC[3] refrigerant R123. The new refrigeration units were designed to reduce electricity consumption, thus reducing harmful emissions. The systems also functioned at low pressure, so that the risk of leakages was less than with the traditional high-pressure systems. In its supply chain operations in France, Carrefour tested natural gas-powered vehicles for both store use and customer home delivery.

All these initiatives were promising but they had not yet been integrated into a corporate-wide sustainability strategy. They remained a diverse assortment of local pilot projects, which created a lot of positive media attention, but were not leveraged

---

[2] Teresa F. Lindeman, "More Retailers Building Environmentally Friendly Stores," *Pittsburgh Post-Gazette*, October 23, 2005.

[3] HCFCs, or hydrochlorofluorocarbons, are of a class of haloalkanes in which not all hydrogen has been replaced by chlorine or fluorine. They are used primarily as chlorofluorocarbon (CFC) substitutes, as the environmental effects are only about 10 per cent of those of CFCs. When the chlorine is reduced to zero, these compounds are known as hydrofluorocarbons (HFCs), with even fewer environmental effects.

corporate-wide. In early 2006, Carrefour established a corporate sustainability department at its headquarters in France, with the mandate to integrate all initiatives into a standardized strategy.

GREEN-BUILDING TRENDS IN CHINA

Although environmental awareness was not yet a critical issue for the emerging Chinese middle class, the Chinese government was growing increasingly more sensitive to the nation's energy problems. Since China began bidding to host the 2008 Olympic Games and was seeking foreign investment in the 1990s, its leaders and urban planners had frequently mentioned environmental issues. However, little action followed, and many environmentalists were unimpressed.

In response, the government worked to develop an environmentally-friendly building standard along with incentives for investors. It was not uncommon to see new developments with names such as "Eco-Town" and "Garden Villa" that had few actual green features, except perhaps the color on the exterior walls. In one case, a Beijing developer claimed having an environmentally-friendly building certification before any construction had even begun. Another concern was that developers used cheaper building practices to offset rising costs, while promising "green" without actually delivering on it. A cynical attitude seemed to prevail among developers: "If it has trees, then it's green."

In early 2006, Xinhua, the official Chinese news agency, announced that harsher punishments for wasting energy were to be enacted in legislation. The construction sector was clearly being targeted, which by some accounts was responsible for one-third of all energy consumption in China. The Financial and Economic Committee of the National People's Congress, in conjunction with the National Development and Reform Commission (NDRC), jointly revised a law on mandatory energy and resources saving for new buildings. While the initial law had been promulgated in 1998, it had failed to halt projects that did not meet energy-saving requirements. As part of its five-year plan in March 2006, the construction ministry issued a regulation that all new constructions had to be 50 per cent more energy-efficient by June of that year, relative to 1980 levels. In six major cities, the regulated level was even higher, with energy consumption being cut by 65 per cent. Construction projects that would not meet those energy-saving requirements would be stopped.

Unfortunately, the actual implementation of energy- and resource-friendly construction in China continued to be mixed, at best. The green objectives of environment-minded policymakers still competed with the realities of aggressive developers, impatient construction firms, and a growing population of several hundred million workers who would need housing in the coming decades. Few Chinese developers felt that the nation would match the 2006 edict for energy efficiency, despite 11 "green city" projects (including 140 buildings) currently under construction.

Similar challenges faced the retail sector. In practice, responsibility for building a greener store fell on the developer, who paid for green building features, but it was the tenant who would benefit through lower operating costs. Ideally, over the long term, lower operating costs for energy, water, and waste disposal should be reflected in higher rents; yet other market forces were not allowing rent increases. Most foreign experts agreed that many of the newest projects would not pass a genuine international environmental sustainability test, which required low energy use, water-recycling systems, and "intelligent" integrated design and material use. The reality in China was that multiple layers of inertia plagued the daily decision process in every area. Despite good intentions by the central government, there was a lack of follow through by local officials. As Monaco recalled:

> In China, we hear a lot about green building standards, but actually, the standards are very flexible. We could define the standard somewhat ourselves, or we could follow a standard from the U.S. However, the Chinese government might pass a law in the future that could be different from our interpretation of "building green." Historically, it has not been uncommon for the Chinese government to promulgate new laws that are stricter than the existing U.S. or European standards.

In general, the limited knowledge of the local supply industry and availability of materials further complicated efforts to implement a green building standard. Moreover, foreign suppliers of energy-saving equipment faced significant hurdles to enter the market, including high import duties, significant transportation costs, and the prevailing practice among many developers to emphasize low capital costs. So, little demand had materialized for the more expensive equipment and materials needed to build "green." Monaco commented:

> You can't just pick up the phone and request standard energy-saving equipment. In addition, people here are used to just doing their own job, and for this kind of project, more than ever, you need people who know how to cooperate with one another.

GREEN MARKET CERTIFICATION

Recently, the Green Market Certification, one of the key components of China's national "Three Greens Project," had been given more attention by the government. Initiated in 1998 by the Ministry of Commerce—in conjunction with the Finance, Sanitation, Railway, Transportation, and Industry Ministries—the Project was undertaken to boost food safety and involved *Green Consumption*, *Green Markets* and the development of *Green Distribution Channels*. A Green Market Certification was given to businesses with high standards for environmental protection, safe facilities, sanitation management, food manufacturing, and other areas. However, energy savings and waste reduction issues were not included.

All wholesale markets, which dealt with vegetables, fruits, meat and eggs, and retail outlets, like supermarkets, hypermarkets, convenience stores and shopping malls, could apply for certification. If approved, the organizations then could use the logo and symbol of the Certification on their products. The "China Certification and Inspection Group" (CCIG) was responsible for issuing Green Market Certification to businesses. The CCIG was an independent legal entity, which was incorporated by voluntary enterprises. The process for obtaining this certification was not entirely clear, and the individual provinces could all use different criteria.

THE LEED GREEN BUILDING RATING SYSTEM

In contrast to China, efforts in Europe and the United States tended to emphasize voluntary approaches. In the United States, the Green Building Council (USGBC) had developed the Leadership in Energy and Environmental Design Green Building Rating System (LEED). The USGBC was a coalition of leaders from the building industry who worked together to promote buildings that were environmentally responsible, profitable and healthy places in which to live and work. USGBC had 7,500 member organizations and a network of 75 regional chapters. LEED was a voluntary standard for the design, construction and operation of green buildings. This rating system focused on five specific categories: sustainable site development, water savings, energy efficiency, materials selection and indoor environmental quality. An objective scale was used to assess a building's performance, which in turn would provide direction for building owners and operators as they evaluated various sustainability initiatives and sought to gain legitimacy with their occupants and community.

To earn the LEED certification, a building project had to meet certain prerequisites and performance benchmarks within each category. The larger the scope, or the greater the number of initiatives undertaken in each category, the higher the number of credits. Projects could be certified at one of four levels based on the number of total credits achieved: *basic, silver, gold* or *platinum.* Moreover, LEED-certified buildings reduced operating costs, created healthier and more productive occupants, and conserved natural resources.

LEED certification standards were not without criticism. Although some items were mandatory, only 26 out of 69 possible points were needed to receive the basic certification (see Exhibit 4). Many areas received equal weight, despite some factors having much greater environmental benefits than others. For example, the point system weighted solar panels about equal with a bicycle-storage room. Thus, it was tempting to seek easy-to-get LEED points at little cost simply to attract a lot of positive media attention. For Carrefour, the *basic* certification was achievable for every store without any additional capital investment for equipment. Selecting a building site that complied with LEED, taking care of proper disposal of construction waste, and installing a certain number of bicycle racks, was already sufficient.

Registration for the LEED assessment process involved a fairly simple project description and a summary of the credits the developer expected to earn. The USGBC's fees for registration ranged from US$750 to US$3,750, and the official recognition ran from US$1,500 to US$7,500, depending on the size of the building. However, the actual certification audit required thorough documentation, review and commissioning, a process that could take many months with considerable cost. For example, energy modeling, commissioning and other mandatory requirements cost often in the range of tens of thousands of dollars and were not included in the registration and certification fees. As a result, developers were forced to trade-off implementing additional eco-friendly features, such as the installation of a solar chiller as an energy-friendly alternative to the traditional air-conditioning system, against increasing audit fees.

Monaco was still not convinced that Carrefour should pursue a LEED certification, and if the company did pursue certification, he was unsure which level the company should aim for. Carrefour wanted to generate both positive public relations effects and real energy savings without inflating the overall construction budget. Monaco also worried that the basic certification was too low a hurdle to merit the green stamp of approval if the Chinese government created its own independent rating system with potentially much more stringent standards. If Carrefour pursued the LEED standard, there was some risk that the building might not become certified before the Olympics, or that the Chinese government might create its own, more stringent standards.

As an alternative, Monaco considered trying to develop or adopt an independent Carrefour "green standard." The company would present specific energy-saving features and environmentally-friendly initiatives, such as the use of shopping trolleys made from recycled materials or a reuse station for cooking oils. However, Monaco's colleagues in France had no specific standards under development to provide guidance.

THE COMPETITION

Carrefour was not alone in considering the environmental impact of its stores. Other large retailers also initiated projects that aimed at greening their businesses. However, while Carrefour focused on the potential for a Beijing Green Store, competitors pursued other strategies including incremental changes to already existing stores, energy saving projects at distribution centers and the merchandising of green products. For example, Wal-Mart China targeted its costumers by launching energy saving centers at 14 Wal-Mart stores in Beijing, Shanghai, Shenzhen, Dongguan and Kunming. Featuring the theme of "building a conservation-minded society together with you," the energy saving centers displayed various environmental lighting products from GE and Wal-Mart's House Brands that tried to help customers save money and reduce energy consumption.

While actions at the individual store level were limited, Wal-Mart decided to test a wider range of environmentally-friendly options at its Tianjin distribution center (renovated in 2006). This pilot project at the distribution center was more effective and less disruptive for customers than developing a green store project, as proposed by Carrefour. The aim was to lower energy and water consumption and to expand the use of recyclable materials. T5 energy saving lighting was installed, reducing energy use by 20 to 30 per cent. Daylight lighting also was increased, and an air conditioning heat-reclaim system was set up. In addition, a 20-square-meter solar panel and two 10-kilowatt wind power generators were installed, capable of generating up to 7,300 kW of electricity per year. Finally, the distribution center was equipped with 10 solar energy water heaters that could provide 1.7 tons of hot water daily, saving up to 25,550 kW per year. Overall, Wal-Mart's Tianjin Distribution Center had the potential to reduce carbon dioxide emission by 31 tonnes per year, equal to the annual emissions produced by 12 average families.

Auchan, another large French hypermarket chain, decided not to improve the energetic footprint of its stores but to launch a range of organic products under its "Auchan Sélection" brand, which consisted of a limited range of vegetables grown using sustainable agriculture methods. The company had previous experience with organically grown produce, and with the recent media attention on healthier food in the build-up to the Beijing Olympics, this appeared to be easy to implement. At first, the company only sold higher priced imported organic produce, but planned to phase in locally grown products. Chinese urban dwellers were increasingly interested in healthier, safer, more wholesome foods—partly fueled by food contamination scandals, e.g. in 2004, transparent "glass" noodles were found bleached with a lead-based whitener. Despite this interest, consumers appeared unready to pay higher prices, as China's first organic supermarket recently closed because of lackluster sales.

Britain's Tesco, which had recently expanded in China with a US$350 million deal to control the local Hymall and now had 44 stores, had not yet implemented any eco-friendly initiatives. However, industry insiders expected that by early 2008, when the company would open its first Tesco-branded store in Beijing, it would transfer some of the eco-initiatives from the United Kingdom to China. This could reduce the expected media hype surrounding the potential opening of Carrefour's own Green Store before the Olympics.

In recent years, many of the local chains, such as industry leading Linhua in Shanghai, had not yet chosen to pursue any environmentally-friendly initiatives. While some top managers might express interest, they invariably were too busy because of the overriding imperatives to expand market share and their store networks. Limited expertise also constrained efforts by local operators to allocate managerial resources and investment into what was perceived to be voluntary, peripheral activities.

However, perceptions were changing, with supermarkets in Shenzhen, in the south of China, initiating new, more environmentally-friendly policies. The intensifying discussion about environmental issues sparked by the more vocal media in neighboring Hong Kong increased the urgency for making changes. Locally owned Rainbow and CR Vanguard Supermarkets had been touting their new shopping bag policies, which limited free bags for consumers. At the Rainbow supermarkets, customers could purchase a fashionable reusable shopping bag for RMB1 (US$0.14) when they spent over RMB100. According to the China Retail and Franchise Association[4], the shopping bags consumed in the entire supermarket industry were worth RMB5 billion annually, with an 8,000 square meter supermarket using up to RMB400,000 worth of shopping bags per year.

TAKING STOCK

Monaco was determined to use this opportunity to change the general direction of how Carrefour would build its stores in China. Initial outcomes were promising, resulting in reductions of average store construction costs by 40 per cent or US$3.5 million. Monaco described his strategy:

> My approach to environmental friendliness and sustainability is threefold. First, I look into the specification of each project and whether the intended size of energy and material consuming equipment is appropriate for the size of the store. Then I look into potential passive energy and material saving measures. Finally, I consider the use of new energy saving equipment, alternative construction materials, and alternative energy generation. All three approaches have to make a positive impact on the bottom line.

Energy Use by Equipment

A typical example of Monaco's approach was the changes he made to the lighting systems for the fresh-food sales areas. The deco lighting in these areas was important because proper illumination was essential for the displayed food items to look fresh and appealing to the customers. The deco lights were individual spotlights, which hung suspended from the ceiling, below the standard general lights that spanned across the entire sales area. Recalling a project he had initiated in North America, he raised the entire deco lighting by about a foot, to illuminate a slightly larger area. At the same time, he removed the redundant general lights above the deco lighting. This

---

[4] ChinaRetailNews.com, June 12, 2007.

adjustment alone provided energy savings of 33 per cent per square meter. In addition, he installed new electronic ballasts instead of the traditional but less efficient magnetic ballasts. The new lights were otherwise no different from the standard deco lights but could save another 33 per cent of energy. Surprisingly with this new set-up, the fresh-food items looked even crisper and fresher. Exhibit 5 shows the energy records of the different set-ups.

Monaco was bothered that several of his early initiatives were no longer a standard part of building projects. One was the heat reclaim system installed to the refrigeration units for hot-water supply. For Monaco, this system was a no-brainer. A heat reclaim system only cost around US$10,000 but could significantly reduce the power consumption of the store. In addition, the heat reclaim system could reduce the required size of the condensers[5] for the refrigeration system, saving immediately between US$2,500 and US$5,000 in capital cost, depending on the size of the overall system.

Energy Management Systems

Another project that Monaco had been working on was the use of an energy management system (EMS). Suppliers for those systems had been knocking at his door for several years, but so far, they had failed to provide evidence to support any real savings. Energy management systems came in different configurations, with the most basic ones featuring only programmable timers for the lighting, refrigeration, and air-conditioning units. These systems cost little, and Monaco could request them as a standard from his main suppliers for no additional cost. But because these systems depended on constant and accurate monitoring and adjustment, he had little confidence that they would save any energy. Instead, his experience was that these systems created more trouble than benefits as inexperienced staff frequently (and incorrectly) adjusted the settings.

More advanced energy management systems measured general store parameters, such as the load on the central refrigeration units and air-conditioning chiller, store temperature and humidity, and incoming daylight. These systems would automatically adjust the performance of individual energy users. For example, they would dim the lights depending on demand. The suppliers claimed potential energy savings of between four per cent and 15 per cent. However, only two companies actually offered to guarantee savings in a contract, and these guarantees were in the range of only six per cent to eight per cent. Those energy management systems could add costs of US$80,000 to a new project.

Building Design

Other measures Monaco had tried included the insulation of the exterior walls and ceilings; the circulation of more cool air from the outside; the reduction of non-sales areas, such as the general office space, preparation areas and cool-rooms; and the use of a central electricity wiring system. He also considered the installation of

---

[5] Condensers were needed to cool the compressed refrigerant inside the refrigeration system so that it could transform from a gas to a liquid state. The liquid pressurized refrigerant would than be released by an expansion valve into an evaporator where it would transform into a cold gas. This gas would cool the evaporator, which was being used to cool down the air inside a cold room or a display case. The gas would then flow back to the central refrigeration unit, where it would be compressed. The compressed gas was hot and was therefore pumped to the evaporator. The waste heat was usually not being used.

alternative-energy generating equipment, including a geo-thermal water and air heater, a solar absorption chiller for the air-conditioning system, a solar rooftop system for electricity, and a carbon dioxide (CO_2) refrigeration system.

The geo-thermal heater was a series of large vertical shafts, which had to be drilled far into the ground to extract heat from the earth. The cost for the geo-thermal project would be US$386,000 with an energy-saving potential of around two per cent of the total energy consumed by the store.

Absorption chillers were developed in Japan in the 1960s, and in 2006, Broad Air Conditioning in China was the world's largest manufacturer of this type of equipment. To power the absorption cycle, solar energy could be used, requiring a series of simple mirror-like solar collectors with integrated water pipes on the rooftop. The heated water was then pumped back to a central unit that used a series of heat exchangers to power the air-conditioning system. For the average Carrefour store, the system had the potential of saving 9.75 per cent of energy, with an incremental cost of US$460,000.

Besides energy savings, Monaco wanted to use environmentally-friendly technologies and materials; for example, by reducing the use of ozone-harming refrigerants. A CO_2 refrigeration system was attractive because in the event of a system leak, harm was avoided to the ozone layer. However, such a system would require a more complicated set-up, including stronger piping and different types of compressors for an additional US$300,000 per store. Potential energy savings were in the range of 1.5 to five per cent. He also considered the installation of a solar energy system. He had received six proposals from three different suppliers (see Exhibit 6). Monaco so far had not been able to convince top management to invest in modern energy-saving equipment, which would initially increase construction costs but would, in return, reduce long-term operating costs significantly.

Monaco had recently received a detailed report about the power consumption of the Yuanchun store in Guangzhou in south China and the Tawan Store in Shenyang, in northern China. Here, he had been experimenting with different material and equipment alternatives (see Exhibit 7) in order to determine the best solution for the Green Store project.

NEXT STEPS

As Monaco prepared for the upcoming meeting in Paris, he wondered how much this project meant to the company as a whole. Was the effort justified or would Carrefour be better served by simply focusing on the media hype surrounding the Olympics? The complex property ownership situation in China and high-profile food safety concerns might convince management at the corporate headquarters in Paris that their time was better focused on issues other than "green" ones in China. Moreover, any efforts to be greener with only one store might be perceived by environmental groups and the media as "green washing," transforming a positive effort into a marketing fiasco similar to Wal-Mart's recent experience. The more Monaco thought about the project the more uncertain he became about how he should proceed. What started as a "no-brainer" had become increasingly complex to manage. However, Monaco had only a few weeks left (and three other stores to complete elsewhere in China) before the management meeting in Paris.

Exhibit 1   Carrefour China Produce Area

Exhibit 2   Carrefour China, Fresh-Food Area Lighthing

Source: Company files.

Exhibit 3   Food-Retail Market Share In China By Number Of Stores*

| Rank | Company | Number of stores | |
		2005	2010
1	China Resources Enterprise	185	283
2	Trust-Mart	98	70
3	Lianhua	97	220
4	Carrefour	73	220
5	Auchan	70	156
6	CP Group / Lotus	69	95
7	Beijing Hualian Supermarket	60	92
8	Shanghai Nonggongshang	55	69
9	Wal-Mart	51	180
10	Tesco	44	120

*Hypermarket format only.
Source: Case writer estimates.

Exhibit 4   Leed Project Checklist

Sustainable Site, 14 Points Possible	
Construction Activity Pollution Prevention	Required
Site Selection	1
Development Density & Community Connectivity	1
Brownfield Redevelopment	1
Alternative Transportation, Public Transportation Access	1
Alternative Transportation, Bicycle Storage & Changing Rooms	1
Alternative Transportation, Low-Emitting & Fuel-Efficient Vehicles	1
Alternative Transportation, Parking Capacity	1
Site Development, Protection or Restoration of Natural Habitat	1
Site Development, Maximize Open Space	1
Storm Water Design, Quantity Control	1
Storm Water Design, Quality Control	1
Heat Island Effect, Non-Roof	1
Heat Island Effect, Roof	1
Light Pollution Reduction	1

Innovation & Design Process, 5 Points Possible	
Innovation in Design: Building Design Better Use of Daylight & Air-circulation	1
Innovation in Design: Provide Specific Title	1
Innovation in Design: Provide Specific Title	1
Innovation in Design: Provide Specific Title	1
LEED Accredited Professional	1

Water Efficiency, 5 Points Possible	
Water Efficient Landscaping, Reduce by 50%	1
Water Efficient Landscaping, No Potable Use or No Irrigation	1
Innovative Wastewater Technologies	1
Water Use Reduction, 20% Reduction	1
Water Use Reduction, 30% Reduction	1

Materials & Resources, 13 Points Possible	
Storage & Collection of Recyclables	Required
Building Reuse, Maintain 75% of Existing Walls, Floors & Roof	1
Building Reuse, Maintain 100% of Existing Walls, Floors & Roof	1
Building Reuse, Maintain 50% of Interior Non-Structural Elements	1
Construction Waste Management, Divert 50% from Disposal	1
Construction Waste Management, Divert 75% from Disposal	1
Materials Reuse, 5%	1
Materials Reuse,10%	1
Recycled Content, 10% (post-consumer + ½ pre-consumer)	1
Recycled Content, 20% (post-consumer + ½ pre-consumer)	1
Regional Materials, 10% Extracted, Processed & Manufactured Regionally	1
Regional Materials, 20% Extracted, Processed & Manufactured Regionally	1
Rapidly Renewable Materials	1
Certified Wood	1

Exhibit 4   (continued)

Energy & Atmosphere, 17 Points Possible	
Fundamental Commissioning of the Building Energy Systems	Required
Minimum Energy Performance	Required
Fundamental Refrigerant Management	Required

Optimize Energy Performance (Compared to Newest Reference Project)	(1 to 10)
10.5% New Buildings or 3.5% Existing Building Renovations	1
14% New Buildings or 7% Existing Building Renovations	2
17.5% New Buildings or 10.5% Existing Building Renovations	3
21% New Buildings or 14% Existing Building Renovations	4
24.5% New Buildings or 17.5% Existing Building Renovations	5
28% New Buildings or 21% Existing Building Renovations	6
31.5% New Buildings or 24.5% Existing Building Renovations	7
35% New Buildings or 28% Existing Building Renovations	8
38.5% New Buildings or 31.5% Existing Building Renovations	9
42% New Buildings or 35% Existing Building Renovations	10

On-Site Renewable Energy	(1 to 3)
2.5% Renewable Energy	1
7.5% Renewable Energy	2
12.5% Renewable Energy	3
Enhanced Commissioning	1
Enhanced Refrigerant Management	1
Measurement & Verification	1
Green Power	1
Minimum IAQ Performance	Required
Environmental Tobacco Smoke (ETS) Control	Required
Outdoor Air Delivery Monitoring	1
Increased Ventilation	1
Construction IAQ Management Plan, During Construction	1
Construction IAQ Management Plan, Before Occupancy	1
Low-Emitting Materials, Adhesives & Sealants	1
Low-Emitting Materials, Paints & Coatings	1
Low-Emitting Materials, Carpet Systems	1
Low-Emitting Materials, Composite Wood & Agrifiber Products	1
Indoor Chemical & Pollutant Source Control	1
Controllability of Systems, Lighting	1
Controllability of Systems, Thermal Comfort	1
Thermal Comfort, Design	1
Thermal Comfort, Verification	1
Daylight & Views, Daylight 75% of Spaces	1
Daylight & Views, Views for 90% of Spaces	1

Points & Certification Levels:
26–32 Certified; 33–38 Silver; 39–51 Gold; 52–69 Platinum

Source: Company files.

Exhibit 5   Fresh Area Lighting Energy Calculation

		Fresh Area Load (W/m2)	Running Time (Hours/Day)	Power Usage (KWh/Day)	Power Usage (KWh /Month)	Power Usage (KWh/Year)
Carrefour Store, 2004	Standard deco lamps (general lighting installed)	45.5	15	682.5	8,190	98,280
Carrefour Store, 2006	Raised deco lamps with magnetic ballasts (general lighting removed)	31.5	15	472.5	5,670	68,040
Carrefour Urumqi Store No. 3, 2006	Raised deco lamps with electronic ballast (general lighting removed)	22.4	15	336	4,032	48,384

Source: Company files.

Exhibit 6   Roof Top Solar System Proposals A and B

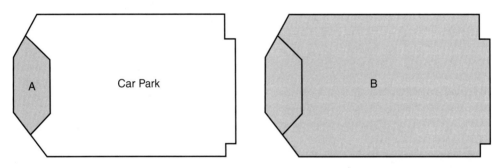

	Suntech		SunDar		Linyang SolarFun		Dawson Solar	
	Proposal A	Proposal B	Proposal A	Proposal B	Proposal A	Proposal B	Proposal A	Proposal B
% of Annual Carrefour Usage	0.9	5.5	0.3	2.3	0.45	1.65	0	1.8
Cost (Million RMB)	8.5	51	2.1	14	3.0	12	0.0	12.8
Payback Period (years)	77	77	57	49	58	60	0	58

Source: Company files.

Exhibit 7   Power Reduction Comparison

Energy Saving by Equipment	CF 2004 North Non-modified Store (A)	CF 2004 South Non-modified Store (B)	CF 2006 North Tawan Test Store (A)	CF 2006 South Yuanchun Test Store (B)	Green Building Estimated Savings Based on Reference Comparison			
					Estimated Savings* (kWh)	Reduction (%) of Total	Annual Savings (RMB)**	Costs (RMB)**
Deco Lighting (balast)		98,280	30,240	30,240	30,240	0.23%	27,216	52,000
Energy Management-System-Lighting			105,333	122,167	246,375	1.84%	221,738	70,000
Energy Management-System-Refrigeration			222,923	259,306	195,000	1.46%	175,500	250,000
Energy Management-System-Air-Conditioning			87,219	195,532	550,460	4.11%	495,414	70,000
Warm Water Heater (heat reclaim)			173,448	115,632	215,496	1.61%	193,946	40,000
Free Cooling (ouside-inside air circulation)			345,474	380,033	1,036,422	7.74%	932,780	770,000
Cold Rooms (size reduction)			6,984	8,970	6,984	0.05%	6,286	−65,000
Preparation Areas (size reduction)			1,314	1,314	1,314	0.01%	1,183	−40,000
Office (size reduction)			51,702	44,928	51,702	0.39%	46,532	−43,000
Sub-total Annual Consumption (kWh)	7,024,637	8,658,122	6,000,000	7,500,000	13,390,000			
Sub-total Annual Cost (RMB at 1 kWh = .9 RMB)	6,322,173	7,792,310	5,400,000	6,750,000	12,051,000			
Geo-thermal Energy Generation					267,800*	2%*	241,020	2,990,000
Solar Chiller Air-Conditioning					1,304,910	9.75%	1,174,419	3,560,000
CO2 System Refrigeration-System					214,240*	1.6%*	192,816	2,330,000
Transformer (capacity reduction)					29,982	0.22%	26,984	−50,000
Busway Cabling Syst. Energy Loss Reduction					19,848	0.15%	17,863	−39,000
Exterior Wall Insulation					93,334	0.70%	84,001	140,000

*Based on pro-rata space and equipment comparison
**Exchange Rate: RMB 1 = US$0.14
Source: Company files.

Case 8

The Prince Edward Island Preserve Company: Turnaround

In April 2008, Bruce MacNaughton, president of Prince Edward Island Preserve Co. Ltd. (P.E.I. Preserves), was focused on turnaround. The company he had founded in 1985 had gone into receivership in May 2007. Although this had resulted in losses for various mortgage holders and unsecured creditors, MacNaughton had been able to buy back his New Glasgow shop/café, the adjacent garden property and inventory, and restart the business. He now needed a viable product-market strategy.

BACKGROUND

Prince Edward Island Preserve Co. was a manufacturing and retail company located in New Glasgow, P.E.I. which produced and marketed specialty food products. The company founder and majority shareholder, Bruce MacNaughton, had realized that an opportunity existed to present P.E.I. strawberries as a world-class food product and to introduce the finished product to an "up-scale" specialty market. MacNaughton had made good on the opportunity he had perceived years earlier. It had not been easy, however.

MacNaughton arrived in Prince Edward Island from Moncton, New Brunswick, in 1978. Without a job, he slept on the beach for much of that first summer. Over the next few years he worked in commission sales, waited tables in restaurants, and then moved to Toronto. There he studied to become a chef at George Brown College. After working in the restaurant trade for several years, he found a job with "Preserves by Amelia" in Toronto. After six months, he returned to Prince Edward Island where he opened a

Nathaniel C. Lupton wrote this case under the supervision of Professor Paul W. Beamish solely to provide material for class discussion. The authors do not intend to illustrate either effective or ineffective handling of a managerial situation. The authors may have disguised certain names and other identifying information to protect confidentiality.

Version: (A) 2008-05-12

restaurant. The restaurant was not successful and MacNaughton lost the $30,000 stake he had accumulated. With nothing left but 100 kilograms of strawberries, MacNaughton decided to make these into preserves in order to have gifts for Christmas 1984. Early the following year, P.E.I. Preserves was founded.

The products produced by the company were priced and packaged for the gift/ gourmet and specialty food markets. The primary purchasers of these products were conscious of quality and were seeking a product which they considered tasteful and natural. P.E.I. Preserves felt its product met the highest standard of quality at a price that made it attractive to all segments of the marketplace.

Over the next few years as the business grew, improvements were made to the building in New Glasgow. The sense of style which was characteristic of the company was evident from the beginning in its attractive layout and design.

In 1989, the company diversified and opened "The Perfect Cup," a small restaurant in Prince Edward Island's capital city of Charlottetown. This restaurant continued the theme of quality, specializing in wholesome, home-made food featuring the products manufactured by the company. The success of this operation led to the opening in 1990 of a small tea room at the New Glasgow location. Both of these locations showcased the products manufactured by P.E.I. Preserves.

In 1989, the company also opened a small (22-square-metre) retail branch in the CP Prince Edward Hotel. MacNaughton hoped this locale would expand visibility in the local and national marketplace, and serve as an off-season sales office. P.E.I. Preserves had been given very favourable lease arrangements and the location would require minimal financial investment. Two years later, the CP hotel location was closed and the company opened the Piece of Cake restaurant and a retail location a short distance away in the Confederation Court Mall. As Table 1 suggests, various forms of diversification had occurred over the years.

Table 1

Operation (Year Opened - Closed)
Charlottetown—Manufacturing and Retail (1985–1987)
New Glasgow—Manufacturing and Retail (1988–Present)
Charlottetown—Restaurant (Perfect Cup) (1989–1990)
Charlottetown—Retail (CP Hotel) (1989–1991)
New Glasgow—Restaurant (Tea Room) (1990–Present)
Charlottetown—Restaurant (Piece of Cake) (1991–1992)
Charlottetown—Retail (1991–1993)
Moncton, N.B.—Retail Franchise (1992–1994)
New Glasgow—Garden (bought 1994, opened 2003)
New Glasgow—Theatre (2003–Present)
Charlottetown—Sweater Shop (2006)

MARKETPLACE

Prince Edward Island was Canada's smallest province, both in size and population. Located in the Gulf of St. Lawrence, it was separated from Nova Scotia and New Brunswick by the Northumberland Strait. The major employer in Prince Edward Island was the various levels of government. Many people in Prince Edward Island worked seasonally in farming (especially potato), fishing, or tourism. During the peak tourist months of July and August, the island population would swell dramatically from its base of 138,000. Prince Edward Island's one million annual visitors came "home" to enjoy the long sandy beaches, picturesque scenery, lobster dinners, arguably the best tasting strawberries in the world, and slower pace of life. Prince Edward Island was best known in Canada and elsewhere for the books, movies and television series about Lucy Maud Montgomery's turn-of-the-century literary creation, Anne of Green Gables. 2008 was a special year for many tourists as it marked the 100th anniversary of the publication of Anne of Green Gables.

P.E.I. Preserves felt it was competing in a global market. Its visitors were from all over the world, and in 2008, it expected the numbers to exceed 150,000 in the New Glasgow location alone. New Glasgow (population 100) was located in a rural setting equidistant (15 kilometres) from Charlottetown and Prince Edward Island's best-known north shore beaches. In its mailings, it planned to continue to promote Prince Edward Island as "Canada's Garden Province" and the "little jewel that was in everyone's heart!" It had benefited, and would continue to benefit, from that image.

MARKETING

Products

The company had developed numerous products since its inception. These included many original varieties of preserves as well as honey, vinegar, mustard and repackaged tea (Exhibit 1 contains a 2008 price list, order form and a page from the mail order catalogue). The company had also added to the appeal of these products by offering gift packs composed of different products and packaging. With over 80 items, MacNaughton felt that a diverse product line had been achieved, and efforts in developing new product lines were expected to decrease in the future. Approximately three-quarters of total retail sales (including wholesale and mail order) came from the products the company made itself. Of these, three quarters were jam preserves.

With the success of P.E.I. Preserves, imitation was inevitable. Several other small firms in Prince Edward Island also retailed specialty preserves. Another company which produced preserves in Ontario emphasized the Green Gables tie-in on its labels.

Price

P.E.I. Preserves was not competing with "low-end" products, and felt its price reinforced its customers' perception of quality. The 13 types of jam preserves retailed for $6.95 for a 250-millilitre jar, significantly more than any grocery store product. However, grocery stores did not offer jam products made with such a high fruit content and with champagne, liqueur or whisky. The food products were not subject to the five per cent national goods and services tax or Prince Edward Island's 10 per cent provincial sales tax, an advantage over other gift products which the company would be stressing.

Promotion

Product promotion had been focused in two areas—personal contact with the consumer and catalogue distribution. Visitors to the New Glasgow location (approximately

125,000 in 2007) were enthusiastic upon meeting MacNaughton "resplendent in the family kilt," reciting history and generally providing live entertainment. MacNaughton and the other staff members realized the value of this "island touch" and strove to ensure that all visitors to New Glasgow left with both a positive feeling and purchased products.

Visitors were also encouraged to visit the New Glasgow location through a co-operative scheme whereby other specialty retailers provided a coupon for a free cup of coffee or tea at P.E.I. Preserves. In 2007, roughly 2,000 of these coupons were redeemed.

Approximately 25,000 people received their mail order catalogue annually. They had experienced an order rate of 7.5 per cent with the average order being $66. They hoped to devote more time and effort to their mail order business in an effort to extend their marketing and production period.

In addition to mail order, the company operated with an ad hoc group of wholesale distributors. These wholesalers were divided between Nova Scotia, Ontario and other locations. For orders as small as $150, buyers could purchase from the wholesalers' price list. Wholesale prices were on average 60 per cent of the retail/mail order price. Total wholesale trade for the coming year was projected at $211,000, under the assumption of a three per cent increase over the previous year.

Over the past few years, the company had received numerous enquiries for quotations on large-scale shipments. Mitsubishi had asked for a price on a container load of preserves. Airlines and hotels were interested in obtaining preserves in 28- or 30-gram single-service bottles. One hotel chain, for example, had expressed interest in purchasing three million bottles if the cost could be kept under $0.40 per unit. (MacNaughton had not proceeded due to the need to purchase $65,000 worth of bottling equipment, and uncertainty about his production costs.) This same hotel chain had more recently been assessing the ecological implications of the packaging waste which would be created with the use of so many small bottles. It was now weighing the hygiene implications of serving jam out of larger, multi-customer use containers in their restaurants.

FINANCIAL

Growth, although indicative of the success of the company's products, had also created its share of problems. Typical of many small businesses, the company had not secured financing suitable to its needs. This, coupled with the seasonal nature of the manufacturing operation, had caused numerous periods of severe cash shortages.

Recent years, however, had been especially difficult for the company. The company had lost over $313,000 to start 2007, and this deficit grew to over $365,000 by the end of March. After going through four different bookkeepers, an unsuccessful attempted acquisition of an unrelated store in Charlottetown which proved costly, and general "distractions" with his garden and other projects, MacNaughton realized his company was not going to be able to manage payments to creditors any longer. The company officially went into receivership on May 10, 2007, after the bank reduced its line of credit to zero. Exhibit 2 presents the balance sheet of the P.E.I. Preserve Co. Ltd. The new company, Prince Edward Island Preserve Co., with a fiscal year end of April 30, opened shortly thereafter.

Sales of the new company up to the end of March 2008 were a little over $1,570,000. These sales were made up of $1,065,000 from retail and wholesale (including mail order) of what they manufactured and/or distributed, $494,000 from the café and dairy bar, and $13,000 in sales and donations from visitors to the garden. Exhibit 3 provides a departmental income statement from these operations, while Exhibit 4 contains a consolidated balance sheet.

At this time, MacNaughton was attempting to provide a sound financial base for the continued operation of the company. Projected sales for the period from May 1, 2008, to April 30, 2009, are summarized in Table 2 (see Exhibit 5 for details).

Table 2

New Glasgow Restaurant	$565,000
Retail (New Glasgow)	$708,000
Wholesale (New Glasgow)	$211,000
Mail Order (New Glasgow)	$163,000
Kiosk (Charlottetown Mall)	$140,000
Garden Donations	$24,600
Gallery and Tea Room	$15,000
Shipping	$50,230
Total	$1,876,830

OPERATIONS

Preserve production took place on site, in an area visible through glass windows from the retail floor. Many visitors, in fact, would videotape operations during their visit to the New Glasgow store, or would watch the process while tasting the broad selection of sample products freely available.

Production took place on a batch basis. Ample production capacity existed for the $30,000 main kettle used to cook the preserves. Preserves were made five months a year, on a single shift, five day per week basis. Even then, the main kettle was in use only 50 per cent of the time.

Only top quality fruit was purchased. As much as possible, P.E.I. raw materials were used. For a short period the fruit could be frozen until it was time for processing.

The production process was labour intensive. MacNaughton was considering the feasibility of moving to an incentive-based salary system to increase productivity and control costs. While there were some minor differences due to ingredients, the variable costs for the 250-ml size are shown in Table 3 for both the traditional line of products and a new certified organic line developed for export to Japan (discussed later). The Japanese retailer required a unique style of jar and shrink-wrapping for the lid which increased the overall cost in addition to the premium price for organically grown fruit.

Café, Gallery and Tea Room

Restaurant operations were the source of many of MacNaughton's headaches. The New Glasgow Restaurant had evolved over time from offering dessert and coffee/tea to its present status where it was also open for meals all day from late May until mid-October. McNaughton spent about 40 per cent of his time on restaurant-related activities.

Table 3

	Traditional Line	Certified Organic
Ingredients	$1.24	$2.37
Labour	$0.47	$0.47
Packaging	$0.40	$0.90
Total	$2.11	$3.74

Retail and Mail Order

Retail accounted for the greatest portion of both sales and income for the company (see Exhibit 3). Most retail took place in the New Glasgow store as visitors stopped in individually or on bus tours. Although road travel vacations were on a steady decline due to record high gas prices, cruise ship travel received a major boost after the opening of a new pier in 2008, as shown in Table 4. With major expansions to the port still under way in Charlottetown, the number of visiting cruise ships was expected to rise to about 80 within two years. In the past, cruise ships would stay in Prince Edward Island for about half a day before heading off to other ports. However, due to the popularity of the location they began staying for a full day in 2007. MacNaughton estimated that about 30 per cent of the ship's passengers would stop in New Glasgow in the morning, and another 30 per cent in the afternoon. Based on this, he forecast that the number of visitors would increase from about 125,000 to 150,000.

Table 4

Year	Cruise Ships	Passengers
2004	28	23,118
2005	23	23,894
2006	25	28,830
2007	16	21,360
2008	40	69,380

Source: http://historiccharlottetownseaport.com/cruiseships/

About 85 per cent of the passengers of these ships were American with the majority of the remaining 15 per cent divided evenly between Canadians and Germans. MacNaughton noted that the European consumers were not interested in purchasing products to take back with them but preferred items they could consume on the premises. American consumers were also beginning to shy away from purchases of preserves and other products as new air travel regulations disallowed liquids and gels in containers with volumes greater than 100-ml in carry-on luggage. When MacNaughton suggested these customers place the bottles in their checked luggage, customers expressed fears about the bottles breaking. For these customers, MacNaughton agreed to ship the products to their homes for the same fee used for mail orders (see Exhibit 1). The goal of P.E.I. Preserves was to operate shipping on a breakeven basis but in actuality it was proving to be an expense (see Exhibit 3).

Some of the customers who purchased products while visiting the New Glasgow location would become repeat customers who would order using the P.E.I. Preserve mail order catalogue or through the company's website (www.preservecompany.com). Shipping to the United States had become difficult over the last few years. The Food and Drug Administration's (FDA) bioterrorism act required that any shipment of food products be announced well in advance of the shipment date. In addition, the FDA notified P.E.I. Preserves early in 2008 that their labels were not compliant with new regulations in terms of the print location and presentation of the size of the container and the ingredients. As a result, the 40,000 labels the company had printed were now useless and mail order was halted for a period of two months while new labels were designed and printed.

In addition to the retail location in New Glasgow and mail order, P.E.I. Preserves Co. opened a small kiosk in the Charlottetown Mall to gain access to the estimated $150,000 local market. MacNaughton felt the kiosk was an efficient way of educating customers about his products. The kiosk operated during the summer months only in 2007, but MacNaughton decided to keep it in operation from July 1 to December 25 in 2008 in order to increase sales during the holiday season.

Wholesale

The company's wholesale operation largely resulted from market pull forces. Prior visitors to the New Glasgow location who did not want the inconvenience and added cost of purchasing products through mail order requested that their local high-end food distributors import P.E.I. Preserves products. The company established several relationships with these distributors in locations from Eastern Ontario to the Maritimes, and a few in Alberta and British Columbia. In general, however, MacNaughton was always worried about how his products were marketed in these stores and how that might affect his brand. He strongly believed customers needed to sample the products, as they regularly did in the New Glasgow shop, in order to be convinced that the premium price was justified. He felt he should visit locations that wished to sell his products, but he did not have the time to do so, given the demands of managing his business.

The Country Garden

P.E.I. Preserves purchased 12 acres of land adjacent to the New Glasgow location in 1994 and committed substantial time, energy and money in landscaping and adding new structures beginning in 2003. One structure was an old church which was donated to the company and was to serve as a gallery for local artists in 2008. Another was a pavilion where local classical musicians were paid to perform on occasion during the summer. The third building was a butterfly observatory which was popular with visitors to the location.

After the first year of operation for the garden, MacNaughton discovered that while visitors truly enjoyed the scenery, most were not willing to pay for the experience. From that point on, the garden was operated on a breakeven basis funded through donations and staffed by local volunteers. In 2007, the garden managed a very slight profit and the company planned to hire back a caretaker on a part time basis in 2008.

The long term plan for the gardens was to build a respite for chronically ill patients and their caretakers. As the land was now designated by the provincial government as a hospice and wildlife park, property taxes were negligible.

Japanese Exports

In 2005, Kosaku Morita visited Prince Edward Island from Japan to meet with MacNaughton and Raymond Loo, a local organic farmer and president of P.E.I. Certified Organic Producers Co-op. Morita was specifically interested in the organic black currants grown by Loo, which Japanese consumers appreciated for their health benefits, most notably their high levels of antioxidants. Morita was so impressed with the quality of P.E.I. Preserves' products he invited both Loo and MacNaughton to Foodex in Japan in March of the following year.

Foodex was an annual event held in Japan in which 2,000 food and beverage producers showcased their wares to roughly 100,000 restauranteurs, caterers, distributors and wholesalers. MacNaughton was impressed with the interest in his preserves, so he decided to extend his line of organics and return the following year in 2007.

P.E.I. Preserves made an initial shipment of 90,000 125-ml and 250-ml bottles of their new organic line of products to a Japanese distributor in 2007. The bottles retailed for ¥1,000 (about $10) and ¥1,800 (about $18), respectively, of which the distributor and retailer took the majority of the margin. P.E.I. Preserves' wholesale price for these organic products was $3.00 for the 125-ml and $4.92 for the 250-ml bottle, both priced to obtain a margin of about $1.00 per bottle. The freight cost of about $0.30 per bottle was paid by the importer. In 2008, the company's Japanese partners were running a two week trial of the organic products during which time they expected to place two orders of 90,000 bottles each.

Together, P.E.I. Preserves, local organic farmers and their Japanese business associates marketed products under the name "Anne's P.E.I. Farm" and created a new Japanese language website (www.annespeifarm.com) which contained information about the products and their health benefits. The website also provided information about the province of Prince Edward Island, including sustainable energy projects, organic farming, photographs capturing the natural beauty of the land and, of course, Anne of Green Gables. In addition, the site recounted the "stories" of the individuals involved in the production and delivery of the end product including the farmers, MacNaughton and P.E.I. Preserves, and the Japanese business associates.

Management

During the peak summer period, P.E.I. Preserves employed 65 people among the restaurants, manufacturing area and retail locations. Of these, five were managerial positions. The company was considered a good place to work, with high morale and limited turnover. Nonetheless, most employees (including some management) were with the company on a seasonal basis. This was a concern to MacNaughton who felt that if he could provide year-round employment, he would be able to attract and keep the best quality staff.

MacNaughton felt that the company had survived on the basis of word-of-mouth. Few follow-up calls on mail order had ever been done, although MacNaughton read every e-mail sent to the customer service address. MacNaughton did not enjoy participating in trade shows—even though he received regular solicitations for them from across North America. He participated in one retail show in 2007 and four in 2008, all of them in or close to Prince Edward Island. He hoped to be able to eventually hire a sales/marketing manager.

The key manager continued to be MacNaughton. He described himself as "a frugal but fair person to deal with when it comes to purchasing. However, I like to spend enough money to ensure that what we do—we do right." Financial and managerial constraints meant that MacNaughton felt stretched ("I haven't had a vacation in years") and unable to pursue all of the ideas he had for developing the business. Other key members of the administrative staff included Lynn Whitlock in charge of production and purchasing, Sian Morris in charge of bookkeeping and administration, retail and human resources manager, Judy Clark, and Don Croiter, chef and product development manager.

THE JAPANESE CONSUMER

Japan was one of Canada's most important sources of foreign tourists. In 2006, there were 364,000 Japanese visitors to Canada. The number of visits by Japanese tourists to each province is shown in Table 5. Most Japanese visitors entered through the Vancouver or Toronto airports. Within Canada, the most popular destination was the Rocky Mountains (in Banff, Alberta, numerous stores catered specifically to Japanese consumers). Excluding airfare, these visitors to Canada spent an estimated $500 million in 2006, making it the third largest international market for tourism. These figures were expected to decline slightly for 2007, and rebound in 2008.

The Japanese fascination with Prince Edward Island could be traced to the popularity of Anne of Green Gables. The Japanese translation of this and other books in the same series had been available for many years. However, the adoption of the book as required reading in the Japanese school system since the 1950s had resulted in widespread awareness and affection for "Anne with red hair" and Prince Edward Island.

Table 5

Province	Japanese Visitors, 2006
Newfoundland	200
Prince Edward Island	4,100
Nova Scotia	5,400
New Brunswick	2,000
Quebec	36,900
Ontario	168,800
Manitoba	7,300
Saskatchewan	1,100
Alberta	87,900
British Columbia	183,000
Yukon	3,000
Northwest Territories	2,300

Source: 2006 facts & figures: Canada Tourism Commission
www.canada.travel/research

The Japanese Jam Market

Japanese annual consumption of jam was approximately 80,000 tons. Imports made up six to nine per cent of consumption, with higher-grade products (¥470 or more per kilo wholesale CIF) making up a third of this total. Several dozen firms imported jam, and utilized a mix of distribution channels. Prices varied, in part, according to the type of channel structure used. Exhibit 6 provides a common structure.

Future Directions

P.E.I. Preserves needed a viable product-market strategy. Many options existed to expand manufacturing and serve a larger market size in order to grow. The factory in New Glasgow was adequate for existing business but too small to meet the demands of a larger market.

One option MacNaughton considered was setting up a manufacturing operation independent of P.E.I. Preserves in which he would be a minority shareholder and would manage initially. Once the operation was up and running, P.E.I. Preserves could continue to license its brand name to the products, provided strict quality standards were maintained. This would allow MacNaughton the freedom to devote his time to the existing New Glasgow operations.

Before expanding production, however, MacNaughton had to decide what product market should be targeted, and to establish what the demand from that market would be. He could attempt to expand one or more of his retail, wholesale, mail order or Japanese export operations. There were also decisions to be made around pursuing his established product lines and the new organic line. He wondered if there were other potential opportunities he had not considered as well.

MacNaughton was the first to acknowledge that, while the business had been "built on gut and emotion, rather than analysis," this was insufficient for the future. The challenge was to determine the direction and timing of the desired change.

Exhibit 1   Prince Edward Island Preserve Co. Mail Order Catalogue

Order Date_____

PRESERVES

Description	250ml	Price	Qty.	250ml	Price	Qty.
Blackcurrant	997	$6.95		9944	$4.95	
Blueberry Raspberry	993	$6.95		9942	$4.95	
Blueberry Lemon	998	$6.95		9949	$4.95	
Cabernet/Sauvignon/Jelly	9918	$6.95		9954	$4.95	
Lemon Ginger/Marmalade	9911	$6.95		9946	$4.95	
Lime Marmalade	9912	$6.95		N/A	$4.95	
Orange Marmalade	9910	$6.95		9945	$4.95	
Raspberry Champagne	992	$6.95		9941	$4.95	
Raspberry Jelly	9919	$6.95		9952	$4.95	
Raspberry Peach	995	$6.95		9943	$4.95	
Sour Cherry Marmalade	999	$6.95		9951	$4.95	
Strawberry Rhubarb	994	$6.95		9947	$4.95	
Strawberry Grand Mariner	991	$6.95		9940	$4.95	
Very Berry	9914	$6.95		9948	$4.95	

Preserves 375ml

	375ml	Price	Qty.
Strawberry Grand Mariner	9930	$9.95	
Raspberry Champagne	9931	$9.95	
Blue Raspberry Champagne	9932	$9.95	
Very Berry	9933	$9.95	
Strawberry Rhubarb	9934	$9.95	
Blueberry Lemon	9935	$9.95	

Gift Boxes

	125ml	Price	Qty
2 x 125ml	99171	$10.95	
3 x 125ml	99172	$15.95	
6 x 125ml	99173	$29.95	
2 x 250ml	99174	$15.95	
3 x 250ml	99175	$22.95	
6 x 250ml	99170	$43.95	
9 x 250ml	99176	$66.95	
2 x 375ml	99177	$23.50	
3 x 375ml	99178	$34.95	

BBQ Sauce 375ml

	375ml	Price	Qty
Tomato & Herb	99140	$6.95	
Smoked Hickory & Maple	99141	$6.95	
Habanero & Mango	99142	$6.95	

Salsa

	250ml	Price	Qty
Peach Salsa 250ml	9923	$6.95	
Cherry Salsa 250ml	9924	$6.95	
Cherry Salsa 375ml	9937	$8.95	
Peach Salsa 375ml	9936	$8.95	

Miscellaneous Items

_____

_____

_____

_____

SOLD TO INFO   Telephone: _____

Name: _____

Address: _____

_____

City: _____

State/Province: _____   ZIP/Postal Code: _____

☐ same as ship to

SHIP TO INFO   Telephone: _____

Name: _____

Address: _____

_____

City: _____

State/Province: _____   ZIP/Postal Code: _____

Gift Message: _____

_____

METHOD OF PAYMENT

☐ Visa   ☐ Mastercard   ☐ American Express
☐ JCB   ☐ Cheque/Money Order ☐ Diners Club

Exp. Date MM/YY   3 Digit Security Code

Name on Card _____

Shipping Cost

STANDARD RATES FOR CANADA AND USA*
For delivery please allow up to 15 business days.

Value or Order	Shipping Cost
$25 – $40.99	$12.00
$41 – $55.99	$13.00
$56 – $65.99	$14.00
$66 – $75.99	$15.00
$76 – $100.99	$16.00
$101 & over	20% of order

*Surcharge of 20% for Northern Canada, Newfoundland Labrador, Alaska and Hawaii.

FREE * SHIPPING with a minimum order per address of 24 jars valued @ $3.50 or more.

Subtotal	$
Shipping IF ASSISTANCE NEEDED CALL 1-800-565-5267	$
GST/HST NO TAX CHARGED TO U.S. DESTINATIONS *Amount paid is set by the province to which the order is being shipped. NF, NB and NS is HST (14%) The rest of Canada is GST (6%)	$
TOTAL ORDER	$

Exhibit 1   (continued)

PRESERVES•JELLY•MARMALADE

Using only the finest and freshest fruits possible, we produce a wonderful low sugar, high fruit content preserve. Our ingredients are only the highest quality and for flavour enhancement we use freshly squeezed orange and lemon juices. No added preservatives! See complete listings at www.preservecompany.com

Strawberry & Grand Marnier
991 250ml   9940 125ml   9930 375ml
Using only Prince Edward Island Strawberries we have created a high in Strawberry flavour product complemented by the addition of Grand Marnier Liqueur. You can taste summer! *Texture: Smooth*

Wild Blueberry and Lemon
996 250ml   9949 125ml   9935 375ml
This recipe has the least amount of sugar and the freshest taste. The fresh lemon and the fresh mint work to enhance the flavour of Wild Blueberries. *Texture: Loose/Smooth*

Raspberries and Champagne
992 250ml   9941 125ml   9931 375ml
This one bursts of fresh raspberry flavour only to be enhanced further by the addition of Champagne. *Texture: Loose/Smooth*

Very Berry
9914 250ml   9948 125ml   9933 375ml
The staff's favourite. Combining Strawberries, Raspberries, Cherries and Wild blueberries, we have created a flavour that is delicious and unique. Great topping as well as preserve. *Texture: Loose/Smooth*

Wild Blueberry and Raspberry w/Champagne
993 250ml   9942 125ml   9932 375ml
My personal favourite. Adding two of the world's most favourite flavours together and adding Champagne to complement is ambrosia in a jar. *Texture: Smooth*

Strawberry and Rhubarb
994 250ml   9947 125ml   9934 375ml
A flavour trip back in time. This combination of flavours is a memory of time past for many people. Delicious! *Texture: Smooth/Loose*

Raspberry and Peach
995 250ml   9943 125ml
This preserve is looser than most and suitable for desserts or ice cream. *Texture: Loose*

Black Currant
997 250ml   9944 125ml
Good morning sunshine! This very flavorful berry and the use of little sugar are sure to wake your mouth up any time of day. Quite tart! *Texture: Smooth*

Lime Marmalade
9912 250ml
Wow! If you like lime and you like marmalade, you will have thought you reached the nirvana of flavour when you taste this marmalade. *Texture: Chunky*

Sour Cherry Marmalade
999 250ml   9951 125ml
Unique, colourful, flavourful are a few words that describe this marmalade. *Texture: Smooth/Chunky*

Lemon and Ginger Marmalade with Amaretto
9911 250ml   9946 125ml
A very unique combination. One of our best selling marmalades. We use fresh lemons, fresh ginger and real Italian Amaretto. *Texture: Smooth/Chunky*

Orange Marmalade with Chivas Regal
9910 250ml   9945 125ml
One way to their hearts. Sweet oranges, a little sugar, time and Chivas Regal is a combination of flavours certain to be enjoyed by anyone who enjoys marmalade.
Texture: Smooth/Chunky/Loose

Cabernet Sauvignon Wine Jelly
9918 250ml   9954 125ml
This is a full bodied wine jelly loaded with flavour. *Texture: Smooth*

Strawberry & Grand Marnier
—our most popular flavour.

$4.95 125ml/4.4oz.

$6.95 250ml/8.8oz.

$9.95 375ml/13.5oz.

2

3

Exhibit 2   P.E.I. Preserve Co. Ltd. Balance Sheet, as at March 31, 2007

Assets	
Current assets	
Accounts receivable	$ 14,927
Accounts receivable—related parties	127,224
Prepaid expenses	6,312
Inventory	358,204
	506,667
Investment tax credits receivable	19,048
Property and equipment	1,642,265
Due from related parties	602,387
Intangible assets	29,787
Funds held on deposit	200,000
	$3,000,154
Liabilities	
Current liabilities	
Bank advances	$ 4,704
Accounts payable and accrued liabilities	248,595
Accounts payable—related parties	86,472
Current portion of capital lease	1,229
Current portion of long-term debt	1,652,814
	1,993,814
Advances from shareholders	155,468
Long-term debt, less current portion	126,748
Deferred government assistance	76,681
Preferred shares	200,000
	2,552,711
Shareholders' Equity	800,000
Capital stock	13,300
Contributed surplus	(365,857)
Deficit	447,443
	$3,000,154

Exhibit 3 Prince Edward Island Preserve Co. (New Company) Departmental Income Statement, May 11, 2007 to March 31, 2008

	Cafe/Dairy Bar	Retail	Wholesale	Mail Order	Garden	Preserves Production	Admin.
Revenue							
Sales	505,369	735,087	180,784	132,409	1,225	0	0
Freight revenue	0	6,325	3,362	27,178	0	0	0
Discounts	(11,209)	(17,266)	(1,976)	(269)	0	0	0
Donations	0	0	0	0	11,830	0	0
Interest/Tax/Other	0	0	0	0	0	0	548
Total Revenue	494,160	724,146	182,169	159,318	13,055	0	548
Direct Costs							
Materials	132,894	0	0	0	0	243,567	0
Supplies	25,952	143,268	0	30,708	0	17,423	0
Wages	186,363	44,125	0	0	0	88,870	0
Repair & maint.	6,991	0	0	0	12,739	2,281	0
Cash over/short	(333)	62	0	(28)	0	0	0
Freight expense	0	6,826	13,017	33,538	0	17,523	0
Opening inventory	0	0	0	0	0	166,172	0
Ending inventory	0	0	0	0	0	(197,610)	0
R & D expense	0	0	0	0	0	4,308	0
Total Direct Costs	351,868	194,280	13,017	64,218	12,739	342,533	0
Admin. Expenses							
Adv. & promotion	0	0	0	0	0	0	29,005
Land & equipment	0	0	0	0	0	0	77,261
Interest expense	0	0	0	709	0	0	58,624
Admin. wages	0	0	0	0	0	0	142,253
Wage & empl. exp.	0	0	0	0	0	0	80,591
Office	0	0	0	0	0	0	57,928
Repairs & maint.	0	0	0	0	0	0	24,074
Other	0	0	0	0	0	0	9,511
Foreign exchange	0	0	0	0	0	0	(447)
TOTAL EXPENSE	351,868	194,280	13,017	64,927	12,739	342,533	478,799
NET INCOME	142,292	529,866	169,152	94,391	317	(342,533)	(478,250)

Exhibit 4   Prince Edward Island Preserve Co. (New Company) Balance Sheet, as at March 31, 2008

ASSETS	
Current assets	
Cash	$ 7,108
Accounts receivable	5,318
Prepaid expenses	49,525
Inventory	197,610
Total Current Assets	259,560
Long Term Assets	
Land	143,840
Building	367,743
Equipment	34,588
Automotive Equipment	2,555
Computer Hardware	2,244
Total Long Term Assets	550,970
TOTAL ASSETS	$810,530
LIABILITIES	
Current Liabilities	
Accounts payable	12,500
Receiver General payable	−290
PST Payable	5
Total Current Liabilities	12,215
Other Liabilities	
Advances from shareholder	−1,918
Loan and Mortgage	685,000
Total Other Liabilities	683,082
TOTAL LIABILITIES	$695,297
EQUITY	
Capital Stock	0
Retained Earnings	115,234
TOTAL EQUITY	115,234
LIABILITIES AND EQUITY	$810,530

Exhibit 5   Prince Edward Island Preserve Co. (New Company) Cash Flow Budget, for the year May 1, 2008–April 30, 2009

Sales	
Café	$ 565,000
Retail	708,000
Wholesale	211,000
Mail order	163,000
Garden donations	24,600
Gallery & Tea room sales	15,000
Charlottetown Mall Location	140,000
Freight (retail—1% sales)	7,080
Freight (wholesale—5% sales)	10,550
Freight (mail order—20% sales)	32,600
TOTAL SALES	**$1,876,830**
Wages & Benefits	
Wages—Management gross	143,000
Wages—Café	184,928
Wages—Retail	69,548
Wages—Mail Order	22,920
Wages—Production	77,358
Wages—Garden Maintenance Gross	6,760
Wages—Maintenance Gross	10,920
CPP, EI, Workers Compensation	40,438
Total Wages & Benefits	**555,872**
Cost of Sales	
Café (28% sales)	158,200
Retail (22% sales + 15% mall)	176,760
Mail order	6,460
Production - preserves	260,800
Freight—production (5% of above)	13,040
Freight—retail (1% sales)	7,080
Freight—wholesale (8% sales)	16,880
Freight—mail order (25% sales)	40,750
Total Cost of Sales	**679,970**
Total Professional Fees	**18,000**
Repairs & Maintenance	**32,000**
Utilities	**61,320**
Insurance	**21,909**
Office	**53,475**
Leases	**16,726**
Advertising & Promotion	**41,200**
Vehicle & Travel	**18,000**
Supplies & Miscellaneous	**75,243**

(continued)

Exhibit 5   (continued)

Interest & Bank Charges	
Interest on operating loan—150k	2,367
Interest on long-term debt + principle	73,707
Bank interest and back charges	16,400
Credit card fees	2,650
Total Banking Charges	**95,124**
Rent	**21,000**
Commission Paid	**5,000**
TOTAL EXPENSES	**$1,694,839**
CASH IN (OUT)	**$ 181,991**
Corporate income taxes, 2008	−15,300
Corporate income tax installments, 2009	−15,300
Cash out to pay creditors	−60,000
Cash from operating line	−55,000
Cash balance—beginning	**0**
Cash balance—ending	**$ 36,391**

Exhibit 6   The Japanese Jam Market

To expand sales of imported jam or enter the Japanese market for the first time, it is necessary to develop products after a precise study of the market's needs. Importers who are making efforts to tailor their products to the Japanese market have been successfully expanding their sales by 10 per cent each year. Based on the analysis of successful cases of imported jam, the following factors may be considered very important.

Diversification of consumer preferences: Strawberry jam occupies about 50 per cent of the total demand for jam and its share is continuing to rise. Simultaneously, more and more varieties of jam are being introduced.

Low sugar content: European exporters have successfully exported low sugar jam that meets the needs of the Japanese market. Jam with a sugar content of less than 65 per cent occupies a share of 65 to 70 per cent of the market on a volume basis.

Smaller containers: Foreign manufacturers who stick to packaging products in large-sized containers (650 grams, 440 grams, 250 grams), even though their products are designed for household use, have been failing to expand their sales. On the other hand, foreign manufacturers who have developed products in smaller containers (14 grams, 30 grams, 42 grams) specifically for the Japanese market have achieved successful results.

Fashionable items: Contents and quantity are not the only important aspects of jam. The shape and material quality of the containers and their caps, label design and product name can also influence sales. It is also important that the label not be damaged in any way.

Development of gift items: Sets of various types of imported jams are popular as gift items. For example, there are sets of 10 kinds of jam in 40-gram mini-jars (retail price ¥2,000) sold as gift sets.

Selection of distribution channel: Since general trading companies, specialty importers and jam manufacturers each have their own established distribution channels, the selection of the most appropriate channel is of the utmost importance.

Pricing Structure: An importer of products typically pays about 50 per cent of the final retail price for the goods and adds about 10-15 per cent when selling to primary and secondary wholesalers. Wholesalers in turn add about 10 per cent of the final cost of the good when selling to retailers, who add the final mark-up of about 30-35 per cent of the retail price to consumers.

Source: Access to Japan's Import Market, *Tradescope*, June 1989.

Case 9

Time Warner Inc. and the ORC Patents

In early July 1992, John Adamson, president of Optical Recording Corporation (ORC), sat depressed and second-guessed his company's decision to sue Time Warner Inc. for patent infringement. An in-house patent counsel from the U.S. Philips Corporation, whose parent firm developed and licensed the compact disc (CD) technology in partnership with Sony Corporation, had just finished his testimony in the Wilmington, Delaware, courtroom.

The Philips attorney had just advised the court that Philips International N.V. had indeed signed a license agreement with ORC but only to "get rid of ORC with a modest nuisance payment." He had gone on to say that in spite of their decision to accept a license from ORC, the Philips engineers and attorneys had never believed that the Russell patents owned by ORC were valid nor that any compact disc products infringed these patents. Adamson watched in shock as the Philips man made his way out of the courtroom.

Given that Time Warner had mounted a very credible defense and that ORC's entire licensing program might be at risk, Adamson needed to decide whether he should make a modest settlement with Time Warner, just to save the licensing program.

BACKGROUND

Optical Recording Corporation (ORC) was incorporated in 1984 to exploit a technology invented by James T. Russell, an American inventor, then working in laboratories in Salt Lake City, Utah. Due to the desperate financial straits of SLC,[1] his employer,

Richard Ivey School of Business
The University of Western Ontario

John Adamson prepared this case under the supervision of Professor Paul Beamish solely to provide material for class discussion. The authors do not intend to illustrate either effective or ineffective handling of a managerial situation. The authors may have disguised certain names and other identifying information to protect confidentiality.

[1] Due to a series of commercial lawsuits lasting 10 years with Russell's former employer, the author prefers to omit any real name reference to this company that had been a party to the technology transfer agreements with ORC. It is referred to here as "SLC." In all other references herein to persons, places or businesses, the actual names are used.

Russell had made little progress in the previous two years and both he and SLC were anxious to secure a buyer for the technology.

Through Wayne White, a fellow MBA 1972 graduate from the University of Western Ontario, then working with Dominion Securities in Toronto, John Adamson was put in contact with Dr. R. Moses and Dr. A. Stein. These two Toronto businessmen had been working for close to a year to buy Russell's technology. By happenstance, Adamson had contacted White looking for business opportunities to start his next business, preferably in electronics or software, just days after Moses and Stein had advised White that they were going to throw in the towel on their Russell project. In spite of the considerable time that they had spent, it appeared unlikely that they would be successful in securing the necessary finances to proceed.

Adamson negotiated an option with these gentlemen to assume their "interests" in the Russell project, on the condition that he secure the necessary funding for a technology transfer by April 1, 1985, a propitious date as it would turn out. In return, Adamson agreed to reimburse their expenses to date and to give to each, a five per cent equity interest in the incorporation formed to exploit the Russell project in Toronto.

After completing a "due diligence" investigation of the Russell technology, with the assistance of Warner Sharkey, an alumnus and friend from the Royal Military College of Canada and a senior technology consultant, who operated from offices in New York and Toronto, Adamson began planning in earnest. He wanted to transfer the Russell technology to Toronto, where he expected a well qualified team of scientists and engineers could be assembled to pursue a cost-effective development of a pocket-portable digital storage device.

For the next nine excruciating months, he worked to find investors for an issue of special debentures from his Toronto start-up. These debentures also offered a very attractive cash-back feature under a research tax credit program of the Canadian government. Funding was secured and the technology transfer agreements were signed on March 28, 1985, only three days before the option agreement with Moses and Stein would have expired. Adamson had resisted the temptation to request an extension of time on his option agreement with Moses and Stein. He feared that, better informed, they might rekindle their interest in the Russell technology and work to obstruct what little chance he still had to find funding prior to the option expiry on the first of April.

With the debenture funding and the transfer agreements signed, the new Toronto company, soon to be called Optical Recording Corporation (ORC), was now ready to hire Russell and transfer SLC's technology to Toronto.

JIM RUSSELL

By 1984, Jim Russell had worked for close to 20 years toward an improvement in recorded music beyond what was possible with the analog magnetic tape technology. This quest was motivated in part by his love of opera and a desire to listen to more accurate playbacks of recorded performances. When Adamson first visited Russell's lab in Salt Lake City, he was treated to the playback of a recording of Richard Wagner's "Ride of the Valkyries" (or "Die Walkure" in the original German). It was a most rousing introduction to a technology!

Russell had accomplished this playback by shining an argon ion laser beam onto a pre-recorded glass plate, the size of an index card. This was the latest of his laboratory prototypes designed to demonstrate his patented techniques. These techniques were claimed in his extensive portfolio of 26 U.S. patents with corresponding foreign issues in seven other countries.

In Russell's way of recording music, the acoustic signal of the music was first pre-processed into a single *digital* bit stream from a series of time-coincident frequency samples. A laser, an *optical* device, was then used as the energy source to mark the music, as digital bits, onto a glass plate in the recording step and then used to read the music, as digital bits, in the playback step. This technology was known as *digital optical audio* recording.

Adamson was not the first to visit Russell's lab, far from it. Over the course of the previous 10 years, both at SLC in Salt Lake City, and at Battelle Northwest Laboratories in Richland, Washington, electronics manufacturers around the world beat a path to Russell's laboratory door and at his invitation. SLC had been trying to sell technology licenses to the Russell technology but with virtually no success. Prominent among the visitors to SLC's labs were representatives from Philips International N.V., the multinational electric/electronics giant headquartered in Eindhoven, the Netherlands. They had made three separate visits over that 10-year period.

Prior to the commercial availability of the diode laser in the early 1980s, Russell's recording and playback devices were operated with the use of a gas ion laser and as such could be made no smaller than the dimensions of an office desk. Gas ion lasers were too bulky, complicated and expensive to be used in consumer products. This may explain SLC's lack of success in licensing and their resultant financial distress. With the advent of the diode laser, essentially a powerful light source on a silicon chip, a light, compact and economical consumer product such as the compact disc was possible. Although never well funded, SLC's money troubles really began in 1981, just as the mass commercialization of a digital optical audio recording device became feasible.

From Adamson's viewpoint, Russell's greatest achievement was not any one of his inventions, but his success in demonstrating the technical feasibility of recording a digital audio signal optically. Before Russell had successfully demonstrated this technical feat in 1975, no one else had even attempted it. By early 1984, however, the electronics trade papers were reporting that Sony and Philips were developing a so-called compact disc player. SLC and Russell must have felt that they were being left on the sidelines in Salt Lake City, a bitter fate for the inventor and his investors who had all contributed so much.

In bringing Russell and his technology to Toronto, Adamson had decided that there was little point in continuing audio research toward a digital optical tape recorder. The opportunity to develop a massive random access data storage device using credit card-sized media was seen as a less ambitious technical challenge and possibly of greater commercial value than a music device like the CD. With the insight of Russell, Adamson envisioned books, medical records, equipment schematics, maintenance instructions and records on this type of device — and all pocket-portable.

In order to determine what protection the existing Russell patents would provide to the new research focus, Adamson employed the services of John Orange, a patent agent, then with the Toronto law firm of McCarthy & McCarthy. (Orange was recommended by Daniel Cooper, a corporate attorney with the same law firm, who earlier had prepared all of the financing and technology transfer agreements for ORC.)

After working with Russell for several months, Orange advised Adamson in early 1986 that the Russell patents may not provide much protection to the new company's research focus, as the most relevant patents appeared to be limited in their claims to audio applications. Adamson had already understood that it was the precise language of the claims within a patent that determined the patent's intellectual property rights.

DISCOVERING A TREASURE

In completing his study of ORC's patents with the assistance of Russell, Orange also concluded that the newly released compact disc players and discs might infringe one or more of the claims in the Russell patents. What a finding!

Russell had mentioned this possibility to Adamson during their first meeting in the Salt Lake City lab; however, Adamson had put little faith in Russell's remark at the time, as no consumer electronics firm had bothered to license the technology, in spite of SLC's efforts. Furthermore there were no CD products on the market then and its commercial success could not be anticipated.

Encouraged by the report from Orange and the early market success of the compact disc by the spring of 1986, Adamson retained the services of Adrian Horne, an established patent licensing professional of Dolby acoustic research fame. With Horne's assistance, ORC set out to advise every electronics firm likely to market a compact disc player anywhere in the world that "they may infringe the Russell patents" by doing so. Horne was most clear on the point that ORC must not appear to threaten legal action in their notice, as it may give grounds to the recipients to file a preemptive request for Declaratory Judgment and thereby force ORC into premature legal proceedings that ORC could ill afford.

In conjunction with the initial contact of alleged infringers, Adamson prepared cost estimates for the licensing effort and started to gain some early information on what it would cost to sue for patent infringement. He knew that once launched, any investment in the licensing program was certain to be incurred, whereas the return by way of royalty revenues would be anything but certain. He also made early estimates of the royalty potential for the licensing program, but these royalty estimates carried an enormous emotional impact.

Simple arithmetic established that if 100 million CD players were sold in ORC's patent-protected territories at an average manufacturer's selling price of US$100 and if ORC licensed their patent rights for this product at two per cent of revenues, ORC's projected royalties would total US$200 million. And this figure ignored the royalties to be earned on the manufacture and sale of the compact disc media itself! It was clear that a successful licensing program could be mounted given these simple estimates. Adamson chose not to dwell on these figures, however, as his typical reaction oscillated between a measured excitement and a raw fear of the business of licensing beyond what little he knew.

ORC's first meeting with a suspected infringer took place in the early summer of 1986 in Tarrytown, New York, in the offices of N.A. Philips Corporation. Legal representatives for both N.A. Philips and their Philips parent in Eindhoven, the Netherlands, and for the DuPont Corporation of Wilmington, Delaware, were in attendance. For ORC there were Cooper, Orange, and Adamson and a lawyer from Battelle Laboratories of Columbus, Ohio, Jim Russell's first employer, and the original owner and assignor of the Russell patents, first to SLC and then to ORC.

This first meeting with the Philips and DuPont people ended three and one-half hours later, after a full exchange of views and some acrimony, but no progress toward a licensing agreement. The attorneys representing both Philips and DuPont were of the view that no patents were infringed and further that there was some question about the validity of the Russell patents in the first place. There seemed little point in a further meeting and it seemed very likely that ORC might get no further without filing a patent infringement suit.

In August 1986, Adamson made a first trip to Tokyo on behalf of ORC, with Horne and Russell. A week-long series of company presentations had been arranged by Horne, with the assistance of Far East Associates, a technology licensing agency based in Tokyo, with whom Mr. Horne had collaborated in his Dolby days. Only one prominent manufacturer was invited to each meeting.

On Horne's advice, ORC had booked conference room space at the prestigious Okura Hotel, located directly across from the American Embassy in Minato-ku, a district of central Tokyo. Adamson choked on the daily expense of US$2,000 per day for a meeting room that comfortably held only six people. Horne, however, had stressed the importance of the location to ensure that the status-sensitive Japanese gained the best initial impression of ORC and its business offering.

The ORC team was overwhelmed by the turnout to their presentations. Each firm sent at least four executives and engineers; and in two instances, a group of over 10 people arrived, forcing the ORC team to scramble for a larger meeting room. Many guests recognized Horne from his previous Dolby research licensing days and more than a few appeared quite knowledgeable of Russell's research and patents. In fact, three firms clearly had comprehensive files on Russell's work and appeared very familiar with the technology.

The ORC presentations were made in English. Horne had advised that the executives in the international departments of all Japanese companies were invariably fluent in English. The younger members, however, tended to be more at ease in English, while some of the more experienced guests appeared to be there simply to witness the process and tone of the meeting and to gage the visitors as adversaries. Adamson concluded that some of the groups had arrived en masse, ready to take notes, in order to do a team translation, once they returned to their corporate offices. This would explain the large numbers of guests from some companies.

Nonetheless, this initial series of meetings convinced the ORC team that their patent infringement claims were being taken seriously by the Japanese firms. Apart from Philips, only the Japanese had announced CD player products by the fall of 1986.

During this initial trip by the ORC team to Tokyo, Yoshihide (Josh) Nakamura, then senior general manager, Intellectual Property, Sony Corporation invited the ORC team to Sony's headquarters for another meeting on their next visit to Japan.

Adamson returned to Tokyo with Orange and Horne in November 1986, for another series of presentations and meetings, but this time at each company's offices as prearranged again by Far East Associates. The most important of these meetings was with Sony Corporation, as the ORC team felt certain that Sony's decision on whether to license the Russell patents, would predetermine ORC's success with all other firms in Japan. (It was a Philips-Sony partnership that had launched the compact disc and taught an industry how to make them.)

On a schedule of two and even three meetings each day, including shuttles between companies located around Tokyo and Osaka, the ORC team made 12 more presentations. All discussions were held in English, again with only a perfunctory objection from the Japanese hosts. Everyone appreciated that the United States represented the largest domestic market for the compact disc industry and as Jim Russell had first filed his patents in the United States, it was also likely to be the site of ORC's most comprehensive patent protection.

In fact, ORC's patents were most comprehensive in the United States, Britain and Canada, but appeared to provide a weaker protection in Germany, France and the Netherlands. The prosecution of ORC's patents before the Japanese Patent Office had been stalled for many years, partly due to SLC's lack of funds. As such, while virtually all of the CD players were being manufactured in Japan, apart from those made by Philips, the greatest exposure of these Japanese manufacturers to ORC's claims of infringement lay in their export shipments to North America and Europe. Their shipments within Japan and to the rest of the world would only be exposed if ORC succeeded in getting the Japanese Patent Office to issue a key patent. (ORC never succeeded at having their Japanese patent issued.)

Some firms, including Sony, had gone to the expense of having an U.S. patent attorney present at all meetings with ORC, but Sony appeared the most ready to enter into substantive discussions. In this second round of discussions, Sony's team of six or seven engineers and executives presented ORC with a package of over 25 U.S. patents, all cited as Prior Art against the Russell patents.

PUBLISHING THE "BLUE BOOK"

Adamson had been warned by both Horne and Orange to expect such a patent defense from Sony. He understood that if the techniques that Russell had claimed in his patents as inventions could be found in any reference that had been published or made public prior to the filing of his patents (i.e. Prior Art), Russell's patents would be found "invalid" and unenforceable. In spite of the warnings, Adamson was highly alarmed and wondered whether ORC was in for a challenge.

On returning to Toronto and on the suggestion of Orange, Adamson tasked him to collaborate with Russell in a review of documents that Sony had provided. Orange prepared a technical response for each reference and compiled these results in a bound booklet for distribution to each prospective licensee. Thus, the so-called "Blue Book" was born. It was thought that by making a general distribution of the "Blue Book," any duplication of effort from one set of technical discussions to another could be minimized, while hopefully speeding all talks toward the signing of licenses.

Adamson had no sense whether one or other of the Prior Art references might hold a "golden arrow" that would pierce the assumed validity for the Russell patents. He knew that a patent was generally assumed to be valid as issued, and therefore enforceable before the courts, but any unanswered Prior Art reference could quickly dispose of ORC's credibility and their licensing prospects.

DISTRACTIONS ALONG THE WAY

Adamson had another more urgent reason to wish the licensing talks to progress quickly. As a research firm, ORC was funding its operations from its initial financing, gained through a tax credit program of the Canadian government. With an initial net investment of just Cdn$6.5 million and a monthly "burn-rate" approaching Cdn$250,000 for the research program, Adamson knew that ORC would likely run out of cash by the end of 1987, at the latest. (Luckily for ORC, the mid-1980s were a period of rampant inflation and ORC was earning 10 per cent, and 12 per cent per annum on its cash hoard.)

To add to the general instability of the situation, the Canadian government, SLC (the firm that had transferred the Russell technology to ORC) and the inventor himself, Russell, were now all objecting to the terms of the agreements that had brought the technology to Toronto. The Canadian government wished to rescind their tax credits and were demanding an immediate cash reimbursement while SLC and Jim Russell were both interpreting their respective agreements in their favor, to secure some respective right to ORC's potential licensing windfall from the compact disc industry.

Adamson remained of the view that all claimants were incorrect in their positions and vowed privately to resist their claims even into bankruptcy. Despite all of these distractions, he also knew that ORC had to maintain the appearance of complete stability, control and competence, in order to avoid "losing face" before their Japanese prospective licensees. Many hours of sleep were lost during this desperate period.

THE SONY PROTOCOL

By their second meeting with ORC, the Sony team were stating that they wished to deal directly with ORC and not through Far East Associates, as Sony reportedly had for their patent licence with the Dolby firm. They also indicated that if Sony agreed to a licence, they would want the right to act as ORC's exclusive agent to license all other manufacturers based in Japan, for their CD player production. As only Japanese manufacturers were then making CD players, apart from Philips in the Netherlands, this was difficult to agree to, given that ORC had resisted a similar proposal from Far East Associates.

Both the services of Horne and Far East Associates had been contracted on a fee-for-service basis, with ORC retaining all licensing rights to the Russell patents. Both could be terminated without cause in the normal course of business. As consultants, their services were required only as long as the client thought they were adding value. Far East Associates had indicated a desire to assume a full agency role on behalf of ORC with the full authority to license ORC's patents on behalf of ORC, but Adamson had resisted this overture, convinced that ORC would be better served by dealing with each manufacturer directly.

Now Sony was asking ORC to terminate Far East Associates and to make presentations directly to Japanese manufacturers, in anticipation of Sony agreeing to a patent licence. This licence, however, would only apply to CD players, with Sony assuming the role of exclusive agent, possibly for all of Asia. Adamson accepted this protocol with Sony, but he had to trust that Sony was in earnest in their desire to be the exclusive agent and not just leading ORC toward a dead end.

Further, as with Far East Associates, he had no idea how ORC was to monitor the work and licensing progress of an exclusive agent based in the Far East, directly licensing Asian manufacturers. How was one to know when a licence signed and royalties collected, if not by the exclusive agent? In any case, as co-licencer with Philips of the CD technology, Sony's support was clearly paramount to ORC.

So a pattern developed. Every four to eight weeks, Adamson and Orange traveled to Tokyo, Osaka and other cities in Japan to hold patent infringement and licensing discussions with the major Japanese consumer electronics firms such as Matsushita (Panasonic), Toshiba, Hitachi, Sanyo, Pioneer, Sharp and particularly Sony.

With each visit, new Prior Art references were put forward by one or other of the manufacturers, and ORC, in the person of Orange, would respond "on the fly" if an obvious separation from the art could be discerned. If not, ORC would fax a response to all participants upon returning to Toronto.

As the months passed, it was becoming increasingly clear to all that the Russell patents as presented by the ORC team, could withstand the invalidity challenges from the Prior Art. Equally important, the compact disc technical standard that ensured manufactured compatibility across all compliant CD products included techniques claimed in the Russell patents. To comply with this CD standard was to infringe the Russell patents! In short it appeared that the Russell patents were valid and infringed by all CD products!

To balance this rosy picture, however, it was equally clear that, month by month, ORC's cash was disappearing into its research program. The company had lost any of the financial strength with which to mount a credible court challenge against even one of the established manufacturers: Sony, Philips or any of the twenty other firms of similar bulk.

THE END GAME?

Finally in the fall of 1987, Adamson realized that neither Sony nor any other firm was likely to accept a license without more pressure being applied and more pressure than ORC could bring to the negotiating table. With nothing left to lose, Adamson flew to Tokyo in mid-January 1988, for a final meeting with Sony Corporation. No other firm was as advanced in discussions with ORC as Sony and Adamson reasoned that Sony had become fairly certain of the profit potential as ORC's master licensee for Japan. Sony would also have something to lose if the talks with ORC failed.

To add to this pressure, he could advise Sony that ORC was close to bankruptcy and, if ORC went into bankruptcy, the Russell patents would revert to their former owner, SLC, a firm that, in his direct experience, proved to be very litigious. The Sony team requested a lunch break.

Over lunch Josh Nakamura asked Adamson whether he would continue to be involved with the Russell patent licensing if ORC went bankrupt. Adamson replied that while his ownership of the patents would be lost, he could no doubt strike a deal with SLC such that the licensing program would not "skip a beat." However the program would then be well financed by a very litigious American backer and, under the circumstances, Adamson would have little interest in favoring Sony in any way. Given his rocky relations with SLC, Adamson painted a most optimistic view of his future.

Returning to the Sony offices after lunch, the Sony team requested a further break and Adamson and Cooper sat quietly for an hour and a half in the meeting room at the Sony corporate head offices in Kita-Shinagawa; Adamson pondering his fate.

ORC'S FIRST LICENSE

Back in the meeting, Nakamura advised that Sony would be ready to sign a license with ORC. The license, however, would only cover CD players, not compact disc media. Further, ORC had to significantly reduce their royalty demands, accept Sony as the exclusive agent with full authority to license all CD player manufacturers based in Asia and pay Sony an administrative fee for their exclusive agency representation out of the royalties to be received. The proposal also required that ORC transfer the right to sue Asian CD player manufacturers for patent infringement to Sony as their exclusive agent. Adamson felt he had no choice but to accept this proposal if he wished to maintain his control of the Russell patents.

It was then agreed that the outline of the license and agency agreements be developed that very afternoon with a final negotiation of royalty rates to occur by telephone in the following week. Cooper took on the task of drafting the required changes to ORC's standard patent license agreement. Negotiations were then completed by telephone the following week and the Sony CD player agreement was signed in early February 1988.

From this shaky last-minute effort, Adamson had managed to retain his full ownership of the Russell patents through ORC. By licensing Sony, ORC now had a royalty cash flow with which to maintain the research program underway in Toronto, as well as the resources to fend off the law suits from the Government of Canada and SLC. For the first time in its existence, ORC was cash flow positive and in that sense, time was now on ORC's side; however, when measured against industry norms, the license with Sony cost ORC plenty. Nakamura and the Sony team had done their job well.

Apart from Sony's hard bargain, they were always gracious but now as business partners, Nakamura and Sony's negotiating team seemed to relish this role even more.

Adamson came to look forward to an invitation to dine at one restaurant in particular. High above Akasaka in central Tokyo, directly overlooking the Diet, Japan's national parliament, there was a restaurant laid out in a series of private dining rooms, each in a unique Western décor of a particular color and at least one Monet or similar Old Master painting dominating the room. Their chefs were trained at the Paul Bocuse culinary school in France and the wine list read like a vintners' award booklet.

Adamson also came to realize that the superb ambiance and staff service of the Hotel Okura was very habit-forming and in spite of the expense, he opted to stay there whenever he was in Tokyo. Horne had been right. Being invited to lunch or dinner at the Hotel Okura, was also a great treat for ORC's licensing prospects and other business associates in Tokyo.

ONWARD

Among the more difficult challenges that ORC faced in mounting the licensing program was the determination of the size of the infringing production unit volumes and sales revenues. A prospective licensee is not about to divulge this data, as it would impair their negotiating position and possibly increase their chances of being sued before one of their competitors. Nevertheless in the case of CD media, it was pretty obvious that the five sisters of sound; Philips (Deutsche Grammophon), Sony (Columbia), Time-Warner (Warner), EMI (London and Angel) and Bertelsmann (RCA) were the largest manufacturers of CD media. After Philips and Sony, Time-Warner was likely to be the largest compact disc maker in the United States.

Government agencies and industry trade associations publish trade statistics, but this data is usually on an industry-wide basis (not by company) and for broad product categories, not for individual products, such as a CD player. Beyond these sources, there are industry consultants of varying usefulness and reliability. Nevertheless the licenser must develop estimates of the production and sales volumes for the infringing product by manufacturer and for each year from the start of the infringement to the expiry of the patent or the end of the infringement, whichever comes first.

Without such numbers it is not possible to decide which companies are the more lucrative licensing prospects and more importantly whether a licensing program is even feasible. Without this data the licenser cannot know which infringer to sue or in which jurisdiction to bring the suit, to ensure the most favorable cost-benefit ratio for such an action.

In the ensuing 12 months, Sony sub-licensed over 50 per cent of the remaining Japanese production for CD players and ORC began to develop a substantial "war-chest." Still unresolved were ORC's equivalent infringement claims against the manufacturers of the discs, the compact disc media. Sony had refused to include this item in the initial license as they advised that they needed more time to study the matter. They also stated the view that the Russell patents were less likely to be infringed by the discs.

In the summer of 1988, however, ORC succeeded in licensing the Philips Corporation for both CD players and media and with this success, somewhat confirming Sony's earlier license commitment, Sony agreed to sign a license for CD media in November 1988. By the end of 1988, ORC had a cash position well in excess of US$10 million and the licensing program was on a roll.

The next largest manufacturer of CD media in the United States, by production volume, after American subsidiaries of Sony and Philips-Dupont, was known to be WEA Manufacturing, a subsidiary of Time Warner Inc. Commencing in 1987, Adamson held several discussions, by mail, telephone and face-to-face meetings, with Time-Warner's in-house counsel. These discussions lead nowhere however as Time Warner's often-repeated view was the standard "non-infringement and invalid patents" position of an alleged infringer.

ENFORCING ORC'S PATENT RIGHTS

In early 1990, ORC had retained Davis Hoxie Faithfull & Hapgood, a patent law firm just next door to Time Warner's corporate head office in the Rockefeller Centre in New York City. Charles Bradley, a senior patent litigating attorney with Davis Hoxie had been recommended to Adamson on a chance encounter, while in Tokyo, with an American attorney who had the misfortune of opposing Bradley in a previous patent case. Bradley and Lawrence Goodwin, his partner, were engaged to pursue ORC's interests with the respect to the alleged infringement by WEA Manufacturing, a subsidiary of Time Warner Inc. Goodwin became the "lead" attorney on the ORC file with Bradley providing oversight, senior counsel and strategic advice to Goodwin.

On ORC's behalf, the Davis Hoxie firm filed a patent infringement complaint against WEA Manufacturing in the Federal District Court in Wilmington, Delaware, in June 1990. Like many other major American corporations, Time Warner and its subsidiary, WEA Manufacturing, were incorporated in the State of Delaware.

Not the least of Adamson's concerns in deciding to sue Time Warner in early 1991, was a looming patent expiry date in July 1992, for a U.S. patent, the key to ORC's infringement claims against CD media manufacturers.

The greatest threat that a patent-holder has against a recalcitrant infringer is a court injunction to stop the infringer's production lines. By 1991, this threat was all but lost to ORC as the July 1992 expiry date of ORC's key U.S. patent was likely to pass before any court could rule on the matter.

Without the threat of a court order to stop an infringing production, the patent-holder's leverage is reduced to the probability of a favorable court award being considerably more arduous for the infringer than the royalty payable if a license had been accepted. Even this leverage is diminished by the reality that, at any time prior to an appeal court ruling on a lower court award, the infringer is free to negotiate a settlement with the licenser, even well past a court decision which declares them to be infringing. The infringer can also hope that the patent-holder will capitulate before the end of a full trial, for lack of sufficient funds.

These considerations were very much on Adamson's mind in March 1992 as he drafted a letter (see Exhibit 1) to be sent directly to Time Warner's in-house counsel with a copy to Goodwin. Goodwin had advised against sending the letter, given that ORC had filed their patent infringement suit against Time Warner almost two years earlier, however, Adamson felt certain that Time Warner should be willing to settle for the modest sum of US$3 million, just to avoid the patent infringement trial now scheduled for June 1992, with all of its costs and disruption. Of no surprise to Goodwin, Time Warner politely declined ORC's settlement proposal, perhaps thinking that the letter was a clear indication that ORC was about to capitulate, if they had not already, with their modest US$3 million settlement offer.

WILL THEY LIKE US IN WILMINGTON?

Now faced with the certainty of a trial in the United States, Adamson had to deal with a personal overriding concern. Could an American jury be prejudiced against a Canadian company such as ORC? Goodwin had told him not to worry about it, but Adamson was concerned that Goodwin simply did not know.

Too embarrassed to advise Goodwin of his continuing concern with a potential American prejudice toward a Canadian company, Adamson hired the New York office of Goldfarb Consultants, a Canadian market survey firm. Their assignment was to conduct an opinion survey on attitudes, toward Canadian companies, of people drawn from the "jury-pool" population around Wilmington, Delaware. The Goldfarb team suggested that they conduct this survey with focus group interviews based on a set of questions pre-cleared by ORC.

In April 1992, Adamson traveled to Wilmington to witness the interviews firsthand by watching the proceedings on a video monitor in an adjacent room. There were three sessions comprising a total of 35 participants, who gave up a part of their evening for the survey in return for dinner and a modest stipend.

The interviews were conducted in two parts. The first part was designed to solicit an unprompted reference to Canada, in its role as a trading partner of the United States. The second part was designed to solicit directly any opinions that they may hold toward Canadian companies and then specifically a Canadian company's right to protect their American rights by suing an American company in Delaware.

The survey was of great benefit to Adamson as it quickly became clear that he should not be concerned about an American prejudice toward Canadian companies. If a prejudice did exist, it could only be positive because the survey, in every focus group, turned into a love-fest for Canada and Canadians.

Each focus group became frustrated with the first part of the survey. In trying to find the trading partner that they might be concerned about, Canada was never mentioned, even in their desperate attempts to finally yell out the "correct answer." This desperation was then followed by groans when Canada was finally noted by the session moderator at the beginning of the second part of the survey. Very few of those surveyed knew that Canada was indeed the largest trading partner of the United States.

With Canada now on the table and not hiding as in a trick question, many positive views were openly expressed. In fact more than a few had vacationed in Canada, some had close Canadian relatives and one woman was so effusive as to simply say, "I love Canadians," quickly adding that she and her husband vacationed regularly in the Montreal area.

A little sheepishly, Adamson returned to Toronto and phoned Goodwin to advise him that "the ball was now in his court" and that ORC would see the Time Warner case through to appeal, if necessary. He did not mention the survey.

THE RUBBER MEETS THE ROAD

Led by Goodwin, the Davis Hoxie team was comprised of one other full-time attorney, Robert Cote, and a support staff of three, all of whom stayed in Wilmington for the duration of the trial (with some weekends at home in New York). This Delaware team worked from the offices of a Wilmington law firm. This law firm in turn provided its own legal and support staff to ORC's team on an as-required basis. At Davis Hoxie in New York, at least one additional full-time attorney, Peter Bucci, and various other support staff were employed in research and document preparation for the duration of the trial. This entire trial effort was monitored and when appropriate, coached by Charles Bradley.

The trial began in the last days of May 1992, and it was to run for five and one-half weeks. Throughout the trial period, the Davis Hoxie team worked a daily double shift, one in courtroom and then a second in their law offices and hotel rooms, debriefing the day's events and preparing for the next day's court sessions. This preparation included a review of salient facts, prior affidavits, deposition testimony and then general court procedures with each individual witness, in preparation for the court appearance.

It also included a daily review of defendant witness testimony for discrepancies. The review of the court plan for the following day might include witness questioning, preparing motions that pulled together now-important facts and revising presentation materials imperiled by the day's events.

Adamson had decided to remain in Wilmington and attend every court session, given the importance of its outcome for ORC. Having watched the jury selection a few days before, he was highly stressed on the morning of the first day of the trial. He took some comfort in the size and evident competence of the Davis Hoxie team until the Time Warner team appeared.

Either by chance or design, 20 minutes prior to the official court start-time, opposing attorneys began to file into the courtroom. First they filled to overflowing the small defendant's bench in front of the commons rail, and then gradually they occupied the entire commons observer section on the defendant side of the courtroom, spacing themselves comfortably. Adamson sat as a lone observer for ORC directly behind the Davis Hoxie team of five on the plaintiff's side until three more groups of attorneys whom he had never met, filed in to sit behind him, also on the plaintiff's side.

Possibly the entire recording industry, including a few Japanese firms with still unlicensed CD plants in the United States, had sent attorneys, some 30 in all, to observe the start of the trial. The contrast between the sizes of the defendant and plaintiff legal teams was so evident that, prior to the jury entrance, lead counsel for Time Warner told the attorneys behind him to scatter into the plaintiff's observer benches.

Apparently unfazed by the obvious imbalance, a few minutes later, Goodwin stood up to address judge, jury and courtroom on behalf of ORC in a calm, humble but masterful tone. He was to continue as he had started through five and one-half weeks of trial, through surprise, setback, equipment failure, client panic and one or two staff confusions.

ORC's case was further strengthened by the skill of a superb expert witness, Leonard Laub. Laub was responsible for explaining ORC's highly technical infringement case, to a jury with no technical training except for one retired man with an engineering degree dating back to the 1930s. This was accomplished with Laub's testimony guided by questioning from Goodwin and with the use of circuit diagram blow-ups and point summaries on white three feet by five feet storyboards. Adamson was satisfied that if there were a chance that the jury could come to understand ORC's case, it would be solely through the ample teaching skills of Goodwin and Laub.

ORC asked the court and jury for an award in lieu of royalty of six cents per disc against Time Warner and their American subsidiaries and a tripling of that award in punitive damages for willful infringement. The decision to ask for six cents per disc was partly based on ORC's initial licensing request of three cents per disc. Legally, licensers are able to change their royalty demands at any point in a negotiation, before or after the filing of a suit, just as infringers are free to agree to previously unacceptable terms.

(In normal licensing practice, it is simply wise to give active infringers, some substantial incentive to sign a license prior to the filing of a suit. This is usually accomplished by increasing the royalty rate by some multiple of the original, say two, three, five or even 10 times. The practical upper limit of a royalty rate is, of course, at that point where the manufacturer can make little profit after paying the royalty, as it is unlikely that any judge or jury would endorse a more onerous royalty request.)

Hearing Goodwin make this request for six cents per disc in open court was a thrilling moment early in the trial. Weeks later the Time Warner attorney was obliged to produce for the court, the unit volumes of their subsidiary's infringing production of compact discs. Their infringement for the period covering the start of production in 1986 through July 1992, the month of the expiry of ORC's patent, totalled over 450 million discs and, at six cents per disc, represented a potential court award for ORC of over US$27 million. The addition of pre-judgment interest and a possible tripling of those damages were more than Adamson could fathom or entertain.

In spite of the good efforts of the Davis Hoxie team with Laub and several other strong witnesses, including Russell, the inventor, and the prospect of an enormous court award, all was not well. After the court appearance by the Philips attorney, Adamson believed that ORC's decision to sue Time Warner might have been taken too lightly.

Goodwin had warned that corporate litigation in the United States was a very expensive enterprise. It was also very demanding of management time, given the need to find, assemble and organize relevant business records, to educate the attorneys in the minutiae of events that usually had happened long ago and to attend court hearings as observers and witnesses. He had also noted that, in the normal course of a robust cross-examination, the combatants and their witnesses could expect personal insults and general verbal abuse. Adamson observed somewhat ruefully that Goodwin had been correct on all counts.

Preliminary motions, production and review of plaintiff and defendant business records and correspondence files, witness depositions, private investigators and trial preparations for the attorneys, company personnel and expert witnesses had already consumed close to US$750,000 of ORC's hard won royalties all before the actual trial had begun. Adamson had budgeted an additional US$1.5 million for fees and expenses to be incurred from the trial itself; however, after the first three weeks of the trial, Adamson saw no end in sight to the trial or its expense.

As was its right as the plaintiff, ORC had chosen to have its case against Time Warner heard before a jury. Even this decision seemed to backfire as it was clear that the jury was putting a good deal of attention and apparent credence into what the defendant's attorneys had to say. The Time Warner litigating team had mounted a very credible defense. They seemed to cloud the technical issues of patent validity and product infringement as these related to the Russell patent claims and the compact disc technology, so that even Adamson found himself confused with ORC's claims from time to time. He had little hope left that the jury would be able to sort through the haze.

With this technical complexity and possible jury confusion, Adamson worried that the direct and damning statements of the Philips attorney toward the Russell patents and ORC's infringement claims could be disastrous for ORC, as these arguments gave the jury, a reasonable and easy "out," from all the confusing technical jargon. Perhaps he was simply someone who knew better about these matters than they could ever hope to know.

Adamson also reflected on the fact that he had been forced to curtail the on-going licensing program for the other CD manufacturers. He had been concerned that some event within ORC's licensing program, such as an agreement with a royalty rate for CD discs below the six cents per disc demanded in the court case, might affect the outcome of the case; however this concern was made mute by the simple fact that the other CD manufacturers had displayed little interest in signing a license with ORC as long as a major record company such as Time Warner was challenging ORC's infringement claims in court.

Should the court case result in anything less than a complete endorsement of ORC's infringement claims, ORC's entire licensing program could collapse including the all important quarterly payments from Sony. The CD player license with Sony may have been a "done deal." As a matter of practicality, Adamson wondered whether ORC would be prudent to take Sony to court, should Sony simply stop paying royalties to ORC after a jury verdict had cleared Time Warner of ORC's patent infringement claims.

Over the course of the six years from 1986 to 1992, Adamson had been drawn away from ORC's research effort and future prospects and ever deeper into patent licensing and then this litigation struggle. As he had testified in the Time Warner trial, "there seems little point in investing in the creation and development of new intellectual property rights if major industrial firms are prepared to ignore and infringe existing patent rights that you already own." Playing somewhat to the jury, he knew that he had purposefully overstated his predicament but the basic truth of his simple observation resonated in the momentary silence of the court that day.

Adamson had made the very difficult decision early in 1991, to temporarily shelve ORC's research program and to reduce the Company's technology development team to a skeleton staff of five team leaders. This move had been made for reasons other than the need to focus the Company's resources on the Time Warner litigation. Nonetheless as he sat in that Delaware courtroom, watching the door close after the hasty exit of the Philips attorney, Adamson felt that he had bet ORC's entire future on the outcome of the court case against Time Warner.

The Richard Ivey School of Business gratefully acknowledges the generous support of John Adamson (MBA '72) in the development of this case as part of the THE JOHN ADAMSON JAPAN CASE SERIES.

Exhibit 1   Draft Letter to Time Warner's In-house Counsel

CONFIRMATION ONLY

FACSIMILE MESSAGE OF TWO PAGES TO: 1 (212) 522-1252

March 4, 1992

<u>WITHOUT PREJUDICE</u>

Dear

<u>RE:</u>   <u>ORC vs Time Warner Inc.</u>

Over the past week, we have prepared estimates on the costs and probable outcome of this case. We share this information with you now, in the hope of developing a common understanding from which a mutually satisfactory settlement might result. Our New York counsel is aware of this communication but, the views expressed here may not necessarily coincide with theirs.

Assuming that your costs to date equal ours, Time Warner has spent US$1,000,000. in out-of-pocket expenses alone,. Assuming that we will each spend another US$1,000,000. to the end of trial and then another US$200,000. on an appeal, we will each have spent another US$1,200,000. for a total of US$2,200,000 on this case. Give or take a few $100,000., these costs have a 100% probability of being incurred, if we proceed.

As to the outcome, it is our view that ORC has a significantly stronger case, as Justice Farnan's recent rulings might suggest. Further, we have substantial confidence in our representation. Nevertheless, we accept that the trial process is highly unpredictable. Therefore, we would attach a conservative estimate of perhaps 50% to the probability of ORC winning at both, trial and appeal.

Our licensing program had been based on the royalty rate of US$0.015 per disk and against the estimated and actual production totals for WEA and Allied of 400 million disks, a royalty amount of US$6,000,000. can be estimated. The size of award by the court could vary up or down from this royalty estimate but, it is our view that US$6,000,000 is a good average to assume of all possible court awards. If we assume a 50% probability that ORC will win, then it follows that there is a 50% probability that Time Warner will be required to pay the average award of US$6,000,000.

.../...

OPTICAL RECORDING CORPORATION

141 JOHN STREET, TORONTO, CANADA M5V 2E4 · TELEPHONE (416) 596-6862 · FAX (416) 596-0452

Exhibit 1   (continued)

OPTICAL RECORDING CORPORATION

- 2 -

To summarize, at this point in time, Time Warner has a 50% probability of paying out $6,000,000 in award and a 100% probability of paying $1,200,000 in continuing litigation costs, if we proceed.

We believe that a final attempt at settlement is in the interest of both companies at this time. Therefore, we now propose a patent license to Time Warner for their manufacture of Compact Disc in the United States, for $3,000,000.; that is, for 50% of the $6,000,000. which we contend that Time Warner has at least a 50% probability of incurring as a court award.

This offer will remain open until 5:00pm, Friday, March 6, 1992, after which, this and all previous offers will be withdrawn.

We would appreciate your comments on the logic presented here, particularly if you have a significantly divergent view on any point. Please feel free to call me directly if you wish to discuss any point in this letter.

Yours very truly,

G. John Adamson
President

GJA/gj

Case 10

Majestica Hotel in Shanghai?

On March 20, 2005, Richard Roy, executive vice-president of Majestica Hotels Inc., was in China, for negotiations with Commercial Properties of Shanghai Limited (CPS). They were discussing a possible management contract under which Majestica would be the operator of a new luxury hotel there owned by Shanghai Industrial Holdings.

Majestica Hotels Inc. was one of the world's leading operators of luxury hotels. The expansion into mainland China had been on management's agenda since 1999. The opportunity emerged in late 2003 when a close friend of Majestica's chief executive officer (CEO) revealed that CPS was looking for an operator for its new luxury hotel under construction in Shanghai. Majestica immediately sent representatives to Shanghai to explore the possibility of becoming the operator. Majestica's proposal was welcomed by CPS, and a letter of intent was signed on August 20, 2004.

However, in discussions regarding the management contract, the two parties had reached a deadlock. The key issues to be resolved were the contract term, and the responsibilities and rights of Majestica as the operator, and CPS as the owner, of the hotel.

This Shanghai deal was important for Majestica's global expansion. It would not only provide Majestica with the opportunity to enter the China market but could also set a precedent for Majestica's future expansion in other emerging markets.

MAJESTICA HOTELS INC.

Majestica was founded in 1970 in western Europe. It focused exclusively on its niche of developing and operating luxury hotels with 200 to 450 rooms. In 1977, Majestica expanded to the United Kingdom. In 1984, Majestica entered the U.S. market via acquisition. Majestica's expansion in the U.S. market continued with properties in seven

Jane Lu prepared this case under the supervision of Professor Paul W. Beamish solely to provide material for class discussion. The authors do not intend to illustrate either effective or ineffective handling of a managerial situation. The authors may have disguised certain names and other identifying information to protect confidentiality.

other major cities. By the end of the 1990s, Majestica had secured a strong position in the luxury hotel industry in North America, competing with such established chains as Four Seasons, Ritz-Carlton, Hilton, Hyatt, Marriott and Westin.

While Majestica expanded quickly in North America, it adopted a gradual expansion strategy in Asia. This gradual expansion strategy shifted when the opportunity arose to acquire a major competitor in Asia in 1998. This acquisition made Majestica one of the world's largest operators of luxury hotels and resort properties. More importantly, it provided Majestica with a much expanded position in Pacific Asia and an immediate presence in the greater China area. Majestica continued its international expansion by amassing a select portfolio of medium-sized luxury hotels in the world's commercial and financial centres. By the end of 2004, Majestica managed 40 properties in 15 countries with approximately 20,000 employees. The contribution of Majestica's properties in North America, Asia and Europe to its consolidated revenue was 54 per cent, 14 per cent and 32 per cent, respectively. Exhibit 1 provides a five-year review of the occupancy rate, average daily room rate (ADR) and average room revenue per available room (REVPAR) of Majestica hotels in these three regions and worldwide.

In 2004, Majestica had a market capitalization of $1.7 billion[1] and generated revenue of more than $2.3 billion (see Exhibit 2). Majestica earned revenue both from hotel management and hotel ownership operations. In the past five years, Majestica shifted away from owning hotels and focused on managing hotels. In 2004, 80 per cent of Majestica's earnings before other operating items were generated by its hotel management business.

Majestica followed a business strategy that offered business and leisure travellers excellent hotel and resort accommodation in each destination it served. Following this strategy, Majestica developed into a luxury hotel chain with service standards among the best in the industry. Majestica hotels and resorts were widely recognized for the exceptional quality of their guest facilities, service and atmosphere. The Majestica brand was generally considered one of the top luxury hotel chain brands in the world, and its hotels and resorts were named frequently among the world's best hotels and travel experiences by Institutional Investor, Condé Nast Traveler, AAA Five Diamond and others. Majestica's success was also reflected in consistently achieving above-market operating results for the properties under its management. During 2003, REV-PAR (revenue per available room) for Majestica core hotels worldwide and in North America was 60 per cent higher than that of its competitors in the luxury segments worldwide and in North America. The room rate for a Majestica hotel in Chicago, for example, averaged $50 higher than those of Hyatt Regency, Hilton, Sheraton and Marriott (see Exhibit 3).

Majestica's superior hotel management results attracted the owners and developers of luxury hotels worldwide. By the end of 2004, in addition to the 40 hotels under its management, Majestica had 16 new hotels and resorts under construction or development, and it was evaluating dozens of additional management opportunities around the world. In summarizing the key success factors, the Majestica management pointed to a service culture that they had fostered for decades.

It emphasized anticipating travellers' needs and meeting those needs with superior hotel structures and a deeply instilled ethic of personal service. This service culture was built into every property, going beyond elegant hotel designs and finishes to the small,

---

[1]All amounts in US$ unless otherwise specified.

thoughtful touches that would add value for the guests. Every detail was deliberate, from mechanical systems that were as quiet as they were efficient to providing a disposable bathing suit in case hotel guests forgot to bring one. In addition, the design of the hotel rooms highlighted a use of space that enhanced the sense of luxury. On average, standard guest rooms in Majestica hotels were 25 per cent larger than those in Hyatt Regency, Hilton, Sheraton and Marriott.

More importantly, the service culture emphasized the depth of personal service. Majestica deemed ultimate luxury as not derived from furnishings but from personal service. The services at Majestica hotels were comprehensive and highly personalized. Guided by the service culture, Majestica's employees treated every interaction with guests as an opportunity to anticipate and satisfy a need. They provided services ranging from room service that felt like a fine dining experience to replacing worn shoelaces. The strong service culture ensured highly reliable services. For example, room service always arrived on time and conference arrangements were in place as promised.

The service culture encouraged surpassing each guest's highest levels of expectation. Majestica employees would do everything possible to accomplish the guests' purpose of the trip. The stories of Majestica employees' responses to unusual requests were legendary.

It took Majestica decades to foster this unique service culture and to achieve the widely recognized outstanding service standards. The challenge Majestica faced in its global expansion was how to replicate the exceptional Majestica guest experience from hotel to hotel, no matter where it operated in the world. Maintaining consistency in the quality of guest experience across its portfolio was regarded as essential to Majestica's continuing success. Decades of experience in the luxury hotel market had taught Majestica that constancy built trust and loyalty. The challenge in Majestica's global expansion was how to export its service culture to new locations. Majestica successfully handled this challenge with the following two policies.

First, Majestica was careful about the pace of adding new hotels and resorts in the portfolio. Whether there was a compatible service culture in the new location was an important criterion in deciding the direction and pace of Majestica's international expansion. In fact, the perceived lack of service culture in Asia was one of the major reasons that Majestica adopted a gradual expansion strategy in Asia in the mid-1990s. This second mover strategy allowed Majestica to profit from the development of a service culture in Asia brought about by the earlier entrants, the major American hotels.

Second, it was Majestica's operating philosophy to have full control of the hotels under its management in order to cultivate its service culture and to maintain service consistency in new markets. Majestica's operating philosophy requested the owners of the Majestica hotels to adopt a hands-off approach, from the planning and designing of the hotels to the daily operating of the hotel such as purchasing hotel equipment, marketing and staffing. The non-interference from the hotel owners was important to the smooth fostering of Majestica's service culture in new markets. For example, the full authority in staffing enabled Majestica to carefully select the right people and imbue them with Majestica's service culture through various training programs and through leadership by example. Following this operating philosophy, Majestica's service culture was passed from one Majestica hotel to another so as to succeed in maintaining consistant service throughout its global expansion.

MAJESTICA IN THE ASIA-PACIFIC REGION

Asia was one of the fastest growing tourism destinations in the world. However, Asia's importance as a travel destination was not recognized by the major hotel companies in the world until the rising of Asia's tigers in the 1980s. Attracted by the unprecedented economic and construction boom in the region, a growing middle class, increases in passenger miles and an expanding economy, major hotel companies rapidly opened new properties in the Asia-Pacific region in an attempt to ensure a strong presence.

Among the major international luxury hotel chains, Hilton was the earliest entrant to the region. After its initial entry in 1948 with the 450-room Nagoya Hilton, Hilton International had 45 properties spreading across the region by 2000.

Through its 1995 acquisition of Westin Hotels & Resorts and ITT Sheraton Corp, Starwood Hotels & Resorts Worldwide gained a strong presence in the Asia-Pacific region. Prior to being acquired, both Westin and ITT Sheraton had been active in the Asia-Pacific region and were managing numerous properties.

Marriott and Hyatt were two of the later entrants to the Asia-Pacific region. Hyatt International managed 56 hotels and 18 resorts in 34 countries. In the Asia-Pacific region, it had 18 hotels in operation and 19 properties under development. Marriott entered the Asia-Pacific region in 1990 with its opening of the JW Marriott Hotel Hong Kong. Four more entries over the next seven years brought Marriott's total to five hotels, with a total of 1,941 rooms. Marriott had also secured management contracts for four additional hotels. The company was looking to add more hotels in the four- and five-star categories.

Another competitor, The Four Seasons, had 15 Asian-Pacific properties, with a total of 4,950 rooms. This total represented one-third of its rooms worldwide. In addition to these hotels, two more were scheduled to open in 2005. The company's Asian-Pacific portfolio was heavily concentrated in India, Indonesia, Singapore and Thailand.

The Ritz-Carlton Hotel Company was another upscale hotel firm that had targeted the region. In 1997, the company opened hotels in Osaka and Kuala Lumpur to complement its existing properties in Singapore, Hong Kong, Seoul and Sydney. The company also opened a resort in Bali, Indonesia, situated near one of Four Seasons' premier properties.

In addition to these competitors, Asian hotel companies such as Mandarin Oriental, Dusit Thani, CDL, Regal Hotels, Marco Polo, New World Hotels International and the Peninsula Group had been exploring opportunities for expansion in and around their bases in Asia. Hong Kong-based Shangri-La Hotels and Resorts was the most active Asian hotel company. It operated 32 hotels and resorts in China and Southeast Asia with plans for more.

Compared with the rapid expansion of these companies, Majestica had kept a low profile in the region. It had not entered Asia in the late 1980s because Majestica was not convinced that the political situation was stable and that a service culture existed there.

However, the 1990s brought a change in Majestica's strategy. In 1994, after two years of negotiation, Majestica acquired two Tokyo hotels, for its first properties in the region. In August 1996, with a solid capital base that had been built on the company's outstanding financial performance, Majestica acquired 100 per cent ownership of Le Roi Resorts, including its management contracts, trade names and trademarks. This transaction provided Majestica with a much expanded position in the Asia-Pacific region.

As 2005 approached, China was becoming the centre of Asia's fiercest competition in the hotel industry. With an annual Gross Domestic Product (GDP) growth rate of nine per cent for the past 20 years, China was the seventh largest economy and the 10th largest trading nation in the world. China's booming economy, coupled with its huge potential market comprising more than 1.2 billion people, had attracted many foreign investors. By the end of 2001, China ranked second to the United States as the largest foreign direct investment recipient in the world.

China's economic development and open door policy also attracted many foreign visitors. With over seven million foreign visitors (including people from Hong Kong, Macao and Taiwan) in 2000, China was the sixth most popular destination for business and leisure travel in the world. The World Tourism Organization predicted that China would become the No. 1 travel destination by 2020.

The hotel industry in China prospered with the boom in tourism. At the end of 2002, China had approximately 5,201 hotels, a growth rate of nearly 20 per cent since 1996. This represented a total of 701,700 available rooms in China. In 2000, the hotels sector recorded growth of over 10 per cent. Over half the hotels in China were categorized as tourist hotels.[2] Of the 1,669 hotels rated by the government, the majority were at the two- and three-star level, while just three per cent had been awarded five-star ratings. Most five-star hotels were operated by international luxury hotel chains such as Shangri-la Hotels & Resorts, ITT Sheraton Asia Pacific Group, Hilton International and Ritz-Carlton Hotels & Resorts.

COMMERCIAL PROPERTIES OF SHANGHAI LIMITED

Commercial Properties of Shanghai Limited (CPS), was a subsidiary of Commercial Properties Shanghai Investment (Holdings) Co., Ltd. (CPSIH), one of several overseas investment arms of the Shanghai municipal government. Incorporated in Hong Kong in October 1985, CPSIH expanded its businesses quickly and became a diversified conglomerate active in a wide range of businesses including international investment, manufacturing, real estate development and investment, banking and finance, trading and cultural activities. By the end of 2001, it was the largest overseas conglomerate wholly owned by the Shanghai municipal government with interests in more than 200 companies in Shanghai, Hong Kong, other parts of China and in cities spanning the Americas, Europe, Australia, Africa and Asia.

Hotel development and management was one of the businesses in which CPSIH was engaged. It owned and managed three hotels: the Oceania Hotel situated on Hong Kong Island, Mandarin United Hotel situated in Pudong, Shanghai, and Peace Garden Hotel located near the Yuyuan Gardens in Shanghai. In addition, it also organized mainland China and Hong Kong tours from its properties. Although hotel development and management was a comparatively small business in the company's 2001 business portfolio, it was one of the focuses of the company's future business development. Development of the hotel industry fit well in the company's mission to promote Shanghai and served the need of the Shanghai municipal government for foreign currency. To strengthen its position in the hotel industry and enter the luxury hotel segment, CPSIH had invested $220 million in building the Oceania Hotel in Hong Kong.

---

[2]In China, there are two basic categories of hotels. Tourist hotels are licensed to receive foreigners. The rest are open only to domestic visitors. Tourist hotels are usually better built and better equipped than domestic hotels.

CPS was listed on the Stock Exchange of Hong Kong in May 2000, and subsequently selected as a Hang Seng Index constituent stock in January 2002. At the time of the listing, the market capitalization of CPS was approximately $700 million. A majority of its shares were held by its parent, CPSIH.

Within the first year after the listing, CPS conducted several successful acquisitions. As well, the parent company also injected assets into CPS. These acquisitions and asset injections together were worth approximately $1.3 billion, making CPS one of the largest "red-chip" stocks listed on the Hong Kong stock market.

For the year ended 31st December, 2001, the company's turnover reached approximately HK$4,978 million (about $795 million), an increase of approximately 60 per cent over that in 2001. Profit for the year amounted to approximately HK$1,421 million (about $227 million), and earnings per share HK$1.79 (about $0.29), representing substantial increases over the results of 2000.

THE HOTEL INDUSTRY IN SHANGHAI

Situated in the middle of China's east coastline, Shanghai was China's economic and trade centre. In 2000, Shanghai had a population of 16.74 million and the highest per capita income in China. Shanghai and the surrounding provinces of Jiangsu and Zhejiang (Shanghai's manufacturing hinterland), formed the Yangtze River delta region. This region had a comprehensive industrial base and accounted for nearly one-third of China's industrial output. Moreover, it was home to one-quarter of all foreign investment in China. For these reasons, Shanghai was regarded not only as one of the main engines of China's economic growth but also as one of the leading markets in China. Given its strategic importance in China's economic development, its huge market potential and its popularity among tourists, Shanghai had long been recognized as a key site for companies that operated in the luxury hotel business.

According to the Shanghai Tourism Administrative Commission, Shanghai had 423 hotels at the end of 2004, with 68,000 rooms. By the end of 2005, the number of hotels was expected to rise to around 470 with the number of guest rooms rising to 75,000. The commission expected more than four million overseas tourists to stay at least one night in the city in 2005, an increase of 11 per cent from 2004. The commission also expected the number of domestic tourists visiting Shanghai to rise by five per cent, hitting 90 million. However, only a handful had a top rating of five-stars (see Exhibit 4). Portman Ritz-Carlton had been originally managed by Shangri-la Hotels & Resorts. However, at the end of 1997, the management contract expired and Ritz-Carlton took over the management of Portman. It was then renamed Portman Ritz-Carlton, and was Ritz-Carlton's first hotel in China.

In 1992, the Chinese government announced its initiative to develop Shanghai's Pudong District into Asia's finance centre. Local government offices, the Shanghai Stock Exchange, the Shanghai Cereal & Oil Exchange, and the Shanghai Real Estate Trading Market were all to move their offices across the Huangpu River to the Pudong District. Hotel developers quickly seized the opportunity created by this initiative and invested in the Pudong area. International luxury hotel chains soon followed and, by mid-1998 Shangri-la opened the first five-star hotel in Pudong. Several months later, in the fall of 1998, Hyatt International opened its first Chinese Grand Hyatt in Pudong. This luxury hotel occupied the top 36 floors of Pudong's 88-story Jin Mao Tower, making it the tallest hotel in the world. Quickly, other luxury hotels followed these entries, and there was some thought among industry observers that the Shanghai luxury hotel market was saturated, even before Majestica's proposed entry.

MAJESTICA—CPS NEGOTIATION

Shanghai was an ideal location for Majestica's expansion into mainland China. First, the Shanghai location met Majestica's preference for locating in major commercial and financial centres. In fact, Shanghai ranked second to Paris on the company's list of attractive international location choices. Shanghai was also attractive for its investment infrastructure, especially in terms of the service mentality of the Shanghai people. The quality of people was important for the development of a service culture.

In addition to being an ideal location, Majestica was interested in the partner. The partner was seen as having both the appetite and resources and could provide the potential to enter into multiple cities in China in the future. Such an owner not only reduced Majestica's concern about the political risk in China but also ensured a long-term commitment to the city and the support of the Shanghai municipal government to the project. The fact that CPS was publicly listed in Hong Kong gave Majestica more confidence about business transparency and independence from government influence. Further, the fact that the hotel was under construction made the opportunity more attractive to Majestica.

Majestica's proposal to operate the luxury hotel satisfied CPS's ambition to build a pre-eminent hotel in Shanghai. Majestica's outstanding financial performance and reputation in the luxury hotel industry convinced CPS that Majestica had the capability to provide the expected rate of return to its investment in the Hotel. CPS's confidence in Majestica was reflected in changing the original hotel design from 600 to 700 rooms (the Sheraton standard) to 375 to 450 rooms to meet the high standard of Majestica.

Majestica and CPS signed a letter of intent on August 20, 2004. After the signing of the letter of intent, the two parties started negotiation on the management contract. With respect to the fee structure, CPS was impressed by Majestica's above-market results for existing properties and was confident that the same could be achieved for the hotel. CPS agreed that Majestica would receive a base fee of three per cent of gross revenues of the hotel, as per its standard arrangement. In addition, Majestica would receive incentive fees based on the hotel's operating performance. Such incentives were in place for 90 per cent of the properties that Majestica managed.

The key issues in the negotiation that required resolution in March 2005 were the length of contract term and the control that Majestica could have over the management of the hotel.

Length of Contract Term

Most of the negotiation time was spent on the issue of the length of contract term. The length of the term of management contract was very important to Majestica. Majestica did not sign short-term management contracts. Based on its typical management contract term of 50 to 60 years elsewhere in the world, Majestica asked for a contract term of 55 years in its negotiation with CPS. CPS was shocked by this request; it had been prepared to offer only 12 years. In China, there were two levels of licensing in hotel development and management. The first level of licensing was from the government to the owner for the use of the land on which the hotel was built. The maximum length of land lease was 50 years. The second level of licensing was from the owner of the hotel to the operator who would manage the hotel on behalf of the owner. The normal hotel management term in China was only 10 years, since one of the objectives of the licensors was to learn hotel management and eventually manage the hotel themselves.

The big gap between the two parties on the contract length was a very difficult issue in the negotiation. After consultation with its parent company and presumably the Shanghai municipal government, CPS countered with an offer of 30 years. Majestica insisted that the hotel management contract term should be at least 50 years, the same as the land use right certificate term that CPS had received from the government. CPS argued that the hotel industry belonged to a sector which limited foreign investment, and government regulations would not allow the duration of hotel operation by foreign investors to be over 30 years. It further suggested that Majestica could enjoy a 30-year operation period, and the operation period could be extended when it expired, if both parties agreed to extend.

Pre-opening Assistance

Majestica assumed a substantial pre-opening role by sending senior people, such as its senior vice-president of design and construction, to help CPS in the design and constructing of the hotel. CPS welcomed Majestica's help but couldn't accept Majestica's request for retaining the approval right over all design aspects relating to the hotel, including the furniture, fixtures and equipment. Majestica argued that it requested this right to keep chain consistency, to make sure that the hotel would be developed and constructed as a world-class luxury hotel and to allow effective functioning of the hotel in operation.

Name of the Hotel

CPS suggested that the hotel be named "Shanghai Oceania – Majestica Hotel." Majestica insisted that the Hotel should be under the name "Majestica Hotel, Shanghai." This was essential to and consistent with Majestica's international strategic expansion program. Majestica believed that the Majestica brand was critical to the successful operation of the hotel as an international luxury hotel. Majestica would not agree to operate the hotel under any other name.

General Manager

Another major issue under debate was staffing the different levels of the hotel management (Exhibit 5). The hotel's general manager was responsible for the overall operation. In general, the two parties agreed that the general manager, upon the opening of the hotel, would be an expatriate. CPS, however, expressed the wish that in the near future, a Chinese general manager would be used. Majestica told CPS that in the selection of a general manager for the hotel, the competence of the general manager was a more important issue than their ethnic background and that while they could make every effort to locate a suitable person with Chinese background, they could not guarantee such an appointment. There was simply no history of Chinese nationals managing world class hotels at or near this level.

Expatriates

In discussions about the number of expatriates to be employed, the localization issue was raised again and was expressed more strongly. CPS could accept the use of any number of expatriates that Majestica considered necessary to get the hotel up and running. But they insisted that the number of the expatriate managers should be gradually reduced and local managers trained to replace them. The reasons were two-fold. First, such a move would cut down the overall operating costs, as it was very expensive to use expatriates. Second, learning how to operate a world class luxury hotel was one of CPS's objectives, and CPS expected Majestica to train the local employees and eventually use them to replace the expatriates.

Specifically, CPS requested that Majestica use a deputy general manager and a deputy financial controller sent by CPS. Majestica told CPS that Majestica would like to fill the positions of senior hotel personnel with local people, both from a cost and a cultural perspective. However, at this time, Majestica did not believe that local people would have the prerequisite experience (i.e. having held an equivalent position successfully in a world class luxury hotel) to perform their duties at the hotel on a basis consistent with its operation as an international world class luxury hotel. In addition, hotel management was a service business, and it took a long time to build a service culture. On average, it took 12 to 15 years for the culture to be absorbed by hotel professionals. Therefore, it was difficult to reduce the number of expatriates in the foreseeable future. In fact, staffing key positions in the new hotels with experienced hotel operations personnel was one of the secrets to Majestica's success. Richard Roy noted: "Exporting the Majestica work ethic does not depend on manuals, but on seeding new markets with those skilled at finding similar people in new places."

General Staffing

Closely related to the issues of the general manager and expatriates was the responsibility and authority of general staffing. Majestica insisted that it must have the exclusive responsibility and authority on the hiring, paying, supervising, relocating and discharging of all personnel of the hotel, and that CPS should unconditionally employ all the personnel selected and pay all the employment expenses. Majestica emphasized that selecting the appropriate employees and developing their attitudes and job performance in the context of Majestica's operating philosophy was critical to maintaining consistently high-quality performance. Therefore, Majestica should have exclusive authority in staffing to achieve a consistency of staff attitude and service standards. CPS argued that it was entitled to share the responsibility and authority in staffing as the ultimate employer of the hotel staff.

Purchasing

Majestica insisted that, commencing on the opening date, the hotel should participate in Majestica's centralized purchasing system for furniture, fixtures, operating equipment and supplies, and CPS should pay Majestica a modest fee relating to such centralized purchasing. Majestica argued that central purchasing could ensure standardized products, economies of scale and control over quality and design. CPS was concerned about the purchase prices and insisted that domestic purchasing should be a first priority.

With regard to personal property, other than the operating equipment and supplies, Majestica agreed that CPS could be responsible for the purchasing, subject to Majestica's approval right over the design of the personal property, as well as the firm used to purchase and install the personal property.

Owners' Access to Hotel Rooms

As the owner of the hotel, CPS requested access to hotel rooms or the use of some hotel rooms as offices. Majestica, however, insisted that the owner should not have any privileges over the use of hotel rooms as such an arrangement would cause confusion for the hotel management.

Arbitration

Another major issue discussed in the negotiation was related to arbitration. While both parties agreed to an arbitration process in the event of future disputes, they disagreed on the location for dispute resolution. Majestica insisted on a third country, following the norm commonly practised by the company. CPS, however, insisted that any arbitration should take place in China.

On top of the various issues in the negotiation of the management contract, CPS asked Majestica to take a minority equity position in the hotel. Generally, Majestica made only minority investments in properties where it was necessary and justified. It sought to limit its total capital exposure to no more than 20 per cent of the total equity required for the new property. The Foreign Investment Law in China, however, had stipulated until recently that the equity holdings by foreign investor(s) in an equity joint venture should be no less than 25 per cent. Thus, the request by CPS exceeded Majestica's upper limit on minority investment policy.

After many rounds of negotiation in the past three months, several issues remained unresolved. While CPS showed its flexibility and made concessions with a counter offer of 30-year contract term, it was clear that Majestica was expected to reciprocate CPS's flexibility and make some concessions in the next round of negotiations. However, Majestica found it difficult to make any concessions. Any requests made in the management contract were based on its operating philosophy for building a service culture, the key success factor in the luxury hotel industry.

THE DECISION

Thinking of the prolonged negotiation, Richard Roy felt disappointed because a lot of management time had been invested in this Shanghai project, but no decision had been reached. Reading through the minutes of the negotiation again, it was clear to Roy that many of the issues under dispute reflected the conflict between Majestica's operating philosophy and CPS's hands-on approach as the owner of the hotel. The Shanghai deal was a great opportunity, particularly if the management contract could be settled quickly. Roy was unsure what position Majestica should take. Given the importance of the China market, should Majestica adopt a contingency approach and relax its operating philosophy at this time, or should it stick with its original philosophy, even if this meant not entering the Shanghai market?

Exhibit 1   Hotel Occupancy, ADR and REVPAR (in US$ millions)

	2004	2003	2002	2001	2000
Worldwide					
Occupancy	75.44%	74.50%	70.30%	69.50%	68.00%
ADR[1]	$380.18	$354.22	$312.24	$286.53	$239.85
REVPAR[2]	$280.38	$265.16	$223.93	$203.20	$162.15
Gross operating margin[3]	32.50%	33.10%	29.10%	26.70%	22.00%
North America					
Occupancy	76.40%	77.50%	78.00%	71.20%	68.90%
ADR	$413.69	$368.73	$328.87	$303.62	$251.84
REVPAR	$311.02	$277.72	$233.04	$211.71	$172.48
Gross operating margin	32.10%	33.10%	31.20%	25.40%	23.80%
Asia-Pacific					
Occupancy	69.90%	74.50%	73.80%	74.10%	67.80%
ADR	$288.44	$299.56	$267.36	$240.39	$195.80
REVPAR	$204.20	$220.02	$193.93	$175.69	$129.27
Gross operating margin	32.30%	34.50%	31.20%	29.60%	25.80%
Europe					
Occupancy	80.10%	82.30%	77.90%	70.10%	64.50%
ADR	$669.40	$637.95	$576.92	$428.95	$515.70
REVPAR	$530.01	$519.36	$455.44	$296.84	$331.49
Gross operating margin	42.10%	41.30%	39.80%	31.70%	34.10%

[1]ADR is defined as average daily room rate per room occupied.

[2]REVPAR is average room revenue per available room. It is a commonly used indicator of market performance for hotels and represents the combination of the average occupancy rate achieved during the period.

[3]Gross operating margin represents gross operating profit as a percentage of gross revenues.

Exhibit 2   Five-year Financial Review (in US$ millions except per share amounts)

	2004	2003	2002	2001	2000
Statements of Operations Data					
Consolidated revenues	268.80	135.18	151.87	143.92	113.23
Hotel Management Operations					
Fee revenues	118.72	106.06	99.12	89.49	67.54
Hotel management earnings before other operating items	71.34	62.38	58.02	51.41	31.25
Hotel Ownership Operations					
Revenues	151.54	19.71	47.60	48.27	42.56
Distribution from hotel investments	6.72	10.30	6.72	7.62	4.37
Hotel ownership earnings before other operating items	16.91	9.74	16.69	15.90	8.06
Earnings before other operating items	88.14	72.02	74.70	67.20	39.31
Net earnings (loss)	45.70	33.49	(83.55)	7.62	(135.30)
Earnings (loss) per share					
Basic and fully diluted	1.86	1.56	(3.92)	0.36	(6.49)
Weighted average number of shares (millions)	24.6	21.5	21.3	20.9	20.9
Balance Sheet Data					
Total assets	507.58	431.54	427.39	550.48	580.27
Total debt	157.02	268.80	299.71	345.63	400.40
Shareholders' equity	285.04	98.67	64.06	153.66	139.66
Other Data					
Total revenues of all managed hotels	2,373.73	2,129.68	2,058.45	1,901.98	1,514.13
Fee revenues as a % of consolidated revenues	44.20%	78.50%	65.30%	62.20%	59.60%
Percentage of Fee revenues derived outside North America	31.20%	38.30%	40.90%	38.80%	35.90%
Hotel management operating margin	60.10%	58.80%	58.50%	57.40%	46.30%
Hotel management earnings before other operating items as a % of earnings before other operating items	80.90%	86.60%	77.70%	76.50%	79.50%
EBITDA	88.14	72.02	74.70	67.20	39.31
Debt, net of cash	128.69	251.55	258.61	335.10	387.07
Market price per share at year-end	50.40	31.08	21.28	18.20	14.56
Shares outstanding (millions)	25.28	21.53	21.38	21.30	20.85
Market capitalization at year-end	1,699.49	892.86	606.26	517.33	404.43
Employees	24,640	23,520	24,080	24,080	22,456

Exhibit 3   Major Luxury Hotels in Chicago (2005) (in US$)

Name of Hotel	Affiliation	Number of Guest rooms	Room rate*
Four Seasons Hotel Chicago	Four Seasons Hotels & Resorts	343	435–535
The Ritz-Carlton Hotel Chicago	Four Seasons Hotels & Resorts	435	395–535
Park Hyatt Chicago	Hyatt International	203	375–425
Renaissance Chicago Hotel	Marriott International	513	204
The Drake	Hilton International	535	255–295
The Peninsula Chicago	Peninsula Hotel Group	339	445–455
Le Meridien	Le Meridien Group	311	249
Majestica Miracle Mile	Majestica Hotels	435	455

*Ratings and pricing were obtained from Frommer's Hotel Guide online as of March 2005.
Source: Company files.

Exhibit 4   Major Luxury Hotels in Shanghai (2005) (in US$)

Name of Hotel	Affiliation	Number of Guest rooms	Room rate*
St. Regis Shanghai	St. Regis Hotels International	318	320–340
Portman Ritz-Carlton Shanghai	Ritz-Carlton Hotels & Resorts	564	250
Westin Shanghai	Westin Hotels	301	320
Sheraton (fka Westin) Tai Ping Yang, Shanghai	Sheraton Hotels & Resorts	578	230–280
Grand Hyatt Shanghai	Hyatt International	555	320–335
Pudong Shangri-la	Shangri-la Hotels & Resorts	606	330–350
Hilton Shanghai	Hilton Hotels International	720	264
Four Seasons Shanghai	Four Seasons Hotels	439	312–362

*Ratings and pricing were obtained from Frommer's Hotel Guide online as of March 2005.
Source: Company files.

Exhibit 5   Hotel Management Chain in Majestica

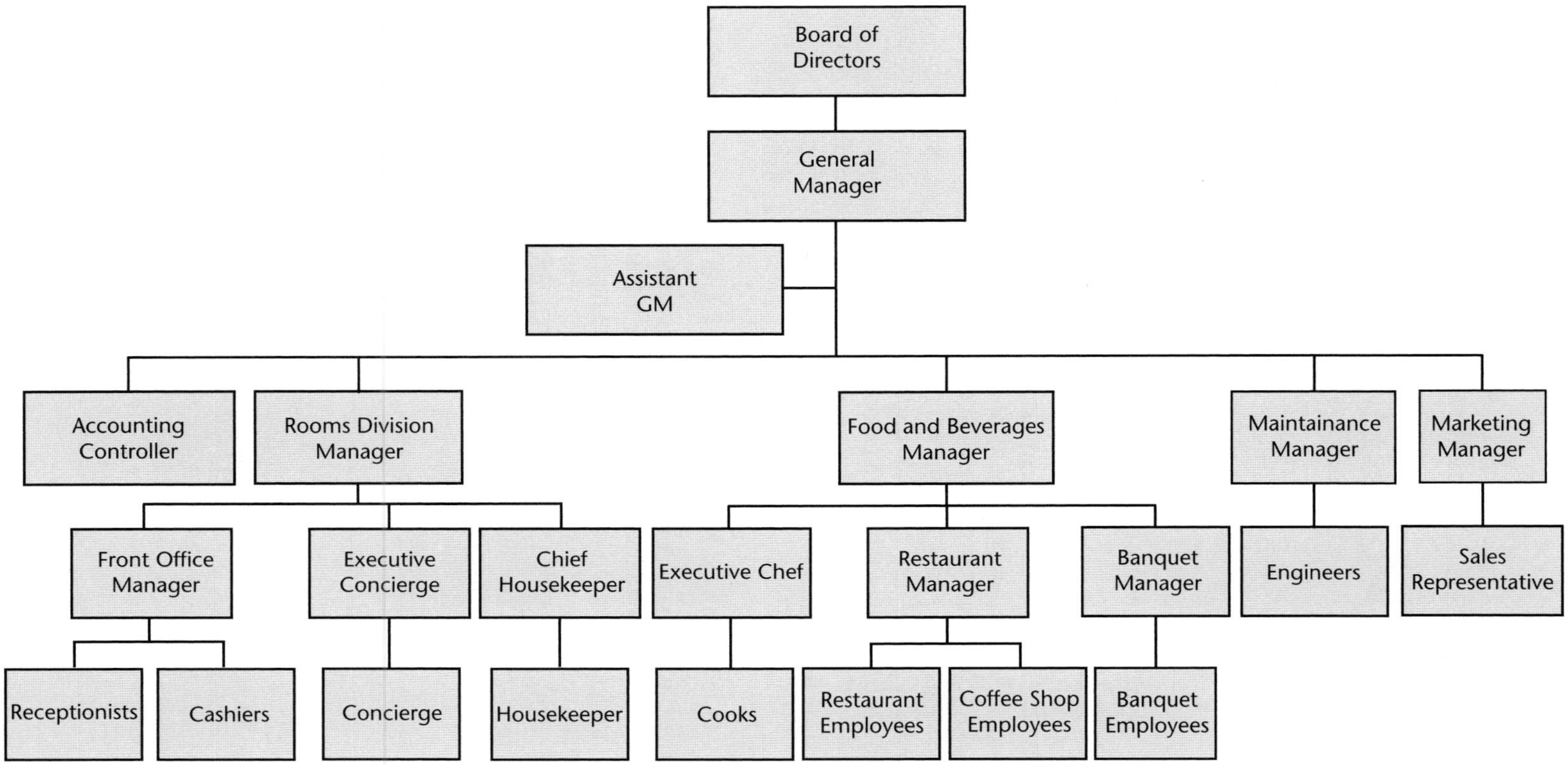

Source: Company files.

Case 11

Kids Market Consulting

Kids have a lot of bright ideas that adults can not know.

Natalia Berezovskaya

In May 2004, Natalia Berezovskaya, founder of Kids Market Consulting (KMC) in Kyiv, Ukraine, was pleased with the success of her business to date. Her niche market research company had enjoyed solid growth and profitability since it began two years ago, and it had developed a strong customer base. Now, Berezovskaya had been presented with last quarter's results, which showed slowing corporate growth. The competition among Ukrainian market research firms was fierce, and Berezovskaya knew that protecting her niche would be increasingly difficult. She had to determine the strategic direction of her company.

UKRAINIAN ECONOMY

The Ukrainian economy expanded by four per cent to eight per cent annually since 2000, due to solid domestic demand, low inflation, and strong investor and consumer confidence. Per capita gross domestic product (GDP) in 2003 was $5,300.[1] The official living minimum for 2004 was $64 per month, and the average monthly wage per employee was $86. Unemployment in Ukraine was four per cent for officially registered workers, but the country had a high number of unregistered or underemployed workers. An estimated 29 per cent of the population lived below the poverty line.

Stephanie Taylor and Oleksiy Vynogradov prepared this case under the supervision of Professor Paul W. Beamish solely to provide material for class discussion. The authors do not intend to illustrate either effective or ineffective handling of a managerial situation. The authors may have disguised certain names and other identifying information to protect confidentiality.

[1]All monies in US$ unless otherwise specified.

UKRAINIAN MARKET RESEARCH INDUSTRY

Market research in Ukraine was a developing industry in the 15 years after the country's independence from the former Union of Soviet Socialist Republics (USSR). Fast moving consumer goods (FMCG), pharmaceutical products, alcohol and tobacco were the most popular market research areas. The most significant development in the industry took place in the past seven years. Opinions about the size of the industry varied. As of 2004, the Ukrainian market research industry was estimated to range from $5 million to $20 million, while the Russian industry was estimated to be at least 10 times larger.

Accurate estimation of the total market size was complicated by poor tax accounting in Ukraine. In 2004, there were three types of companies: white, gray and black market businesses.

The companies that fully reported their revenues in the Ukrainian market research industry were considered part of the "white market," which was estimated to be $5 million to $8 million. The "black market" referred to those businesses disguising their revenue for tax purposes, while the "gray market" consisted of companies whose business practices straddled both areas. The exact size of the black and gray markets was unknown, but experts estimated them to be $8 million to $10 million altogether. As legislative changes began to take place, over time, the black and gray market companies were expected to join the white market.

Most domestic firms tended to focus their marketing strategies on advertising efforts, rather than on market research. As a result, spending on advertising was significantly more than spending on market research. However, the market research industry in Ukraine had made much progress over the past years. The sophistication of the industry could be seen through the development of self-regulating organizations. For example, the Ukrainian Marketing Association (UMA) developed an ethical code and regulations that were designed to stabilize pricing policies in market research, diminish unfair competition and promote legal companies. White market firms adhered to these regulations and tended both to be more professional and to deliver better quality work.

There were approximately 30 market research companies operating in Ukraine. The major firms included Gfk-USM, ACNielson Ukraine LLC, IPSOS S.A., Consumer Insights Ukraine (CIU) and Comcon Ukraine. Gfk, a German-based firm, had global sales of $747 million and net income of $41.8 million in 2003. Revenue for the French-based IPSOS S.A. was $564.3 million, and its net income was $7.5 million for the same year. ACNielson was part of VNU N.V. from the Netherlands, the largest market research firm in the world. VNU N.V. had revenue of $4.9 billion in 2003, and net income of $163.1 million. The largest firms were all part of the prestigious European Society for Opinion and Marketing Research (ESOMAR), a global community of market research professionals which was founded in 1948. While there were many niche players, none of the firms operating in Ukraine was solely dedicated to market research focusing on children.

There were several sources of competition in market research. Traditionally, advertising agencies contracted market research work to a separate firm, but they had begun conducting their own market research in response to their customers' demands. There was increasingly less and less differentiation between advertising, branding and marketing agencies, as they each worked to satisfy all of their clients' needs.

Other competition in the market research industry existed besides the large firms competing for contracts, such as independent consultants who were soliciting market research work. In between election periods, companies that conducted research for political blocs would conduct commercial market research as well. The quality of work among these firms tended to be poorer than that of full-time consumer market research firms.

KIDS, TWEENS AND TEENS IN UKRAINE

The segment of the population that ranged from birth to 19 years of age was identified by KMC as an unserved niche. None of the other market research firms in Ukraine focused on this particular niche. Brands oriented toward kids were relatively new to local companies as they had largely ignored the purchasing power possessed by this segment. Panel research conducted by KMC, in 2004, showed that disposable income was, in fact, available to kids, tweens and teens (see Exhibit 1). Furthermore, owners of adult brands began to recognize that the kids, tweens and teens segments would eventually become their target consumers, and were, therefore, an important audience.

The Ukrainian population was centered in seven major cities, including Kyiv, the capital of Ukraine, with a population of 3.5 million. These cities were called "millionniki" since they each had populations in excess of one million, and they accounted for approximately 20 per cent of the Ukrainian population. Kids, tweens and teens made up roughly 25 per cent of the total population of 47 million (see Exhibit 2). Studies by KMC showed that the kids, tweens and teens in Kyiv were representative of these segments in most of the other Ukrainian urban centres. Advertisers and marketers in Ukraine generally ignored the rural areas of the country.

GETTING STARTED

Natalia Berezovskaya started KMC in September 2002 with her partner, Vitaly Ocheretyanyi. Her studies in mass media and communications at Dnipropetrovsky State University sparked her interest in the advertising and marketing industries. With more than 10 years' experience as a radio anchor and author for youth programs, director of programming at a national radio station and coordinator at a Ukrainian advertising agency, Berezovskaya was able to identify kids, tweens and teens as unserved segments in the Ukrainian marketplace.

Prior to starting at KMC, Berezovskaya made contact with market research firms serving the kids, tweens and teens segments in other countries, such as Yeladim, Teenage Research Unlimited and Doyle Research. Along with this research, Berezovskaya monitored media sources, such as magazines, the Internet and business publications, to determine the value of such a niche market research firm in Ukraine. The presence of Western children's brands, the appearance of low-quality national Ukrainian brands, as well as the general lack of information regarding the consumer psychology of children were encouraging indications of the success of such a niche business. Berezovskaya's contacts in the Ukrainian advertising community further helped to ensure the success of KMC.

KIDS MARKET CONSULTING

The agency was formed as part of Dynamic Development and Innovation Group (DDI), a 100 per cent Ukrainian-owned business, co-founded in 1995, by Vitaly Ocheretyanyi. DDI consisted of five specialized companies representing the entire scope of marketing services. In 2004, SC-DOM, a market research firm focusing on adult consumers, accounted for 50 per cent of DDI's revenue, KMC represented 40 per cent, with the other businesses representing the remaining 10 per cent (see Exhibit 3).

Being a part of DDI provided many advantages for KMC. Berezovskaya has commented that "being a part of DDI is very comfortable for KMC." A variety of corporate resources were available to KMC from other DDI businesses at significantly reduced rates. These resources included access to both DDI's network of interviewers for market research and their tools to collect sociological, market and consumer behavior information. KMC was able to enter the market with access to DDI's customer base and experience. A further advantage was the cost-efficiency of sharing physical office space with SC-DOM in Kyiv. Rental costs accounted for 10 per cent of KMC's total expenses, utilities and web hosting were 12 per cent, and miscellaneous office expenses were three per cent. The cost savings of shared advertising to promote DDI's collection of businesses as well as leveraging the well-known DDI brand have proven significant for KMC over the past two years. KMC's expenses for promoting the business were five per cent of its overall expenses. DDI benefited from KMC because it expanded DDI's area of specialization and became another source of customers for all of DDI's companies.

Challenges arose for KMC in the beginning, due to its first-mover position in the kids, tweens and teens niche. There was initially a low level of acknowledgement from potential clients, due to the lack of information surrounding this specific segment in Ukraine. In order to promote the business, KMC worked to increase prospects' knowledge about the advantages of marketing to children and addressing segmentation in general. KMC organized seminars and presentations and introduced information at various meetings, including free specialized workshops called "Child-targeted Marketing." The company promoted consolidated research, whereby it offered one package of market research to several buyers. It was important to educate Ukrainian businesses of the value of market research, and to emphasize the varying levels of research, in terms of quality. Traditional market research services were offered, with the focus of each service on kids, tweens and teens. Services included:

- Surveys and questionnaires for quantitative studies
- "Delicate Age" study, a regular investigation of lifestyles and consumer preferences of children and teenagers
- Focus group discussions
- One-on-one, in-depth interviews (IDI) with children to better understand their feelings towards brands
- Child-and-parent pair interviews to understand the psychology of child-parent interaction in purchasing
- Creative groups (brainstorming groups with children to develop ideas about names, heroes, slogans, etc.)
- Observation and immersion experiences

- Desktop studies (analysis of secondary information and its assessment by different experts)
- Hall-test and home-test (assessment of the target group's reaction to the product at its point of sale, or practical use of the study subject in the target group's routine life)

KMC's customers included both Ukrainian and international firms seeking to better target kids, tweens and teens. Project costs for KMC varied, based on the type of project and customer requirements. KMC's Kyiv-based operation provided a competitive advantage because of its close proximity to Ukraine's largest market. Non-Ukraine-based firms that specialized in the kids, tweens and teens segment could not offer the same level of expertise for the Ukrainian business environment.

Difficulties involved in working in this niche included collecting information from children, who were often unable to clearly articulate their thoughts. With the use of child psychologists specially trained by KMC in concepts of marketing and market research, KMC was able to study the market awareness of kids, tweens and teens in Ukraine. KMC was the only market research company in both Ukraine and the former U.S.S.R. that focused exclusively on kids, tweens and teens.

By 2004, KMC was a relatively small business compared to its global competitors, with annual revenues of approximately $100,000. The company had five full-time employees in Kyiv, including Berezovskaya, and their salaries accounted for 70 per cent of KMC's expenses. The company hired freelance workers to fulfill the demands of its larger projects. KMC's relationship with DDI Group enabled the business to be profitable by controlling costs and to provide the best services at competitive rates for the loyal customer base it had developed. In its first year, KMC used 50 per cent of its revenue for new computer equipment and project planning activities. Re-investment in the business was 15 per cent to 20 per cent of revenue in subsequent years.

NEXT STEPS AT KMC

Increasingly the non-specialized Ukrainian firms began competing for KMC's niche business. KMC's growth appeared to have stabilized (see Exhibit 4), and the expected growth of the children's market was uncertain.

Berezovskaya had told Ocheretyanyi that she would brainstorm ideas to take KMC forward to protect its niche or expand its business. Was it a viable option to expand to other geographical areas? Were there additional services KMC could offer its clients? Could another niche be targeted? Berezovskaya had to make a decision and let him know by the end of the week, and there seemed to be a large range of possibilities she had yet to consider.

Exhibit 1 Weekly Disposable Funds Available to Each Group
Kids, Tweens and Teens (in UAH)

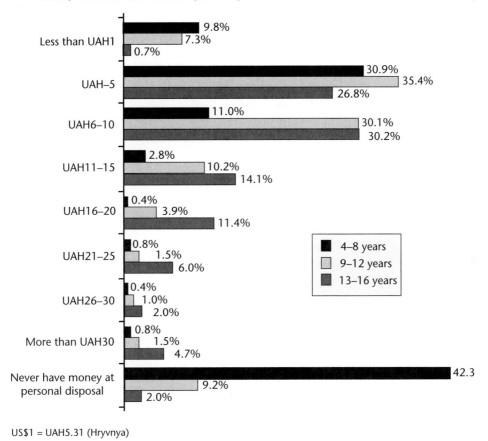

Less than UAH1
- 9.8%
- 7.3%
- 0.7%

UAH–5
- 30.9%
- 35.4%
- 26.8%

UAH6–10
- 11.0%
- 30.1%
- 30.2%

UAH11–15
- 2.8%
- 10.2%
- 14.1%

UAH16–20
- 0.4%
- 3.9%
- 11.4%

UAH21–25
- 0.8%
- 1.5%
- 6.0%

UAH26–30
- 0.4%
- 1.0%
- 2.0%

More than UAH30
- 0.8%
- 1.5%
- 4.7%

Never have money at personal disposal
- 42.3
- 9.2%
- 2.0%

Legend:
- ■ 4–8 years
- ▨ 9–12 years
- ▨ 13–16 years

US$1 = UAH5.31 (Hryvnya)

Exhibit 2 Kids, Tweens and Teens Population in Ukraine 2001

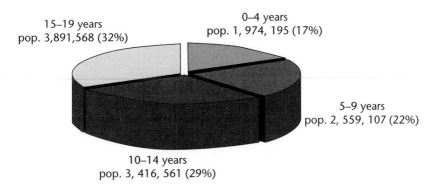

15–19 years
pop. 3,891,568 (32%)

0–4 years
pop. 1, 974, 195 (17%)

5–9 years
pop. 2, 559, 107 (22%)

10–14 years
pop. 3, 416, 561 (29%)

Source: "Goscomstat," National Committee of Statistics, population census 2001.

Exhibit 3   DDI Group's Companies

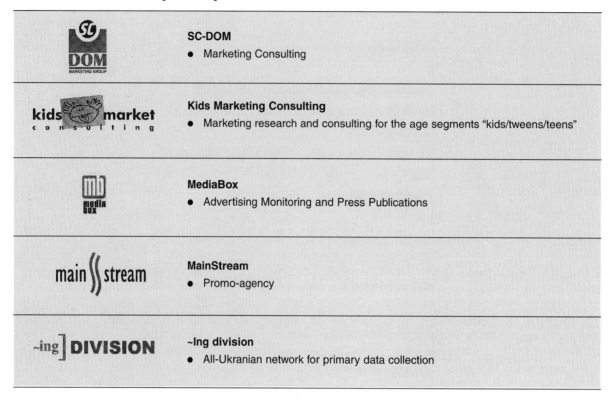

SC-DOM
- Marketing Consulting

Kids Marketing Consulting
- Marketing research and consulting for the age segments "kids/tweens/teens"

MediaBox
- Advertising Monitoring and Press Publications

MainStream
- Promo-agency

~Ing division
- All-Ukranian network for primary data collection

Exhibit 4   Revenue Growth at KMC 2003 to 2004

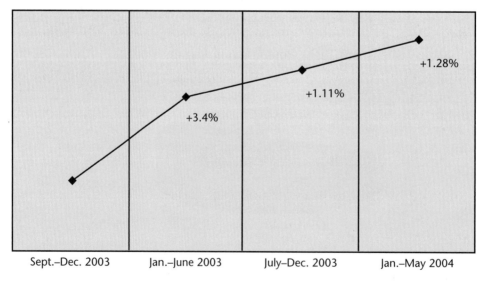

Source: Company files.

Eli Lilly in India: Rethinking the Joint Venture Strategy

In August 2001, Dr. Lorenzo Tallarigo, president of Intercontinental Operations, Eli Lilly and Company (Lilly), a leading pharmaceutical firm based in the United States, was getting ready for a meeting in New York, with D. S. Brar, chairman and chief executive officer (CEO) of Ranbaxy Laboratories Limited (Ranbaxy), India. Lilly and Ranbaxy had started a joint venture (JV) in India, Eli Lilly-Ranbaxy Private Limited (ELR) that was incorporated in March 1993. The JV had steadily grown to a full-fledged organization employing more than 500 people in 2001. However, in recent months Lilly was re-evaluating the directions for the JV, with Ranbaxy signaling an intention to sell its stake. Tallarigo was scheduled to meet with Brar to decide on the next steps.

THE GLOBAL PHARMACEUTICAL INDUSTRY IN THE 1990s

The pharmaceutical industry had come about through both forward integration from the manufacture of organic chemicals and a backward integration from druggist-supply houses. The industry's rapid growth was aided by increasing worldwide incomes and a universal demand for better health care; however, most of the world market for pharmaceuticals was concentrated in North America, Europe and Japan. Typically, the largest four firms claimed 20 per cent of sales, the top 20 firms 50 per cent to 60 per cent and the 50 largest companies accounted for 65 per cent to 75 per cent of sales (see Exhibit 1). Drug discovery was an expensive process, with leading firms

Nikhil Celly prepared this case under the supervision of Professors Charles Dhanaraj and Paul W. Beamish solely to provide material for class discussion. The authors do not intend to illustrate either effective or ineffective handling of a managerial situation. The authors may have disguised certain names and other identifying information to protect confidentiality.

Version: (A) 2004-05-25

Richard Ivey School of Business
The University of Western Ontario

spending more than 20 per cent of their sales on research and development (R&D). Developing a drug, from discovery to launch in a major market, took 10 to 12 years and typically cost US$500 million to US$800 million (in 1992). Bulk production of active ingredients was the norm, along with the ability to decentralize manufacturing and packaging to adapt to particular market needs. Marketing was usually equally targeted to physicians and the paying customers. Increasingly, government agencies, such as Medicare, and health management organizations (HMOs) in the United States were gaining influence in the buying processes. In most countries, all activities related to drug research and manufacturing were strictly controlled by government agencies, such as the Food and Drug Administration (FDA) in the United States, the Committee on Proprietary Medicinal Products (CPMP) in Europe, and the Ministry of Health and Welfare (MHW) in Japan.

Patents were the essential means by which a firm protected its proprietary knowledge. The safety provided by the patents allowed firms to price their products appropriately in order to accumulate funds for future research. The basic reason to patent a new drug was to guarantee the exclusive legal right to profit from its innovation for a certain number of years, typically 20 years for a product patent. There was usually a time lag of about eight to 10 years from the time the patent was obtained and the time of regulatory approval to first launch in the United States or Europe. Time lags for emerging markets and in Japan were longer. The "product patent" covered the chemical substance itself, while a "process patent" covered the method of processing or manufacture. Both patents guaranteed the inventor a 20-year monopoly on the innovation, but the process patent offered much less protection, since it was fairly easy to modify a chemical process. It was also very difficult to legally prove that a process patent had been created to manufacture a product identical to that of a competitor. Most countries relied solely on process patents until the mid-1950s, although many countries had since recognized the product patent in law. While companies used the global market to amortize the huge investments required to produce a new drug, they were hesitant to invest in countries where the intellectual property regime was weak.

As health-care costs soared in the 1990s, the pharmaceutical industry in developed countries began coming under increased scrutiny. Although patent protection was strong in developed countries, there were various types of price controls. Prices for the same drugs varied between the United States and Canada by a factor of 1.2 to 2.5.[1] Parallel trade or trade by independent firms taking advantage of such differentials represented a serious threat to pharmaceutical suppliers, especially in Europe. Also, the rise of generics, unbranded drugs of comparable efficacy in treating the disease but available at a fraction of the cost of the branded drugs, were challenging the pricing power of the pharmaceutical companies. Manufacturers of generic drugs had no expense for drug research and development of new compounds and only had limited budgets for popularizing the compound with the medical community. The generic companies made their money by copying what other pharmaceutical companies discovered, developed and created a market for. Health management organizations (HMOs) were growing and consolidating their drug purchases. In the United States, the administration under President Clinton, which took office in 1992, investigated the possibility of a comprehensive health plan, which, among other things, would have

---

[1]Estimates of industry average wholesale price levels in Europe (with Spanish levels indexed at 100 in 1989) were: Spain 100; Portugal 107; France 113; Italy 118; Belgium 131; United Kingdom 201; The Netherlands 229; West Germany 251. Source: T. Malnight, "Globalization of an Ethnocentric Firm: An Evolutionary Perspective," *Strategic Management Journal*, 1995, Vol. 16, p.128.

allowed an increased use of generics and laid down some form of regulatory pressure on pharmaceutical profits.

THE INDIAN PHARMACEUTICAL INDUSTRY IN THE 1990s

Developing countries, such as India, although large by population, were characterized by low per capita gross domestic product (GDP). Typically, healthcare expenditures accounted for a very small share of GDP, and health insurance was not commonly available. The 1990 figures for per capita annual expenditure on drugs in India were estimated at US$3, compared to US$412 in Japan, US$222 in Germany and US$191 in the United Kingdom.[2] Governments and large corporations extended health coverage, including prescription drug coverage, to their workers.

In the years before and following India's independence in 1947, the country had no indigenous capability to produce pharmaceuticals, and was dependent on imports. The Patent and Designs Act of 1911, an extension of the British colonial rule, enforced adherence to the international patent law, and gave rise to a number of multinational firms' subsidiaries in India, that wanted to import drugs from their respective countries of origin. Post-independence, the first public sector drug company, Hindustan Antibiotics Limited (HAL), was established in 1954, with the help of the World Health Organization, and Indian Drugs and Pharmaceutical Limited (IDPL) was established in 1961 with the help of the then Soviet Union.

The 1970s saw several changes that would dramatically change the intellectual property regime and give rise to the emergence of local manufacturing companies. Two such key changes were the passage of the Patents Act 1970 (effective April 1972) and the Drug Price Control Order (DPCO). The Patents Act in essence abolished the product patents for all pharmaceutical and agricultural products, and permitted process patents for five to seven years. The DPCO instituted price controls, by which a government body stipulated prices for all drugs. Subsequently, this list was revised in 1987 to 142 drugs (which accounted for 72 per cent of the turnover of the industry). Indian drug prices were estimated to be five per cent to 20 per cent of the U.S. prices and among the lowest in the world.[3] The DPCO also limited profits pharmaceutical companies could earn to approximately six per cent of sales turnover. Also, the post-manufacturing expenses were limited to 100 per cent of the production costs. At the World Health Assembly in 1982 Indira Gandhi, then Prime Minister of India, aptly captured the national sentiment on the issue in an often-quoted statement:

> The idea of a better-ordered world is one in which medical discoveries will be free of patents and there will be no profiteering from life and death.

With the institution of both the DPCO and the 1970 Patent Act, drugs became available more cheaply, and local firms were encouraged to make copies of drugs by developing their own processes, leading to bulk drug production. The profitability was sharply reduced for multinational companies, many of which began opting out of the Indian market due to the disadvantages they faced from the local competition. Market

---

[2]Organization of Pharmaceutical Producers of India Report.
[3]According to a study from Yale University, Ranitidine (300 tabs/10 pack) was priced at Rs18.53, whereas the U.S. price was 57 times more, and Ciprofloxacin (500 mg/4 pack) was at Rs28.40 in India, whereas the U.S. price was about 15 times more.

share of multinational companies dropped from 80 per cent in 1970 to 35 per cent in the mid-1990s as those companies exited the market due to the lack of patent protection in India.

In November 1984, there were changes in the government leadership following Gandhi's assassination. The dawn of the 1990s saw India initiating economic reform and embracing globalization. Under the leadership of Dr. Manmohan Singh, then finance minister, the government began the process of liberalization and moving the economy away from import substitution to an export-driven economy. Foreign direct investment was encouraged by increasing the maximum limit of foreign ownership to 51 per cent (from 40 per cent) in the drugs and pharmaceutical industry (see Exhibit 2). It was in this environment that Eli Lilly was considering getting involved.

ELI LILLY AND COMPANY

Colonel Eli Lilly founded Eli Lilly and Company in 1876. The company would become one of the largest pharmaceutical companies in the United States from the early 1940s until 1985 but it began with just $1,400 and four employees, including Lilly's 14-year-old son. This was accomplished with a company philosophy grounded in a commitment to scientific and managerial excellence. Over the years, Eli Lilly discovered, developed, manufactured and sold a broad line of human health and agricultural products. Research and development was crucial to Lilly's long-term success.

Before 1950, most OUS (a company term for "Outside the United States") activities were export focused. Beginning in the 1950s, Lilly undertook systematic expansion of its OUS activities, setting up several affiliates overseas. In the mid-1980s, under the leadership of then chairman, Dick Wood, Lilly began a significant move toward global markets. A separate division within the company, Eli Lilly International Corporation, with responsibility for worldwide marketing of all its products, took an active role in expanding the OUS operations. By 1992, Lilly's products were manufactured and distributed through 25 countries and sold in more than 130 countries. The company had emerged as a world leader in oral and injectable antibiotics and in supplying insulin and related diabetic care products. In 1992, Lilly International was headed by Sidney Taurel, an MBA from Columbia University, with work experience in South America and Europe, and Gerhard Mayr, an MBA from Stanford, with extensive experience in Europe. Mayr wanted to expand Lilly's operations in Asia, where several countries including India were opening up their markets for foreign investment. Lilly also saw opportunities to use the world for clinical testing, which would enable it to move forward faster, as well as shape opinion with leaders in the medical field around the world; something that would help in Lilly's marketing stage.

RANBAXY LABORATORIES

Ranbaxy began in the 1960s as a family business, but with a visionary management grew rapidly to emerge as the leading domestic pharmaceutical firm in India. Under the leadership of Dr. Parvinder Singh, who held a doctoral degree from the University of Michigan, the firm evolved into a serious research-oriented firm. Singh, who joined Ranbaxy to assist his father in 1967, rose to become the joint managing director in 1977, managing director in 1982, and vice-chairman and managing director in 1987. Singh's visionary management, along with the operational leadership provided by Brar, who joined the firm in 1977, was instrumental in turning the family business into a global corporation. In the early 1990s, when almost the entire domestic pharmaceutical industry was opposing a tough patent regime, Ranbaxy was accepting it as given. Singh's argument was unique within the industry in India:

> The global marketplace calls for a single set of rules; you cannot have one for the Indian market and the other for the export market. Tomorrow's global battles will be won by product leaders, not operationally excellent companies. Tomorrow's leaders must be visionaries, whether they belong to the family or not. Our mission at Ranbaxy is to become a research based international pharmaceutical company.[4]

By the early 1990s, Ranbaxy grew to become India's largest manufacturer of bulk drugs[5] and generic drugs, with a domestic market share of 15 per cent (see Exhibit 3).

One of Ranbaxy's core competencies was its chemical synthesis capability, but the company had begun to outsource some bulk drugs in limited quantities. The company produced pharmaceuticals in four locations in India. The company's capital costs were typically 50 per cent to 75 per cent lower than those of comparable U.S. plants and were meant to serve foreign markets in addition to the Indian market. Foreign markets, especially those in more developed countries, often had stricter quality control requirements, and such a difference meant that the manufacturing practices required to compete in those markets appeared to be costlier from the perspective of less developed markets. Higher prices in other countries provided the impetus for Ranbaxy to pursue international markets; the company had a presence in 47 markets outside India, mainly through exports handled through an international division. Ranbaxy's R&D efforts began at the end of the 1970s; in 1979, the company still had only 12 scientists. As Ranbaxy entered the international market in the 1980s, R&D was responsible for registering its products in foreign markets, most of which was directed to process R&D; R&D expenditures ranged from two per cent to five per cent of the annual sales with future targets of seven per cent to eight per cent.

THE LILLY RANBAXY JV

Ranbaxy approached Lilly in 1992 to investigate the possibility of supplying certain active ingredients or sourcing of intermediate products to Lilly in order to provide low-cost sources of intermediate pharmaceutical ingredients. Lilly had had earlier relationships with manufacturers in India to produce human or animal insulin and then export the products to the Soviet Union using the Russia/India trade route, but those had never developed into on-the-ground relationships within the Indian market. Ranbaxy was the second largest exporter of all products in India and the second largest pharmaceutical company in India after Glaxo (a subsidiary of the U.K.-based firm).

Rajiv Gulati, at that time a general manager of business development and marketing controller at Ranbaxy, who was instrumental in developing the strategy for Ranbaxy, recalled:

> In the 1980s, many multinational pharmaceutical companies had a presence in India. Lilly did not. As a result of both the sourcing of intermediate products as well as the fact that Lilly was one of the only players not yet in India, we felt that

---

[4]Quoted in *Times of India*, June 9, 1999.

[5]A bulk drug is an intermediate product that goes into manufacturing of pharmaceutical products.

we could use Ranbaxy's knowledge of the market to get our feet on the ground in India. Ranbaxy would supply certain products to the joint venture from its own portfolio that were currently being manufactured in India and then formulate and finish some of Lilly's products locally. The joint venture would buy the active ingredients and Lilly would have Ranbaxy finish the package and allow the joint venture to sell and distribute those products.

The first meeting was held at Lilly's corporate center in Indianapolis in late 1990. Present were Ranbaxy's senior executives, Dr. Singh, vice-chairman, and D.S. Brar, chief operating officer (COO), and Lilly's senior executives including Gene Step and Richard Wood, the CEO of Lilly. Rickey Pate, a corporate attorney at Eli Lilly who was present at the meeting, recalled:

> It was a very smooth meeting. We had a lot in common. We both believed in high ethical standards, in technology and innovation, as well as in the future of patented products in India. Ranbaxy executives emphasized their desire to be a responsible corporate citizen and expressed their concerns for their employees. It was quite obvious Ranbaxy would be a compatible partner in India.

Lilly decided to form the joint venture in India to focus on marketing of Lilly's drugs there, and a formal JV agreement was signed in November 1992. The newly created JV was to have an authorized capital of Rs200 million (equivalent of US$7.1 million), and an initial subscribed equity capital of Rs84 million (US$3 million), with equal contribution from Lilly and Ranbaxy, leading to an equity ownership of 50 per cent each. The board of directors for the JV would comprise six directors, three from each company. A management committee was also created comprising two directors, one from each company, and Lilly retained the right to appoint the CEO who would be responsible for the day-to-day operations. The agreement also provided for transfer of shares, in the event any one of the partners desired to dispose some or its entire share in the company.

In the mid-1990s, Lilly was investigating the possibility of extending its operations to include generics. Following the launch of the Indian JV, Lilly and Ranbaxy, entered into two other agreements related to generics, one in India to focus on manufacturing generics, and the other in the United States to focus on the marketing of generics. However, within less than a year, Lilly made a strategic decision not to enter the generics market and the two parties agreed to terminate the JV agreements related to the generics. Mayr recalled:

> At that time we were looking at the Indian market although we did not have any particular time frame for entry. We particularly liked Ranbaxy, as we saw an alignment of the broad values. Dr. Singh had a clear vision of leading Ranbaxy to become an innovation driven company. And we liked what we saw in them. Of course, for a time we were looking at the generic business and wondering if this was something we should be engaged in. Other companies had separate division for generics and we were evaluating such an idea. However, we had a pilot program in Holland and that taught us what it took to be competitive in generics and decided that business wasn't for us, and so we decided to get out of generics.

The Start-up

By March 1993, Andrew Mascarenhas, an American citizen of Indian origin, who at the time was the general manager for Lilly's Caribbean basin, based in San Juan, Puerto Rico, was selected to become the managing director of the joint venture. Rajiv

Gulati, who at the time spearheaded the business development and marketing efforts at Ranbaxy, was chosen as the director of marketing and sales at the JV. Mascarenhas recalled:

> Lilly saw the joint venture as an investment the company needed to make. At the time India was a country of 800 million people: 200 million to 300 million of them were considered to be within the country's middle class that represented the future of India. The concept of globalization was just taking hold at Lilly. India, along with China and Russia were seen as markets where Lilly needed to build a greater presence. Some resistance was met due to the recognition that a lot of Lilly's products were already being sold by Indian manufacturers due to the lack of patent protection and intellectual property rights so the question was what products should we put in there that could be competitive. The products that were already being manufactured had sufficient capacity; so it was an issue of trying to leverage the markets in which those products were sold into.
>
> Lilly was a name that most physicians in India did not recognize despite its leadership position in the United States, it did not have any recognition in India. Ranbaxy was the leader within India. When I was informed that the name of the joint venture was to be Lilly Ranbaxy, first thing I did was to make sure that the name of the joint venture was Eli Lilly Ranbaxy and not just Lilly Ranbaxy. The reason for this was based on my earlier experience in India, where "good quality" rightly or wrongly, was associated with foreign imported goods. Eli Lilly Ranbaxy sounded foreign enough!

Early on, Mascarenhas and Gulati worked getting the venture up and running with office space and an employee base. Mascarenhas recalled:

> I got a small space within Ranbaxy's set-up. We had two tables, one for Rajiv and the other for me. We had to start from that infrastructure and move towards building up the organization from scratch. Rajiv was great to work with and we both were able to see eye-to-eye on most issues. Dr. Singh was a strong supporter and the whole of Ranbaxy senior management tried to assist us whenever we asked for help.

The duo immediately hired a financial analyst, and the team grew from there. Early on, they hired a medical director, a sales manager and a human resources manager. The initial team was a good one, but there was enormous pressure and the group worked seven days a week. Ranbaxy's help was used for getting government approvals, licenses, distribution and supplies. Recalled Gulati:

> We used Ranbaxy's name for everything. We were new and it was very difficult for us. We used their distribution network as we did not have one and Lilly did not want to invest heavily in setting up a distribution network. We paid Ranbaxy for the service. Ranbaxy was very helpful.

By the end of 1993, the venture moved to an independent place, began launching products and employed more than 200 people. Within another year, Mascarenhas had hired a significant sales force and had recruited medical doctors and financial people for the regulatory group with assistance from Lilly's Geneva office. Mascarenhas recalled:

> Our recruiting theme was 'Opportunity of a Lifetime' i.e., joining a new company, and to be part of its very foundation. Many who joined us, especially at senior level, were experienced executives. By entering this new and untested company, they were really taking a huge risk with their careers and the lives of their families.

However, the employee turnover in the Indian pharmaceutical industry was very high. Sandeep Gupta, director of marketing recalled:

> Our biggest problem was our high turnover rate. A sales job in the pharmaceutical industry was not the most sought-after position. Any university graduate could be employed. The pharmaceutical industry in India is very unionized. Ranbaxy's HR practices were designed to work with unionized employees. From the very beginning, we did not want our recruits to join unions. Instead, we chose to show recruits that they had a career in ELR. When they joined us as sales graduates they did not just remain at that level. We took a conscious decision to promote from within the company. The venture began investing in training and used Lilly's training programs. The programs were customized for Indian conditions, but retained Lilly's values (see Exhibit 4).

Within a year, the venture team began gaining the trust and respect of doctors, due to the strong values adhered to by Lilly. Mascarenhas described how the venture fought the Indian stigma:

> Lilly has a code of ethical conduct called the Red Book, and the company did not want to go down the path where it might be associated with unethical behavior. But Lilly felt Ranbaxy knew how to do things the right way and that they respected their employees, which was a very important attribute. So following Lilly's Red Book values, the group told doctors the truth; both the positive and negative aspects of their drugs. If a salesperson didn't know the answer to something, they didn't lie or make up something; they told the doctor they didn't know. No bribes were given or taken, and it was found that honesty and integrity could actually be a competitive advantage. Sales people were trained to offer product information to doctors. The group gradually became distinguished by this "strange" behavior.

Recalled Sudhanshu Kamat, controller of finance at ELR:

> Lilly from the start treated us as its employees, like all its other affiliates worldwide. We followed the same systems and processes that any Lilly affiliate would worldwide.

Much of the success of the joint venture is attributed to the strong and cohesive working relationship of Mascarenhas and Gulati. Mascarenhas recalled:

> We both wanted the venture to be successful. We both had our identities to the JV, and there was no Ranbaxy versus Lilly politics. From the very start when we had our office at Ranbaxy premises, I was invited to dine with their senior management. Even after moving to our own office, I continued the practice of having lunch at Ranbaxy HQ on a weekly basis. I think it helped a lot to be accessible at all times and to build on the personal relationship.

The two companies had very different business focuses. Ranbaxy was a company driven by the generics business. Lilly, on the other hand, was driven by innovation and discovery.

Mascarenhas focused his effort on communicating Eli Lilly's values to the new joint venture:

> I spent a lot of time communicating Lilly's values to newly hired employees. In the early days, I interviewed our senior applicants personally. I was present in the two-day training sessions that we offered for the new employees, where I shared

the values of the company. That was a critical task for me to make sure that the right foundations were laid down for growth.

The first products that came out of the joint venture were human insulin from Lilly and several Ranbaxy products; but the team faced constant challenges in dealing with government regulations on the one hand and financing the affiliate on the other. There were also cash flow constraints.

The ministry of health provided limitations on Lilly's pricing, and even with the margin the Indian government allowed, most of it went to the wholesalers and the pharmacies, pursuant to formulas in the Indian ministry of health. Once those were factored out of the gross margin, achieving profitability was a real challenge, as some of the biggest obstacles faced were duties imposed by the Indian government on imports and other regulatory issues. Considering the weak intellectual property rights regime, Lilly did not want to launch some of its products, such as its top-seller, Prozac.[6] Gulati recalled:

> We focused only on those therapeutic areas where Lilly had a niche. We did not adopt a localization strategy such as the ones adopted by Pfizer and Glaxo[7] that manufactured locally and sold at local prices. India is a high-volume, low price, low profit market, but it was a conscious decision by us to operate the way we did. We wanted to be in the global price band. So, we did not launch several patented products because generics were selling at 1/60th the price.

Product and marketing strategies had to be adopted to suit the market conditions. ELR's strategy evolved over the years to focus on two groups of products: one was off-patent drugs, where Lilly could add substantial value (e.g. Ceclor), and two, patented drugs, where there existed a significant barrier to entry (e.g. Reopro and Gemzar). ELR marketed Ceclor, a Ranbaxy manufactured product, but attempted to add significant value by providing medical information to the physicians and other unique marketing activities. By the end of 1996, the venture had reached the break-even and was becoming profitable.

The Mid-Term Organizational Changes

Mascarenhas was promoted in 1996 to managing director of Eli Lilly Italy, and Chris Shaw, a British national, who was then managing the operations in Taiwan, was assigned to the JV as the new managing director. Also, Gulati, who was formally a Ranbaxy employee, decided to join Eli Lilly as its employee, and was assigned to Lilly's corporate office in Indianapolis in the Business Development — Infectious Diseases therapeutic division. Chris Shaw recalled:

> When I went to India as a British national, I was not sure what sort of reception I would get, knowing its history. But my family and I were received very warmly. I found a dynamic team with a strong sense of values.

Shaw focused on building systems and processes to bring stability to the fast-growing organization; his own expertise in operations made a significant contribution during this phase. He hired a senior level manager and created a team to develop standard

---

[6]Used as an antidepressant medication.

[7]An industry study by McKinsey found that Glaxo sold 50 per cent of its volume, received three per cent of revenues and one per cent of profit in India.

operating procedures (SOPs) for ensuring smooth operations. The product line also expanded. The JV continued to maintain a 50-50 distribution of products from Lilly and Ranbaxy, although there was no stipulation to maintain such a ratio. The clinical organization in India was received top-ratings in internal audits by Lilly, making it suitable for a wider range of clinical trials. Shaw also streamlined the sales and marketing activities around therapeutic areas to emphasize and enrich the knowledge capabilities of the company's sales force. Seeing the rapid change in the environment in India, ELR, with the support of Mayr, hired the management-consulting firm, McKinsey, to recommend growth options in India. ELR continued its steady performance with an annualized growth rate of about eight per cent during the late 1990s.

In 1999, Chris Shaw was assigned to Eli Lilly's Polish subsidiary, and Gulati returned to the ELR as its managing director, following his three-year tenure at Lilly's U.S. operations. Recalled Gulati:

> When I joined as MD in 1999, we were growing at eight per cent and had not added any new employees. I hired 150 people over the next two years and went about putting systems and processes in place. When we started in 1993 and during Andrew's time, we were like a grocery shop. Now we needed to be a company. We had to be a large durable organization and prepare ourselves to go from sales of US$10 million to sales of US$100 million.

ELR created a medical and regulatory unit, which handled the product approval processes with government. Das, the chief financial officer (CFO), commented:

> We worked together with the government on the regulatory part. Actually, we did not take shelter under the Ranbaxy name but built a strong regulatory (medical and corporate affairs) foundation.

By early 2001, the venture was recording an excellent growth rate (see Exhibit 5), surpassing the average growth rate in the Indian pharmaceutical industry. ELR had already become the 46th largest pharmaceutical company in India out of 10,000 companies. Several of the multinational subsidiaries, which were started at the same time as ELR, had either closed down or were in serious trouble. Das summarized the achievements:

> The JV did add some prestige to Ranbaxy's efforts as a global player as the Lilly name had enormous credibility while Lilly gained the toehold in India. In 10 years we did not have any cannibalization of each other's employees, quite a rare event if you compare with the other JVs. This helped us build a unique culture in India.

THE NEW WORLD, 2001

The pharmaceutical industry continued to grow through the 1990s. In 2001, worldwide retail sales were expected to increase 10 per cent to about US$350 billion. The United States was expected to remain the largest and fastest growing country among the world's major drug markets over the next three years. There was a consolidation trend in the industry with ongoing mergers and acquisitions reshaping the industry. In 1990, the world's top 10 players accounted for just 28 per cent of the market, while in 2000, the number had risen to 45 per cent and continued to grow. There was also a trend among leading global pharmaceutical companies to get back to basics and concentrate on core high-margined prescription preparations and divest non-core businesses. In addition, the partnerships between pharmaceutical and biotechnology companies were growing rapidly. There were a number of challenges, such as escalating R&D costs, lengthening development and approval times for new products, growing competition from generics and follow-on products, and rising cost-containment pressures, particularly with the growing clout of managed care organizations.

By 1995, Lilly had moved up to become the 12th leading pharmaceutical supplier in the world, sixth in the U.S. market, 17th in Europe and 77th in Japan. Much of Lilly's sales success through the mid-1990s came from its antidepressant drug, Prozac. But with the wonder drug due to go off patent in 2001, Lilly was aggressively working on a number of high-potential products. By the beginning of 2001, Lilly was doing business in 151 countries, with its international sales playing a significant role in the company's success (see Exhibits 6 and 7). Dr. Lorenzo Tallarigo recalled:

> When I started as the president of the intercontinental operations, I realized that the world was very different in the 2000s from the world of 1990s. Particularly there were phenomenal changes in the markets in India and China. While I firmly believed that the partnership we had with Ranbaxy was really an excellent one, the fact that we were facing such a different market in the 21st century was reason enough to carefully evaluate our strategies in these markets.

Ranbaxy, too, had witnessed changes through the 1990s. Dr. Singh became the new CEO in 1993 and formulated a new mission for the company: to become a research-based international pharmaceutical company with $1 billion in sales by 2003. This vision saw Ranbaxy developing new drugs through basic research, earmarking 20 per cent of the R&D budget for such work. In addition to its joint venture with Lilly, Ranbaxy made three other manufacturing/marketing investments in developed markets: a joint venture with Genpharm in Canada ($1.1 million), and the acquisitions of Ohm Labs in the United States ($13.5 million) and Rima Pharmaceuticals ($8 million) in Ireland. With these deals, Ranbaxy had manufacturing facilities around the globe. While China and Russia were expected to remain key foreign markets, Ranbaxy was looking at the United States and the United Kingdom as its core international markets for the future. In 1999, Dr. Singh handed over the reins of the company to Brar, and later the same year, Ranbaxy lost this visionary leader due to an untimely death. Brar continued Singh's vision to keep Ranbaxy in a leadership position. However, the vast network of international sales that Ranbaxy had developed created a large financial burden, depressing the company's 2000 results, and was expected to significantly affect its cash flow in 2001 (see Exhibit 8). Vinay Kaul, vice-chairman of Ranbaxy in 2001 and chairman of the board of ELR since 2000, noted:

> We have come a long way from where we started. Our role in the present JV is very limited. We had a smooth relationship and we have been of significant help to Lilly to establish a foothold in the market here in India. Also, we have opened up a number of opportunities for them to expand their network. However, we have also grown, and we are a global company with presence in a number of international markets including the United States. We had to really think if this JV is central to our operations, given that we have closed down the other two JV agreements that we had with Lilly on the generics manufacturing. It is common knowledge that whether we continue as a JV or not, we have created a substantial value for Lilly.

There were also significant changes in the Indian business environment. India signed the General Agreement on Tariffs and Trade (GATT) in April 1994 and became a World Trade Organization (WTO) member in 1995. As per the WTO, from the year 2005, India would grant product patent recognition to all new chemical entities (NCEs), i.e., bulk drugs developed then onward. Also, the Indian government had made the decision to allow 100 per cent foreign direct investment into the drugs and pharmaceutical industry in 2001.[8] The Indian pharmaceutical market had grown at an average of 15 per cent through the 1990s, but the trends indicated a slowdown in growth, partly due to intense price competition, a shift toward chronic therapies and the entry of large players into the generic market. India was seeing its own internal consolidation of major companies that were trying to bring in synergies through economies of scale. The industry would see more mergers and alliances. And with India's entry into the WTO and its agreement to begin patent protection in 2004-2005, competition on existing and new products was expected to intensify. Government guidelines were expected to include rationalization of price controls and the encouragement of more research and development. Recalled Gulati:

> The change of institutional environment brought a great promise for Lilly. India was emerging into a market that had patent protection and with tremendous potential for adding value in the clinical trials, an important component in the pharmaceutical industry. In Ranbaxy, we had a partner with whom we could work very well, and one which greatly respected Lilly. However, there were considerable signals from both sides, which were forcing us to evaluate the strategy.

Dr. Vinod Mattoo, medical director of ELR commented:

> We have been able to achieve penetration in key therapeutic areas of diabetes and oncology. We have created a high caliber, and non-unionized sales force with world-class sales processes. We have medical infrastructure and expertise to run clinical trials to international standards. We have been able to provide clinical trial data to support global registrations, and an organization in place to maximize returns post-2005.

EVALUATING STRATEGIC OPTIONS

Considering these several developments, Tallarigo suggested a joint task force comprising senior executives from both companies:

> Soon after assuming this role, I visited India in early 2000, and had the pleasure of meeting Dr. Brar and the senior executives. It was clear to me that both Brar and I were in agreement that we needed to think carefully how we approached the future. It was there that I suggested that we create a joint task force to come up with some options that would help us make a final decision.

A task force was set up with two senior executives from Lilly's Asia-Pacific regional office (based in Singapore) and two senior executives from Ranbaxy. The task force did not include senior executives of the ELR so as to not distract the running of the day-to-day operations. Suman Das, the chief financial officer of ELR, was assigned to support the task force with the needed financial data. The task force developed several scenarios and presented different options for the board to consider.

---

[8]In order to regulate the parallel activities of a foreign company, which had an ongoing joint venture in India, the regulations stipulated that the foreign partner must get a "No objection letter" from its Indian partner, before setting up a wholly owned subsidiary.

There were rumors within the industry that Ranbaxy expected to divest the JV, and invest the cash in its growing portfolio of generics manufacturing business in international markets. There were also several other Indian companies that offered to buy Ranbaxy's stake in the JV. With India recognizing patent protection in 2005, several Indian pharmaceutical companies were keen to align with multinationals to ensure a pipeline of drugs. Although there were no formal offers from Ranbaxy, the company was expected to price its stakes as high as US$70 million. One of the industry observers in India commented:

> I think it is fair for Ranbaxy to expect a reasonable return for its investment in the JV, not only the initial capital, but also so much of its intangibles in the JV. Ranbaxy's stock has grown significantly. Given the critical losses that Ranbaxy has had in some of its investments abroad, the revenue from this sale may be a significant boost for Ranbaxy's cash flow this year.

Gerhard Mayr, who in 2001, was the executive vice-president and was responsible for Lilly's demand realization around the world, continued to emphasize the emerging markets in India, China and Eastern Europe. Mayr commented on Ranbaxy:

> India is an important market for us and especially after patent protection in 2005. Ranbaxy was a wonderful partner and our relationship with them was outstanding. The other two joint ventures we initiated with them in the generics did not make sense to us once we decided to get out of the generics business. We see India as a good market for Lilly. If a partner is what it takes to succeed, we should go with a partner. If it does not, we should have the flexibility to reconsider.

Tallarigo hoped that Brar would be able to provide a clear direction as to the venture's future. As he prepared for the meeting, he knew the decision was not an easy one, although he felt confident that the JV was in a good shape. While the new regulations allowed Lilly to operate as a wholly owned subsidiary in India, the partnership has been a very positive element in its strategy. Ranbaxy provided manufacturing and logistics support to the JV, and breaking up the partnership would require a significant amount of renegotiations. Also, it was not clear what the financial implications of such a move would be. Although Ranbaxy seemed to favor a sell-out, Tallarigo thought the price expectations might be beyond what Lilly was ready to accept. This meeting with Brar should provide clarity on all these issues.

Exhibit 1   World Pharmaceutical Suppliers 1992 and 2001 (US$ millions)

Company	Origin	1992 Sales*	Company	Origin	2001 Sales**
Glaxo	US	8,704	Pfizer	USA	25,500
Merck	UK	8,214	GlaxoSmithKline	UK	24,800
Bristol-Myers Squibb	US	6,313	Merck & Co	USA	21,350
Hoechst	GER	6,042	AstraZeneca	UK	16,480
Ciba-Geigy	SWI	5,192	Bristol-Myers Squibb	USA	15,600
SmithKline Beecham	US	5,100	Aventis	FRA	15,350
Roche	SWI	4,897	Johnson & Johnson	USA	14,900
Sandoz	SWI	4,886	Novartis	SWI	14,500
Bayer	GER	4,670	Pharmacia Corp	USA	11,970
American Home	US	4,589	Eli Lilly	USA	11,540
Pfizer	US	4,558	Wyeth	USA	11,710
Eli Lilly	US	4,537	Roche	SWI	8,530
Johnson & Johnson	US	4,340	Schering-Plough	USA	8,360
Rhone Poulenc Rorer	US	4,096	Abbot Laboratories	USA	8,170
Abbot	US	4,025	Takeda	JAP	7,770
			Sanofi-Synthélabo	FRA	5,700
			Boehringer Ingelheim	GER	5,600
			Bayer	GER	5,040
			Schering AG	GER	3,900
			Akzo Nobel	NTH	3,550

*Market Share Reporter, 1993.
**Pharmaceutical Executive, May 2002.

Exhibit 2   India Economy at a Glance

	1992	1994	1996	1998	2000
Gross domestic product (GDP) at current market prices in US$	244	323	386	414	481
Consumer price index (June 1982=100) in local currency, period average	77.4	90.7	108.9	132.2	149.3
Recorded official unemployment as a percentage of total labor force	9.7	9.3	9.1	9.2	9.2
Stock of foreign reserves plus gold (national valuation), end-period Foreign direct investment inflow	8,665	23,054	23,784	29,833	48,200
(in US$ millions)[1]	252	974	2,525	2,633	2,319
Total exports	19,563	25,075	33,055	33,052	43,085
Total imports	23,580	26,846	37,376	42,318	49,907

Year	Population[2]
1991	846
2001	1,027

[1]United Nations Commission on Trade and Development.
[2]1991, 2001 Census of India (in millions).
Source: The Economist Intelligence Unit.

Exhibit 3   Top 20 Pharmaceutical Companies in India by Sales 1996 to 2000 (Rs billions)

Company	1996*	Company	2000
Glaxo-Wellcome	4.97	Ranbaxy	20.00
Cipla	2.98	Cipla	12.00
Ranbaxy	2.67	Dr. Reddy's Labs	11.30
Hoechts-Roussel	2.60	Glaxo (India)	7.90
Knoll Pharmaceutical	1.76	Lupin Labs	7.80
Pfizer	1.73	Aurobindo Pharma	7.60
Alembic	1.68	Novartis	7.20
Torrent Pharma	1.60	Wockhardt Ltd.	6.80
Lupin Labs	1.56	Sun Pharma	6.70
Zydus-Cadila	1.51	Cadilla Healthcare	5.80
Ambalal Sarabhai	1.38	Nicholas Piramal	5.70
Smithkline Beecham	1.20	Aventis Pharma	5.30
Aristo Pharma	1.17	Alembic Ltd.	4.80
Parke Davis	1.15	Morepen Labs	4.70
Cadila Pharma	1.12	Torrent Pharma	4.40
E. Merck	1.11	IPCA Labs	4.20
Wockhardt	1.08	Knoll Pharma	3.70
John Wyeth	1.04	Orchid Chemicals	3.60
Alkem Laboratories	1.04	E. Merck	3.50
Hindustan Ciba Geigy	1.03	Pfizer	3.40

*1996 figures are from ORG, Bombay as reported in Lanjouw, J.O., www.oiprc.ox.ac.uk/EJWP0799.html, NBER working paper No. 6366.
Source: "Report on Pharmaceutical Sector in India," *Scope Magazine*, September 2001, p.14.

Exhibit 4   Values at Eli Lilly-Ranbaxy Limited

PEOPLE

"The people who make up this company are its most valuable assets"

- Respect for the individual
  - Courtesy and politeness at all times
  - Sensitivity to other people's views
  - Respect for ALL people regardless of case, religion, sex or age
- Careers NOT jobs
  - Emphasis on individual's growth, personal and professional
  - Broaden experience via cross-functional moves

"The first responsibility of our supervisors is **to build men, then medicines**"

ATTITUDE

"There is very little difference between people. But that difference makes a BIG difference. The little difference is attitude. The BIG difference is... Whether it is POSITIVE or NEGATIVE"

"Are we part of the PROBLEM or part of the SOLUTION?"

TEAM

"*None of us* is as smart *as all of us*"

INTEGRITY

- Integrity outside the company
  a) "We should not do anything or be expected to take any action that we would be ashamed to explain to our family or close friends"
  b) "The red-faced test"
  c) "Integrity can be our biggest competitive advantage"
- Integrity inside the company
  - With one another: openness, honesty

EXCELLENCE

- Serving our customers

  "In whatever we do, we must ask ourselves: how does this serve my customer better?"
- Continuous improvement

  "Nothing is being done today that cannot be done better tomorrow"
- Become the Industry Standard

  "In whatever we do, we will do it so well that we become the Industry Standard"

Exhibit 5   Eli Lilly-Ranbaxy India Financials 1998 to 2001 (Rs'000s)

	1998–1999	1999–2000	2000–2001
Sales	559,766	632,188	876,266
Marketing Expenses	37,302	61,366	96,854
Other Expenses	157,907	180,364	254,822
Profit after Tax	5,898	12,301	11,999
Current Assets	272,635	353,077	466,738
Current Liabilities	239,664	297,140	471,635
Total Assets	303,254	386,832	516,241
No. of Employees	358	419	460
Exchange Rate (Rupees/US$)	42.6	43.5	46.8

Note: Financial year runs from April 1 to March 31.
Source: Company Reports.

Exhibit 6   Lilly Financials 1992 to 2000 (US$ millions)

	1992	1994	1996	1998	2000
Net sales	4,963	5,711	6,998	9,236	10,862
Foreign sales	2,207	2,710	3,587	3,401	3,858
Research and development expenses	731	839	1,190	1,739	2,019
Income from continuing operations before taxes and extraordinary items	1,194	1,699	2,131	2,665	3,859
Net income	709	1,286	1,524	2,097	3,058
Dividends per share*	1.128	1.260	0.694	0.830	1.060
Current assets	3,006	3,962	3,891	5,407	7,943
Current liabilities	2,399	5,670	4,222	4,607	4,961
Property and equipment	4,072	4,412	4,307	4,096	4,177
Total assets	8,673	14,507	14,307	12,596	14,691
Long-term debt	582	2,126	2,517	2,186	2,634
Shareholder equity	4,892	5,356	6,100	4,430	6,047
Number of employees*	24,500	24,900	27,400	29,800	35,700

*Actual value
Source: Company files.

***Exhibit* 7**   Product Segment Information Lilly and Ranbaxy 1996 and 2000

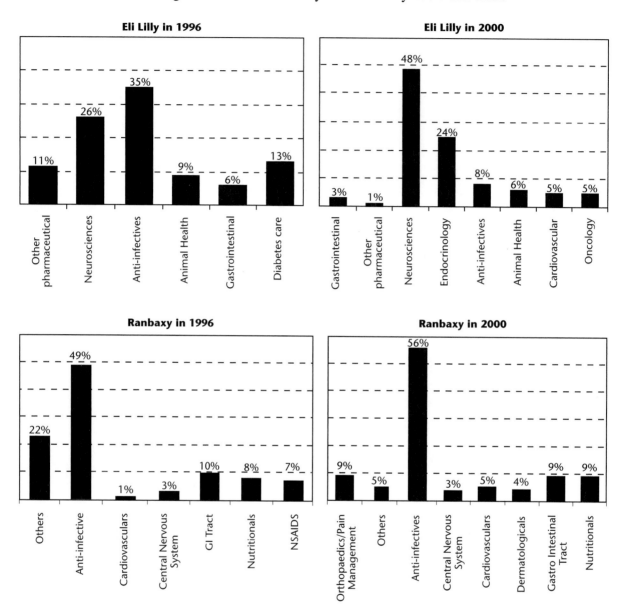

Exhibit 8   Ranbaxy Financials 1992 to 2000 (Rs millions)

	1992–93	1994–95	1996–97	*1998	2000
Sales	4,607	7,122	11,482	10,641	17,459
Foreign sales	1,408	3,019	5,224	4,414	8,112
Profit before tax	358	1,304	1,869	1,240	1,945
Profit after tax	353	1,104	1,604	1,170	1,824
Equity dividend	66.50	199.80	379.10	560.10	869.20
Earnings per share (Rs)	16.21	25.59	32.47	13.46	15.74
Net current assets	1,737	5,790	9,335	8,321	8,258
Share capital	217.90	430.50	494.00	1,159.00	1,159.00
Reserves and surplus	1,028	6,000	11,056	12,849	16,448
Book value per share (Rs)	57.16	149.08	233.70	120.90	136.60
No. of employees	4,575	4,703	6,131	5,469	5,784
Exchange rate (US$1 = Rs)	29.00	31.40	35.90	42.60	46.80

*The financial year for Ranbaxy changed from April 1 to March 31 to calendar year in 1998. Also, the company issued a 1:2 bonus issue (see the changes in share capital and book value per share). The 1998 figures are based on nine months April to December 1998.

Source: Company files.

Case 13

Maple Leaf Consumer Foods—Fixing Hot Dogs (A)

Kelly Gervin hardly had the chance to get things straightened around in her new office. It was June 5, 2001, and Gervin had been the senior marketing director of the packaged meats group in the consumer foods division of Maple Leaf Foods (MLF) for all of four hours. She was still unpacking boxes in her office when the division's vice-president of marketing, Pat Jacobs, came flying in. He tossed a pile of papers on her desk (see Exhibits 2 to 7).

> Kelly . . . these reports I received this morning are scary. We have a serious problem in our hot dog business. Of our nine hot dog brands, five are losing significant market share and another one is down marginally. We've lost as much as 45 per cent relative to last year in one category . . . and that's just the start of it! Kelly, I need you to figure out what is going on and solve this problem, and I need you to do it quickly.

MAPLE LEAF FOODS

The MLF brand had been around in Canada for over 100 years. The organization had grown and evolved out of a number of mergers and amalgamations, but its origins could be traced as far back as 1836 when Grantham Mills opened a flour production and distribution facility in St. Catharines, Ontario. In 1991, U.K.-based Hillsdown Holdings PLC amalgamated with MLF through the purchase and merger of Canada Packers and Maple Leaf Mills. In 1995, McCain Capital Corporation and the Ontario Teachers' Pension Plan Board came together to acquire controlling interest of MLF. Between 1995 and 2001, new systems were introduced, operations streamlined, and several new acquisitions were completed.

Richard Ivey School of Business
The University of Western Ontario

Scott Hill prepared this case under the supervision of Professor Allen Morrison solely to provide material for class discussion. The authors do not intend to illustrate either effective or ineffective handling of a managerial situation. The authors may have disguised certain names and other identifying information to protect confidentiality.

Ivey Management Services prohibits any form of reproduction, storage or transmittal without its written permission. This material is not covered under authorization from CanCopy or any reproduction rights organization. To order copies or request permission to reproduce materials, contact Ivey Publishing, Ivey Management Services, c/o Richard Ivey School of Business, The University of Western Ontario, London, Ontario, Canada, N6A 3K7; phone (519) 661-3208; fax (519) 661-3882; e-mail cases@ivey.uwo.ca.

Copyright © 2002, Ivey Management Services   Version: (A) 2004-05-07

By 2001, MLF was Canada's largest and most dominant food processor, generating nearly $4.8 billion in annual sales. The MLF organization and its products were also gaining significant momentum on the international scene. The company's operations focused on three core areas of business: bakery products, meat products and agribusiness. Each core business was composed of several independent operating companies (IOCs) and each IOC was run by a president who controlled the overall profitability and competitive strategy of the business. Under the direction of MLF chief executive officer (CEO), Michael McCain, IOCs were encouraged to follow a common set of values and strategic principles that emphasized the importance of brand equity, operating efficiencies, market leadership and continuous improvement (see Exhibit 1).

The meat products group was by far the largest of the company's core groups, with 2000 sales of nearly $2.5 billion and EBITDA (earnings before interest, taxes, depreciation and amortization) of $26.5 million. The group consisted of all the company's meat and meat-related businesses and included four distinct IOCs: Maple Leaf Pork, Maple Leaf Poultry, Maple Leaf International and Maple Leaf Consumer Foods. While each IOC operated independently, efforts were under way in 2001 to optimize the vertical co-ordination of IOCs within the broader MLF organization.

The packaged meats division, in which Kelly Gervin worked, was part of the Consumer Foods IOC. Consumer Foods had full responsibility for the production and distribution of all branded and value-added prepared meat products. This included bacon, ham, hot dogs, cottage rolls, a wide variety of delicatessen products, prepared turkey products, sliced meats, cooked sausage products, frozen entrees, lard and canned meats. In 2000, Consumer Foods generated in excess of half a billion dollars in sales, representing over 10 per cent of MLF's overall revenues.

Excluding commodities, the MLF hot dog portfolio of products was by far the largest meat category at MLF Consumer Foods, with over twice the dollar sales of any other MLF branded, value-added or prepared meat category within the IOC. The MLF organization had been acquiring expertise in the production and distribution of hot dogs for nearly 75 years. The organization first entered the hot dog business when Canada Packers began producing hot dogs in 1927. At that time, hot dog and sausage production was seen as a financially viable method to dispose of beef, pork and chicken trimmings. It was this profitable opportunity to use up raw material—in combination with the increasing momentum the hot dog was gaining as a cultural icon in the marketplace—that traditionally drove the business.

In 2000, total MLF hot dog sales were approximately $50 million. Industry professionals used both dollar sales and volume by weight to measure sales performance, and these sales correlated with a total of approximately 10.5 million kilograms of hot dogs sold. In the preceding year, total MLF hot dog sales were also approximately $50 million, but volume by weight had actually been approximately 11.2 million kilograms. In Gervin's words, "Our average price per kilo was going up, but there was no question we were selling less. We were losing market share and this became our primary concern."

THE HOT DOG INDUSTRY

A good deal of disagreement exists over the origin of the hot dog. People in Frankfurt, Germany, claim they discovered the hot dog in 1487. Others argue that it was Johan Georghehner, a butcher from Coburg who travelled to Frankfurt to promote this product—which he called the "dachshund" because of its shape—in the late 1600s. Others in Vienna point to the name "wiener" as evidence of the product's Austrian roots.

In the United States, the origins of the hot dog industry can be traced to the arrival of a German immigrant by the name of Charles Feltman who opened up the first Coney Island hot dog stand in 1871. In 1893, Chris Ahe, the owner of the St. Louis Browns baseball team, started selling hot dogs in his ball park. This laid the groundwork for what would become an inseparable connection between hot dogs and the game of baseball.

The actual phrase "hot dog" was coined in 1901. It all started on a cold April day in New York City when concessionaire Harry Stevens became frustrated with losing money selling ice cream and soda. He ordered his assistant to go out and buy all the long, skinny sausages he could find and to sell them from portable hot-water tanks while yelling "get your red hot dachshund while they last!" Sports cartoonist Ted Dorgan became quite amused with the scene, and did a cartoon strip on it. When he had trouble spelling "dachshund," he substituted the term "dog," and the rest, as they say, is history.

THE INDUSTRY TODAY

At the aggregate level, per capita demand for hot dogs was slightly higher in the United States than in Canada. In 2000, consumers in the United States spent nearly $1.7 billion on hot dogs in retail outlets. The average U.S. household purchased 7.65 pounds of hot dogs annually, which translated into about 65 hot dogs per person per year. In 2000, total Canadian hot dog market sales were just over $220 million, which represented approximately 52.5 million kilograms of hot dogs. This translated into an annual consumption rate of about 52 hot dogs per person in Canada. Sixty-four per cent of hot dogs sold in Canada were pork and meat combinations, 24 per cent were all-beef hot dogs, and 12 per cent were made from poultry.

Demand for hot dogs was consistently strongest during the summer months. Since the turn of the century, hot dogs in buns at baseball games, summer picnics, backyard barbecues and roadside diners had become a tradition in North American culture. Hot dog sales from May to August represented more than 44 per cent of the annual total, with July—National Hot Dog Month in the United States—leading the pack. In both Canada and the United States, hot dogs were popular at barbecues and entertainment events. Four hot dogs were consumed for every 10 baseball tickets sold, so it was projected that there would be more than 26 million hot dogs consumed in major league ballparks in 2001.

Hot dog consumption preferences were subject to significant regional differences in Canada. Western Canadian consumers had the strongest demand in Canada for beef hot dogs. The Quebec market was partial to hot dogs in a specific (lower) price segment—due to the influence of "steamies" or "toasties"—hot dogs that were prepared using unique cooking methods. (In this market, lower-priced hot dogs were considered adequate since any hot dog could be prepared in the preferred manner.) Atlantic Canada had the largest per capita consumer of low-fat hot dogs, due in part to the higher average age of the population versus other parts of Canada.

Hot dog consumption was consistently uniform throughout all income levels. Wealthy and low-income Canadians appeared to consume approximately the same volume of hot dogs on an annual basis. Larger families with five or more members tended to eat larger numbers of hot dogs, as did younger families where heads of households were under the age of 35. Children were heavy influencers in hot dog purchase decisions.

Despite their broad consumption, hot dogs had always been subject to considerable consumer scrutiny concerning their content and manufacture. For some time, consumers had been concerned about the presence of "mystery" meat in hot dogs. Both the Canadian and U.S. Departments of Agriculture required by law that meats used in hot dogs include only muscle meat. In addition to meeting this requirement, there was a movement in the industry to introduce all-meat, byproduct-free hot dogs.

COMPETITIVE LANDSCAPE

In 2001, the competitive landscape of the hot dog industry in Canada was dominated by two organizations: MLF and Schneider Foods (JMS). Each had over 20 per cent share of the national market (see Exhibit 2). Other competitors were relatively small (less than one-quarter the size of MLF and JMS) and were regionally focused.

Based in Kitchener, Ontario, JMS had over 110 years of experience in producing and distributing meat products throughout the Canadian marketplace. JMS also had a reputation as a tough competitor; it fought for every inch of shelf space and was tactically reactive and retaliatory. It also knew the hot dog business well and had loyal employees.

In June of 2001, JMS led the industry, possessing over 28 per cent of the dollar share of the hot dog market in Canada. The company was not only the largest hot dog producer in Canada, it was the fastest growing. Between mid-2000 and mid-2001, JMS's dollar sales increased by nearly three per cent; in contrast, MLF's overall sales declined by just over two per cent. JMS had strong national brands that it supported with consistently effective promotional campaigns. It was also very aggressive on pricing. While MLF raised hot dog prices in both 2000 and 2001, JMS held firm to is prices and picked up market share.

In assessing JMS's performance in the Canadian hot dog market, one MLF insider commented:

> Schneider has done a great job of managing its product line from a quality perspective and overall consistency. It has done very little to its hot dog product line over the years. It has not proliferated sub-brands as we did. It did not change packaging on a regular basis as we did. It has also had great consistency in its sales and marketing staff—as we did not. Also, Schneider has done a great job managing its trade relations.
>
> Consumers consistently tell us that JMS means quality, heritage and great-tasting products. This is something that Consumer Foods has to overcome!

HOT DOG SEGMENTATION

For marketing purposes, MLF segmented the hot dog market in two ways: 1) by target consumer (adult or family), and 2) by price (premium, mainstream and value/economy). While there were plenty of small niche players, both JMS and MLF competed in all major hot dog markets in Canada.

Target Segment

The adult segment consisted of franks and sausages. Franks had a larger diameter, slightly more coarse emulsion (meat blend), larger particle definition and more spices than wieners. Also, franks were at least six inches long and by weight were usually about six per pound (2.5 ounces each). Sausages were curved and by weight were three to five per pound (three to five ounces each). Unlike franks, which were always sold pre-cooked, sausages could be sold either uncooked or pre-cooked. In 2001, the adult segment was growing at a rate of about 11 per cent industrywide, but this segment still represented approximately only 16 per cent of the total hot dog industry. In the adult segment, MLF's brands included *ML 100s, Overlander* and *Shopsy's Original Recipe*. JMS's primary adult segment hot dog was *Juicy Jumbos*.

Products targeted towards the family segment were called wieners and represented 84 per cent of overall industry sales. Wieners were also six inches long, but had a finer emulsion than franks and by weight were generally about 12 per pound (1.3 ounces each). Across the industry, the family segment was growing at a rate of about two per cent per year. Industry observers believed that, increasingly, consumers were trading up towards adult categories. In the family segment, JMS offered *Red Hots* (in Ontario) and an identical product simply called *Wieners* for the rest of Canada. MLF's brands in the family segment included *Top Dogs* (Regular and BBQ), *Lean 'n Lite* (Regular and all-Beef), *Beef Dogs* and *Shopsy's Beef*.

Price Segment

Premium hot dogs sold at a price point greater than $3.50 per pound and contained franks and sausages. In addition, Maple Leaf competed in this segment with *Top Dogs Singles*, which were premium priced to reflect the quality of their ingredients and high packaging and high labor costs. Mainstream hot dogs were the largest price segment and included all hot dogs priced between $2.50 and $3.50. MLF's *Top Dogs, Lean 'n Lite, Beef Dogs* and *Shopsy's Beef* fit into this segment. Hot dogs in the value segment sold for between $1.89 and $2.50 per pound. MLF's products in this segment included *Maple Leaf Original* (Regular and Beef), *Burns* (Regular, Beef, and 6+6), *Hygrade* (Regular and Beef), and *Shopsy's* (Regular and BBQ). Wieners in the economy segment were priced under $1.89 per pound; MLF produced several retail brands in this segment including *No-Name* and *Smart Choice*. JMS's *Red Hots* and *Wieners* were both considered mainstream hot dogs. However, during 2001, both products were heavily discounted (to $1.99), which gave them about a 10 per cent to 20 per cent price advantage over MLF's value-price products.

MLF'S CURRENT BRAND STRATEGY

In mid-2001, MLF had nine different brands competing in the Canadian marketplace. Exhibit 3 summarizes the positioning of each of the Maple Leaf hot dog brands. While MLF had strong regional brands, none of the company's brands had a strong national presence. Instead, *Shopsy's* brands were sold only in Ontario, *Burns* and *Overlander* brands competed only in Western Canada, and *Hygrade* was distributed only in Quebec.

For some time, MLF had emphasized different brands for different geographic regions within Canada. This development had resulted in strong brand equity in each of Canada's major regions. The *Burns* brand was strong in Western Canada. In the late 1990s, *Burns* lost substantial market share due to a cost-plus pricing structure which drove prices substantially higher than key competitors. MLF had recently fixed the pricing formula and had moved to reduce production costs, thereby stabilizing the brand. The *Hygrade* brand was a leader in the Quebec hot dog marketplace, possessing a 25 per cent share in that province (eight per cent nationally). The *Shopsy's* brand boasted an eight per cent market share in Ontario (two per cent nationally). All MLF hot dog products were produced at the company's manufacturing facility in Stoney Creek, Ontario. Despite brand distinctions and minor taste differences, there were essentially no major differences in the hot dog products within each price segment. At MLF, the senior marketing director did not have direct authority over, or responsibility for manufacturing.

When interviewing for her current position, Gervin had asked about the origins of regional hot dog branding at MLF. To her surprise, no one in MLF could fully explain why the company had so many regional brands. Some believed it was the result of the company's numerous mergers and acquisitions and the desire to preserve the strength in each new brand that was acquired. Others felt the brand differences could be traced to the different consumer preferences in each region. Notwithstanding these explanations, one of the first things that Gervin noticed about the MLF hot dog portfolio was that often as many as six different MLF brands competed for shelf space in any given retail outlet at the same time.

In 1994, MLF launched *Lean 'n Lite* brand hot dogs. The product was introduced in an effort to meet increasing consumer demands for low-fat food products. The initial launch was very successful and produced strong profit margins for the company. However, sales for *Lean 'n Lite* peaked in 1997, and between 1998 and 2001, sales dropped every year. Many at MLF believed that the decline was the result of growing consumer unwillingness to compromise taste for low fat. However, this belief had not been substantiated with market research. Furthermore, the company was familiar with national consumer research that showed that 70 per cent of consumers were interested in low-fat products with acceptable taste.

In 1999, MLF introduced *Top Dogs* as a national hot dog. The launch was in response to consumer trends that seemed to emphasize healthy and natural food products and ingredients. The all-meat product was designed to appeal to both children and parents, and was initially launched with vitamins and protein added. *Top Dogs* were the first—and only—hot dogs sold in North America that were nutritionally enhanced. The product was launched with a value price of $1.99 per package, and initial consumer demand was strong. However, in the summer of 2000, the price was increased to $2.49, and sales declined noticeably. The perception was that the new price alienated many price-sensitive shoppers. Also, during this period, the formulation for *Top Dogs* was altered several times in an attempt to lower per-unit costs. The result was a product that was priced too high and that, in the minds of many consumers, lacked good taste. By June 2001, *Top Dogs* had captured just 2.8 per cent of the national market (4.6 per cent in Western Canada, 2.6 per cent in Ontario, 2.3 per cent in the Maritimes and 1.7 per cent in Quebec).

Based on the initial success of *Top Dogs*, MLF launched *Beef Dogs* in 2000. The launch was designed to replace the company's existing beef hot dog product called *Maple Leaf All Beef Hot Dogs*. *Beef Dogs* were fortified with calcium and iron. Initial taste tests were positive. However, the product's formulation came under the scrutiny of the Canadian Food Inspection Agency (CFIA), which raised concerns over the sourcing of calcium for *Beef Dogs*. *Beef Dogs* were then reformulated to incorporate a new source of calcium. Several internal taste panels concluded that the newly refor-mulated *Beef Dogs* tasted chalky and somewhat artificial. By June 2001, *Beef Dog* sales were down seven per cent from 2000 levels.

Kelly Gervin

Kelly Gervin had a solid professional marketing management background. Prior to joining the MLF organization, Gervin had been North American director of marketing for Moulinex, a French appliance manufacturer. She had joined Moulinex after gradu-ating from the University of Toronto with a bachelor of science degree in microbiol-ogy. She decided to leave Moulinex after it became apparent that her opportunities for professional growth were stagnating.

Gervin first applied for a job with MLF in 1996 in response to a newspaper ad-vertisement. Always one to embrace a challenge, she jumped at the opportunity to join an organization she could grow with. She initially accepted the position of category manager within Consumer Foods and then spent five years in sales and 18 months in purchasing, where she was presented with the opportunity to take over her cur-rent position as senior marketing director. Reporting directly to the vice-president of marketing, Gervin had responsibility for overseeing all marketing decisions (product, price,[1] promotions, packaging and marketing communications strategies) for Maple Leaf's lines of hot dogs, sliced meats and meat snack products. While success in all categories was critical, hot dogs represented by far the largest portion of the portfolio of products over which Gervin was responsible.

Recent Developments

From 1995 through 1999, MLF went through a period of reorganization of the meats business, refocusing on vertically co-ordinating both its pork and poultry protein value chains. By 2000, Consumer Foods had a new president and vice-president of marketing. The president, Rick Young, had built a very successful career in sales and general management while working within the Maple Leaf Companies. The vice-president, Pat Jacobs, had just arrived at Maple Leaf Consumer Foods, having built a marketing career in the packaged goods industry. During 2000, Young focused on strengthening the management team, while Jacobs concentrated on organizing a strong marketing team. As 2001 approached, it was becoming clear to Young that the team was not coming together, and he began to pay increasing attention to the marketing operations. In 2001, Young came to the conclusion that marketing needed additional changes in leadership. It was through this decision that Gervin arrived in her new role.

In Gervin's mind, the market-share reports that had come to Jacobs' attention unquestionably reflected the lack of stability in the packaged meats group. Although she knew MLF's hot dog business was struggling, she was hoping that additional market analysis and customer survey data would provide her with the information needed to make appropriate decisions. On her first morning as the new marketing director, she was troubled to find many of the data she needed were simply not avail-able. During the late 1990s, considerable research had been carried out on brands culminating with the introduction of *Top Dogs*. But the individual who conducted

---

[1]Pricing responsibility also fell under Category Management, which set price in consultation with Gervin.

this research had since been promoted and transferred out of the IOC. The data were now a couple of years old and had not been updated. In addition, there was essentially no consumer research relating to what drove consumers to buy MLF's hot dog products.

In addition to segment sales numbers and market-share data referred to by Jacobs, Gervin found two notes of interest. One was written by the previous marketing director, suggesting that his group had been working diligently to become the low-cost producer in the value segment. On this matter, Gervin did a couple of quick calculations and realized that they weren't even close to achieving this goal. The second document of interest was a hand-written note from an unidentified source that indicated growing concerns over recent losses in market share in the adult segment. That was it.

To complicate matters, the group did not seem to have a business plan. Being new to the team, Gervin was unsure of the backgrounds, skills and commitments of her direct reports. Also, she could sense that morale was low—not surprising, given the recent declines in market share and changes in staff. Beyond the organizational concerns, MLF hot dogs were having real problems in the marketplace. Earlier in the morning, Gervin had placed a call to a major grocery retailer to get a sense of what that customer thought of MLF's hot dog products. The retailer was surprisingly cool to Gervin and offered the following observation: "MLF has an uncompetitive product portfolio. Quite frankly, some of your hot dogs taste lousy." Gervin had no idea whether these sentiments were shared across all of MLF's retail customers, whether this retailer was dissatisfied for other reasons, or whether the retailer was, in fact, satisfied but was playing games with her to win later concessions on price or service.

In organizing a business plan, Gervin knew that she would have to work within the constraints of the broader Consumer Foods organization. As senior marketing director, she had full profit and loss accountability for hot dogs. But, others in the organization were also responsible for various determinants of profit. For example, the sales team in the field—account managers, directors, and the vice-president of sales for the IOC—were in part measured by hot dog profits. Manufacturing also had a stake in the game. So, while she was responsible for profits, people outside her direct control impacted how far she could go and whether her overall approach would succeed.

Decisions

As soon as Jacobs left her office, Gervin closed the door and put her phone on voice mail. She needed time to think. There was clearly good news and bad news in what she had learned on her first day on the job. The bad news was MLF's hot dog business was a mess in almost every sense of the word, and if not handled deftly, the business could go from bad to worse. The good news was that Gervin felt the business could be turned around and that it had huge up-side potential for growth and profitability. She knew this, and she believed that Jacobs and Young also believed in the huge up-side potential in hot dogs. Reversing the negative trends and moving MLF to a leadership position in the marketplace would have positive spill-over effects on the entire Consumer Foods product line and would almost certainly capture the attention of the broader MLF organization.

As the challenges of turning the hot dog business around were becoming more and more apparent, Gervin recognized the need for short-term "fixes" and a clear strategy for the future. She pulled out a pen and scratched down two questions: (1) Which hot dog segments do we most want to be in? and (2) How are we going to grow the business in these segments?

While these were simple questions, the answers would be much more difficult. As Gervin contemplated her next steps, additional questions came to mind. Should MLF even "make" hot dogs? Gervin was aware that an increasing number of companies like Nike, IBM and Matsushita were contracting all or part of their manufacturing over to others. Should hot dogs be any different? She also wondered whether the fact that MLF was Canada's largest supplier of pork and poultry products should influence a decision on the composition of hot dogs and their overall positioning in the marketplace. Gervin was also uncertain how the positioning of hot dogs might influence other products manufactured and sold by Consumer Foods. For example, how might an emphasis on the value segment affect the sales of branded lunch meats? Finally, she wondered what role brands should play in growing hot dog sales in a chosen segment? Should she emphasize a national brand or brands, and if so, what impact might national branding have on existing regional brands?

The more Gervin thought about the challenges she faced, the more questions came to her mind. She had no idea how to answer them, but she knew that a number of senior executives were waiting to hear what she had to say.

Exhibit 1   Maple Leaf Foods Core 7 Principles

Maple Leaf Foods' broad strategic direction is shaped by the Core 7 strategic principles. Continuously evolving, these seven principles are strongly grounded in the Maple Leaf culture and provide the guiding framework for the planning and execution of the company's corporate and competitive strategies.

1. Build high potential leadership.
2. Focus on markets and categories where we can lead.
3. Develop brand equity.
4. Create customer value with Six Sigma processes and products.
5. Be the lowest-cost producer.
6. Execute with precision and continuous improvement.
7. Think global.

Source: Company files.

Exhibit 2   Canadian Market Share Analysis (as of June 5, 2001)

| Company | Latest 52 Weeks | | | |
	Share in Weight	Share Point Change in weight	$ Share	Share Point Change in $
MLF	19.3	−1.6	22.9	−2.1
Hub Larsen	5.0	−0.1	4.0	0.0
JM Schneider	22.6	2.7	28.2	2.9
Fleetwood	1.4	0.2	2.2	0.3
Freybe	0.8	0.2	1.5	0.3
Grimms	0.6	0.0	1.2	−0.1
Harvest	1.0	0.2	1.4	0.2
Fletchers	1.7	0.0	2.1	0.0
Lafleur	3.6	0.0	3.4	0.1
Lesters	0.4	−0.2	0.4	−0.1
Lilydale	0.2	−0.2	0.4	−0.1
Maple Lodge	4.2	−1.5	2.7	−0.7
Mitchells	3.9	0.8	5.0	1.1
Olymel	1.3	−0.2	1.3	−0.2
Control Label	32.3	−0.3	22.9	−0.2

Source: Company files.

Exhibit 3   Maple Leaf Foods Hot Dog Product Line (segmentation)

	Family (Wieners)	Adult (Franks & Sausages)
Premium (>$3.50)	● Top Dogs Singles (450g)	
Mainstream ($2.50 to $3.50)	● Top Dogs (Reg. & BBQ) ● Lean 'n Lite (Reg. & Beef) ● Beef Dogs ● Shopsy's Beef	● Maple Leaf 100's ● Overlander ● Shopsy's Original Recipe
Value ($1.89 to $2.50)	● Maple Leaf Original (& BBQ) ● Burns (Reg., Beef, & 6+6) ● Hygrade (Reg. & Beef) ● Shopsy's (Reg. & BBQ)	
Economy (<$1.89)	● Control/Private Label	

Source: Company files.

Exhibit 4   Canadian Hot Dog Market Review (as of June 5, 2001)

	Total	Family	Adult
Last 52 Weeks	Category: +2.5% ML: −5.0% JMS: +18.2%	Category: +0.7% ML: +0.7% JMS: +14.5%	Category: +11.2% ML: −44.8% JMS: +35%
Last 12 Weeks	Category: +3.2% ML: −8.8% JMS: +9.6%	Category: +2.6% ML: −4.9% JMS: +10.0%	Category: +1.0% ML: −38.4% JMS: +15.5%
Last 4 Weeks	Category: +4.0% ML: −9.3% JMS: +10.6%	Category: +3.1% ML: −6.5% JMS: +10.4%	Category: −1.0% ML: −30.5% JMS: +16.4%

Source: Company files.

Exhibit 5 Current Brand Share (as of June 5, 2001)

	1998 Volume	Share	1999 Volume	Volume Variance To PY	National Share	Share Variance To PY	2000 Volume	Volume Variance To PY	National Share	Share Variance To PY	2001 LE Volume	Volume Variance To PY	National Share*	Regional Share	National Share Variance To PY
Burns	1,071,903	1.7	1,033,266	-4%	1.5	-0.2	810,295	-22%	1.1	(0.4)	711,491	(0.1)	0.9	3.8	-28%
Hygrade	2,065,039	4.6	2,171,784	5%	4.6	0	2,449,504	13%	5.1	0.5	2,630,840	0.1	5.0	22.5	16%
Lean 'n Lite	588,071	1.1	597,365	2%	1.2	0.1	448,795	-25%	0.9	(0.3)	328,384	(0.3)	0.6		-24%
ML Reg./BBQ	2,917,099	4.9	2,512,953	-14%	3.8	-1.1	2,087,457	-17%	3.7	(0.1)	2,291,438	0.1	3.9		-1%
ML Beef	932,830	1.7	868,634	-7%	1.3	-0.4	798,928	-8%	1.5	0.2	687,283	(0.1)	1.2		-7%
Top Dogs		0	1,467,889		2.6	2.6	1,199,268	-18%	2.6	–	1,243,616	0.0	2.2		-6%
ML 100's	1,019,974	2.4	1,139,581	12%	2.4	0	710,382	-38%	1.5	(0.9)	600,205	(0.2)	1.0		-45%
Top Dogs Singles		0			0		123,572		0.2	0.2	215,655	0.8	0.3		N/A
Overlander	394,373	0.9	470,076	19%	1	0.1	416,278	-11%	0.8	(0.2)	365,957	(0.1)	0.6	2.9	-28%
Shopsy's	2,058,655	3.7	2,230,319	8%	3.5	-0.2	2,154,001	-3%	3.7	0.2	2,255,999	0.1	3.5	9.2	6%
TOTAL	11,047,944	21.4	12,491,867	13%	22.1	0.7	11,198,480	-10%	20.9	(0.8)	11,330,868	0.0	19.3		-5%

Source: Latest 52 weeks, June 2001.

Exhibit 6   Maple Leaf Consumer Foods: Hot Dog Margins

	Projected 2001	Actual 2000
Hot Dog Margins by Category		
Regular	$0.44	$0.56
Adult	0.16	0.37
Beef	0.24	0.27
Better for You	0.60	0.75
Total	0.38	0.59
Hot Dog Margins by Brand		
Maple Leaf Regular	$0.71	$0.92
Maple Leaf 100%'s	0.31	0.47
Maple Leaf Beef Dogs	0.10	0.27
Lean 'n Lite	0.35	0.33
Top Dogs	0.60	0.78
Overlander	(0.14)	0.20
Hygrade	0.23	0.20
Burns	(0.14)	0.23
Shopsy's	0.43	0.50
Total	0.39	0.49

GP – = Gross Profit

Exhibit 7   TL Wieners—National Tonnage Trends

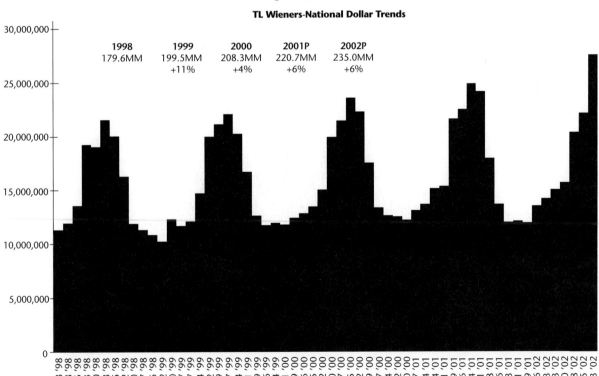

TL Wieners-National Dollar Trends

1998	1999	2000	2001P	2002P
179.6MM	199.5MM	208.3MM	220.7MM	235.0MM
	+11%	+4%	+6%	+6%

Source: Company files.

Case 14

Ganong Bros. Limited

On March 30, 1995, David Ganong, president of Ganong Bros. Limited (GBL), walked out of the annual board meeting gravely concerned. Ganong Bros. Limited was a small, private family confectionery firm in St. Stephen, New Brunswick, with a wide variety of sugar confectionery and chocolate product lines. The board of directors had just reviewed the year-end financial statements, which essentially showed two consecutive years of financial losses. The board had pressed Ganong hard for a solution and had given him six weeks to return with a recommendation that would restore the company to profitability. The board had also challenged Ganong to develop a growth plan that would increase company revenues by 50 per cent. Furthermore, this growth was required to take place above and beyond changes that were made to the main business lines, and was to be driven by business models, products or services that were not currently considered to be part of the core business.

THE CONFECTIONERY INDUSTRY IN CANADA[1]

The confectionery industry was divided into sugar confectionery, chocolates and other cocoa-based products, and chewing gum. The major products in Canada consisted of chocolate bars (34 per cent), boxed and bulk chocolates (28 per cent), hard and soft candies (18 per cent), gum (15 per cent), and other products (five per cent). Most Canadian confectionery goods were produced in Ontario, accounting for 67 per cent of industry employment and 65 per cent of shipments; Quebec followed closely behind.

Richard Ivey School of Business
The University of Western Ontario

Vanessa M. Strike prepared this case under the supervision of Professor Eric Morse solely to provide material for class discussion. The authors do not intend to illustrate either effective or ineffective handling of a managerial situation. The authors may have disguised certain names and other identifying information to protect confidentiality.

Ivey Management Services prohibits any form of reproduction, storage or transmittal without its written permission. This material is not covered under authorization from CanCopy or any reproduction rights organization. To order copies or request permission to reproduce materials, contact Ivey Publishing, Ivey Management Services, c/o Richard Ivey School of Business, The University of Western Ontario, London, Ontario, Canada, N6A 3K7; phone (519) 661-3208; fax (519) 661-3882; e-mail cases@ivey.uwo.ca.

Copyright © 2004, Ivey Management Services   Version: (A) 2005-06-14

---

[1]Industry, Science and Technology Canada; Agriculture and Agri-Food Canada.

Profits tended to be higher in the sugar confectionery industry than in the chocolate industry. Furthermore, return on sales in the chocolate bar industry was less in Canada than in the United States. Canada was the only country in which the four major multinational chocolate bar companies, all essentially equal in size, co-existed in the same market. The intensely competitive market conditions caused by this unique situation kept profits low. In addition, the demand for many domestic confectionery products had decreased recently, due to a lower proportion of children in Canada and to a growing number of health-conscious Canadians; conversely, exports showed a slight increase.

Production facilities ranged in size from small one- and two-person operations to several plants with more than 1,000 employees at each plant. Operations with fewer than 20 employees accounted for 70 per cent of total establishments, but only five per cent of the industry's employment and three per cent of shipments. About 52 per cent of total industry employment was shared among 15 per cent of the firms that contributed 85 per cent of total shipments. Approximately 44 per cent of all products sold at retail made their way from the manufacturers to the final outlets through wholesale distributors. Most of the rest was sold directly to retail stores.

It was estimated that the industry operated at about 75 per cent of production capacity, in large part because specialized equipment was used only for seasonal product lines. Managing production, full-time employees, inventory, marketing and cash flow could thus be particularly challenging for smaller firms.

THE CHANGING CANADIAN ENVIRONMENT

The industry in Canada originally consisted mainly of independents, but in the late 1980s, consolidation led to greater concentration of market shares, resulting in the increased plant efficiencies necessary to compete internationally. There were still several large independent firms but their numbers were dwindling. Many brand-name acquisitions were also being made by American parent firms. These acquisitions were not meant to build international distribution or gain market share, but they provided a way for multinationals to prevent the erosion of their domestic market share.

There were two additional main issues facing confectionery firms in the late 1980s. The first one was free trade. Prior to free trade the industry was protected behind a tariff wall. Canadian firms had protection from confectioneries coming into the country. Some of the product lines had tariffs as high as 15 per cent and Canadian firms going into the United States faced tariffs as low as five per cent to 7.5 per cent; with free trade the Canadian industry lost this tariff differential.

The second issue was the belief that Canadian firms would find it difficult to penetrate the U.S. market. Canadian plants typically faced scale disadvantages compared with U.S. and European firms; they were smaller, had less capacity and served smaller markets. As a result, their unit costs of production were higher. Even if Canadian firms were able to penetrate the U.S. market, they often did not have the capacity to cope with orders of the magnitude that the market dictated.

In the late 1980s, the growth of retail gourmet candy shops, such as Laura Secord, pointed to a consumer trend toward purchasing high-quality, specialty products at premium prices. While many shops sold imported merchandise, they would also sell high-quality domestic products. The industry began to adapt to the more open global trading environment through a series of rationalizations that resulted in more efficient and specialized operations.

By 1994, there were 87 confectionery plants in Canada that employed almost 9,500 people and manufactured products worth more than $1.5 billion. Approximately $400 million of these were exported outside of Canada, and $540 million worth of confectionery products were imported into Canada, mainly from the United States and Europe. Foreign ownership of the industry was high, as multinationals had a major position in the industry. Approximately 60 per cent of industry shipments were accounted for by foreign-controlled enterprises located in Canada, and the number was growing.

THE CHOCOLATE GANONGS

Ganong Bros. Limited was founded in 1873 by two brothers in St. Stephen, New Brunswick (Exhibit 1). The town, situated on the U.S. border, had a population of approximately 5,000 people and was officially named "Canada's Chocolate Town."

GBL was Canada's oldest confectionery company. It had invented the widely imitated chicken bone—a cinnamon-flavored, pink, hard candy jacket over a chocolate centre—and was the first company in Canada to make lollipops using butchers' wooden skewers. It had invented the first five-cent chocolate nut bar in North America (originally made to take along on fishing trips), and it was the first in Canada to sell Valentine heart boxes. All GBL products were made with great professional care using only the finest ingredients.

GBL was a small company compared to the international giants, but it had done a good job of becoming "Canadian competitive." It had built a name for itself in boxed chocolates, competing with similar Canadian firms such as Moirs, Laura Secord, Smiles and Chuckles, Neilson and Lowney. GBL maintained its traditional regional markets through local allegiances and seasonal products; for example, the firm enjoyed a 30 per cent market share for its Valentine's Day chocolates in heart-shaped boxes. Yet, although GBL was a strong player in boxed chocolates in Atlantic Canada, it was a fringe player in other product lines.

PRIVATE OWNERSHIP

GBL had survived four generations remaining a private, family firm. Private ownership was important to GBL as it ensured that they could remain committed to its community and employees, it provided them with the ability to make long-term decisions, and it avoided the time investment of a public company. The firm's success in large part was due to its unique business ethic, where the commitment to both the community and to its workers ranked above all else, including, on occasion, profitability.

As with many family firms in Atlantic Canada, GBL's strong commitment to the community played a significant role in the firm's business decisions over the years. For example, there were several opportunities to sell the firm, but the commitment to the community and to the employees who worked in the company came first. Historically, in other small towns in Atlantic Canada, when the ownership left the community, the firm eventually left as well, and those from the town employed with the company lost their jobs. The economic benefit to Atlantic Canada provided through the location of head offices in that region could not be overstated.

While GBL was "Canadian competitive," it was not North American competitive. Several years earlier, Nicholas Highfield had expressed concerns for the future of GBL. Highfield was the president of the leading manufacturer and marketer of boxed chocolates and chocolate bars in Canada; he was also the president of the Confectioners Association and knew the industry well. Nicholas had said that GBL was an "anachronism," having lived beyond its time. It was dated, the world had changed, and GBL was too small. He asserted that due to its lack of critical mass, research and development capabilities, financial capacity and managerial capabilities, GBL was not big enough to compete in the world of global giants.

THE GBL BOARD OF DIRECTORS

For a family firm, GBL had a robust governance process. The board of directors was a strong diverse board consisting of six external members and two family members. Ganong was the only person from the management team on the board, and he reported directly to the board's non-executive chairman. The board approved all business plans, financial statements and compensation. The philosophy for having such a disciplined governance structure came from Arthur Ganong two generations earlier, who said "when ownership and management are the same, you need a board of directors to protect you against yourself; it is important to not get carried away with your own ideas, and the board fills the essential role of providing a sobering second thought." Several of the board members had been selected because they owned and led firms of their own; as a result they were able to provide valuable insights based on their own successes.

DISTRIBUTION

GBL used both its own sales force and independent brokers to sell its chocolate across Canada (see Exhibit 2). In Western Canada, Ontario and the Atlantic Provinces, GBL had its own sales operation with a sales force of 29 personnel. The company employed 10 sales people and two managers in the west, nine sales people and a manager in Ontario, and 10 sales personnel and two managers in Atlantic Canada. Having its own sales force resulted in fixed costs that would be incurred whether sales were doing well or not; these fixed costs averaged about 10 per cent of sales.

In Quebec, GBL used a broker, which resulted in variable costs of approximately five per cent of sales. Typically, brokers, who carried hundreds of lines of products, were most successful with grocery goods. Brokers were less successful, however, with drug-related goods, a category in which chocolates were usually sold. As a result, despite the lower cost of using brokers, there was sometimes hesitancy to use them for confectionery products.

GANONG'S RESPONSE TO CHANGES IN THE ENVIRONMENT

St. Stephen Factory

The series of rationalizations within the industry in the late 1980s resulted in more efficient operations for most large and mid-sized firms. The modernization of competing plants and the establishment of free trade were the key determinants to build a new factory in St. Stephen. GBL felt it needed to make a quantum change and had initially looked at dramatic expansion to the old facility, but it didn't have the long-term growth prospects. In the modern world, the original factory could not compete effectively. The firm required more automation, more buying leverage for supplies and more volume to cover fixed costs. In 1988, GBL began building the new St. Stephen plant, and it moved into the facility in 1990. GBL now had a facility with the potential for expansion and growth and the ability to reduce unit costs so it could compete with the onslaught of U.S. confectioners that would come with free trade.

The near term results of the expansion were modest. GBL had had a very solid box chocolate performance in the 1980s, and felt that it could capture more of the Canadian market based on extrapolating the success of boxed chocolates. While variable costs fell, fixed costs from the new facility were higher, and the company did not build sales as quickly as projected. GBL had also thought there would be an opportunity to capture some of the U.S. market as a result of changes that were taking place in the U.S. confectionery industry. The U.S. market offered potential for specialty products, particularly in large border markets. Unfortunately, GBL was not successful in extracting the customer support it anticipated and it experienced a direct profit loss from the U.S. drive.

Overseas Market

The domestic market exhibited very little real growth in the late 1980s. As a result, GBL realized it needed to become more aggressive in the export market. The company decided to go into partnership with a firm in Thailand that would provide an opening into the growing Asian market. On Halloween Day in 1989, GBL opened the new Bangkok factory, which coincided with the building of the St. Stephen plant.

The Thailand factory produced several products that were brought back to Canada. It also produced chocolates that were exported to the Middle East and Japan, where chocolate imports were increasing and there was a strong demand for Western consumer products. The Thailand operation did well; while it did not create purchasing synergies, it made money. It provided a small amount of royalties and dividends, and accounted for approximately seven per cent of total sales with a four per cent total cost of goods sold.

In conducting business in Asia, the relationship with the partner was critical, and it took time to maintain. Ganong was the primary contact, and he spent significant time traveling to and from Bangkok to nurture the relationship.

Ganong in the 1990s

As GBL entered the mid-1990s, the competitive environment intensified across all lines of business from both U.S. and Canadian producers. GBL employed 207 in the factory and 15 staff. The factory was operating at 50 per cent of capacity, and none of the individual product lines was pushing its capacity limits. As a result, GBL had to apply twice the amount of fixed cost to its products. Overhead costs were making GBL uncompetitive in various markets. For example, jelly beans were only made part of the year, but the fixed costs associated with maintaining the floor space (depreciation, interest and taxes) still had to be paid for the entire year, resulting in slim margins and fixed costs that were high, relative to the competitors. David Ganong wondered if the firm should cut selling prices to try to increase volume or increase prices to try to cover fixed costs.

In total, GBL had 400 lines of product in seven product categories (see Exhibit 3). The firm wanted to use its labor force, equipment and capacity to build volume; consequently it ended up with very broad and diverse product lines. Not all of the lines were profitable, and some were more profitable than others (Exhibit 4). With so many independent lines it was difficult to achieve economies of scale. In addition to its own brands, GBL also made products for private labels. GBL was fairly reactive in this market, providing its services occasionally and only when asked.

ALTERNATIVES

As David Ganong walked out of the meeting, he tried to figure out what his options were, given the board mandate; he recalled some of the strategies board members had previously shared with him, ones that they had used for their own firms. He wasn't sure which ones, if any, made sense for GBL.

Alternative Financing

As a private firm, GBL had limited financial flexibility; the past two years of losses had tapped the financial resources that it required to take the business where it needed to go, and obtaining additional funds was a challenge. In addition, GBL had a covenant with the bank where all of its assets were secured, thus it was difficult to pursue other lines of financing. The firm had hit a crisis point (see Exhibits 5, 6 and 7).

Recently, GBL had been approached by an international chocolate firm who was interested in becoming a partner with a minority position. To accept such an offer was a defensive strategy, a "rear guard action," but Ganong felt they had their back in the corner. He thought this option may be feasible as the company could keep the business in St. Stephen and build the firm, while establishing an umbilical cord for the resources it lacked. Ganong's one concern was whether the partner would continue to be satisfied with a minority position. He had seen too often the detrimental results on the community when a family firm was purchased by an outsider, and he was wary of such offers.

Contract Packs

One of the board members had explained how he had built his business by focusing on contractual business lines. These contract packs were with firms who required a reliable source of supply that would meet certain specifications for a particular product. In return for adhering to such specific terms, these firms would sign a long-term contract that allowed the supplying firm to obtain the financing required to purchase the necessary specialized manufacturing equipment and raw materials. Such arrangements were very common in the auto industry. For example, Ford would sign a long-term contract with a car-part supplier to have that firm manufacture parts that met Ford's specific requirements.

Private Labels

The management team had also explored the possibility of becoming more proactive in the private label sector as they felt the private label trend would grow in Canada. Private label products, also known as in-house or store brands, were products that carried a store's name as its brand or another name owned by the store, where the selling prices were relatively lower. For example, Loblaw's private label, President's Choice, produced by George Weston Ltd., accounted for 80 per cent ($23 billion) of Weston's sales.

Private labels offered wide product lines, including budget, value and premium products. The market for private-label foods was driven both by a desire on the part of retailers to increase their profit margins and by consumer demand for good quality foods at prices lower than those of brand-name products. Retailers retained a greater portion of the margin for private-label products than for brand-name products. This increased gross margin allowed them to pass on savings to their customers, who typically saved from 10 per cent to 25 per cent.

For the manufacturer, private labels provided an opportunity for increased volume and limited competition. This ability to deliver high-quality products at a reduced price was due to lower marketing, lower overhead and lower logistical costs. To keep up with private labels, brand names had to make greater marketing efforts and keep introducing new, value-added products.

Moving the Factory

Another option Ganong considered was to move the GBL operations. As the majority of the Canadian population and a large portion of the company's market were located in Ontario, it could move the enterprise and build a new factory to a more central location. Ganong wondered if such a move would help to increase the firm's presence and thereby increase sales.

Consolidation of Manufacturing and Shared Ownership

The previous year, GBL, along with two other confectionery firms, had hired an outside consultant to complete an extensive study on the prospect of consolidating the operations of the three firms. The purpose of the study was to determine which of the firms were the lowest cost producers for their shared product lines, and then to explore the possibility of having the lowest cost producer complete the production runs for all three firms for that particular product. Once produced, the product would be marketed under each separate company name.

A variation of this idea was to go a step further and share the ownership of the confectionery assets that each firm had in common. The three firms would consolidate their candy production and form a new independent company that each would have stake in. While each firm shared product lines with the other firms, they also had their own unique lines. One company, for example, produced biscuits, which the other two did not, and GBL produced chocolate, while the other two did not. The companies would continue with their own independent product lines under their original firm. GBL, for example, would continue to produce chocolate in its own premises and under the Ganong name.

MARCH 30, 1995

Ganong realized he had to convince the board of a solid plan going forward to solve these issues. At the end of the first year of losses, the management team had convinced the board they did not need to change the business model, that they would do a better job of executing the current strategy. The board was losing patience with its ability to pull out of the red. Ganong realized they had to make fundamental changes to the business model to bring the firm back to profitability and to develop a new $10 million block of business. It was already several months into the new fiscal year, and Ganong was unsure of where to go next. The gravity of the results was apparent, and he had committed to get back to the board within six weeks. The leadership of Ganong Bros. Limited in chocolate making went back four generations, and David Ganong wanted to preserve and perpetuate the firm's rich heritage.

As he left the board meeting, Ganong thought back to his conversation with Nicholas Highfield. Highfield's comment on GBL being an "anachronism" had stuck with Ganong over the years. This comment had challenged his fundamental belief system and pushed him to succeed. Until this time, he had proven Highfield wrong, but now the words came back to haunt him as he wondered how their small independent firm, based in the middle of nowhere, could possibly compete among the international giants.

Exhibit 1   St. Stephen, New Brunswick, Head Office Location

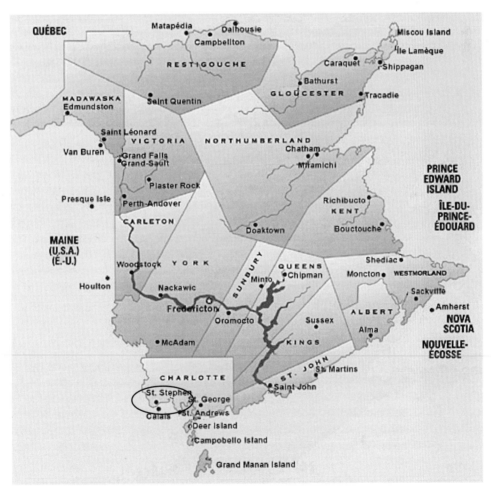

Source: National Geographic Maps, www.nationalgeographic.com/xpeditions/atlas/index.html.

Exhibit 2   Sales Analysis for 1994 (in $000s)

	1994
Ganong Brand Sales	
Atlantic	$ 7,082
Quebec	1,798
Ontario	4,485
Prairies	2,013
British Columbia	980
National Accounts	3,855
Private Label	1,450
Domestic Ganong Sales	$21,663
Export	950
United States	577
Total Ganong Sales	$23,190
Distributor Line Sales	
Atlantic	$ 40
Quebec	3
Ontario	50
Prairies	93
British Columbia	42
Special	39
Private Label	15
Domestic Distributor Line Sales	$ 282
Export	–
United States	–
Total Distributor Line Sales	$ 282
Total Sales	$23,472

Exhibit 3   Description of Product Categories

Packaged Chocolates	Boxed or packaged chocolates; sold as gifts for birthdays, Christmas, Valentine's Day, etc.
Portable Confections	Non-chocolate sugar confection bars sold for less than $1; e.g., mint rolls.
Chocolate Bars	Chocolate pre-packed snack that sold for less than $1.
Cellos	Sugar confectionery such as jelly beans, jujubes, mints packaged in flexible packaging.
Staples	Bulk product.
Fruit Snacks	Portable nutritional snack with real fruit content, generally marketed in the cereal section of grocery stores.
Distributor Lines	Products purchased and resold by Ganong Bros. Limited under another firm's name; these helped to reduce sales cost and allowed the company to employ more sales people.
National Accounts	Accounts with centralized warehousing where the product was shipped to a customer who redistributed it (e.g. Wal-Mart).

Exhibit 4   Parital Income Statement for 1994 (in $000s)

	1994
Sales—Packaged Chocolates	$11,817
COGS	7,326
Gross Margin $	4,491
Gross Margin %	38.0%
Sales—Portable Confections	447
COGS	286
Gross Margin $	161
Gross Margin %	36.0%
Sales—Chocolate Bars	1,056
COGS	542
Gross Margin $	514
Gross Margin %	48.7%
Sales—Cellos	4,804
COGS	3,167
Gross Margin $	1,637
Gross Margin %	34.1%
Sales—Staples	2,485
COGS	1,731
Gross Margin $	754
Gross Margin %	30.3%
Sales—Fruit Snacks	2,580
COGS	1,624
Gross Margin $	956
Gross Margin %	37.1%
Sales—Distributor Lines	283
COGS	249
Gross Margin $	34
Gross Margin %	12.0%
Total Sales	23,472
Total COGS	14,925
Pre-Discount Gross Margin $	8,547
Pre-Discount Gross Margin %	36.4%
Discounts	796
Net Gross Margin $	7,751
Net Gross Margin %	33.0%

Exhibit 5   Partial Balance Sheet (in $000s)

	1994	1993	1992
Current Assets			
Cash	$ 48	$ 21	$ 15
Accounts Receivables	4,263	5,049	4,155
Inventories:			
Raw Materials	2,590	2,254	2,399
Work in Process	245	215	260
Finished Goods	1,581	1,727	1,708
Prepaid Expenses	446	370	477
Total Current Assets	**9,173**	**9,636**	**9,014**
Long Term Assets			
Land & Building—Net	8,583	8,953	9,464
Machinery & Equipment—Net	3,517	3,818	4,065
Notes & Misc. Receivables	71	70	68
Investments In/Due from Affiliates	16	16	16
Other Investments	199	189	189
Deferred Charges (Pension, Startup)	496	513	470
Total Assets	**22,055**	**23,195**	**23,286**
Current Liabilities			
Notes Payable—Bank	1,479	1,478	1,238
Accounts Payable	3,821	3,620	3,920
Income Taxes	203	225	146
Current Portion—LTD	399	422	311
Current Liabilities	**5,902**	**5,745**	**5,615**
Long-term Liabilities			
Long-term Debt	6,236	6,593	7,029
Deferred Government Grants	5,027	5,372	5,663
Deferred Taxes	1,135	1,317	1,097
Total Liabilities	**18,300**	**19,027**	**19,404**
Capital Stock	83	83	83
Retained Earnings	1,463	1,864	1,569
Subordinated Debt	2,209	2,221	2,230
Net Worth	**3,755**	**4,168**	**3,882**
Total Liabilities & Net Worth	**$22,055**	**$23,195**	**$23,286**

Exhibit 6   Key Operating Ratios

Key Operating Ratios	1994	1993	1992	Industry Medians*
Liquidity				
Current Ratio	1.6	1.7	1.6	2.5
Quick Ratio	0.7	0.9	0.7	1.1
Days' Receivables	61 days	71 days	59 days	21 days
Inventory Turnover	3.2	3.3	3.0	4.2
Coverage				
EBIT/Interest	(0.0)	1.2	1.5	9.5
Leverage				
Fixed assets/net worth	3.2	3.1	3.5	0.5
Total debt/net worth	4.9	4.6	5.0	0.6
Operating				
Profit before taxes/net worth	−14.9%	13.3%	9.7%	13.3%
Profit before taxes/ total assets	−2.5%	2.4%	1.6%	7.7%
Net sales/fixed assets	1.8	1.9	1.7	5.4
Net sales/total assets	1.0	1.0	1.0	1.6

* For firms $10 million to $50 million in assets.
Source: Robert Morris Associates Annual Statements

Exhibit 7   Statement of Operations 1992 to 1994 (in $000s)

	1994	1993	1992
Net Sales	22,346	23,803	23,554
Cost of Sales	14,075	13,706	13,182
Gross Profit $	8,271	10,097	10,372
Gross Profit %	37.0%	42.4%	44.0%
Admininstration and Selling Expenses	8,279	9,368	9,239
Operating Profit $	(8)	729	1,133
Operating Profit %	0.0%	3.1%	4.8%
Interest Expense	651	625	770
Other (Income) Expenses—Net*	(98)	(452)	(15)
Net Profit (Loss) Before Taxes	(561)	556	378
Income Taxes	(159)	261	167
Net Profit After Taxes $	(402)	295	211
Net Profit After Taxes %	−1.8%	1.2%	0.9%

* Includes sale of old factory in 1993.

Case 15

Yunnan Baiyao: Traditional Medicine Meets Product/Market Diversification

In 2003, following an introduction through the State Food and Drug Administration of China, 3M Company, a major U.S. multinational corporation, initiated contact with Yunnan Baiyao Group Co., Ltd. (YB) to discuss potential cooperative opportunities in the area of transdermal pharmaceutical products. YB, the namesake of one of its main products, Yunnan Baiyao, was a household brand in China for its unique traditional herbal medicines that were effective in the treatment of open wounds, fractures, contusions and strains. (Hereafter, we refer to the group company as YB and the product as Baiyao.) In recent years, the company had been engaged in a series of corporate reforms and product / market diversification strategies to respond to the sea change in the Chinese pharmaceutical industry and competition at a global level. By 2003, YB was already a vertically integrated, product-diversified group company with an ambition to become an international player.

The proposed cooperation with 3M was an attractive option to YB: it was not only an opportunity for domestic product diversification but also an opportunity for international diversification. YB had been attempting to internationalize its products for some time: an overseas department had been established in 2002, specifically for this purpose. On the other hand, YB had also been considering another option for some time; namely, whether to extend its brand to toothpaste and other healthcare products. YB had to decide which of the two options to pursue and whether it would be feasible to pursue both.

Richard Ivey School of Business
The University of Western Ontario

George Z. Peng wrote this case under the supervision of Professor Paul Beamish solely to provide material for class discussion. The authors do not intend to illustrate either effective or ineffective handling of a managerial situation. The authors may have disguised certain names and other identifying information to protect confidentiality.

THE HISTORY OF YUNNAN BAIYAO: 1902–1998[1]

Stage 1: 1902–1955 (Qu Huanzhang Panacea Period)

In 1902, Baiyao, originally know as Qu Huanzhang Panacea, was formulated from various natural herbs by Qu Huanzhang, a highly respected practitioner of Chinese medicine. However, he did not develop the medicine solely on his own. Some stories say that he benefited from the Yi, Hani and Yao ethnic minority medicine in Yunnan Province; while others say that he may have developed his herbal formula based on the traditional medicines used by the trading caravans that traveled on the Tea and Horse Caravan Road (known in Chinese as *Chamadao*), an ancient trade route that connected Southwest China and India, and functioned as the so-called Silk Road of Southwest China.

Baiyao was destined, to a certain degree, to be formulated in Yunnan Province, a mountainous area characterized by high and dangerous terrain. In old times, it had been routine for local people to suffer injuries, fractures, contusions and strains from work or travel. Local people looked for ways to cure injuries, and herbal medicine was the usual solution. In addition, Yunnan Province was famous for its herbal diversity: 6,500 out of the 11,000 medicinal herbs in China were grown there, and many were unique to Yunnan Province. The combination of the need for medicine and the herbal diversity resulted in a higher likelihood of the formulation of herbal medicines in Yunnan Province.

When Baiyao was first formulated, it was known as Qu Huanzhang Panacea. The name Baiyao translates as white powder, referring to the original form of the product. Because of its effectiveness in the treatment of open wounds, muscular strains, bruising and arthritis, and its ability to invigorate blood circulation, this formulation gained rapid fame. It became a household name, initially in Yunnan Province and then throughout the rest of China. In 1916, the Chinese Nationalist government allowed the public sale of the product. By the 1930s, it could be found, in its powder form, on the shelves of many Chinese homes.

In 1937, Qu, the creator of the formulation, donated 30,000 bottles of Baiyao to the Chinese army, who were fighting the Japanese in the Anti-Japanese War. The medical power of Baiyao was further spread through word of mouth of the soldiers. The product proved so effective that from that time on, it became part of the first-aid kit of the Chinese armed forces.

The formula and manufacturing process of Baiyao had been kept secret since its formulation in 1902. Because of his refusal to reveal the formula of Baiyao, Qu was imprisoned and tortured by the then ruling party, the Chinese Nationalist government. Before his death in captivity in 1938, at the age of 58, he secretly passed the details of the formula and manufacturing process over to his wife, Miao Lanying. In order to guard the formula, she closed down their shops and ceased the production of Baiyao.

On the fall of the Chinese Nationalist government in 1949, the new government led by the Chinese Communist Party assisted Miao Lanying in re-establishing the business. She was so grateful for this assistance that, on her death, she left the formula and manufacturing process to the government.

---

[1] Please refer to Exhibit 1, Yunnan Baiyao Timeline.

Stage 2: 1956–1992 (Baiyao Period)

After Miao Lanying transferred the formula and manufacturing process to the government in 1955, the production of Baiyao was started by Kunming Pharmaceutical Factory under the original name of Qu Huanzhang Panacea. One year later, the name was changed to Baiyao, and the formula and the manufacturing process were listed as a top national secret and placed under national protection. At that time, Baiyao was of military importance due to the adverse international environment China was facing. Baiyao was so highly guarded and regarded by the central government that, in 1970, former premier Zhou En-lai himself gave instructions that efforts should be made "to construct a specialized pharmaceutical factory to expand the production; to establish research institutes to deepen the research into Baiyao; and to establish a herb planting base for Baiyao."

Subsequently, in 1971, Yunnan Baiyao Pharmaceutical Factory, the predecessor of the current YB, was established on the foundation of the fifth workshop of Kunming Pharmaceutical Factory. Since then, Baiyao had seen rapid development in its mass production, research and application.

Yunnan Baiyao Pharmaceutical Factory carried out a series of product development and product diversification moves. Various forms of Baiyao and related products were developed and mass produced:

- 1975: Baiyao Capsule (for internal use)
- 1984: Baiyao Plaster and Baiyao Tincture
- 1985: Gong Xue Ning Capsule (for vaginal bleeding)
- 1992: Baiyao Aerosol

In the meantime, the active ingredients of Baiyao and its source herbs had been identified, and their pharmacologic activity had been determined. This stage also saw the use of Baiyao in the treatment of a wider spectrum of diseases. Baiyao moved from being an herbal medicine with narrow usage in caring for wounds and injuries to a wide-spectrum medical product line. Baiyao products were widely used in caring for more than 300 applications in areas such as internal medicine, gynecology, pediatrics and dermatology.

Stage 3: 1993–1998

In 1993, Yunnan Baiyao Pharmaceutical Factory was reformed toward a modern enterprise system through the establishment of Yunnan Baiyao Limited Co., which was listed on the Shenzhen Securities Exchange through a successful A-Share initial public offering. This public listing not only brought in much needed funds for technological upgrading, but it also standardized operations and management practices, which were prerequisites for a public company.

Despite efforts to modernize Yunnan Baiyao Pharmaceutical Factory, problems hindered its development. One of the most serious problems was the lack of unified branding. Because of historical reasons, Baiyao was also produced by three other companies in Wenshan, Dali and Lijiang under different trademarks. As a result, there was a vicious price competition that weakened the brand reputation of Baiyao as a whole. Companies sacrificed product quality to lower costs and gain market share, resulting in over-production and predatory use of wild herbal resources.

To strengthen the brand reputation of Baiyao, Yunnan Baiyao Limited Co. and the other three producers were integrated into Yunnan Baiyao Group Co. (YB) through joint shareholding in 1996. Through what was referred to as the five U's—unified production planning, unified permit number, unified trademark, unified quality standards and unified sales management—YB became the sole producer of Baiyao and the sole proprietor of intellectual property related to Baiyao. Production was reduced from 50 million vials/packages to 20 million vials/packages, alleviating the pressure on the wild herbal resources. The acquisition of the other three companies also served a product diversification purpose because all of the other three companies also marketed a series of other products.

The unified sales management approach also enhanced product standardization and market concentration, transforming the original price competition into a competition based on quality, brand and service. As a result, the brand image and market price of Baiyao recovered quickly. Baiyao subsequently raised the prices of Baiyao products several times to position them as quality products. The five U's also effectively curbed the counterfeiting of Baiyao, and the interest of customers was better protected.

During this period, YB took the first step in its corporate strategy by adopting both a modern enterprise system and a unified management of production and branding. The integration of the companies also diversified YB's products. This stage laid the foundation for the subsequent corporate strategies in product and market dimensions. It should be noted that even though YB was trying to reform toward a modern enterprise system and move toward a market-oriented economy, the strategic moves made during this period were basically directed by the government. It was the government that pushed for the integration of the Baiyao-producing companies and the production of Baiyao by a single company. Without government support, YB could not have repeatedly raised the prices of Baiyao products amid generally declining drug prices as a result of intensified competition and China's rapid transition toward market economy.

THE REFORM, RESTRUCTURING AND DIVERSIFICATION OF YUNNAN BAIYAO: 1999–2003

Year 1999 (Share Diversification, Vertical Integration and Product Diversification)

In 1999, the Chinese pharmaceutical industry entered an era of drastic transition. The requirements of Good Manufacturing Practices (GMP) and Good Supply Practices (GSP) certification resulted in further industry concentration. Several diversified and vertically integrated pharmaceutical companies had appeared, shaping the industry landscape. Firms faced the fact that they needed to either grow bigger through integration and diversification or they would be eliminated through competition.

Regardless of Baiyao's reputation and various efforts made in the past to move YB toward a market-oriented economy, by 1999, YB was still basically a state-owned company. Its resources were mainly allocated to production, and its sales department consisted of only a dozen staff members waiting for customers to come. YB could not respond to the rapidly changing market situation. As a consequence, revenue in 1998 dropped RMB 8 million compared with the previous year. In 1999, the chief executive officer (CEO) of YB was replaced by Wang Minghui.

Under Wang's leadership, YB underwent a series of reforms, restructurings and strategic moves toward product and market diversification. In 1999, Hongta Group became YB's second largest shareholder, and as a result, YB diversified its share structure. YB also acquired Yunnan Pharmaceutical Trading Co. and Tian Zi Hong Pharmaceutical Co. Through the distribution channels of the former, YB achieved forward vertical integration into distribution; while through the latter, YB diversified its offerings into the production of decocted (concentrated) pieces. These simultaneous activities moved YB in the direction of becoming a diversified and vertically integrated player in the Chinese pharmaceutical industry.

In the same year, YB established its e-Commerce Co. Ltd. to build its nationwide sales network. Previously, YB had a negligible sales force and its resources were mainly allocated to production, like many other state-owned companies. Because Wang had a background in sales, he saw the importance of a sales network during a time when China was moving toward a market economy. YB used the e-Commerce Co. Ltd. as a platform on which to build its sales offices across the country. The e-Commerce Co. Ltd. also served as a platform for internal entrepreneurship: YB regarded the 800-plus salespersons as internal entrepreneurs who used YB's e-commerce platform to set up sales offices in an entrepreneurial spirit. These salespersons were hired based on competition and were motivated to compete with each other through a benchmarked incentive plan on a yearly basis. With the establishment of a sales network, YB allocated more resources to marketing, which played a decisive role in YB's competition with other pharmaceutical companies.

Year 2000 (Research & Development Reforms)

In 2000, YB also made efforts to build its research and development (R&D) system, based on the belief that a competitive enterprise must have strong R&D capabilities. In September, YB established a Medicinal Herb Research Institute (MHRI) by integrating its three originally independent R&D entities: the National Postdoctoral Research Station, the Technology Center and the Research Institute. The integration of the originally dispersed units pooled their resources and laid the foundation for future R&D to exploit synergy and scale.

With the establishment of MHRI, YB also adopted new ways of R&D operation, including the Chief Scientist System and the R&D Cooperative System. The Chief Scientist System motivated scientists by linking their income to their scientific output. A series of awards was set up for the purpose of motivating scientists and spurring their creativity, including the stage output award, the subproject award, the risk reduction award for timely termination of unfruitful projects, the cost reduction award, the project early / on-time delivery award, etc. Chief scientists and their team members who made significant R&D contribution would be given a substantial reward. Through the R&D Cooperative System, YB in fact established a society-wide and open R&D system, maximally using society-wide resources and successfully implementing a "brain-borrowing" strategy. YB cooperated with a number of universities and research institutes in a series of cooperative agreements. A number of national experts were hired by YB to serve as chief scientists. Through new ways of R&D operation, YB solved more than 20 technical problems and developed a series of new products.

Year 2001 (Organizational Restructuring and Management Reform)

On the foundation of achievements made in 1999 and 2000 in marketing and R&D reform, YB forged ahead to carry out fundamental organizational restructuring in 2001. First, YB streamlined its structure by reducing the number of its departments. Functional departments with overlapping functions were either eliminated or merged, and administrative departments were reduced. In all, the number of departments was reduced from 17 to 12, resulting in higher functional and administrative efficiency.

Secondly, YB underwent drastic management reform by adopting a compensation point system, an enterprise resource planning (ERP) system and a production order system. Through cooperation with Tsinghua University, YB clarified 158 jobs by assigning compensation points for each job position, based on detailed job descriptions. YB broke away from the traditional egalitarian compensation system and made a transition toward a skills-based and contribution-based compensation system. YB also established eight cost centers and implemented an ERP system to carry out cost and benefit accounting for these cost centers. The ERP system was also linked to the compensation point system to serve the purpose of employee compensation accounting. The adoption of ERP and the compensation point system greatly motivated employees on a fair basis.

Traditionally, YB had been focused on production and lacked cost and market competition awareness. As a result, the production was not oriented toward market demand, which greatly affected YB's core competence and competitiveness, resulting in high costs, low product quality, and low levels of flexibility and agility in production. To change this passive situation, YB decided to adopt a production order system. Through this system, the production became demand-oriented, resulting in better use of resources, cost reduction and production flexibility. The production order system was subsequently introduced in YB in 2003.

In 2001, YB also established Shanghai Yunnan Baiyao Transdermal Technology Ltd. to develop the market for Baiyao Bandage and Baiyao Plaster. In June 2001, Baiyao Bandage appeared on the market and was an immediate success. In this year, YB also made another product diversification move by bringing to market a hemorrhoid ointment. YB succeeded again in extending its brand by leveraging its brand reputation.

Year 2002 (100-Year Anniversary and a New Strategy)

The year 2002 was significant for YB. Not only was it YB's 100-year anniversary, it was also the first year since China had been accepted as a member of the World Trade Organization (WTO). The end of 100 years was a convenient moment to take stock. Looking back, the leadership felt that the progress YB had made was remarkable; and the progress made in the last three years since the current leadership took office had occurred in leaps and bounds. The combination of a rapidly changing market situation and the mission falling upon YB leadership to carry the firm into a new century called for new strategies.

However, YB was facing some problems. The first was how to respond to the significant changes in the Chinese pharmaceutical industry. The reform of the Chinese pharmaceutical industry and China's accession to the WTO brought about drastic changes in the competitive landscape. Several diversified and vertically integrated pharmaceutical companies had appeared, shaping the industry landscape. Firms faced the decision to either grow bigger through integration and diversification or be eliminated through competition. YB had been essentially a producer of a medicine for the treatment of minor injuries. It would become a minor niche player if it did not follow a diversification and integration strategy. With the opening up of the Chinese market to world competition, YB either had to become a world brand or it would fade out from competition. Even though YB had pursued bold corporate strategies in the past decade, more needed to be done to keep up with global competition.

Secondly, many of YB's products had reached or were reaching maturity. To grow this traditional medicine firm, YB had to look for new growth areas; diversification of its products and markets and vertical integration could help YB extend its life cycle and stabilize its profits.

To respond to these challenges, YB established a series of strategies titled "one core and four growth areas." The "one core" referred to the headquarters of YB, its group companies (the other three production-oriented companies acquired in 1996) and its sales network, which was basically what YB had in 2002. The four growth areas—the industrialization of herbal resources, the industrialization of research and development, vertical integration and internationalization—are described below.

Growth Area 1: The Industrialization of Herbal Resources

The market for herbs and decocting pieces had been growing at an annual rate of 20 per cent both for the domestic market and the export market. Yunnan Province was one of main source of herbs with its more than 6,500 species. However, the potential of rich herbal resources was not exploited in a managed way. There was no quality assurance system in place. Herbal resources products originating from Yunnan Province lacked not only bioactivity fingerprint standards, which ensured consistency in the identification, chemical separation, and quality monitoring of the characteristic chemical substances of the herbs, but also branding and product quantity control. This lack of standards and quality control greatly affected the profitability of these herbal resources.

YB believed that it could benefit from Yunnan's rich herbal resources by industrializing the herbal resources. To achieve this goal, YB decided to set up an herb planting base and establish a quality assurance system and bioactivity fingerprint standards. The herb planting base could be used as a platform upon which herbal resources could be industrialized based on established quality systems and fingerprint standards. Herbs would be purchased from farmers through a system of purchase orders. YB could help farmers plant herbs in quantity according to the established quality standards. YB would then use its brand and sales network to market the herbal resources, ensuring consistent quality, controlled quantity and compliance with the fingerprint standards.

Growth Area 2: The Industrialization of Research and Development

The development of new medicines had become the rule of the game in the international pharmaceutical industry. In addition, the transfer of intellectual property rights and new medicine certificates was more profitable than producing and selling pharmaceutical products themselves. For example, the annual net profit of the National Institute of Health (NIH), a U.S. medical research institute, was approximately US$12 billion. YB aspired to become a big player in pharmaceutical research by adopting similar approaches to those of NIH. These approaches included research contracts, grants and findings. YB's research institute could serve as a platform for industrializing R&D.

YB had already become a target of those who had herbal know-how for potential cooperation and knowledge transfer. By leveraging its reputation into research, YB believed that further growth could be expected.

Growth Area 3: Vertical Integration into Distribution through the Operation of Chain Stores

With competition intensifying as a result of the drastic changes in the Chinese pharmaceutical industry, many companies diversified into distribution. Even though YB had made similar moves by acquiring Yunnan Pharmaceutical Trading Co. in the past, the distribution channels so obtained were not fine-grained and extensive. YB felt the need to strengthen its foothold in Yunnan Province by establishing Baiyao Da Yao Fang (a drugstore chain) to cover the whole province.

Growth Area 4: Internationalization

Even though Baiyao was well-known in China and in Singapore, Malaysia, Thailand and Vietnam, where there were visible overseas Chinese communities, Baiyao was not known to customers in other countries, especially those in the two biggest markets, the European Union (EU) and North America. To ultimately become a world player, YB had to internationalize its products. Therefore, YB saw internationalization as another growth area.

Once its strategies had been determined, YB was aggressive in pursuing them. In 2002, the Wuding Traditional Chinese Herb Planting Base was set up for the planting and domestication of wild herbs. The planting base later obtained a Good Agricultural Practices (GAP) certificate. On the foundation of the Wuding base, the industrialization process of wild herbal resources was sped up. Under the auspices of state funding, two companies, Traditional Chinese Herbal Seed Breeding Company and Yunnan Baiyao State Key Laboratory, were established that attracted a group of top scientists and were key in the construction of a planting base that met the Good Laboratory Practice (GLP) standards. YB hoped that through quality assurance it could offer the domestic and international markets safe, reliable and consistent herbal products, thus laying the foundation for the modernization and internationalization of traditional Chinese herbal medicine.

Even though the Wuding planting base was set up to industrialize herbal resources, there was another reason for YB to backward integrate into herbal planting. Throughout the past couple of decades, the herbs from which Baiyao was produced had been exploited without regulation. Some herbal medicine species were very rare, and due to increasing demand in alternative treatment, they were getting closer to extinction. Because of over-exploitation, it became questionable whether the supply of herbal sources could keep pace with YB's growth. To a certain degree, YB's move in this direction was a necessity.

The backward integration also was motivated by the associative branding effect for YB because the herbal resources produced through the planting base would be exported using the YB brand name. YB hoped that through the export of good quality herbs it could build its reputation overseas for its pharmaceutical products.

Also in 2002, Baiyao Da Yao Fang Ltd. (a drugstore chain) was established, and it had since been making smooth progress. YB also integrated the operations of the drugstore chain and Yunnan Pharmaceutical Trading Co. because the two strategies shared the same goal of forward vertical integration and had many synergies.

The moves YB made in 2002 were all strategic in nature. Both the Wuding Planting Base and the Baiyao Da Yao Fang drugstore chain were long-term investments because they would not contribute to YB's profit within the first five years after their establishment.

In summary, during the 1999 to 2002 period, YB had been pursuing systematic reform, restructuring, vertical integration and diversification strategies to modernize the state-owned enterprise. This period coincided with the assumption of office by Wang Minghui. With these strategic moves, YB had been seeing dramatic improvement in its performance (see Exhibits 2, 3 and 4).

THE OPTION OF MARKET AND PRODUCT DIVERSIFICATION: THE 3M PROPOSAL

Consistent with the "one core and four growth areas" strategy, YB had been exploring the possibilities of overseas markets. In 2002, the Yunnan Baiyao Overseas Department was set up to develop international markets. The goal of the department was to solidify Yunnan Baiyao's markets in Southeast Asia and to develop markets in the United States, the European Union and Japan.

YB wasted no time in its internationalization strategy. In 2003, YB registered and received approval from Vietnam and Thailand authorities to market its products. YB adopted the path of least resistance by first exploring geographic regions of low cultural distance and low entry barriers. The company was deliberating about how to enter the United States, the European Union and Japan, and at this juncture, 3M proposed to cooperate with YB in the area of transdermal products. YB had to decide whether to pursue this opportunity.

3M Company

3M Company (NYSE: MMM; formerly Minnesota Mining and Manufacturing Company until 2002) was founded at Two Harbors, Minnesota, in 1902. The company had since become a gigantic multinational enterprise with a worldwide presence. By 2003, 3M was one of the 30 companies included in the Dow Jones Industrial Average, and was ranked number 110 on the 2003 Fortune 500 listing. The company had 132 plants and more than 67,000 employees around the world, with sales offices in more than 200 countries.

Out of 3M's more than a dozen core competencies, adhesives was one of its major successes. Over the years, 3M had leveraged its competencies in adhesives technologies to many industries, including health care, automotive, construction and telecommunications. In health care, 3M's adhesive technology was mainly used in transdermal drug delivery systems. 3M's Drug Delivery Systems Division was a global leader in transdermal drug delivery with a 30-year proven track record, and more than 80 per cent of the transdermal drug delivery products in the United States contain a 3M transdermal component. The Drug Delivery Systems Division utilized nearly 50 per cent of the 3M corporate core technologies to meet customer needs. Transdermal products developed and manufactured by 3M were registered in more than 60 countries.

3M's technology in transdermal delivery systems offered many advantages over other products: they were breathable adhesives, offered pain-free removability and were waterproof. 3M solutions to transdermal delivery were also hypo-allergenic, thus reducing skin irritation.

3M's transdermal technologies could be utilized by pharmaceutical and biotech companies by forming partnerships with 3M. 3M Drug Delivery Systems technology, product development, global regulatory expertise and commercial manufacturing provided pharmaceutical and biotech companies with differentiated products, speed to market and increased probability of technical and commercial success. For example, 3M had been involved in the development and manufacturing of the following products:

- Minitran™ ([nitroglycerin] transdermal delivery system)[2]
- Climara® (estradiol transdermal system)[3]
- ClimaraPro® (estradiol transdermal system)[4]
- Menostar® (estradiol-levonorgestrel transdermal system)[5]

YB's Experiments with Transdermal Products

The History of Chinese Traditional Transdermal Products

Transdermal drug delivery through a plaster (or plaster bandage) was an important branch of traditional Chinese medicine. The Chinese term for plaster, Bo Tie, appeared in the year 682 for the first time in Sun Si-Miao's *Thousand Golden Prescriptions*, an important medical book containing the main medical achievements before the Tang dynasty [AD 618–907]. In later dynasties, the application of plasters was further developed and perfected with the development in acupuncture and moxibustion (a therapy using moxa, or mugwort herb). According to Chinese medical theory, plasters were applied on acupoints for better curative effect. There were many plaster recipes collected in the famous Ming Dynasty book, *Compendium of Materia Medica* (or Great Pharmacopoeia), compiled by Li Shi-Zhen in 1578.

The application of plasters culminated in Qing Dynasty with the publication of *Li Yue Pian Wen* in 1864. Written by Wu Shi-Ji, this book focused on the cutaneous and external applications of various plasters. Wu Shi-Ji, regarded as the master of plasters, used plaster as the main way of drug delivery for most diseases and achieved significant curative effects on patients. Many Chinese doctors learned from his masterpiece of plasters and spread the use of plasters across China.

As a result, plasters were a well accepted form of medicine in China. In an online survey, 99 per cent of respondents answered that they had used plasters before. However, due to the disadvantages of traditional rubber adhesive plasters and the inroads of Western medicine, Chinese plaster medicine had been under pressure and many thought plasters were a so-called sunset form of treatment. Plasters occupied a very small share in the Chinese pharmaceutical market, and market competition of plaster products was not intense. Within the small market share of plasters in the whole pharmaceutical industry, the share occupied by Baiyao plasters was almost negligible.

However, plasters, as a medium of transdermal drug delivery, were still an attractive alternative drug delivery. Compared to oral medication and hypodermal injection, transdermal drug delivery had the advantage of direct application to the afflicted areas,

---

[2] Minitran™ is a trademark of 3M Company.
[3] Climara® is a registered trademark of Schering AG.
[4] Climara Pro® is a registered trademark of Schering AG
[5] Menostar® is a registered trademark of Berlex Laboratories.

thus avoiding both the degradation of medicine in the digestive tract and toxic effects on the liver. The apprehensions people held about plasters were largely caused by non-medicinal components, such as skin allergies to the adhesives, the adhesive's lack of breathability, the pain associated with removing the adhesive from the skin and the failure of the adhesives when they became wet. If these disadvantages could be overcome with technological advances, more and more people would embrace plasters. An online survey showed that 95 per cent of respondents thought that plasters had huge market potential.

YB's History in Transdermal Products

YB's interest in diversifying into transdermal products dated back to 1997, when a product called Baiyao Bandage (a product similar to Band-Aid) was developed in the laboratory. Seeing the great market potential of transdermal products, Shanghai Yunnan Baiyao Transdermal Technology Ltd. was consequently established in 2001, charged with the market development for Baiyao Bandage and Baiyao Plaster. In the beginning, the company adopted the concept of a virtual firm, with only an investment of RMB 5 million and three persons from Yunnan Baiyao: one responsible for general management, one responsible for sales and the third responsible for technology.

Prior to Baiyao Bandage, the Chinese bandage market had been monopolized by Johnson & Johnson. To compete with such a strong competitor, speed and strategy were needed. If Yunnan Baiyao had adopted its traditional way of doing business by sequentially acquiring land, constructing production workshops and purchasing production facilities, it would have taken at least two years for Baiyao Bandage to go to market. By outsourcing the production of Baiyao Bandage to a French firm, Yunnan was able to not only bring Baiyao Bandage to market within only three months but also to concentrate on brand and market development.

In June 2001, Baiyao Bandage appeared on the market and was an immediate success. In June alone, YB achieved sales of RMB 4 million and a profit of RMB 1.88 million. From June to December, YB realized sales revenue of RMB 30 million. In only a short time, Baiyao Bandage became the most formidable competitor of Band-Aid. This accomplishment was attained not only because YB had adopted a strategy of using second-grade cities to encircle first-grade cities to avoid direct market competition but more importantly because YB had a deep grassroots brand image. In addition, Baiyao Bandage came in two forms, one without medicinal contents sold in supermarkets to compete with Johnson & Johnson, and the other with medicinal contents sold in pharmacies. Compared to Band-Aid, Baiyao Bandage with medicinal contents could not only cover the wounds but also had antiphlogistic (inflammation-reducing) and haemostatic (blood-stopping) effects.

The Potential of the 3M Proposal

The Potential for Product Diversification

The cooperative opportunity with 3M could potentially be an effective way of diversifying YB's product line into the transdermal market. 3M had numerous transdermal solutions that could overcome customer concerns in terms of the adhesive's breathability, removability, skin irritation and waterproofness. By solving these problems, YB could better serve customers and increase its market share.

The potential cooperation with 3M also had several advantages. First, if YB decided to use 3M transdermal drug delivery systems to deliver its Baiyao medicinal contents, the cooperation would improve the likelihood of success because the proposed products were proven from both sides.

Secondly, YB would enjoy speed to market with low R&D costs. Because the 3M contents were proven products, only minimal R&D would be necessary to tailor 3M's product to YB's medicinal contents. R&D would cost much less and consume less time, resulting in higher speed to market. In addition, most of the R&D was to be carried out by 3M because it had the core competence. 3M would carry out the pre-feasibility assessment, the feasibility study, the product development and the commercialization with input from YB.

The Potential for Internationalization

The cooperation with 3M offered not only an opportunity for product diversification but also an opportunity for YB to diversify its markets. 3M's transdermal products were widely registered, and 3M had global regulatory expertise. 3M's global presence and expertise would serve as a platform for YB to internationalize its products, beginning with its transdermal products. 3M had shown interest in helping YB to gain access to the U.S. market using its reputation. This opportunity was just what YB has been looking for.

It was very difficult for a traditional herbal medicine to enter a market like the United States because of the regulatory barriers. Through 3M's regulatory expertise and its status as a reputed American company, YB might gain easier access to the U.S. market. In addition, the regulatory barrier for transdermal products was lower than that for products that were delivered either orally or directly into the bloodstream.

By first introducing transdermal products into the U.S. market, YB could build its brand internationally while incurring minimal risk. If the launch of a transdermal product were successful, there would be potential for brand synergy for YB's other pharmaceutical products in the future.

However, there were also a series of challenges YB had to face. The first challenge was cultural distance, which YB had to overcome in many respects. American customers had different consumer behaviors, and they were not very comfortable with traditional herbal medicine that lacked modern scientific substantiation. Even though the YB transdermal products adopted a form North Americans were familiar with, there was still high potential of customer rejection due to skepticism regarding its herbal contents.

YB also lacked international marketing experience. Even though YB had been building up its marketing capabilities, these efforts were confined within China. Despite an overseas department that was established in 2002, the scope of business of the department was still very limited. This lack of international experience could prove to be a big hurdle to surmount by a long-time domestic firm. Even if YB hired local sales personnel, the management of these personnel could still be a big challenge. On the other hand, entering into a foreign market could provide YB an opportunity to gain precious overseas operations experience.

Yet another challenge was the gap between the levels of economic development between China and the United States. Thus, the marketing expense would be very high in the U.S. market, imposing a burden on a developing country firm that was defending and expanding along both the product and market dimension.

THE PRODUCT DIVERSIFICATION OPTION: ESTABLISHING A HEALTHCARE DEPARTMENT

Concurrent with the 3M option, YB was also faced with another option. According to the "one core and four growth areas" strategy, YB should not ignore further strengthening its core business. Even though internationalization was one of its growth strategies, YB had to be cautious because it lacked the necessary international experience. In the foreseeable future, the majority of its revenue would still be generated from the Chinese market. Therefore, YB had to maintain a focus on its domestic market. Because many of YB's products had reached or were reaching maturity, YB needed to further diversify its product line and extend its brand to seek new growth opportunities.

In 2003, YB was considering the feasibility of establishing a healthcare department to diversify into healthcare products. One such product was Baiyao toothpaste. YB came up with this idea based on two facts: 1) many customers already used Baiyao powder to deal with dental bleeding, and 2) many multinational pharmaceutical companies offered healthcare products, including toothpaste.

First, even though Baiyao had been formulated for the purpose of curing wounds and injuries, customers had been extending its use in innovative ways. Since its formulation, Baiyao had been used by people for every kind of disease related to blood or bleeding. People had been using Baiyao in its powder form for curing periodontitis and gingivitis for many years, even though the powder form was very inconvenient to use in these cases. By formulating a toothpaste as the carrier to deliver the medicinal content, the customer needs could be better served.

Secondly, many international pharmaceutical companies had healthcare products. Johnson & Johnson (J&J), which had very strong presence in China, was one such example. The sales of J&J in healthcare products made up approximately 18 per cent of its total sales, and the net revenue had been increasing steadily. Healthcare products did not cannibalize J&J's main products; on the contrary, they strengthened J&J's brand equity by brand synergy. J&J's healthcare brands, such as Johnson's Baby, Band-Aid, Neutrogena and Tylenol, made J&J even more visible to customers. YB thought that it could learn from these multinationals by leveraging its own brand. A successful healthcare product (such as a Baiyao toothpaste) affiliated with YB could potentially add to YB's brand equity. If multinationals all adopted this approach, they reasoned it might work in the case of YB, too.

Diversifying into healthcare products could also increase YB's economy of scope and/or economy of scale because a Baiyao toothpaste would share some value chain activities with its original products. Brand extension might bring about greater production and marketing efficiency and lower promotion costs.

Another potential benefit of product diversification was that it offered an opportunity for YB to build its capabilities. Because YB aspired to be a Chinese multinational in the global pharmaceutical industry, it had to build capabilities. In the past decade, YB had been building up its capabilities in both the product and market dimensions and along the value chain. To compete in the new area of affiliated health care, YB needed to build capabilities in this area, otherwise YB would not be on par with the multinationals, even in the Chinese market.

However, this option did have several weaknesses. Although Baiyao toothpaste would have medicinal content the value chain activities that could be shared were few.

Few healthcare products were related to YB's current businesses. New production facilities would have to be built sooner or later for each healthcare product.

Healthcare products did not even share sales channels with the existing products. YB was a traditional herbal medicine firm, and it was not familiar with the sales practices in the Chinese daily chemical industry. YB would have to establish new distribution channels different from that for its medicine-related products.

In addition, the potential intense competition could not be ignored. The toothpaste industry was dominated by multinational firms, such as Colgate and Procter & Gamble (P&G). The competition was already intense and profit margins were very low. YB was in no position to compete with these giants on their turfs as a new entrant. On the other hand, if YB tried to avoid direct competition by pricing the toothpaste to target the higher end, it would then only occupy a niche market.

Yet another potential problem was product cannibalism. Toothpaste had been used by Chinese customers for various topical uses in the past. Some even used toothpaste to clean utensils. There was no guarantee that consumers of Baiyao toothpaste would not use it for other external uses, and consequently cannibalize the markets of existing products.

Lastly, there was the problem of brand contagion. Because toothpaste was not in YB's core competence, potential failure of toothpaste might cause damage to YB's reputation overall. As such, YB had to make sure that the new product would succeed. The success of Baiyao toothpaste would not only affect the fate of the healthcare department, but would also affect YB's brand equity.

THE DECISION

The year 2003 was an important one for YB: It marked one year since YB had established its "one core and four growth areas" strategy, and 2003 had been scheduled for implementing those strategies. The company's leadership was also very ambitious to achieve even higher goals.

The possibilities of the cooperative arrangement with 3M and the diversification into healthcare products were both opportunities and threats to YB. After careful deliberation, YB came to a point where a decision had to be taken. Should YB pursue the 3M option or the toothpaste option? Was it feasible to pursue both? YB had to come up with a decision soon.

Exhibit 1

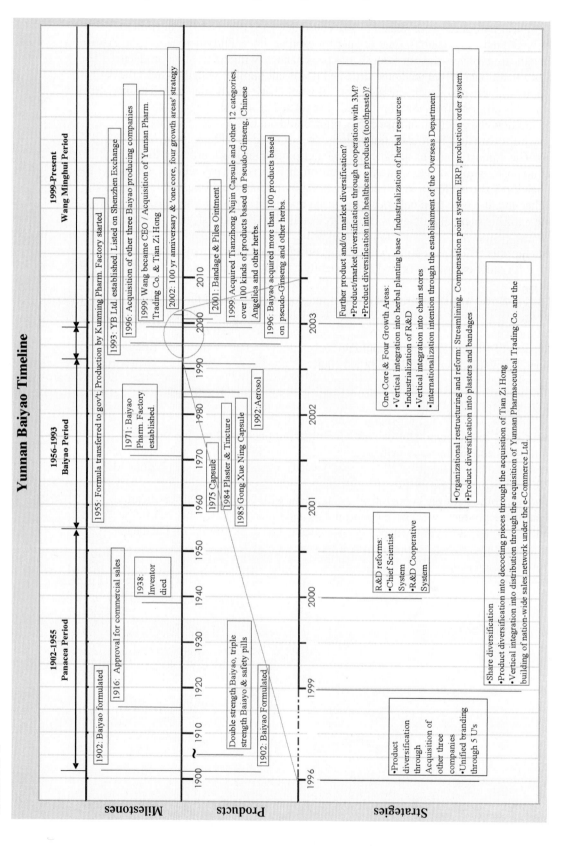

Yunnan Baiyao Timeline

Milestones

1902–1955 Panacea Period | 1956–1993 Baiyao Period | 1999–Present Wang Minghui Period

1902: Baiyao formulated

1916: Approval for commercial sales

1938: Inventor died

1955: Formula transferred to gov't; Production by Kunming Pharm. Factory started

1971: Baiyao Pharm. Factory established.

1993: YB Ltd. established. Listed on Shenzhen Exchange

1996: Acquisition of other three Baiyao producing companies

1999: Wang became CEO / Acquisition of Yunnan Pharm. Trading Co. & Tian Zi Hong

2002: 100 yr anniversary & 'one core, four growth areas' strategy

Products

Double strength Baiyao, triple strength Baiayo & safety pills

1902: Baiyao Formulated

1975 Capsule

1984 Plaster & Tincture

1985 Gong Xue Ning Capsule

1992: Aerosol

2001: Bandage & Piles Ointment

1999: Acquired Tianzihong Nujin Capsule and other 12 categories, over 100 kinds of products based on Pseudo-Ginseng, Chinese Angelica and other herbs.

1996: Baiyao acquired more than 100 products based on pseudo-Ginseng and other herbs.

Strategies

•Product diversification through Acquisition of other three companies
•Unified branding through 5 U's

R&D reforms:
•Chief Scientist System
•R&D Cooperative System

One Core & Four Growth Areas:
•Vertical integration into herbal planting base / Industrialization of herbal resources
•Industrialization of R&D
•Vertical integration into chain stores
•Internationalization intention through the establishment of the Overseas Department

•Organizational restructuring and reform: Streamlining, Compensation point system, ERP, production order system
•Product diversification into plasters and bandages

Further product and/or market diversification?
•Product/market diversification through cooperation with 3M?
•Product diversification into healthcare products (toothpaste)?

•Share diversification
•Product diversification into decocting pieces through the acquisition of Tian Zi Hong
•Vertical integration into distribution through the acquisition of Yunnan Pharmaceutical Trading Co. and the building of nation-wide sales network under the e-Commerce Ltd

1900 1910 1920 1930 1940 1950 1960 1970 1980 1990 2000 2010

1996 1999 2000 2001 2002 2003

Exhibit 2 Total Annual Revenue of Yunnan Baiyao, 1990–2003

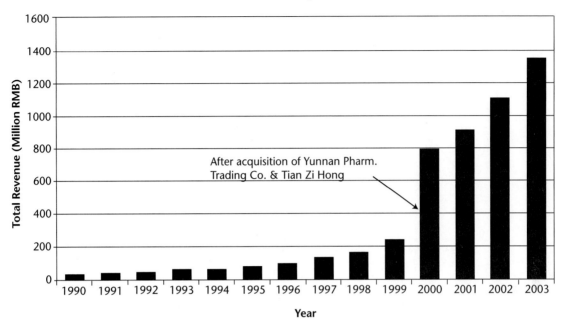

Source: Authors' calculation based on: Yunnan Baiyao Group Co. (various years), *Annual Report of Yunnan Baiyao Group Co.* and Jing Luo, "Yunnan Baiyao Company Analysis," Shenyin & Wanguo Securities Co., Ltd., February 13, 2006.

Exhibit 3 Annual Net Profit Of Yunnan Baiyao, 1993–2003

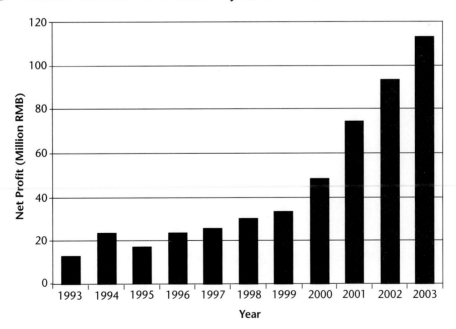

Source: Authors' calculation based on: Yunnan Baiyao Group Co. (various years), *Annual Report of Yunnan Baiyao Group Co.* and Jing Luo, "Yunnan Baiyao Company Analysis," Shenyin & Wanguo Securities Co., Ltd., February 13, 2006.

Exhibit 4   Return on Equity of Yunnan Baiyao, 1993–2003

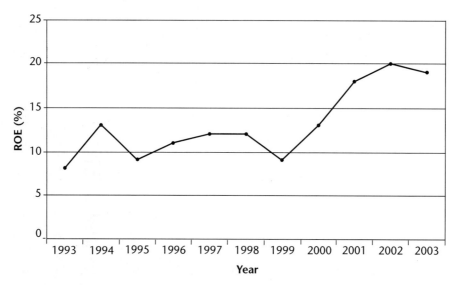

Source: Authors' elaboration based on Jing Luo "Yunnan Baiyao Company Analysis," Shenyin & Wanguo Securities Co., Ltd., February 13, 2006.

Case 16

Gillette's Energy Drain (A): The Acquisition of Duracell[1]

It was February of 2001, and James Kilt, newly elected chief executive officer (CEO) of Gillette, was preparing for his first strategy session with Gillette's board of directors. Kilt pondered what actions to propose in order to satisfy the board, as well as investors, that he had an effective turnaround plan for Gillette's Duracell division.

Kilt, 52, had been the president and CEO of Nabisco just one week previously and was widely credited with dramatically increasing its performance. Gillette's board, which included investor Warren Buffett, hired Kilt to take charge of a company that "had gone nowhere for four years."[2] Gillette's stock price, at $34, had fallen 45 per cent since its high in 1999.

Kilt's biggest challenge in the strategy session, which was just two weeks away, was to lay out a plan for Duracell. Gillette had originally acquired Duracell in September of 1996 for $7.3 billion in stock. Gillette's earnings had been growing at 17 per cent annually for the six years prior to the acquisition. "People are going to be surprised by how well we do," stated then CEO, Alfred M. Zeien in regard to the acquisition, "[Duracell will] make the next five years [at Gillette] even better than the last five."[3]

Professor Frank C. Schultz and Michael T. McCune prepared this case solely to provide material for class discussion. The authors do not intend to illustrate either effective or ineffective handling of a managerial situation. The authors may have disguised certain names and other identifying information to protect confidentiality.

IVEY

Richard Ivey School of Business
The University of Western Ontario

[1] This case has been written on the basis of published sources only. Consequently, the interpretation and perspectives presented in this case are not necessarily those of Gillette or any of its employees.
[2] Banc of America Securities analyst William Steele.
[3] "Can Gillette Regain its Voltage?" *BusinessWeek*, October 16, 2000, p.102.

THE GILLETTE COMPANY[4]

When King C. Gillette founded the Safety Razor Company in 1901 in a small office located over a fish store in Boston, he sold only 58 razors and 168 blades in his first three years of operation. One century later, the company that still carries his name totalled more than $9.2 billion in revenues in 2000. During those 100 years, Gillette became one of the most recognizable name brands from the United States to Europe to the Far East. Even as early as 1926, King C. Gillette said of the safety razor that he invented, "There is no other article for individual use so universally known or widely distributed."

Gillette has introduced a number of new razor shaving systems during the last 30 years, beginning with the Trac II shaving system in 1971 and followed by a new system in 1977 known as the Gillette Atra. Between 1977 and 1988, new disposable razors with pivoting heads and twin blades were introduced along with an updated version of the original Trac II razor. Then, in 1990, the company introduced the Sensor shaving system and followed its release several years later with the Sensor Excel and the Sensor for Women. In 1998, Gillette brought another new shaving system to the market—the Mach3 razor. In 2001, the Mach3 and the Sensor were the top two shaving systems in the United States.

During its first 100 years, Gillette diversified its businesses to include more than razors. At the beginning of 2001, the Gillette Company comprised four distinct business segments: personal-grooming products, small appliances, oral care products and portable power.

The personal grooming segment included men's and women's razors, shaving creams and lotions, and deodorants. In this segment, Gillette operated under the name brands of Gillette, Right Guard, Soft & Dri and Dry Idea. In 2000, Gillette ranked fifth in personal care manufacturers. It has been the world leader in shaving products over the last century, holding a 77.2 per cent market share in the razor blade refill market and 52.4 per cent market share in the disposable razor market. Gillette had become the world's second largest deodorant producer, behind Proctor & Gamble. In 2000, personal grooming products generated $4.385 billion in revenues. This segment also accounted for $1.42 billion of Gillette's operating margin (see Exhibits 1 and 2 for Gillette Company's balance sheets and income statements; Exhibit 3 for the stock price performance of Gillette, ticker symbol "G").

In the area of small appliances, Braun became part of the company in 1964. Some products that carried the Braun logo were electric razors, coffee makers and hair dryers. In 2000, Braun held 16 per cent of the men's electronic shaver market and ranked fifth in the production of coffee makers. This segment produced total revenues of $1.65 billion in 2000 and an operating margin of $218 million.

Gillette was also involved in the oral hygiene market since its acquisition of Oral-B laboratories in 1994. Oral B and Braun combined their capabilities to create the best selling powered toothbrush, the Braun Oral-B 3D. In 2000, Oral-B generated $676 million in revenues for Gillette, along with a $75 million profit margin.

In the portable power segment, the company acquired Duracell, the United States' leading producer of alkaline batteries, in 1996. In 2000, Duracell accounted for $2.6 billion of Gillette's total revenues and $439 million of its total operating margin.

Gillette also had a stationery division during a large portion of its history, mainly consisting of Paper Mate, which manufactured pens and other similar items. Gillette sold this division to Newell Rubbermaid for a loss of $428 million in 2000.

---

[4]Portions of this section adapted from the Gillette Company website: *www.gillette.com.*

THE ACQUISITION OF DURACELL

During the later half of the 20th century, the Gillette Company diversified into a number of businesses. Its acquisitions ranged from Paper Mate to Braun to Oral-B. During the 1990s, it was rumored that Gillette was seeking another product line that would fit well within its current worldwide distribution network and would offer significant market growth. In September of 1996, Gillette announced the purchase of the Duracell Corporation for $7.3 billion in stock. The purchase was overwhelmingly approved by Gillette stockholders at an annual meeting in December of the same year. The acquisition was highly regarded in the investing community as well with investment analyst Connie Maneaty, who stated, "This is a brilliant deal for Gillette. The opportunity to take two global franchises like Gillette razors and Duracell batteries comes along so infrequently."[5]

Before its acquisition by Gillette, Duracell had been the leading producer of alkaline batteries in the United States. Between 1991 and 1996, the company had experienced consistent growth in revenues of about eight per cent per year and had increased total revenues by 46 per cent during that time frame. The company also increased operating margins by more than 75 per cent. At the time, 20 per cent of Duracell's sales were outside of the United States. In 1996, 37 per cent of Gillette's revenues came from the United States; 32 per cent from Western Europe; 11 per cent from Latin America; and 20 per cent from other global areas.

The Gillette Company was known for its solid relationships with vendors around the world, especially drug stores and retailers. Analyst Amy Low said at the time of the merger, "There's a perfect fit between the two companies in terms of channels of distribution."[6] Gillette was determined to make a smooth transition for Duracell and its employees. Charles R. Perrin, the chairman and CEO of Duracell at the time of the acquisition, was offered a job at Gillette as head of Duracell operations. Gillette also offered generous departure terms for any Duracell employee whose job would be eliminated because of the combination. At the time of the acquisition, the restructuring of Duracell was estimated to result in cost savings of $80 million to $120 million per year.

BATTERIES AND THE BATTERY INDUSTRY

A battery is simply an electrochemical container of stored energy that is used on demand. The use of batteries can be traced back to as early as the late 18th century when Alessandro Volta began to experiment with zinc and silver plates. He would create what would become the world's first dry battery, in which solid metals interacted with each other to create a chemical reaction. Soon after, Georges Leclanche developed the first working battery, which was widely used in the telegraph system. His "wet cell" battery, which used a liquid substance to create a chemical reaction, was contained in a porous pot and was the prelude to what would become the zinc-carbon battery. Since then, most batteries used in today's society are dry cell batteries including the familiar alkaline battery that, as an industry, generated $2.6 billion in U.S. domestic sales in 2000.

Batteries can generally be divided into two separate categories: primary and secondary. It is important to note that these categorizations do not necessarily refer to

---

[5]William M. Bulkely, "Duracell Pact Gives Gillette an Added Source of Power—Purchase of Battery Maker for $7.3 billion Promises Distribution Advantages" *Wall Street Journal.* September 13, 1996, A3.
[6] Ibid.

a battery's use in a device. Instead, they mainly refer to the battery's ability to be recharged. Primary batteries could not easily be recharged so they were made for one-time use; once the battery had discharged its energy, it was discarded. On the other hand, secondary batteries were those that could be recharged multiple times over the course of their life. Primary and secondary batteries each offered their own advantages and disadvantages. Primary batteries tended to hold their charge for longer amounts of time and were less expensive than secondary batteries. However, secondary batteries had a higher energy density and were more usable in extreme temperatures. The difference between these batteries often came down to their applications.

Primary batteries mainly consisted of alkaline and zinc-carbon cells. Companies such as Duracell and Energizer concentrated on the disposable market because they believed that consumers were more apt to want a convenient, no hassle, portable power source. Alkaline batteries became the standard in the United States due to the fact that they lasted six times longer than the outdated zinc-carbon. However, in countries outside the United States, zinc-carbon batteries still held a majority of the market share. Conversion to alkaline outside the United States was much slower than originally expected, and hindered international sales of some U.S. battery companies. For example, in India, alkaline batteries made up only three per cent of the battery market compared to 70 per cent in developed countries. This has been attributed to tough economic conditions and the high cost of building new battery manufacturing facilities capable of handling the production of alkaline batteries.

The secondary battery market also had a variety of different types of batteries. This battery market consisted of lead-acid, nickel-containing (NiCd and NiMH), and lithium-ion batteries. Lead-acid batteries were most commonly found in automobiles and other transportation uses. Nickel-containing and lithium-ion batteries were used in electronic consumer products that utilized a rechargeable battery. Lithium batteries have increased in popularity for high drain devices such as laptop computers and cellular phones due to their high energy density and weight. However, most other rechargeable consumer products used a nickel-containing secondary battery.

Batteries also came in a variety of sizes and shapes. The International Electrotechnical Commission was responsible for creating standardized numbers for the different sizes of batteries; these numbers incorporated both a battery's size and electrochemical makeup. These standardization codes differed from those often printed on a manufacturer's packaging. Although the American National Standards Institute's designations for batteries officially no longer existed, they were still used by manufacturers for battery labelling in relation to their size. For alkaline batteries, the most popular sizes that were available on the market were AAA, AA, C, D and 9-Volt. The AA size accounted for almost half of all alkaline battery sales. (Exhibit 4 shows dollar sales volume by battery size in 2000). Other primary battery types in use today included miniature batteries used for hearing-aids and electronic watches.

It was estimated by industry experts that about 75 per cent of all alkaline battery sales were a result of impulse purchases.[7] Batteries ranked as 25th in sales in the top 200 products of general merchandise/health and beauty aids for retailers. The distribution of alkaline batteries occurred through three main channels in the United States: supermarkets, drug stores and discounters. These retailers often marketed alkaline batteries at impulse buying locations such as the checkout lane and then complemented those with other displays in separate departments. An unidentified director of marketing services of a battery supplier has said, "It's critical for manufacturers to assist

---

[7]Mass Market Retailers (MMR), September 20, 1999.

merchants in effectively maximizing their retail floors. Providing merchandising and display avenues that enable retailers to market the high impulse nature of batteries would be a useful step."[8] As a result, battery manufacturers have tried to meet the diverse needs of the retailers by providing different displays and other tools such as clip-strips, which are small hangers attached on the end of a grocery or merchandise aisle, to place batteries in limited spaces.

In 2000, discounters were responsible for 52.5 per cent of total dollar sales of alkaline batteries (see Exhibit 5). This figure has increased steadily during the previous four years from 48.7 per cent in 1996. Drug stores and supermarkets were the other two main suppliers for alkaline batteries in the market place. They held 23.8 per cent and 23.7 per cent of total dollar alkaline sales in 2000, respectively.

ALKALINE BATTERY INDUSTRY COMPETITORS

The alkaline battery industry had three main manufacturers: Duracell, Energizer and Rayovac (see Exhibit 6). While Energizer and Duracell had been competing for many years, Rayovac was a relatively new force in the industry. In 1996, these three companies combined to total $4.8 billion in revenues and operating margins of $832 million. Since then, revenues have increased by seven per cent to $5.2 billion and operating margins have decreased by three per cent to $807 million in 2000. In the context of the two main brands, Duracell and Energizer, revenues increased 1.3 per cent during those four years, and operating margins dropped by more than 10 per cent. The only company to experience growth in both revenues and operating margins from 1996 to 2000 was Rayovac.

Energizer Holdings Incorporated

Energizer Holdings Incorporated was the world leader in the manufacturing of dry cell batteries, selling more than six billion batteries each year. The company's wide variety of products included alkaline, carbon zinc, miniatures and rechargeable batteries as well as flashlights. Energizer currently produced two general brands of batteries: Energizer and Eveready.

Energizer Holdings Inc., which had been its own publicly traded company, was acquired by Ralston-Purina in 1986. At that time, battery products were separated into two divisions by brand. Zinc carbon batteries were sold under the Eveready brand, while Energizer became the major brand for the company in the alkaline market. In 2000, Ralston Purina completed a spin-off of its battery segment, and Energizer Holdings became a publicly traded company again.

In the alkaline market, Energizer had two major brands, the original Energizer battery and the more recent release of the Energizer e^2. The e^2 was launched in 2000 as a power source for more "high tech" devices such as digital cameras, CD players and cellular phones. While the original e^2 was available only in smaller sizes, both brands soon become available in AA, AAA, C and D sizes. Energizer also manufactured rechargeable batteries for electronic devices as well as watch and hearing aid batteries. In 1997, Energizer held a 36.5 per cent market share of all alkaline battery sales. Since, then market share has dropped to just below 30 per cent in 2000. In 1994, the company

---

[8]Quoted in MMR, September 20, 1999.

generated $2.1 billion in revenues and an operating margin of $312 million. In 2000, the company reported $1.9 billion in revenues and an operating margin of $279 million. In the four years between 1997 and 2000, Energizer's revenues decreased, every year, and operating margins decreased three of the four years.

The Rayovac Corporation

The Rayovac Corporation was originally founded in 1903 as the French Battery Company in Madison, Wisconsin. Rayovac still had its world headquarters in that location and had grown to 3,300 employees. Significant growth was catalyzed by Thomas H. Lee's decision to purchase Rayovac in 1996 and to take it public. In 1997, an initial offering was made at $14 per share on the New York Stock Exchange. This was followed by a major facelift to the company's packaging and marketing practices.

Rayovac's main brand of disposable alkaline battery was the Rayovac Maximum. It was comparable to the products of Duracell and Energizer, but cost approximately 15 per cent less. Rayovac also engaged in the rechargeable battery market, selling NiMH and rechargeable alkaline batteries for consumer use. In the year 2000, Rayovac's revenues increased by 25 per cent and its operating margin was 66 per cent higher than that of 1999. Since its initial offering, Rayovac has had 16 straight quarters of increased growth in revenues. Before becoming a public company, revenues for the company were approximately $400 million a year. In 2000, Rayovac generated more than $700 million in revenues. During that same time period, Rayovac increased its total market share of alkaline batteries from 10 per cent to 12 per cent.

Other Competitors

During the 1990s, electronics manufacturers also began to enter the battery market. Sony was the largest supplier of secondary batteries to original equipment manufacturers (OEMs) and was also involved with the alkaline market. Sony's Stamina line of alkaline batteries was test-marketed in several areas. Sony claimed that these batteries performed better in the company's electronic devices. Kodak also promoted this type of concept with camera batteries. Another large electronics producer, Panasonic, produced consumer-orientated secondary batteries and was slowly entering the alkaline market. Other smaller producers of alkaline batteries included RCA, Gold Peak and the more recent brand, Star Struck. Major retailers and supermarkets also began selling their own private label brands of batteries. However, these batteries were often manufactured by outside companies, including Duracell and Energizer, and then sold under the private label brand. In 1997, the total market share of brands outside of Duracell, Energizer and Rayovac totalled 11.7 per cent. In 2000, their market share had increased to 13.3 per cent and generated $350 million in revenues.

COMPETITIVE DYNAMICS IN THE ALKALINE BATTERY INDUSTRY

In May of 1997, Gillette announced restructuring plans at Duracell with an estimated charge of $283 million and anticipated layoffs of 1,700 jobs. A year later, Gillette made its first competitive move with its new battery business. At the same time as it was introducing its new Mach3 razor technology, Gillette made its first upgrade to Duracell's offerings. The "Duracell Ultra" was rolled out in May of 1998 in the AA and

AAA sizes and featured 50 per cent longer life on "high-drain" devices such as digital cameras and portable CD players. Ultra did not replace Duracell's original "Copper Top" line, but instead the two brands were allowed to co-exist on retailer shelves. As it had regularly done with shaver technology upgrades, Ultra was priced at a 20 per cent premium over the older technology. In January of 1997, Gillette fired the long-time advertising agency associated with Duracell (Ogilvy & Mather) and hired BBDO (Gillette's advertising agency) to assist with the $60 million launch of the Duracell Ultra. The campaign promoted "More Power, More Life" (see Exhibit 7).

Duracell, however, was not the only player to upgrade its alkaline battery technology. Two smaller players, Sony and Panasonic had previously entered the market in the hope of leveraging their reputation in consumer electronics. Sony, which had never been a significant player in the alkaline segment but had long been involved in the development of battery technology—including the initial development and commercialization of the lithium ion rechargeable battery—introduced its Stamina line in AA size in February of 1997. Its introduction was supported by television, radio and concert sponsorships and used the message "So the beat goes on." Panasonic followed two months later with the Panasonic Plus alkaline in AA size for high drain devices, which it claimed was better than the industry leader. Like Sony, Panasonic was a highly recognized brand in consumer electronics and offered a full range of batteries including carbon zinc and lithium ion.

Rayovac also beat its two larger counterparts to the punch with its alkaline upgrade. It replaced its existing battery with the Rayovac "Maximum" in August 1997. The new battery was priced 20 per cent below Duracell and Energizer levels. Prior to the introduction of Maximum, Rayovac had employed basketball great Michael Jordan to promote its rechargeable line of batteries, Renewal. With the launch of Maximum, Rayovac spent $25 million on a new advertising campaign with the Chicago Bulls star and the tagline "Maximum Power, Maximum Value." An additional $30 million was spent one year later on the "Duracell Challenge," in which customers would receive their money back if Rayovac Maximum did not outlast Duracell and Energizer (see Exhibit 8).

Energizer, which had previously upgraded its AA and AAA batteries in August and November of 1997, announced in May of 1998 that it would come out with a new "Energizer Advanced Formula" battery in AA, AAA, C, D and 9-volt sizes. In contrast to Gillette's targeting of its upgraded offering, Energizer indicated that Advanced Formula was not designed exclusively for high drain devices but instead incorporated more active ingredients and patented resistors that made them applicable for all devices. According to Energizer internal testing and independent research, Advanced Formula could last 60 per cent longer than ordinary alkaline batteries and nine per cent longer than Duracell Ultra. A $150 million worldwide (US$70 million) advertising campaign employing the Energizer Bunny was used to help launch the product upgrade. In contrast to the launch of Ultra, Advanced Formula was introduced at the same price point as its previous alkaline, which it now replaced.[9] As one analyst pointed out: "It's a classic example of two rivals trying to one-up each other. Duracell's going to have to reassess its strategy now."[10]

In February of 1999, Duracell announced the introduction in June of a "new" Ultra with a 20 per cent improvement in performance over the original Ultra and now

---

[9]Energizer had raised the price of its alkaline lineup four per cent in April of 1998.

[10]Tony Vento, Edward Jones analyst quoted in "Energizer Steps up Battle of the Battery; Its Long-Life Formula Follows Duracell's," *St Louis Post Dispatch*, May 27, 1998.

available in C, D and 9-volt sizes as well. Duracell research showed that the new Ultra lasted up to 80 per cent longer in digital cameras, 60 per cent longer in flash cameras, 80 per cent longer in mobile phones, two hours longer in super boom boxes and up to three hours longer in halogen torches. The new Ultra also had an extended shelf life of seven years, up from the previous five, and was promoted with a $140 million advertising spend. According to A. Bruce Cleverly, senior vice-president, business management and business development, stated:

> Duracell intends to continue delivering technological innovation that electronic device manufacturers can capitalize on as they design the next generation of high-tech devices. Offering this superior performing line of high-tech batteries will only fuel the growth potential of the high-tech device base, particularly as it expands to include power-hungry devices, which use all of the Duracell Ultra battery sizes.[11]

Just three months after the announcement of the new Ultra, Duracell took the competitive battle to the courtroom, charging Energizer with false advertising claims. A judge ordered the ads removed, claiming that the ads raised "serious questions as to the accuracy." Energizer's parent, Ralston-Purina complied. This was not the first time, however, that competitors in the battery industry had met in court. In August of 1998, Rayovac had filed a lawsuit to bar a former engineer from working for Duracell. In April of 1999, Rayovac sued Gillette, alleging patent infringement over hearing aid battery technology. Gillette ultimately prevailed with the judge nullifying Rayovac's patents.

In September of 1999, Gillette announced a round of layoffs and a restructuring. Gillette cut 4,700 jobs and shut down 14 plants, saving $200 million. Gillette indicated that the move was brought on by slumping sales in Asian and Latin American markets.

The series of technology upgrades and escalating performance claims by the major battery manufacturers caught the eye of the independent consumer testing organization that publishes Consumer Reports. In December of 1999, it published its findings on the relative superiority of the various brands, and concluded:

> The moral on battery shopping is simple: buy by price. Most of the time, the cheaper brand will work as well as costlier ones, whether they're powering portable stereos, toys, wall clocks or flashlights. Don't be put off by store brands; the ones we tested are as good as the big names for most bread and butter uses . . . . Sales and bulk packs can also save you money on many brands, big and small.

Consumer reports also commented that the "look" of many of the store brands (the dimples and indentations) matched those of the major brands. When asked about the potential connections between the store brands and the major manufacturers, an Energizer spokeswoman commented, "The relationship we might have with retailers is proprietary."[12]

The next competitive battery technology upgrade came in February of 2000 when Energizer introduced a "super premium" line of batteries named e^2 Titanium. The

---

[11]"Duracell Successfully Establishes High-Tech Alkaline Battery Segment," *PR Newswire*, November 2, 1999.

[12] The case authors traced the patent numbers found on selected store brands to the major battery manufacturers.

product launched in June of 2000 and this time was meant as a line extension rather than a replacement to its Advanced Formula brand. The $100 million introduction of e^2 Titanium did not employ the Energizer Bunny, which was to remain associated with Advanced Formula only, but it did encourage customers to "take power to the next level." According to Energizer, e^2 could, in some cases, last twice as long as normal alkalines and 78 per cent longer than regular batteries in regular cameras and 240 per cent longer than regular batteries in digital cameras. e^2 was priced at approximately a 32 per cent premium to Advanced Formula and four per cent to six per cent higher than Ultra. In that same month, Energizer targeted the lower end of the market by introducing a value priced Eveready alkaline battery.

In the same month that Energizer announced e^2 Titanium, Duracell announced its third generation of Ultra. Ultra with M3 technology would be introduced in September of 2000. M3 technology was "Packed with Power," and offered "More Fuel, More Efficiency and More Power." "More Fuel" as inactive ingredients were removed and more active ingredients added, "More Efficiency" due to reformulated ingredients that facilitated electron flow and "More Power" from patented and patent pending technologies that extended life and enhanced performance. A $70 million advertising campaign was used. Ultra with M3 technology arrived on store shelves with redesigned packaging but no increase in price.

Just prior to Kilts arrival at the beginning of 2001, Gillette attended to its traditional Copper Top line by announcing a new Duracell Plus that would be available in June of 2001. A $100 million advertising campaign touted that the improved "Copper & Black" technologies were designed to "Deliver Longer-Lasting Performance," marking the first change to the traditional Copper and Black line in nine years.

THE BOARD OF DIRECTORS MEETING

As Kilt considered the strategic options available to Duracell, he couldn't help but remember that his predecessor, Michael Hawley, had been fired after only 18 months as CEO, due in large part to an inability to reverse the trends at Duracell. It was apparent that, despite the initial optimism expressed by the company and the accolades from the investment community, Duracell had become a drain on Gillette's performance and had brought to an end Gillette's impressive earnings growth history. While selling off Duracell was certainly an option, would the board be willing to accept the implicit acknowledgement that the acquisition had been ill-advised? Were there other options, short of divesture, that Kilt could recommend to the board in two weeks that would turn Duracell around and return the Gillette Company to its former reputation as a dependable financial performer?

Exhibit 1   Gillette Company Financial Statements
Balance Sheet (for years ending December 31) (in US$ millions)

	2000	1999	1998	1997
Assets				
Current Assets				
Cash and cash equivalents	$ 62	$ 80	$ 102	$ 105
Receivables, less allowances	2,506	2,527	2,943	2,522
Inventories	1,162	1,392	1,595	1,500
Deferred income taxes	566	309	517	320
Other current assets	386	1,489	283	243
Total Current Assets	4,682	5,797	5,440	4,690
Property, plants, and equipment, net of accumulated depreciation	3,550	3,467	3,472	3,104
Intangible assets, less accumulated amortization	1,574	1,897	2,448	2,423
Other Assets	596	625	542	647
Total Assets	**$10,402**	**$11,786**	**$11,902**	**$10,864**
Liabilities and Stockholders' Equity				
Current Liabilities				
Loans payable	$ 2,195	$ 1,440	$ 981	$ 552
Current portion of long-term debt	631	358	9	9
Accounts payable and accrued liabilities	2,346	2,149	2,170	1,794
Income taxes	299	233	318	286
Total Current Liabilities	$ 5,471	$ 4,180	$ 3,478	$ 2,641
Long-term debt	1,650	2,931	2,256	1,476
Deferred income taxes	450	423	411	359
Other long-term liabilities	767	795	898	1,101
Minority interest	41	38	39	39
Contingent redemption value of common stock put options	99	359	277	407
Total Liabilities	**$ 8,478**	**$ 8,726**	**$ 7,359**	**$ 6,023**
Stockholders' Equity				
8.0% cumulative series C ESOP convertible preferred, without par value	$ —	$ 85	$ 90	$ 93
Unearned ESOP compensation	—	(4)	(10)	(17)
Common stock, par value $1 per share	1,365	1,364	1,358	1,353
Additional paid-in capital	973	748	621	309
Retained earnings	5,853	6,147	5,529	5,021
Accumulated other comprehensive Income				
Foreign currency translation	(1,280)	(1,031)	(826)	(790)
Pension adjustment	(34)	(30)	(47)	(20)
Treasury stock	(4,953)	(4,219)	(2,172)	(1,108)
Total Stockholders' Equity	**$ 1,924**	**$ 3,060**	**$ 4,543**	**$ 4,841**
Total Liabilities and Stockholders' Equity	**$10,402**	**$11,786**	**$11,902**	**$10,864**

Source: Company files.

Exhibit 2   Gillette Company Financial Statements
Income Statements (for years ending December 31) (in US$ millions)

	2000	1999	1998
Net sales	$9,295	$9,154	$9,200
Cost of sales	3,384	3,392	3,499
Gross profit	**5,911**	**5,762**	**5,701**
Selling, general and administrative expenses	3,827	3,675	3,485
Restructuring and asset impairment charges	572	—	440
Profit from operations	**1,512**	**2,087**	**1,776**
Nonoperating charges (income)			
Interest income	—	—	—
Interest expense	223	136	94
Other charges - net	6	46	34
	224	175	120
Income from continuing operations before income taxes	1,288	1,912	1,656
Income taxes	467	664	583
Loss on disposal of discontinued operations, net of tax	(428)	—	—
Income (loss) from discontinued operations, net of tax	(1)	12	8
Net Income	**$392**	**$1,260**	**$1,081**
Net income (loss) per common share, basic			
Continuing operations	$0.78	$1.14	$0.95
Disposal of discontinued operations	(0.41)	—	—
Discontinued operations	—	0.01	0.01
Net Income	**$0.37**	**$1.15**	**$0.96**
Net income (loss) per common share, assuming full dilution			
Continuing operations	$0.77	$1.13	$0.94
Disposal of discontinued operations	(0.40)	—	—
Discontinued operations	—	0.01	0.01
Net Income	**$0.37**	**$1.14**	**$0.95**
Weighted average number of common shares outstanding			
Basic	1,054	1,089	1,117
Assuming full dilution	1,063	1,111	1,144

Source: Company files.

Exhibit 3   Stock Price of Gillette Company (G) Compared to S&P 500 Index

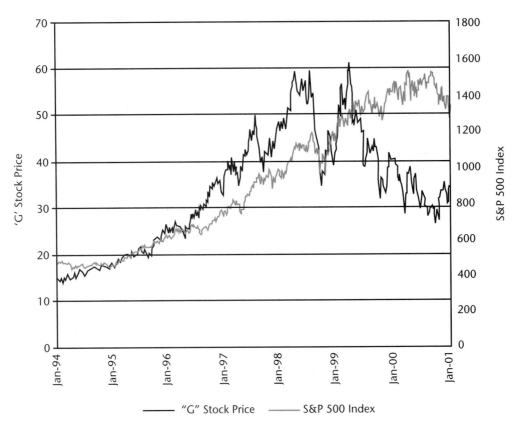

Exhibit 4   Sales by Battery Size in 2000 (in US$)

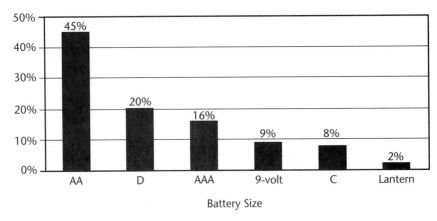

Source: Market Share Reporter.

Exhibit 5   Sales by Retailer Type (in US$)

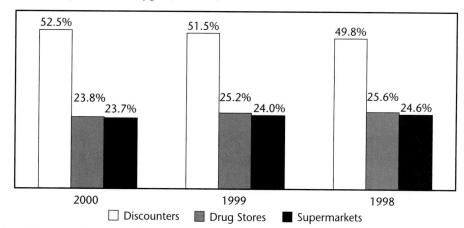

Source: AC Neilson data reported in mass market retail.

Exhibit 6   Comparative Financial and Trend Data

Duracell

Year	Revenues	Operating Margin	Operating Margin	Growth-Revenues	Growth-Operating Margin
1995	$2,079	$409	19.67%		
1996	$2,251	$450	19.99%	8.27%	10.02%
1997	$2,478	$526	21.23%	10.08%	16.89%
1998	$2,576	$597	23.18%	3.95%	13.50%
1999	$2,726	$606	22.23%	5.82%	1.51%
2000	$2,577	$439	17.04%	−5.47%	−27.56%

Energizer

Year	Revenues	Operating Margin	Operating Margin	Growth-Revenues	Growth-Operating Margin
1995	$2,168	$345	15.89%		
1996	$2,184	$352	16.10%	0.70%	2.00%
1997	$2,178	$342	15.70%	−0.26%	−2.73%
1998	$2,071	$324	15.62%	−4.90%	−5.38%
1999	$2,000	$275	13.76%	−3.44%	−14.93%
2000	$1,914	$279	14.58%	−4.30%	1.38%

Rayovac

Year	Revenues	Operating Margin	Operating Margin	Growth-Revenues	Growth-Operating Margin
1995	$415	$32	7.60%		
1996	$423	$30	7.16%	1.93%	−3.97%
1997	$432	$35	7.99%	2.13%	14.03%
1998	$496	$41	8.18%	14.75%	17.44%
1999	$564	$54	9.51%	13.84%	32.29%
2000	$704	$89	12.69%	24.74%	66.54%

Source: Company files.

***Exhibit* 7**   Market Share of Duracell Products (in US$)

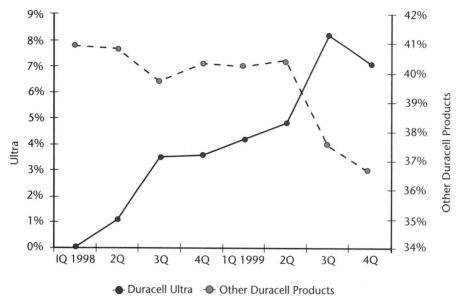

Source: Market Share Reporter.

***Exhibit* 8**   Market Share by Brand (in US$)

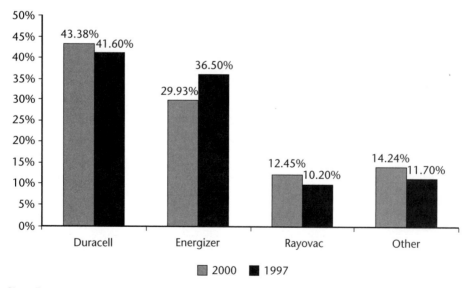

Source: Market Share Reporter.

Vincor and the New World of Wine

On September 16, 2002, Donald Triggs, chief executive officer (CEO) of Vincor International Inc. (Vincor) was preparing for the board meeting to discuss the possible acquisition of Goundrey Wines, Australia. Vincor had embarked upon a strategic internationalization plan in 2000, acquiring R.H Phillips and Hogue in the United States. Although Vincor was the largest wine company in Canada and the fourth largest in North America, Triggs felt that to be a major player, Vincor had to look beyond the region. The acquisition of Goundrey Wines in Australia would be the first step. Convincing the board would be difficult, as the United States was a close and attractive market where Vincor had already spent more than US$100 million on acquisitions. In contrast, Australia was very far away.

THE GLOBAL WINE INDUSTRY

Wine-producing countries were classified as either New World producers or Old World producers. Some of the largest New World producers were the United States, Australia, Chile and Argentina. The largest of the Old World producers were France, Italy and Spain (see Exhibit 1). The world's top 10 wine exporters accounted for more than 90 per cent of the value of international wine trade. Of those top 10, half were in western Europe, and the other half were New World suppliers, led by Australia (see Exhibit 2).

France

France had been a long-time world leader in the production of wine, due to historical and cultural factors. France was the top producer of wine in the world (see Exhibit 1).

Nikhil Celly prepared this case under the supervision of Professor Paul W. Beamish solely to provide material for class discussion. The authors do not intend to illustrate either effective or ineffective handling of a managerial situation. The authors may have disguised certain names and other identifying information to protect confidentiality.

Richard Ivey School of Business
The University of Western Ontario

The French had developed the vins d'appellation d'origine contrôlée (AOC) system centuries ago to ensure that the quality of wine stayed high. There were many regions in which quality grapes could be grown in France. Some of their better-known appellations were Bordeaux, Burgundy and Champagne. France was the second largest exporter of wine (see Exhibit 2).

Italy

Italy, like France, also had a very old and established wine industry that relied on the appellation method to control the quality. Italy was the second largest producer of wine in the world (see Exhibit 1) and the largest exporter (see Exhibit 2).

Australia

Grape vines were first introduced to Australia in 1788. The wine "industry" was born in the 1860s when European immigrants added the skilled workforce necessary to develop the commercial infrastructure. The Australian wine industry grew after 1960 with the development of innovative techniques to make higher quality wine while keeping costs down. Australia was the sixth largest producer of wine in the world (see Exhibit 1). Australia had 5.5 per cent of the total export market and was ranked fourth in the world for its export volume (see Exhibit 2).

Chile

The first vines were introduced to Chile in the 16th century. Due to political and economic instability, the wine industry was not able to develop and take on a global perspective until 1979 when Chile began to focus on the exporting of natural resources to strengthen its economy. Despite being only the 10th largest producer, Chile had 4.5 per cent of the total export market and was ranked fifth in the world (see Exhibit 2).

Argentina

Argentina had a long history of making wine. However, the quality of the wine from Argentina was never as high, due to the small area of land that was capable of producing high quality grapes. Argentina was the fifth largest producer of wine in the world (see Exhibit 1), but did not feature in the top 10 exporters of wine.

All of the countries, with the exception of Argentina, were capable of shipping brands that could compete at a wide range of price points. The French wines typically were capable of competing in the higher price classes, and could retail for more than US$100 per bottle.

MAJOR WORLD MARKETS

After a 2.2 per cent gain in 2001, the global wine market was estimated to have increased another 1.2 per cent in 2002 to 2.55 billion cases, according to *The Global Drinks Market: Impact Databank Review and Forecast 2001 Report*. Wine consumption was projected to expand by 120 million cases by 2010. Most of the growth was expected to come from major wine-consuming nations, such as the United States, United Kingdom, Australia and South Africa, as well as from less developed wine markets, such as China and Russia.

Wine imports were highly concentrated. The 10 top importing countries accounted for all but 14 per cent of the value of global imports in the late-1980s. In 2001, half the value of all imports was purchased by the three biggest importers: the United Kingdom (19 per cent), the United States (16 per cent) and Germany (14 per cent).

France and Italy were the number one and two countries in the world for per capita consumption (see Exhibit 3). However, the consumption rate in France was relatively stagnant, while Italy was showing a decrease. Italy, unlike France, had a very small market for imported wines. The import market sizes for France and Italy were respectively 13.4 per cent and 2.8 per cent in 2001, based on volume.

The United Kingdom's wine market was considered to be the "crucible" for the global wine market (Wine Market Report, May 2000). The United Kingdom had very small domestic wine production and good relationships with many of the wine-producing countries in the world. This coupled with the long history of wine consumption, resulted in an open and competitive market. The United Kingdom was ranked number seven for consumption in 2001 with a trend of increasing consumption. The United Kingdom wine market was dominated by Old World country imports; however, New World imports had grown as Australian wines replaced French wines as the number one import (see Figure 1).

Other Countries

In 2001, Canada was ranked number 30 in the world for per capita consumption, with an increasing trend. Japan had seen a steady increase in the size of its imported wine market. Asia presented a great opportunity for wine producers around the world because it had populous markets that had yet to be tapped.

Figure 1   United Kingdom Wine Market Share

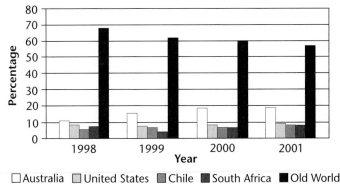

Source: Company files.

THE U.S. WINE INDUSTRY

The international image of the U.S. wine industry until the mid 1970s was that of a low-quality jug wine producer. This changed in 1976 during a blind wine-tasting contest in France where California wines from Napa Valley beat out several well-established European wines for the top honors. From that time forward, there has been a focus on developing high-quality wines that could compete in the international market from the northern California appellations, such as Napa Valley and Sonoma County. The United States was the fourth largest producer of wine (1.98 billion litres) in 2001 (see Exhibit 1), with California wines accounting for 90 per cent of production volume. There were more than 3,000 wineries in all 50 states. The nation's top wine-producing states were California, New York, Washington and Oregon.

The United States saw huge gains in the total volume and value of its wine exports, increasing from US$85 million in 1988 to US$548 million in 2002. The major markets for U.S wines included the United Kingdom, Canada and Japan. Together they represented 66 per cent of the total export market value for the United States (see Exhibit 4).

The United States was the third largest wine market in the world, consuming 2.13 billion litres a year in 2001. It was also one of the biggest untapped wine markets in the world; seven per cent of the U.S. population accounted for 86 per cent of the country's wine consumption. The total wine market in the United States in 2001 was $21.1 billion, with an average growth rate of six per cent since 1994. Of this, approximately $10 billion were sales of New World wines.

While California wines dominated the domestic market (67 per cent market share) due to the ideal growing conditions and favorable marketing and branding actions taken by some of California's larger wineries, imports were on the rise. The United States had one of the most open markets in the world for wine, with low barriers to entry for imports. Imports represented 530 million litres for a 25 per cent share of the market. By 2002, wine imports grew by 18 per cent (see Figures 2 and 3).

Figure 2   United States Wine Markets 1998 to 2001

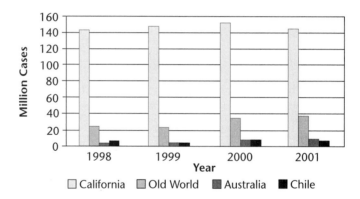

Source: Company files.

Figure 3   United States Wine Market Growth Rates

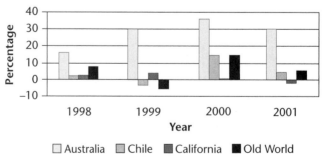

Source: Company files.

Wine was the most popular alcoholic beverage in the United States after beer, which accounted for 67 per cent of all alcohol consumed. The table wine category represented 90 per cent of all wine by volume, dessert wine was six per cent and sparkling wine accounted for four per cent. U.S.-produced table wine held an 83 per cent share of the volume and 78 per cent of the value. Premium wine ($7 and more per 750 ml bottle) sales increased eight per cent over 2001, accounting for 30 per cent of the volume, but a sizeable 62 per cent of winery revenues. Everyday value-priced wines selling for less than $7 per bottle grew about 1.5 per cent by volume. This segment represented 70 per cent of all California table wine shipments and 38 per cent of the value.

The United States wine industry was fragmented, with the largest producer, E. & J. Gallo, supplying 30 per cent and no other producer supplying more than 15 per cent by volume in 2002.

In the United States, a law mandated the implementation of a three-tier distribution system. The wine producers were required to sell to a wholesaler, who then sold to an established customer base of grocery stores, liquor stores, hotels and restaurants. Wineries were capable of using a two-tier distribution system, which allowed wineries to sell directly to the customers through gift shops located at the winery. The role of the distribution channel was growing and taking on greater strategic importance as the trend towards international and domestic consolidation grew.

THE CANADIAN WINE INDUSTRY

Canadians had been making wine for more than two centuries, but Canada's modern-day success in the production of high-quality vinifera-based wines went back only a quarter century. The signing of the North American Free Trade Agreement in 1988, together with a ruling under the General Agreement on Tariffs and Trade (GATT), required Canada to abandon the protection it offered its wine industry. While many producers felt threatened, many more responded by reaffirming their belief in their capacity to produce premium wines, and redoubled their efforts to prove it. New vineyards were planted with only the finest varieties of grapes: Chardonnay, Riesling, Sauvignon Blanc, Pinot Gris, Gewürztraminer, Pinot Noir, Cabernet Sauvignon, Merlot and others.

During 1988, the Vintners Quality Alliance (VQA) was launched in Ontario, culminating six years of voluntary initiatives by the leaders of Ontario's wine industry. This group set the standards, to which they agreed to comply, to elevate the quality of Canadian wines and provide quality assurances to the consumer. British Columbia adopted similar high standards in 1990, under the VQA mark.

The 1990s was a decade of rapid growth. The number of commercial wineries grew from about 30 in 1990 to more than 100 by the end of the decade, and consumers began to recognize the value represented by wines bearing the VQA medallion. Canadian vintners continued to demonstrate that fine grape varieties in cooler growing conditions could possess complex flavors, delicate yet persistent aromas, tightly focused structure and longer aging potential than their counterparts in warmer growing regions of the world.

In Canada, despite increasing import competition, sales of Canadian quality wines were increasing as consumers moved up the quality and price scale (see Figure 4).

Canadian quality wines began to capture both domestic and international recognition not only in sales but also by garnering an impressive list of significant wine awards, beginning in 1991 when Inniskillin won the Grand Prix d'Honneur for its 1989

Figure 4   The Canadian Wine Market

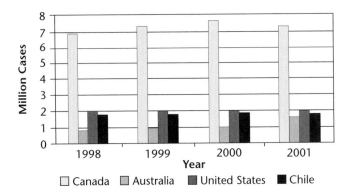

Source: Company files.

icewine at the prestigious VinExpo, in Bordeaux, France. New access for Canadian wines, especially icewine, in the European market, and expanding market opportunities in the United States and Asia were giving Canadian wines greater market exposure.

THE AUSTRALIAN WINE INDUSTRY

The Australian wine industry was structured to be able to deliver large quantities of high-quality branded wine to the world's major markets, at costs less than many of their Old World and New World competitors. Since Australia had a very limited domestic market (population of only 17 million), the wineries realized that if the industry was to continue to grow it would have to do so internationally.

As a result, Australian wineries had gained, and were expected to continue to gain, market share. Growth had been in exports as well as domestic sales (see Exhibits 5 and 6). Australia had recently overtaken France as the largest exporter to the United Kingdom, where seven of the top 10 wine brands were Australian. Exports to North America had grown at 27 per cent by volume in 2001. Consumption of Australian wine in Canada was up 24 per cent and in the United States consumption was up 35 per cent. The growth trends were expected to continue. Export growth had been driven by sales of premium red wine which accounted for 53 per cent of Australia's wine exports.

Domestic wine consumption had grown from 296 million litres in 1991 to 398 million litres in 2001, an annual growth rate of four per cent. The Australian domestic market was relatively unregulated compared to North America, although alcohol taxes were high (42 per cent). Wineries were allowed to have their own retail outlets and sell directly to retailers or on-premise customers. The 7,500 licensed liquor retail outlets, accounted for 56 per cent of wine sales while the 28,000 licensed on-premise outlets accounted for 44 per cent of wine sales.

Although there were 1,300 wineries in Australia, the industry was the most concentrated of any major wine region, with 80 per cent of production being accounted for by four players: Southcorp Wine, Beringer Blass, BRL Hardy and Orlando Wyndham. The large wineries had their own sales forces, as well as warehouses in the major markets.

Southcorp Wines was Australia's largest winery and vineyard owner, with sales of AUD$1.5 billion. Beringer Blass was owned by the Fosters Group and had wine revenues of approximately AUD$800 million (seven million cases). The purchase of Beringer (for AUD$2.6 billion) provided the company with significant growth and U.S. market access.

BRL Hardy had revenues of more than AUD$700 million. The company had several top brands and a very strong U.K. market position. A recent joint venture in the United States with Constellation brands had improved their United States market access. Orlando Wyndham was owned by Pernod Ricard, a French publicly traded spirits company.

TRENDS IN THE GLOBAL WINE INDUSTRY

Wine was unique among alcoholic beverages in that its top 25 brands represented only seven per cent of the global market. In 2002, Martini vermouth was the world's most widely distributed wine, while Gallo's E. & J. Wine Cellars was the largest-selling brand, at 25 million cases annually, with most of those sales in the United States.

Globally, vermouth and other fortified wines were projected to continue their long-term decline, but this would be more than offset by expected growth in table wines, which accounted for more than 90 per cent of total wine consumption. The hottest sales category was Australian wines, with brands such as Rosemount Estate, Jacob's Creek and Lindemans showing double-digit growth rates.

The North American market was expected to exhibit annual growth rates of three per cent. There were positive demographics, with the 20 to 39 age group having a per capita consumption at 7.9 litres and the 40+ age group having a per capita of 14.0 litres. The ongoing trends were a shift in consumer preference to red wines and premium wines (see Exhibits 7, 8).

The global wine market was consolidating in terms of its retail, wholesale and production operations. One key to success seemed to be distribution and marketing. Globalization was also altering the structure of firms both within the wine industry and among those distributing and retailing wine. Rapid growth in supermarkets and in concentration among distributors was driving wine companies into mergers and acquisitions to better meet the needs of those buyers and their customers. Since information about the various niches and the distribution networks in foreign markets was expensive to acquire, new alliances between wine companies were being explored with a view to capitalizing on their complementarities in such knowledge.

Recent examples of such alliances included the purchase by the owner of Mildara Blass (Fosters Brewing Group) of Napa Valley-based Beringer, the alliance between Southcorp/Rosemount and California's Mondavi, BRL Hardy's joint venture with the second largest U.S. wine company, Constellation Brands (to operate as Pacific West Partners) and the purchase by New Zealand's biggest wine firm (Montana) of the country's second largest winery (Corbans). See Exhibit 9 for the 10 largest wine companies worldwide.

VINCOR INTERNATIONAL INC.

Vincor International Inc. (Vincor) was formed as a combination of a number of Canadian wineries—Barnes Wines, Brights Wines, Cartier Wines, Inniskillin Wines and Dumont—over the period from 1989 to 1996. Vincor began operations in 1989 with a management buyout of Ridout Wines (Ridout) from John Labatt Ltd. The Ridout management team, led by Allan Jackson, Peter Graigner and John Hall, sought out Donald Triggs to lead the purchase and become CEO. They raised more than Cdn$2 million in equity, largely from personal finances, and borrowed $25 million to buy out Ridout. The new company was renamed Cartier Wines and Beverages.

Vincor had grown in three stages to become Canada's largest wine company in 2002. The first stage of growth had been a leveraged buyout (LBO) in turbulent times,

1989 to 1995, followed by a period of consolidation and rationalization—Building Canada's Wine Company (1990 to 2000). The third stage of growth was Building an International Wine Company (2000 onwards).

The first stage had seen the formation of Vincor and wine company acquisitions. From 1995 to 2000, Vincor acquired eight wineries, integrated its sales, marketing, production and accounting, and merged two wine-kit companies. This lead to economies of scale and a 21 per cent market share in 2000.

During this period, Vincor developed Canada's first premium wine brands: Jackson-Triggs, Inniskillin and Sawmill Creek. The Canadian wine market had seen a shift from popular (less than $7 retail price) to premium ($7 to $10 retail price), leading Vincor to start focusing on the premium and super-premium ($10 to $15 retail price) segments. They developed vineyards and re-capitalized wineries to support premium growth. Product coverage was also achieved in the growing ultra-premium ($15 to $20 retail price) and specialty (more than $20 retail price) segments. The year 2000 saw Vincor at a strategic crossroads. Triggs recalled:

> We were faced with three options. We could choose to be a cash cow by further developing our dominant Canadian position. A second option was to develop a diversified Canadian beverage conglomerate. A third option was to expand to the United States and perhaps beyond.
>
> We went for option 3. The move was driven by opportunities as well as threats. In terms of opportunities, the global trend was one of strong growth and premiumisation. There was an industry consolidation favoring global brands. The market was fragmented with the largest player only having one per cent market share. The markets for New World wine were growing. The dynamics in the U.S. market were highly profitable with very high profit margins. We were already #5 in North America and #22 globally.
>
> On the risk side, wine was an agricultural industry and as such susceptible to changing weather conditions. A diversified portfolio in terms of production and markets would only be an asset.

Triggs and Vincor decided to go international. The company's mission statement was drafted to reflect the new strategic plan:

> To become one of the world's top-10 wine companies, producing Vincor-owned New World, premium branded wines, which are marketed and sold through Vincor-controlled sales and distribution systems in all major premium wine consuming regions.

Where Were the Big Markets?

According to Triggs:

> The United States was the largest market with New World wine sales of $10 billion followed by the United Kingdom and Australia at $3.7 billion each. Canada and the rest of Europe were next at $700 million. Japan was the sixth largest with sales of about $500 million. To be a New World market player, Vincor needed to be in five to six markets.

In 2002, the company's strategy was formulated for each region. In Canada, the aim was to build share in premium segments, to develop export capability and to generate cash and improve return on capital employed. In the United States, Vincor decided to focus on portfolio migration to high-end super-premium, enhancement of sales capability, product innovation and a shift to consumer marketing. Vincor's international strategy was to develop new geographic markets for core brands, specifically for icewine, a signature product for Canada that had attained world recognition. It was a luxury product in terms of pricing and margins and one of the top-five wine brands in select Asian duty-free stores. The U.S. launch was in F'01 in 1,850 high-end restaurants. By 2002, Inniskillin was being sold in 3,300 premium restaurants across the United States. The European launch of Inniskillin was slated for F'02.

U.S. ACQUISITIONS
R.H. Phillips

On October 5, 2000, Vincor acquired R.H. Phillips, a leading California estate winery, which produced a range of super-premium wines. The aggregate purchase price, including acquisition costs, was US$56.7 million. In addition, R.H. Phillips' debt of US$33.8 million was assumed and refinanced by the company. The Phillips acquisition and the refinancing of the assumed debt were funded entirely through borrowing from the company's senior lender.

R.H. Phillips was established in 1981 by John and Karl Giguiere. It was located in the Dunnigan Hills Viticultural Region near the wine regions of Napa and Sonoma. R.H. Phillips specialized in the production of super-premium wines, marketing its products under the brands R.H. Phillips, Toasted Head, EXP and Kempton Clark. Its wines were sold throughout the United States and in several other countries, including Canada. In 2001, its brands generated sales revenues of approximately US$25 million for Vincor. Its wines were distributed across the United States by a network of 13 sales executives, distributors and brokers.

The Phillips acquisition established a presence for Vincor in the U.S. wine market, in addition to adding strong brands, which were well-positioned in the super-premium category, one of the fastest growing segments of the wine market. With its national network of distributors and sales professionals, R.H. Phillips provided a platform for future acquisitions in the United States (such as the Hogue acquisition), while also facilitating the marketing of Vincor's products in the United States.

The Hogue Cellars

On September 1, 2001, Vincor acquired Hogue Cellars for US$36.3 million. Hogue was the second largest wine producer in Washington state, well-known for its super premium wine. Hogue was a family-controlled and family-operated winery founded in 1982 by Mike and Gary Hogue.

The Washington state wine industry had emerged as the second largest producer of premium wines in the United States, after California. Hogue produced red varietals, including Cabernet Sauvignon, Merlot and Syrah, as well as white varietals, including Chardonnay, Sauvignon Blanc, Riesling and Pinot Gris. In 2001, sales of Hogue-produced premium wine were 415,400 cases. In addition to its owned brands, Hogue was the U.S. agent for Kim Crawford wines of New Zealand and Heritage Road wines from Brian McGuigan wines of Australia.

The Hogue acquisition added 11 sales people nationally and immediately increased Vincor's annual U.S. sales volume to more than one million cases and its annual U.S. revenues to more than US$60 million.

INTEGRATION WITH R.H. PHILLIPS

Vincor's management believed that Hogue was an excellent complement to the R.H. Phillips portfolio, as Hogue was primarily a super-premium brand, with approximately 88 per cent of its volume in the super-premium category. The strength of the Hogue product range lay in different varietals from the R.H. Phillips range. Different appellations greatly reduced portfolio overlap, as the character and taste of the wines were clearly distinct. Given the price and quality positioning of both businesses, customers were similar, and opportunity existed to improve the efficiency and effectiveness of the sales force, while simultaneously developing incremental sales for all brands in the combined portfolio. Vincor incurred expenses of US$4 million from the integration of Hogue and R.H. Phillips and from transaction costs related to the Hogue acquisition. It was management's objective that the integration of Hogue and R.H. Phillips would result in the realization of annual synergies of US$2.8 million.

VINCOR IN 2002

In 2002, Vincor was Canada's largest producer and marketer of wines, with leading brands in all segments of the market in Canada. Vincor had a 22 per cent market share and sales of Cdn$376.6 million (see Exhibit 11 for Financials). Andrés Wines Ltd., the second largest winery in Canada, had approximately an 11 per cent market share. Vincor was North America's fourth largest wine producer in terms of volume and the world's 22nd largest wine producer in terms of revenue.

The company had wineries in British Columbia, Ontario, Quebec, New Brunswick, California and Washington state, marketing wines produced from grapes grown in the Niagara Peninsula of Ontario, the Okanagan Valley of British Columbia, the Dunnigan Hills of California, the Columbia Valley of Washington state and other countries. The company's California and Washington wines were available throughout the United States and in parts of Canada (see Exhibit 10 for corporate structure).

Canada's government liquor distribution systems and the company's 165-store Wine Rack chain of retail stores sold Vincor's well-known and industry-leading brands: Inniskillin, Jackson-Triggs, Sumac Ridge, Hawthorne Mountain, R.H. Phillips, Toasted Head, Hogue, Sawmill Creek, Notre Vin Maison, Entre-Lacs, L'Ambiance, Caballero de Chile, Bellini, Spumante Bambino, President Canadian Champagne, Okanagan Vineyards, Salmon Harbor and other table, sparkling and fortified wines, Vex and the Canada Cooler brands of coolers, and the Growers and Vibe brands of cider.

In the United States, R.H. Phillips, Toasted Head, EXP, Kempton Clark and Hogue wine brands were distributed through a national network of more than 127 distributors, supported by eight brokers and 40 sales managers. The company's icewines were sold in the United States through a dedicated team of sales managers and internationally, primarily through the duty-free distribution channel. The company had seven employees outside of Canada engaged full-time in the sale of icewine.

Vincor's portfolio had evolved as per Table 1.

Table 1 Evolution of Vincor's Portfolio—Table Wine

	F'95		F'02	
	% By Vol	% by $	% By Vol	% by $
Popular	83	80	47	28
Premium	17	20	53	72

Source: Company files.

The company's objectives in 2002 were to obtain a top quartile return on capital employed (ROCE) of 16 per cent to 20 per cent and to achieve sales of Cdn$1 billion and an earnings per share (EPS) increase of more than 15 per cent. At the time these objectives were to be met as per Table 2.

Table 2   Company Sales Objectives (Cdn$ millions)

	Current	5 Years
Canada	300	400
United States	100	200
Icewine	15	50
Acquisitions	0	350
Total	415	1,000

Source: Company files.

GOUNDREY WINES PTY. LTD.

Goundrey Wines was one of the pioneer winery operations in Western Australia. The Goundrey family had established the vineyard in 1972, and the first vintage was produced in 1976. By 1995, the business had grown to approximately 17,000 cases in annual sales and was sold to Perth businessman Jack Bendat. Bendat expanded both the vineyards and the winery to reach 2002 sales levels of 250,000 cases annually and revenues of AUD$25 million. Goundrey was one of the largest wineries in Western Australia, selling under two labels, Goundrey and Fox River (see Exhibit 12 for financials).

Bendat was 77 years old, and health and family concerns had resulted in his recent decision to sell the business. Vincor believed it would be able to purchase the assets of Goundrey for AUD$46 million plus working capital at close (estimated at AUD$16.5 million) plus transaction costs of AUD$2 million for an enterprise value of AUD$64.5 million.

The majority of the Goundrey brand volume (85 per cent) was sold in the AUD$15 to AUD$30 super-premium segment of the Australian market. The ultra-premium segment ($30 to $50) accounted for seven per cent of sales and the premium ($10 to $15) for the remaining eight per cent. The company's sales were almost entirely in the domestic market, with three per cent export sales. When asked what was Goundrey's export strategy, Bendat said, "I answer the phone."

Goundrey employed its own sales force in Queensland and New South Wales, with a total of 13 sales reps and four sales managers in two states. In other states, Goundrey had appointed distributors. In all regions, Goundrey was the most important winery for the distributor. Goundrey had tighter control of its distribution capability in Australia than most of its competitors. Goundrey consumption was running at more than 26 per cent year-over-year growth versus 2001.

Located 350 km south of Perth, the winery could process 3,500 tonnes of grapes. The winery also had its own bottling capability, enabling it to support an export business where each export market has different labeling requirements.

Triggs felt the Goundrey acquisition would be an important strategic move for Vincor. He saw several major advantages. First, the acquisition would be a significant step in achieving Vincor's strategy of converting from a North American to a global player. The Australian wine industry had captured market share in the world's new wine markets and was poised to continue to do so. Second, the Western Australia region had an established reputation for super- and ultra-premium wines. Although the grape harvest was a mere four per cent of the Australian total, more than 25 per cent of Australia's super-premium wines were sourced from that state. Third, the company had developed its own sales force in Queensland and New South Wales. Triggs wanted the proposal to go through.

Exhibit 1   Top 10 Producers of Wine in the World—2001

Country	Wine Production* (million litres)	Share of World Production (%)
France	5,330	19.9
Italy	5,090	19.0
Spain	3,050	11.4
United States	1,980	7.4
Argentina	1,580	5.9
Australia	1,020	3.8
Germany	900	3.4
Portugal	770	2.9
South Africa	650	2.4
Chile	570	2.1
World	27,491	

* Does not include juice and musts (the expressed juice of fruit and especially grapes before and during fermentation; also the pulp and skins of the crushed grapes).
Note: 1 litre = 0.26 gallons; each case contains 12 × 750 ml bottles = 9 litres.
Source: G. Dutruc-Rosset, Extract of the Report on World Vitiviniculture, June 24, 2002.

Exhibit 2   Top 10 Exporters of Wine in the World—2001

Country	Wine Production* (million litres)	Share of World Exports (%)
Italy	1,830	26.5
France	1,580	22.9
Spain	990	14.4
Australia	380	5.5
Chile	310	4.5
United States	300	4.3
Germany	240	3.5
Portugal	200	2.9
South Africa	180	2.6
Moldavia	160	2.3
World	6,897	

Source: G. Dutruc-Rosset, Extract of the Report on World Vitiviniculture, June 24, 2002.

Exhibit 3   Top 10 Wine-Consuming Nations—2001

Country	Wine Consumption (million litres)	Share of World Consumption (%)
France	3,370	15.4
Italy	3,050	13.9
United States	2,133	9.7
Germany	1,966	9.0
Spain	1,400	6.4
Argentina	1,204	5.5
United Kingdom	1,010	4.6
China	580	2.6
Russia	550	2.5
Romania	470	2.1
World	21,892	

Source: G. Dutruc-Rosset, Extract of the Report on World Vitiviniculture, June 24, 2002.

Exhibit 4   U.S. Wine Exports—Top Countries (by Dollar Value in 2002)

Country Ranking by 2002 Dollar Value	Value ($000)	Volume (litres 000)
United Kingdom	188,895	95,446
Canada	92,571	50,348
Japan	81,199	32,342
Netherlands	53,201	26,388
Belgium	18,791	10,884
France	13,326	5,943
Germany	11,818	8,634
Ireland	10,153	5,380
Switzerland	7,199	3,914
Denmark	5,710	3,933
Mexico	5,001	3,705
Taiwan	4,868	2,736
South Korea	3,865	2,439
China	3,370	2,537
Singapore	3,002	1,822
Sweden	2,782	1,145
Hong Kong	2,393	1,140

Source: Wine Institute and Ivie International using data from U.S. Dept. of Commerce, USA Trade Online. History revised. Numbers may not total exactly due to rounding.

Exhibit 5   Australia Wineries

	1998 to 1999	2000 to 2001
Wineries (number)	1,150	1,318
Hectares under vine	122,915	148,275
Wine grape production	793	1,035
Wine consumption	373	398
Wine exports		
million litres	216	339
AUD$ million	$ 991	$ 1,614
Wine imports		
million litres	24	13
AUD$ million	$ 114	$ 92

Source: Company files.

Exhibit 6   Australia—Top Export Markets—2001

	Million Litres	AUD$ Million
United Kingdom	183	762
United States	78	457
Canada	17	106
New Zealand	23	83
Germany	13	55
Other	61	301
All Markets	375	1,764

Source: Company files.

Exhibit 7   The Wine Market—Canada—Fiscal 2002

	Retail Price	% By Volume	Trend	% By Sales
Popular	< $7	33%	−5%	20%
Premium	$7–$10	35%	5%	30%
Super-Premium	$10–$15	24%	19%	33%
Ultra-Premium	$15–$20	6%	31%	15%
Specialty	>$20	2%	45%	6%

Source: Company files.

Exhibit 8   The U.S. Market for California Wine—Fiscal 2002

	Retail Price	% By Volume	F'02 Trend*	% By Sales
Jug	<$3	36%	–4%	12%
Premium	$3–$7	36%	–2%	27%
Super-Premium	$7–$15	18%	8%	28%
Ultra-Premium	>$15	10%	3%	33%

* Total U.S. table wine market +1%; imports +9%; states other than California +4%
Source: Company files.

Exhibit 9   Top 10 Wine Companies and Sales in 2002 (US$)

Company	Country	Wine Sales ($ Million)
E. & J. Gallo Winery	United States	1,500
Foster's Group	Australia	818
Seagram	Canada	800
Constellation Brands	United States	712
Southcorp	Australia	662
Castel Freres	France	625
Diageo	Britain	590
Henkell & Sonlein	Germany	528
Robert Mondavi	United States	506

Note: Excludes France's LVMH, which earned more than 75 per cent of its $1.6 billion in wine sales from champagne.
Source: Direction des Etudes/Centre Français du Commerce Exterieur.

Exhibit 10   Vincor's Significant Legal Subsidiaries—2001 (all wholly owned)

Subsidiary	Jurisdiction of Incorporation
Hawthorne Mountain Vineyards (2000) Ltd	Canada
The Hogue Cellars, Ltd	Washington
Inniskillin Wines Inc	Ontario
Inniskillin Okanagan Vineyards Inc	British Columbia
R.H. Phillips, Inc	California
Spagnol's Wine & Beer Making Supplies Ltd	Canada
Sumac Ridge Estate Winery (2000) Ltd.	Canada
Vincor (Quebec) Inc	Quebec

Source: Company files.

Exhibit 11 Vincor Consolidated Financials (1998 to 2002) (Cdn$ millions)

	F'98	F'99	F'00	F'01	F'02	Average Annual Growth	
						F'01-02	F'98-02
Revenue	206.4	253.2	268.2	294.9	376.6	27.7%	17.7%
EBITDA	28.1	35.0	37.9	49.5	70.5	42.4%	26.1%
% Revenue	13.6%	13.8%	14.1%	16.8%	18.7%		
Net Income	10.8	11.7	13.3	14.3	26.9	40.1%	25.6%
Avg.Capital Empl'd	145.5	191.6	222.1	310.4	468.2		
ROCE (EBIT)	14.5%	13.8%	12.7%	13.1%	12.5%		
Funds Employed							
Receivables	30.4	33.3	35.7	37.4	55.1		
Inventory	65.1	83.1	70.7	125.9	175.6		
Working Capital	57.8	73.3	67.9	111.9	184.9		
Net Fixed Assets	45.2	60.0	73.3	165.9	178.8		
Other Assets	59.8	87.1	82.7	133.4	161.5		
Funds Employed	162.8	220.4	223.9	411.2	525.2		
Turnover	1.2x	1.1x	1.2x	.7x	.7x		
Financing							
Debt (net)	50.9	92.5	80.5	254.5	110.1		
Deferred Tax	9.6	12.1	14.1	11.4	18.3		
Equity*	102.3	115.8	129.3	145.3	396.8		
Financing	162.8	220.4	223.9	411.2	525.2		

Note: EBITDA — Earnings Before Interest, Taxes, Depreciation and Amortization
*Increased in 2002 due to the fact that two equity issues were completed that year.
Source: Company files.

Exhibit 12 Goundrey Financials (for years ending June 30) (000s)

	1999	2000	2001
Sales (000)	16,280	21,509	20,942
EBITDA	3,102	6,014	3,548
EBITDA%Sales	19.1%	28.0%	16.9%

Source: Company files.

CIBC–Barclays: Should Their Caribbean Operations Be Merged?

At the end of 2001, the Canadian Imperial Bank of Commerce (CIBC) and Barclays Bank PLC were in advanced negotiations regarding the potential merger of their respective retail, corporate and offshore banking operations in the Caribbean. Motivated in part by a mutual desire to achieve greater economies of scale, the negotiations had gained momentum ever since the possibility had been raised a year earlier.

Notwithstanding the progress to date, some members of each board could not help but wonder whether this was the best direction to take. Would the combined company be able to deliver superior returns? Would it be possible to integrate, within budget, companies that had competed with each other in the region for decades? Would either firm be better off divesting regional operations instead? Should the two firms just continue to go-it-alone with an emphasis on continual improvement? These and other issues and options continued to be discussed by the executives at CIBC, and their counterparts at Barclays.

Decision time was fast approaching. Both executive teams knew that to prolong discussion further would increase employee, investor and customer anxieties and perhaps do serious harm to both firms. A decision needed to be made within the coming week; there was little time for additional research.

Don Wood and Professor Paul W. Beamish prepared this case solely to provide material for class discussion. The authors do not intend to illustrate either effective or ineffective handling of a managerial situation. The authors may have disguised certain names and other identifying information to protect confidentiality.

Version: (A) 2004-09-30

Richard Ivey School of Business
The University of Western Ontario

AN OVERVIEW OF BANKING IN THE CARIBBEAN

Banking in the Caribbean can best be described as complex and dynamic. Most of the Caribbean countries are islands, with the consequent natural isolation from each other and the main continental world (see Exhibit 1).

Most Caribbean countries were colonies until the latter half of the 20th century. Caribbean banks were originally largely a convenience for the colonial governments and their representatives, and focused on savings, some lending and financing trade. In colonial times, branches of international banks such as Barclays were set up in the region to finance the production and export of commodities such as bananas, sugar, rum, bauxite and petroleum. These banks viewed the Caribbean as a small part of their global operations, and they typically focused on maximizing profits and shareholder returns. They were an oligopoly, involving a small number of players with limited government control. Consequently, the banks co-operated in setting interest rates and terms of credit and were able to make significant profits.

In the post-colonial period, there was an effort by governments in the region to exert greater control over the economies, and some governments nationalized a number of industries, including the banking sector. By the 1980s, the limitations of state ownership had become evident, and many state-owned banks were privatized. The most significant result was increased competition and an improvement in customer service and product innovation.

The Caribbean banking industry is currently undergoing structural change characterized by mergers and strategic alliances. These mergers and alliances have been driven by the need for economies of scale and scope and the need to be more competitive in the light globalization in the overall industry. Mergers are complicated, however, because of the many central banks and different currencies—many countries have individual central banks and their own currency, the exception being the Organization of Eastern Caribbean Countries (OECS), comprising eight countries,[1] which share a central bank and currency.

CURRENT OPERATIONS IN THE CARIBBEAN

Barclays PLC (total assets of US$500 billion) and CIBC (total assets of US$200 billion) have extensive operations throughout the Caribbean. Although neither has branches in all countries, between the two, they cover most of the English-speaking Caribbean, as illustrated in Exhibit 2.

CIBC CARIBBEAN OPERATIONS

CIBC Canada is one of North America's leading financial institutions, measured by assets, with more than eight million personal banking and business customers worldwide. It has provided banking services in the West Indies[2] since 1920 and employs approximately 1,600 staff serving 350,000 retail and commercial clients at 42 branches and four commercial banking centres.

---

[1]The Eastern Caribbean comprises Anguilla, Antigua and Barbuda, the Commonwealth of Dominica, Grenada, Montserrat, St. Kitts and Nevis, St. Lucia, and St. Vincent and the Grenadines.
[2] For the purpose of this case, the terms "West Indies" and "the Caribbean" are used interchangeably.

The West Indies comprises 29 countries with four major language groups. The countries in which CIBC operates represent nine per cent of the total population of the Caribbean, and 57 per cent of the English-speaking population. Although the West Indies is a small market, it is growing faster than North America on a population basis. Economic measures, such as GDP per capita, unemployment and inflation, vary widely across the region.

CIBC is the only major bank serving the Caribbean as a separate, integrated unit, CIBC West Indies Holdings Limited (WIHL). Exhibit 3 displays WIHL and its subsidiaries.

CIBC's Caribbean operations showed net income of US$67.8 million, and total assets were US$4.6 billion for the year ended October 31, 2001. The Company is listed on three regional stock exchanges: the Jamaica Stock Exchange, the Barbados Stock Exchange and the Trinidad and Tobago Stock Exchange. In addition, two subsidiaries, CIBC Bahamas Limited and CIBC Jamaica Limited, are also listed on their local stock exchanges. Caribbean headquarters for CIBC is in Barbados.

During 1999 through 2001, CIBC had invested US$48 million in a new banking system, FISERV's International Banking System (ICBS), and related technology and operational improvements. While the conversion to the new system had created operational and customer service problems in the 1999 through 2001 period, the system and its operational platform were now stable and working effectively. The capacity of the ICBS system, however, was built for a bank roughly twice the size of CIBC WI, and full efficiencies would not be realized at the current size of the bank.

CIBC views its strengths and weaknesses in Exhibit 4.

BARCLAYS BANK PLC—CARIBBEAN OPERATIONS

Barclays Caribbean Banking Operations had a net income of US$72.6 million and total assets of US$5.2 billion for the year ended December 31, 2001. Barclays Caribbean branch network employed 1,584 staff: 157 were management staff, 738 were in front office functions and 846 were in back office functions. Staff were unionized in six countries: Antigua & Barbuda, Barbados, Dominica, Grenada, St. Lucia, and St. Vincent & the Grenadines. Apart from salaries and a fully funded pension scheme, local staff received benefits in the form of a medical scheme, loans at preferential rates, 20 to 30 days annual leave, uniforms and profit sharing. Management grades also participated in a bonus scheme, received the use of bank cars, and many had club memberships provided.

Corporate and business services are offered in all 14 countries (see Exhibit 5), and offshore banking services are offered in the Bahamas, Barbados, Cayman, the British Virgin Islands (BVI), and Turks & Caicos. Corporate banking accounts for 45 per cent of corporate income, personal banking 27 per cent and offshore banking 28 per cent.

Barclays' current Caribbean strategy has been rationalization, alongside focused development of the onshore business, together with controlled development of offshore business. Increasing focus has been placed on managing the level of operational risk. Specifically this has meant:

- Organic growth of the corporate and retail presences in existing countries;
- Focus on increased share of existing customers through improvement of consumer lending propositions;

- Limited investment to rationalize the operating model through centralization initiatives and closure of marginal branches.

Barclays' view of current competitive conditions and their strengths and vulnerabilities can be summarized as follows:

Competition is increasing. For example:

- Traditional Canadian bank competitors are marketing aggressively;
- Regional indigenous banks are expanding their footprints;
- Competitors with new business models (e.g. niche players like CitiGroup) are increasingly entering Barclays' markets;
- In the onshore and retail and corporate businesses, competition comes from large Canadian banks (principally CIBC, Royal Bank of Canada and Scotiabank) and from regional indigenous banks (e.g. Republic Bank of Trinidad);
- Barclays' strong customer relationships have been key to maintaining the bank's market position and have helped to maintain margins;
- Price and convenience are becoming increasingly important as buying factors; as markets become more crowded, price erosion can be expected to reduce currently relatively high margins;
- Barclays sees its delivery channel "gaps" of real-time electronic banking for corporate accounts and full telephone and Internet offerings for retail customers as becoming increasingly significant.

With no player having an obvious opportunity to develop a sustainable competitive advantage, Barclays believes that the player that achieves the best productivity (and can match the best customer service) is likely to succeed in the medium term. This has led Barclays to increase its focus on how to maximize the cost effectiveness of its operating model.

Barclays' information technology (IT) approach focuses on its Caribbean Regional Data Processing Centre (RPC), located in Nassau, Bahamas. One reason for locating the centre in the Bahamas is the strong Bahamian secrecy laws, which protect confidential client data from being disclosed to third parties. The RPC operates the core banking applications for 13 of the 14 countries in the region.[3] It performs the following:

- BRAINS (Barclays Retail Accounting and Information System), the retail banking software package, which is also used by Barclays Africa;
- Interlink connection for the ATM network (55 units);
- Gateways to the MasterCard and VISA networks;
- BusinessMaster, online access to information and customer service for corporate and offshore customers; and
- BarclayCall, online access to information and customer service for retail customers (available only in the Bahamas and Barbados).

All the applications above are run on stand-alone Caribbean systems, with no dependency on the United Kingdom except for contingency arrangements.

The BRAINS system had been installed about 10 years previously and lacked the ability to consolidate projects by customer as to facilitate Internet and telephone

---

[3]The remaining country is British Virgin Islands, which, for historic reasons, uses a stand-alone accounting system.

banking. Barclays operations in both Africa and the Caribbean were faced with a costly decision on whether to replace BRAINS with a more modern banking system. Moreover, Barclays operations tended to be more manually intensive and costly than those of its competitors, Royal, BNS and CIBC, who had installed more modern technology.

THE COMPETITION

The four major international players identified in Exhibit 6 have each developed a different market niche in which to compete successfully in the retail and commercial markets in the West Indies. The Royal Bank is considered the best performer across the region. CIBC summarized its competitive niches as shown in Exhibit 6.

Banking oligopolies existed across the West Indies, with the five largest banks in each country controlling more than 80 per cent market share. CIBC estimated market shares in the various national markets it serves as shown in Exhibit 7.

In addition to the retail and commercial services, major banks in the Caribbean also serve the US$1.1 billion capital markets in the region. The capital markets business in the West Indies is composed mainly of debt financing arrangements. It is considered a new and emerging sector comprising eight players in this marketplace (see Exhibit 8).

The capital market segment began to develop in the 1980s and is expected to grow at about 10 per cent annually for the next few years. The majority of debt financing is government borrowing, government divestitures of banks, hotels and utilities, and large multinational corporations' projects. More recently, the resource sector has brought more sophisticated arrangements to the West Indies capital markets sector. The market is driven mainly by the large economies of Jamaica and Trinidad & Tobago. Revenue in this sector is generated by a typical one per cent fee and a 3.5 per cent lending spread. In 2000, the total size of all CIBC WI Capital Markets deals was estimated at US$118 million generating about US$3 million of revenue and US$1.5 million in profits.

A few large competitors like CS First Boston, Citibank and ABN AMRO have entered the market and basically manage the region through local relationships with business and government leaders, augmented by head office expertise to complete the transactions. These key relationships are important to gaining business, and many other large competitors like DLJ, Merrill Lynch, and Smith Barney have not been able to enter the market successfully. Exhibit 8 summarizes the main players in the West Indies Capital Markets.

Both CIBC and Barclays now need to assess their options, evaluate the factors and select the best strategy for their respective firms. They must consider whether to merge or not, and determine the implications for merging in this complex environment. Exhibits 9 and 10 provide financial information on the two firms' Caribbean operations.

Exhibit 1   Map of the West Indies

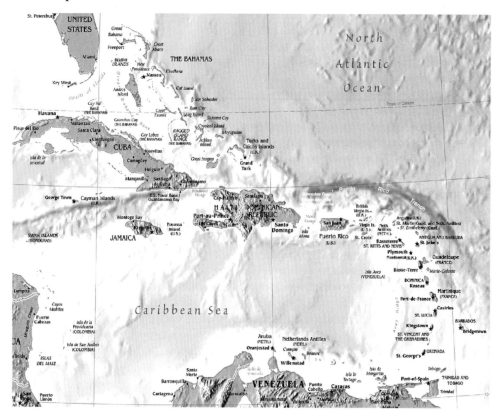

Source: CIA World Factbook, 2004.

Exhibit 2   Caribbean Presence

Country	Population	GDP/Capita (US$)	CIBC	Barclays
Anguilla	10,000	4,000		●
Antigua and Barbuda	70,000	8,419	●	●
The Bahamas	280,000	13,847	●	●
Barbados	270,000	7,750	●	●
Belize	230,000	2,688		●
British Virgin Islands	20,000	12,000		●
The Cayman Islands	30,000	24,000	●	●
Dominica	70,000	3,233		●
Grenada	100,000	877		●
Jamaica	2,570,000	1,756	●	
St. Kitts and Nevis	40,000	5,761		●
St. Lucia	160,000	3,581	●	●
Netherlands Antilles	200,000	N/A		●
St. Vincent and the Grenadines	110,000		●	●
Turks and Caicos Islands	20,000	6,000	●	●

Source: CIBC Economics, World Fact Book, Americas Review 1999—Economic Indicators.

Exhibit 3   Current Situation—CIBC West Indies Holdings Limited (WIHL) and
Subsidiaries

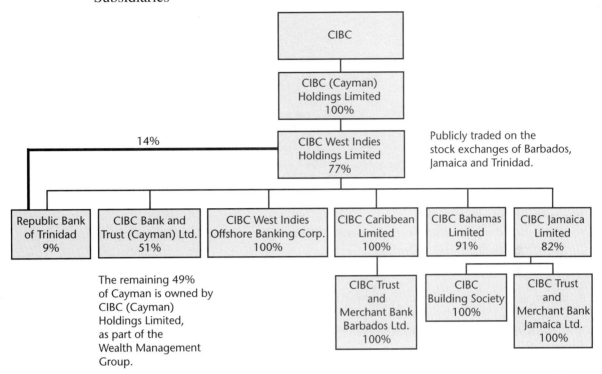

Operating Units:

1. Bahamas—CIBC Bahamas Limited.
2. Jamaica—consists of CIBC Jamaica Limited, CIBC Building Society and CIBC Trust and Merchant Bank Jamaica Limited.
3. Barbados—consists of CIBC Caribbean Limited and CIBC Trust and Merchant Bank Barbados Limited, which includes our operations in Barbados, Antigua, St. Lucia, St. Vincent and Turks & Caicos.
4. Cayman—Fifty-one per cent of operations of CIBC Bank and Trust (Cayman) Ltd., which relate to the Retail and Commercial Operations in Cayman.

Exhibit 4   CIBC Internal Analysis

STRENGTHS

CIBC Ownership
- Strong brand and public image
- Expertise in retail banking
- Effective mix of delivery channels
- High loyalty ratings
- Excellent relationships with governments, important business players and the public
- Enormous value in WIHL franchise on local equity markets – currently selling at 26 X earnings

Management
- New leadership with strong management support from CIBC in Canada
- Extensive knowledge of the region (economic and political)
- Important relationships with business and political leaders

Products and Delivery Channels
- An established strength in product lines currently experiencing tremendous growth in the region (mortgages, cards, ABMs)
- Ability to leverage expertise in all products and services from the Canadian organization

Operations
- Co-ordinated regional operations strengthened by strong linkages to CIBC
- Established branch network with 40 branches in eight countries
- Ability to leverage CIBC Canadian operations expertise from Intria Items Inc., O&T and National Operations Support

Technology
- An integrated banking system (ICBS) that will enable consistent and efficient operations in the WI and will allow new channels such as Internet banking
- An extended wide area network (EWAN) will provide a dependable robust real-time environment
- Ability to leverage CIBC Canadian technology expertise from Intria Corporation and O&T

WEAKNESSES — Issues (all of which were being resolved)

Credit Risk Management
- During the conversion period, Retail Loan losses have increased substantially.
- Recent audits have revealed weaknesses in lending practices.
- There was not a consistent view on credit risk appetite between local management and the credit risk group, which is largely seconded from CIBC Canada.

Items Processing
- Three item processing centres have been found to be inefficient and lacking in reliable processes.

Systems and Technology
- Two years ago, systems were antiquated and not Y2K compliant; however, the new platform is stable and operating effectively.
- The investment in technology exceeds the scale of the current operations.

Organization
- Until recently the West Indies operations were organized geographically.
- Inefficiencies and overlaps.

Jamaica
- Very inefficient operations with high NIX ratios and low returns.
- Poor credit risk management.

Exhibit 5   Barclays Caribbean Business Base

Country	Operating Income—1999 (US$ millions)	No. of Accounts ('000)			No. of Outlets*
		Personal	Business	Total	
Anguilla	2	4.3	0.1	4.4	1
Antigua and Barbuda	8	28.5	0.7	29.2	1
The Bahamas	49	50.1	2.4	52.5	9
Barbados	42	101.0	2.9	103.9	6
Belize	8	16.9	3.1	19.9	4
British Virgin Islands	16	17.6	1.6	19.2	3
The Cayman Islands	34	11.9	3.4	15.3	2
Dominica	4	20.0	0.7	20.7	2
Grenada	6	23.6	1.3	24.9	4
St. Kitts and Nevis	5	14.1	0.4	14.5	2
St. Lucia	12	43.1	1.1	44.2	4
Netherlands Antilles	3	5.7	0.6	6.3	3
St. Vincent and the Grenadines	4	20.8	0.4	21.1	1
Turks and Caicos Islands	12	11.0	2.3	13.2	3
Totals	**205**	**368.6**	**21.0**	**389.3**	**45**

*In addition, there is a Card & Mortgage Centre and a Regional Processing Centre in the Bahamas, as well as a Card and Operations Centre in Barbados.

Exhibit 6   External Analysis—Retail and Commercial

Each of the four major international players has developed a different market niche in which to compete successfully in the retail and commercial market in the West Indies. Royal Bank is considered the best performer across the Region.

Player	Operations	How They Compete in West Indies
CIBC	• 40 branches in eight countries serving 350,000 retail and commercial customers • Core business is retail banking with trust, offshore and capital market activities as other lines of business	• Strong in Retail and Small Business and Merchant services across the West Indies Region, particularly in Bahamas which has a sizeable market share • Market leader in credit card sales in Barbados but lags behind in Bahamas and Jamaica • Good reputation for corporate and capital markets activities • Newest technology in the region • Only major competitor to manage the West Indies as a separate, integrated unit
ScotiaBank	• 158 branches in 24 countries with a balance sheet of Cdn$6.9 billion built primarily on consumer products, hospitality financing and loans to government • Very efficient at managing expenses • In 1998, Bank of Nova Scotia Jamaica earned $73 million, five per cent of total BNS profit • In 1999, International retail operations were larger than domestic operations—the West Indies accounts for the majority of international operations.	• Leader in consumer loans, particularly vehicle loans • Competitive advantage by having hard currency lending operations maintained out of Puerto Rico, giving them access to inexpensive government funding, which they have leveraged throughout the West Indies Region • Focus on product offering and strong marketing efforts • Very successful operations in Jamaica • Good development of local staff using secondments to Canada, consistent
Royal Bank	• 33 branches in nine countries with the most comprehensive convenience delivery channels in those countries and are leaders in the offshore industry	• Active high value strategy and a leader amongst high value clients • Considered best performer of retail banks • Significant offshore and international presence in Barbados and Bahamas • Dominating in certain products in each country
Barclays PLC	• 45 branches in 17 countries and have recently invested US$30 million in new technology for the region	• Strong remittance and offshore business • Strong corporate banking connections • Good Cards business run by Barclaycard US • Offers telephone banking • Strong client relationship building system, (Premiere Service), targeted to its working professional client base

Exhibit 7   Selected Market Share Measures

	Measure	CIBC	Barclays	Scotiabank	Royal Bank	NCB*	Others
Antigua	% total assets						
	% deposits	12		14	10	24	40
	% loans	11	9	22	7	20	31
	No. branches	1	3	4	3		15
	No. ATMs	1	3	4	2		10
Barbados	% total assets						
	% deposits	18	22	13	21	17	9
	% loans	19	21	21	10	18	11
	No. branches	10	6	8	7		15
	No. ATMs	11	8	8	13		14
Jamaica	% total assets						
	% deposits	7		41		36	16
	% loans	9		50		27	14
	No. branches	13		45			100
	No. ATMs	8		31			55
St. Lucia	% total assets						
	% deposits	10	23	16	10	24	19
	% loans	12	24	17	10	21	17
	No. branches	2	4	4	4		10
	No. ATMs	3	4	7	3		12
St. Vincent	% total assets	14	14	13			59
	% deposits						
	% loans						
	No. branches	1	1	1			10
	No. ATMs	1	1	1			5
The Bahamas	% total assets	19		15	21		45
	% deposits						
	% loans						
	No. branches	8	10	17	21		27
	No. ATMs	9	11	21	21		18
The Cayman Islands	% total assets	25	25	15			35
	% deposits						
	% loans						
	No. branches	2	2	4	2		10
	No. ATMs	4	3	3	2		16
Turks & Caicos	% total assets		70	16			14
	% deposits						
	% loans						
	No. branches	1	2	2			
	No. ATMs	1	2	1			

*National Commercial Banks.

Exhibit 8   External Analysis—Capital Markets

The West Indies Capital Markets business is dominated by a small number of players. Citibank is the dominant competitor in the Region and is estimated to have earned profits of US$20 million in the Capital Markets sector in each of the last five years.

Financial Services Company	Industry Focus[1]	Product Focus[2]	Level of Relationship with Foreign Parent/ Partner[3]	Level of Physical Caribbean Presence	Market Share (approx)	Level of Offshore Booking (approx)
CIBC	E&P, H&R, A, Cong. PS	Bnd U/W, PF, LS	Medium	High	10%	100%
Citibank	E&P, PS, A	Bnd U/W, D, CBF, LS, S	High	Low	50%	80%
Royal Merchant Bank (Trinidad)	E&P, H&R, A, Cong. PS	Bnd U/W, E U/W, S. PF	Medium	High	15%	50%
Republic Bank (Fincor)	E&P, H&R, A, Cong. PS	PF, Bnd U/W, E U/W, LS	Low	Medium	10%	60%
Scotia Bank	E&P, H&R, A, Cong. PS	Bnd U/W, LS	High	High	5%	70%
Credit Swiss First Boston	E&P, PS	Bnd U/W, LS	High	None	5%	100%
ABN Ambro	E&P	LS	High	None	4%	100%
Chase	E&P, PS	Bnd U/W, LS	High	None	1%	100%

1. Energy and Petrochemicals; (E&P), Hotel and Resorts; (H&R), Agriculture; (A), Conglomerates; (Cong), Public Sector; (PS).

2. Bond Underwriting: (Bnd UW), Project Financing (PF), Equity Underwriting (E U/W), Derivatives; (D), Commodity Based Financing: (CBF), Loan Syndication; (LS), Securatization, (S), Advisory Services; (AS).

3. This variable measures the relationship with the foreign partner in terms of advisory assistance on financial products structuring.

Exhibit 9   Five Year Statistical Review—CIBC West Indies Holdings Condensed Consolidated Balance Sheets (as of October 31) (Bds $000s)

	2001	2000	1999	1998	1997
Assets					
Cash resources	2,743,877	1,849,630	1,961,285	813,025	772,552
Securities	2,417,865	2,249,992	1,578,942	458,508	450,235
Loans	3,760,574	3,411,184	3,162,052	2,424,544	2,030,889
Customer's liability under acceptances	11,587	42,880	1,651	1,600	4,532
Net Investment in leases	3,055	4,221	5,396	6,817	6,061
Fixed assets	138,114	123,427	120,401	75,175	62,281
Other assets	113,982	127,393	127,179	118,460	67,039
	9,189,054	7,808,727	6,956,906	3,898,129	3,393,589
Liabilities and Shareholders' Equity					
Deposits	8,191,737	6,716,869	6,016,367	3,285,774	2,895,778
Acceptances	11,587	42,880	1,651	1,600	4,532
Other liabilities	101,172	303,874	279,636	173,236	97,697
Minority interests	232,282	195,375	170,298	39,829	37,321
Shareholders' equity common shares	316,380	316,380	316,380	274,980	274,980
Retained earnings	335,896	233,349	172,574	122,710	83,281
	9,189,054	7,808,727	6,956,906	3,898,129	3,393,589

Consolidated Statements of Income (as of October 31) (Bds $000s)

	2001	2000	1999	1998	1997
Interest income	601,309	594,914	497,534	348,231	317,178
Interest expense	(316,737)	(313,945)	(252,750)	(149,632)	(147,423)
Net interest income	284,572	280,969	244,784	198,599	169,755
Non-interest income	128,378	126,846	120,286	71,640	63,020
Total income	412,950	407,815	365,070	270,239	232,775
Non-interest expenses	218,519	224,891	210,402	159,211	136,167
Provision for credit losses	10,287	28,602	23,908	15,342	10,277
Total Expenses	228,806	253,493	234,310	174,553	146,444
Net income before income taxes	184,144	154,322	130,760	95,686	86,331
Income taxes	8,616	7,038	4,027	12,980	15,228
Net income before exception/extraordinary items and minoirty interests	175,528	147,284	126,731	82,706	71,103
Exceptional/Extraordinary items	–	–	(2,171)	–	583
Minority interests	(39,919)	(29,702)	(29,536)	(7,690)	(4,563)
Net income	135,609	117,582	95,024	75,016	67,123

Exhibit 10 Financial Information—Barclays Profit and Loss/Balance Sheets (for years ending December 31) (US$ millions)

	1995	1996	1997	1998	1999
Net interest income	103	107	116	134	153
Commission inocme	41	42	46	51	54
Total operating income	**144**	**149**	**162**	**185**	**207**
Staff Costs	(53)	(57)	(58)	(61)	(66)
Property, equipment and other expenses	(36)	(34)	(42)	(48)	(50)
Depreciation/amortisation	–	(6)	(8)	(8)	(10)
Operating costs	**(89)**	**(97)**	**(108)**	**(117)**	**(126)**
Net operating income	**55**	**52**	**54**	**68**	**80**
Provisions	**(8)**	**(11)**	**(2)**	**(1)**	**(9)**
Profit before Tax	**47**	**41**	**52**	**67**	**71**
	1,995	**1,996**	**1,997**	**1,998**	**1,999**
ASSETS					
Loans to banks	54	50	168	55	87
Loans to customers	1,141	1,240	1,360	1,618	1,884
Other assets	255	572	593	752	860
Accruals and prepayments	–	3	14	21	23
Due from BBPLC	2,270	2,017	2,188	2,897	2,855
Property & Equipment	54	62	61	60	79
Total assets	**3,774**	**3,944**	**4,384**	**5,403**	**5,788**
LIABILITIES AND CAPITAL					
Customer deposits	3,469	3,513	3,836	4,654	4,972
Other liabilites	108	206	279	161	180
Due to BBPLC	166	194	235	549	580
Revenue reserve	31	31	34	39	56
Total liabilities	**3,774**	**3,944**	**4,384**	**5,403**	**5,788**

2000 Full Year Forecast (US$ millions)

	H1 2000 Actual	H2 2000 Forecast	2000 Forecast
Net interest income	91	91	182
Fees and commission	30	29	59
Total operating income	**121**	**120**	**241**
Staff Costs	(32)	(30)	(62)
Property and equipment	(11)	(11)	(22)
Other expenses	(14)	(11)	(25)
Depreciation/amortisation	(4)	(5)	(9)
Operating costs	**(61)**	**(57)**	**(118)**
Net Operating Income	**60**	**63**	**123**
Provisions	**(4)**	**(4)**	**(8)**
Profit before Tax	**56**	**59**	**115**

* Income analysed between Net interest, fees and commissions and other.

Mattel and the Toy Recalls (A)[1]

It's sad to say that the most safe product coming out of China these days is fireworks.

—Jay Leno, U.S. Talk Show Host

Jay Leno aptly reflected the mood of U.S. consumers during the summer of 2007. Many Chinese-made goods such as pet food, toothpaste, seafood, and tires had been recalled in recent weeks. These recalls began to severely erode the confidence of U.S. consumers in Chinese-made goods. On July 30, 2007, the senior executive team of Mattel under the leadership of Bob Eckert, CEO received reports that the surface paint on the Sarge Cars made in China contained lead in excess of U.S. federal regulations.[2] It was certainly not good news for Mattel, which was about to recall 967,000 Chinese-made children's character toys such as Dora, Elmo, and Big Bird, because of excess lead in the paint. Not surprisingly, the decision ahead was not only about whether to recall the Sarge Cars and other toys that might be unsafe, but also how to deal with the recall situation.

TOY INDUSTRY—OVERVIEW

The global toy market was estimated to be a $71 billion business in 2007—an increase of about six per cent over the previous year.[3] About 36 per cent of the global market

---

Professors Hari Bapuji and Paul Beamish wrote this case solely to provide material for class discussion. The authors do not intend to illustrate either effective or ineffective handling of a managerial situation. The authors may have disguised certain names and other identifying information to protect confidentiality.

Richard Ivey School of Business
The University of Western Ontario

---

[1] This case has been written on the basis of published sources. Consequently, the interpretations and perspectives presented are not necessarily those of Mattel and other organizations represented in this case or any of their employees.

[2] Mattel, Inc.'s communication (dated September 5, 2007) to the Subcommittee on Commerce, Trade and Consumer Protection.

[3] Source: International Council of Toy Industries and NPD.

was concentrated in North America (about $24 billion), but annual sales in this region were growing at a slower pace—about one per cent. European markets accounted for about 30 per cent of the global toy sales and were growing at about five per cent each year. In contrast, the markets in Asia grew at 12 per cent in 2006, and were expected to grow by 25 per cent in 2007.[4] A large part of this growth was expected to occur in China and India, whose burgeoning middle-classes were thriving on the double-digit economic growth in their countries.

The toy industry in the United States had a large number of players. About 880 companies operated in the dolls, toys, and games manufacturing industry in 2002. This figure was about 10 per cent less than the 1,019 companies that operated in 1997. Approximately 70 per cent of the toy companies employed less than 20 persons.[5] The industry was dominated by a few key players such as Mattel, Hasbro, RC2, JAAKS Pacific, Marvel, and Lego. The industry leaders were Mattel and Hasbro, whose combined sales in 2006 were about US$8.7 billion. The sales of many other major players were under a billion dollars. Exhibit 1 contains key financial data of some major U.S. toy makers.

Big retailers like Wal-Mart and Target had become major players in the U.S. toy market. They not only sold the products of other toy companies such as Mattel, Hasbro, and Lego, but also sourced toys directly from China. These toys were often sold under their own brand names. For example, Wal-Mart sold toys under its Kid-Connection brand while Target sold toys under its PlayWonder brand.[6] It was estimated that Wal-Mart accounted for about 25 per cent of the toy sales in the United States[7]. As a result of the entry of big-box retailers in the toy industry, specialty toy retailers such as Toys'R'Us had steadily lost market share.[8] The top five retailers sold about 60 per cent of all the toys sold in the United States.[9]

Toy markets in the United States were categorized into multiple segments such as Action Figures & Accessories, Arts & Crafts, Building Sets, Dolls, Games/Puzzles, Infant/Preschool Toys, Youth Electronics, Outdoor & Sports Toys, and Plush Vehicles. Of these, the infant/preschool toy segment was the largest, followed by outdoor and sport toys, and dolls. These segments had largely remained stagnant over the years. As a result of kids getting old younger (KGOY), the only segment with noticeable growth was youth electronics. By contrast, video games which were outside the traditional toy industry had been experiencing remarkable growth. For segment-wise sales of toy in the United States, see Exhibit 2.

While the major markets for toys existed in the United States and Europe, production was concentrated in Asia, primarily China. About 60 per cent of the toys sold in the world were made in China. More than 10,500 toy makers operated in China.[10] These companies typically had contacts with large Western toy companies. The toy companies in China formed a complex web of supply chains, with contractors themselves sub-contracting production of components, and often, entire products to various companies.

---

[4] Ibid.

[5] Source: U.S. Census Bureau.

[6] Doug Desjardins. Target to leapfrog over Toys 'R' Us into no. 2 spot. *Retailing Today*. 2006. 45(7):36.

[7] Allan Drury. Concerns about China-made toys hurt holiday sales. *The Journal News*, January, 2008.

[8] Kelly Nolan. Toys 'R' Us not playing games with success. *Retailing Today*. Sep 10, 2007. Vol. 46, Iss. 13; p. 24.

[9] Lazich, Robert S. *Market Share Reporter*. Farmington Hills, MI: Gale Group, 2004.

[10] David Barboza. China Bars Two Companies From Exporting Toys. *New York Times*. Aug. 10, 2007.

TOY PRODUCTION IN CHINA

Over the years, U.S. toy companies shifted their production overseas and focused their domestic operations on product design, marketing, research and development, and other high-value activities. As a result, employment in the domestic toy industry declined from 42,300 workers in 1993, to 17,400 workers in 2005, while toy imports increased.[11] Approximately 10 per cent of the demand for toys in the U.S. market was met by domestic production, while the rest was met through imports, primarily from China (see Exhibit 3).[12]

Chinese toy imports accounted for a full 86 per cent of toy imports to the United States in 2006, up dramatically from 41 per cent in 1992. The rise of China came at the expense of other toy exporting countries, whose combined share of toy imports to the United States plummeted from 59 per cent to 14 per cent during the same period. For instance, Japan remained a strong exporter of toys to the United States until a substantial drop around 2001. Despite its proximity to the United States, Mexico had not been able to sustain the up-tick it experienced in 2002. Further, Taiwan and Hong Kong toy exports had both been in decline for over a decade.

China's rising share of U.S. toy imports, and more generally China's position in the global toy industry, can be attributed to the lower cost business environment in China. China had attracted tremendous foreign direct investment and outsourcing of manufacturing operations. While analysts have often pointed to the phenomenal economic growth in China, they have also noted the resultant pressure on the physical, technical, and human resource infrastructures.[13] These pressures, some analysts argue, have resulted in the Chinese manufacturers compromising on the product safety.

According to American regulators, tainted pet food imported from China was responsible for deaths of, or injuries to, about 4,000 cats and dogs. As a result, regulators initiated the biggest pet food recall in U.S. history. This was followed by worldwide recalls of Chinese toothpaste laced with anti-freeze called diethylene glycol, which was found to be responsible for nearly 200 deaths in Haiti and Panama. Shortly thereafter, Chinese-made tires were linked to two deaths in an accident in the United States and recalled. The tires lacked a safety feature that prevented tire treads from splitting and falling apart.[14] The spate of recalls of Chinese-made goods began to erode consumer confidence in products made in China.

TOY SAFETY

The safety of consumer goods in the United States is managed by four federal agencies: (i) the Food and Drug Administration (FDA) has jurisdiction over foods, drugs and cosmetics, (ii) the Department of Transportation oversees the safety of cars, trucks, motorcycles, and their accessories such as tires and car seats, (iii) the Department of Treasury has jurisdiction over alcohol, tobacco and firearms, and (iv) the U.S. Consumer Product Safety Commission (CPSC) has jurisdiction over about 15,000 types of consumer products, from microwave ovens to cribs to lawn mowers.[15]

---

[11] Toy industry outlook 2006 http://www.ita.doc.gov/td/ocg/outlook06_toys.pdf
[12] Ibid.
[13] Paul Beamish. The High Cost of Cheap Chinese Labor. *Harvard Business Review*. June: 23, 2006.
[14] David Barboza. China Steps up its Safety Efforts. *New York Times*, July 7, 2007.
[15] Source: CPSC.

The safety of toys and other children's products falls within the jurisdiction of CPSC, which was created in 1972 by Congress in the Consumer Product Safety Act to "protect the public against unreasonable risks of injuries and deaths associated with consumer products." In 2007, the CPSC had an operating budget of $66 million and a staff of 393 full-time equivalent employees. Its strategic goals for the year were to reduce deaths and injuries by fire hazards, carbon monoxide poisoning hazard, and hazards from children's products.[16] According to CPSC, 22 toy-related deaths and an estimated 220,500 toy-related injuries occurred in 2006.[17] Based on its analysis, CPSC identified the Top Five Hidden Home Hazards. These hazards were listed on the CPSC website to make consumers aware of the hazards and avoid injuries due to those. In 2007, CPSC listed the following as the top hazards: magnets, recalled products, tip-overs, windows and covering, pool and spa drains.

The CPSC collects information about product safety issues from sources such as hospitals, doctors, newspaper reports, industry reports, consumer complaints, investigations conducted by its staff, and reports from companies. When a company becomes aware of hazards associated with the products it sold, it is required by law to immediately inform the CPSC. Based on the information it received, CPSC worked in coordination with the companies involved to recall the hazardous products from the market. Exhibit 4 presents the number of toy recalls made by CPSC since 1988. Not surprisingly, the majority of recalls in recent years involved toys made in China. See Exhibit 5 for a list of the toys recalled in the United States since the beginning of 2007. All the toys recalled, with one exception, were made in China. Seven of the recalls were a result of excess lead in the surface paint of the toys.

Lead in children's products poses a serious hazard because exposure to lead can affect almost every organ and system in the human body. Children exposed to high levels of lead can suffer from damage such as IQ deficits, attention deficit hyperactivity disorder, motor skills, and reaction time. Considering the damages that lead can cause to humans, particularly children, the U.S. government limited the permissible amount of lead in products. Under the Consumer Safety Product Act 1972, lead in products accessible to children should not be greater than 600 parts per million (ppm). The standards for permissible lead in other products vary depending on the usage and amount of lead in the product that is accessible.

Although lead use is banned or restricted in many developed countries, the same is not true for developing countries. In developed countries, the only source of lead exposure to children is from paint. In contrast, lead exposure in developing countries occurs due to lead gasoline, ceramics, mining, batteries, and even medication and cosmetics. Manufacturers use paint with a high percentage of lead because it is highly resistant to corrosion, extremely malleable, and has poor electrical conductivity. In addition, paint with higher lead is heavy and bright, making the products such as jewelry more appealing to consumers.

While excess lead in toys and other children's products is an issue of concern, CPSC has identified another major hazard associated with small magnets in toys. Due to the availability of powerful rare-earth magnets at cheap prices, the manufacturers began to use them in many toys such as building blocks and jewelry. On some of these products, the magnets came loose. If a child swallowed more than one magnet, they could attach to each other and cause intestinal perforations and blockage, which can

---

[16] CPSC. Performance and accountability report. 2007. http://www.cpsc.gov/cpscpub/pubs/reports/2007par.pdf

[17] CPSC. Toy related deaths and injuries. 2006. http://www.cpsc.gov/library/toymemo06.pdf

be fatal. In April 2006, CPSC and Rose Art Industries recalled 3.8 million Magnetix magnetic building sets following the death of a 20-month-old boy after he swallowed magnets that twisted his small intestine and created a blockage. In addition, several other children required surgery and intensive care to remove the magnets they swallowed.[18]

Following the recall of Magnetix building sets, Rose Art Industries redesigned its building sets to cover the magnets and reinforced these with resins so that the magnets could not be detached from the building set. Further, they changed the age suitability of their product to six years or older and provided new warnings about the dangers associated with ingesting magnets.[19] The recall of Magnetix was followed by another five recalls of toys that contained small magnets that detached. One of those recalls involved 2.4 million Polly Pocket play sets (an additional 2 million sets were sold worldwide), which was prompted by 170 reports of magnets coming loose and three children who swallowed the magnets requiring surgical care.[20] The Polly Pocket play sets, recalled on November 21, 2006, were made by Mattel and sold between May 2003 and September 2006.

MATTEL—THE NO.1 TOY MAKER IN THE WORLD

With a vision to provide "the world's premier toy brands—today and tomorrow," Mattel "designs, manufactures, and markets a broad variety of toy products worldwide through sales to its customers and directly to consumers."[21] Mattel's position as a leader in the global toy industry was so formidable that Mattel's international business division with gross sales of $ 2.7 billion in 2006 would be the industry's third largest company, if it was a separate company, and Mattel's U.S. business with $3.4 billion would still be No.1.[22]

Mattel was an industry leader not only by its sales, but also through its pioneering efforts to be a good corporate citizen. In 1996, Mattel initiated its Global Manufacturing Principles, which aimed to ensure responsible management practices were used in Mattel's factories as well as by its vendors. Mattel's factories were audited by the International Center for Corporate Accountability, an independent body, and its results made publicly available by Mattel. Mattel engaged in philanthropic activities through Mattel Children's Foundation in 37 countries. It was named one of the top 100 Best Corporate Citizens by CRO Magazine in 2006. More saliently, Mattel's corporate governance received the highest global rating of 10 by Governance Metrics International (GMI), which placed the company among the top one per cent of more than 3,400 global companies.

The journey of Mattel, however, began modestly in 1944, when Harold Matson and Elliot Handler began to make toys out of a converted garage in California. They named the company Mattel, using letters from their last and first names. Matson sold his share to Elliot Handler and his wife, Ruth Handler, who incorporated the company in 1948. Mattel's first products were picture frames and doll house furniture.[23] Their first big

---

[18] http://www.cpsc.gov/cpscpub/prerel/prhtml06/06127.html
[19] U.S. PIRG Education Fund. Trouble in Toyland. 21st Annual Toy Safety Survey.
[20] http://www.cpsc.gov/cpscpub/prerel/prhtml07/07039.html
[21] *Mattel Annual Report*, 2006, p.3.
[22] Letter to Shareholders by Bob Eckert, Mattel CEO, *Mattel Annual Report*, 2006.
[23] J. Amerman. *The story of Mattel, Inc.: Fifty years of innovation.* 1995.

product was a mass-produced, and thus, inexpensive music box, which established Mattel firmly in the toy business. The introduction of Barbie in 1959, and Ken two years later, propelled company growth. The products introduced later such as Hot Wheels went further to establish Mattel's position as an industry leader. Mattel went public in 1960.

Mattel's products were organized in three different business groups: (i) Mattel Girls & Boys Brands that includes brands like Barbie dolls and accessories, Polly Pocket, Hot Wheels, Matchbox, Batman, CARS, and Superman. (ii) Fisher-Price Brands consisting of brands such as Fisher-Price, Little People, Sesame Street, Dora the Explorer, Go-Diego-Go!, Winnie the Pooh, and Power Wheels. (iii) American Girl Brands, with brands such as Just Like You and Bitty Baby. In the United States alone, the sales of these three groups in 2006 were: Mattel Girls & Boys Brands—$1.57 billion, Fisher-Price Brands—$1.47 billion, and American Girl Brands—$0.44 billion.

About 45 percent of Mattel's sales were accounted for by three major buyers: Wal-Mart, Toys'R'Us, and Target. In addition to Mattel's principal competitors, it also competed with a large number of smaller companies that made toys, video games, and consumer electronics, and published children's books.

In the 1990s, Mattel made a number of significant acquisitions, including Fisher-Price (1993, leader in pre-school segment), Kransco (1994, made battery-powered ride-on vehicles), Tyco (1997, made Tickle Me Elmo and Matchbox cars), Pleasant Company (1998, mail-order firm that made American Girl-brand books, dolls, and clothing), and Bluebird Toys (1998, made toys such as Polly Pocket and The Tiny Disney Collection). Mattel's acquisition of The Learning Company, a leading educational software maker, in 1999 at a cost of $3.6 billion proved to be troublesome. The company lost money and was later sold. Mattel also made a hostile bid to acquire Hasbro, the second largest toy company. This bid, made in 1996, failed to materialize.

The toy industry is different from other industries on two major counts. First, toy sales are seasonal. Most sales occurred during the third and last quarter of the year, which coincide with the traditional holiday period. Second, there is a lot of uncertainty around new product success. It was difficult, almost impossible, to predict whether a particular toy would be liked by children. Not surprisingly, many companies in the toy industry made millions with one successful toy and also went bankrupt with one big failure.

Over a long period, Mattel had managed the peculiarities of the toy industries well with a number of innovative and often revolutionary ideas. Traditionally, the retailers promoted toys during the holiday season and toy manufacturers had little, if any, role to play. In 1955, Mattel tied-up with ABC Television and sponsored a 15-minute segment of Walt Disney's Mickey Mouse Club for one full year. At that time, Mattel's revenues were only $5 million, but it paid $500,000 for the sponsorship. The sponsorship quickly established a continuous connection for Mattel with the kids and gave it an opportunity to influence the buying habits of its consumers. Not surprisingly, this move changed the nature of marketing in the toy industry. Also, for Mattel, it paved the way for further partnerships with entertainment companies to produce character toys.

Mattel entered into licensing agreements to make toys based on the characters owned by companies such as Disney, Warner Brothers, Viacom (Nickelodeon), Origin Products, and Sesame Workshop. These agreements gave the company access to characters such as Winnie the Pooh, Disney Princesses, CARS, Dora the Explorer, Go-Diego-Go!, Sponge Bob SquarePants, Polly Pocket, Batman, Superman, and Elmo.

In 2005, Mattel partnered with Scholastic Entertainment to produce educational learning systems.

Not only did Mattel license characters, but also licensed some of its core brands to other non-toy companies to design and develop an array of products sporting the core brand names. These deals included Barbie eyewear for little girls (with REM Eyewear), Hot Wheels apparel and accessories (with Innovo Group), Barbie video games (with Activision), and CD Players, learning laptops, and MP3 players. Recently, Mattel was trying to reduce its reliance on its big customers such as Wal-Mart, Target, and Toys'R'Us through internet and catalogue sales.[24]

Traditionally, toy companies relied on point-of-sale (POS) data to forecast demand for toys. With its Hot Wheels brand, Mattel realized that variety was the key driver of the sales and introduced a rolling mix strategy. This strategy involved changing the physical 72-car assortment mix by seven to eight per cent every two weeks. This changed the nature of its practices and instead of relying on POS data, Mattel only needed to design the varieties and supply an assortment pack to the retailer.[25]

Mattel designed and developed toys in the corporate headquarters. In 2006, Mattel spent US$174 million on in-house product design and development. In contrast, the company spent US$261 million on royalties and US$651 million on advertising. Mattel manufactured products in its own factories as well as through third-party manufacturers. Also, it marketed the products purchased from unrelated companies that designed, developed, and manufactured those products.

Offshoring the Toy Production

Mattel's principal manufacturing facilities were located in China, Indonesia, Thailand, Malaysia, and Mexico. It closed its last toy factory in the U.S., originally part of its Fisher-Price divisions, in 2002.[26] Mattel produced its core brands such as Barbie and Hot Wheels in company-owned facilities, but used third-party manufacturers to produce its non-core brands. It used third-party manufacturers in a number of countries, including the United States, Mexico, Brazil, India, New Zealand, and Australia. This manufacturing mix minimized Mattel's risk and gave it focus and flexibility. The core brands were a staple business, while the non-core brands tended to be those products that were expected to have a short market life. The non-core brands were typically associated with popular movie characters and had a life of one year.[27]

The development of new toys was done at Mattel's corporate headquarters. Outsourcing for the manufacturing of non-core brand toys followed a strict multi-step process. The design teams created a bid package containing the new product's blueprint and engineering specifications. It often contained a physical model. After the selection of a vendor, the company established the vendor's production infrastructure. At this point, Mattel assumed responsibility for the cost of tooling. The vendor then produced 50 units as "First Shots" to verify if any tool modifications were required. This was followed by one or more "Engineering Pilot," depending on the toy's complexity, and the "Final Engineering Pilot." After this, a "Production Pilot" of 1,000 units was run

---

[24] Hoover Company Report on Mattel.

[25] Eric Johnson and Tom Clock. *Mattel, Inc: Vendor Operations in Asia*. Tuck School of Business at Dartmouth. 2002.

[26] Louis Story, After stumbling, Mattel cracks down in China. *New York Times*. August 29, 2007.

[27] Company annual reports and chat excerpts of Mattel India CEO on CNN-IBN.

using the entire assembly line to run the product. Finally, the "Production Start" phase began only when the new toy met design compliance.[28]

Mattel and its vendors manufactured about 800 million products each year. Approximately half of the toys Mattel sold were made in its own plants, a higher proportion than other large toy makers. Also, Mattel made a larger percentage of its toys outside China than other large toy companies. Mattel's manufacturing and offshoring strategy was developed over a period of five decades. The company made its first Barbie doll in Asia in 1959. Since then, Mattel managed the risks of offshored operations by employing a mix of company-owned and vendor-owned manufacturing facilities all over Asia.

In China alone, Mattel had contracts with approximately 37 principal vendors who made toys for the company.[29] The principal vendors further used smaller companies for the full or partial production of toys. As a result, the supply chains in China were long and complex. According to some estimates, about 3,000 Chinese companies made Mattel products.[30] However, Mattel had direct contact only with the principal vendors.

A RECALL UNDERWAY

In June 2007, a French direct importer of Mattel's products, Auchan, performed pre-shipment tests with the help of Intertek, an independent laboratory. These tests revealed that Mattel's toys, made by a vendor Lee Der Industrial Company, contained lead above permissible limits. Intertek sent the test results, on June 8, 2007, to Mattel employees in China. Consequently, Mattel employees contacted Lee Der instructing it to correct the problem and provide another sample for testing. Another test by Intertek on June 29, for Auchan, on the same toy produced by Lee Der had passed the test.

On June 27, 2007, Mattel's call center in the United States received a report from a consumer, who informed them that a home test kit found excessive lead in Mattel's toys. These were also manufactured by Lee Der. Following this, Mattel tested five samples of Lee Der toys and found on July 6 that three of them contained excess lead. As the testing was underway, Auchan informed Mattel on July 3 about lead violations in another toy made by Lee Der. As soon as the test results were out, Mattel employees in China notified Lee Der and stopped accepting products made by Lee Der. Further tests on the toy samples collected from Lee Der were conducted on July 9 in Mattel's own laboratories, which revealed that nine of the 23 samples of Lee Der toys contained excess lead in surface paint.

Mattel's employees in China notified the senior management team at corporate headquarters on July 12 about the issues with Lee Der products. Following this, Mattel management ordered an immediate suspension of all shipments of products made by Lee Der. Further investigations by Mattel revealed that the nonconforming lead levels were because of a yellow pigment in paint used on portions of toys manufactured by Lee Der.[31]

---

[28] Op. cit. Johnson and Clock. 2002.
[29] Testimony of Robert Eckert, CEO, Mattel, to the Sub-committee on Commerce, Trade, and Consumer Protection of the Committee on Energy and Commerce. September 19, 2007.
[30] David Barboza, Scandal and Suicide in China: A Dark Side of Toys. *New York Times*. August 23, 2007.
[31] Mattel's response to the information request from the Sub-committee on Commerce, Trade, and Consumer Protection of the Committee on Energy and Commerce. September 5, 2007.

Lee Der Industrial Company was located in Foshan City of Guangdong Province, where thousands of small toy factories existed. The company was founded by two Chinese entrepreneurs, Cheng Shu-hung and Xie Yuguang. Mattel first used Lee Der for making a small batch of educational toys in 1993. By July 2007, Lee Der employed approximately 2,500 people and made toys almost exclusively for Mattel. With annual sales of about $25 million, Lee Der was about to open a new $5 million plant.[32]

Lee Der had purchased its paint from Dongxing New Energy Co. since 2003. The owner of Dongxing was a good friend of Cheng Shu-hung. When Dongxing ran out of yellow pigment in April 2007, it sourced about 330 pounds of it for $1,250 from Dongguan Zhongxin Toner Powder Factory. Then, Dongxing supplied the paint to Lee Der, which used it in Mattel's toys. Initial reports suggested that Dongguan Zhongxin Toner Powder Factory was fake and that its owners were not traceable.[33]

An essential component of Mattel's contracts with its vendors is that the products made by vendors comply with applicable safety standards. Mattel had systems which required the vendors to either purchase paint from a list of eight certified vendors in China or test for compliance each batch of the paint purchased from a non-certified vendor. Mattel also conducted audits of certified paint suppliers and vendors to ensure that Mattel's requirements were being followed. The frequency of audits depended on Mattel's prior experience with the suppliers and vendors.

Following its investigations, Mattel filed an initial report with the CPSC on July 20 and followed it up with another on July 26, indicating that it would like to issue a recall of all the products manufactured by Lee Der between April 19, 2007 (the date when Lee Der took delivery of the lead-tainted paint from its supplier), and July 6, 2007, the date when Mattel stopped accepting products from Lee Der.[34] Work on this recall was underway and Mattel and the CPSC were scheduled to announce the recall on August 2, 2007. See Exhibit 6 for the press release announcing the recall, expected to be issued by the CPSC. Mattel had already informed big retailers such as Wal-Mart and Toys'R'Us of the impending recall. The retailers pulled the toys off their shelves and flagged the cash registers so that customers could not buy the toys from the stores.[35]

ANOTHER INSTANCE OF LEAD AND FURTHER REPORTS OF LOOSE MAGNETS

While Mattel was preparing to announce its recall, on July 30, 2007, it found that paint on Sarge cars contained excess lead. The Sarge cars were made for Mattel by Early Light Industrial Company, Ltd. of Hong Kong, which made them in its manufacturing facility located in Pinghu, China.[36] Early Light had supplied toys to Mattel for 20 years.[37] Only further investigation would be able to clarify where exactly in the supply chain the problem originated and why. Initial reports indicated that approximately 250,000 Sarge cars made between May 2007 and August 2007 may have been affected with lead paint.

---

[32] http://www.ckgsb.edu.cn:8080/article/600/3051.aspx
[33] Ibid.
[34] Testimony of Robert Eckert, CEO, Mattel, to the Sub-committee on Commerce, Trade, and Consumer Protection of the Committee on Energy and Commerce. September 19, 2007.
[35] http://www.reuters.com/article/domesticNews/idUSN0230401920070802
[36] Ibid.
[37] Op. cit. Louis Story. 2007.

After the November 2006 recall of eight different Polly Pocket play sets made in China for the problem of magnets coming loose, Mattel reinforced the magnets by locking them in the toys rather than gluing them. Nonetheless, in recent months Mattel had received a few hundred reports of magnets coming loose from a number of play sets sold before November 2006. The play sets affected with magnet problems were: (i) fifty additional models of Polly Pocket play sets (about five million of these play sets were sold between March 2003 and November 2006), (ii) Batman and One Piece action figures (about 350,000 toys sold between June 2006 and June 2007), (iii) Barbie and Tanner play sets (about 683,000 toys sold between May 2006 – July, 2007), and (iv) Doggie Day Care play sets (about one million sold between July 2004 and July 2007).

Recalls are a nightmare to companies for several reasons. First, the recalls pose major logistics challenges as the company needs to establish a set-up to handle the recalls. Second, the company has to deal with regulators who tend to push the company to ensure that not only a recall is issued, but the products in consumers' hands are actually returned to the company. Third, recalls are often viewed as an admission of guilt and open the company to consumer litigations. Finally, recalls damage the reputation of the company and result in increased costs, lost sales, and stock price erosion.

Mattel and Fisher-Price were not new to recalls. In their long history, they had recalled products in the past (see Exhibit 7). Nevertheless, the current situation seemed entirely new, complex, and challenging. It was not clear if and which products needed to be recalled. As importantly, how could the company minimize the negative consequences which are germane to any product recall? Finally, how could the company ensure such recalls did not recur?

Exhibit 1   Key Financial Data of Toy Majors (All figures in thousands of U.S. dollars, except number of employees)

	Mattel		Hasbro		RC2		JAAKS Pacific	
	2006	2005	2006	2005	2006	2005	2006	2005
Sales	5650156	5179016	3151481	3087627	518829	504445	765386	661536
Net Profits	592927	417019	230055	212075	34094	53130	72375	63493
Total Assets	4955884	4372313	3096905	3301143	614640	629736	881894	753955
Debt/ Liabilities	940390	807395	494917	528389	22438	82647	98000	98000
Stockholder Equity	2432974	2101733	1537890	1723476	451926	398951	609288	524651
R & D Expenses	173514	182015	171358	150586	N.A.	N.A.	N.A.	N.A.
Marketing/Advertising and Promotion	650975	629115	368996	366371	N.A.	N.A.	N.A.	N.A.
Number of employees (worldwide)	32000	N.A.	5800	N.A.	821	842	N.A.	N.A.
Property, Plant & Equipment	536749	547104	181726	164045	38991	47039	16883	12695
Capital Expenditure	314784	82191	83604	120671	8319	6643	121914	9467

Source: Company Annual Reports

Exhibit 2   U.S. Toy Sales by Product Category (All figures in billion USD)

Product Category	2006	2005
Action Figures & Accessories	1.3	1.4
Arts & Crafts	2.6	2.5
Building Sets	0.67	0.68
Dolls	2.7	2.7
Games/Puzzles	2.4	2.5
Infant/Preschool	3.2	3.2
Youth Electronics	1.1	0.91
Outdoor & Sports Toys	2.9	2.9
Plush	1.3	1.4
Vehicles	2.1	2.0
All Other Toys	2.0	2.1
Total (Traditional Toy Industry)	**22.3**	**22.2**
Total Video Games	**12.5**	**10.5**

Source: Toy Industry Association / NPD Group.

Exhibit 3   U.S. Toy Imports—Total vs. China (1989–2006)

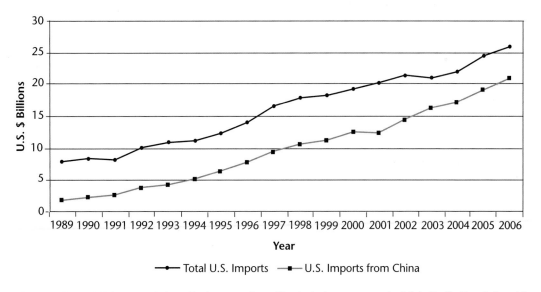

Source: Bapuji H, Beamish P, Laplume A. 2007. Toy import and recall levels: Is there a connection? Asia Pacific Foundation of Canada: Vancouver, Canada.

Exhibit 4   Toy Recalls by CPSC (1988–2006)

Year	Total Number of Recalls	Recalls of Chinese-made Toys	
		Number	Percentage
1988	29	1	3
1989	52	4	8
1990	31	14	45
1991	31	8	26
1992	25	13	52
1993	20	8	40
1994	29	16	55
1995	35	19	54
1996	26	13	50
1997	22	9	41
1998	29	12	41
1999	20	4	20
2000	31	15	48
2001	23	12	52
2002	25	11	44
2003	15	10	67
2004	15	13	87
2005	19	16	84
2006	33	26	79

Source: Bapuji H, Beamish P. 2007. Toy recalls: Is China really the problem? Asia Pacific Foundation of Canada: Vancouver, Canada.

Exhibit 5   Toy Recalls in The United States (January 2007–July 24, 2007)

1. Risk of Explosion and Hearing Damage Prompts Recall of Remote Control Airplanes (July 24)
2. New Easy-Bake Oven Recall Following Partial Finger Amputation; Consumers Urged to Return Toy Ovens (July 19)
3. AAFES Expands Recall of "Soldier Bear" Toy Sets Due to Lead Poisoning Hazard (July 18) – Made in Hong Kong
4. Serious Intestinal Injury Prompts Kipp Brothers Recall of Mag Stix Magnetic Building Sets (July 5)
5. Infantino Recalls Children's Toy Castles Due to Choking Hazard (July 3)
6. Target Recalls Toy Barbeque Grills Due to Laceration Hazard (June 28)
7. RC2 Corp. Recalls Various Thomas & Friends™ Wooden Railway Toys Due to Lead Poisoning Hazard (June 13)
8. Gemmy Industries Corp. Recalls Flashing Eyeball Toys Due to Chemical Hazard (June 7)
9. Toy Drums Recalled by The Boyds Collection Ltd. Due to Lead Poisoning Hazard (May 30)
10. AAFES Recalls "Soldier Bear" Toy Sets Due to Lead Poisoning Hazard (May 23) – Made in Hong Kong
11. Tri-Star International Recalls Children's Toys Due to Choking Hazard (May 23)
12. Bookspan Recalls Discovery Bunny Books Due to Choking Hazard (May 17)
13. Bookspan Recalls Clip-on Baby Books Due to Choking Hazard (May 17)
14. Small World Toys Recalls Children's Take-Apart Townhouse Toys; Detached Magnets Pose Aspiration and Intestinal Hazards (May 3)
15. Battat Inc. Recalls Parents® Magazine Toy Cell Phones for Choking Hazard (May 3)
16. Graco Children's Products Recalls to Replace Soft Blocks Towers on Activity Centers Due to Choking Hazard (May 2)
17. Target Recalls Anima Bamboo Collection Games Due to Lead Poisoning Hazard (May 2)
18. Magnetix Magnetic Building Set Recall Expanded (April 19)
19. Small World Toys Recalls Children's Wooden Sound Puzzles with Knobs for Choking Hazard (April 11)
20. Target Recalls Activity Cart Toys Due to Choking Hazard (April 4)
21. OKK Trading Recalls Baby Dolls Due to Choking Hazard (April 4)
22. Regent Products Corp. Recalls Stuffed Ball Toys Due to Lead Hazard (March 28)
23. Estes-Cox Radio Control Airplanes with Lithium Polymer Batteries Recalled for Fire Hazard (March 27)
24. Toys "R" Us Recalls "Elite Operations" Toy Sets Due to Lead and Laceration Hazards (March 13)
25. Sportcraft Recalls Inflatable Bounce Houses Due to Impact Injury Hazard (February 27)
26. Jazwares Inc. Recalls Link-N-Lite™ Magnetic Puzzles, Ingested Magnets Pose Aspiration and Intestinal Hazards (February 15)
27. Fisher-Price Recalls "Laugh and Learn" Bunny Toys Due to Choking Hazard (February 15)
28. Battery Packs for Toy Vehicles Recalled by JAKKS Pacific Due to Fire Hazard (February 13)
29. Easy-Bake Ovens Recalled for Repair Due to Entrapment and Burn Hazards (February 6)
30. Geometix International LLC Recalls MagneBlocks™ Toys, Ingested Magnets Pose Aspiration and Intestinal Hazards (January 18)
31. Target Recalls Baby Rattles and Ornaments for Choking Hazard (January 18)

Source: CPSC

Exhibit 6   Recall Notice of Mattel's Character Toys for Lead Paint Violations

U.S. Consumer Product Safety Commission

Office of Information and Public Affairs   Washington, DC 20207

FOR IMMEDIATE RELEASE
August 2, 2007   Firm's Recall Hotline: (800) 916-4498
Release #07-257   CPSC Recall Hotline: (800) 638-2772
                                                       CPSC Media Contact: (301) 504-7908

Fisher-Price Recalls Licensed Character Toys Due To Lead Poisoning Hazard

WASHINGTON, D.C.—The U.S. Consumer Product Safety Commission, in cooperation with the firms named below, today announced a voluntary recall of the following consumer product. Consumers should stop using recalled products immediately unless otherwise instructed.

Name of Product: Sesame Street, Dora the Explorer, and other children's toys

Units: About 967,000

Importer: Fisher-Price Inc., of East Aurora, N.Y.

Hazard: Surface paints on the toys could contain excessive levels of lead. Lead is toxic if ingested by young children and can cause adverse health effects.

Incidents/Injuries: None reported.

Description: The recalled involves various figures and toys that were manufactured between April 19, 2007 and July 6, 2007 and were sold alone or as part of sets. The model names and product numbers for the recalled toys, which are all marked with "Fisher-Price," are listed below. The toys may have a date code between 109-7LF and 187-7LF marked on the product or packaging.

Sold at: Retail stores nationwide from May 2007 through August 2007 for between $5 and $40.

Manufactured in: China

Remedy: Consumers should immediately take the recalled toys away from children and contact Fisher-Price. Consumers will need to return the product and will receive a voucher for a replacement toy of the consumer's choice (up to the value of the returned product).

Consumer Contact: For additional information contact Fisher-Price at (800) 916-4498 anytime or visit the firm's Web site at www.service.mattel.com

Product List: A list of about 50 different toys. The case authors excluded this list in the interest of space.

Source: CPSC

Exhibit 7   Product Recalls in Mattel–Fisher-Price History (Up to July 2007)

Mattel Recalls

1. Serious Injuries Prompt Recall of Mattel's Polly Pocket Magnetic Play Sets (November 21, 2006)
2. Children's Jewelry Sold at American Girl Stores Recalled for Lead Poisoning Hazard (March 30, 2006)
3. Mattel, Inc. Recall of Batman Batmobile Toy Vehicle (April 14, 2004)
4. Fisher-Price Intelli-Table Toy Recall (March 29, 2001)
5. Barbie Sunglasses Recalled by IMT Accessories (February 21, 2001)
6. Cabbage Patch Kids Snacktime Dolls Refund (January 6, 1997)
7. Disney Play 'N Pop Activity Toy Recalled by Arcotoys (February 23, 1995)
8. Mattel Voluntarily Recalls Disney Poppin' Sounds Pull Train (November 18, 1991)
9. Battlestar Galactica Space Toys Replaced by Mattel (January 11, 1979)

Fisher-Price Recalls

10. Fisher-Price Rainforest Infant Swings Recalled Due to Entrapment Hazard (May 30, 2007)
11. Fisher-Price Recalls "Laugh and Learn" Bunny Toys Due to Choking Hazard (February 15, 2007)
12. Fisher-Price Recalls Infant Musical Toy Chair Posing Strangulation Hazard (January 18, 2006)
13. Fisher-Price Recall of Scooters and Mini Bikes (June 14, 2005)
14. Fisher-Price Recall of Push Toys (May 10, 2005)
15. Fisher-Price Recall of Pogo Sticks (May 10, 2005)
16. Scooters and Mini Bikes Recalled by Fisher-Price (November 13, 2003)
17. Crib Mobile Toys Recalled by Fisher-Price (June 19, 2003)
18. Little People® Animal Sounds Farms Recalled by Fisher-Price (April 23, 2003)
19. Fisher-Price Recall for In-Home Repair of Infant Swings (April 10, 2002)
20. Fisher-Price Portable Bassinet Recall (July 31, 2001)
21. Basketball Sets Recalled by Fisher-Price (May 10, 2001)
22. Fisher-Price Intelli-Table Toy Recall (March 29, 2001)
23. McDonald's "Scooter Bug" Happy Meal Toy Recall (March 5, 2001)
24. Children's Riding Vehicles Recalled by Fisher-Price (August 31, 2000)
25. Swings and Toys Recalled by Fisher-Price (August 23, 2000)
26. Baby Jumper Seats & Construction Toys Recalled by Fisher-Price (July 21, 2000)
27. Swings & Domes Recalled by Fisher-Price (April 7, 2000)
28. Toy Basketball Nets Recalled by Little Tikes, Today's Kids & Fisher-Price (December 22, 1998)
29. Power Wheels Ride-On Battery-Powered Vehicles Recall to Repair (October 22, 1998)
30. Infant Toys Recalled by Fisher-Price (March 2, 1998)
31. Toy Police Car s Recalled by Fisher-Price (May 19, 1997; Revised October 29, 2002)
32. Baseball Training Toy Recall/Repair by Fisher-Price (July 7, 1995; Revised October 29, 2002)
33. Fisher-Price Recalls Kiddicraft Racing Rover Car (August 17, 1993; Revised October 29, 2002)
34. Fisher-Price Recalls Snuggle Light Doll (August 12, 1993; Revised October 29, 2002)
   Fun Bus Safety Modification Program by Fisher-Price (March 15, 1990; Revised October 29, 2002)
35. "Pop-Up Playhouse" Modification by Fisher-Price (July 27, 1988; Revised October 29, 2002)
36. Strollers Repair by Fisher-Price (November 24, 1987; Revised October 29, 2002)
37. Crib Toy Safety Alert issued by Fisher-Price (October 10, 1984; Revised October 29, 2002)
38. "Splash & Stack Bluebird" Toys Recalled by Fisher-Price (July 26, 1984; Revised December 2, 2005)

Source: CPSC

Case 20

Guest-Tek Interactive Entertainment: International Sales

GUEST-TEK AND THE GLOBAL OPPORTUNITY

The chief executive officer (CEO) of Calgary-based Guest-Tek Interactive Entertainment Ltd. (Guest-Tek) considered whether and how his company should grow its business overseas. Ninety-seven per cent of Guest-Tek's 2003 revenue was derived from North American hotels—a market he knew would eventually become saturated. Guest-Tek had listed publicly several weeks earlier, in January 2004. Both internal and external investors now demanded results. Other geographic markets held the promise of new growth and competitors were already pursuing those opportunities. The CEO had to decide on a course of action.

COMPANY BACKGROUND

Guest-Tek was founded in Calgary, Canada, in March 1997, and since then had established itself as a leading provider of high-speed Internet access in hotels in North America and, to a lesser extent, abroad. Guest-Tek sold its Internet solution, which was branded as GlobalSuite, to three-, four- and five-star hotels and installed access points in guest rooms, meeting rooms and common areas. Guest-Tek then maintained a post-installation network and provided technical support for GlobalSuite users through a toll-free, 24-hour telephone line. Users were typically business travelers

Richard Ivey School of Business
The University of Western Ontario

Nigel Goodwin prepared this case under the supervision of Professor Laurie Milton solely to provide material for class discussion. The authors do not intend to illustrate either effective or ineffective handling of a managerial situation. The authors may have disguised certain names and other identifying information to protect confidentiality.

who connected with their own laptop computers. GlobalSuite was a premium high-speed Internet access solution that was easy to use for travelers and convenient for hotel managers.

GlobalSuite's industry-leading 99 per cent user success rate,[1] together with Guest-Tek's comprehensive service package for both guests and hotel managers, had secured some of the world's finest hotel chains and management groups as clients (see Exhibit 1 for Guest-Tek's client list). The company had also raised sales to $17.2 million[2] for the nine months ending December 31, 2003 (see Exhibit 2 for Guest-Tek's income statement) and successfully completed an initial public offering (IPO) of $44.6 million. Virtually all of the company's activities were run from the head office in Calgary with a staff of fewer than 150 (see Exhibit 3 for an allocation of Guest-Tek's staff by department).

THE HOSPITALITY INDUSTRY

The hospitality industry encompassed many segments, including hotels, rental properties, military housing, student housing and timeshare units, plus bars, coffee shops, restaurants, airports and train stations. Guest-Tek focused its efforts on serving hotels and, more specifically, on those in the three-, four- and five-star range. To this point in time, the company had concentrated almost exclusively on its home continent, North America (see Exhibit 4 for Guest-Tek's revenue by geographic region). The company had left the other geographic markets in Europe, Asia-Pacific and South America largely unexplored, with limited direct sales to date.

Business travelers who frequented North American three-, four- and five-star hotels had come to expect or even require Internet access. One industry survey found that as many as 87 per cent of business travelers checked email or accessed the Internet from their laptops on a daily basis while on the road. There was general agreement in the industry that these travelers preferred high-speed Internet access to dial-up access for speed, convenience and cost effectiveness. Many travelers cited broadband services as an important factor in selecting accommodations. As a result, hotel managers were adopting high-speed Internet access as a way of attracting guests, competing with other properties and deriving additional revenue. This competitive edge had been particularly important for hotel managers during the recent downturn in the industry when Severe Acute Respiratory Syndrome (SARS), global security concerns and other political, social and economic events had raised anxiety about travel. Hotel managers hoped that high-speed Internet access would position them to capitalize on the expected recovery.

THE NORTH AMERICAN MARKET

With 64,500 hotels and more than five million hotel rooms, North America was second only to Europe on both dimensions. More importantly from Guest-Tek's perspective, though, was the fact that 40 per cent of the world's business travel was conducted in North America—more than in any other geographic region.

---

[1] Guest-Tek measured user success as the percentage of users achieving a high-speed Internet connection when using GlobalSuite; user success rates among Guest-Tek's competitors were typically much lower, and in some cases were as low as 50 per cent.
[2] Financial figures in this case are presented in Canadian dollars, unless otherwise noted.

North America led the world in terms of both the proportion of total hotels equipped with high-speed Internet access (referred to as the penetration rate) and the frequency with which the service was used by guests (referred to as the usage rate). Both penetration and usage rates were rising sharply. Also, hotel managers increasingly viewed such access as a competitive necessity or a guest amenity and were cutting user fees or offering access for free.

High-speed Internet access-enabled properties were typically in the four- and five-star hotel categories. These hotels normally installed the service in all of their guestrooms as well as in meeting rooms and common areas. When installation in four- and five-star hotels approached saturation (which was expected to happen within two to three years), several access providers planned to reach out to the two- and three-star categories for more growth opportunities. Fewer hotels in those categories could afford 100 per cent installation. Consequently, many opted to install services in a portion of rooms, to be used either on a trial basis or in rooms reserved for business travelers.

North America was home to 85 different hotel brands (see Exhibit 5 for more information on the North American hotel industry) as well as independent boutique hotels. Guest-Tek was a certified supplier to eight of those brands: Accor, Carlson Hospitality, Choice, Hilton, Hyatt, InterContinental Hotel Groups, Marriott and Starwood. In total, GlobalSuite had been installed with 35 different brands and 40 independent hotels. In fiscal year (FY) 2003, no single brand represented more than 11 per cent of Guest-Tek's revenue.

GLOBALSUITE SOLUTION

To answer the demand for high-speed Internet access, Guest-Tek's research and development team had developed GlobalSuite as an easy-to-use or "plug-and-play" solution. In other words, hotel guests could connect their own laptops and gain access to the Internet, corporate email and other applications quickly and without changing their settings. Guests typically connected by plugging their laptops into ports or "nodes" located in the guestrooms and public areas, including conference rooms and business centers; those ports were in turn connected to a network throughout the hotel.

Wireless solutions were becoming increasingly common in the industry, allowing guests with wireless network interface cards to connect from hotspots located in lobbies, bars and other public areas and sometimes in the guestrooms themselves. Not only were wireless solutions convenient for guests, they were less demanding in terms of infrastructure and were therefore less expensive for hotels. By February 2004, 70 per cent of Guest-Tek's installations involved some degree of wireless functionality.

The wide variety of laptop configurations and network settings often made access difficult, but GlobalSuite's technology was reliable and easy to use regardless of laptop settings and technical challenges. Guests who still experienced difficulty could call the technical support desk and receive help in a variety of languages, including English, French, Spanish, Dutch, Cantonese, Mandarin, Japanese, Arabic and Hindi. GlobalSuite was also a secure solution suitable for business use. The proprietary software was regarded as best-in-class technology and was guarded closely as intellectual property.

GlobalSuite had been developed with the hotel manager in mind as a complete or "turnkey" system requiring little knowledge or effort on the manager's part. Installation services were provided by Guest-Tek's highly skilled operations and deployment teams. Network equipment was sourced from high-quality manufacturers, including

Cisco Systems, Hewlett Packard, Dell and Paradyne Networks. Following an installation, Guest-Tek trained hotel staff to use the system, monitored and managed the system, acted as an Internet service provider (ISP) and offered free software upgrades. Guest-Tek thus offered a complete solution designed for high-quality service and peace of mind.

Additional features and benefits were designed to appeal to hotel managers who had the option to set access prices or provide the service free of charge, to track and report on usage and to customize the user interface with the hotel's own brand. GlobalSuite was a best-in-class solution designed for clients who were willing to pay a premium. Depending on the size of an installation and the user fees that a hotel manager was willing to pay, payback for the system could be achieved within 12 to 18 months.

BUSINESS MODEL

Once a hotel had signed a contract to purchase GlobalSuite, Guest-Tek deployed its own project managers and installation professionals to the hotel to set the system up. By managing the installation with its own people, Guest-Tek maintained control over the timelines, costs and quality. Installation work required only a few days and typically took place within four to six weeks of a contract being signed. The company could install the solution in 40 to 50 hotels per month. Installation capacity had doubled over the previous year, due to better processes and the addition of new staff.

An installation typically generated one-time revenues for Guest-Tek from the software license, installation services and networking equipment. These revenues could total between US$100 and US$350 per room, depending on the hardware involved, with a gross margin of 35 to 45 per cent. Guest-Tek also derived recurring revenues from ongoing software and hardware maintenance and from call center support. Recurring revenues totaled between US$3 and US$4 per room, per month. A 99 per cent customer retention rate ensured the sustainability of the recurring revenue.

NORTH AMERICAN COMPETITION

Guest-Tek faced direct competition in North America from a number of other Internet solution providers. Chief among these were Wayport and STSN. These companies were running systems in approximately 600 North American hotels each, as of December 2003, as compared to Guest-Tek's roughly 360 installations at that time. Other providers trailed behind (see Exhibit 6 for a breakdown of the competition in North America).

Wayport, based in Austin, Texas, provided wired access but was also a leader in wireless solutions. Wayport had preferred vendor status with Four Seasons and was also building the Wayport brand by providing access in airports and 75 McDonald's restaurants in California. STSN, of Salt Lake City, Utah, was partially owned by Marriott and most of STSN's installations were at Marriott hotels. GoldenTree Communications, a spin-off of a Korean hardware manufacturer, was also a notable competitor in North America. With low prices and what Guest-Tek's executives believed to be a more basic solution, GoldenTree appealed to three-star hotels as well as budget-conscious four-star hotels. StayOnline, another notable North American provider, was similar to Wayport in its focus on wireless applications.

In-room entertainment companies, cable companies, ISPs, data networking companies and local telephone network operators also offered Internet access. These companies used different technology and offered a variety of benefits to various segments of the market. In-room entertainment companies, for example, provided Internet access through television sets outfitted with keyboards. This rudimentary solution did not allow users to connect with their own laptops. Some of these companies, particularly the telecommunications companies (telcos), were attempting to include hotels in their broader strategy to set up wireless public access points, known as hotspots. Hotspots could be set up at virtually any location, including coffee shops, airports, office buildings and shopping malls. Guest-Tek, as a niche solution provider, recognized that these companies were penetrating the market but did not consider them to be direct competitors.

In the CEO's estimation, Guest-Tek was very strong compared to its competitors on key competitive elements, which included comprehensive solutions, ease of deployment, wireless capability, security, connectivity rates and end-user support. The subsequent supplier certification from various hotel brands, including Hilton, Hyatt and Marriott, gave Guest-Tek a strong competitive message. Finally, Guest-Tek was reasonably priced, relative to other premium service providers.

GUEST-TEK'S SALES AND MARKETING DEPARTMENT

Guest-Tek's revenue generation was overseen by the vice-president of Sales and Marketing. He held an undergraduate finance degree and an MBA in Enterprise Development from the University of Calgary. Known as an ambitious and energetic entrepreneur, he was keenly interested in growing Guest-Tek.

The VP of Sales and Marketing had a staff of 24 and was responsible for all geographic regions. Within North America, the VP had the help of a sales director; the sales director managed the sales staff directly while the VP managed the region at a strategic level and actively participated in major deals. The VP also had the help of a consultant who provided advice on the European market. There were no sales and marketing staff allocated to the other geographic regions.

Sales were pursued through direct and indirect channels, with direct being the principal channel in North America and indirect being the principal channel in the other geographic regions. Direct sales were conducted by Guest-Tek sales representatives working at Guest-Tek's head office and traveling to visit potential customers. Indirect sales were pursued through partnerships and alliances with complementary service providers and through independent agents who sold GlobalSuite on a freelance basis.

A marketing director reported to the VP of Sales and Marketing and supported the sales activities by managing the Guest-Tek brand and creating demand for GlobalSuite. Marketing activities included telemarketing, direct mail, communication with media and industry analysts, advertising and trade shows. The marketing director had a total staff of eight.

The VP of Sales and Marketing additionally oversaw a value-added solutions director. This manager was charged with finding ways to sell new products and services to existing clients. This function was seen as a way to derive additional revenue in a market that was becoming saturated. Value-added solutions were also viewed as tools for enhancing customer loyalty and ensuring recurring service and maintenance revenue for GlobalSuite installations. The value-added solutions director was assisted by two other staff members.

DIRECT SALES

The direct sales process began with Guest-Tek inside sales representatives contacting groups of hotels that shared common ownership or common management and contacting individual hotels. The inside sales representatives' objective was to generate leads for Guest-Tek's direct sales representatives. There were five inside sales representatives working under the direction of a coordinator. The direct sales representatives followed up on those leads, promoted GlobalSuite to the hotel owners and managers and attempted to close deals. Guest-Tek employed 10 direct sales representatives. All inside and direct sales representatives reported to the sales director for North America. The direct sales method was the exclusive method employed in North America, and the sales team was now extending this method to Latin America as well. All direct sales activities were managed out of Guest-Tek's head office.

Inside and direct sales representatives preferred to work with hotel ownership and management groups rather than individual hotels. Convincing one such group to purchase GlobalSuite usually resulted in sales to multiple properties. The sales representatives also targeted hotels that fell under brands such as Hilton, Hyatt and Marriott, which had granted Guest-Tek preferred vendor status and wished to see consistency across their properties. While the hotels under these brands did not necessarily have to follow advice from the brand level, preferred vendor status was a strong selling point for Guest-Tek.

Inside and direct sales employees had revenue quotas and were compensated partly through commission. All North American sales were priced and recorded in U.S. dollars but overseas sales could also be priced and recorded in local currency.

The direct sales approach had driven Guest-Tek's rapid growth despite an inherently long sales cycle. A contract required a significant capital commitment from the hotel's decision maker, who typically had to obtain approval from many layers of ownership and management. The direct sales approach allowed Guest-Tek representatives to build relationships with clients and influence them throughout the decision-making process. The full process, from generating interest to building a relationship and finally signing a contract, could take between four and 12 months and occasionally even longer.

INDIRECT SALES THROUGH RESELLERS

The indirect sales method most commonly involved partnerships with technology resellers who licensed GlobalSuite software as part of their own solution. In this case, Guest-Tek collected one-time revenue for the software license but took no other part in the deal and undertook no other efforts for marketing, operations or otherwise. Guest-Tek's only activity in this process was to manage the relationship with the reseller. This method had been employed in Europe, the Middle East and Africa through French technology reseller Locatel.

The relationship with Locatel had been relatively easy to manage. Initial meetings to broker the deal had been conducted at Guest-Tek's office in Calgary and at Locatel's office in Paris, France, and a Guest-Tek technical representative had later been sent to Paris to train Locatel personnel. The relationship was managed by Guest-Tek's business development team, and since Locatel installed the solution, Guest-Tek project managers and operations teams were not involved.

The reseller channel was a low-cost and low-risk method of entering new markets, particularly when Guest-Tek did not have expertise or presence in those markets. As the CEO explained, "Inbound demand mitigates risk, because a knowledgeable partner is coming to us with opportunities." However, the reseller retained a significant portion of the revenue and Guest-Tek had no control over the installation or support aspects of the solution and consequently could not control the quality, the customer experience or the user experience. Furthermore, the CEO felt that this channel was too passive.

INDIRECT SALES THROUGH AGENTS

Guest-Tek also sold GlobalSuite indirectly through agents, although this method was less common. Agents were independent technology salespeople selling the full GlobalSuite solution as well as other products and solutions from other vendors. They were self-employed freelancers who took a percentage of the revenue from each sale. Agents were familiar with GlobalSuite but under no obligation to sell it over other solutions.

Guest-Tek did not drive this strategy and any sales generated this way were essentially viewed as bonus sales. The company's efforts were limited to providing the agents with information to help them sell GlobalSuite and offering the agents better commissions to encourage them to favor it. There were currently two agents operating for Guest-Tek in the Latin American region: one in Argentina and the other in Trinidad.

THE EXPANSION CHALLENGE

Guest-Tek's share offering, completed on February 6, 2004, brought the company net proceeds of $28.3 million (see Exhibit 7 for the intended allocation of the funds). These funds would allow Guest-Tek to grow by eliminating some of the financial constraints that had inhibited the company in the past. However, public status brought new shareholders and higher expectations and the CEO knew that these people were watching Guest-Tek's market position very closely. The company's sales had grown quickly over the past two years, and the CEO felt pressure to continue that pace.

One promising avenue for growth was the international market. "Guest-Tek has established a strong position with the industry in North America," the CEO stated in a recent earnings release. "We are working aggressively to repeat this success on a global scale." To that end, $3.0 million of the IPO proceeds had specifically been allocated for international sales and marketing initiatives. Guest-Tek had young, energetic and entrepreneurial leaders and employees, and there was a general feeling within the ranks that the company could "take on the world." Also, the company's executives believed that they could make up for their lack of international experience with their superior technology, turnkey solution, technical expertise, sales skills and hotel market expertise.

However, international sales could be framed as both an opportunity and a competitive requirement because the North American branches of hotel brands wanted the solutions they chose to also be available to their international branches. In other words, hotel brands wanted to deal with global players. Finally, international sales could also be considered as a risk because Guest-Tek was unfamiliar with those markets.

KEY DECISION MAKERS

As a rapidly growing company with expectations to match, Guest-Tek's business decisions were driven principally by the sales, marketing and business development personnel. The CEO would ultimately make the decision with substantial input from the VP of Sales and Marketing, who viewed international expansion as an excellent opportunity and the most natural avenue for growing the company.

Guest-Tek's founder, who was also the former CEO and the former executive vice-president of Business Development, would also have some input in the decision-making process. While no longer an executive of the company, the founder held a seat on the board of directors. He held a bachelor of commerce degree specializing in the hospitality industry. Prior to founding Guest-Tek, he had spent several years as an analyst for economic diversification and business development. The founder strongly favored international expansion. The founder and the VP of Sales and Marketing had known each other for years, even before the VP of Sales and Marketing joined the company, and the two had held many positive conversations about international expansion.

Feasibility and practical aspects had to be considered as well as market potential; therefore, the CEO would also consider the opinions of several other executives. These executives were supportive of international expansion but cautioned that there would be challenges. There was a general feeling that risks could be mitigated by working with partners such as Locatel and by selling to international hotel management groups, ownership groups and brands that were already customers in North America.

Guest-Tek's vice-president of Operations was an industrial engineer with an MBA from the same graduating class as the VP of Sales and Marketing. She had joined Guest-Tek in 2000. With her dual training, she provided a balanced opinion of both operations and business. She believed that the required changes to the software would be minimal but cautioned that hardware standards and prices would vary considerably between countries. The company would face a learning curve upon entering each new region and each new country. The VP of Operations accepted these challenges and was supportive of international expansion.

The vice-president of Research and Development was also supportive of international expansion. With a doctorate in computer science from the University of Calgary, postdoctoral fellowships at both MIT and Stanford University and experience with several high-tech startups, he had a deep understanding of the technological ramifications facing Guest-Tek. He suggested that his department's only challenge would lie in translating GlobalSuite's user and manager interfaces into multiple languages. GlobalSuite's user interface was already available in English, French and Spanish, and additional translation would be a straightforward task. Translation of the management interface—that part of the solution used by hotel managers for pricing and billing, reporting and other administrative work—would be a much more complicated, expensive and time-consuming project.

There was also the question of multilingual service through Guest-Tek's user support hotline. Support was currently offered in the same three languages—English, French and Spanish—on a full-time basis and only partial coverage was available in other languages.

Guest-Tek's chief financial officer was also an important figure in the decision-making process and a supporter of international expansion. She was a chartered accountant with a strong business background. She was keenly aware of the expectations that Guest-Tek now faced from investors and analysts and recognized the need for revenue growth. Additional funds from the IPO had been allocated to expanding Guest-Tek's operational capacity, so growth could be achieved profitably.

GEOGRAPHIC CHOICES

The outstanding questions to those involved revolved around which markets were the most attractive, how those markets should be pursued and how the overseas business should be managed. These were difficult questions to answer because Guest-Tek had only basic information on the overseas markets and had no staff with overseas experience or expertise aside from a recently retained consultant for the European region. The CEO preferred to gather as much information as possible before making a decision in an unfamiliar area, but in this case adequate information was not to be found internally. Without reasonable information, he was more reactive and preferred to entertain proposals from knowledgeable partners, but as explained previously, that was considered a passive strategy. The CEO had set an ambitious goal of deriving 15 to 20 per cent of new installation revenue outside North America in FY2005—a goal that might require more proactive efforts. With this in mind, the CEO considered what he did know about the opportunities before him.

EUROPEAN MARKET

Guest-Tek had historically looked beyond North America to the European market as a possible avenue for expansion. Europe featured 67,500 hotel properties and nearly six million hotel rooms, which were often combined with the 14,000 properties and roughly 670,000 rooms in the Middle East and Africa, and referred to as the broader Europe, Middle East and Africa (EMEA) region. However, a higher concentration of hotels and steeper demand for high-speed Internet access made the United Kingdom and continental Europe the focus.

Penetration and usage rates were growing in Europe, but trailed behind North American rates and were not expected to fully catch up. In general, there was less business travel in Europe than in North America, and guests demanded less Internet service. However, European hotel managers were beginning to perceive high-speed Internet access as a necessary service offering, and the market was becoming more demand-driven, with strong growth expected for 2004 and beyond. European hotel managers were also more inclined to pay higher prices for better solutions. Industry sources suggested that growth in high-speed Internet access in homes and offices was particularly noticeable in France and Italy. The CEO also knew that within Europe, the busiest destinations for both European and American business travelers were the United Kingdom and Germany. The proliferation of wireless technology was expected to bolster the European industry since many of Europe's hotels were historic and managers preferred less intrusive and less damaging infrastructure.

Guest-Tek's CEO resisted the temptation to discuss Europe as a single market since he perceived little homogeneity across the continent. Countries varied considerably in culture, language, business practices, the balance between business and pleasure travel, Internet use and broadband penetration among the general population (see Exhibit 8 for a comparison of broadband access in OECD [Organisation for Economic Co-operation and Development] countries). Adoption of high-speed Internet access in hotels also varied accordingly. Hotel communities in different countries varied in the extent to which they welcomed a solution provider from North America. Some did not mind, while others preferred to deal with local providers or at least local offices of global providers.

European countries also differed from Canada and the United States in terms of hotel structure. Firstly, the majority of European hotels were independent or affiliated with voluntary chains that demanded less in terms of conformity and standards. Guest-Tek's preferred provider approach might not be as effective in these situations.

Secondly, European hotels tended to be smaller than North American hotels, resulting in smaller sales. It was often more difficult to convince a manager of a small hotel to accept the high price of a premium high-speed Internet access solution. Furthermore, the CEO believed that the European property and room totals had been inflated by small lodging establishments catering only to leisure travelers. Thus, while the totals for Europe were higher than those for North America, the CEO believed that the effective market for Guest-Tek was actually smaller in Europe.

A variety of providers were now targeting Europe, most notably European telcos, such as British Telecom and France Telecom, offering hotspots and other technologies. However, Guest-Tek perceived its most direct competition in the European market as coming from North American solution providers who viewed Europe as a natural growth area as the North American market approached saturation. As the most notable example, STSN was believed to have at least 100 European installations. Wayport was smaller than STSN in Europe but also had a presence. Several Asian niche providers were also entering Europe. One such company, inter-touch, had completed 36 installations by mid-2003.

Guest-Tek had so far approached EMEA sales indirectly through a partnership with Locatel, which had a relationship with the Accor hotels and had installed Global-Suite in 33 hotels as of January, 2004. As explained previously, indirect sales had been a low-cost and low-risk method of introducing GlobalSuite to the market. The CEO wondered whether the time had come to sell more proactively. Guest-Tek was not prohibited from selling directly in markets where Locatel had a presence.

LATIN AMERICAN MARKET

High-speed Internet access penetration and usage rates among Latin America's 21,000 hotels and nearly one million hotel rooms were widely believed to trail behind North America's rates, although exact figures for Latin America were unavailable. A higher ratio of pleasure travel to business travel in Latin America resulted in lower demand for high-speed Internet access among travelers. Lower penetration in Latin homes and offices also limited demand in hotels. The low demand was exacerbated by a poor communications infrastructure that raised the cost for a solution. Hotel managers charged higher users fees to fund cost recovery, and this practice further discouraged use.

In a more positive light, the CEO viewed Latin America as a relatively easier market to approach than Europe or Asia-Pacific because he believed Latin America had more internal homogeneity. However, in his experience, this internal homogeneity sometimes led Latin American clients to favor Latin American vendors.

Guest-Tek has thus far approached South America as an extension of the company's North American activities. Activity had been modest to date. Since beginning direct sales efforts to Latin America from its Calgary headquarters in June 2003, Guest-Tek had sold at least one major hotel in Aruba, Chile, Costa Rica, Dominican

Republic, Mexico, Panama and Puerto Rico. Some additional demand came from Hilton and other existing customers and from the two agents who sold GlobalSuite among other solutions. Each opportunity was carefully and individually evaluated and only accepted if it presented a comfortable return on investment. In this way, Guest-Tek had mitigated its risk by reacting to inbound opportunities. In total, Guest-Tek had nearly a dozen installations in Latin America. Based on these results, the CEO considered the establishment of a regional office with a larger direct sales force.

ASIA-PACIFIC MARKET

The Asia-Pacific region, with 54,700 hotel properties and nearly four million hotel rooms, also caught the CEO's attention. Its usage rate actually rivaled that of North America and both usage and penetration rates were expected to rise quickly in a revived economy. Guests were demanding high-speed Internet access in spite of user fees that doubled or even tripled North American fees. Many foreign and local providers were stepping in to answer the demand.

The Asia-Pacific region, like Europe, was diverse. Cultures, languages, business communication styles and high-speed Internet access penetration and usage varied widely. Some countries or districts within the region, including Hong Kong, were approaching hotel high-speed Internet access saturation while the market in other countries was still nascent. Countries with high residential and business broadband adoption reportedly had high hotel adoption as well, and Japanese hotel managers in particular demanded the service.

Unfortunately, Guest-Tek had little knowledge of the region and detailed assessments of the various countries were not available; in fact, the CEO ventured to say that this was the region that Guest-Tek understood least. Guest-Tek had few relationships in the area and no staff members with Asian expertise. This lack of familiarity and knowledge had clearly influenced Guest-Tek's approach to the region in the past. Guest-Tek had not proactively pursued deals and had only installed services when approached by hotels. As with opportunities in Latin America, inbound opportunities were carefully evaluated on an individual basis and only accepted on the grounds of a comfortable return on investment. Although the CEO didn't know for certain, Guest-Tek's experience in Asia-Pacific so far supported the widely held belief that it was a difficult market for foreigners to enter.

The Asian preference for a different business model was one aspect of the market that was known to Guest-Tek. In this region, solution providers were often expected to provide the solution, including software, hardware and installation services, at no charge in exchange for a share of the user fees. This model, usually referred to as "revenue share," required a great deal of capital and involved a high degree of risk for the solution provider. This model had been commonplace in North America five years earlier, but had proved to be unsustainable, and many providers following that model had filed for bankruptcy. In fact, Guest-Tek had employed that model to some degree in the company's early stages, but had abandoned it before shifting to its current model. The demand for revenue share contracts on the part of Asian hotel managers ran counter to Guest-Tek's proven strategy, and the CEO was reluctant to revisit the matter.

Most of the high-speed Internet access solutions in Asia were provided by larger telcos, including China Mobile, China Telecom, NTT Communications, Japan Telecom and Yahoo Broadband Japan, and most of the solutions were based on different technologies including hotspots. There were only a few providers in the region that were similar to Guest-Tek, in terms of their solution and business model. They were generally locally based, like Australia's inter-touch, which had more than 100 installations in the region.

MANAGEMENT OF INTERNATIONAL BUSINESS

International expansion not only posed questions of how and where to sell GlobalSuite but also how to manage the business and actually install the solution. Up to that time, Guest-Tek's direct sales activities had been conducted from Guest-Tek's head office in Calgary with personal visits by sales and account managers to the hotel properties as necessary. When a contract was signed, a project manager and an operations team were dispatched from the Calgary office to the hotel property to install the solution. Travel to overseas properties for both sales and installations could be costly due to the time and distance involved. Since, to date, international sales were relatively rare, coordination from the head office had been wise and feasible.

This situation could change, however, if Guest-Tek were to make a more concerted effort overseas. The option that immediately came to mind was to set up local offices with local presence, knowledge, connections and acceptance. Such offices, though difficult to staff, might provide a competitive advantage. An overseas office could be built with transplanted North American personnel, local personnel or some mix of the two. Present Guest-Tek employees had little overseas experience. None of the executives had worked overseas, and beyond the one direct salesperson pursuing Latin America and the consultant providing advice on Europe, there were no employees with significant international knowledge. The CEO preferred to promote people from within the company but knew also that international expansion would require an international experience base.

The establishment of overseas offices would also force questions about management and control. International offices could operate as closely managed extensions of the North American office under the CEO or the VP of Sales and Marketing, or they could be run as relatively autonomous units. The CEO wanted to replicate the Guest-Tek culture and ensure quality of operations, but with limited information about the markets, he was unsure of how well the North American management style would translate into the regions in question. He was also unsure of what level of overseas activity could effectively be managed by executives in the head office and at what point a region required or deserved its own autonomous leadership.

Of course, the option of pursuing indirect sales was still available and was somewhat attractive. Reseller and agent relationships were relatively easy to manage and would not require a buildup of staff levels. Resellers and agents would already have presence and expertise in the markets in question. However, the CEO was not certain that the more passive nature of indirect sales would fulfill his mandate for expansion.

THE CEO'S CHALLENGE

Understanding the new investors' demands for revenue growth, the CEO had to decide whether or not Guest-Tek should pursue overseas opportunities. He felt he had to decide quickly, given that the North American market would eventually become saturated and competitors were already pursuing international opportunities. Should Guest-Tek expand overseas? If so, which markets should it enter? And how should the overseas operations be managed?

Exhibit 1   Guest-Tek Client List, 2003

Ownership Group / Chain	Properties
Marriott International	132
Hyatt Corporation / Hyatt International Corporation	42
InterContinental Hotels Group	37
Hilton Hotels Corporation	34
Starwood Hotels & Resorts Worldwide	20
Accor Hotels	20
Carlson Companies	18
Best Western International	8
Ritz-Carlton Hotel Company	6
Independent, boutique and other	87
Total	404

Geographic Region	Properties
North America	358
International	46
Total	404

Guestrooms	80,700

Note: Figures as of November 30, 2003.
Source: Guest-Tek Prospectus, January 30, 2004.

Exhibit 2 Guest-Tek Income Statement, FY2001–FY2003, (in Cdn$)

	Year ended March 31			Six months ended September 30	
	2003	**2002**	**2001**	**2003**	**2002**
Revenue:					
New installations	$7,294,666	$ 2,733,589	$ 1,134,780	$9,705,524	$2,615,911
Recurring revenue	1,406,428	810,783	400,917	1,333,641	591,972
	8,701,094	3,544,372	1,535,697	11,039,165	3,207,883
Expenses:					
Cost of goods and services sold	4,597,565	2,032,882	1,194,804	6,147,837	1,633,172
Selling, general and administrative	2,694,619	1,922,727	1,728,720	1,897,504	1,130,086
Research and development	551,216	556,804	456,467	273,488	270,079
Foreign currency loss	37,558	1,320	—	175,144	1,942
Interest expense (income), net	37,726	(6,468)	171,277	53,256	15,464
Write-down of property and equipment	—	—	810,544	—	—
Amortization of property and equipment	151,687	122,100	264,360	85,964	67,644
	8,070,371	4,629,365	4,626,172	8,633,193	3,118,387
Income (loss) from operations	630,723	(1,084,993)	(3,090,475)	2,405,972	89,496
Government assistance for research & development	175,709	—	—	—	54,803
Income (loss) before income taxes	806,432	(1,084,993)	(3,090,475)	2,405,972	144,299
Income taxes (recovery)	(440,000)	—	—	(185,122)	—
Net income (loss)	$1,246,432	$(1,084,993)	$(3,090,475)	$2,591,094	$ 144,299

Note: Six month figures are unaudited.
Source: Guest-Tek Prospectus, January 30, 2004.

Exhibit 3   Guest-Tek Staff by Department

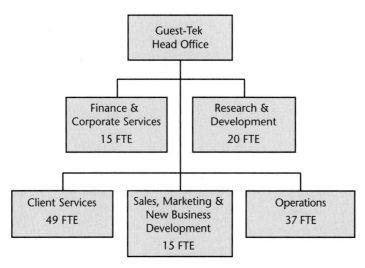

Exhibit 4   Guest-Tek Revenue by Geographic Region, FY2001–FY2003

| | Year ended March 31 | | | Six months ended September 30 | |
	2003	2002	2001	2003	2002
Canada	$1,192,855	$ 977,309	$ 907,240	$ 781,478	$ 812,562
United States	7,203,772	2,567,063	628,457	10,021,236	2,343,616
Other	304,407	—	—	236,451	51,705
Total	$8,701,034	$3,544,372	$1,535,697	$11,039,165	$3,207,883

Source: Guest-Tek Prospectus, January 30, 2004.

Exhibit 5   North American Hotel Industry By Segment, (as of November 2003)

Segment	Upper Upscale	Upscale	Midscale w/ F&B	Midscale w/out F&B	Economy	Independent
Rating	5 - 4 star	4 star	3 star	3 star	2 star	Various
Representative brands	Four Seasons Hilton Hyatt InterContinental Ritz-Carlton	Crown Plaza Doubletree Novotel Radisson Residence Inn	Best Western Four Points Holiday Inn Park Plaza Ramada	Amerihost Comfort Inn Country Inn Hampton Inn Signature Inn	Budget Inn Days Inn Econo Lodge Motel 6 Super 8	Various
Target client	Luxury/corporate	Corporate	Ec. bus. traveler	Ec. bus. traveler	Traveling sales	Various
Hotels	1,794	2,370	5,097	6,980	10,330	29,271
Rooms	658,316	380,236	643,490	628,155	810,445	1,728,300
Rooms per hotel	367	160	126	90	78	59

Notes: Figures for US and Canada only. F&B refers to food and beverage service. Ec. bus. traveler refers to economy business traveler.
Source: Smith Travel Research Database, November 26, 2003. Cited in Guest-Tek Prospectus, January 30, 2004.

Exhibit 6   HSIA Installations in North America, by Company,
(as of November/December 2003)

	Upper upscale	Upscale	Mid w/ F&B	Mid w/out F&B	Economy	Unclassified	Total
Wayport	296	101	78	53	12	56	596
STSN	254	277	7	28	-	24	590
Guest-Tek	100	145	21	26	9	57	358
GoldenTree	17	95	25	78	8	21	244
Stay Online	8	79	17	7	1	11	123
Broadband Hospitality	4	37	8	63	-	4	116
V-Link	78	-	-	-	-	1	79
Suite Speed	3	4	4	9	-	10	30
Indirect competitors	368	350	469	581	209	418	2,395
Total	1,128	1,088	629	845	239	602	4,531

Note: Figures for US and Canada only. GoldenTree had 142 pending installations under construction. F&B refers to food and beverage service.
Source: Roger Sharma, "North American Market Analysis", *Guest-Tek*, December 2003.

***Exhibit* 7**   Intended Allocation of Proceeds from Guest-Tek's IPO, (figures in Cdn$)

Millions	Allocation
$2.0	Increasing operational capacity for deployments
3.0	Expanding international sales and marketing initiatives
5.0	Advancing new product offerings
15.0	Funding disciplined, strategic acquisitions
3.3	Supplying working capital for general corporate purposes
$28.3	Proceeds to the corporation

***Exhibit* 8**   Broadband Access in OECD Countries, (as of June 2003)

Country	Penetration
Korea	23.2%
Canada	13.3%
Iceland	11.2%
Denmark	11.1%
Belgium	10.3%
Netherlands	9.2%
Sweden	9.2%
Switzerland	9.1%
Japan	8.6%
United States	8.3%
Austria	7.0%
Finland	6.6%
OECD	6.1%
Norway	5.4%
Germany	4.8%
EU	4.6%
Spain	4.2%
France	4.1%
Portugal	3.7%
United Kingdom	3.6%
Italy	2.8%
Luxembourg	2.3%

Note: Penetration figures per 100 inhabitants. Only countries with at least 1.0% penetration are shown.
Source: OECD.

Activplant: The European Opportunity

MONDAY MORNING

On Monday January 30, 2006, Dennis Cocco, chief executive officer (CEO), and Chuck Frosst, chief operating officer (COO) of Activplant Corporation, sat debating the European market opportunity. Frosst wondered aloud:

> Can we financially afford to enter Europe? Can we afford to put substantial human resources into developing and implementing that market at all? I mean, we can get the financing, but that doesn't mean it's the best idea.

Of Activplant's current customers, more than 90 per cent were located in North America. Recently, many larger customers had been attempting to pull Activplant into the European market so that the company could provide more extensive support. Cocco responded:

> Listen, we have now proven ourselves in the North American auto manufacturing market. I don't understand what we're waiting for. We know that our product is easily transferable to Europe. We also know that our current "doggy-paddle-to-Europe" strategy isn't going to build us the market. Potential customers are not going to meet us in the middle of the Atlantic. We have to go get them and we have to do it before our competitors do.

Frosst responded:

> I don't know, Dennis. It sounds like a lot of risk for a company our size. Don't forget that it's not just our customers we have to pay attention to. Our investors are watching closely as well.

Brodie B. Christ prepared this case under the supervision of Professor Stewart Thornhill solely to provide material for class discussion. The authors do not intend to illustrate either effective or ineffective handling of a managerial situation. The authors may have disguised certain names and other identifying information to protect confidentiality.

Richard Ivey School of Business
The University of Western Ontario

BACKGROUND

Activplant Corporation was a London, Ontario-based software firm specializing in manufacturing intelligence (MI). Essentially, MI is the ability to monitor, measure and analyse the performance of factory automation systems. Activplant was founded by a group of technology entrepreneurs in 1998. It was a privately held company supported by significant investments from world-class companies, such as Ford Motor Company, Ventures West Management, the Canadian Science and Technology Growth Fund and the Bank of Montreal Capital Corporation.

Activplant had installations all over the world, the majority within North America. It controlled 80 per cent of the automotive original equipment manufacturer (OEM) plants that had MI software in North America. Much of the North American market was still unexplored, as were Europe and Asia. Current customers included Toyota, Gillette, Ford, Honda, Chrysler, Visteon and Magna. Historically, Activplant had acquired customers on a plant-by-plant basis. In the future, they looked forward to gaining sales for installations across an entire enterprise, which had become the focus of the current sales process.

THE ACTIVPLANT PRODUCT

Activplant was a web-deployed, fully scalable enterprise manufacturing intelligence solutions designed to work across an entire operation from the smallest to the largest plants. Activplant collected data from any source on the factory floor and integrated it with business logic, reporting capabilities, analysis and intelligent discovery via alerts. From the integration of these elements, managers and decision-makers across the enterprise had a tool to identify constraints on the plant floor with the goal of maximizing throughput. The software worked on fundamental manufacturing process principles and had been proven useful for automotive, consumer goods, and food and beverage manufacturers with discrete and hybrid manufacturing processes.

THE PRODUCT/SERVICE OFFERING IN NORTH AMERICA

Licensing

Activplant sold its software on a license basis. The license fee was paid one time and was followed with an annual maintenance fee that included upgrades, bug fixes and access to a support help desk. License fees were the major source of revenue for Activplant, which had placed greater emphasis on the product than on services as a driver for growth. As well, the service revenue was dependent on the license being purchased.

The software license allowed the customer to have the Activplant software suite installed and set up to begin monitoring any manufacturing equipment that the suite was attached to. The larger the installation and the more manufacturing machines that were being monitored, the more license revenue Activplant generated. However, for larger deals, Activplant would lower its per-installation price, making the return-on-investment proposition more attractive for the customer.

Maintenance/Support

Activplant North America currently had staff available by phone for customer service to provide both knowledge support and assistance with maintenance and upgrades. The web-based platform allowed Activplant staff in London to see precisely what was occurring on the factory floor, assess the situation and offer assistance, all without being physically present.

Training

From its headquarters, Activplant ran a training facility for customers to learn the specifics and details of the software. Activplant offered an extensive array of training programs to ensure customers could maximize their Activplant investment. Courses were designed to train customers in implementing, supporting, administering and effectively using various Activplant solutions. The courses were instructor led and used hands-on labs and examples to reinforce the course material provided. The training options included courses at the London headquarters, customized on-site training and, where required, training in prominent U.S. locations. Training for the software could take a number of weeks to complete.

The Sales Process

The Activplant sales method could be a grueling six- to 12-month process, due to the complexity of clearly illustrating the product's value and the substantial investment required from potential customers. Activplant had sales managers who visited potential clients and provided pitches, as well as inside sales representatives who generated and qualified leads. There was a very technical aspect to selling the product that required a technical expert. While the sales managers targeted the decision makers in an organization (CEOs, COOs, VPs), the technical sales representative needed to convince the internal engineers and technical staff of ease of integration and the aspects of the product that would improve production.

The Services Process

The value proposition of the services process was to provide customers with timely and effective services, such as installation and customization of the product, to best suit the customer's needs. All of Activplant's services in North America were supplied by internal staff at Activplant. The complexity of the product was such that having internal staff providing services ensured the requisite level of quality.

This component of the Activplant solution was complex and required substantial resource commitment for both Activplant and the customer. Services at Activplant could be broken into a number of different categories: installation, training and support. The installation process could be broken down into three further subsections: Discovery, the survey of the plant by an Activplant consultant to assess specifically how the installation would proceed; Delivery, the installation of the software, including tests to ensure that it was communicating with the line machinery; and Maintenance, Activplant's updates and software "tweaking" to suit the specific needs of the company. The personnel and resources required could fluctuate substantially, depending on the size of the implementation.

THE EUROPEAN OPPORTUNITY

Activplant currently had some customers in Europe, none of which had been actively pursued by sales. Activplant had either been pulled into Europe by current customers (e.g. Ford and Visteon) or had been pursued by proactive companies (e.g. Gillette and Duracell in the United Kingdom). The offerings had been provided on an ad hoc basis.

A European go-to-market strategy would require a product that supported multiple languages in some fashion. This requirement could be partially satisfied by the pre-installation customization/configuration, by which labels (text on the screen) of the local language were entered into the system. Although this solution might have been adequate as a temporary means to enter the European market, a complete internationalization could be required in order to compete effectively with local and global companies.

Full internationalization of the Activplant Software Suite would likely cost more than $2 million as a one time cost and approximately $300,000 per language to translate the interface.[1] Internationalization of the software would enhance the product in three ways: it would allow administration of the software in local languages; enable local dependent representation of data (for example, currency, date and time values), and cover all the necessary character sets, including double-byte character sets that would be required for markets in Asia. Among these three objectives, being able to display data in a format consistent with the appropriate locale was the most important.

Operating since 1998 on investments from venture capitalists (VCs), Activplant had just achieved its first year of profitability in fiscal year 2006. A European strategy would be funded entirely by Activplant's cash and operating income currently on hand, since the current investors were not committing any additional funds at this time.

Services

Existing European customers had experienced slow responses when problems were encountered, partly due to the time zone difference between Europe and North America. In addition, reliance on partners in the past to deliver quality services had yielded mixed results, since there had not been a vigorous partnership program to ensure the quality of services. Therefore, being able to provide quality services more consistently and more timely by having a local presence would make Activplant a better vendor for customers' business needs.

To deliver this value proposition, Activplant would need to deploy its own resources, or work with partners. Either option would require active management and execution by Activplant.

Maintenance/Support

For reasons similar to that of installation services, European customers would value local on-going support. Running a support center in Europe from the first year would likely be too expensive for the relatively small volume of sales; however, pager or phone support by local Activplant personnel could satisfy customers' needs

---

[1] All funds in U.S. dollars unless otherwise specified.

for responsiveness. A protocol needed to be developed to standardize the process by which support requests through the support personnel in Europe were handled, so that responsiveness and cost would be well balanced. For example, requests could be classified into multiple levels, but it remained to be determined which issues staff in Europe would be responsible for and which issues staff in North America would need to address.

Training

Activplant could provide training to customers through its certified partners in Europe; alternatively, it could attempt to provide training itself, either locally at the customer's site or in Canada. A partnership training strategy provided an opportunity for the partners to learn about Activplant's products in depth, strengthening the partners' ability to provide services and support in the future. One of the difficulties regarding outsourcing services and support tasks to the partners was their lack of knowledge of the product. By offering European partners the training business, Activplant received a greater benefit of educating the partners themselves, allowing more flexibility in its operations in the future. For example, if the operation needed to be scaled up rapidly due to market demand, Activplant might need to offload some of the tasks to its partners since it may not be able to expand its capacity as drastically.

COMPETITORS ACROSS THE GLOBE

Manufacturing software had yet to be clearly defined as a market, and it was difficult to determine whether a company offered solutions that overlapped or complemented Activplant's solutions in this growing and convoluted solution space.

Some of the competitors to be aware of in Europe included the following:

Wonderware/Invensys
- Performance management solutions with real-time capability. Claimed 30 per cent of the factories in the world used Wonderware software.

Rockwell
- A global provider of manufacturing hardware and software systems. Recently acquired Manufacturing Execution Systems (MES) provider Datasweep.

SAP/Lighthammer
- A German enterprise resource planning (ERP) solution provider driving toward manufacturing solutions. Acquisition of Lighthammer had provided portal capabilities for manufacturing.

OSIsoft
- A manufacturing intelligence company with a joint venture in Germany.

Matrikon
- A provider of manufacturing intelligence solutions for process, hybrid and discrete manufacturing with offices in Ireland and Germany

UGS
- Broad scope of product lifecycle management solutions, including some MES products. A global company with presence in Europe.

Iconics

- A provider of manufacturing intelligence solutions from the HMI/SCADA end of the space with many locations throughout Europe

Citect

- An MES provider with strong global approach based in Australia.

In general, the market growth for manufacturing intelligence and performance management solutions was accelerating. As some of the larger brand-name global players, such as Rockwell, GE and SAP, acquired smaller well-developed software platforms, Activplant needed to maintain adequate market share and size or it would risk being pushed out of the market. In addition, as competitive platforms increased their scope, the value proposition in Activplant's discrete manufacturing software solution became less distinctive.

PARTNERS

Solution Partners

Activplant had engaged in two relationships with other firms in order to sell its product in Europe. These relationships were developed based on the desire of these two firms —ATS and Systema—to sell Activplant software. A commission was paid based on the amount of sales that Activplant received from these partners.

These two partners fell into separate areas of expertise. ATS had competencies in the smaller details of the installation and provided additional services to the end customer. ATS's motivation was to either include Activplant products as an add-on to increase revenues or as a selling feature to help ATS secure contracts.

Systema approached the customer in a manufacturing consultant capacity, using the Activplant software data to supplement its own consultancy services. Activplant's relationship with Systema was established recently and had not yet generated any deals, although Systema had indicated that several were in the pipeline.

The solution partners did not have the sales expertise to make the enterprise deals that were Activplant's current focus. These types of solution partners often had a number of different software products that they could offer to their clients. Changes in the levels of commission or preferences of the client could affect a partner's desire to sell one product over another. The Activplant software suite was not a significant portion of either partner's revenue. Partners did not have exclusivity agreements, but ATS has been hinting that such an arrangement would "enable" them to sell more Activplant product.

Integration/Technology Partners

Initially, customer installations, support and other services would not be sufficient to cover the costs of a complete services team in Europe, although many functions would still be required. Some functions could be covered by the North American office. Other functions, such as installation and multi-language support, would need to be provided in Europe. Integration partners had proven capable in the past, and Activplant was wise to continue to utilize them to make up for the lack of infra-structure in Europe. Installation was also not one of Activplant's core competencies. The services components of the Activplant process could be coordinated by staff in

Europe, remotely from Canada with frequent flights to Europe or managed by the partners in Europe.

Channel Partners

There were advantages to creating, growing and strengthening relationships with either large players in the business solutions industry who would have interconnected software products, such as Microsoft, Oracle and SAP, or larger consulting firms, such as Accenture or Tata.

There was a potential to leverage Activplant's current relationship with Microsoft by engaging Microsoft to promote Activplant solutions as part of its portfolio for manufacturing clients. However, Microsoft did not participate in direct sales; Microsoft did not even sell its own product directly. Since the outcome of a Microsoft-dependant strategy was questionable, and, outside of Activplant's control, sales needed to be generated by a sales force to ensure that targets were met. A Microsoft partner strategy would likely become a greater source of lead generation in the future, but it was still unproven.

Revenue

According to past sales experience, it was estimated that one Activplant sales representative in Europe could, on average, conclude two deals in one quarter. The average size of one deal was US$100,000 (excluding services and support contract). Since a typical sales cycle was six to eight months, the first deal closed by the European operation, excluding deals currently in the sales process, would likely occur in the third quarter after entry. Partners in Europe pursuing their selling efforts were also assumed to be able to conclude two deals per quarter.

Market Size

The estimated automotive market for Activplant in Europe was $343 million as compared to the estimated $300 million market in North America. Suppliers outnumbered OE manufacturers by a ratio of 22 to one. The automotive industry comprised nearly 80 per cent of Activplant's current revenues.

	North American Plants	European Plants
OEMs	90[2]	94
Suppliers	1,910	1,986[3]
Total	2,000[4]	2,080

The average deal size for Activplant was $100,000, but the range could range from $30,000 for small single plant deals to $3 million for enterprise-wide installations.

---

[2] Automotive News http://www.autonews.com/assets/PDF/CA31631024.PDF for NA OEM.
[3] http://www.emcc.eurofound.eu.int/automotivemap/
[4] Activplant Market Sizing and Roadmap, October 18, 2005.

Staffing

The most significant factor affecting profitability in the European market was employee payroll. Salaries for various positions could be assessed first as if the employees were hired in Canada and worked in Canada, then a 30 per cent premium could be added to account for the higher wage level and benefits in Europe. Finally, the premium-added cost was converted to U.S. dollars to be comparable with revenue figures.

Financial assumptions are detailed in Exhibit 4.

ALTERNATIVES

There were two main components to the decision to launch Activplant in Europe from personnel and operations perspectives.

The first component involved the method used to sell the product. This selection answered questions such as the following: Will Activplant involve partners in the selling process? Will Activplant have sales staff full-time in Europe? If so, how many? Will enterprise deals be managed from Europe or Canada? This part of the decision is known as the Sales Process.

The second component was the method by which Activplant would deliver the sold services in Europe. It would answer such questions as: Who will deliver support, and from where? How will services be provided? How will Activplant deal with training? This piece was known as Services.

The selected option from the Sales Process with the selected option from Services would combine to form the basis of a European Entrance Strategy.

Sales Alternatives

Activplant would like to sell both single plant deals and large deals, which would involve multiple plants across an entire enterprise. Given those segments, Activplant could decide who would be responsible for single plant sales (solution partners, full-time staff in Europe or sales staff in Canada) and who would be responsible for enterprise deals.

Using solution partners to pursue enterprise deals would require the development of a partner management strategy to ensure consistent messaging and quality of the sales process. This approach would require a partnership manager. If Activplant had staff directly in Europe, these staff would require a senior account manager and a regular account manager.

Staff Requirements

Option	Title	Cost CDN$)
Solution Partners	Partnership Manager	$150,000 × 130% = $195,000
Activplant Staff in Europe	Account Manager, Senior Account Manager	$125,000 × 130% + $150,000 × 130% = $357,500

Services Alternatives

Similarly, the services that Activplant performed after an installation comprised two components: Project Delivery and Solution Consulting. Project delivery referred to lower-end work, such as machine programming and product installation, but also the coordination and management of these tasks. Currently, these tasks were mostly performed by integration partners where they performed the work and managed the project. It was lower margin work that required substantial human resources. Solution Consulting was higher end, knowledge- and expertise-intensive fine-tuning of the product so that the client could glean the most benefit. Occasionally, clients preferred to do take on this task themselves, believing that they could do it better than Activplant and/or their partners.

Each services component, Project Delivery and Solutions Consulting, could be performed either by Activplant staff in Europe, remotely by Activplant staff in Canada or by integration partners (for project delivery) and solution partners (for solution consulting). The latter often allowed solution partners to upsell their own consulting services or software add-ons and could add quite substantially to their revenue on an Activplant installation.

Option	Title	Cost (CDN$)
AP Europe manages project delivery and consulting	Project Manager	$150,000 × 130% = $195,000
AP Europe project manages all service components and performs project delivery	Project Manager, Project Delivery Personnel	$150,000 × 130% + $90,000 × 130% = $312,000
AP Canada manages services remotely	None	Travel, contracting partners to do delivery
Partners manage services	None	$0

The Sales and Services staffing and strategy decisions are exclusive of each other.

CRITERIA

The principal objectives of a European entrance were to ensure revenue growth (approximately $1.5 million in year one), and achieve profitability by the end of year two. To evaluate the alternatives for sales and services operations, Activplant began to review the options based on the following considerations:

- Quality of Execution
- Risk of Brand Damage
- Feasibility
- Governance and Control

WHAT NOW?

Should Activplant develop a partnership strategy and spend resources supporting partners in the selling process in Europe, or should it perform the selling process directly and build a European sales team? A partnership development strategy would require investment in new training and additional incentives for solution partners, but a new European operation could bring with it higher costs and greater risk.

As Frosst and Cocco sat discussing the various main issues involved, they knew that each issue could essentially be broken down into three options: going it alone, utilizing partners or temporarily not going. Each option had its benefits and drawbacks. Now all they had to do was decide, keeping in mind that this decision could have major effects on the future of the company.

Exhibit 1   Sales Cycle

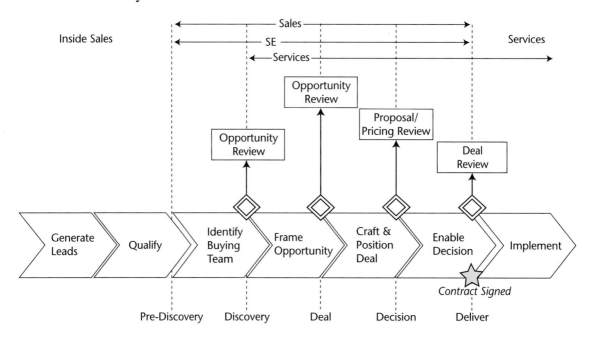

Exhibit 2   Revenue by Sector

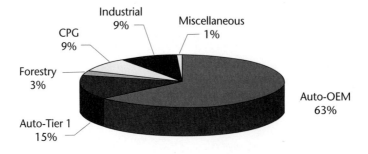

Exhibit 3 Competitive Landscape

Software Provider	Operational Scope	Geographic Focus	Manufacturing Focus
Activplant	Data Acquisition/Performance Analysis	NA/Minimal EU	Discrete
Wonderware	Data Acquisition/Automation Software	EU/Some NA	Process/Hybrid
Rockwell	Data Acquisition/Process Mgmt/ Automation software	NA/EU	All
SAP/Lighthammer	Portal/Dashboard/Middleware/ ERP	EU/NA	Discrete
OSIsoft	Data Acquisition/Performance Analysis	NA/Some EU	Process/Some Hybrid
Citect	MES and Discrete	AMEA	Process/Some Hybrid
Iconics	Dashboard/Performance Analysis	EU	Discrete
UGS	Product Tracking/ERP/CRM	Europe	Hybrid/Discrete
Matrikon	Data Acquisition/Performance Analysis	NA/Some EU	Process/Some Hybrid

Company documents.

Exhibit 4 Financial Assumptions

Average Number of Deals per Account Manager per quarter = 2

This figure is to be discounted for Year 1 because of the effort required to build the infrastructure, time required for training, as well as setting up the operation.

Salary difference between Canadian market and the European Market = + 30%

Office Related Expense = US$500 per month per person
HQ.com rate

Cost for the following positions in Canada:
Director/Senior Account Manager: Cdn$150,000 + commission (5%) of up to $100,000
Account Manager: Cdn$125,000 + commission (5%) of up to $100,000
Sales Engineer: Cdn$150,000
Project Manager: Cdn$150,000
Service Personnel: $80,000 – $100,000 (Cdn$90,000)
Partnership Manager: Cdn$125,000 + bonus

Salary difference between Canadian market and the European Market = + 30%

Service Margin: 20%
Potential Service Revenue / License Revenue = 100%

Sales Cycle: Six months to eight months

(continued)

Exhibit 4   (continued)

Average Deal Size—License: US$100,000
Average Deal Size—Support: US$15,000

Exchange Rate Cdn$/US$ = 1.15
2-year range = 1.40 to 1.15
- The value of the U.S. dollar is still under downward pressure, due to the economic conditions of the United States. For example, the United States has been running a current account deficit for many years, which suppresses the value of the U.S. dollar. There is a common belief that the U.S. dollar is due for a downward correction. Thus we expect the U.S. dollar to remain in its low level at Cdn$1.15 per US$1.00.

Exchange Rate Euro/US$ = 0.82
2-year range = 0.74 to 0.86
- We expect the euro to fluctuate between its 2-year range. The current exchange rate is 0.82 euro per US$1.00, which will be used in our projection.

The Global Branding of Stella Artois

In April 2000, Paul Cooke, chief marketing officer of Interbrew, the world's fourth largest brewer, contemplated the further development of their premium product, Stella Artois, as the company's flagship brand in key markets around the world. Although the long-range plan for 2000-2002 had been approved, there still remained some important strategic issues to resolve.

A BRIEF HISTORY OF INTERBREW

Interbrew traced its origins back to 1366 to a brewery called Den Hoorn, located in Leuven, a town just outside of Brussels. In 1717, when it was purchased by its master brewer, Sebastiaan Artois, the brewery changed its name to Artois.

The firm's expansion began when Artois acquired a major interest in the Leffe Brewery in Belgium in 1954, the Dommelsch Brewery in the Netherlands in 1968, and the Brassiere du Nord in France in 1970. In 1987, when Artois and another Belgian brewery called Piedboeuf came together, the merged company was named Interbrew. The new company soon acquired other Belgian specialty beer brewers, building up the Interbrew brand portfolio with the purchase of the Hoegaarden brewery in 1989 and the Belle-Vue Brewery in 1990.

Interbrew then entered into a phase of rapid growth. The company acquired breweries in Hungary in 1991, in Croatia and Romania in 1994, and in three plants in Bulgaria in 1995. Again in 1995, Interbrew completed an unexpected major acquisition by purchasing Labatt, a large Canadian brewer also with international interests. Labatt had operations in the United States, for example, with the Latrobe brewery, home of the Rolling Rock brand. Labatt also held a substantial minority stake in the second

Professors Paul W. Beamish and Anthony Goerzen prepared this case solely to provide material for class discussion. The authors do not intend to illustrate either effective or ineffective handling of a managerial situation. The authors may have disguised certain names and other identifying information to protect confidentiality.

Version: (A) 2002-11-22

IVEY

Richard Ivey School of Business
The University of Western Ontario

largest Mexican brewer, Femsa Cervesa, which produced Dos Equis, Sol, and Tecate brands. Following this major acquisition, Interbrew went on, in 1996, to buy a brewery in the Ukraine and engaged in a joint venture in the Dominican Republic. Subsequently, breweries were added in China in 1997, Montenegro and Russia in 1998, and another brewery in Bulgaria and one in Korea in 1999.

Thus, through acquisition expenditures of US$2.5 billion in the previous four years, Interbrew had transformed itself from a simple Belgian brewery into one of the largest beer companies in the world. By 1999, the company had become a brewer on a truly global scale that now derived more that 90 per cent of its volume from markets outside Belgium. It remained a privately held company, headquartered in Belgium, with subsidiaries and joint ventures in 23 countries across four continents.

THE INTERNATIONAL MARKET FOR BEER

In the 1990s, the world beer market was growing at an annual rate of one to two per cent. In 1998, beer consumption reached a total of 1.3 billion hectolitres (hls). There were, however, great regional differences in both market size and growth rates. Most industry analysts split the world market for beer between growth and mature markets. The mature markets were generally considered to be North America, Western Europe and Australasia. The growth markets included Latin America, Asia, Central and Eastern Europe including Russia. Although some felt that Africa had considerable potential, despite its low per capita beer consumption, the continent was not considered a viable market by many brewers because of its political and economic instability (see Exhibit 1).

Mature Markets

The North American beer market was virtually stagnant, although annual beer consumption per person was already at a sizeable 83 litres per capita (lpc). The Western European market had also reached maturity with consumption of 79 lpc. Some analysts believed that this consumption level was under considerable pressure, forecasting a decline to near 75 lpc over the medium term. Australia and New Zealand were also considered mature markets, with consumption at 93 lpc and 84 lpc, respectively. In fact, volumes in both markets, New Zealand in particular, had declined through the 1990s following tight social policies on alcohol consumption and the emergence of a wine culture.

Growth Markets

Given that average consumption in Eastern Europe was only 29 lpc, the region appeared to offer great potential. This consumption figure, however, was heavily influenced by Russia's very low level, and the future for the large Russian market was unclear. Further, some markets, such as the Czech Republic that consumed the most beer per person in the world at 163 lpc, appeared to have already reached maturity. Central and South America, on the other hand, were showing healthy growth and, with consumption at an average of 43 lpc, there was believed to be considerable upside. The most exciting growth rates, however, were in Asia. Despite the fact that the market in this region had grown by more than 30 per cent since 1995, consumption levels were still comparatively low. In China, the region's largest market, consumption was only 16 lpc and 20 to 25 lpc in Hong Kong and Taiwan. Although the 1997 Asian financial crisis did not immediately affect beer consumption (although company profits from the region were hit by currency translation), demand in some key markets, such as Indonesia, was reduced and in others growth slowed. The situation, however, was expected to improve upon economic recovery in the medium term.

BEER INDUSTRY STRUCTURE

The world beer industry was relatively fragmented with the top four players accounting for only 22 per cent of global volume—a relatively low figure as compared to 78 per cent in the soft drinks industry, 60 per cent in tobacco and 44 per cent in spirits. This suggested great opportunities for consolidation, a process that had already begun two decades prior. Many analysts, including those at Interbrew, expected that this process would probably accelerate in the future. The driver behind industry rationalization was the need to achieve economies of scale in production, advertising and distribution. It was widely recognized that the best profit margins were attained either by those with a commanding position in the market or those with a niche position. However, there were several factors that mitigated the trend towards rapid concentration of the brewing industry.

One factor that slowed the process of consolidation was that the ratio of fixed versus variable costs of beer production was relatively high. Essentially, this meant that there was a limited cost savings potential that could be achieved by bringing more operations under a common administration. Real cost savings could be generated by purchasing and then rationalizing operations through shifting production to more efficient (usually more modern) facilities. This approach, however, required large initial capital outlays. As a result, in some markets with "unstable" economies, it was desirable to spread out capital expenditures over a longer period of time to ensure appropriate profitability in the early stages. A second factor that may have had a dampening effect on the trend towards industry consolidation was that local tastes differed. In some cases, beer brands had hundreds of years of heritage behind them and had become such an integral part of everyday life that consumers were often fiercely loyal to their local brew. This appeared to be a fact in many markets around the world.

INTERBREW'S GLOBAL POSITION

Through Interbrew's acquisitions in the 1990s, the company had expanded rapidly. During this period, the company's total volumes had increased more than fourfold. These figures translated to total beer production of 57.5 million hls in 1998 (when including the volume of all affiliates), as compared to just 14.7 million hls in 1992. Volume growth had propelled the company into the number four position among the world's brewers.

Faced with a mature and dominant position in the declining Belgian domestic market, the company decided to focus on consolidating and developing key markets, namely Belgium, the Netherlands, France and North America, and expansion through acquisition in Central Europe, Asia and South America. Subsequently, Interbrew reduced its dependence on the Belgian market from 44 per cent in 1992 to less than 10 per cent by 1998 (total volumes including Mexico). Concurrently, a significant milestone for the company was achieved by 1999 when more than 50 per cent of its total volume was produced in growth markets (including Mexico). Interbrew had shifted its volume so that the Americas accounted for 61 per cent of its total volume, Europe added 35 per cent, and Asia Pacific the remaining four per cent.

Taken together, the top 10 markets for beer accounted for 86 per cent of Interbrew's total volume in 1998 (see Exhibit 2). The Mexican beer market alone accounted for 37 per cent of total volume in 1998. Canada, Belgium, the United States and the United Kingdom were the next most important markets. However, smaller, growing markets such as Hungary, Croatia, Bulgaria, and Romania had begun to increase in importance.

Adding to its existing breweries in Belgium, France and the Netherlands, Interbrew's expansion strategy in the 1990s had resulted in acquisitions in Bosnia-Herzegovina, Bulgaria, Canada, China, Croatia, Hungary, Korea, Montenegro, Romania, Russia, the Ukraine, the United States, in a joint venture in South Korea, and in minority equity positions in Mexico and Luxembourg. Through these breweries, in addition to those that were covered by licensing agreements in Australia, Italy, Sweden and the United Kingdom, Interbrew sold its beers in over 80 countries.

INTERBREW'S CORPORATE STRUCTURE

Following the acquisition of Labatt in 1995, Interbrew's corporate structure was divided into two geographic zones: the Americas and Europe/Asia/Africa. This structure was in place until September 1999 when Interbrew shifted to a fully integrated structure to consolidate its holdings in the face of industry globalization. Hugo Powell, formerly head of the Americas division, was appointed to the position of chief executive officer (CEO). The former head of the Europe/Africa/Asia division assumed the role of chief operating officer, but subsequently resigned and was not replaced, leaving Interbrew with a more conventional structure, with the five regional heads and the various corporate functional managers reporting directly to the CEO.

RECENT PERFORMANCE

1998 had been a good year for Interbrew in terms of volume in both mature and growth markets. Overall, sales volumes increased by 11.1 per cent as most of the company's international and local brands maintained or gained market share. In terms of the compounded annual growth rate, Interbrew outperformed all of its major competitors by a wide margin. While Interbrew's 1998 net sales were up 29 per cent, the best performing competitor achieved an increase of only 16 per cent. Of Interbrew's increased sales, 67 per cent was related to the new affiliates in China, Montenegro and Korea. The balance was the result of organic growth. Considerable volume increases were achieved also in Romania (72 per cent), Bulgaria (28 per cent), Croatia (13 per cent), and the United States (14 per cent). While volumes in Western Europe were flat, duty-free sales grew strongly. In the U.S. market, strong progress was made by Interbrew's Canadian and Mexican brands, and Latrobe's Rolling Rock was successfully relaunched. In Canada, performance was strong, fuelled by a two per cent increase in domestic consumption. Labatt's sales of Budweiser (produced under license from Anheuser Busch) also continued to grow rapidly.

Given that the premium and specialty beer markets were growing quickly, particularly those within the large, mature markets, Interbrew began to shift its product mix to take advantage of this trend and the superior margins it offered. A notable brand success was Stella Artois, for which total global sales volumes were up by 19.7 per cent.

That growth came from sales generated by Whitbread in the United Kingdom, from exports, and from sales in Central Europe where Stella Artois volumes took off. The strong growth of Stella Artois was also notable in that it was sold in the premium lager segment. In Europe, Asia Pacific and Africa, Interbrew's premium and specialty beers, which generated a bigger margin, increased as a proportion of total sales from 31 per cent in 1997 to 33 per cent in 1998. This product mix shift was particularly important since intense competition in most markets inhibited real price increases.

Success was also achieved in the United States specialty beer segment where total volume had been growing at nine per cent annually in the 1990s. In 1998, Interbrew's share of this growing market segment had risen even faster as Labatt USA realized increased sales of 16 per cent. The other continuing development was the growth of the light beer segment, which had become over 40 per cent of the total sales. Sales of Labatt's Blue Light, for example, had increased and Labatt Blue had become the number three imported beer in the United States, with volumes up 18 per cent. Latrobe's Rolling Rock brand grew by four per cent, the first increase in four years. Interbrew's Mexican brands, Dos Equis, Tecate and Sol, were also up by 19 per cent.

Following solid volume growth in profitable market segments, good global results were realized in key financial areas. Net profit, having grown for each of the previous six consecutive years, was 7.7 billion Belgian francs (BEF) in 1998, up 43.7 per cent from the previous year. Operating profit also rose 7.9 per cent over 1997, from 14.3 to 15.4 BEF; in both the Europe/Asia/Africa region and the Americas, operating profit was up by 8.5 per cent and 4.9 per cent respectively. Further, Interbrew's EBIT margin was up 58.1 per cent as compared to the best performing competitor's figure of 17.0 per cent. However, having made several large investments in Korea and Russia, and exercising an option to increase its share of Femsa Cerveza in Mexico from 22 per cent to 30 per cent, Interbrew's debt-equity ratio increased from 1.04 to 1.35. As a result, interest payments rose accordingly.

Interbrew also enjoyed good results in volume sales in many of its markets in 1999. Although Canadian sales remained largely unchanged over 1998, Labatt USA experienced strong growth in 1999, with volumes up by 10 per cent. There was a positive evolution in Western European volumes as well, as overall sales were up by 6.5 per cent overall in Belgium, France and the Netherlands. Central European markets also grew with Hungary showing an increase of 9.6 per cent, Croatia up by 5.5 per cent, Romania by 18.9 per cent, Montenegro by 29 per cent, and Bulgaria with a rise of 3.6 per cent in terms of volume. Sales positions were also satisfactory in the Russian and Ukrainian markets. Further, while South Korean sales volume remained unchanged, volumes in China were 10 per cent higher, although this figure was still short of expectations.

INTERBREW CORPORATE STRATEGY

The three facets of Interbrew's corporate strategy, i.e., brands, markets and operations, were considered the "sides of the Interbrew triangle." Each of these aspects of corporate strategy was considered to be equally important in order to achieve the fundamental objective of increasing shareholder value. With a corporate focus entirely on beer, the underlying objectives of the company were to consolidate its positions in mature markets and improve margins through higher volumes of premium and specialty brands. Further, the company's emphasis on growth was driven by the belief that beer industry rationalization still had some way to go and that the majority of the world's major markets would each end up with just two or three major players.

Operations Strategy

Cross fertilization of best practices between sites was a central component of Interbrew's operations strategy. In the company's two main markets, Belgium and Canada, each brewery monitored its performance on 10 different dimensions against its peers. As a result, the gap between the best and the worst of Interbrew's operations had narrowed decisively since 1995. Employees continuously put forward propositions to improve processes. The program had resulted in significantly lower production costs, suggesting to Interbrew management that most improvements had more to do with employee motivation than with pure technical performance. In addition, capacity utilization and strategic sourcing had been identified as two areas of major opportunity.

Capacity Utilization

Given that brewing was a capital-intensive business, capacity utilization had a major influence on profitability. Since declining consumption in mature markets had generated excess capacity, several of Interbrew's old breweries and processing facilities were scheduled to be shut down. In contrast, in several growth markets such as Romania, Bulgaria, Croatia and Montenegro, the opposite problem existed, so facilities in other locations were used more fully until local capacities were increased.

Strategic Sourcing

Interbrew had begun to rationalize its supply base as well. By selecting a smaller number of its best suppliers and working more closely with them, Interbrew believed that innovative changes resulted, saving both parties considerable sums every year. For most of the major commodities, the company had gone to single suppliers and was planning to extend this approach to all operations worldwide.

Market Strategy

The underlying objectives of Interbrew's market strategy were to increase volume and to lessen its dependence on Belgium and Canada, its two traditional markets. Interbrew dichotomized its market strategy into the mature and growth market segments, although investments were considered wherever opportunities to generate sustainable profits existed. One of the key elements of Interbrew's market strategy was to establish and manage strong market platforms. It was believed that a brand strength was directly related to a competitive and dedicated market platform (i.e., sales and distribution, wholesaler networks, etc.) to support the brand. Further, Interbrew allowed individual country teams to manage their own affairs and many felt that the speed of success in many markets was related to this decentralized approach.

Mature Markets

Interbrew's goals in its mature markets were to continue to build market share and to improve margins through greater efficiencies in production, distribution and marketing. At the same time, the company intended to exploit the growing trend in these markets towards premium and specialty products of which Interbrew already possessed an unrivalled portfolio. The key markets in which this strategy was being actively pursued were the United States, Canada, the United Kingdom, France, the Netherlands and Belgium.

Growth Markets

Based on the belief that the world's beer markets would undergo further consolidation, Interbrew's market strategy was to build significant positions in markets that had long-term volume growth potential. This goal led to a clear focus on Central and Eastern Europe and Asia, South Korea and China in particular. In China, for example, Interbrew had just completed an acquisition of a second brewery in Nanjing. The Yali brand was thereby added to the corporate portfolio and, together with its Jingling brand, Interbrew became the market leader in Nanjing, a city of six million people.

In Korea, Interbrew entered into a 50:50 joint venture with the Doosan Chaebol to operate the Oriental Brewery, producing the OB Lager and Cafri pilsener brands. With this move, Interbrew took the number two position in the Korean beer market with a 36 per cent share and sales of 5.1 million hls. The venture with Doosan was followed in December 1999 by the purchase of the Jinro Coors brewery. This added 2.5 million hls and increased Interbrew's market share to 50 per cent of total Korean volume. Thus, the Interbrew portfolio in Korea consisted of two mainstream pilsener brands, OB Lager and Cass, the two local premium brands, Cafri and Red Rock, and Budweiser, an international premium brand.

In Russia, Interbrew expanded its presence by taking a majority stake in the Rosar Brewery in Omsk, adding the BAG Bier and Sibirskaya Korona brands. Rosar was the leading brewer in Siberia with a 25 per cent regional market share, and held the number four position in Russia. New initiatives were also undertaken in Central Europe with acquisitions of a brewery in Montenegro and the Pleven brewery in Bulgaria, as well as the introduction of Interbrew products into the Yugoslavian market. Finally, although Interbrew had just increased its already significant investment in Mexico's second largest brewer from 22 per cent to 30 per cent, Latin America remained a region of great interest.

Brand Strategy

A central piece of Interbrew's traditional brand strategy had been to add to its portfolio of brands through acquisition of existing brewers, principally in growth markets. Since its goal was to have the number one or two brand in every market segment in which it operated, Interbrew concentrated on purchasing and developing strong local brands. As it moved into new territories, the company's first priority was to upgrade product quality and to improve the positioning of the acquired local core lager brands. In mature markets, it drew on the strength of the established brands such as Jupiler, Belgium's leading lager brand, Labatt Blue, the famous Canadian brand, and Dommelsch, an important brand in the Netherlands. In growth markets, Interbrew supported brands like Borsodi Sor in Hungary, Kamenitza in Bulgaria, Ozujsko in Croatia, Bergenbier in Romania, Jingling in China, and OB Lager in Korea. In addition, new products were launched such as Taller, a premium brand in the Ukraine, and Boomerang, an alternative malt-based drink in Canada.

A second facet of the company's brand strategy was to identify certain brands, typically specialty products, and to develop them on a regional basis across a group of markets. At the forefront of this strategy were the Abbaye de Leffe and Hoegaarden brands and, to a lesser extent, Belle-Vue. In fact, both Hoegaarden and Leffe achieved a leading position as the number one white beer and abbey beer in France and Holland. The Loburg premium pilsener brand also strengthened its position when it was relaunched in France. Further, in Canada, Interbrew created a dedicated organization for specialty beers called the Oland Specialty Beer Company. In its first year of operation, the brands marketed by Oland increased its volumes by over 40 per cent. More specifically, sales of the Alexander Keith's brand doubled and the negative volume trend of the John Labatt Classic brand was reversed. The underlying message promoted by Oland was the richness, mystique and heritage of beer.

To support the regional growth of specialty beers, Interbrew established a new type of café. The Belgian Beer Café, owned and run by independent operators, created an authentic Belgian atmosphere where customers sampled Interbrew's Belgian specialty beers. By 1999, Belgian Beer Cafés were open in the many of Interbrew's key markets, including top selling outlets in New York, Auckland, Zagreb and Budapest, to name a few. The business concept was that these cafés were to serve as an ambassador of the Belgian beer culture in foreign countries. They were intended to serve as vehicles to showcase Interbrew's specialty brands, benefiting from the international appeal of European styles and fashions. Although these cafés represented strong marketing tools for brand positioning, the key factors that led to the success of this concept were tied very closely to the individual establishments and the personnel running them. The bar staff, for example, had to be trained to serve the beer in the right branded glass, at the right temperature, and with a nice foamy head. It was anticipated that the concept of the specialty café would be used to support the brand development efforts of Interbrew's Belgian beers in all of its important markets.

The third facet of Interbrew's brand strategy was to identify a key corporate brand and to develop it as a global product. While the market segment for a global brand was currently relatively small, with the bulk of the beer demand still in local brands, the demand for international brands was expected to grow, as many consumers became increasingly attracted to the sophistication of premium and super-premium beers.

THE EVOLUTION OF INTERBREW'S GLOBAL BRAND STRATEGY

Until 1997, Interbrew's brand development strategy for international markets was largely *laissez faire*. Brands were introduced to new markets through licensing, export and local production when opportunities were uncovered. Stella Artois, Interbrew's most broadly available and oldest brand, received an important new thrust when it was launched through local production in three of the company's subsidiaries in Central Europe in 1997. This approach was consistent with the company's overall goals of building a complete portfolio in high growth potential markets.

By 1998, however, the executive management committee perceived the need to identify a brand from its wide portfolio to systematically develop into the company's global brand. Although the market for global brands was still small, there were some growing successes (e.g., Heineken, Corona, Fosters and Budweiser) and Interbrew believed that there were several basic global trends that would improve the viability of this class of product over the next couple of decades. First, while many consumers were seeking more variety, others were seeking lower prices. It appeared that the number of affluent and poor consumer segments would increase at the expense of the middle income segments. The upshot of this socioeconomic trend was that eventually all markets would likely evolve in such a way that demand for both premium and economy-priced beers would increase, squeezing the mainstream beers in the middle. A second trend was the internationalization of the beer business. As consumers travelled around the world, consuming global media (e.g., CNN, Eurosport, MTV, international magazines, etc.), global media were expected to become more effective for building brands. A global strategy could, therefore, lead to synergies in global advertising and sponsoring. In addition, the needs of consumers in many markets were expected to converge. As a result of these various factors, Interbrew believed that there would be an increasing interest in authentic, international brands in a growing number of countries.

Interbrew had a wide portfolio of national brands that it could set on the international stage. The two most obvious candidates were Labatt Blue and Stella Artois.

The Labatt range of brands included Labatt Blue, Labatt Blue Light and Labatt Ice. To date, however, the exposure of these brands outside of North America had been extremely limited and they were not yet budding global brands. Of the total Labatt Blue volume in 1998, 85 per cent was derived from the Canadian domestic and U.S. markets, with the balance sold in the United Kingdom. The Labatt brands had been introduced to both France and Belgium, and production had been licensed in Italy, but these volumes were minimal. The only real export growth market for Labatt Blue appeared to be the United States, where the brand's volume in 1998 was some 23 per cent higher than in 1995, behind only Corona and Heineken in the imported brand segment. The Labatt Ice brand was also sold in a limited number of markets and, after the appeal of this Labatt innovation had peaked, its total volume had declined by more than 25 per cent since 1996. Total Labatt Ice volume worldwide was just 450,000 hls in 1998, of which 43 per cent was sold in Canada, 33 per cent in the United States, and 21 per cent in the United Kingdom.

STELLA ARTOIS AS INTERBREW'S INTERNATIONAL FLAGSHIP BRAND

The other potential brand that Interbrew could develop on a global scale was Stella Artois, a brand that could trace its roots back to 1366. The modern version of Stella Artois was launched in 1920 as a Christmas beer and had become a strong market leader in its home market of Belgium through the 1970s. By the 1990s, however, Stella's market position began to suffer from an image as a somewhat old-fashioned beer, and the brand began to experience persistent volume decline. Problems in the domestic market, however, appeared to be shared by a number of other prominent international brands. In fact, seven of the top 10 international brands had experienced declining sales in their home markets between 1995 and 1999 (see Exhibit 3).

Stella Artois had achieved great success in the United Kingdom through its licensee, Whitbread, where Stella Artois became the leading premium lager beer. Indeed, the United Kingdom was the largest market for Stella Artois, accounting for 49 per cent of total brand volume in 1998. Stella Artois volume in the U.K. market reached 2.8 million hls in 1998, a 7.6 per cent share of the lager market, and came close to 3.5 million hls in 1999, a 25 per cent increase over the previous year. By this time, over 32,000 outlets sold Stella Artois on draught.

Apart from the United Kingdom, the key markets for Stella Artois were France and Belgium, which together accounted for a further 31 per cent of total brand volume (see Exhibit 4). With these three markets accounting for 81 per cent of total Stella Artois volume in 1999, few other areas represented a significant volume base (see Exhibit 5). Beyond the top three markets, the largest market for Stella Artois was Italy, where the brand was produced under license by Heineken. Stella Artois volume in Italy had, however, declined slightly to 166,000 hls in 1998. Licensing agreements were also in place in Sweden and Australia, but volume was small.

Stella Artois was also produced in Interbrew's own breweries in Hungary, Croatia and Romania, with very pleasing 1998 volumes of 84,000 hls, 120,000 hls, and 60,000 hls, respectively. After only three years, the market share of Stella Artois in Croatia, for example, had reached four per cent—a significant result, given that the brand was a premium-priced product. In all Central European markets, Stella Artois was priced at a premium; in Hungary, however, that premium was lower than in Croatia and Romania where, on an index comparing Stella's price to that of core lagers, the indices by country were 140, 260 and 175 respectively.

Promising first results were also attained in Australia and New Zealand. Particularly in New Zealand, through a "seeding" approach, Interbrew and their local partner, Lion Nathan, had realized great success in the Belgian Beer Café in Auckland where the brands were showcased. After only two years of support, Stella Artois volume was up to 20,000 hls, and growing at 70 per cent annually, out of a total premium segment of 400,000 hls. Interbrew's market development plan limited distribution to top outlets in key metropolitan centres and priced Stella Artois significantly above competitors (e.g., 10 per cent over Heineken and 20 per cent over Steinlager, the leading domestic premium lager brand).

The evolution of the brand looked very positive as world volumes for Stella Artois continued to grow. In fact, Stella Artois volume had increased from 3.4 million hls in 1992 to a total of 6.7 million hls in 1999, a rise of 97 per cent. Ironically, the only market where the brand continued its steady decline was in its home base of Belgium. Analysts suggested a variety of reasons to explain this anomaly, including inconsistent sales and marketing support, particularly as the organization began to favor the rising Jupiler brand.

Overall, given Interbrew's large number of local brands, especially those in Mexico with very high volumes, total Stella Artois volume accounted for only 10 per cent of total Interbrew volume in 1999 (14 per cent if Femsa volumes are excluded). Interbrew's strategy of nurturing a wide portfolio of strong brands was very different as compared to some of its major competitors. For example, Anheuser-Busch, the world's largest brewer, focused its international strategy almost exclusively on the development of the Budweiser brand. Similarly, Heineken sought to centre its international business on the Heineken brand and, to a lesser extent, on Amstel. While the strategies of Anheuser-Busch and Heineken focused primarily on one brand, there were also great differences in the way these two brands were being managed. For example, Budweiser, the world's largest brand by volume, had the overwhelming bulk of its volume in its home U.S. market (see Exhibit 6). Sales of the Heineken brand, on the other hand, were widely distributed across markets around the world (see Exhibit 7). In this sense, Heineken's strategy was much more comparable to that of Interbrew's plans for Stella Artois. Other brands that were directly comparable to Stella Artois, in terms of total volume and importance of the brand to the overall sales of the company, were Carlsberg and Foster's with annual sales volumes in 1998 of 9.4 million hls and 7.1 million hls, respectively. While Foster's was successful in many international markets, there was a heavy focus on sales in the United Kingdom and the United States (see Exhibit 8). Carlsberg sales volume profile was different in that sales were more widely distributed across international markets (see Exhibit 9).

STELLA'S GLOBAL LAUNCH

In 1998, Interbrew's executive management committee settled on Stella Artois, positioned as the premium European lager, as the company's global flagship brand. In fact, the Interbrew management felt that stock analysts would be favorably disposed to Interbrew having an acknowledged global brand with the potential for a higher corporate valuation and price earnings (P/E) multiple.

As the global campaign got under way, it became clear that the organization needed time to adapt to centralized co-ordination and control of Stella Artois brand marketing. This was, perhaps, not unexpected given that Interbrew had until recently operated on a regional basis; the new centralized Stella brand management approach had been in place only since September 1998. In addition, there were often difficulties in convincing all parties to become part of a new global approach, particularly the international advertising campaign that was the backbone of the global plan for Stella Artois. Belgium, for example, continued with a specific local advertising program that positioned Stella as a mainstream lager in its home market, and in the United Kingdom, Whitbread maintained its "reassuringly expensive" advertising slogan that had already proved to be so successful. For other less-established markets, a global advertising framework was created that included a television concept and a series of print and outdoor executions. This base advertising plan was rolled out in 1999 in 15 markets, including the United States, Canada, Italy, Hungary, Croatia, Bulgaria, Romania, New Zealand and France (with a slightly changed format) after research suggested that the campaign had the ability to cross borders. The objective of this campaign was to position Stella Artois as a sophisticated European lager. It was intended that Stella Artois should be perceived as a beer with an important brewing tradition and heritage but, at the same time, also as a contemporary beer (see Exhibit 10).

In 1998, an accelerated plan was devised to introduce Stella Artois to two key markets within the United States, utilizing both local and corporate funding. The U.S. market was believed to be key for the future development of the brand since it was the most developed specialty market in the world (12 per cent specialty market share, growing 10 per cent plus annually through the 1990s), and because of the strong influence on international trends. Thus, Stella Artois was launched in New York City and Boston and was well received by the demanding U.S. consumer and pub owner. Within 1999, over 200 pubs in Manhattan and 80 bars in Boston had begun to sell Stella Artois on tap. To support the heightened efforts to establish Stella Artois in these competitive urban markets, Interbrew's corporate marketing department added several million dollars to Labatt USA's budget for Stella Artois in 2000, with commitments to continue this additional funding in subsequent years.

CURRENT THINKING

Good progress had been made since 1998 when Stella Artois was established as Interbrew's global brand. However, management had revised its expectations for P/E leverage from having a global brand. The reality was that Interbrew would be rewarded only through cash benefits from operational leverage of a global brand. There would be no "free lunch" simply for being perceived as having a global brand. In addition, in an era of tight fiscal management, it was an ongoing challenge to maintain the funding levels required by the ambitious development plans for Stella Artois. As a result, in early 2000 the prevailing view at Interbrew began to shift, converging on a different long-range approach towards global branding. The emerging perspective emphasized a more balanced brand development program, focusing on the highest leverage opportunities.

The experience of other brewers that had established global brands offered an opportunity for Interbrew to learn from their successes and failures. Carlsberg and Heineken, for example, were two comparable global brands that were valued quite differently by the stock market. Both sold over 80 per cent of their total volumes outside their domestic market, and yet Heineken stock achieved a P/E ratio of 32.4 in 1999 versus Carlsberg's figure of only 17.1. According to industry analysts, the driving force behind this difference was that Heineken maintained a superior market distribution in terms of growth and margin (see Exhibit 11). The key lesson from examining these global brands appeared to be that great discipline must be applied to focus resources in the right places.

In line with this thinking, a long range marketing plan began to take shape that made use of a series of strategic filters to yield a focused set of attractive opportunities. The first filter that any potential market had to pass through was its long-term volume potential for Stella Artois. This volume had to trace back to a large and/or growing market, the current or potential sizeable premium lager segment (at least five per cent of the total market), and the possibility for Stella Artois to penetrate the top three brands. The second screen was the potential to achieve attractive margins after an initial starting period of approximately three years. The third filter was whether or not a committed local partner was available to provide the right quality of distribution and to co-invest in the brand. The final screen was the determination that success in the chosen focus markets should increase leverage in other local and regional markets. For example, the size and stature of Stella Artois in the United Kingdom was a significant factor in the easy sell-in of Stella Artois into New York in 1999.

Once filtered through these strategic market development screens, the global branding plans for Stella Artois began to take a different shape. Rather than focus on national markets, plans emerged with an emphasis on about 20 cities, some of which Interbrew was already present in (e.g., London, Brussels, New York, etc.). This approach suggested that the next moves should be in such potential markets as Moscow, Los Angeles and Hong Kong. Some existing cities would receive focused efforts only when distribution partner issues had been successfully resolved to solidify the bases for sustained long term growth. The major cities that fit these criteria provided the right concentration of affluent consumers, who would be attracted to Stella's positioning, thus providing scale for marketing and sales, investment leverage, as well as getting the attention and support of motivated wholesalers and initial retail customers. These venues would thereby become highly visible success stories that would be leveragable in the company's ongoing market development plans.

Thus, the evolving global branding development plan required careful planning on a city-by-city basis. Among the demands of this new approach were that marketing efforts and the funding to support them would have to be both centrally stewarded and locally tailored to reflect the unique local environments. A corporate marketing group was, therefore, established and was charged with the responsibility to identify top priority markets, develop core positioning and guidelines for local execution, assemble broadly based marketing programs (e.g., TV, print advertising, global sponsorships, beer.com content, etc.), and allocate resources to achieve the accelerated growth objectives in these targeted cities. To ensure an integrated development effort the company brought all pivotal resources together, under the leadership of a global brand development director. In addition to the brand management team, the group included regional sales managers who were responsible for licensed partner management, a customer services group, a Belgian beer café manager, and cruise business management group. Another significant challenge that faced the corporate marketing group was to ensure that all necessary groups were supportive of the new approach. This was a simpler undertaking among those business units that were wholly owned subsidiaries; it was a more delicate issue in the case of licensees and joint ventures. A key element of managing brands through a global organizational structure was that the head office team had to effectively build partnerships with local managers to ensure their commitment.

Fortunately, much of the initial effort to establish Stella Artois as a global brand had been done on a city-by-city basis and, as such, there was ample opportunity for Interbrew to learn from these experiences as the new global plan evolved. In the late 1990s, for example, Stella Artois was introduced to various Central European cities (e.g., Budapest, Zagreb, Bucharest and Sofia). In each of these cities, Interbrew's marketing efforts were launched when the targeted premium market was at an early stage of development. Further, distribution and promotion was strictly controlled (e.g., product quality, glassware, etc.) and the development initiatives were delivered in a concentrated manner (e.g., a media "blitz" in Budapest). In addition, results indicated that the presence of a Belgian Beer Café accelerated Interbrew's market development plans in these new areas. These early successes suggested that brand success could be derived from the careful and concentrated targeting of young adults living in urban centres, with subsequent pull from outlying areas following key city success.

The key lessons of these efforts in Central Europe proved to be very valuable in guiding the market development plan in New York City. In this key North American city, the rollout of Stella Artois was perceived by the analysts as "one of the most promising introductions in New York over the last 20 years" and had generated great wholesaler support and excitement. Among the tactics used to achieve this early success was selective distribution with targeted point of sale materials support. In addition, a selective media campaign was undertaken that included only prestigious outdoor advertising (e.g., a Times Square poster run through the Millennium celebrations). Similarly, the sponsoring strategy focused only on high-end celebrity events, Belgian food events, exclusive parties, fashion shows, etc. Finally, the price of Stella Artois was targeted at levels above Heineken, to reinforce its gold standard positioning. This concerted and consistent market push created an impact that resulted in the "easiest new brand sell" in years, according to wholesalers. The success of this launch also built brand and corporate credibility, paving the way to introductions in other U.S. cities as well as "opening the eyes" of other customers and distribution partners around the world.

To pursue this new global development plan over the next three years, a revised marketing budget was required. Given that the corporate marketing department was responsible for both the development of core programs as well as the selective support of local markets, the budget had to cover both of these key elements. To achieve these ends, total spending was expected to more than double over the next three years.

While great progress had been made on the global branding of Stella Artois, Cooke still ruminated on a variety of important interrelated issues. Among these issues was the situation of Stella Artois in Belgium—would it be possible to win in the "global game" without renewed growth in the home market? What specific aspirations should Interbrew set for Belgium over the next three years? Further, what expectations should Interbrew have of its global brand market development (e.g., volumes, profit levels, number of markets and cities, etc.)? How should global success be measured? With respect to Interbrew's promotional efforts, how likely would it be that a single global ad campaign could be successful for Stella Artois? Was there a particular sponsorship or promotion idea that could be singled out for global leverage? And what role should the Internet play in developing Stella Artois as a true global brand?

Exhibit 1   The World Beer Market in 1998

Region	% of Global Consumption	Growth Index ('98 Vs 92)	Per Capita Consumption
Americas	35.1%	112.6	57
Europe	32.8%	97.7	54
Asia Pacific	27.2%	146.2	11
Africa	4.6%	107.7	8
Middle East/Central Asia	0.4%	116.0	2

Source: Canadean Ltd.

Exhibit 2   Interbrew's 1998 Share of the World's Top 10 Markets

Rank	Country	Volume (000 HL)	Market Share
1	USA	3,768	1.6%
2	China	526	0.3%
3	Germany	–	–
4	Brazil	–	–
5	Japan	–	–
6	UK	3,335	5.5%
7	Mexico	21,269	45.0%
8	Spain	–	–
9	South Africa	–	–
10	France	1,915	8.4%
Total		30,813	3.6%

Source: Canadean Ltd.

Exhibit 3   Domestic Sales History of Major International Brands (million hectolitre)

	1995	1996	1997	1998
Budweiser (incl. Bud Light until '98)	69.48	71.10	72.43	40.00
Bud Light	n/a	n/a	n/a	30.00
Heineken	3.87	3.78	3.85	3.78
Becks	1.68	1.71	1.72	1.78
Carlsberg	1.47	1.39	1.31	1.22
Stella Artois	1.08	1.00	0.96	0.92
Fosters	1.48	1.11	1.40	1.43
Kronenbourg	5.65	5.53	5.35	5.60
Amstel	2.30	2.23	2.21	2.18
Corona	12.89	14.09	14.80	15.18

Exhibit 4   1999 World Sales Profile of Stella Artois

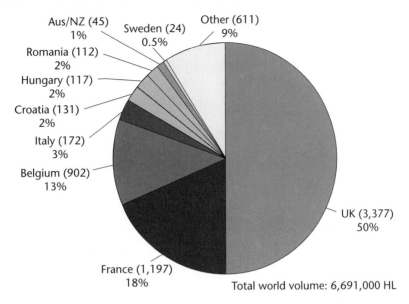

Total world volume: 6,691,000 HL

Exhibit 5   Stella Artois Sales Volume Summary (000 hectolitre)

	1997	1998	1999
Production:			
Belgium	965	921	902
France	1,028	1,110	1,074
Hungary	59	84	117
Croatia	54	120	133
Romania	17	60	112
Bulgaria	–	–	3
Bosnia-Herzegovina	–	–	2
Montenegro	–	–	0
Total Production	**2,123**	**2,295**	**2,343**
License Brewing:			
Italy	162	166	172
Australia	6	11	22
New Zealand	7	11	22
Sweden	29	27	24
Greece	7	7	10
UK	2,139	2,815	3,377
Total Licensed	**2,350**	**3,037**	**3,627**
Export:			
USA	–	–	7
Canada	–	–	5
Other Countries	92	49	202
Duty Free	245	389	507
Total Export	**337**	**438**	**721**
Overall Total	**4,810**	**5,770**	**6,691**

Exhibit 6 Top 10 Brewers by International Sales

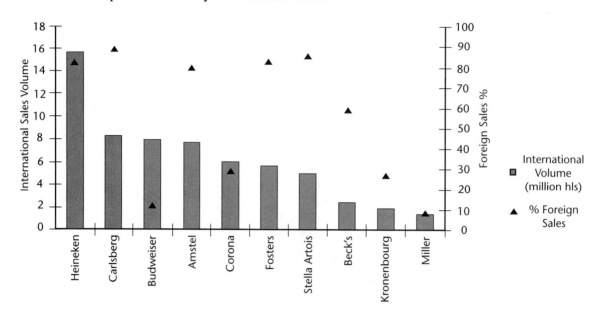

Exhibit 7 1998 Heineken World Sales Profile

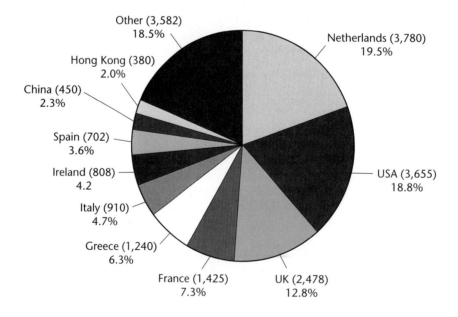

Exhibit 8   1998 Foster's World Sales Profile

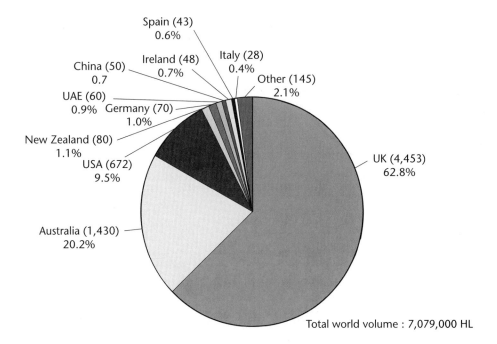

Total world volume : 7,079,000 HL

Exhibit 9   1998 Carlsberg World Sales Profile

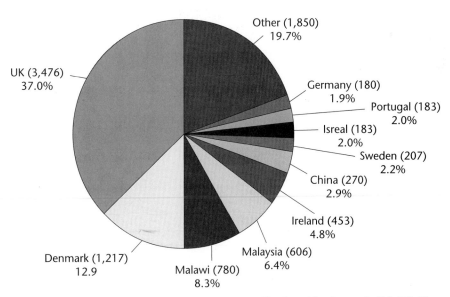

Total world volume : 9,405,000 HL

Exhibit 10 Global Positioning Statement

Brand Positioning

To males, between 21 to 45 years of age, that are premium lager drinkers, Stella Artois is a European premium lager beer, differentially positioned towards the product.

Stella Artois offers a modern, sophisticated, yet accessible drinking experience with an emphasis on the very high quality of the beer supported by the noble tradition of European brewing.

The accent is on the emotional consequence of benefit: a positive feeling of self esteem and sophistication.

Character, Tone of Voice

Sophistication
Authenticity, tradition, yet touch of modernity
Timelessness
Premium quality
Special, yet accessible
Mysticism
European

Exhibit 11 A Comparison of Carlsberg and Heineken

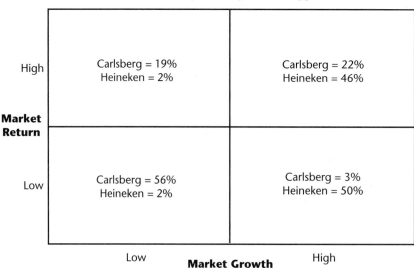

Profit Exposure by Market Type

	Low Market Growth	High Market Growth
High Market Return	Carlsberg = 19% Heineken = 2%	Carlsberg = 22% Heineken = 46%
Low Market Return	Carlsberg = 56% Heineken = 2%	Carlsberg = 3% Heineken = 50%

Palliser Furniture Ltd.: The China Question

In September 2003, Art DeFehr, president of Canada's second largest furniture company, Palliser Furniture Ltd. of Winnipeg, Manitoba, was pondering whether to significantly expand the company's relationship with China. Ever since Palliser set up a plant in Mexico in 1998, the company had faced increasing competitive pressures from Asia, especially from China.

THE MEXICO INVESTMENT 1998

In 1998, Palliser set up a leather furniture manufacturing facility in Saltillo, Coahuila, Mexico, to serve the mid-west and southern North American market. Palliser continued to ship products from its Winnipeg plants to the northern United States and Canadian markets. The Mexican facility would expand Palliser's leather manufacturing capacity, which was also part of its strategic shift from producing wood furniture to more leather products.

In 1997, DeFehr had considered the China option. Beginning in the mid-1990s, Taiwan furniture manufacturers started to establish plants in Mainland China, and China's household furniture exports to the U.S. market had increased quickly. However, in 1997, China was not making much leather furniture. This would have been a proactive move to respond to the emerging low-cost Asian furniture-manufacturing sector. DeFehr nonetheless chose Mexico over China for several reasons:

1. The Mexican location, which was close to the Texas border, would provide a lower distribution cost structure for Palliser. Prior to 1998, Palliser had difficulties absorbing the higher freight cost when the company shipped products from Winnipeg, Canada, across the U.S.–Canadian border to the south.

Jing'an Tang prepared this case under the supervision of Professor Paul W. Beamish solely to provide material for class discussion. The authors do not intend to illustrate either effective or ineffective handling of a managerial situation. The authors may have disguised certain names and other identifying information to protect confidentiality.

Version: (A) 2004-02-25

IVEY

Richard Ivey School of Business
The University of Western Ontario

2. At the time, China's leather furniture sector was small and inexperienced. Tanneries in China were not suitable for making leather furniture, and the leather had to be imported. Moreover, although there had been leather cutting and sewing workers in the garment business in China, they had little experience in producing leather furniture. In Mexico, there were more industry skills. One other major firm in the volume furniture business, Leather Trend, built products in Tijuana (a Mexican city near San Diego, California) and shipped across the continent to other cities in the United States. Other firms in Mexico were all very small businesses.

3. At that stage, the foreign investments in China were mainly joint venture operations. DeFehr wanted to own a business; he did not want a joint venture (JV) and he did not want to contract the work.

> I did not feel comfortable owning something in China. I still have certain discomfort. There are millions of examples of joint ventures in China. The JV partners were pushed out after some time. In contrast, in Mexico it was easy to wholly own a business.

4. Palliser had manufactured its products mainly in Canada with only a small portion of products being assembled in the United States in 1997. As a first stage of expansion, Palliser considered Mexico an ideal choice because it was closer to the U.S. market, and it was more manageable compared with offshore sites.

Since being established, the Mexican facility had been working well, operationally. It started to ship products to the United States, especially to the southern states, in 1999. Because of reduced costs and similar quality, Palliser's Mexican-made products were well accepted.

There had been some problems however, with the Mexico investment. Palliser had issues with the Mexican taxation practices and had disagreements with the local taxation authorities. According to Kliewer, senior vice-president in finance,

> (Their) way of interpreting the law was just so discretionary. What they allow and what they don't allow were not clear. For example, the inflation adjustment was very problematic . . . It is a bit hard to plan for that. These are things you learned as you go on.

It had taken longer than planned to recover the initial investment. For instance, Palliser did not anticipate all the shipping costs accurately. The company had not anticipated the extra tariff fees associated with cross-border shipments leaving Mexico. Moreover, there had been other costs involved in shipping products across the Mexico–U.S. border because the trucks from Mexico could not cross the border; goods had to be transferred to U.S. trucks which resulted in extra charges. DeFehr called it a "friction cost." According to Palliser calculations, the friction costs of crossing the Canadian border were around US$1[1] for a leather sofa, but the friction costs for the same sofa built in Mexico would be US$12. (The friction costs from China would have been approximately $10.)

As another example, the order allocation process initially favored the Canadian facility. While the Mexico plant essentially produced the same products, orders were given to the Winnipeg plants first and the balance was allocated to Mexico. As a result, the Mexico plant had to fight with headquarters for orders. Palliser acknowledged and corrected the issue, a move that had a positive impact on the Mexican overhead recovery rate.

---

[1]All currency in Cdn$ unless otherwise specified.

It could also be noted that the decision to set up a facility in Mexico had relied upon the competitiveness resulting from the North American Free Trade Agreement (NAFTA). Palliser had yet to focus on how to lower the costs through changes in its Mexican supply chain. Mexico was, in a sense, trying to build its competitiveness on a more limited framework.

THE FURNITURE INDUSTRY SINCE 1998

Since the late 1990s, the world furniture industry had undergone tremendous change. The most significant trend was the rise of China. In 2002, China's total furniture output value was US$20 billion, accounting for 10 per cent of the world's total furniture output value. In the past five years, China's furniture export had grown at an annual rate of over 30 per cent. Countries with heavy demand for furniture products had flocked to China to make purchases. China's export of household furniture to the United States accounted for almost 40 per cent of the market, while exports to Japan accounted for about 15 per cent of Japan's total furniture demand. IKEA, the top selling furniture company in the world, had shifted its purchasing centre from Singapore to Mainland China.

With the prospect of cheaper labor and high-quality workers in China, American, Japanese and Italian firms had established factories in China. Natuzzi, an Italian firm who was the No. 1 furniture manufacturer in the world, built a plant in Shanghai. DeCoro, another Italian furniture company, set up a plant in DongGuan, Gongdong province. Taiwanese firms had also built more than 500 furniture plants in Mainland China. Three U.S. office furniture firms with annual production values of US$1.5 billion, US$2.7 billion and US$3 billion, respectively, had all constructed production bases in Shanghai. China's furniture capacity had increased dramatically. Guangdong province, the biggest furniture manufacturing province, produced one-third of China's total furniture production.

The rise of China had shifted the world furniture market competition structure. It had affected most furniture firm's profit margins. Natuzzi's income dropped 70 per cent, and sales dropped 10 per cent in the second quarter 2002. Firms in the North America furniture industry felt the pressure most. The market share of all household furniture imports in the U.S. domestic market increased between 1993 and 2002 from 20.4 per cent to 38.9 per cent, while the market share of all office furniture imports increased from 9.1 per cent to 23.8 per cent during the same period. U.S. furniture imports in 2002 grew 13 per cent to US$14.2 billion. China fuelled much of that growth, accounting for 40 per cent of total U.S. imports in 2002. That year also marked the fifth out of the last six years in which total Chinese furniture exports to the United States jumped 30 per cent or more (see Exhibits 1, 2, 3 and 4).

The contributing factors were multifold, including China's cheaper labor and comparable product quality and design. Palliser managers estimated that the labor cost in China was around US$3 day, in Mexico about US$32, while in Canada it was around US$90 a day. Chinese workers usually worked more than 10 hours a day, six days a week. There were no unions nor union pressure. The leather furniture business in China did not need to deal with any environmental problems, although there were many concerns with tannery operations. Chinese firms did not pay much income tax, nor did they bear many social costs, such as health and insurance costs for employees. The Chinese currency was pegged to the U.S. dollar and, to many people, was arguably undervalued. The combination of these factors gave China a strongly competitive position. Furniture from China could be 20 per cent to 30 per cent cheaper than the same products that were produced in North America. Exhibit 5 provides the comparison of cost bases for some wood furniture components.

Under the weight of the competitive pressure, many U.S. firms moved manufacturing sites offshore. In July 2003, some furniture makers in America jointly protested to the American government about the severe impact the Chinese furniture manufacturers were having on the American wood bedroom furniture industry. They submitted anti-dumping applications seeking industry protection.

Total Canadian shipments of furniture and bedding hit a record $4.76 billion in 2002, capping 10 years of almost continuous growth (see Exhibit 6). According to a survey conducted by Statistics Canada, there were 630 residential furniture and bedding manufacturers in Canada in 1999—the last year for which figures were available. Canada's furniture and bedding producers could be segmented into four categories: exporters, non-exporters, bedding producers and importers. The exporters were by far the largest group. While the 19 exporters did some business in Europe, South America and the Middle East, more than 95 per cent of all Canadian furniture exported was sold to U.S. retailers.

Canadian furniture producers were employing a variety of strategies to remain competitive in an increasingly uncertain North American economy. The impact of China had not been felt as deeply in Canada as it had been in the United States. Unlike their American counterparts, many of which had moved much of their production offshore, almost every one of the top 10 Canadian producers (see Exhibit 7) had recently made, or was making, a big investment in their business.

While others followed a balancing act to remain as low-cost manufacturers, some Canadian manufacturers became active importers, focusing on specialized lines not being produced domestically. Two examples illustrate this approach. Dorel Industries tried to develop a strong capability to source a wide variety of products designed by Dorel and manufactured in Asia. In 2002, the company established a new division called Dorel Asia, whose mission was to develop product suitable for North America that was built cheaply and efficiently in the Pacific Rim. A second company Shermag Inc., launched a new import division to expand its offerings of labor-intensive, traditionally styled bedroom and dining room furniture. These goods complemented the more technology-driven, casual contemporary furniture that Shermag made in its factories in Quebec and New Brunswick, Canada.

PALLISER'S STRATEGY SINCE 1998

Cost Leadership

The Mexico investment was part of Palliser's cost leadership strategy. Palliser negotiated with its Brazilian partners to be part of its supply chain for the Mexico plant. Brazil was the No. 1 source of leather in the world. Raw leather was delivered from Brazil to Mexico, where Palliser processed the leather (cutting and sewing) for redistribution to its U.S. and Canadian locations. Although it was more expensive than that in China, processing leathers in Mexico was still much cheaper than producing in Canada.

Quick Delivery

Quick delivery was another strategy. Purchasing from China meant a minimum delivery time of six to seven weeks, which translated into high inventory cost for those importers buying Asian products. Alternatively, Palliser focused on a custom manufacturing strategy with a delivery time of three weeks. Custom business was Palliser's premium business. The company was able to charge a slight premium for the service that could eliminate customers' inventory cost. According to DeFehr, Palliser was still making most of its money from the plants in Canada, which were strong at specialty order businesses. As the China threat developed, more and more competitors established factories offshore. However, in doing so, they became less flexible, either in time or in variety. For example, the cycle time of the specialty businesses of the Italian producers DeCoro and Natuzzi was around 90 days.

The quick delivery strategy had been working very well until September 11, 2001 (9/11). After 9/11, because the airlines cut their flights, airfares had risen, it became very expensive to ship leather from Brazil to Mexico by air. If shipping by ocean, the quick delivery advantages over China would soon disappear. Palliser was working with Brazilian suppliers seeking solutions.

Value Enhancement

Palliser was committed to delivering annual value improvements to its customers. For instance, if the company offered some products for $500 last year, it would try to offer the equal value of products at $400 this year. Such improvements were driven by process and product redesign. The first step was to identify those products where Palliser had absolute advantages or relative advantages in the North American market. Palliser still considered the North American market to be its first priority. Palliser considered developing a product using oak in Canada. Oak had a similar price around the world. Products could be built with a rustic and low grade of oak, with rough and simple machine-driven designs. By leveraging the low-cost material and leveraging the machine-driven design, the value would be similar to that produced in China.

At the same time, Palliser tried to remain a volume producer. Using Mexico and China to do cutting and sewing, Palliser was still doing low-price business. Beyond Mexico, the company was sourcing substantial quantities of finished goods from Asian countries, such as China, Thailand and Indonesia. Another way to enhance value was to produce machine-made and capital-intensive products instead of labor intensive-furniture. The new products that Palliser was going to produce were all less labor-intensive.

EQ3, a New Marketing Initiative

In the late 1990s, Palliser started a new marketing program called EQ3. Palliser realized that there was an opportunity in the market place, which had been underserved. A trend in the furniture industry was that consumers were becoming more fashion conscious, design conscious and more educated. EQ3 was a new concept that was designed to meet this market trend. It was not about one piece of furniture, but about everything in the home with fashionable designs. Palliser recruited some product managers from IKEA and designers from many regions over the world, such as Sweden, Hong Kong, and Italy. Most people in the new EQ3 team were in their late 20s and early 30s.

After two years of market research. Palliser introduced in-store EQ3 galleries through its traditional retailers in the United States and Canada in October 2001, but these galleries did not work well in the traditional stores channels which did not understand or draw in the target customer. In late 2002, Palliser started building new channels. The company set up the first two dealer-owned EQ3 stores—one in Toronto, Ontario, and the other in Grand Rapids, Michigan. These stores started offering unique storefront with the new image and the right advertising and catalogues, which customers could identify with. This distribution channel was developed outside of the traditional channel and had been very successful.

Motion Business

In the North American marketplace, the motion business was one of the fastest growing categories. Motion products referred to furniture that could be adjusted, such as recliners. Palliser started to make motion products at the same time it started to make leather furniture. Several years ago, Palliser's sales in motion products were around $26 million dollars. In 2003, sales were expected to be nearly $100 million.

Previously, motion products were mainly considered to be products that would go in the basement, not something that could be a focal point in the living room or family room. But in recent years, with better leathers and the popularity of leather furniture in the market place, furniture companies had been able to utilize leather to make motion products more attractive, fashionable and contemporary. People were willing to put them in their living room, family room and home theatres. Leather had made motion products more fashionable. For example, the leather recliner became one of the most popular household furniture products for every American family and sofas and love seats were becoming more fashionable too.

On average, from a labor perspective, motion products required 25 per cent to 30 per cent more labor than standard products. Motion products were more technical and required more skill to produce.

Palliser had motion product factories in Winnipeg, Manitoba; Airdrie, Alberta and Saltillo, Mexico. The latter plant called "Las Colinas" was set up in 2000. Each of these factories operated at the same scale, but production costs in Mexico were much cheaper. The lower labor rate in Mexico might translate into a $75 savings for a sofa ($1,000 in retail value). If making the same product in Asia, the possible savings could be $120 to $130 dollars for a product with a retail value of $1,000.

Currently, Palliser realized advantages in the North American marketplace by offering good value in motion products with color options, good service, delivery and good quality. Traditionally, even the large Asian companies, which had considerable exports to North America, had not been successful in the motion business. The lengthy lead time had been a contributing factor, but in the last year, motion products were starting to come from Asia. For instance, DeCoro now produced motion products in China. In the last international furniture show, DeCoro displayed around 10 new motion product styles.

Palliser's approach to motion products was vinyl-leather match design. DeCoro's approach was all-leather style. By producing in China, DeCoro was able to provide the same product at a lower cost than Palliser offered. For example, Palliser could offer a leather-vinyl sofa at $999 retail, while DeCoro could offer $999 for an all-leather sofa retail. Thus, for the same product, DeCoro would have approximately a $200 advantage over Palliser's retail price. In the stationary category, several years ago, Palliser was providing leather-vinyl products. As a result of competition from Asia, which was offering all-leather products at the same price point, Palliser stopped producing leather-vinyl stationary products. The same shift might be anticipated in the motion product market.

Rach, director of motion products at Palliser, pointed out that contributing factors to cheap production in Asia were not only the leather for less money, but other components were cheaper too, such as the wood for the frame, the foam and the packaging materials.

PALLISER'S ASIAN PRESENCE

Palliser had several small factories in Indonesia, did contract work in Thailand and China, and had an office in Taiwan and two offices in Mainland China, (one in Shanghai and another in Guangzhou).

Taiwan

Furniture exports from Asia were driven by people from Taiwan, who developed the expertise first, starting around 20 years ago. Palliser set up an office in Taiwan in 1985. It mainly imported final furniture products to the North American market.

Taiwanese firms were the first investors to go to Mainland China. In contrast to Palliser, Taiwanese firms did not go to Indonesia because Mainland China was closer and the culture was the same, therefore they preferred to invest in Mainland. Also the Chinese had had a bad experience in Indonesia in the 1960s, and there had been a recent reoccurrence of this experience. Many Chinese people who were sent there to do quality work flew to Indonesia in the morning and flew back home to China at night. Some people considered Indonesia an investment place with a lot of uncertainty.

Indonesia

Palliser had several factories in Indonesia. Some were owned, some used 100 per cent contracting and others used partial contracting. Palliser provided loans to one of the plants in 1997 when the plant experienced financial difficulties during the Asian financial crisis. The loan ended up with Palliser's controlling interests in that factory. The other two plants were owned by Palliser. Compared with Palliser's production facilities in Canada and in Mexico, these operations were very small. The total investment amount was approximately Cdn$500,000. Indonesia was more like a training ground for Palliser in Asia. Palliser sent full-time Canadian staff in those local operations.

DeFehr had worked and kept in touch with Indonesia for almost 20 years, and he felt comfortable investing there. In terms of the risk concerns in Indonesia, DeFehr provided the following logic,

> By going to Indonesia, I separate myself from the face-to-face competition with these Chinese businesses for factory space, materials and other things. As a result, I am not competing with the best capital in the business. Will Indonesia be better than China in five years? I don't know, and you don't know either. So we make the bet . . . . We try to go to places that others might consider difficult. Because we are alone, you may get a little bit of a premium by being there.

Thailand and Mainland China

Beyond Indonesia, Palliser had a lot of contract work in Thailand as well. Local plants manufactured furniture components or finished products according to the design provided by Palliser.

Currently, Palliser contracted cutting and sewing work to a Chinese factory in Haiyin, a city south of Shanghai. The factory processed leather covers for its motion products. According to Rach, director of Palliser motion products,

> Chinese workers were very good at making leathers now. One of the advantages came from their larger tannery and their experience in the garment industry, especially the leather garment industry.

These leather covers were shipped back to Winnipeg, where they were upholstered. Almost $1 million of monthly sales were from Asia. Cutting and sewing covers from China had enabled Palliser to make a leather sofa at eight per cent to 10 per cent less than that in Canada. In retail, there is around one price point ($100) difference. That was the only component that Palliser outsourced from China for motion products. For a sofa with a total cost of $625, the cutting and sewing cost was around $250. It cost approximately $30 to $33 per seat to transport a sofa from China to North America.

DeFehr had certain concerns about doing business in China. Although many foreign firms had set up plants in China, few of them had been successful.

Finding the right partner was another concern. DeFehr felt that Chinese partners were not committed, long-term OEM suppliers. He was not comfortable building long-term relationships in China. This might be due to the fact that a level of trust had not been established yet.

DeFehr was also concerned about the product itself. If a product had a well-established brand, no one else could easily make it and sell to the market. But a sofa and chair usually were not branded products. People could easily imitate and sell them. Therefore, if the products were exclusive, either technologically or brand-wise, the partnership relationship could work. Most furniture products were not exclusive.

Realistically, Palliser could not ignore China anymore. The resources in China were phenomenal, both in labor quantity and quality. People in China were working more and more efficiently than people in North America and in other developing countries. According to Tielmann, senior vice-president of marketing,

> If you look at India, Indonesia and Thailand, there are real differences. The value you get from China is one of the best worldwide. Another interesting thing was the Chinese Yuan, which was tied to the U.S. dollar. It had stayed that way for a while and might be that way for a long time yet. This could avoid currency fluctuations, which is different from Indonesia and Thailand. Also, the exchange rate was very advantageous for export.

TOP MANAGEMENT'S ASIAN EXPERIENCE

DeFehr had been to China many times, both on political and business issues. His first visit to China was with his family in 1983 as guests of the government. He had started visiting Taiwan regularly on furniture business since 1985. He had regularly visited Mainland China since 1992. Most recently, he had visited Beijing, Shanghai, Shenzheng, Dongguan, Qsingdao, Tianjin and other coastal cities. Those were cities where the Chinese furniture businesses were concentrated.

DeFehr had extensive experience with Asian culture. He had lived in Asia, but he had never lived in Mexico. His two children were born in Asia. He had lived in Bangladesh, Thailand, and he travelled to Cambodia, India and many other Asian countries. Asia, to DeFehr was very much home. However, because both of his parents were from the former Soviet Union and he had experienced dealing with communist governments, he did not think he was comfortable doing business in a communist environment.

Most members of Palliser's top management had been to China. As the director of motion products, Rach visited China more frequently. He went to China at least three times a year. As China's furniture business had become stronger in recent years, the top management team had shifted much more attention to Asia.

THE DECISION

Products from China had increasingly become threats to most furniture manufacturers in North America and the pressures on Palliser had been increasingly felt. In April 2003, Palliser conducted its first layoff in the Winnipeg factory.

Palliser had production facilities in Canada, Mexico and Indonesia, and the company experimented with cutting and sewing leather in China. DeFehr had to decide whether to significantly expand Palliser's relationship with China and discern what form that relationship might follow. Should it be an investment, either wholly or partly owned? Should it be through subcontracting? To build Palliser's competitive advantages, DeFehr summarized:

> What we are considering right now is how to take advantage of our particular organizational and geographic situation to counter the advantages that the people in lower cost environments have.

Exhibit 1   All Household Imports by Significant Countries in the U.S. Market (US$ millions)

	1998	1999	2000	2001	2002	CAGR
China	1,550.5	2,235.6	3,001.6	3,423.2	4,832.8	37.9%
Canada	1,301.4	1,584.7	1,837.4	1,744.2	1,739.6	16.4%
Italy	760.3	917.8	1,140.1	1,107.7	1,139.3	14.5%
Mexico	641.0	704.7	764.2	699.9	729.1	13.1%
Indonesia	323.1	407.3	450.7	445.4	492.0	16.0%
Taiwan	687.2	722.1	701.1	502.1	477.6	−7.5%
Malaysia	384.0	443.1	452.3	407.9	467.4	10.8%
Thailand	165.2	210.5	253.7	261.1	338.3	9.5%
Philippines	214.0	241.1	269.2	223.8	217.7	8.4%
Brazil	53.4	74.8	96.9	135.2	209.5	23.6%

CAGR—Compounded Annual Growth Rate.
Source: Company files.

Exhibit 2   Wood Household Imports by Significant Countries in the U.S. Market (US$ millions)

	1998	1999	2000	2001	2002	CAGR
China	794.0	1,141.0	1,650.7	1,897.6	2,893.6	40.1%
Canada	947.5	1,182.9	1,368.5	1,306.7	1,267.7	17.1%
Italy	306.4	392.6	460.4	453.6	484.3	15.2%
Malaysia	340.4	396.4	399.5	364.4	414.5	11.3%
Indonesia	254.6	332.2	373.4	376.7	414.2	19.2%
Mexico	353.7	371.9	392.8	372.2	372.1	10.8%
Thailand	149.7	188.2	225.8	226.7	297.7	9.7%
Taiwan	381.7	402.7	349.4	280.5	260.2	−8.7%
Brazil	52.0	70.3	92.6	126.1	187.9	23.3%
Philippines	83.9	99.6	118.6	109.8	109.2	15.0%

Source: Company files.

Exhibit 3   Upholstered Household Imports by Significant Countries in the U.S. (US$ millions)

	1998	1999	2000	2001	2002	CAGR
Italy	363.6	412.9	559.3	529.0	528.6	14.5%
China	46.6	83.6	127.6	172.8	312.9	53.8%
Mexico	111.8	139.0	170.5	172.3	208.6	27.3%
Canada	95.8	122.8	156.2	161.5	184.3	19.7%

Source: Company files.

Exhibit 4   Metal and Other Household Imports by Significant Countries in the U.S. Market (US$ millions)

	1998	1999	2000	2001	2002	CAGR
China	541.3	766.7	938.7	1,033.6	1,235.5	44.0%
Canada	181.9	185.4	205.2	167.7	183.4	13.0%
Taiwan	240.9	256.7	282.4	177.2	178.0	−6.0%
Mexico	150.6	164.8	171.0	126.2	121.0	8.0%
Italy	61.3	85.4	82.0	85.9	85.0	15.0%

Source: Company files.

Exhibit 5   Wood Furniture Cost Comparison

	American Made[1]	Chinese Made[2]	Difference
Bed headboard	100.00	89.00	11%
Nightstand	95.00	80.22	16%
Chest	109.00	88.76	19%
Entertainment centre	211.00	159.54	24%
Armoire	474.00	330.00	30%
Rolltop desk	275.00	181.50	34%

[1]Costs are as if the product were in a U.S. warehouse, ready to ship to retailers.
[2]For the Chinese, shipping is included.
Source: Furniture/Today, May 26, 2003.

Exhibit 6 The Canadian Furniture Market (Cdn$ millions)

	2002	2001	2000	2001–2002 Change	1997–2001 Change
Total industry shipments	4,760	4,307	4,106	10.5%	54.9%
Total exports	2,153	2,018	1,924	6.7%	87.9%
Export to the United States	2,036	1,911	N/A	6.5%	N/A
Total imports	1,443	1,252	1,134	15.3%	54.7%
Imports from the United States	489	509	N/A	–3.9%	N/A
Total domestic shipments	2,607	2,289	2,182	13.9%	34.2%

Source: Statistics Canada.

Exhibit 7 Canada's Top 25 Furniture and Bedding Producers (Cdn$ millions)

Rank	Company Name	Home Base	Furniture & Bedding Shipments		Change
1	Dorel Inds.	Montreal, Quebec	712.9	701.7	1.6%
2	Palliser Furniture	Winnipeg, Manitoba	518.8	493.6	5.1%
3	Shermag Inc.	Sherbrooke, Quebec	188.0	163.2	15.2%
4	Canadel Furniture	Louiseville, Quebec	155.0	135.0	14.8%
5	Sealy Canada	Toronto, Ontario	139.7	121.1	15.4%
6	Simmons Canada Inc	Mississauga, Ontario	130.9	120.1	9.0%
7	La-Z-Boy Canada Ltd.	Waterloo, Ontario	117.9	100.9	16.8%
8	Magnussen Home Furnishings	New Hamburg, Ontario	106.8	N/A	N/A
9	Gusdorf Canada	Montreal, Quebec	105.0	94.0	11.7%
10	South Shore Inds.	Sainte-Croix, Quebec	100.0	100.0	0.0%

Source: Furniture/Today, June 2, 2003.

Case 24

West Lake Home Furnishings Ltd.

INTRODUCTION

It was May 23, 2007, and Charles Bowman, the chief executive officer (CEO) of West Lake Home Furnishings Ltd. (West Lake), was thinking about a proposal one of his top three wholesale customers had made to him: if Bowman would reduce the retail price of a signature line of decorative lamps from $69.99 to $29.99 for a period of one year, the wholesaler would give the product prominent shelf space and the potential to more than quintuple unit sales. This customer, a large U.S.-based retail chain, accounted for about one-third of West Lake's wholesale business in 2006. On the one hand, Bowman found the prospect of boosting sales attractive. On the other hand, Bowman knew that agreeing to a reduction in retail price of this signature product for one customer could force prices down in his wholesale, retail and Internet businesses. Still, Bowman wondered if this was an offer he could afford to refuse.

THE CANADIAN RETAIL MARKET

In 2006, with sales of more than $200 billion[1] and a wide selection of products offered by retailers, the Canadian retail market was highly competitive. Large chains, such as U.S.-based Wal-Mart Stores Inc., Canadian Tire, Hudson's Bay Company and Sears Canada, accounted for about one-third of the retail market. The chains offered consumers a wide variety of home furnishings, generally carrying three or four national brands and a private-label line. The other two-thirds of the market consisted of thousands of small retailers, most of which had local or regional presence. These smaller

Richard Ivey School of Business
The University of Western Ontario

---

[1] All currency in Canadian dollars unless specified otherwise.

retailers rarely had private-label lines in home furnishings, preferring to carry national brands. Smaller retailers typically had limited shelf space, which meant that they could carry only a small selection of items and ordered in small volumes.

Sales in the home furnishings category had grown from $7.6 billion in 2002 to $9.7 billion in 2006, a compounded average growth rate of 6.1 per cent. For some statistics on the Canadian retail market see Exhibit 1. However, average prices for home furnishing items had fallen significantly in the same period, suggesting that the increase in unit sales was greater than the overall growth rate indicated, perhaps as high as 15 per cent.

During this period, there were several significant trends in the home furnishings market. The baby boomers, a population bulge in Canada, were now between the ages of 45 and 64. People between the ages of 45 to 64 generally earned higher incomes and had higher levels of home ownership. As home ownership rates rose, so did spending on home improvements, including home furnishings, since consumers tended to spend more money on home products in the first two or three years following the purchase of their home (see Chart 1).

Because of the consumer's growing interest in home furnishings, many new competitors had entered the industry. Due to the increasing awareness of Asia as a low-cost production base, many North American manufacturers had been shifting manufacturing to Asia, especially China. Many large retail chains also opened sourcing offices in Asian countries, bypassing intermediaries by buying directly from local manufacturers. The effect of these trends at the retail level was that consumers had access to a wider variety of merchandise at lower prices. However, as retailers sought to manage their supply chain costs by ensuring that merchandise arrived at stores "just in time," manufacturers—whether North American or Asian—had to adjust by holding higher inventory levels in warehouses.

Chart 1　The Home Products Purchasing Cycle[2]

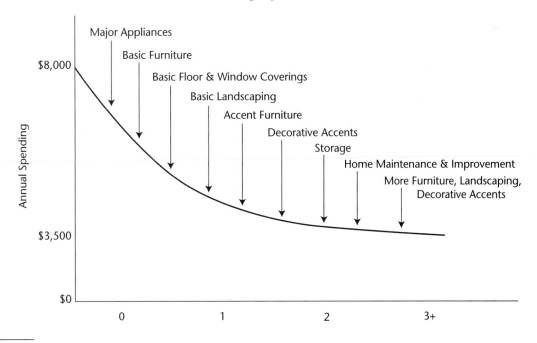

---

[2] Source: Adapted from BB&T Capital Markets, *Home Décor Industry Report,* September 23, 2005, p. 4.

Consumers of home furnishings typically patronized a small set of retailers when making purchase decisions. Large "big-box" retailers were usually among this set, because they offered a "one-stop" shopping experience. Consumers also visited retailers who were focused on providing product depth and expertise in one area—lighting stores, for example.

Lighting and Light Fixtures

The market for lighting and lighting fixtures in Canada, at retail, was $900 million in 2006, with no retailer accounting for more than 20 per cent of the market. The key reason why retailers retained suppliers was because their products sold well. Less important reasons included responsiveness and a record of on-time delivery. Chain retailers represented three or four lighting brands, along with the retailer's own private-label brand if it had one. It was common for retailers to change suppliers frequently if their products were not selling well.

Suppliers to retailers could be grouped into two categories: importers of ready-made, standard products operating in the lower price-point market, and North American manufacturers (mostly small firms focused on high-end or custom products) that offered attractive designs and high quality at higher price points. Lighting was a fragmented market and the top five major competitors had a combined share of 20 per cent of the market. None of the top five competitors manufactured in North America. Private-label lighting accounted for about 40 per cent of the market, with small firms accounting for the remaining 40 per cent. Here were some characteristics of lighting manufacturers in Canada Bowman identified in his market research:

Competitor	Market Share	Positioning	Competitive Strengths
Salisbury	5%	Functional, value for money	Cost leadership
Court Meadow	5%	Traditional, elegant	Design
Kilchberg	5%	Modern, minimalist	Design
Luxon	3%	Decorative, bright colors	Design
Tudor Country	2%	Traditional, elegant	Cost and design
Private label	40%	Varied	Varied
Others	40%	Varied	Varied
Total	100%		

Bowman knew of at least five major competitors in the Canadian market, with another two new entrants in 2006. To attract business from retailers, the new entrants, who had some designs similar to West Lake's, were competing primarily on price and targeting West Lake's retail accounts.

WEST LAKE HOME FURNISHINGS LTD.

Based in Toronto, Ontario, West Lake had its beginnings in 1970 as a manufacturer of table lamps. In the three decades since its founding, West Lake had broadened its wholesale line to include floor lamps and lighting fixtures, opened a retail location and started selling from its own website.

Bowman had been involved in the business since 1992, when he took over from his father, the founder. At that time, West Lake manufactured the majority of its decorative lamps in Canada, with a main factory east of Toronto. Bowman, recognizing that Asian sourcing was about to have an impact on prices, started the process of shifting production overseas. By 1999, half of West Lake's production was sourced from China, and West Lake opened its China sourcing office that year. In 2006, only 10 per cent of West Lake's production remained in Canada.

West Lake had 30 employees in total, 20 of whom worked in the retail store. From a financial perspective, West Lake had no external long-term debt (it had an interest-free loan from its shareholders, the Bowman family) and was consistently profitable. In the last two years, however, due to increasing levels of inventory in its warehouse (required by wholesale customers, to ensure that merchandise could be delivered on time), operating cash flows were negative (Exhibit 2 shows West Lake's financial statements for 2005 and 2006). Bowman did not want to increase his exposure to inventory, which was $1.6 million at the end of 2006. The typical cost for a line of credit (secured by assets of the business) was six per cent in mid-2007).

For customized orders or short runs, West Lake maintained a small manufacturing facility, on a leased plot of land located next to its warehouse. Producing for all three of its business segments—wholesale, retail and Internet—West Lake's manufacturing facility allowed it to experiment with new designs, identify and fix quality issues, and produce short runs of customized lamps or fixtures without having to wait the six to eight weeks it took to ship from its Chinese suppliers factories. Many customers to its retail store watched the skilled workers with fascination as they cut, soldered and painted the lights and fixtures. Maintaining this small manufacturing facility consumed about one-third of West Lake's sales, general and administrative (SG&A) expenses.

Wholesale

West Lake's products were sold in three national chains and in smaller retailers across Canada. The three chains' business together accounted for approximately 71 per cent of the company's wholesale (supplier to retail) business in 2006. For wholesalers, generally speaking, it was more cost-efficient to deal with the large chains. Consumers were drawn to West Lake's products because of their modern designs and reasonable price points. The purchase of a table lamp or floor lamp helped home owners update the look of their home for under $150 per item. Priced at retail between $45 and $195, West Lake lamps and lighting fixtures were generally mid- to premium-priced. For certain chain retailers, West Lake produced a private-label (high-end) line, generally retailing for between $50 and $80. In 2006, West Lake's wholesale business generated $3.1 million in gross margin from $8 million in sales.

Retail Store

In addition to the wholesale business, West Lake had built up a factory outlet store east of Toronto, selling a broad line of lighting and other accent home decor products, including its own products. West Lake products accounted for approximately 50 per cent of stock keeping units at its retail store. The retail store featured 17,000 square feet of selling space. A window between the store and the manufacturing facility next door allowed visitors to see some decorative and custom lamps being assembled onsite. In addition to serving retail customers, the store had begun to serve a small but growing list of Toronto-based interior decorators. Since 1980, West Lake had employed two designers and one engineer at its manufacturing facility. In addition, production and sales staff were on hand to meet with potential and current customers. Bowman estimated that an additional $300,000 in annual retail sales could be generated by hiring a sales consultant dedicated to attracting business from home designers. Total employment costs for this sales consultant would be about $80,000 per year.

Internet Sales

At the end of 2005, West Lake had started an Internet-based business selling its products directly to consumers. With prices similar to those found in retail stores, West Lake's Internet sales, though small at $200,000, enjoyed gross margins in the 70 per cent range. Bowman felt he had not allocated enough marketing dollars to make West Lake's Internet presence as well-known as it could be.

Generally speaking, expenses incurred for the various businesses, such as SG&A and shipping and warehousing (S&W), were proportional to sales. Bowman intended to stay at the helm of the business and was eager to grow it. He stated:

> I want to be the best-in-class, most recognizable name in my category. I want to be innovative in new designs and to be price competitive. In the past five years, we've steadily grown our retail store sales. I have been aggressively going after the Internet business for the past four years with advertisements in national magazines [and] paid search spending on Google, and [have been] offering promotional pricing. I think we can do better, though, at promoting the Internet business. For example, I don't think our paid search advertising is doing as well as we thought it would.

As for the overall business, Bowman preferred to be based in Canada and wanted to achieve steady growth rates of about 10 to 15 per cent per year. One potential avenue of growth was to increase sales in the custom lighting and fixtures department. West Lake had yet to put significant effort toward attracting business from interior decorators in Toronto. "There are so many luxury homes in Toronto," stated Bowman. "I'm sure we can do a better job at attracting business from interior decorators looking for customized lighting."

THE DECISION

Bowman thought about the success of West Lake's signature line at this retailer's growing network of stores. The signature line, which accounted for all of West Lake's sales at this retailer, was not sold anywhere else. He remembered the many presentations he had made to the retailer's buyer; he had shared detailed information about costs, and specifications, and even the name of the Chinese factory that manufactured the line. He was certain that the retailer had already contacted similar suppliers in Asia who would be willing to manufacture a similar-looking private-label line.

He knew that this retailer had gross margins of about 30 per cent and was willing to drop its gross margins to 15 per cent for this special one-year promotion.

Bowman had done some research, and preliminary feedback from his manufacturing contact in China suggested that, for an order this large, West Lake's cost of goods sold (COGS) for this signature line would drop to $20 from about $30. Although the units sold would quintuple at this retail account, associated expenses were expected to rise more slowly. For example, SG&A and S&W expenses specific to this retail account would increase by 20 per cent and 150 per cent, respectively. After taking into account the drop in COGS, the dollar value of West Lake's inventory associated with this retail account would rise by 30 per cent. Unfortunately, Bowman knew that the other two wholesale accounts West Lake served would soon learn about this concession and, within a short period of time, West Lake's gross margin for its wholesale business would end up to be the same across the three accounts.

Reviewing the product buyer's suggestion in his mind, Bowman wondered if this was an offer he could afford to *accept*.

Exhibit 1   Canadian Retail Industry (in $ millions)

	2002	2003	2004	2005	2006	CAGR
Food	51,658	53,904	56,652	59,473	62,132	4.72%
Non-alcoholic beverages	3,983	4,171	4,488	4,653	4,986	5.77%
Alcoholic beverages	14,408	15,209	15,729	16,324	17,220	4.56%
Cosmetics and fragrances	1,853	1,870	1,970	2,025	2,132	3.57%
Other toiletries and personal care products and home health care	6,152	6,374	7,166	7,323	7,703	5.78%
Drugs (prescription and over-the-counter), vitamins and supplements	16,259	17,689	18,848	19,865	21,760	7.56%
Women's clothing and accessories	11,564	11,780	12,371	12,981	13,861	4.63%
Men's clothing and accessories	6,288	6,301	6,574	6,838	7,252	3.63%
Girls', boys' and infants' clothing and accessories	2,880	2,907	2,839	2,829	2,882	0.02%
Footwear	4,015	4,097	4,090	4,415	4,760	4.34%
Indoor furniture	6,190	6,485	7,005	7,379	8,118	7.01%
Household appliances	4,340	4,612	4,812	5,119	5,760	7.33%
Home electronics, computers and cameras	10,301	10,873	11,399	11,872	12,434	4.82%
Home furnishings	7,616	7,905	8,389	8,832	9,660	6.12%
Housewares	6,778	7,039	7,287	7,480	7,865	3.79%
Hardware and home renovation products	14,816	16,610	18,370	19,639	21,454	9.70%
Lawn and garden products, equipment and plants	3,997	4,388	4,819	5,167	5,814	9.82%
Sporting goods	3,837	3,882	3,845	3,959	4,218	2.40%
Toys, games and hobby supplies	2,532	2,596	2,643	2,797	3,026	4.56%
Pre-recorded CDs, DVDs and video and audio tapes	1,758	1,831	1,941	2,069	2,073	4.22%
Books, newspapers and other periodicals	2,597	2,658	2,740	2,863	2,923	3.00%
Tobacco products and supplies	8,092	8,883	8,844	8,540	8,295	0.62%
Total	191,911	202,062	212,820	222,441	236,325	5.34%

Source: http://www40.statcan.ca/l01/cst01/trade52.htm, accessed August 20, 2007.

Exhibit 2   West Lake Home Furnishings Ltd., Financial Statements

INCOME STATEMENTS	2006			2006	2005
	Store	**Wholesale**	**Internet**		
Sales	$3,000,000	$8,000,000	$200,000	$11,200,000	$11,100,000
COGS	2,100,000	4,900,000	57,000	7,057,000	7,000,000
Gross margin	900,000	3,100,000	143,000	4,143,000	$4,100,000
As a % of sales	30.00%	38.75%	71.50%	36.99%	36.94%
Sales, General, Administrative Expenses				3,000,000	3,000,000
Shipping and Warehouse				830,000	830,000
Operating income				313,000	270,000
Income taxes				109,550	94,500
Net earnings				$ 203,450	$ 175,500

BALANCE SHEETS	2006	2005
Assets		
Current assets	4,200,000	4,830,000
Fixed assets	265,000	280,000
Other assets	175,000	175,000
Total	$ 4,640,000	$ 5,285,000
Liabilities		
Current liabilities	1,150,000	2,581,200
Future income taxes	5,000	13,500
Interest-free loan due to parent company	3,300,000	2,500,000
Total	4,455,000	5,094,700
Shareholders' equity		
Share capital	37,500	37,500
Retained earnings	147,500	152,800
Total	185,000	190,300
Total liabilities and shareholders' equity	$ 4,640,000	$ 5,285,000

Source: West Lake Home Furnishings Ltd. Annual Reports (disguised)

Barrie Charity Bingo

It was June 2002, and Kevin Bubel was concerned about the financial drain placed on his company by his latest strategic move. Three months earlier, Bubel had purchased Mayfair Bingo, his only competitor in Barrie, Ontario, due to the threat of an impending smoking bylaw that would have placed both businesses in jeopardy. After purchasing Mayfair, Bubel was left with a 20,000-square-foot building, for which he had little use. Financing the building, utilities and property taxes was now costing him almost $500 a day.

KEVIN BUBEL AND BARRIE CHARITY BINGO

In 1996, at the age of 26, Kevin Bubel assumed managerial control of Barrie Charity Bingo (BCB). The business had been in operation for a total of four years and was making only a small profit. Over the course of the next several years, Bubel bought out all other BCB owners and, by 2001, he held 100 per cent of the business. There were two bingo halls in the Barrie area in 1996: BCB and Mayfair Bingo. Due to its convenient location, high prize giveaways and aggressive marketing, Mayfair Bingo owned 70 per cent of the market, while BCB held the remaining 30 per cent. During Bubel's first year as manager, BCB earned just over $60,000. By 2001, however, BCB was netting over $400,000, and by June 2002, BCB had eaten into Mayfair's market share, with each firm now holding about 50 per cent of the market. With profits increasing each year, Barrie Charity Bingo had become a great investment.

In 1999, BCB moved from its original location to a prime building in downtown Barrie. The building comprised 17,000 square feet, including one restaurant that was integrated into the bingo hall plus a separate restaurant that provided additional rental revenue for BCB. The city of Barrie was experiencing tremendous growth, which had contributed to BCB's success; the population of Barrie was well over

Joe Bubel prepared this case under the supervision of Professor Eric Morse solely to provide material for class discussion. The authors do not intend to illustrate either effective or ineffective handling of a managerial situation. The authors may have disguised certain names and other identifying information to protect confidentiality.

Richard Ivey School of Business
The University of Western Ontario

100,000 and the city was forecasted to be one of the fastest growing cities in Canada over the next 10 years.

Under the Ontario Gaming Control Act, charities were responsible for running each program (i.e. bingo session) for which they receive 60 per cent of the gaming revenues. The bingo hall owner (in this case, BCB) received the remaining 40 per cent of the revenue but is responsible for the running of the actual bingo hall, including all related costs such as rent, utilities, labor and debt servicing. Bubel established good relationships with all the charities he worked with, and the charities were especially grateful for the substantially increased revenues during Bubel's years as BCB manager.

The Barrie Smoking Bylaw and Response

In August 2001, Bubel was informed that the City of Barrie was considering the introduction of a bylaw that would prohibit smoking in all public places. As approximately 75 per cent of all bingo players are smokers, Bubel was very concerned that these players would be spending considerably less time and money at BCB if this bylaw were to be implemented. Bubel estimated that the new bylaw would reduce revenues to both of Barrie's bingo halls by 50 per cent.

Bubel concluded that, if this bylaw were to pass, it would be very difficult for both bingo halls to survive. Taking a proactive stance, Bubel immediately called the owner of Mayfair Bingo, and within two days he had signed a purchase agreement for $1.5 million. Bubel believed that the business was worth roughly $400,000, meaning he paid $1.1 million for a 20,000-square-foot building on two acres of prime land in Barrie. One condition of this purchase was that Mayfair would close its doors immediately, leaving BCB a monopoly in the Barrie bingo market.

It seemed very likely that the bylaw would be passed; however, the one remaining requirement was a majority vote from the city's aldermen (area representatives). Taking the argument that this bylaw would result in a $1.5 million loss of revenue for the city's charities, Bubel protested at weekly city council meetings, gave numerous interviews, wrote editorials for the city's newspapers and appeared on the local news. Bubel's argument was well received and, as a result, he was able to convince two aldermen to change their vote, resulting in a final tally of 6 – 4, giving BCB the only exemption from the bylaw.

BCB would therefore be the only building in the city of Barrie where smoking was not prohibited, and this unique status was guaranteed until at least 2007. Bubel had successfully kept his business alive. Now he had to decide what to do with the empty Mayfair building on Bellfarm Road.

Opportunities

The building on Bellfarm Road was costing Bubel almost $500 a day. He had hoped for a quick sale, but this had not materialized, and approximately $40,000 had already been spent on costs such as debt servicing, property taxes and utilities for the building. Although Bubel was not happy with this financial drain, he felt that the bingo monopoly would net him a further $250,000 per year.

The building itself was in excellent shape and in a good location with ready access to traffic (roughly 6,000 cars passed by daily) and close proximity to Highway 400. Any signage or addition added to the back of the building could be seen from the highway. It was carpeted, heated and fully furnished, with numerous tables and chairs, and it contained an office and a kitchen.

The building sat on two acres of prime land that could be conservatively valued at $400,000 per acre. The building would cost approximately $50 per square foot to build new, and leasehold improvements to fixture the interior in a like manner would cost another $15 per square foot.

Bubel considered his options: the first option would be to sell the building, relieving him of further losses. The second option would be to rent the space, which would cover the cost of holding the building. The third option was to keep it and use it himself. Bubel had done some research on self-storage, and he thought the building might be a good fit for this purpose.

Opportunity No. 1: Sell

When Bubel purchased Mayfair Bingo, his goal was to sell the building and continue running his own bingo hall. A few potential buyers had viewed the building during the past few months, but only one showed even mild interest in its purchase. The asking price was $1.35 million, although Bubel felt that any price over $1.1 million would be acceptable. Clearly the building was not going to be easy to sell. It was difficult to convince retail users that they needed 20,000 square feet, and industrial users were not willing to pay the asking price. Bubel would either have to drop the price or wait for the right buyer.

A slight deviation on the sell option surfaced when the owners of the building next door showed interest in purchasing the back parking lot to expand their own business. They were willing to pay $500,000 for the one acre lot. This was attractive in that it would relieve some of Bubel's exposure, but it would work only if any new tenant would not need the back parking lot. Another disadvantage of selling the back lot was that the back part of the property could be seen from the highway. Moreover, Bubel was not sure how this deviation would affect the value of the remaining property.

Opportunity No. 2: Rent

Renting the building was another viable option. One possible prospect considered using the building as a large pool hall and bar. This potential tenant was a viable option. However, the tenant was demanding certain provisions, which included leasing only 10,000 square feet at a cost of $14 per square foot, as well as asking for $350,000 in leasehold improvements. Furthermore, they were asking for one year of free rent on a five-year lease.

This option was advantageous as the rental income would cover the cost of holding the property. It was possible that, with a good tenant, the property value might actually increase in the future, and Bubel could perhaps sell it for a higher figure than the $1.35 million he was currently asking. On the other hand, if the new tenant was unsuccessful, the property may carry the stigma of housing failed businesses, and the building may ultimately be worth less than its current market value. There would certainly be upfront costs incurred in order to transform the building to the desired look required by any new tenant. These costs were estimated to be roughly $25 per square foot in leasehold improvements.

Another potential tenant considered using the building as a banquet hall. Bubel had approached all banquet facilities in the Barrie area and attempted to sell them on the benefits of leasing the building. The fit for a banquet hall was perfect. The building was carpeted and had numerous tables, chairs, a large kitchen and plenty of parking. It could seat approximately 600 people and could be divided into two or even three separate large rooms. Although a few banquet halls had showed serious interest, none had made an offer. Typically, a retailer in the Barrie area would pay around $12 per square foot per year for a large space. However, given the amount of total space involved, Bubel felt that a discount would be necessary, putting the price at around $9 a square foot.

Opportunity No. 3: Self-Storage

A third and totally different alternative involved Bubel opening a self-storage facility in the vacant building. Self-storage is the term used for a facility offering storage units on a month-to-month basis where the tenant can lock up their possessions for a monthly rental fee. A typical storage facility might be on two to five acres of land and would be anywhere in the range of 10,000 to 100,000 square feet. Many facilities offered large roll-up doors and direct drive-up access to conventional (outside) units. Facilities offering climate controlled premises usually offered interior hallways for access to the units.

Barrie had five main storage facilities, ranging in size from 10,000 square feet to 40,000 square feet. Presently, all facilities were at least 85 per cent occupied and were grossing on average $14 per square foot per year. The main niche that Bubel felt he could target would be indoor, heated/cooled mini storage. Only one competitor offered indoor facilities, and they were charging close to $18 per square foot per year in an inferior location. The advantages of an indoor facility included a better atmosphere for an individual's possessions, the ability to target commercial customers due to the sprinkler system and better security.

The building on Bellfarm seemed ideal for self-storage, but there were some reservations. The major concern was that, in order to take advantage of economies of scale, the building should be 40,000 square feet. Of the 40,000 square feet, only about 75 per cent of it would be leaseable due to hallways, an office and other necessary requirements. An expansion to 40,000 square feet would cost $1.1 million for the new construction and another $300,000 for leasehold improvements on the original structure. This financing would be difficult to obtain due to most bank's reluctance to finance self-storage facilities. The other main obstacle was the fact that a new self-storage facility would have difficulty obtaining initial customers. The main advertising source of self storage was the Yellow Pages, which did not print again until August of 2003.

Now that Bubel had examined these options, he was wondering whether there were other alternatives that he had not yet considered. Would he be able to use the vacant building in another way? Many of his friends and advisors had suggested a banquet hall, while others remained skeptical about retail use for 20,000 square feet. The financial burden continued, and he hoped to come up with something sooner rather than later.

The Richard Ivey School of Business gratefully acknowledges the generous support of the K.W. Lemon and Ernst & Young Endowment Funds at Foundation Western in the development of these learning materials.

Coral Divers Resort (Revised)

Jonathon Greywell locked the door on the equipment shed and began walking back along the boat dock to his office. He was thinking about the matters that had weighed heavily on his mind during the last few months. Over the years, Greywell had established a solid reputation for the Coral Divers Resort as a safe and knowledgeable scuba diving resort that offered not only diving but also a beachfront location. Because Coral Divers Resort was a small but well-regarded, all-around dive resort in the Bahamas, many divers had come to prefer Greywell's resort to the other crowded tourist resorts in the Caribbean.

However, over the last three years, revenues had declined; for 2008, bookings were flat for the first half of the year. Greywell felt he needed to do something to increase business before the situation worsened. He wondered whether he should add some specialized features to the resort to help distinguish it from the competition. One approach would be to focus on family outings.

Rascals in Paradise (Rascals), a travel company that specialized in family diving vacations, had offered to help him convert his resort to specialize in family diving vacations. Rascals had shown him the industry demographics indicating that families were a growing market segment (see Exhibit 1) and suggested the changes that would need to be made at the resort. Rascals had even offered to create children's menus and to show the cook how to prepare the meals.

Another potential strategy for the Coral Divers Resort was to focus on adventure diving. Other resort operators in the Bahamas were offering adventure-oriented deep-depth dives, shark dives and night dives. The basic ingredients for adventure diving (i.e., reef sharks in the waters near New Providence and famous deep-water coral walls) were already in place. However, either of these strategies, creating a family vacation resort or an adventure diving resort, would require changes and additions to

Professors Paul W. Beamish and Kent E. Neupert prepared this case with assistance from Andreas Schotter solely to provide material for class discussion. The authors do not intend to illustrate either effective or ineffective handling of a managerial situation. The authors may have disguised certain names and other identifying information to protect confidentiality.

Copyright © 2008, Ivey Management Services   Version: (A) 2008-05-02

Ivey

Richard Ivey School of Business
The University of Western Ontario

the current operations. Greywell was not sure whether any of the changes was worth the time and investment or whether he should instead try to improve on what he was already doing.

A final option, and one that he had only recently considered, was to leave New Providence and relocate elsewhere. At issue here was how much he might be able to recover if he sold Coral Divers Resort and whether better opportunities existed elsewhere in the Bahamas or around the Caribbean.

SCUBA DIVING INDUSTRY OVERVIEW

Skin diving was an underwater activity of ancient origin in which a diver swam freely, unencumbered by lines or air hoses. Modern skin divers used three pieces of basic equipment: a face mask for vision, webbed rubber fins for propulsion and a snorkel tube for breathing just below the water's surface. The snorkel was a J-shaped plastic tube fitted with a mouthpiece. When the opening of the snorkel was above water, a diver was able to breathe. When diving to greater depths, divers needed to hold their breath; otherwise, water entered the mouth through the snorkel.

Scuba diving provided divers with the gift of time to relax and explore the underwater world without surfacing for their next breath. Scuba was an acronym for self-contained underwater breathing apparatus. Although attempts to perfect this type of apparatus dated from the early 20th century, it was not until 1943 that the most famous scuba, or Aqualung, was invented by the Frenchmen Jacques-Yves Cousteau and Emil Gagnan. The Aqualung made recreational diving possible for millions of non-professional divers. Although some specially trained commercial scuba divers descended below 100 meters (328 feet) for various kinds of work, recreational divers never descended below a depth of 40 meters (130 feet) because of increased risk of nitrogen narcosis, an oxygen toxicity that causes blackouts and convulsions.

The scuba diver wore a tank that carried a supply of pressurized breathing gas, either air or a mixture of oxygen and other gases. The heart of the breathing apparatus was the breathing regulator and the pressure-reducing mechanisms that delivered gas to the diver on each inhalation. In the common scuba used in recreational diving, the breathing medium was air. As the diver inhaled, a slight negative pressure occurred in the mouthpiece, prompting the opening of the valve that delivers the air. When the diver stopped inhaling, the valve closed, and a one-way valve allowed the exhaled breath to escape as bubbles into the water. By using a tank and regulator, a diver could make longer and deeper dives and still breathe comfortably.

Along with scuba gear and its tanks of compressed breathing gases, the scuba diver's essential equipment included a soft rubber mask with a large faceplate; long, flexible swimming flippers for the feet; a buoyancy compensator device (known as a BC or BCD); a weight belt; a waterproof watch; a wrist compass and a diver's knife. For protection from colder water, neoprene-coated foam rubber wet suits were typically worn.

Certification Organizations[1]

Several international and domestic organizations trained and certified scuba divers. The most well-known organizations were PADI (Professional Association of

---

[1] Information on the certifying agencies has been drawn from materials published by the various organizations.

Diving Instructors), NAUI (National Association of Underwater Instructors), SSI (Scuba Schools International) and NASDS (National Association of Scuba Diving Schools). Of these, PADI was the largest certifying organization.

Professional Association of Diving Instructors

The Professional Association of Diving Instructors (PADI), founded in 1967, was the largest recreational scuba diver training organization in the world. PADI divers comprised 70 per cent of all divers. The diving certificate issued by PADI through its instructors was acknowledged worldwide, thus enabling PADI-certified divers wide access to diving expeditions, tank filling, and diving equipment rental and purchase. Worldwide, PADI had certified more than 16.5 million recreational divers. In 2007, PADI International issued nearly 1 million new certifications.

In addition to PADI's main headquarters in Santa Ana, California, PADI operated regional offices in Australia, Canada, Switzerland, Japan, Sweden, the United Kingdom and the United States. PADI offices served more than 130,000 individual professional members and more than 5,300 dive centers and resorts in more than 180 countries and territories. Translations of PADI materials were available in more than 26 languages. PADI comprised four groups: PADI Retail Association, PADI International Resort Association, professional members and PADI Alumni Association. The three association groups emphasized the "three E's" of recreational diving: education, equipment and experience. By supporting each facet, PADI provided holistic leadership to advance recreational scuba diving and snorkel swimming to equal status with other major leisure activities, while maintaining and improving the organization's excellent safety record. PADI courses ranged from entry levels (such as scuba diver and open water diver certifications) to master scuba diver certification and a range of instructor certificates. Via its affiliate, Diving Science and Technology (DSAT), PADI also offered various technical diver courses, including decompression diving, Trimix diving and gas blending for deep sea diving. In 1995, PADI founded Project AWARE to help conserve underwater environments. Project AWARE information was integrated into most courses, and divers were offered the opportunity to exchange their standard certificate for an AWARE certificate by making a donation to the program when applying for a new certificate.

National Association of Underwater Instructors

The National Association of Underwater Instructors (NAUI) first began operation in 1960. The organization was formed by a nationally recognized group of instructors known as the National Diving Patrol. Since its beginning, NAUI had been active worldwide, certifying sport divers in various levels of proficiency from basic skin diver to instructor. NAUI regularly conducted specialty courses for cave diving, ice diving, wreck diving, underwater navigation, and search and recovery.

Industry Demographics[2]

Scuba diving had grown steadily in popularity over the last 20 years. From 1989 until 2001, certifications had increased an average of 10 per cent each year; and increases had continued to be steady, despite more difficulties surrounding air travel because of

---

[2] This section draws from results of surveys conducted by scuba diving organizations and publications for the years 1991 to 2007.

the events of September 11, 2001, and the bleaching impact of climate change on coral reefs. In 2007, the total number of certified divers worldwide was estimated to be more than 22 million. The National Sporting Goods Association, which conducted an annual sports participation survey, projected the number of active divers in the United States at 2.1 million, and market share data from resort destinations showed 1.5 million active traveling U.S.-based scuba divers, not including resort divers.

Approximately 65 per cent of the certified scuba divers were male, 35 per cent were female and about half of all scuba divers were married. Approximately 70 per cent of scuba divers were between the ages of 18 and 34, and approximately 25 per cent were between the ages of 35 and 49 (see Exhibit 2). Scuba divers were generally well educated: 80 per cent had a college education. Overwhelmingly, scuba divers were employed in professional, managerial and technical occupations and earned an average annual household income of $75,000, well above the national average. Forty-five per cent of divers traveled most often with their families, and 40 per cent traveled most often with friends or informal groups.

People were attracted to scuba diving for various reasons; seeking adventure and being with nature were the two most often cited reasons (identified by more than 75 per cent of divers). Socializing, stress relief and travel also were common motivations. Two-thirds of all divers traveled overseas on diving trips once every three years, whereas 60 per cent traveled domestically on dive trips each year. On average, divers spent $2,816 on dive trips annually, with an average equipment investment of $2,300. Aside from upgrades and replacements, the equipment purchase could be considered a one-time cost. Warm-water diving locations were generally chosen two to one over cold-water diving sites. Outside of the continental United States, the top three diving destinations are Cozumel in Mexico, the Cayman Islands and the Bahamas.

According to a consumer survey, the strongest feelings that divers associated with their scuba diving experiences were excitement and peacefulness. In a recent survey, these two themes drew an equal number of responses; however, the two responses had very distinct differences. The experience of excitement suggested a need for stimulation, whereas experience of peacefulness suggested relaxation and escape. Visual gratification (beauty) was another strong motivation for divers, as were the feelings of freedom, weightlessness and flying.

Under PADI regulations, divers needed to be at least 10 years old to be eligible for certification by the majority of scuba training agencies. At age 10, a child could earn a junior diver certification. Divers with this certification had to meet the same standards as an open water diver but generally had to be accompanied on dives by a parent or another certified adult. At age 15, the junior diver certification could be upgraded to open water status, which required a skills review and evaluation. Youth divers required pre-dive waiver and release forms signed by a parent or guardian until they reached age 18. Recently, PADI added a so-called bubble-maker program, which allowed children as young as age 8 to start scuba diving at a maximum depth of two meters (six feet). The program was conducted by PADI instructors in sessions that typically lasted one hour, and no pre-training was required. However, few dive centers had adopted the program because of the additional investment in special child-sized equipment and the low student-to-instructor ratio, which made the program uneconomical. On the other hand, children's programs increased the family friendliness of scuba diving.

In general, most dive centers maintained a cautious approach to young divers, based on the concept of readiness to dive. An individual's readiness to dive was determined by physical, mental and emotional maturity. Physical readiness was the easiest factor to assess: Was the child large enough and strong enough to handle scuba equipment? A regular air tank and weight belt can weigh more than 40 lb. (18 kilograms). Mental readiness referred to whether the child had the academic background and conceptual development to understand diving physics and perform the arithmetic required for certification. The arithmetic understanding was needed to determine a diver's allowable bottom time, which required factoring in depth, number of dives and length of dives. Emotional readiness was the greatest concern. Would the junior diver accept the responsibility of being a dive buddy? Divers never dived alone, and dive buddies needed to look out for and rely on each other. Did young divers comprehend the safety rules of diving and willingly follow them? Most dive centers therefore accepted students from age 10, but the final determination of readiness to dive rested with the scuba instructor. Instructors were trained to evaluate the readiness of all students before completion of the course work and would only award a certification to those who earn it, regardless of age.

DIVING IN THE BAHAMAS[3]

New Providence Island, the Bahamas

New Providence Island was best known for its major population center, Nassau, a community whose early development was based on its superb natural harbor. As the capital of the Bahamas, it was the seat of government and home to 400 banks, elegant homes, ancient forts and a wide variety of duty-free shopping. Nassau had the island's most developed tourist infrastructure exemplified by its elegant resort hotels, casinos, cabaret shows and cruise ship docks. More than two-thirds of the population of the Bahamas lived on the island of New Providence, and most of these 180,000 people lived in or near Nassau, on the northeast corner of the island.

Because thousands of vacationers took resort-based diving courses (introductory scuba courses taught in resort pools), Nassau had become known as a destination for both an exploratory first dive and more advanced diving. As a result, many professional dive operations were located in the in the Nassau area (see Exhibit 3). Although all dive operations offered resort courses, many also offered a full menu of dive activities designed for more advanced divers. Within a 30-minute boat ride of most operations were shipwrecks, beautiful shallow reefs and huge schools of fish.

In contrast to the bustle of Nassau, the south side of New Providence Island was quieter and more laid back. Large tracts of pine trees and rolling hills dominated the central regions, while miles of white sand beach surrounded the island. At the west end of the island was Lyford Cay, an exclusive residential area. Nearby, the Coral Harbour area offered easy access to the sea. Although golf and tennis were available, the primary attractions were the good scuba diving and the top-quality dive operators.

The southwest side of the island had been frequently used as an underwater film set. The "Bond wrecks" were popular diving destinations for divers and operators. The Vulcan Bomber used in the James Bond film *Thunderball* had aged into a framework draped with colorful gorgonians and sponges. The freighter, Tears of Allah, where

---

[3] The content in this section is based on information drawn from *The Islands of the Bahamas Dive Guide*, published by the Bahamas Ministry of Tourism, Commonwealth of the Bahamas, in conjunction with The Bahamas Diving Association, retrieved from http://www.bahamasdiving.com/6729/with_flash/html/index-5.html on April 10, 2008.

James Bond eluded the Tiger Shark in *Never Say Never Again*, remained a popular dive attraction in just 40 feet of water. The photogenic appeal of this wreck had improved with age as marine life increasingly congregated on this artificial reef.

Natural underwater attractions, such as Shark Wall and Shark Buoy, were popular dive spots. Drop-off dives, such as Tunnel Wall, featured a network of crevices and tunnels beginning in 30 feet of water and exiting along the vertical wall at 70 or 80 feet. Southwest Reef offered magnificent coral heads in only 15 to 30 feet of water, with schooling grunts, squirrelfish and barracuda. A favorite of the shallow reef areas was Goulding Cay, where Elkhorn coral reach nearly to the surface.

TYPES OF DIVING

A wide array of diving activities was available in the Bahamas, including shark dives, wreck dives, wall dives, reef dives, drift dives and night dives. Some illustrative examples follow.

Shark Diving

The top three operators of shark dives in the Caribbean were located in the Bahamas. Although shark diving trips varied depending on the dive operators, one common factor was shared by all shark dives in the Bahamas: the Caribbean reef shark (Carcharhinus perezi). When the dive boat reached the shark site, the sound of the motor acted as a dinner bell. Even before the divers entered the water, sharks gathered for their handouts.

Long Island in the Bahamas was the first area to promote shark feed dives on a regular basis. This method began 20 years ago and had remained relatively unchanged. The feed was conducted as a feeding frenzy. Sharks circled as divers entered the water. After the divers positioned themselves with their backs to a coral wall, the feeder entered the water with a bucket of fish, which was placed in the sand in front of the divers, and the action developed quickly. At Walker's Cay, in Abaco, the method was similar except for the number and variety of sharks in the feed. Although Caribbean reef sharks made up the majority of sharks seen, lemon sharks, bull sharks, hammerhead sharks and other species also appeared.

The shark feed off Freeport, Grand Bahama, was an organized event in which the sharks were fed either by hand or off the point of a polespear. The divers were arranged in a semi-circle with safety divers guarding the viewers and the feeder positioned at the middle of the group. If the sharks became unruly, the food was withheld until they calmed down. The sharks then went into a regular routine of circling, taking their place in line and advancing to receive the food. Although the sharks often came within touching distance, most divers resisted the temptation to reach out.

Shark Wall, on the southwest side of New Providence, was a pristine drop-off decorated with masses of colorful sponges along the deep-water abyss known as the Tongue of the Ocean. Divers positioned themselves along sand patches among the coral heads in about 50 feet of water as Caribbean reef sharks and an occasional bull shark or lemon shark cruised mid-water in anticipation of a free handout. During the feeding period, the bait was controlled and fed from a polespear by an experienced feeder. Usually six to 12 sharks were present, ranging from four to eight feet in length. Some operators made two dives to this site, allowing divers to cruise the wall with the sharks in a more natural way before the feeding dive.

The Shark Buoy, also on the southwest side of New Providence, was tethered in 6,000 feet of water. Its floating surface mass attracted a wide variety of ocean marine life, such as dolphin fish, jacks, rainbow runners and silky sharks. The silky sharks were typically small, three to five feet long, but swarmed in schools of six to 20, with the sharks swimming up to the divemaster's hands to grab the bait.

From the operator's standpoint, the only special equipment needed for shark dives were a chain mail diving suit for the feeder's protection, feeding apparatus and intestinal fortitude. The thrill of diving among sharks was the main attraction for the divers. For the most part, the dives were safe; only the feeder took an occasional nip from an excited shark.

Recently, shark feeding had come under attack from environmentalists for causing a change in the feeding behavior of sharks, which had led to the loss of their natural fear of humans. In addition, some rare but fatal accidents had been prominently exposed through TV news channels and newspapers. For example, in 2001, Krishna Thompson, a 34-year-old New York banker, lost a leg and very nearly his life, when he was attacked just off the beach at Lucaya Golf and Beach Resort in Freeport, Grand Bahama. Thompson successfully sued the resort for failing to warn guests that local dive operators sold shark-feeding tours at sites located less than a mile from the hotel beach. In April 2002, TV shark show daredevil Erich Ritter went into severe shock and nearly lost his left leg after he was bitten by a bull shark that he had attracted to shallow water with fish bait.

In spite of opposition from a small but well-funded group of U.S. dive industry insiders including PADI, DEMA, *Scuba Diving* magazine and *Skin Diver* magazine, the Florida Fish and Wildlife Conservation Commission banned shark feeding in 2001. However, shark feeding remained legal in the Caribbean, and despite its dangers, was on the rise. Divers participating in shark dives were required to sign waivers before the actual dive. As noted by the fine print in most life insurance and travel insurance policies, claims for scuba-related accidents were excluded.

Wreck Diving

Wreck diving was divided into three levels: non-penetration, limited penetration and full penetration. Full penetration and deep wreck diving should be attempted only by divers who had completed rigorous training and have extensive diving experience. Non-penetration wreck diving referred to recreational diving on wrecks without entering an overhead environment that prevented direct access to the surface. Divers with open water certification were qualified for this type of diving without any further training provided they were comfortable with the diving conditions and the wreck's depth. Limited penetration wreck diving was defined as staying within ambient light and always in sight of an exit. Full penetration wreck diving involved an overhead environment away from ambient light and beyond sight of an exit. Safely and extensively exploring the insides of a wreck involved formal training and mental strength. On this type of dive, a diver's first mistake could be a diver's last.

Wall Diving

In a few regions of the world, island chains, formed by volcanoes and coral, have been altered by movements of the earth's crustal plates. Extending approximately due east-west across the central Caribbean Sea was the boundary between the North American and Caribbean crustal plates. The shifting of these plates had created some of the most spectacular diving environments in the world, characterized by enormous cliffs, 2,000 to 6,000 feet high. At the cliffs, known as walls, divers could experience, more than in any other underwater environment, the overwhelming scale and dynamic forces that shape the ocean. On the walls, divers were most likely to experience the feeling of free motion, or flying, in boundless space. Many of the dives in the Bahamas were wall dives.

Reef Diving

Reefs generally were made up of three areas: a reef flat, a lagoon or bay, and a reef crest. The depth in the reef flat averaged only a few feet with an occasional deeper channel. The underwater life on a shallow reef flat could vary greatly in abundance and diversity within a short distance. The reef flat was generally a protected area, not exposed to strong winds or waves, making it ideal for novice or family snorkelers. The main feature distinguishing bay and lagoon environments from a reef flat was depth. Caribbean lagoons and bays could reach depths of 60 feet but many provided teaming underwater ecosystems in as little as 15 to 20 feet, making this area excellent for underwater photography and ideal for families because it was a no decompression stop diving site.[4] The reef's crest was the outer boundary that sheltered the bay and the flats from the full force of the ocean's waves. Since the surging and pounding of the waves was too strong for all but the most advanced divers, most diving took place in the protected bay waters.

FAMILY DIVING RESORTS

The current average age of new divers was 36. As the median age of new divers increased, families became a rapidly growing segment of the vacation travel industry. Many parents were busy and did not spend as much time with their children as they would have preferred. Thus, many parents who dived would have liked to have a vacation that would combine diving and spending time with their children. In response to increasing numbers of parents traveling with children, resort operators had added amenities ranging from babysitting services and kids' camps to dedicated family resorts with special facilities and rates. The resort options available had greatly expanded in recent years. At all-inclusive, self-contained resorts, one price included everything: meals, accommodations, daytime and evening activities, and water sports. Many of these facilities offered special activities and facilities for children. Diving was sometimes included or available nearby.

For many divers, the important part of the trip was the quality of the diving, not the quality of the accommodations, but for divers with families, the equation changed. Children, especially younger children, could have a difficult time without a comfortable bed, a television and a DVD player, no matter how good the diving promised to be. Some resorts that were not dedicated to family vacations, made accommodations for divers with children. Condos and villas were an economical and convenient vacation option. The additional space of this type of accommodation

---

[4] A decompression stop is a safety requirement for dives below 30 feet. It lasts typically between 1 to 5 minutes at 3 to 6 meters (10 to 20 ft). During the stop, "micro-bubbles" in the bloodstream that are present after every dive leave the diver's body safely through the lungs. If they are not given enough time to leave safely, it can cause the symptoms and injuries known as decompression sickness.

allowed parents to bring along a babysitter, and the convenience of a kitchen made the task of feeding children simple and economical. Most diving destinations in the Bahamas, the Caribbean and the Pacific offered condo, villa and hotel-type accommodations. Some hotels organized entertaining and educational activities for children while parents engaged in their own activities.

Because the number of families vacationing together had increased, some resorts and dive operators started special promotions and programs. On Bonaire, an island in the Netherlands Antilles, August had been designated family month. During this month, the island was devoted to families, with a special welcome kit for children and island-wide activities, including eco-walks at a flamingo reserve, snorkeling lessons and evening entertainment for all ages. In conjunction, individual resorts and restaurants offered family packages and discounts. Similarly, in Honduras, which had very good diving, a resort started a children's dolphin camp during summer months. While diving family members were out exploring the reefs, children aged eight to 14 spent their days learning about and interacting with a resident dolphin population. The program included classroom and in-water time, horseback riding and paddle boating.

Rascals in Paradise

One travel company, Rascals in Paradise (Rascals), specialized in family travel packages. The founders, Theresa Detchemendy and Deborah Baratta, were divers, mothers and travel agents who had developed innovative packages for diving families. According to Detchemendy, "The biggest concern for parents is their children's safety, and then what the kids will do while they're diving or enjoying an evening on the town." The Rascals staff worked with a number of family-run resorts all over the world to provide daily activities, responsible local nannies and child-safe facilities with safe balconies, playgrounds and children's pools.

Rascals also organized family weeks at popular dive destinations in Belize, Mexico and the Cayman Islands. Family week packages accounted for more than 50 per cent of Rascals' bookings each year. On these scheduled trips, groups of three to six families shared a teacher/escort, who tailored a fun program for children and served as an activities director for the group. Rascals' special family week packages were priced based on a family of four (two adults and two children, aged two to 11) and included a teacher/escort, one babysitter for each family, children's activities, meals, airport transfers, taxes, services and cancellation insurance (see Exhibit 4) but not airfare. For example, in 2007, a seven-night family vacation at Hotel Club Akumal, on the Yucatan coast, cost US$2,080 to US$3,100 per family. Rascals also packaged independent family trips to 57 different condos, villas, resorts and hotels, which offered scuba diving. An independent family trip would not include a teacher/escort and babysitter (see Exhibit 5) and a 7-night family trip to Hotel Club Akumal would cost between US$624 and US$1,779, depending on the season and the type of room. Here also, the airfare was not included.

Rascals personally selected the resorts with which the company worked. "We try to work with small properties so our groups are pampered and looked after," says Detchemendy. "The owners are often parents and their kids are sometimes on the property. They understand the characteristics of kids." Typically, Detchemendy and Baratta visited each destination, often working with the government tourist board to identify potential properties. If the physical structure were already in place, adding the resort to the Rascals booking list was easy. If modifications were needed, the Detchemendy and

Baratta met with the property's management to outline the facilities needed to include the resort in the Rascals program.

Rascals evaluated resorts according to several factors:

- Is the property friendly toward children and does it want children on the property?
- How does the property rate in terms of safety?
- What facilities does the property have? Is a separate room available that could be used as a Rascals room?
- Does the property provide babysitting and child care by individuals who are screened and locally known?

A successful example of this approach was Hotel Club Akumal, in Akumal, Mexico. Detchemendy and Baratta helped the resort expand its market reach by building a family-oriented resort that became part of the Rascals program. Baratta explained:

> In that case, we were looking for a place close to home, with a multi-level range of accommodations, that offered something other than a beach, that was family friendly, and not in Cancun. We found Hotel Club Akumal, but they didn't have many elements in place, so we had to work with them. We established a meal plan, an all-inclusive product and designated activities for kids. We went into the kitchen and created a children's menu and we asked them to install a little kids' playground that's shaded.

The resort became one of Rascals' most popular family destinations.

Rascals offered two types of services to resort operators interested in creating family vacations. One was a consulting service. For a modest daily fee plus expenses, Baratta or Detchemendy, or both, would conduct an on-site assessment of the resort, which usually took one or two days. They would then provide a written report to the resort regarding needed additions or modifications to the resort to make it safe and attractive for family vacations. Physical changes might include the addition of a Rascals room and child-safe play equipment and modifications to existing buildings and structures, such as rooms, railings and docks, to prevent child injuries. Rascals always tried to use existing equipment or equipment available nearby. Other non-structural changes could include the addition of educational sessions, play times and other structured times for entertaining children while their parents were diving. The report also included an implementation proposal. Then, after implementation, the resort could decide whether or not to list with Rascals for bookings.

Under the second option, Rascals provided the consulting service at no charge to the resort; however, any requests for family bookings were referred to Rascals. Rascals would then list and actively promote the resort through its brochures and referrals. For resorts using the Rascals booking option, Rascals provided premiums, such as hats and T-shirts, in addition to the escorted activities. This attention to the family differentiated a Rascals resort from other resorts. Generally, companies that promoted packages received net rates from the resorts, which were 20 per cent to 50 per cent lower than the rack rates. Rascals, in turn, promoted these special packages to the travel industry in general and paid a portion of its earnings out in commissions to other travel agencies.

Rascals tried to work with its resorts to provide packaged and prepaid vacations, an approach that created a win-win situation for the resort managers and the vacationer. Packaged vacations, also known as all-inclusive vacations, followed a cruise ship approach that allowed the inclusion of many activities in the package. For example, such a package might include seven nights' lodging, all meals, babysitting, children's activities and scuba diving. This approach allowed the vacationer to know, upfront, what to expect. Moreover, the cost would be included in one set price, so that the family would not have to pay for each activity as it came along. The idea was to remove the surprises and make the stay enjoyable. The resort operator could bundle the activities together, providing more options than might otherwise be offered. As a result, the package approach was becoming popular with both resort owners and vacationers.

In its bookings, Rascals required prepayment of trips, which resulted in higher revenues for the resort since all activities were paid for in advance. Ordinarily, resorts that operated independently might require only a two- or three-night room deposit. The family would then pay for the balance of the room charge on leaving, after paying for other activities or services they used. Although vacationers might think they had a less expensive trip this way, in fact, pre-paid activities were generally cheaper than a la carte activities. Moreover, purchasing individual activities potentially yielded lower revenues for the resort. Rascals promoted prepaid vacations as a win-win, low-stress approach to travel. Rascals had been very successful with the resorts it listed. Fifty per cent of its bookings were repeat business, and many inquiries were based on word-of-mouth referrals. All in all, Rascals provided a link to the family vacation market segment that the resort might not otherwise have access to. It was common for Rascals-listed resorts to average annual bookings of 90 per cent.

CORAL DIVERS RESORT

Coral Divers Resort (Coral Divers) had been in operation for 10 years. Annual revenues had reached as high as $554,000. Profits generally had been in the two per cent range, but for the past two years, the business had experienced losses. The expected turnaround in profits in 2007 had never materialized (see Exhibit 6). Although the resort was not making them rich, the business had provided an adequate income for Greywell and his wife, Margaret, and their two children, Allen, age 7, and Winifred, age 5. However, revenues had continued to decline. From talking with other operators, Greywell understood that resorts with strong identities and reputations for quality service were doing well. Greywell thought that the Coral Divers Resort had not distinguished itself in any particular aspect of diving or as a resort.

The Coral Divers Resort property was located on a deep-water channel on the southwest coast of the island of New Providence in the Bahamas. The three-acre property had beach access and featured six cottages, each with its own kitchenette, a full bath, a bedroom with two full-sized beds and a living room with two sleeper sofas. Four of the units had been upgraded with new paint, tile floors, a microwave, a color TV and a DVD player. The two other units ranged from "adequate" to "comfortable." Greywell tried to use the renovated units primarily for families and couples and housed groups of single divers in the other units (see Exhibit 7). Also on the property was a six-unit attached motel-type structure. Each of these units had two full-sized beds, a pull-out sofa, sink, a refrigerator, a microwave and a television. The resort had the space and facilities for a kitchen and dining room, but neither a kitchen nor a dining room was in use. A small family-run restaurant and bar was available within walking distance.

Greywell had three boats that could each carry from eight to 20 passengers. Two were 40-foot fiberglass V-hull boats powered by a single diesel inboard with a cruising speed of 18 knots and a protective cabin with dry storage space. The third was a 35-foot covered platform boat. Greywell also had facilities for air dispensing, equipment repair, rental and sale, and tank storage.

Coral Divers Resort, which was affiliated with PADI and NAUI, had a staff of 11, including two boat captains, two mates, a housekeeper, a groundskeeper, a person who minded the office and the store, and four scuba diving instructors. Greywell, who worked full-time at the resort, was a diving instructor certified by both PADI and NAUI. The three other diving instructors had various backgrounds: one was a former U.S. Navy SEAL working for Coral Divers as a way to gain resort experience, another was a local Bahamian whom Greywell had known for many years and the third was a Canadian who had come to the Bahamas on a winter holiday and had never left. Given the size of the operation, the staff was scheduled to provide overall coverage, with all of the staff rarely working at the same time. Greywell's wife, Margaret, worked at the business on a part-time basis, taking care of administrative activities, such as accounting and payroll. The rest of her time was spent looking after their two children and their home.

A typical diving day at Coral Divers began around 7:30 a.m. Greywell would open the office and review the activities list for the day. If any divers needed to be picked up at the resorts in Nassau or elsewhere on the island, the van driver would need to leave by 7:30 a.m. to be back at the resort for the 9 a.m. departure. Most resort guests began to gather around the office and dock about 8:30 a.m. By 8:45 a.m., the day's captain and mate began loading the diving gear for the passengers.

The boat left at 9 a.m. for the morning dives that were usually "two tank dives," that is, two dives utilizing one tank of air each. The trip to the first dive site took 20 to 30 minutes. Once there, the captain would explain the dive, the special attractions of the dive, and tell everyone when they were expected back on board. Most dives lasted 30 to 45 minutes, depending on the depth. The deeper the dive, the faster the air consumption. On the trip down, divers were always accompanied by a divemaster, who supervised the dive. The divemaster was responsible for the safety and conduct of the divers while under water.

After the divers were back on board, the boat would move to the next site. Greywell tried to plan two dives that had sites near each other. For example, the first dive might be a wall dive in 60 feet of water, and the second might be a nearby wreck 40 feet down. The second dive would also last approximately 40 minutes. If the dives went well, the boat would be back at the resort by noon, which allowed time for lunch and sufficient surface time for divers who might be interested in an afternoon dive. Two morning dives were part of the resort package. Whether the boat went out in the afternoon depended on the number of non-resort guest divers contracted for afternoon dives. If enough paying divers were signed up, Greywell was happy to let resort guests ride and dive free of charge. If there were not enough paying divers, no afternoon dive trips were scheduled, and the guests were on their own to swim at the beach, sightsee or just relax. When space was available, non-divers (either snorkelers or bubble-watchers) could join the boat trip for a fee of $15 to $25.

Greywell's Options

Greywell's bookings ran 90 per cent of capacity during the high season (December through May) and 50 per cent of capacity during the low season (June through November).

Ideally, he wanted to increase the number of bookings for the resort and dive businesses during both seasons. Adding additional diving attractions could increase both resort and dive revenues. Focusing on family vacations could increase revenues because families would probably increase the number of paying guests per room. Break-even costs were calculated based on two adults sharing a room. Children provided an additional revenue source since the cost of the room had been covered by the adults, and children under 10 incurred no diving-related costs. However, either strategy, adding adventure diving to his current general offerings or adjusting the focus of the resort to encourage family diving vacations, would require some changes and cost money. The question was whether the changes would increase revenue enough to justify the costs and effort involved.

Emphasizing family diving vacations would probably require some changes to the physical property of the resort. Four of the cottages had already been renovated. The other two also would need to be upgraded, which would cost $15,000 to $25,000 each, depending on the amenities added. The Bahamas had duties of up to 35 per cent, which caused renovation costs involving imported goods to be expensive. The attached motel-type units also would need to be refurbished at some point. The resort had the space and facilities for a kitchen and dining area, but Greywell had not done anything about opening these facilities.

The Rascals in Paradise people had offered to help set up a children's menu. He could hire a chef, prepare the meals himself or offer the concession to either the nearby restaurant or someone else. He would also need to build a children's play structure. An open area with shade trees between the office and the cottages would be ideal for a play area. Rascals would provide the teacher/escort for the family vacation groups, and it would be fairly easy to find babysitters for the children as needed. The people who lived on this part of the island were very family-oriented and would welcome the opportunity for additional income. From asking around, Greywell determined that between $5 and $10 per hour was the going rate for a sitter. Toys and other play items could be added gradually. The Rascals people had said that, once the program was in place, Greywell could expect bookings to run 90 per cent capacity annually from new and return bookings. Although the package prices were competitive, the attraction was in group bookings and the prospect of a returning client base.

Adding adventure diving would be a relatively easy thing to do. Shark Wall and Shark Buoy were less than an hour away by boat. Both of these sites featured sharks that were already accustomed to being fed. The cost of shark food would be $10 per dive. None of Greywell's current staff was particularly excited about the prospect of adding shark feeding to their job description. But these staff could be relatively easily replaced. Greywell could probably find an experienced divemaster who would be willing to lead the shark dives. He would also have to purchase a special chain mail suit for the feeder at a cost of about $15,000. Although few accidents occurred during shark feeds, Greywell would rather be safe than sorry. His current boats, especially the 40-footers, would be adequate for transporting divers to the sites. The other shark dive operators might not be happy about having him at the sites, but they could do little about it. Shark divers were charged a premium fee. For example, a shark dive would cost $115 for a two-tank dive, compared with $65 for a normal two-tank dive. He figured that he could add shark dives to the schedule on Wednesdays and Saturdays without taking away from regular business. Although he needed a minimum of four divers on a trip at regular rates to cover the cost of taking out the boat, 10 or 12 divers would be ideal. Greywell could usually count on at least eight divers for a normal dive, but he did not know how much additional new and return business he could expect from shark diving.

A third option was for Greywell to try to improve his current operations and not add any new diving attractions, which would require him to be much more cost efficient in his operations. For example, he would have to strictly adhere to the policy of requiring a minimum number of divers per boat, and staff reductions might improve the bottom line by five per cent to 10 per cent. He would need to be very attentive to materials ordering, fuel costs and worker productivity in order to realize any gains with this approach. However, he was concerned that by continuing as he had, Coral Divers Resort would not be distinguished as unique from other resorts in the Bahamas. He did not know the long-term implications of this approach.

As Greywell reached the office, he turned to watch the sun sink into the ocean. Although it was a view he had come to love, a lingering thought was that perhaps it was time to relocate to a less crowded location.

Exhibit 1   U.S. Population Demographics, 1980, 1990 and 2000

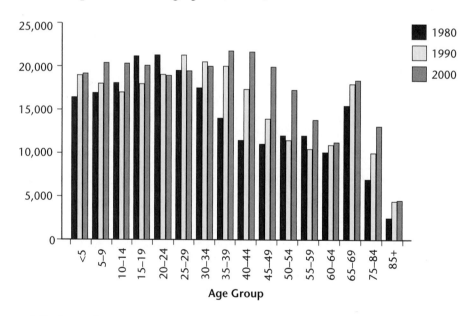

Note: Numbers are in the thousands.

Source: U.S. Bureau of the Census, 2000. Retrieved from http://factfinder.census.gov/servlet/QTTable?_bm=y&-geo_id=01000US&-qr_name=DEC_2000_SF1_U_DP1&-ds_name=DEC_2000_SF1_U on April 10, 2008.

Exhibit 2   U.S. Diver Demographics: Age of Divers

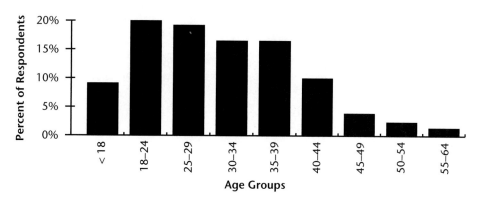

Source: PADI Diver Survey Results and Analysis.

Exhibit 3   Names and Location of Diving Operators in the Bahamas

Abaco
Above and Below Abaco
Brendal's Dive Center International
Dive Abaco
Dive Guana
Froggies Out Island Adventures, Ltd.
Treasure Divers

Andros
Coral Caverns Dive Resort
Kamalame Cay Resort
Seascape Inn
Small Hope Bay Lodge
Tiamo Resort

Bimini
Bill & Nowdla Keefe's Bimini Undersea
Scuba Bimini

Cat Island
Hawk's Nest Resort & Marina

Eleuthera/Habour Island
Cape Eleuthera Divers
Ocean Fox Divers
Valentine's Dive Center

Exuma
Exuma Scuba Adventures

Live-Aboard Dive Boats
Aqua Cat Cruises
Blackbeard's Cruises
Cat Ppalu Cruises
Explorer Ventures
Juliet Sailing and Diving
Nekton Diving Cruises
Sea Dragon
The Dream Team, Inc.

Long Island
Cape Santa Maria Beach Resort
Reel Divers at Grotto Bay
Stella Maris Resort Club

New Providence Island/Nassau
Bahama Divers Ltd.
Coral Divers Resort
Land Shark Divers
Stuart Cove's Dive South Ocean

San Salvador
Riding Rock Resort

Source: The Bahamas Diving Association membership.

Exhibit 4   Rascals In Paradise Pricing Guide, Rascals Special Family Weeks

Destination	Price	Notes
Bahamas		
South Ocean Beach	$3,120 to $3,970	Lunch not included
Small Hope Bay	$3,504	Scuba diving included. Local host only.
Mexico		
Hotel Buena Vista	$2,150 to $2,470	
Hotel Club Akumal	$2,080 to $3,100	Lunch and airport transfer not included.

Note: Prices are based on a family of four with two adults and two children aged two and 11. Rates are per week (seven nights) and include (except as noted): accommodations, Rascals escort, meals, babysitter, children's activities, airport transfers, taxes and services, and a $2,500 cancellation insurance per family booking. Airfares not included.

Exhibit 5   Rascals In Paradise Pricing Guide, Independent Family Trips

Destination	Price	Notes
Bahamas		
South Ocean Beach	$1,355 to $1,771	
Small Hope Bay	$2,860 to $3,560	All meals, bar service, babysitter and diving included.
Hope Town Harbour Lodge	$962 to $1,121	
Treasure Cay	$875 to $1,750	
Stella Maris, Long Island	$1,547 to $2,597	
Mexico		
Hotel Buena Vista	$1,232 to $1,548	All meals included
Hotel Club Akumal	$624 to $1,779	
Hotel Presidente	$1,120 to $1,656	
La Concha	$655 to $963	
Plaza Las Glorias	$632 to $1,017	

Note: Prices are based on a family of four with two adults and two children aged two and 11. Rates are per week (seven nights) and include accommodations and applicable taxes. These rates are to be used as a guide only. Each booking is quoted separately and the amount charged depends on season, type of accommodation, ages and number of children, meal and activity inclusions. All prices are subject to change. Some variations apply. Airfares not included.

Exhibit 6 Comparative Balance Sheets, as at June 30 (US$)

	2007	2006	2005
Assets			
Current Assets			
Cash	$ 5,362	8,943	15,592
Accounts Receivable	2,160	8,660	2,026
Inventories	5,519	6,861	9,013
Prepaid Expenses	9,065	8,723	8,195
Total Current Assets	22,106	33,187	34,826
Fixed Assets			
Land	300,000	300,000	300,000
Building	200,000	200,000	200,000
Less: Accumulated Depreciation	(70,000)	(60,000)	(50,000)
Boats	225,000	225,000	225,000
Less: Accumulated Depreciation	(157,500)	(135,000)	(112,500)
Vehicles	54,000	54,000	54,000
Less: Accumulated Depreciation	(32,400)	(21,600)	(10,800)
Diving Equipment	150,000	150,000	150,000
Less: Accumulated Depreciation	(90,000)	(60,000)	(30,000)
Total Fixed Assets	579,100	652,400	725,700
Total Assets	601,206	685,587	760,526
Liabilities			
Current Liabilities			
Accounts Payable	1,689	4,724	1,504
Bank Loan	20,000	-	2,263
Mortgage Payable, current portion	25,892	25,892	25,892
Note Payable, current portion	40,895	40,895	40,895
Total Current Liabilities	88,476	71,511	70,554
Long-term Liabilities			
Mortgage Payable, due in 1996	391,710	417,602	443,494
Note Payable, 5-year	81,315	122,210	163,105
Total Long-term Liabilities	473,025	539,812	606,599
Total Liabilities	561,501	611,323	677,153
Shareholders' Equity			
Jonathan Greywell, Capital	44,879	44,879	44,879
Retained Earnings	(5,174)	29,385	38,494
Total Shareholders' Equity	39,705	74,264	83,373
Total Liabilities and Shareholders' Equity	$601,206	685,587	760,526

(continued)

Exhibit 6   (continued)

	2007	2006	2005
Revenue			
Diving and lodging packages	$482,160	507,670	529,820
Day diving	11,680	12,360	14,980
Certifications	5,165	5,740	7,120
Lodging	2,380	1,600	1,200
Miscellaneous	1,523	1,645	1,237
Total Revenues	**502,908**	**529,015**	**554,357**
Expenses			
Advertising and promotion	15,708	15,240	13,648
Bank charges	1,326	1,015	975
Boat maintenance and fuel	29,565	31,024	29,234
Cost of goods sold	762	823	619
Depreciation	73,300	73,300	73,300
Dues and fees	3,746	4,024	3,849
Duties and taxes	11,405	18,352	17,231
Insurance	36,260	34,890	32,780
Interest, mortgage, note and loan	40,544	40,797	41,174
Management salary	31,600	31,600	31,600
Office Supplies	12,275	12,753	11,981
Professional fees	11,427	10,894	10,423
Repairs and maintenance, building	15,876	12,379	9,487
Salaries, wages and benefits	196,386	194,458	191,624
Telephone and fax	9,926	9,846	7,689
Trade shows	14,523	14,679	14,230
Utilities	20,085	19,986	17,970
Vehicles, maintenance and fuel	12,753	12,064	11,567
Total Expenses	**537,467**	**538,124**	**519,381**
Net Income	**(34,559)**	**(9,109)**	**(34,976)**
Retained Earnings, beginning	**29,385**	**38,494**	**3,518**
Retained Earnings, ending	**$ (5,174)**	**29,385**	**38,494**

Note: Bahama$1 = US$1

Exhibit 7   Coral Divers Resort Pricing Guide, Family Dive Vacations

Destination	Duration	Price	Notes
Bahamas			
Coral Divers Resort		$1,355 to 1,455	Standard accommodations, continental breakfast and daily two-tank dive included.
Coral Divers Resort		$1,800 to $1,950	Deluxe accommodations, continental breakfast and daily two-tank dive included.

Note: Prices are based on a family of four with two adults and two children ages two and 11. Rates are per week (7 nights) and include accommodations and applicable taxes. Rates will be dependent on season, type of accommodation, ages and number of children. All prices are subject to change. Airfares not included. Prices dropped to $600 to $700 per week for the standard package and $800 to $900 for deluxe accommodation if diving was excluded.

Vancity Credit Union —Strategy in Financial Services

In February 2004, Dave Mowat, chief executive officer of Vancouver City Savings Credit Union (Vancity), pondered his organization's competitive future. Founded in Vancouver in 1946, Vancity had become the largest credit union in Canada, operating 41 branches in Greater Vancouver, the Fraser Valley and Victoria with $9 billion in assets and more than 300,000 members.[1] In the past, Vancity had achieved success by focusing on three elements: member experience, employee experience, and community leadership to create membership growth, to deepen relationships and to enhance financial sustainability. However, as powerful financial services institutions continued to press for a greater share in Vancity's core market and as market characteristics appeared to be changing significantly, Dave Mowat decided that now was an opportune time to examine Vancity's strategy as well as the resources and capabilities that underpin it.

BACKGROUND ON CREDIT UNIONS AND CHARTERED BANKS

Vancity was part of the financial institution sector, which included commercial (or investment) banks, trust companies, brokerage houses, insurance companies, credit unions and other types of financial intermediaries. A credit union is a co-operative financial institution, owned and controlled by the members who use its services. The benefits include improved member service and, in some cases, better interest rates on

Professor Anthony Goerzen prepared this case solely to provide material for class discussion. The author does not intend to illustrate either effective or ineffective handling of a managerial situation. The author may have disguised certain names and other identifying information to protect confidentiality.

Ivey Management Services prohibits any form of reproduction, storage or transmittal without its written permission. This material is not covered under authorization from CanCopy or any reproduction rights organization. To order copies or request permission to reproduce materials, contact Ivey Publishing, Ivey Management Services, c/o Richard Ivey School of Business, The University of Western Ontario, London, Ontario, Canada, N6A 3K7; phone (519) 661-3208; fax (519) 661-3882; e-mail cases@ivey.uwo.ca.

Richard Ivey School of Business
The University of Western Ontario

---

[1]Vancity Financial Report, www.vancity.com/menuId/50083, accessed December 31, 2003.

deposits and loans. In addition, an attractive feature for some people is the opportunity to influence the institution's operating policies by nominating and voting for the board of directors and participating in the annual general members' meeting.

Credit unions serve groups that often share a common bond, such as where they work or where they live. They are not-for-profit organizations, existing to provide a safe, convenient place for members to save money and to obtain loans and other financial services at reasonable rates. Thus, credit unions are different from for-profit financial institutions, as credit unions exist to serve their members whereas other financial institutions, such as chartered banks, exist to maximize shareholder wealth. Credit unions' earnings are returned to the members in various forms, including dividends, higher interest on savings, lower interest on loans and other services. A major similarity between credit unions and the major chartered banks, however, is that they both provide comparable financial services to both retail and business members—savings and chequing accounts, youth and senior accounts, multi-purpose loans, wealth management services, insurance and convenient access to funds.

In 1999, there were 2,453 credit unions that served, for the most part, particular geographic areas, such as small towns; others were used exclusively by members of an association or by employees of a certain company. The credit union sector in Canada had the world's highest per capita membership; there were more than 10 million credit union members, which account for approximately one-third of the population in Canada.[2] In British Columbia, credit unions have combined assets of more than $25 billion and return to their members an average of $32 million annually by the way of dividends and patronage refunds.[3] Credit unions, democratically managed through locally elected directors, also made up the largest financial network in British Columbia with more than 7,000 employees. Since 2001, the credit union industry had been growing in assets by an average of 7.2 per cent in Canada, and 6.3 per cent within British Columbia on a yearly basis.[4] However, while the number of branches had continued to increase, in recent years there had been a decrease in the overall number of credit unions, due mainly to mergers and acquisition and resulting in an increase in the average asset size of individual credit unions.

Under the Co-operative Credit Associations Act, the national central Credit Union Central of Canada was chartered and regulated by the federal government.[5] While provincial legislative and regulatory structures were similar to those of federal financial institutions, credit unions in Canada are subject to provincial government regulations and, therefore, credit unions could not extend their activities beyond their own provincial borders.

Credit unions' biggest competitors in Canada were the chartered banks. Collectively, chartered banks held about one-third of all assets in the financial sector in 2000. At that time, 48 chartered banks were operating in Canada through a highly developed system of branch networks (approximately 8,000 branches) and more than 12,500 automated teller machines. It is the traditional "Big Six," however, that continue to dominate the industry: the Canadian Imperial Bank of Commerce, the Royal Bank of Canada, the Bank of Nova Scotia, the Bank of Montreal, the Toronto Dominion Bank and the National Bank of Canada, which together account for 92 per cent of chartered bank total assets. Moreover, five of the 100 largest financial institutions in the world are Canadian chartered banks.

---

[2] "Financial Consumer Agency of Canada," www.fcac-acfc.gc.ca, accessed November 13, 2003.
[3] "Credit Union Central BC," www.cucbc.com, accessed November 7, 2003.
[4] "Credit Union Central of Canada," www.cucentral.ca, accessed November 7, 2003.
[5] "World Council of Credit Unions, Inc." www.woccu.org, accessed November 17, 2003.

VANCITY

Goals and Performance

By several measures, Vancity's performance has been very good in recent years. Membership, for example, has grown by approximately five per cent as compared to its competitors, who have grown at three per cent per year.[6] Growth is essential, in both dollars and members, since this enables Vancity to create closer and stronger ties to its local communities. Further, while employee turnover has been high at certain points in the past (reaching a peak of 16 per cent in 1999), turnover was still less than at other BC credit unions.[7] In addition, Vancity had a higher efficiency ratio (73.6 per cent) relative to its bank competitors (by 15 to 20 points). This ratio reflects Vancity's "Triple Bottom Line" approach to business.

As a credit union, the main focus at Vancity is not on profits, as is the case at other financial institutions, but rather it is on creating a positive experience for the members, employees and communities, i.e., "People before Profits."[8] Vancity's earned profits are distributed to its members through its Shared Success Program. Vancity generates its revenues mainly from interest income (interest on mortgages and loans), service charges, foreign exchange fees, building and safety deposit rentals, and fees from insurance, credit cards, loan administration and other fee-generating products (see Exhibit 3).

Vancity's core competencies underpin its approach to member and employee experience, and its commitment to the local community. In the pursuit of these elements, Vancity has created a level of differentiation that allows it to sell financial services in a very competitive marketplace.[9]

Membership Experience—Customer Service

In 2002, Vancity had a remarkable year, ranking the highest in a Customer Service Index survey by Synovate, surpassing major banks and other credit unions. "Service excellence is always the highest priority with the Vancity board of directors who are elected by our members. It is that consistency and support which empowers us to ingrain service into everything we do."[10]

To meet customers' changing demands for financial products, Vancity had developed the ability to effectively and flexibly bundle its more than 200 products. In this way, it could offer the same types of accounts offered at other financial institutions at a competitive cost, bundling products to meet specific occupational groups, such as teachers or health-care workers. Vancity also offered specialized, innovative products, including Living by Water loans, Clean Air Car loans, (International) Community Investment Deposits (CIDs) and the EnviroFund VISA Card. The Living by Water loan is a joint program with Vancity's CID to help residents improve the shoreline and salmon streams. The CID investments are unique to Vancity: they are term deposits that yield a lower interest rate, but the funds are used to improve the local or global communities. Through emerging data mining techniques, Vancity's marketing department is using its

---

[6] Five Year Business Plan: 2003 Business Plan, p.4.

[7] Vancity 2000–01 Accountability Report, www.vancity.com/Community/About Us/Corporate Reports/2000–01, p.29.

[8] Email interview with Dave Mowat, CEO of Vancity, November 11, 2003.

[9] Ibid.

[10] "Vancity Beats Out Big Banks for Top Spot in Customer Service in BC," www.vancity.com/menuId/53218, accessed November 10, 2003.

improving customer knowledge to create new bundles of products and innovative services to facilitate competitive differentiation.

Vancity is also the owner of Citizens Bank, a full-service electronic bank, which was founded in 1997 and provides its members with financial services through the Internet and by telephone. Vancity along with two other credit unions launched Credential Securities, a full-service brokerage firm, in 1995, a wholly owned subsidiary of Credit Union Central of Canada. The company also purchased Real Assets Investment Management Inc. and has taken the initiative to provide its members with investment products from companies that are socially and environmentally responsible. The other subsidiaries of Vancity include Vancity Insurance Services Ltd., Vancity Investment Management, Vancity Enterprises, Vancity Capital Corporation, as well as the arms-length Vancity Community Foundation. These various operations allow Vancity to offer a more complete array of financial services to satisfy customer demands.

Employee Experience

A critical resource that has underpinned Vancity's success resides in its human capital. In fact, in 2003, Vancity was named by *Maclean's* magazine one of the Top 100 Canadian Employers in Canada.[11] While Vancity's turnover rate reached as high as 16 per cent, its employee retention rate was favorable as compared to other credit unions[12] leading to a lower cost of hiring. To improve the employee retention rate, the Human Resource Department had created various programs to motivate employees and to increase their dedication to the organization. Some of these initiatives include Empowerment, Recognition Night, Mount Kudos, special leaves to attain other personal goals, Living Leadership, and Profit-Sharing programs. Empowerment provided employees with greater involvement in day-to-day business decisions that relate to customer service. Mount Kudos was an online system designed to recognize various achievements on a daily basis. Further, Recognition Night was a yearly party intended to create a collective sense of value and accomplishment which, in turn, promoted employee commitment to the organization.

The structure of Vancity was hierarchical, much like most financial institutions. It was, however, somewhat flatter which allowed for faster communication between departments and levels in the organization. The company frequently asked for feedback, suggestions, and comments from employees to involve them in various decision-making processes. For example, Vancity had developed a survey tool called "Employee Engagement" through which the corporation gained feedback on employee sentiment towards the company and elicited feedback on how the work environment could be improved. Past surveys found that the influential drivers of employee engagement are "culture and values, leadership and opportunity."[13] The information generated through these efforts helped the human resource department to devise programs and strategies for employee attraction and retention and their relatively flat organizational structure allowed for faster implementation of new ideas.

Vancity executives also formed "Corporate Teams" to deal with the various issues ranging from employee engagement to retail and business member satisfaction. There were 19 different targets and actions plans set out in the five-year plan, in which individual members of the executive team had been assigned. The respective executive

---

[11] "Vancity," www.vancity.com, accessed November 5, 2003.
[12] Vancity 2000–01 Accountability Report, p.29.
[13] Five Year Business Plan: 2003 Business Plan (internal document), Vancity Intranet, p.21.

member then put together a team or focus group to deal with the issue at hand. This practice brought together employees from all departments to contribute their skills, expertise, competencies and relationships to devise plans to achieve Vancity's goals. Again, involving employees and members promoted a sense of belonging and achievement.

New information technologies (e.g. intranet and e-mail) were implemented to enable quick exchange of information about problems, opportunities, successes, activities and decisions, which, in turn, allowed employees to engage more efficiently with members and to provide outstanding service. Furthermore, at least twice a year, members of the executive team would visit the branch or department to meet with the employees, share experiences, launch new products or programs, and share the success of the organization. Meeting with the executive team made employees feel more a part of the organization and its strategic direction.

Community Involvement

In 2002, as in previous years, Vancity donated to its local communities a "success bonus," i.e., 30 per cent of its net profits. They also awarded its second annual $1 million grant, this time to the Vancouver East Cultural Community. In 2003, the award went to WISH (Women's Information Safe House). This award was initiated in 2001 to provide an organization in Vancity's community, decided by membership vote, with significant funds to finance its own projects. Vancity is also founder of the successful Youth Credit Union program, in which local schools operate a credit union under the leadership teachers and Vancity employees, to instill in students the value of saving for the future.

The majority of Vancity's suppliers were local companies as support of businesses in the community considered a major factor in its purchasing decision. By purchasing locally, Vancity may save the costs of transportation and, in turn, deepen community relationships. Vancity also chose its suppliers based on their employee relations, their contributions to their own communities and evidence of their commitment to environmental responsibility. "We aim to be fair and ethical in our dealings with suppliers while also making our purchasing decisions efficient and cost-effective."[14]

Through initiative such as these, Vancity's brand recognition had become a critical strategic resource. Both members and non-members in the Vancouver community recognize Vancity's name and logo. As one non-member put it, "every time I turn my head, I see the Vancity logo (in our community). You really deserve and have earned the name Vancity, because this city would not be the same without you."[15] Vancity had developed a reputation on which it had become possible to capitalize.

The Changing Competitive Terrain—The Role of Information Technology

A key strategic issue for Vancity, and others in the financial services industry was the clear shift away from the traditional business model that had centred on branches and tellers. Further, the major banks had historically focused primarily on the delivery of basic products while the credit unions had emphasized greater service (see Exhibit 2); customer preferences had forced a shift by all parties to greater service, broader product

---

[14] Vancity Web site: Corporate Reports: 2000–01 Accountability Report—Commitment Six, www.vancity.com/menuId/53218, accessed November 10, 2003.
[15] Vancity Five Year Plan 2004-2008 (internal document) p.1.

offerings and flexibility. At the same time, customers were demanding lower transaction costs, forcing financial institutions to maintain a keen focus on cost-efficiency.

A major trend in the financial services industry had been electronic banking. When banking through personal computers was introduced in the 1980s, forecasters predicted it would revolutionize the way people handle their personal finances. Optimistic industry analysts at the time posited that, by the year 2000, nearly everyone in North America would bank online. The e-commerce revolution largely failed to materialize—at least, not at the pace that was first envisioned. Nonetheless, the Internet has created great change in the banking industry in recent years.

Companies from outside the traditional banking industry (e.g. supermarket chains) have taken advantage of the low barriers to entry, made possible by the Internet, to encroach into the banking and bill presentment marketplace. Meanwhile, new legislation had opened the door to competition from brokers, insurance companies and other financial service competitors, all of whom were fighting banks for their customers.

Estimates vary for the numbers using home banking options today. Data from eMarketer's eBanking Report[16] indicated that that the number of online banking consumers in North America will steadily grow from three million in 2000 to more than 18 million by 2004. Further, Jupiter Media Metrix[17] estimates that 95 per cent of all North American homes would be running their accounts online by 2010. The report goes on to say that traffic to all banks grew 77.6 per cent between July 2000 and July 2001, compared with overall Web traffic, which increased only 19.8 per cent in the same period. Further, Celent Communications[18] surveyed people in the generation X age group (people born between 1966 and 1981) and found that 67 per cent of those that do not have a financial planner intended to look for one online and, of those respondents who already had financial planners, 47 per cent indicated that they preferred to communicate with their planners online. According to Harris Interactive's YouthPulse study,[19] Generation Y (people born between 1982 and 1995—the second largest generation in history) consider digital technology no more intimidating than a toaster and would likely conduct all their future financial business, from checking and investments to mortgages and insurance, online. Taken together, these trends clearly indicated that online banking is becoming an increasingly potent force in the financial services business.

In addition to these online trends, the ways in which people were interacting with online financial information is changing. Increasingly, people were accessing computer banking via programs such as Quicken, through intermediary servers. This allowed people to find a house loan from one bank and a car loan or insurance deal from another. This trend could turn banks into little more than wholesalers of financial services. Salomon Brothers, the Wall Street investment house, recently suggested that "this may not sever an institution's ties with its retail customer base, but will weaken the ties, lower brand value and steal much of the remaining profits." In this scenario, customers would have a far stronger relationship with a personal finance program than with a single financial institution. In fact, Intuit, the owner of Quicken, had been swamped by banking transactions and had recently agreed to sell its online banking and bill paying service to CheckFree for $227.6 million. Like VISA Interactive, CheckFree will become a major force in the financial industry, providing home banking and bill payment services to 180 financial institutions and to more than a million customers.

---

[16] www.emarketer.com

[17] www.comscore.com

[18] www.celent.com

[19] www.harrisinteractive.com

At the same time margins will come under sharper pressure with banking commissions and other charges are falling rapidly in every area. These new technologies threatened to make traditional client relationships redundant in the mass retail market, as more people become detached from their area branches and bank managers. Banks were responding by moving upmarket as fast as they could, chasing premium "relationships" in private banking and corporate finance sectors. Differentiating through service rather than just price was expected to be a key feature of corporate banking throughout to 2010. These premium customers, however, had not been within the traditional domain of credit unions.

Many of the established players in the financial services business were faced with several huge and urgent challenges. The first challenge was making the significant investments in both people and infrastructure to enable e-commerce. The second was that of winding down and closing branches with the attendant social, political, and image issues. At the same time, all companies were forced to deal with the complex post-merger problems of culture, product and information technology integration. Many of the larger banks were finding that their capacity to evolve was limited by these post-merger issues.

One response by Vancity to the increased demand for and usefulness of information technologies has been the creation of the MRM (Member Relationship Management) system. This is a software system that was created to enable sales staff to efficiently sell products the member(s) need and to create a seamless organization view for the credit union's members. This tool replaced the four or five databases that stored information about members' interactions. The information was used jointly with the marketing department as a communication stream to feed information about potential marketing campaigns to members' entitled in the current campaign for selling opportunities. With all the profile information in one location, employees have more knowledge and competence in responding when making their outbound calls regarding mortgage and term retentions, loan applications, follow-up calls or member inquiries. This harnessing of information enabled the identification of opportunities, the deepening of relationships and further extended service levels.

Since technologies are often very expensive, some credit unions had begun to share various solutions to reduce the cost of developing and managing them alone. For example, for a period of time, Vancity shared Inventure Solutions with Surrey Metro Savings Credit Union to share expertise on technology-based services and to reduce costs. In addition, Vancity has one call centre for both Vancity and Citizen members, which reduced costs by serving members of both establishments. Further, as an added value to members, credit unions shared their automated teller machine (ATM) networks so that members could make deposits and withdrawals from any credit union ATM without service charges—in contrast to the major chartered banks that levied fees on all but their own customers.

THE WAY FORWARD

Vancity's traditional approach has been to provide high levels of customer service. However, technological changes (e.g. rising percent of houses with computers, invention of Internet banking) and social changes (e.g. busier lifestyles, increasing acceptance of technology) appear to be leading to changes in the requirements of "service." Whereas service was once thought to be one-on-one attention, it is now moving to include the concepts of convenience and ease of use through ATMs, Internet services, etc. Unfortunately for Vancity and other credit unions, the major banks may be better positioned to satisfy the emerging demands for online services because these demands require large initial investments in computer infrastructure and specialized personnel. Provincially-based credit unions are at a disadvantage because they are simply smaller and, therefore, have fewer resources to devote to technology installation and maintenance. Further, the large banks have a larger base of customers over which investments can be averaged.

Growth may be one solution to this competitive threat; unfortunately, credit unions are limited in their prospects for growth because they are not allowed to expand outside their home provinces. Further, significant growth could compromise their primary focus—that of personal service—without guaranteeing an improvement in customer convenience through improved technological capability. Notwithstanding the credit union's dilemma, the major banks on the other hand are becoming more like credit unions by offering more products and improving customer service through customer relation management. Banks are moving up the pyramid from being the "nuts and bolts" of banking to providing customized services, creating and achieving social value-based approaches, and gaining respect in their respective communities.

If Vancity takes up the challenge of growth, they can expand via new locations in suitable geographic locations (i.e. increase their market share) or attempt to increase their product offering (i.e. grow their "wallet share" per customer). To grow through new branches is capital intensive, however, as it costs $400,000 to $1.4 million to open a new branch (building, training, equipment, and supplies) plus an additional $1.4 million of operating capital. One risk of this tactic is that it could cause them to become overextended, both financial and managerially, without necessarily creating additional value at the new locations.

By competing on technological capability, Vancity would risk the daunting prospect of locking horns with the major banks. In addition, any dramatic move to expand and reinforce its traditional service offerings through new products and locations in British Columbia will certainly attract the attention of Coast Capital, Vancity's rival (see Exhibit 5). Thus, no easy remedies exist and any solution to their competitive dilemmas entail a number of risks and tradeoffs.

Exhibit 1   Membership and Number of Locations

	Credit Unions		Locations		Members	
	1999	2003	1999	2003	1999	2003
British Columbia	76	61	333	340	1,434,632	1,509,221
Canada	2,034	1,335	3,636	3,572	10,240,773	10,484,028
Total	2,110	1,396	3,969	3,912	11,675,405	11,993,249

Source: www.cucentral.ca

Exhibit 2   Traditional Service Differences Between Credit Unions and Banks

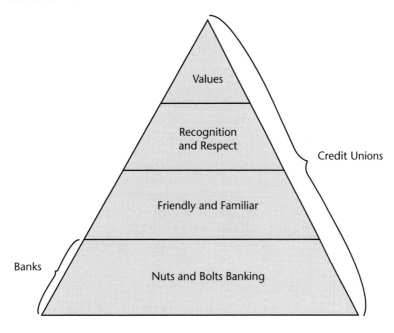

Exhibit 3   Vancity's Sources of Revenue ($000s)

	2002	2001	2002	2001
Interest Income				
Residential Mortgages	$259,314	$283,320	52.01%	53.55%
Commercial Mortgages	55,939	49,321	11.22%	9.32%
Other Loans	105,693	110,955	21.20%	20.97%
Cash and Securities	19,819	26,996	3.98%	5.10%
Total Interest Income	440,765	470,592	88.41%	88.94%
Other Income				
Account Service Fees	$ 17,094	$ 17,131	3.43%	3.24%
Building Rentals	813	805	0.16%	0.15%
Credit Card Fees	7,922	7,684	1.59%	1.45%
Foreign Exchange	5,731	8,392	1.15%	1.59%
Insurance Fees	5,696	5,442	1.14%	1.03%
Loan Administration Fees	4,055	4,551	0.81%	0.86%
Loan Application Fees	1,481	2,636	0.30%	0.50%
Safety Deposit Box Rentals	1,085	968	0.22%	0.18%
Trust & Wealth Management Fees	6,958	6,495	1.40%	1.23%
Other	6,953	4,393	1.39%	0.83%
Total Other Income	$ 57,788	$ 58,497	11.59%	11.06%
Total Income	$498,553	$529,089		

Source: Company 2002 Annual Report, pp. 24–25.

Exhibit 4   Vancity's Financial Statements, for the year ending December 31, 2002
            (1998 to 2002) ($000s)

	2002	2001	2000	1999	1998
Assets					
Cash and Securities	$ 943,270	$ 618,455	$ 649,715	$ 604,078	$ 550,722
Loans	7,071,926	6,706,487	6,054,379	5,639,893	5,212,914
Other Assets	187,624	186,947	185,415	167,007	161,873
Total Assets	$8,202,820	$7,511,889	$6,889,509	$6,410,978	$5,925,509
Liabilities and Members' Equity					
Deposits and Equity Shares	$7,591,664	$6,744,487	$6,191,577	$5,673,801	$5,359,291
Debentures and Loans Payable	53,000	250,315	221,759	309,645	187,710
Other Liabilities	219,514	218,016	203,029	172,771	147,489
Retained Earnings	338,642	299,071	273,144	254,761	231,019
Total Liabilities and Members' Equity	$8,202,820	$7,511,889	$6,889,509	$6,410,978	$5,925,509
Statement of Earnings					
Net Interest Income	$ 230,379	$ 178,837	$ 157,799	$ 150,381	$ 149,751
Charge for Impairment of Loans	(32,220)	(17,141)	(17,742)	(7,407)	(5,516)
Other Income	57,788	58,497	59,458	55,362	52,282
Net Interest and Other Income	255,947	220,193	199,515	198,336	196,517
Salaries and Employee Benefits	104,285	92,745	81,141	81,161	78,415
Other Operating Expenses	83,997	85,286	82,483	76,996	77,841
Total Operating Expenses	188,282	178,031	163,624	158,157	156,256
Earnings from Operations	67,665	42,162	35,891	40,179	40,261
Distributions to Community and Members	13,625	8,999	7,242	7,927	7,967
Income Taxes	14,469	7,236	7,648	8,510	8,194
Net Earnings for the Year	$ 39,571	$ 25,927	$ 21,001	$ 23,742	$ 24,100

Source: Company 2002 Annual Report, p.22.

Exhibit 5   Background Information on Coast Capital Savings

Coast Capital Savings is the result of two recent mergers, Richmond Savings and Pacific Coast Savings merged in 2000 to form Coast Capital Savings, and then Coast Capital Savings and Surrey Metro Savings merged in June of 2002.

Facts About Coast Capital Savings

- Established: December 31, 2000
- Founding Credit Unions Established: Pacific Coast Savings 1940; Richmond Savings 1948; Surrey Metro Savings 1947
- Rank: Second largest credit union in Canada
- Members: 300,000
- Assets: $6.4 billion
- Head Office: Surrey, BC
- Employees: 2,000
- Branches: 42 branches: 30 in Lower Mainland and 12 on Vancouver Island
- ATMs: 76 across the Lower Mainland, Fraser Valley and southern Vancouver Island

Subsidiaries

- Coast Capital Insurance Services Ltd.
- U-Select Financial and Insurance Service Ltd.
- Coast Capital Real Estate Services Ltd.
- Coast Appraisals
- Coast Capital Investments

Distinctions

- Ethics in Action Community Care Award.
- YM-YWCA Women Of Distinction Award
- Community Champion Award
- Victoria Chamber of Commerce Business Leadership Award
- CBSR GoodCompany Award
- A Caring Company Award
- Canada's 50 Best Managed Companies List
- Solicitor General Emergency Preparedness Award

Community Involvement

Coast Capital Savings' community investments supports causes in the areas of education, life skills, advancement of youth, health, wellness and arts/heritage through the Rising Tide and ABLED loans.

Case 28

CQUAY Technologies Corp.

It was April 2004, and Calvin McElroy had just closed the CQUAY ("seek way") financials for the quarter. A year earlier, the board had asked McElroy to shape the company into an acquisition target over the next 18 to 24 months. There were no imminent acquisition discussions, and recent customer traction and the sales pipeline seemed to merit raising growth capital instead of following the acquisition-focused plan. McElroy wanted to keep his stockholders and board happy by executing the plan they had given him, but he did not want to jeopardize possible customer growth. If he refocused the plan, McElroy feared it might change acquisition opportunities. Without further contracts, the existing cash would sustain the company for only another six to eight months. McElroy thought the most likely outcome was to sell the company, but he needed to make the company more attractive. He planned to present options and a recommendation to the board of directors later that month.

THE COMPANY

CQUAY Technologies Corporation ("CQUAY") was a privately held Canadian company with offices in Toronto, Calgary and Washington, D.C. CQUAY marketed a patented location intelligence engine, called Common Ground®[1] to enterprise customers, software developers and systems integrators. The company's technology was designed for an emerging, multibillion-dollar segment of the spatial information management (SIM) market, as defined by International Data Corporation (IDC).

Richard Ivey School of Business
The University of Western Ontario

Kevin K. Boeh prepared this case under the supervision of Professor Paul W. Beamish solely to provide material for class discussion. The authors do not intend to illustrate either effective or ineffective handling of a managerial situation. The authors may have disguised certain names and other identifying information to protect confidentiality.

[1]Common Ground is a registered trademark of CQUAY Technologies Corp.

CQUAY History and Board of Directors

CQUAY's predecessor company was founded in 1995 as a data management consultancy with customers in the telecom, utility, and oil and gas industries. The projects undertaken by the company evolved into complex Web-enabled databases and applications. Management identified an opportunity, in 1998, to jointly develop a technology platform to manage address and mapping information with a major Canadian telecommunications company. An initial Cdn$1.2 million was secured for the initial technology research and application prototype. This funding was provided by this telecommunications customer, as well as profits from the company's consulting business and certain private investors close to the company. In 2001, the company raised Cdn$5.6 million in an external venture capital round of financing. In January 2002, the company entered into a marketing and implementation agreement with Telus Corporation, the second largest Canadian telecommunications company. In March 2002, the company achieved a significant milestone by demonstrating its Common Ground location services platform using an open location services (OpenLS) compliant interface. The company was the first in the world to demonstrate an online geo-coding and map portrayal service based on this important new specification. In 2002, this predecessor company became illiquid and was unable to raise additional growth capital in the depressed capital markets environment.

Founded in 2002, CQUAY secured its technology, patent interests, trademarks and team from the predecessor company and thereafter offered commercial products and services in Canada and the United States.

A year before, in early 2003, McElroy and his board of directors had decided to pursue a strategy that would prepare the company for its eventual sale. It was agreed that then-current market and economic conditions constrained the possible valuation and likelihood of a near-term acquisition outcome, and, as such, the company should instead lay the groundwork for its sale in 18 to 24 months. The tactics laid out for the company included:

1. keeping operational costs minimal;
2. minimizing future-focused research and development expenditure;
3. securing three to five lead customers;
4. creating a recurring revenue stream;
5. validating the pricing models; and
6. keeping the company structure flexible, if not virtual, so as to facilitate a merger or acquisition.

Industry—The Business Problem

Business and government organizations had created a massive and rapidly growing amount of information in databases, Web pages and files. Inaccurate or outdated information were negatively affecting operational efficiency, customer satisfaction and business decision-making. In areas of public safety and national security, these costs were substantially higher and could include non-financial costs. For many, data quality had become a cornerstone of organizational efficiency.

> By 2005, Fortune 1000 enterprises will lose more money in operational inefficiency due to data quality issues than they will spend on data warehouse and CRM initiatives combined.
>
> The Gartner Group

One of the most pervasive data quality problems related to address information. An "address" was commonly attached as an "attribute" to computerized records about people, places, and things. An estimated 80 per cent of all databases and 15 per cent to 20 per cent of all Web pages in the world contained address data. Address errors and discrepancies were common due to:

- The lack of a standard format for storing address data;
- Duplication of address data in a myriad of systems, in varied, incompatible formats;
- "Free form" data entry fields in applications and databases, with little or no validation;
- Spelling and transposition errors made and liberties taken during data entry (e.g. "West Pender Street" versus "Pender St. W"); and
- Constantly changing "real world" data due to new building construction, building subdivision, boundary changes and street name changes.

Address problems were universal and a major issue for most organizations. Technologies and tools that improved address data quality were in high demand.

> Address data errors alone cost U.S. businesses US$611 billion a year in postage, printing and staff costs related to re-work.
>
> The Data Warehousing Institute

In addition to data quality issues, information technology (IT) organizations were faced with a major challenge in linking and integrating disparate data sources to support many business processes. The integration of two or more databases required a "common key" to join records. This key could be a customer name, customer identification (ID) number, or asset ID number as long as the reference was unique and consistent. An address match was seemingly another obvious key. Unfortunately, due to errors, discrepancies and the lack of a standard format, address fields were not reliable as a unique key for data integration.

The Location Dimension

Location is an abstract concept associated with:

1. Places and things (e.g. buildings, oil wells, cellular towers, street intersections and other physical structures);
2. Geographic areas with boundaries (e.g. cities, countries, postal codes, sales territories or census tracts); or
3. Positions (e.g. the latitude and longitude coordinates for a mobile device or vehicle).

Most things have a location. A location is simply the point or extent of space that is occupied by a person, place or thing. As such, a location always has geographic context and dimensions. Location intelligence is about understanding where locations are in the real world and knowing how one location relates to another in a geographic sense.

An address record contained numbers or words that identified a place and referred to its associated boundaries (e.g. building numbers as well as street, city, postal, state or province, and country names or codes). However, these were simply location references and did not encode, enable or provide location intelligence.

Understanding the geographic relationship between places and boundaries was important. Those relationships were hard-coded in databases by replicating location references within address records. This approach was inefficient and caused data quality problems whenever a boundary changed. McElroy's idea was that humans have spatial intelligence and enough geographic knowledge to look at an address record and understand location context. Even if not familiar with the street-level address, the reference to "Canada," "USA" or "Europe" enabled a rudimentary level of location intelligence. In comparison, the average computer did not understand that White Plains, New York, was in the United States, and that the state of New York was adjacent to Canada.

An address referred to a unique location. Therefore, address data quality and location intelligence were inter-related. These relationships between addresses and locations were important to certain industries and to organizations with geographically dispersed operations. For example:

- Telecom: determining available network capabilities for a particular service address;
- Wireless Telecom Carriers: determining tax zones and tariffs for telephone calls and services;
- Utilities: ensuring valid addresses and postal service formats on bills;
- Call Centres: entering valid addresses on orders or trouble tickets;
- Oil and Gas: retrieving public and private data regarding a geographic area of interest;
- Retailers: associating customer locations to stores and service centres;
- Public Safety: identifying geographic patterns associated with emergencies and events;
- Marketing: linking demographic, census and lifestyle data to customer sales records;
- Technical Services: tracking staff, equipment and parts in regard to field service calls;
- Financial Services: using address as a key to create a single view of a customer; and
- Real Estate: buying, selling and renting based on location.

Virtually all information technology (IT) systems contained location references but lacked location intelligence. Computer system users had access to computerized address records but had to use manual methods to determine location.

Until the advent of CQUAY's Common Ground product, the only way to organize, search for and analyse business information based on location context was to extract data from operational systems and upload them into a mapping system. This approach was costly, technically complicated and raised many concerns about data security and integrity. As such, less than five per cent of knowledge workers used a location-enabled application or analysis tool that was dynamically linked to proprietary business data sources.

> The real value of location technology lies in better customer relationships and improved business processes.
>
> IDC

One of the three or four big trends in software is location-enabled applications.

Bill Gates, Microsoft

The CQUAY Common Ground Solution

Over US$5 million had been invested in developing this innovative system that solved the address data quality problem while at the same time enabling IT staff to simply "plug in" location intelligence to existing applications or system. Common Ground was based on the notion that a unique "key" in databases, application systems, files and Internet content could be used to encode location context. The goal was that such a key could uniquely identify a place along with its location in the world.

Research into this idea led to a breakthrough concept called a "location object." In Common Ground, locations were modeled as intelligent "objects." The location objects incorporated a robust addressing model supporting 11 different methods (e.g. civic (street) address, aliases (Empire State Building), municipal survey (lot/block/plan), section/township/range). The object model also incorporated location context. As such, each place could "respond" to a range of address queries, "know" where it was in the world and "understand" its geographic relationships with other location objects.

Common Ground could be used as a master repository to store and maintain the valid locations that mattered to an organization. Customers could register the locations of buildings, assets (e.g. oil wells, cell towers), or boundaries (e.g. geopolitical, taxation, sales territory or serving area boundaries) in the Common Ground Location Registry.

The platform also incorporated a patented index method, where every registered location was assigned a unique key called a Universal Spatial Locator™ (USL). The USL provided the link between an external data source or application and the location intelligence contained in Common Ground. Common Ground, along with the Location Registry and USLs, served as a location intelligence engine that understood location context and the relationships among any registered locations.

A location intelligence engine was similar to a search engine like Google™. A search engine registered and cross-referenced key words, in Web pages, to an associated URL or Internet address. Common Ground registered and cross-referenced "location references" in database records, Web pages and files to the associated USL. The platform provided a secure, centralized, location-smart index to widely distributed data sources (see Exhibit 1).

The Common Ground platform came bundled with a subscription to high-quality mapping and address data for the customer's geographic area of interest. This simplified deployment as well as ongoing updates and maintenance. The engine and its location data were licensed to enterprise customers or online application service providers. The platform was based on highly scalable Web services architecture and used standard XML-based interfaces (compatible with IBM, SUN Microsystems and Microsoft) to link securely, through firewalls, to other applications and systems.

A Java-based Web Services Kit (WSK) enabled easy and rapid integration with existing customer relationship management (CRM), enterprise resource planning (ERP), asset or inventory management (AM/IM), workforce management (WFM) systems, or custom developed Web applications, in order to:

- Match, cleanse and reconcile address data discrepancies within existing systems;
- Provide dynamic address validation and address standardization (e.g. U.S. Postal Service and Canada Post standards) to external applications (e.g. Siebel CRM);
- Tag enterprise databases, Web pages and files with USLs;
- Pass a USL from one system to another as an address proxy to avoid propagating address errors through mechanized interfaces;

- Register the places, things and boundaries used by the enterprise within the Location Registry;
- Index, integrate, correlate, search, analyse and visualize widely distributed data sources based on location-centric or geographic criteria (e.g. within a boundary, nearest, within five miles, adjacent); and
- Dynamically associate the real-time position of wireless devices and fleet vehicles to places, things and boundaries registered with Common Ground, thereby linking mobile resources to back office enterprise applications.

CQUAY generated revenue in four ways:

1. Software licence fees for the Common Ground® platform;
2. Recurring annual software maintenance and support fees;
3. Recurring annual location data subscription services; and
4. Professional services to assist customers in implementing the platform.

CQUAY was the first company to integrate tools for address data management and quality assurance with location intelligence capabilities in a single platform.

The CQUAY Value Proposition

McElroy felt the potential for Common Ground was enormous. It cut across virtually all industries, business functions, processes and application systems. An estimated 80 per cent of all databases in the world contained either address or some other location reference. These estimates did not include Web content and the billions of electronic documents that had been created by organizations. The problems and costs associated with address data quality were well understood by most organizations and were a cause of great concern. Common Ground could help customers:

- Reduce operational costs through reducing address data errors;
- Increase revenue through cross-selling, based on better customer information and knowledge;
- Improve customer satisfaction through reduced errors on orders and invoices, more predictable and reliable delivery and installation timeframes and faster responses to inquiries with more accurate information;
- Achieve strategic advantage through insights provided by the "lens" of location intelligence;
- Improve business decision-making through access to more accurate information; and
- Optimize the management of mobile assets, equipment and staff resources by rationalizing workload and task assignments based on location context.

Client Case Studies

Bell West Inc., a division of Bell Canada, was experiencing a 30 per cent customer cancellation rate on new service orders caused by address data errors and an inability to accurately associate a customer location to network boundaries and associated telecom facilities. The company implemented Common Ground and integrated the engine with Bell West's existing Siebel CRM, Metasolv (equipment inventory and provisioning planning) and data warehouse systems. The project was completed in six months and dramatically reduced order cancellation rates and operating costs, with a return on investment of just over eight months.

The U.S. National Sheriff's Association was implementing a secure, national messaging and information sharing network. Over 500 disparate databases in 220 different organizations were indexed and cross-referenced using Common Ground and USLs. In a subsequent phase, location intelligence was planned to be used to navigate a massive multi-agency and multi-jurisdictional resource directory and to generate alerts and notification lists based on location context (e.g. all agencies within 500 miles of an emergency or incident).

The Market and Competition

Systems with location intelligence were not new. According to Daratech, the global Geographic Information Systems (GIS) market size was approximately US$7 billion, including software, map data, related hardware and consulting services. However, 75 per cent of this revenue was attributed to back-office engineering systems in telecom and government organizations. IDC had identified a US$1.5 billion spatial information management (SIM) market (software only) that was very fragmented and had three segments:

- Traditional GIS and Mapping Software: Focused on engineering users, characterized as mature, saturated and dominated by established vendors, such as Intergraph, ESRI and Autodesk with growth rates of two per cent to five per cent per year;

- Web Mapping Services: Currently less than five per cent of total SIM revenue, viewed as a nascent but potentially large market that had consolidated into a battle between Microsoft's MapPoint and AOL's MapQuest services; and

- Spatially enabled Business Support Systems (BSS): An emerging high-growth segment, projecting 30 per cent to 60 per cent annualized growth to US$1.2 billion in software by 2006, without a dominant player. This market extended to support mobile applications as well.

According to IDC and other industry experts, traditional GIS and mapping software vendors had been unsuccessful at moving into the Web mapping and emerging location-enabled BSS segments. The high-growth BSS segment was projected to overtake the traditional GIS market within three years. CQUAY was exclusively focused on this SIM market segment and its extension into "mobilized" applications. Common Ground, as a master repository and Web services platform, provided a complementary capability to data quality tools from companies like First Logic, Group 1, Trillium, QAS and Ascential, as well as integration technologies from companies like WebMethods, BEA, Vitria and TIBCO. There were perhaps 5,000 to 7,000 companies or government agencies in North America that had licensed software products from these companies that could also benefit from location technology. An average licence price of US$250,000 per customer supported the projected US$1.2 billion market identified by IDC.

Data quality tool vendors were starting to augment address data with latitude/longitude coordinates through a technique called "geo-coding" but did not offer an engine for location-centric data indexing, integration and search. Online mapping services could resolve a building number on a street to a valid "address range" only and could show the place on a map but had limited knowledge of "real world" places, things, or boundaries (e.g. customer or facilities data). See Exhibit 2 for a summary of market competition.

CQUAY Intellectual Capital

In August of 2003, CQUAY was granted a broad patent by the United States Patent and Trademark Office (Number 6,611,751) for the USL concept. The Location Object model and technology platform had required US$5 million to develop the proprietary technology. The robust address model (not duplicated by any of the traditional mapping or GIS vendors, nor by Oracle or IBM) included substantial intellectual property created in a joint venture research project with TELUS Communications.

CQUAY Marketing Strategy

Virtually any application, database, Web site or document with location references could be parsed and tagged with USLs and enhanced with Common Ground Web services. However, CQUAY planned to focus on the telecom and utility markets, specifically on supporting business areas and applications:

- Applications: CRM, WFM, and AM/IM were large and growing enterprise application segments. Users recognized address data problems as well as the lack of location intelligence in current solutions. These areas also represented cross-industry market extension potential;

- Industry: Telecom and utility companies had been early adopters of CRM, WFM, and AM/IM applications and, as users of traditional GIS systems, also recognized the value of location intelligence. Wireless carriers were starting to leverage the power of location-based services; and

- Relationships: The CQUAY principals, board of directors and advisors had extensive experience and relationships within the telecom and utility marketplaces.

CQUAY's market entry and development strategy involved three key elements:

- Direct Sales to Enterprise Customers: Direct sales, supported by consulting and systems integration (SI) partners, were used to sell and implement Common Ground for enterprise customers. A potential customer's current investment in systems encouraged relationships with certain independent software vendors (ISVs) and SI firms. The direct sales program was supported by seminar and trade show marketing as well as by analyst and media tours;

- Leverage ISV Alliances: CQUAY used its enterprise customer success stories to build support from ISVs for collaborative development and co-marketing agreements. Through these partnerships CQUAY leveraged the ISV direct sales forces as a channel; and

- Enterprise Application SI Channel: CQUAY planned to recruit the implementation partners of ISVs to extend the reach of its direct marketing efforts.

McElroy thought that success in the CRM/WFM/AM in the telecom and utility spaces would lead to a horizontal extension into other verticals, by leveraging the same ISV and channel partnerships. The successful integration of Common Ground with a CRM, WFM or AM solution would lead to projects involving other applications such as data warehouse, ERP, supply chain management, workflow, document management or wireless applications.

A secondary, but high-profile market opportunity existed in public safety under the auspices of Homeland Security in the United States. CQUAY had secured a significant contract as part of a consortium bid in the United States. CQUAY planned to leverage this in direct sales and marketing, as well as SI partnerships within the state and federal government markets, with an emphasis on Homeland Security and public safety.

CQUAY had also established collaborative marketing relationships with a number of related companies, including:

- Viewpoint Support—A Canadian systems integrator in the telecom and utility markets. Also, the prime contractor on Bell West;
- eLabs—Canadian Billing/CRM software platform vendor, partner on National Sheriff's Association;
- Coronado Group—U.S. federal government-focused systems integrator, with a joint proposal to a major U.S. federal agency;
- Visionquest—Atlanta-based vendor of project information management, with joint proposals to several telecom prospects; and
- UMA Group—A Canadian consulting engineering firm with a joint proposal under development to a large municipal government prospect.

The company was also in early stages of partnering discussions with several other technology and systems integration partners.

The Team

The CQUAY management and technical team had extensive experience in the SIM industry and within the initial target vertical markets. The company's chief executive officer and chairman, Calvin McElroy, had over 24 years of successful sales, operational and executive management experience with companies, including Oracle and Intergraph. Both Oracle and Intergraph were successful marketing traditional SIM technologies in telecom, utility, emergency 911, and public safety markets. Vice-President and Chief Operating Officer Peter Lee, had over 19 years of experience with Intergraph and Enghouse Systems, both companies in the SIM market. The team also included Vice-president of Research and Development and Chief Technical Office David Warren, who had 25 years of experience in similar roles with Intergraph, Encor and Texaco. The executives had worked together with McElroy for several years. All company employees were located in Calgary and Toronto, with a sales office in Washington, D.C. The three key executives plus the technology development team were dedicated staff, but other workers were hired as independent contractors as needed to fulfil customer integration requirements.

Capitalization

CQUAY Technologies Corporation was incorporated in March 2002 and raised US$150,000 in seed capital from management and other founding stockholders. With this seed funding, the company secured the Common Ground technology, patent interests and trademarks in a liquidation sale by the predecessor company. CQUAY had subsequently generated over US$350,000 in positive cash flow from two commercial contracts. In the fiscal year ending March 31, 2004, the company had generated US$1 million in revenue and was slightly profitable (see Exhibit 3). As of December 31, 2003, CQUAY had a total of 78.8 million common shares outstanding and had neither issued nor granted any preferred shares, warrants or options and had no debt.

The Future of CQUAY

Over the past year, McElroy had been able to secure two major customer implementations with a handful more in various stages of discussion. While each new contract generated positive cash flow, he knew that aggressive growth would require additional capital. The predecessor company had intended to grow using private capital until it was large enough to undertake an initial public offering; unfortunately the capital markets were depressed at the time. McElroy and the board that had been newly formed with the refounding of CQUAY decided that the company should instead focus on being bought, since the ability to raise capital was unpredictable. Without further contracts, the existing cash would sustain the company for only another nine to 12 months. McElroy thought the most likely outcome would be to sell the company, but he wanted to ensure he maximized its valuation in the current market environment (see Exhibit 4). McElroy had to decide what to recommend to the board.

Exhibit 1   Location-Centric Data Integration

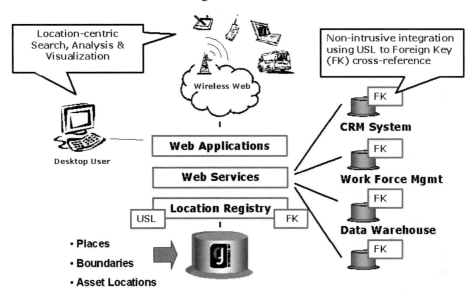

Source: CQUAY Business Plan—March 2004.

Exhibit 2   Competitive Landscape in Location Technology

	CQUAY	Intergraph ESRI MapInfo	Group 1 1st Logic Ascential	MapPoint MapQuest	IBM Oracle
Robust address model	✓		✓		
OGC geometry model	✓	✓			✓
Location index (e.g. USL)	✓				
Web services API	✓	Map	Address	Map	
Enterprise scalability	✓			✓	✓
Location object database	✓				
Address geo-coding	✓	✓	✓	✓	
Bundled address & map data subscription	✓	Map	Address	Map	
Address validation & standardization	✓		✓		

Source: CQUAY Business Plan—March 2004.

Exhibit 3   CQUAY, Inc. Financial Projections (in US$)

Fiscal Year End March 31	2004	2005e	2006e	2007e	2008e
Revenue					
Software licence	$ 312,000	$ 350,000	$ 2,050,000	$ 6,150,000	$14,350,000
Professional services	586,139	500,000	615,000	1,537,500	2,870,000
Data subscription	62,563	110,000	520,000	1,750,000	4,620,000
Maintenance	48,263	95,000	402,500	1,325,000	3,477,500
	1,008,964	1,055,000	3,587,500	10,762,500	25,317,500
Cost of Revenue					
Cost of services	618,837	610,000	1,013,500	2,612,500	5,687,500
Data royalties	11,700	55,000	260,000	875,000	2,310,000
	630,537	665,000	1,273,500	3,487,500	7,997,500
Operating Margin	$ 378,427	$ 390,000	$ 2,314,000	$ 7,275,000	$17,320,000
Operating Expenses					
General and admininstration	203,697	205,000	538,125	968,625	1,519,050
Sales and marketing	17,625	165,000	1,363,250	3,121,125	6,329,375
Research and development	108,987	175,000	538,125	968,625	1,519,050
	330,309	545,000	2,439,500	5,058,375	9,367,475
EBITDA	48,118	(155,000)	(125,500)	2,216,625	7,952,525
Interest, depreciation and taxes	4,358	(2,000)	5,000	789,088	3,192,138
Net Income	$ 43,760	$ (153,000)	$ (130,500)	$ 1,427,537	$ 4,760,387

e = estimates

Summary Balance Sheet, FY March 31, 2004

Cash	$158,188
Accounts receivable	76,861
Other	10,000
Net capital assets	29,942
Total Assets	**$274,991**
Accounts payable	88,112
Other	22,799
Debt	—
Total Liabilities	**$110,910**
Share capital	204,874
Retained earnings	(40,794)
Stockholders' Equity	**$164,080**
Total Liabilities and Stockholders' Equity	**$274,991**

Exhibit 4   Selected Comparable Market Data (as of March 31, 2004) (in US$ millions)

	Ticker	Market Cap	Price	Shares O/S (M)	Cash	Debt	Sales (ttm)	EBITDA (ttm)
Traditional GIS and Mapping Software								
Intergraph	INGR	$ 886	$24.26	37	$ 251	$ —	$ 540	$ 46
ESRI	Private							
Map Info	MAPS	259	12.81	20	36	18	118	13
Business Support Systems (BSS) Providers								
Group 1	GSOF	249	16.36	15	60	1	119	25
First Logic	Private							
Ascential	ASCL	1,294	21.82	59	510	—	212	10
QAS	Private						71	
BSS Integration Technologies								
Webmethods	WEBM	495	9.36	53	120	1	195	(20)
BEA	BEAS	5,180	12.72	407	1,560	766	1,040	228
Vitria	VITR	194	5.88	33	91	—	72	(14)
Tibco	TIBX	1,621	8.17	198	379	53	295	42
Database Vendors								
IBM	IBM	155,210	91.84	1,690	8,500	23,670	91,320	15,190
Oracle	ORCL	$ 62,040	$12.00	5,170	$8,590	$ 172	$10,160	$ 4,100
Web Mapping Services								
MapPoint	Owned by Microsoft							
MapQuest	Owned by Time Warner Inc (America Online)							

ttm = trailing twelve months.

Case 29

Governance Challenges at Good Hands Healthcare (A)

In mid-2000, the board of directors of Good Hands Healthcare (Good Hands), a $3 billion company trading on the New York Stock Exchange, was pondering its current situation. It had become increasingly discouraged by the downward spiral of Good Hands' stock and financial performance and by the continuing explanations of the situation by the company's chief executive officer (CEO), George Jackson. Jackson, who had been Good Hands' CEO for the past 30 years, had attributed the slide of Good Hands' performance to "external factors beyond their control."

The health-care industry was indeed subject to a great deal of environmental factors, not the least of which was the reliance on government reimbursement for services. One of the major issues facing the industry was significant reductions in federal funding of health and eldercare. In addition, the industry had experienced an increasing number of lawsuits filed by patients' families and attention by the media to incidents of poor care, especially of the elderly. Good Hands, one of the largest U.S. nursing home providers, was no exception to these lawsuits and, along with other industry players, was experiencing escalating patient care liability costs.

The board of directors wondered, however, why Good Hands' major competitors, HealthUS, ElderCare and Aged Services, Inc., were able to increase their profitability and market share at the same time that Good Hands' was slipping. After all, wasn't the whole industry affected by the same "external factors"? Was there something else to explain Good Hands' recent troubles beyond these industry threats?

In addition to questions regarding management's assessment of the firm's performance woes, the board of directors of Good Hands was concerned with the absence of a succession plan within the company. While Jackson was recognized as an industry leader, would he be able to stop the current downward spiral and perform a turnaround of the firm? And, if not, who would be able to step into his shoes? The lack of a

Professors Amy Hillman and Marilyn Seymann prepared this case solely to provide material for class discussion. The authors do not intend to illustrate either effective or ineffective handling of a managerial situation. The authors may have disguised certain names and other identifying information to protect confidentiality.

succession plan at Good Hands coupled with no formal internal effort to develop leadership for the future cast an ominous shadow over the future of the company.

The board knew it didn't have a lot of time to waste. Good Hands was sliding precipitously towards bankruptcy. In fact, several of its competitors had already filed Chapter 11, and as a result of their restructuring, they were more nimble than Good Hands to weather the industry threats. The board set its sight on its next meeting, in two months, to address these important issues. All of the board members knew this meeting would be a critical turning point for the future of Good Hands.

THE COMPANY

Good Hands Healthcare was founded as a small nursing home business in 1970, in Brownsville, Texas. Through rapid expansion, the company went public in 1978 and now represented more than 400 facilities in 25 states. Good Hands operated facilities in three areas of operations: 285 nursing homes, 74 assisted living and outpatient facilities, and 47 care units for people with Alzheimer's disease. George Jackson, the current CEO, had founded the business and had served as its president/CEO and chairman of the board for 30 years.

While originally founded as a nursing home company, Good Hands diversified into assisted living and outpatient facilities in the early 1990s and later, in 1995, into care facilities for people with Alzheimer's disease. Nursing home facilities now provided residents with long-term care, including daily skilled nursing and nutritional services, along with the social and recreational services that accompany a long-term residence facility. Pharmacy and medical supplies were also provided to residents. Good Hands saw themselves as an "extension of patients' families." The Good Hands culture had long emphasized that employees treat each resident as they would their own family and that each Good Hands facility was akin to a family community. For example, in 1999, Good Hands began redesigning several of its facilities to reflect the newest trend in nursing homes, home-centric design.

Similarly, assisted living and facilities for people with Alzheimer's disease, while emphasizing a different mix of traditional services, also promoted a communal experience and a loving, caregiving environment. Assisted living centers were targeted at those elderly whose health did not necessitate daily nursing per se, but who were less able to safely live an independent lifestyle. These facilities resembled apartment complexes with a collection of small efficiency-like living spaces where residents could bring their own furniture and belongings. Access in and out of these facilities was not restricted; residents could come and go as they please. Meals were typically offered in communal dining halls or in-suite, while social activities included a full range of classes and excursions outside of the facility. The advantage of these living facilities was that a full-time nursing staff was always on hand should a resident require assistance. Residents were monitored throughout the day. This level of service was in stark contrast to that received by the elderly who lived alone in single-family residences. In addition to the availability of professional nursing help, assisted living centers provided many elderly with social interaction with other residents and the staff, something that was often lacking for elderly living at home.

The facilities for people with Alzheimer's disease, on the other hand, were centers meant to specifically meet the needs of the elderly suffering from the dementia and other indications of Alzheimer's disease. These patients required much more intensive supervision than both the assisted living or nursing home residents and Good Hands' facilities allowed for specialized treatment of these needs. Good Hands saw the need for more specialized care for people with Alzheimer's disease beyond the typical nursing home environment and was rolling out more such facilities as a part of its expansion plan.

By the end of 1999, more than 85 per cent of Good Hands' net operating revenues came from nursing home facilities, with 10 per cent and five per cent coming from assisted living and facilities for people with Alzheimer's disease, respectively. Occupancy of its 406 facilities in 1999 was 86 per cent, with Medicare patients representing 21 per cent of total patient days and 43 per cent of revenue.

Good Hands' facilities were staffed by more than 61,000 employee caregivers. Typically, 30 per cent to 34 per cent of the staff at a given facility were certified, skilled nursing professionals. The remainder were typically staff paid little more than minimum-wage, such as custodians and housekeepers ($7 per hour), aides ($9 per hour) and office personnel, cooks and maintenance workers ($12 per hour). More than 98 per cent of Good Hands' employees were female with an average of a high-school education for non-certified staff. Turnover among Good Hands' employees averaged 80 per cent a year for non-certified staff, and 47 per cent for certified staff, and the company encountered periodic difficulty attracting and retaining registered and licensed nurses, certified nurses' aides and other facility personnel. Approximately 21 per cent of the employees in more than 150 facilities were represented by various labor unions, the largest of which was the AFL-CIO. While relations with these unions had been generally good (Good Hands had not experienced any work stoppages as a result), the unions had commonly targeted Good Hands because of its visible position as one of the largest companies in the U.S. eldercare industry.

Good Hands' financial position had deteriorated in the last three years (see Exhibit 1). Most notably, for each of the previous three years, Good Hands had experienced declining sales growth and net income. In 1999, this loss was 10.3 per cent in sales from the previous year and a loss of $143.7 million in net income. Its competitors' experiences in recent years were much more robust. HealthUS grew sales from 1998 to 1999 by 44.2 per cent despite a drop of 33 per cent in net income, while ElderCare's one-year sales growth was 5.7 per cent with a 90.7 per cent increase in net income. Aged Services, Inc. posted an eight per cent loss in sales over the previous year, but had a total net income of more than $1 billion.

As a result of Good Hands' declining performance, the company was in a critical cash position, with cash at the end of 1999 of only $21 million. The funds needed to sustain its business were provided largely through revolving credit that increased overall short-term borrowing to $173 million. Total debt, on and off balance sheet, had grown by early 2000 to nearly $1 billion, and, along with it, the cost of debt for Good Hands had also risen considerably. This put Good Hands at a substantial disadvantage vis-à-vis its major competitors, HealthUS and Aged Services, Inc., who as a result of coming out of Chapter 11 bankruptcy had restructured their debt and were much less encumbered than Good Hands.

THE ELDERCARE INDUSTRY

Health care and general care for the elderly was a highly regulated industry and a fragmented industry with a significant number of "mom and pop" facilities. While Good Hands Healthcare was one of the largest companies in the industry, and they had the largest share of the nursing home market, this only represented 3.8 per cent of the market. It was estimated that in the also very fragmented assisted-living industry, the top 25 players accounted for only two per cent to five per cent of the market. The leader in the home health-care industry, Sullivan Services, similarly had only four per cent of the market.

Increasing life expectancies and aging baby boomers were driving U.S. revenues for long-term health care. U.S. revenues for long-term health care were estimated to total $225.8 billion by 2003, versus $149.4 billion in 1998. Revenues for nursing homes were expected to rise to $115.4 billion in 2003, versus $87.3 billion in 1998 when home-care revenues were expected to rise to $48.7 billion from $33.2 billion.

Despite the healthy forecasts for growth in revenue, the 1995 National Nursing Home Survey suggested that elderly Americans were reducing their use of nursing home care. The changes from 1985 to 1995 per thousand elderly are illustrative. In 1985, 219.4 per thousand elderly aged 65 to 74 used nursing homes, whereas by 1995, this number dropped to 198.6 per thousand. For ages 75 to 85 this number dropped from 57.5 per thousand to 45.9 per thousand, and for ages 85 and older, from 12.5 to 10.1 per thousand. The gap left by decreasing nursing home use was being filled by alternatives, such as assisted living and home health care.

Health-care service providers were subject to various federal, state and local health-care statutes and regulations. State licenses were required to operate health-care facilities and to participate in government health care funding programs, such as Medicaid and Medicare. Medicaid was operated by individual states, funded by the federal government and designed to provide health care to the indigent. Medicare, on the other hand, was a health insurance program for the elderly and other disabled people and was operated by the federal government. Increasingly, the government and general public had been concerned with not only improving the quality of care provided but, paradoxically, also with cutting overall expenses.

Payments for services provided by companies such as Good Hands typically were funded by the states, via Medicaid; the government, under Medicare and other programs, such as the Department of Veteran Affairs; and from private payers, such as insurance companies and managed care providers. For the past three years, Good Hands' percentage from each source has varied from 52 per cent to 55 per cent from Medicaid, representing 70 per cent of patient days; from 21 per cent to 26 per cent from Medicare or 11 per cent of patient days; and 19 per cent to 23 per cent from private and other payers, or 17 per cent to 18 per cent of patient days.

Most of the state Medicaid programs operated on a cost-based reimbursement system, with some states including efficiency incentives subject to certain cost limits. Cost reimbursement in these programs typically covered the administrative, general, property and equipment costs in addition to the direct and indirect allowable costs the company incurred in providing routine patient services. State Medicaid programs varied in the level of allowable costs reimbursed to operators.

In 1999, health-care reform measures, resulting from concern over the rising cost of Medicaid and Medicare programs, were passed, requiring nursing facilities to continue to provide care to Medicaid residents as well as those who might qualify for Medicaid in the future, even if the facility decided to withdraw from the program. In addition, cuts were made to the payments made for acute nursing care, initially put in place by the 1997 Balanced Budget Act. In 1997, efforts to balance the federal budget led Congress to cut reimbursements for Medicare patients. The 1999 cuts only added more problems for the industry, and, to make matters worse, further cuts were anticipated for 2000.

In addition to the reliance of the industry on government revenues, government regulations also strictly enforced quality standards for patient care. Government authorities periodically inspected facilities to ensure compliance with standards set for continued licensing and Medicare and Medicaid participation. Deficiencies could result in the imposition of fines, temporary suspension of new patient admissions into the facility, decertification from Medicare or Medicaid and, in extreme circumstances, revocation of a facility's license.

General liability and professional liability costs of the long-term care industry had become quite expensive in recent years. The past decade had seen a tremendous increase in the number and size of claims and lawsuits against the industry. The Florida Healthcare Association estimated that in Florida alone, in 1999, seven out of every 10 facilities had open claims against them, and nine out of 10 faced potential new lawsuits. Not only were there more claims, but they were growing in size. The 1999 average litigation claim in Florida was $279,000, a 250 per cent increase over the year prior.

This growing number and size of claims led to dramatically more expensive liability costs. For example, liability insurance per bed in 1999 ranged between $100 and $200 annually, but this number was estimated to grow by 100 per cent to 200 per cent per year. In some states, these numbers were considerably higher: in Texas, this rate was $2,000 to $3,000 per bed per year, and in Florida, it could reach as high as $7,000 per bed per year. Primarily as a result of these increases, insurance companies were ceasing to insure long-term care companies or were limiting their liability insurance severely. Substantially increased premiums and increased liability retention levels for reduced coverage were the norm when insurance coverage was available.

Other important industry trends included an overbuilding of nursing facilities in states that had eliminated the certificate of need process for new construction; the growing availability of eldercare delivered to the home; rapid expansion of assisted living facilities; and the expansion of acute care hospitals into long-term care.

GOOD HANDS' CEO AND MANAGEMENT TEAM

George Jackson, president, CEO and chairman of Good Hands Healthcare, founded the company and helped build the firm over its 30-year history. In early 2000, Jackson was 62 years of age and frequently discussed with the board his desire to work past the age of 65. A well-loved and admired industry expert, Jackson received his bachelor's degree in business administration from the University of Texas at Austin. Prior to founding Good Hands Healthcare, Jackson had worked in the banking industry for 12 years.

Jackson was a charismatic figure, handsome and personable. From Good Hands' beginning, he saw the company as an extension of himself, often blurring the line between the profession and the person. This created issues with his top management team and board in that he often perceived questioning of his strategies as a lack of confidence in his personal abilities. His top management team soon learned that it was prudent from a career perspective to play a supportive role to Jackson's vision. In early 2000, this cadre of Jackson's top management team represented a variety of people he had personally chosen for their positions.

A primary concern of Good Hands' board was the lack of succession planning within the firm. In mid-1999, the board raised its concern with Jackson and recommended he consider not only developing a formal succession plan, but that he consider bringing in some new leadership from outside the firm and industry to jump-start the company and try to turnaround the situation so that Good Hands could regain its leadership position.

At the next meeting, the board received a complex chart of all the CEO's direct reports and their proposed successors. Each was accompanied by an appropriate development plan. Noticeably absent from this plan, however, was the CEO's succession plan. When the board queried Jackson about this, he stated he intended to keep working "as long as possible" and that if the proverbial bus ran him over, he was confident the current team, with help from the board, could run the company while a search was conducted for a successor.

One of Jackson's other responses to the succession plan discussion was to argue for substantial year-end bonuses for his top management team, despite the deteriorating financial conditions of the firm. His argument was that these individuals were underpaid given industry standards and that large bonuses were needed to retain them. He hinted that a large increase in his own compensation would also be appropriate although he did not go so far as to threaten to quit.

Chief Financial Officer (CFO) Bob Wayman (age 61) joined Good Hands in 1976. Wayman had experience with a Wall Street investment company prior to joining Good Hands. He had a bachelor's degree and a master's degree in business administration from Minnesota State University. A highly competent but extremely competitive person, especially with Chief Legal Counsel David Baker, the board was concerned that Wayman lacked the personality to be an effective leader. Wayman frequently commented that the numbers were the heart of the business. On multiple occasions, the board had questioned Wayman's ability to strategically manage the balance sheet to reflect the needs of the cash flow situation. The board questioned whether he was "old school" cautious since he refused to discuss any use of derivatives or any of the other financial instruments available to smooth out the peaks and valleys in the reimbursement stream. In addition, when asked questions by the board on routine financial issues, he tended to be defensive and often treated the question as if it were stupid. Another issue that arose with some frequency was that he did not see his role as reporting to the board's Audit Committee and often circumvented the committee to resolve an issue with the CEO without bringing it to the board's attention. However, the marked lack of financial expertise among the rest of the senior management team had made him indispensable to the CEO, especially in his dealings with Wall Street.

Chief Operating Officer (COO) James O'Malley (age 64) joined Good Hands in 1987 after working for a competitor in the health-care industry for eight years. Since that time, O'Malley had risen up the ranks of Good Hands through the operations division and, in 1990, was appointed both COO and a member of the board of directors. While O'Malley was well-liked and respected throughout the company, he was nearing retirement and was not likely to continue employment with Good Hands for more than another year or two. O'Malley was also well-liked by the board but had been questioned frequently about his resistance to making changes to the operating model. His responses were typically a stream of explanations and excuses, mostly attributable, in his estimation, to "causes outside his control." However, given the quality-of-care issues and the difficulty finding more experienced people in the industry, the board had not pursued any aggressive questioning of his effectiveness.

Chief Legal Counsel (CLC) David Baker (age 54) was a close confidant of Jackson. The two of them were social acquaintances before Jackson persuaded Baker to leave his law firm to become in-house counsel for Good Hands in 1989. Baker often played the role of smoothing over the CEO's behavior when it was questioned by the board, and he was quick to defend Jackson's actions. While Baker was an accomplished attorney and had valuable expertise in the health-care arena, he lacked any management experience beyond the legal areas of the business. The board commonly regarded him as "a thorn in their side" and often questioned his handling of legal matters. His exclusive use of only one outside law firm, regardless of the matter, had caused many late-night discussions among board members. The board's concern over his competence had been discussed with the CEO in several executive sessions and had become a point of contention between the board and the CEO, who ardently defended his friend. Baker had also been the key person to structure all of the employment contracts of the senior management team and was, therefore, held in high regard by his peers in the company.

GOOD HANDS' BOARD

Good Hands Healthcare's board was composed of 10 members total: eight outside members with varied lengths of tenure and two inside members, Good Hands' CEO and Chair George Jackson and COO James O'Malley. Five of the board members had been on the board since it was founded and were handpicked by Jackson. The three newer members joined the board within months of each other in 1998 when the existing board realized that there were too few members to effectively handle all of the board committees. When there were only five independent directors, they found they were all attending every committee meeting and, as a result, they were either devoting too much or not enough time to the issues at hand. Not wanting to be remiss, they decided that the addition of three new members, each with the ability to chair one of the committees, would be the appropriate number. They hired a search firm and recruited three directors within one year of beginning the search.

Since adding the last three members to the board, no new directors had been added. The board discussed frequently the need for "new ideas and diversity" but had made no progress in replacing the more senior directors.

Howard Learned was the dean of the School of Business at Minnesota State University. He was 62 years old and had been on the board for nine terms of three years each. He was a professor of business when the CFO of the company was in business school getting an MBA. When the company went public and was recruiting a board, the CFO thought of his old professor. Learned brought good experience and knowledge to the board and added the prestige of having a business school dean on the board. Learned had chaired a number of committees over his board tenure, but, perhaps most importantly, he had chaired the Compensation Committee for the past 20 years. He also had served on the local board of a national bank

Steven Scales was 60 years old, from a small town near the corporate headquarters and was the managing partner of a small law firm. He was known to the former CEO through years of golfing together, and his wife and the CEO's wife had been longtime friends. Steven Scales' legal knowledge had been essential in keeping Good Hands in regulatory compliance as they grew. Scales had chaired the Governance Committee, the Nominating Committee and the Audit Committee over his terms as a director. He did not serve on any other public board but was active on many civic boards in his community.

Norm Current, age 61, was a banker from Brownsville, Texas, where the corporation was founded. Although the corporate headquarters had since relocated, Current decided to stay on and maintained an excellent contact base among employees and legislators. He had chaired the Compensation and Audit Committees during his tenure and was a close, personal friend of the CEO. His behavior in board meetings had been very unpredictable and he tended to be somewhat volatile. He either contributed very little or contributed on issues he felt strongly about in an aggressive fashion, using terms that were sometimes inappropriate in the board setting. Current served on a variety of local civic boards and on the board of the community hospital.

Don Anson was 63 years old, an attorney and a former U.S. congressman. He had been friends with Jackson since college. They frequently went on fishing trips, hunting trips and vacations together with their wives. His national clout had been an important factor in getting things done in Washington in a highly regulated industry. He had chaired the Nominating Committee for most of the years he was on the board and also had chaired the Compensation Committee for several years. He was active in national politics and, since his retirement from Congress, served on the boards of various political organizations.

Frank Fowler, age 61, was an investment banker whose company did the earliest financing of Good Hands. Fowler's company also took the company public and held a significant position of Good Hands' stock. He and Jackson had been hunting buddies for many years. Fowler was probably the board member who was the closest business advisor/confidant of the CEO. He served on the boards of various companies that his company had financed.

The three newer members of the board had been recruited by executive search firms and had no prior relationship with anyone on the board or on the management team.

Gerry Comco, age 62, was the retired CEO of a telecommunications company and lived in Boca Raton, Florida. He had been recruited during the time when the board was discussing a change to its strategy and wanted additional "out of industry" perspective. Comco was aggressive and outspoken, respected and liked by the rest of the board. He had recently been named chair of the Governance Committee and undertook a thorough review of the committee charters, calendars and board composition. Prior to leaving his company, he had served on its board of directors.

Mark Andrews was 58 years old, and was the senior vice-president (SVP) of a global company. This was his first experience on a public board but his professional background made him an excellent board member. He was well-liked and spoke up about the most important issues. He had particular expertise in operations and could make some significant contributions as the company expanded its operating model beyond nursing home operations. He was the chairman of the Compensation Committee and had initiated an exhaustive review of the company's compensation policies and philosophy upon accepting the chairmanship. He served on the board of one of the subsidiaries of his company and was a competitive athlete.

Greg Simon, age 59, was a consultant, a former banker and presidential appointee to the board of a national regulatory agency. He was also an expert in the areas of corporate governance, strategy and risk. He had been asked to chair the Nominating Committee shortly after joining the board. In this capacity he had initiated a formal process for evaluating the board and CEO. He sat on the boards of four public companies.

THE DECISION

Good Hands' board of directors knew the company was at a crossroads. Was the industry environment really the cause of Good Hands' sliding financial performance? What strategies would be necessary to stop the slide and regain Good Hands' dominant position? How would Good Hands weather the changing regulatory climate and reimbursement cuts? These were among many questions that the board knew had to be addressed to keep the company afloat and to ensure its survival as a viable entity in the future.

But, perhaps more pragmatically, was Jackson still the best CEO to lead Good Hands? Did he have the management team in place that could help chart a new course for the future? If not, who would take Jackson's place?

The board saw three primary alternatives. First, they could keep Jackson on as CEO and see how Good Hands fared in the coming months. But, could they continue to do so in light of the company's precarious financial position? Jackson had grown the company to its heights but also had presided over its recent decline. Had conditions changed so much that a new leader was needed? Most pragmatically, keeping Jackson in place would be the lowest cost option due to the nature of his employment contract. In 1997, the board (then consisting of Learned, Scales, Current, Anson and Fowler) had approved an employment contract for Jackson that would grant him in excess of $25 million (including severance, salary, options, benefits, etc.) if he were removed from his position as CEO (see Exhibit 2).

Second, the board could ask for Jackson's resignation and undertake a search for his replacement. Asking Jackson, the company's founder and leader for more than 30 years, to step down would be no easy task. If he left Good Hands, what would be the effect on the culture? How would the company make up for the loss of his experience and guidance? How would the board handle his severance payments when the company was already short on cash? Would they find a suitable replacement within Good Hands' top management team or would they need to look outside the company and/ or industry? On the one hand, promoting from within would minimize the lack of additional losses in the top management team who may resign if they were overlooked for promotion. And, continuity in experience, strategy, etc. would be achieved by promotion within. On the other hand, was the board satisfied that any of the current top management team could tackle the job and work well with them? Going outside could bring in some fresh perspectives that may be much needed as well as one potentially improving Good Hands' competitiveness via the insights into other company's best practices and operating models.

Finally, the board saw a compromise position. Could they ask Jackson to give up his position as CEO yet stay on as chairman of the board? This option would be much easier than a total resignation and overcome the loss of his expertise, etc. Under this option, the board expected to keep Jackson's current compensation package, which totaled just over $3 million annually, intact but they would not be liable for any additional compensation because such a move would not trigger any additional severance under the terms of his agreement. But even at this generous pay package for a reduction in duties, would Jackson accept this? How much could a new CEO accomplish with Jackson still around and leading the board? And, what message would this send to Wall Street?

The board members knew the answers to these questions were not going to come easily. But, they felt they had to resolve the issues and resolve them quickly. They set their sights on their next board meeting in two months' time to make a succession decision on which alternative was the best to adopt.

Exhibit 1

CONSOLIDATED BALANCE SHEETS ($000s) (for years ending December 31)		
	1999	**1998**
ASSETS		
Current Assets:		
Cash and cash equivalents	$ 21,086	$ 67,984
Accounts receivables- patient, less allowance for doubtful accounts	248,443	190,504
Accounts receivables- nonpatient, less allowance for doubtful accounts	48,005	30,890
Notes receivables, less allowance for doubtful notes	2,799	16,930
Operating supplies	34,320	44,534
Deferred income taxes	70,057	25,666
Prepaid expenses and other	17,654	18,643
Total current assets	$ 442,364	$ 395,151
Property and equipment, net	901,649	910,065
Other assets:		
Goodwill, net	201,111	265,443
Deferred income taxes	38,744	10
Other, less allowance for doubtful accounts and notes	123,338	23,393
Total other assets	363,193	255,802
	$1,732,206	$1,561,018
LIABILITIES AND STOCKHOLDERS' EQUITY		
Current Liabilities:		
Accounts payable	$ 109,420	$ 89,040
Accrued wages and related liabilities	134,002	78,094
Accrued interest	26,550	19,448
Other accrued liabilities	60,628	163,292
Short-term debt and current portion of long-term debt	240,513	28,990
Total current liabilities	$ 571,113	$ 378,864
Long-term debt	438,039	335,605
Deferred income taxes payable	—	—
Other liabilities and deferred items	170,374	325,432
Total Liabilities	$1,154,526	$1,039,901
Stockholders' equity:		
Preferred stock, shares authorized: 20,000,000	—	—
Common stock, shares issued: 1999- 112,808,705; 1998- 120,382,356	11,844	11,038
Additional paid-in capital	776,981	775,637
Accumulated deficit	(81,081)	(139,429)
Accumulated other comprehensive income	953	1,054
Treasury stock, at cost: 1999-18,954,450 shares; 1998- 16,807,800 shares	(131,057)	(127,183)
Total stockholders' equity	577,680	521,117
Total liabilities and stockholders' equity	1,732,206	1,561,018

(continued)

Exhibit 1   (continued)

CONSOLIDATED STATEMENTS OF OPERATIONS ($000s) (for years ending December 31)	1999	1998	1997
Net operating revenues	2,764,034	2,801,339	3,346,556
Interest income	2,650	4,335	10,708
Total revenues	2,766,684	2,805,674	3,357,264
Costs and expenses:			
Operating and administrative:			
Wages and related	1,886,990	1,846,363	1,914,452
Provision for insurance and related items	72,456	117,215	177,407
Other	645,889	708,183	936,246
Interest	121,990	53,105	19,349
Depreciation and amortization	100,061	109,076	107,780
Asset impairments, workforce reductions and other unusual items	43,033	38,602	89,578
Total costs and expenses	2,870,419	2,872,544	3,244,813
Net income/(loss) before benefit from income taxes, extraordinary charge and cumulative effect of change in accounting	(103,735)	(66,870)	112,451
Income taxes	31,121	26,138	(25,936)
Net income/(loss) before extraordinary charge and cumulative effect of change in accounting	(72,615)	(40,732)	86,515
Special charges related to settlements of regulatory claims and disputes	(82,510)	(1,865)	—
Extraordinary charge, net income tax benefit	11,420	653	1,985
Cumulative effect of change in accounting designation			550
Net Income/(Loss)	(143,705)	(41,944)	89,050
Basic and diluted loss per share of common stock:			
Before extraordinary charge and cumulative effect of change in accounting	(0.70)	(0.39)	0.83
Extraordinary charge	(0.68)	(0.01)	0.02
Cumulative effect of change in accounting			(0.04)
Net income/(loss)	(1.38)	(0.40)	0.86
Shares used to compute per share amounts	103,864	103,574	103,762

Exhibit 2 Key Provisions of George Jackson's Employment Contract

1. Proscription of responsibilities, duties and location of performance	Specifies Executive's obligations under the agreement
2. Duration	5 years, automatically renewed annually
3. Compensation and benefits treatment	Total package is composed of base salary, long- and short-term incentives and benefits (1999 approximately $3 million total)
4. Hold harmless/indemnification	Provides financial protection to the Executive for costs incurred in event of legal action and/or judgment against Executive as Director, Officer, employee or agent of the Corporation

5. Termination protection	Specifies protection provided in event of termination
	• Causes (defined)… payment of all accrued bonuses and vested long-term incentives
	• Without cause… payments equal to remaining term plus one year times salary, short-term bonuses and FMV of long-term incentives in event of:
	  – Diminution
	  – Office Move
	  – Change in control… single trigger; includes Excise tax
	  – Material breach by Good Hands
	• Disability/death…same as without cause
	• Benefit extension/credits and accelerated vesting of long-term incentives/equity in case of w/out cause term.
	• Lump sum payment option (trust arrangement)

6. Non compete, non-solicitation and confidentiality	2 years
7. Attorney's fees	Reimbursement of all costs associated with legal actions taken to enforce/interpret agreement, if Executive prevails
8. Arbitration	Requires arbitration to settle all contractual disputes

Case 30

CCL Industries Inc.: Building and Maintaining an Effective Board

"I have to work harder to ensure stakeholders don't think of CCL as a 'controlled' company. As CEO, *I* am accountable for the outcome of our decisions, not the board."

Donald Lang reflected on the relationship between himself, president and chief executive officer (CEO) of CCL Industries Inc. (CCL), and the CCL board of directors. CCL had recently undertaken a major change in strategy when the planned and publicly announced sale of one of CCL's major divisions was abruptly cancelled.

"We had specific conditions and they ultimately were not met, so I decided to cancel the deal. I then had to explain the rationale to the board." Fortunately for Lang, he and the CCL board had an excellent and effective working relationship. It was not always this way. In the past, the CCL board was much less involved and less effective. Through hard work, the CEO/board team was on pace to meet its goal of being the world's premier packager of consumer products by 2005. In order to ensure this goal was attained, Lang and the board felt that there were issues that needed to be addressed to further the improvements they had made over the years.

CCL INDUSTRIES INC.

CCL was founded in 1951 by Stuart Lang Sr., his brother and Stuart's two sons, Gordon and Jim.[1] It was Gordon, however, who built CCL into the preeminent aerosol, custom

Richard Ivey School of Business
The University of Western Ontario

Trevor Hunter prepared this case under the supervision of Professor Larry Tapp solely to provide material for class discussion. The authors do not intend to illustrate either effective or ineffective handling of a managerial situation. The authors may have disguised certain names and other identifying information to protect confidentiality.

[1]For a comprehensive history of CCL Industries, see D.B. Davies, *Magic in the Mist: The exciting and improbable saga of CCL Industries 1951-2001*, CCL Industries Inc., 2001.

manufacturing, rigid packaging and labeling business in North America. Fifty years after its founding, sales topped (see Exhibit 1) $1.6 billion, and CCL employed 7,500 people around the world.

CCL was originally named Connecticut Chemicals Limited and originated as a joint venture with an American company. Under the leadership of Gordon Lang, Conn-Chem (as it was more widely known in the early days) eventually outgrew its American parent and repatriated the balance of the equity it didn't own.

Through a number of acquisitions, the lines of business expanded beyond aerosols. To reflect this change of direction, the company's name was further shortened to CCL Industries Inc. in 1980.

Essentially an outsourcer to major packaged goods and consumer products firms, CCL produced some of the best-known name brands in the world, yet was largely unknown to the general public. The company produced its various products in close association with its customers and was divided into four divisions:[2]

1. CCL Custom Manufacturing—was the largest contract manufacturer of outsourced consumer products in North America and the United Kingdom. Products included some of the best-known brand names in the world for personal care, household, over-the-counter (OTC) pharmaceutical, oral care and specialty food products.

2. CCL Container—provided packaging solutions to the major global consumer products manufacturers from locations in North and Central America. Products included aluminium aerosol containers, tubes and jars.

3. CCL Plastic Packaging—from operations in the United States, this division produced plastic tubes, tamper-evident closures, dispensing closures, lined closures and jars.

4. CCL Label—was the largest North American printer of identification and information labels (paper and film pressure sensitive), with plants located in the United States, Canada, Europe, Mexico and Puerto Rico.

CCL first went public in 1972. Its shares consistently performed well on the Toronto Stock Exchange (TSE) until the 1976 "ozone scare." Reports issued by the Environmental Protection Agency (EPA) and the Food and Drug Administration (FDA) had suggested that chloro-fluorocarbons (CFCs), the propellant in aerosol cans, lead to depletion of the earth's ozone layer. These reports seriously injured the global aerosol market. By this time, CCL had both diversified its product line (sufficiently that a decrease in aerosol sales did not cripple the firm) and converted away from use of CFCs (which were ultimately banned in the United States in 1978 and in Canada in 1979). Nevertheless, the "ozone scare" significantly depressed CCL's share price.

Sensing an opportunity, management repurchased all outstanding shares and took CCL private. The firm went public again in 1980 and has remained public since then.

DONALD LANG

Although he was the son of the man who built CCL, Donald Lang was not automatically given the job of president and CEO.

After graduating from the HBA program at the Richard Ivey School of Business (formerly Western Business School), Lang worked at Nabisco Canada for two years.

---

[2]This information was taken from the CCL Web site, www.cclind.com.

He knew that he wanted to eventually work at CCL, but felt it was important to gain some management experience in a larger, more formalized organization prior to joining CCL Industries.

He entered the business in a plant operations role in 1982. By 1993, he had been appointed president of CCL Custom Manufacturing and later, president and chief operating officer (COO) of CCL. Finally, he became CEO in 1999. Although by 2002 he had held the top management position in CCL for only three years, he had been involved with the corporation's governance as a member of the board of directors since 1991.

During his time as a board member, Lang had been considered a catalyst for change. He had often not agreed with the processes or extent of involvement of the CCL board. He had been only a minority voice, however, and was unable to effect change. When Lang wrote a letter that suggested he might resign from the board should change not be forthcoming, the board responded by agreeing to some initial modifications.

THE CCL BOARD

From its incorporation, CCL has had only three board chairs. The first was Gordon Lang. In discussion with the board, a succession plan was developed whereby he would step down from his position but would be recognized for his contributions with the new title, founder chairman. The chairman title and corresponding responsibilities were appointed to the then-current president and CEO, a longtime senior CCL manager. In 1999, the first independent board chair, Jon Grant, was appointed (see Exhibit 2).

In the heyday of CCL's rapid growth in the 1960s and 1980s, the board could arguably have been characterized as a rubber stamp to management. The senior management of CCL was composed of longtime employees who had been hired by Gordon Lang and had worked their way up the ladder through hard work. There was no doubt that they were exceedingly hard-working and competent, but decisions were made with the expectation that once made, they would have to be approved by the board.

A quote from Edward W. Dobson, former executive vice-president and chief administrative officer and one of the builders of CCL, illustrates this point well. "We didn't have time for regular meetings, memos, reports or a rigid management structure. We just talked about it, made a decision and did it."[3]

Donald Lang recalls:

> After we went public we were trying to make the bridge to a public structure but we still clung to our past. We brought in outside directors, but we were still only providing a rubber stamp. The firm's managers were not being held accountable for their actions. Then we had U.S. directors who were getting frustrated with the situation and pushed for a change. I was in a better position as COO and together we were able to make the necessary changes.

It was Donald Lang who ultimately instigated a formal evolution of the board, including a change in the nominating and governance committee chairman, the hiring of a search company for new directors and a succession plan for his father to retire as chairman with the long-term plan of separating the chairman and CEO roles.

Lang commented, "Unfortunately business performance has to get pretty bad before the board is compelled to take any action against a CEO. When I was appointed

---

[3]Quoted in D.B. Davies, *Magic in the Mist: The exciting and improbable saga of CCL Industries 1951–2001*, CCL Industries Inc., 2001, pg. 49.

CEO, I wanted to make sure the CEO was held accountable to the board." The separation of the CEO and chairman roles was advocated by Lang, even though he was the incoming CEO.

The focus on accountability went beyond management however. In 1994, the board itself decided to bring in a consultant to assist in a board self-evaluation. The purpose of the evaluation was to improve the process and contribution the board made to the operations of CCL to ensure it was acting as more than a rubber stamp. Three annual evaluations followed until 1997, when they were stopped. Lang suggested that the evaluations were both not welcomed by the board members and had received negative feedback:

> During that time (i.e., the period between 1994 and 1997) the company's strategy lacked focus. There was a need for the board to work better together and to be more aligned. They were not interested in being evaluated when there were other issues that were considered a higher priority.

Lang was convinced that self-evaluation was critical to the success of the board as an effective group. "The intention (of the evaluations) was good, but the execution was wrong. We needed to find a better way to make them a priority and make them work," said Lang. A new evaluation process was introduced in 2000 that received more positive feedback. The addition of new directors, with differing opinions than those on the board from 1994 to 1997, helped improve the reception and effectiveness of the evaluations.

In order to give structure to CCL's governance policies, a document titled "Statement of Governance Policies of the Board of Directors of CCL Industries Inc." was prepared in 1994. This document was updated regularly and was given to every current and new director. Its purpose was to:

> Set forth the mandates and principles adopted by the board of directors of CCL Industries Inc. for the good stewardship of the company. It is intended as guidance for the board, for each director and for the committees of the board in the exercise of their respective responsibilities in the governance of the company.

The document contained policies on the following:

- The mandate of the board as a whole,
- The mandates of the audit, human resources, nominating and governance, and environment and occupational health and safety committees,
- The composition of the board,
  - Related and unrelated directors
  - The role of the chair
  - The composition of committees
- The role of a director,
  - Access to management and independent counsel
- New directors,
  - Criteria for new director selection
  - Orientation and training for new directors
- Duties of the president and CEO,
- Performance assessment procedure for the president and CEO,
- Proceedings and meetings,
  - Meeting procedures
  - Information

The following is a list of some of the specific activities undertaken by the board that Lang felt significantly improved the performance of the board after his appointment as CEO in 1999:

1. The appointment of a non-executive board chair. Aside from the skills and experience Board Chair Jon Grant brought to the position, the fact that there was independence at the top allowed for constructive challenging of the CEO and other senior executives that pushed for performance, clarity and accountability.

2. Grant, like Lang, was interested in bringing in more unrelated directors to further enhance the independence of the board. Members were selected strategically. The contribution and skill set each potential member could bring and how each prospect could help improve CCL's performance were heavily considered.

3. On average, Lang expected that directors should spend one day's worth of preparation briefing themselves on the materials the corporation sent them one week in advance of meetings for each four-hour board meeting, aside from their additional roles on the various committees.

4. Board committees were chaired by outside directors with functional executives acting as secretaries. There was thus more direct contact between board members and other senior executives. Senior executives were also required to make presentations to the board on topics of business plans. This gave the board more freedom to critique their strategies directly and assess the ability of the senior executives the CEO had hired and promoted.

5. A two-day board member retreat entirely devoted to strategic planning was instituted. Day one involved presentations from the divisional presidents that included an exchange of ideas and opinions. Day two was reserved for the board and the CEO only. The CEO was challenged and pushed, while at the same time, the experience and skills of the board members were leveraged.

6. One board meeting per year would be held at one of the manufacturing sites as an opportunity to better understand the business details.

7. One half-hour was set aside at every meeting for the board to meet without the CEO present. This time allowed for frank discussion on such issues as CEO performance, compensation, evaluation or any other sensitive topic.

8. It was usual for the board members to meet for dinner informally the night preceding the CCL board meeting with, and sometimes without, management, which offered another opportunity for directors to converse and build a stronger relationship.

9. The splitting of the CEO and chair positions was a shift from the way the roles had been conceived and institutionalized at CCL in the past. There was frequent contact between Lang and Grant, and a good working relationship was fostered. Lang was accountable to Grant, but while Lang often consulted Grant, decisions were made by Lang. As a non-executive chair, Grant was an "outsider." Although the two worked together closely, Lang ran the business.

10. Board agendas were very detailed and included:
    * Scheduled time for outside directors' discussions
    * General background information
    * Consent agenda items;
      – Items that could be approved with one motion, past board minutes, for example,
    * Committee reports
    * Operations update

All pertinent information was included in advance briefing books, including a summary of the resolutions to be proposed.

11. The amount and type of documentation directors received was revamped. Agendas were set one month before the meeting, and materials were delivered to directors no less than one week before the meeting. If an item missed the agenda, it had to be held for the next meeting (emergencies excepted). Thus, senior executives that wanted something on the board agenda had to be sure that their timing was on schedule. Meetings were scheduled on a two-year rotating basis to ensure full attendance. There was a conscious attempt to strike a balance between providing too much detail (thus overwhelming the directors) and too little information.

These and other measures had led many of the directors to feel that the CCL board was one of the most effective on which they had served.

MOVING FORWARD

Although the CCL board and Lang had made an effective team and understood and fulfilled their roles with accountability, there were still issues that needed improvement. The latest board evaluation had resulted in some concerns that needed to be addressed.[4]

Three main areas in which the board could be strengthened emerged from the evaluation: the strategic planning process, succession planning and board composition.

Strategic Planning

While the directors noted that this process had improved over the years and that the value of the two-day retreat was clear, they felt that more of their time should be spent on reviewing strategic opportunities and risks, and the plans for execution, rather than management reports. There was concern over a lack of clarity and direction on the part of the board. While unanimity was not the goal, greater consensus was desired. Concerns as to how to reach a consensus in a timely and effective manner were raised. The directors felt that in order to effectively aid in the strategic planning process they needed to be involved in the process on a more regular basis. The content, amount and timing of the information they received regarding strategic planning needed to be reviewed. Did they need more information? Should they meet more often? Who should be at the meetings? What sort of information should they receive? These questions needed to be addressed.

Succession Planning

Nearly all the directors felt that more time needed to be spent on the issue of succession planning. Many felt that this issue was often considered secondary, which is why it had not been given its due attention. An annual discussion regarding potential successor candidates for all senior positions was suggested. The discussion would center on their readiness, development plans, retention risk and compensation.

Another issue of key personnel involved a lack of clarity of the role of the board's HR committee and the degree of support the committee received. The HR committee

---

[4]This information is drawn from a report prepared by Patrick O'Callaghan & Associates for CCL Industries Inc.

saw part of its role as challenging the CEO on whether the senior executives were not only experts in their area, but also strategic thinkers and could take work off the desk of the CEO. This followed the philosophy of CCL founder Gordon Lang who said "I hired good people and then got out of their way. I had no time to constantly look over people's shoulders or question their every decision."[5] Perhaps the content of the annual reviews needed to be changed. Perhaps the HR committee needed a broader scope for potential candidates.

A further important issue that needed attention was the development of an emergency plan in case of an accident involving the CEO or other senior executives.

Board Composition

Although the majority of board members was composed of "outside and non-related" directors, there was a concern regarding the skills and experience that were needed at the board level to assist with strategic planning in the coming years. Criteria for future directors included:

- U.S. or international background (with a concern regarding the logistics problem for international directors)
- Experience in corporate finance and mergers and acquisitions
- Information technology experience
- A current CEO of a significant-sized public corporation operating internationally
- Human resources experience

Although the board was always looking for the best candidate, there was a clear recognition of the lack of women and visible minorities at the board level. While not looking to fulfill a quota, there was a desire to break away from the "white male" stereotype characteristics of many boards.

THE CURRENT SITUATION

After the change in strategy, Lang recognized the need and potential for greater board involvement in the strategic activities of CCL. As this sort of activity could be the norm in the future, the need for flexible, nimble strategic planning, along with informed governance, would only increase in the face of competition and global uncertainty.

In 2002, CCL operated in nine countries around the world. There was a global economic slowdown and decreased consumer confidence. The effects of the terrorists' attacks on September 11 had further exacerbated the poor economic conditions. Acquisitions and divestitures, keys to CCL's growth strategy, would be difficult in the coming years, particularly in new markets around the world.

The challenge was to develop and execute strategy and appropriately develop and leverage the skills and experience of the board. Clearly, the board was working well now; however, there were issues regarding strategic planning, succession planning and composition that needed to be addressed if it was going to fulfill its role as steward in the future business environment facing CCL. Making changes to the board as an anticipatory change tended to be difficult, especially when the change affected something

---

[5]Quote taken from in D.B. Davies, *Magic in the Mist: The exciting and improbable saga of CCL Industries 1951–2001*, CCL Industries Inc., 2001, Prologue.

that was working well. What needed to be done to increase the involvement of the board? How could the board's concerns be handled? Was it time to update or overhaul CCL's governance policies? There was a fine line between governing and running the firm; and neither Lang, nor Grant, wanted to cross that line.

The Richard Ivey School of Business gratefully acknowledges the generous support of CCL Industries Inc. in the development of these learning materials.

Exhibit 1   Selected Financial Data from the CCL 2001 Annual Report for Years Ending 2000 and 2001 (in thousands of dollars except for per-share data)

	2001	2000
Sales	1,600,497	1,589,087
EBITDA	159,879	183,295
Depreciation, amortization of other assets	73,439	75,351
Interest	32,415	36,560
Income from operations before unusual items, income tax and goodwill amortization	54,025	71,384
Unusual item (net)	7,684	18,776
Earnings before income taxes and goodwill amortization	46,341	52,608
Income taxes	7,993	13,156
Earnings before goodwill amortization	38,348	39,452
Goodwill amortization, net of tax	13,457	12,798
Net earnings	24,891	26,654
Per class B share		
Earnings before goodwill amortization	1.08	1.04
Earnings before unusual item	0.83	1.10
Net earnings	0.70	0.70
Cash flow before unusual item	3.39	3.47
At year end		
Total assets	1,454,991	1,392,820
Net debt	435,755	486,139
Shareholders' equity	563,704	558,201
Net debt to equity ratio	0.77	0.87
Return on average equity	4.4%	4.7%
Net debt-to-total capitalization	43.6%	46.5%
Book value per share	16.52	15.22

Exhibit 2   Profile of CCL Industries Inc. Board of Directors

Jon Grant – Chairman of the Board of CCL Industries Inc.

Chairman of the board of the Laurentian Bank of Canada and former chairman of Canada Lands Company Limited and a director of CCL since 1994. Former chairman and CEO of the Quaker Oats Company of Canada Limited, former chairman of Scott Paper Limited and former chairman of the board of governors of Trent University. Mr. Grant is also a director of AXA Pacific Insurance Company. He is currently chairman of the Ontario Board of the Nature Conservancy of Canada.

Donald G. Lang – President and CEO, CCL Industries Inc.

CEO of CCL Industries since June 1999 in addition to his previous role as president. Mr. Lang was appointed president and chief operating officer of CCL in April 1998. Prior to his appointment as COO, he was president of the company's largest division, CCL Custom Manufacturing. Mr. Lang has served on CCL's Board of Directors since 1991. Additionally, he is a member of the Advisory Committee at the Richard Ivey School of Business. Mr. Lang holds an Honours Bachelor of Arts degree from the Richard Ivey School of Business, University of Western Ontario.

Stuart W. Lang – President of CCL Label International

Mr. Lang has held progressively senior positions throughout the Custom and Label Manufacturing divisions in Canada, Mexico and Europe since joining the company in 1982, and has served as a director of CCL Industries since 1991. Mr. Lang has a BSc in Chemical Engineering from Queen's University. Prior to this he played for the CFL's Edmonton Eskimos for eight years.

Paul J. Block

Chairman and CEO of Proteus Capital Associates. Previously, Mr. Block was chairman and president of Revlon International. Mr. Block is a board member of the China Retail Fund and the Shanghai-Syracuse University International School of Business. He is also a member of the Advisory Board of the Syracuse University School of Management. Mr. Block has served as a director of CCL since 1997.

Dermot G. Coughlan

Former chairman and chief executive officer of Derlan Industries Limited. A director of CCL Industries Inc. since 1991, Mr. Coughlan is also a director of Mackenzie Financial Corporation and chairman of a number of North American and international manufacturing companies.

Stephan J. Friedman

Senior partner with the international law firm of Debevoise & Plimpton. Mr. Friedman was previously executive vice president and general counsel of the Equitable Companies Inc. He served as commissioner of the Securities and Exchange Commission and as deputy assistant secretary of the Treasury for Capital Markets Policy. Mr. Friedman also serves on the boards of the American Ballet Theatre, the Practising Law Institute and the United Way of New York City.

Albert Gnat

Partner at Lang Michener, a Toronto law firm. A director of CCL since 1973, Mr. Gnat also serves on the boards of CamVec Corporation, GEAC Computer Corporation Limited, Leitch Technology Corporation, IKEA Limited, MDC Corporation, Rogers Communication and Vitran Corporation.

Jean-René Halde

President and chief executive officer of Irwin Toys and was president and CEO of Livgroup Investments which succeeded Livingston Group where he was president and CEO from 1995–2000. Prior to this he served as president and CEO to Culinar Inc. Mr. Halde's other directorships include the boards of Bracknell Corporation and the Institute of Corporate Directors.

Lawrence G. Tapp

Dean of the Richard Ivey School of Business since 1995. He also served as executive-in-residence and adjunct professor, Faculty of Business, University of Toronto from 1993–1995, vice chairman, president and CEO of Lawson Mardon Group Ltd. (a packaging conglomerate) from 1985–1992. He has served as a director of CCL since 1994.

Source: CCL Industries Inc. Web site, http://www.cclind.com/corp_profile_directors_bio.html.

ING Insurance Asia/Pacific

In June 2003, Jacques Kemp, newly appointed chief executive officer (CEO) of ING Insurance Asia/Pacific (ING A/P) was reviewing the regional operating structure, performance, and growth strategy. After arriving in Asia in July 2002 as regional general manager, Kemp traveled extensively throughout the region, in order to gain many insights into the existing ING A/P organization, the individual business units (countries) and their strategies. He also solicited ideas from major consulting firms on how to further strengthen ING A/P. The company was doing well, but he felt that ING's existing market position, strategy and operations in Asia/Pacific could be enhanced.

Kemp was concerned that ING needed to prepare for the time when the general market growth in Asia slowed and the competitive pressure intensified. He also was determined to make a difference during his tenure as ING's Asia/Pacific chief executive officer and to take the company to the next level.

INTERNATIONAL NETHERLANDS GROUP (ING)

ING was a global financial services company of Dutch origin, with more than 150 years of history. The company provided an array of banking, insurance and asset management services in more than 50 countries. With over 120,000 employees, ING served a broad customer base, including individuals, families, small businesses, large corporations, institutions and governments. Based on market capitalization, ING was one of the 20 largest financial institutions globally and ranked in the top 10 in Europe. The company was organized along six major business lines, which included both regions and product groups. While the banking business was divided into wholesale, retail and direct banking with a global management structure, the insurance business

Richard Ivey School of Business
The University of Western Ontario

was organized into three regional business lines, including the Americas, Europe and Asia/Pacific (see Exhibit 1).

JACQUES KEMP

Jacques Kemp started his career on the banking side of ING in 1974, in risk management at a local office in the Netherlands, and later moved to the foreign division at the head offices in Amsterdam. He was involved in setting up the ING Los Angeles office in 1982, and from 1984 to 1990, he was general manager in Brazil. In 1990, he returned to Amsterdam to take a general manager position, and one year later, became chairman of ING Bank International. One of his main achievements was the set-up of the emerging market banking network. After the merger and integration with Barings Bank in the mid-1990s, he became a member of the executive committee with responsibility for ING's general banking activities and the international banking network worldwide. In 2000, Kemp became Global Head of e-Business for ING Group, and was responsible for initiating and coordinating ING's strategy on Web-enabling, integrated financial services on a global basis. He joined the executive committee of ING Insurance Asia/Pacific in July 2002 and became CEO for Asia/Pacific on April 1, 2003.

THE INSURANCE INDUSTRY IN ASIA

The insurance industry in Asia was expected to expand dramatically, driven by rapid economic growth and a general increase in the popularity of insurance products, resulting from rising incomes. Gradual deregulation and the opening up of the Asian insurance markets were making them increasingly accessible to foreign insurers.

The proportion of gross domestic product (GDP) accounted for by life insurance premiums in Asia was relatively high when measured against income levels. The demand for life insurance in Asian markets was greater than in other countries at a comparable stage of development. Japan and South Korea, in fact, displayed the second- and third-highest degrees of insurance penetration in the world.

There were several reasons for the popularity of life insurance in Asia. Life insurance (like every other form of saving) profited from the high rates of saving in Asia. In this respect, insurers in some Asian countries had stolen the march on the banks by intensively marketing whole life policies.[1] Further, in most Asian nations, state or company pensions were modest, and private insurance products filled the gap. Life insurance enjoyed slight tax advantages in most Asian countries. Premium volume in Asia (excluding Japan) was expected to experience real growth of more than 10 per cent per year between 2003 and 2008. Global premium volume was expected to increase by about four per cent during the same period.

At the end of 2002, approximately 900 insurance companies (about 265 of them foreign) were operating in 12 Asian insurance markets. The size of the companies, their capital assets and the share of the market in foreign hands varied considerably from country to country. Regulations on the part of the supervisory bodies also had highly varying effects on market activities. The liberal regulations of Hong Kong ensured adherence only to minimum capital regulations, while the additional (and in some cases far-reaching) regulations of other countries covered the licensing of

---

[1] Unlike term insurance which only paid out when the principal died (or was disabled); whole life policies had an insurance component and a savings component.

companies, products and prices. However, under pressure from the World Trade Organization (WTO), these Asian markets were expected to become more open.

ING IN ASIA/PACIFIC

ING Insurance Asia/Pacific was responsible for the life insurance operations and asset/wealth management activities of ING throughout Asia Pacific. ING was the first European company to enter the life insurance markets of Japan, Taiwan and South Korea. By the beginning of 2003, ING was ranked among the top five foreign financial services providers in Asia/Pacific with more than six million clients. The portfolio consisted of large businesses across six mature markets —Australia/New Zealand, Taiwan, Malaysia, Hong Kong, Japan and Korea—some smaller, semi-mature markets, such as the Philippines and Singapore, as well as newly emerging life insurance markets, including China, India, Indonesia and Thailand.

ING Insurance Asia/Pacific's business units offered various types of life insurance, wealth management, retail and institutional asset management products (including annuity, endowment, disability/morbidity insurance, unit linked/universal life, whole life, participating life, group life, accident and health, term life and employee benefits) and services (see Exhibits 2 and 3). In Hong Kong and Malaysia, non-life insurance products (including employees' compensation, medical, motor, fire, marine, personal accident and general liability) were also offered. ING Asia/Pacific's distribution channels included tied or career agents, independent agents, financial planners, bancassurance,[2] telemarketing and e-business channels. In several countries, ING had strategic alliances with local companies to enhance distribution capacity.

In 2002, several regional shared service centers were established to lower operating costs. With 60,000 points of distribution in Asia, ranging from tied agents, independent agents and brokers/dealers to banks, ING's strategy was able to access its clients through the channel of their choice.

ING had leading positions in Australia, Taiwan, Korea and Malaysia, and it was a fast-growing niche player in Japan. In New Zealand, ING managed about 16 per cent of all mutual funds, making it the number-three player in terms of assets under management. ING was well positioned in the two largest Asian growth markets, China and India. It had two joint venture operations in life insurance in China and a 44 per cent stake in ING Vysya Bank, India's fifth largest private bank, as well as a life insurance joint venture and a mutual funds business.

ING was doing well in Asia Pacific (see Exhibit 4). Although 2002 was marked by continuing declines in global equity markets, the aggregate financial results of ING Asia/Pacific showed robustness against this market volatility. ING Asia/Pacific's regional results exceeded its financial expectations for the year with the businesses in Australia, Japan and Korea delivering the most outstanding results.

THE AETNA INTEGRATION

By 2003, the integration of Aetna, a major acquisition undertaken during 2000, was accomplished, and rebranding was completed in almost all countries. This challenging integration was the major achievement of Kemp's predecessor.

---

[2] Bancassurance is a French term referring to the selling of insurance through a bank's established distribution channels.

ING Group acquired the life insurance activities of American-based Aetna International, which at the time had a much stronger position and an insurance organization that was four times larger in Asia than ING. The integration caused the departure of many of Aetna's top managers but there were also examples of non-disruptive transitions, such as the one in Hong Kong, where the local general manager of Aetna embraced the opportunities provided by the merger and led the local joint operation to become the most recognized foreign financial services provider in Hong Kong. Overall, the business remained strong, and ING Asia/Pacific benefited substantially from the Aetna acquisition. The merger helped ING became one of the largest life insurance companies in Asia-Pacific.

To rebalance the portfolio, ING sold its life and non-life operations in the Philippines, Singapore and Indonesia. ING felt these three countries would not produce enough "substance" in premiums to allow foreign insurance companies to make decent returns and profits, and the business units in these countries would need huge amounts of resources to manage these markets properly and to meet ING's standards of risk and compliance. Strategically ING decided that it had enough substance and growth potential in the other 12 Asian countries in which it operated while retaining the asset management operations in the Philippines and Singapore.

REGIONAL STRUCTURE

ING A/P's activities were organized by business units (countries). The regional office in Hong Kong fulfilled the role as monitoring center. The regional goal was to be a top player in the key markets of Australia, Hong Kong, Japan, Korea, Malaysia and Taiwan, while further developing the major growth markets of China and India. What this goal meant and how it could be achieved was left largely to the local country business units.

Individual business units (countries) had a relatively high level of autonomy. This culture created a very entrepreneurial environment, but also some frictions between the regional office in Hong Kong and the country business units. The functional managers at the regional office had difficulties maintaining common standards across the region. As one regional office manager stated:

> All business units have different ideas, standards and priorities. It is hard to keep track of activities, especially since the business unit managers only report to the regional managers and not to us, who are supposed to be in charge for the coordination of the operational activities.

The region was divided into four country clusters, each under the nominal supervision of either one of two regional general managers or one of two executive members who then reported to the regional CEO (see Exhibit 5). The regional CEO reported directly to the chairman of the executive committee. The regional office had several regional office professionals reporting to the chief of staff, including actuarial staff, the controller, as well as professionals engaged in the areas of legal issues, compliance issues, information technology (IT), investment product development, human resources (HR), E-business, security and finance. The chief of staff, the executive members and the regional managers were part of the regional management committee. The regional functional department managers did not have direct responsibility for their respective counterparts within each business unit. For example, the IT manager in Thailand reported to the Thailand country manager, not to the regional IT manager. The regional IT manager received information from the country manager by request.

The individual business units varied greatly in terms of their internal organizational characteristics and operating styles. Some business units, like Taiwan, Japan and Hong Kong, were organized along product lines. Other business units were organized as "do it alls," such as Australia, which marketed itself as a total financial solution provider. In each country, the local management followed their own instincts. There was no corporate-wide approach. By and large the units were successful, and the potential benefits of a more common approach were rarely explored.

KEMP'S SIZE-UP

Although the latest results had been solid and ING Insurance Asia/Pacific appeared to be doing well, something bothered Kemp. During off-site meetings, where the senior line and functional managers of the regional office and the local business units discussed what could be improved to get to better performance, Kemp received clear calls for better coordination between the regional office and the individual business units. The executives asked specifically for more aligned plans and procedures improved communication, and more delegated authority (see Exhibit 6). There was a clear belief that a detailed roadmap was needed to get things done. Kemp pondered:

> Would it be an operating model, a business model, or a process framework and whatever the name, where can I find it. Could the head office provide me with one; or perhaps I should try to involve consulting firms?

Regional reports were characterized by a multitude of different formats, which made comparisons difficult. Functional heads at the regional office spent several days each month preparing consolidated presentations. Business unit managers defined their own performance benchmarks and agendas for regional meetings. As the chief of staff recalled:

> Sometimes it appears that we speak totally different languages and that nobody understands one another. This is frustrating for us at the regional office and I believe that this is the reason why the business unit managers do not really buy into ideas proposed by the regional office's functional groups.

Kemp sensed the difficulties with the existing level of organizational heterogeneity. Strategic objectives were set according to business unit preferences and they were not formally aligned with regional strategy. Pay for performance was difficult to implement, since results were reported in local formats and not measured against group benchmarks. Local marketing campaigns did not always reflect existing corporate identity standards. In fact, many business unit managers did not even know the current corporate standards.

Each country had its own ideas where the best business opportunities could be found, and thought its own market was special. Consequently, it was difficult to identify commonalities across the region. As Kemp recalled from some of the feedback that he received during his initial tour of the region:

> There are no clear mission statements, despite that every country wants to be the leader in something. For example India wants to be the leader in asset management but without presenting a clear plan, outlining how to get there with for example acquisition, organic growth or through partnerships and what this means for the organization, marketing and so on.

Another problem was the ambiguity in terms of the roles of the managers at the regional office. The managers knew their titles but nobody was really clear how the roles tied into the operational structure. During the last couple of months, Kemp heard many times the question: "What is the actual function of the regional office?" This issue caused frustration especially with the functional managers at the regional office who felt disconnected from the operations of the business units.

As Kemp observed:

> Strategic actions are mainly characterized by reactions and less by planning. As the new CEO I have to handle all kinds of strategic plans for the various business units, most are different, inconsistent, incomplete, not aligned with the overall goals of ING, and short of details and specifics. I am therefore wondering what is the "better" way for getting from strategy to execution. I have checked the literature, I checked with consultants and my own study papers and I have not come across any solid and pragmatic operating model or framework for getting close to what I think we need.

THE CONSULTANTS

Kemp exchanged ideas with several top international consulting firms, including McKinsey & Company, Monitor, and Boston Consulting Group (BCG) about ING Insurance Asia/Pacific's situation. The inputs were initial overviews and not detailed analyses, but Kemp wanted to get a feeling for the thought processes of these firms and whether it would be worthwhile to engage one of them for follow-on work. Each firm identified different key issues (see Exhibit 7).

McKinsey & Company identified strategic portfolio management and pro-active human resource management as the key areas for improvement. Kemp could see the importance of these issues but he noted the lack of marketing and operational recommendations. For him, the proposal did not get to the day-to-day operational issues. He did not see how a different approach to HR management could solve the operational issues that he had already identified. He believed that ING Insurance Asia/Pacific had a great talent pool and that HR management could not be the only key driver for further improvement.

Monitor Group, on the other side, focused on branding as the key driver for improvements in all areas, including, finance, HR, sales, marketing, manufacturing and operations, distribution and research and development (R&D). Kemp was aware of the importance of branding, which, in fact, was a core strength of ING globally. However, he did not think that branding could or should overwhelm the other key drivers for success.

BCG's proposal focused on building professional capabilities and identified six functional categories in which capabilities should be improved or developed. These categories included strategy and business planning, sales and distribution, products and marketing, finance management, operational processes and infrastructure, and human resources and organization. Kemp liked the approach of BCG but he still noted the lack the important issue of reputation management and compliance. Like the other consulting firms, BCG applied a generic framework to ING. Kemp still thought that the solution was detached from ING Insurance Asia/Pacific's specific operational issues. After all, the company was doing well, so if he started a change process, he needed the full support of his team; and the consultants' proposals, though interesting, did not provide a clear pathway for involving ING Insurance Asia/Pacific's managers.

Kemp summarized:

> Even if BCG gets the closest, the model lacks completeness and comprehensiveness (specific operational drivers). It is also incomplete in that it does not follow through with clear "objectives and key performance measures." For me it comes to the question how to get from strategy to execution, especially in an aligned way and how to list and connect all the "dots" needed to build (and keep building) a "lasting" and efficient organization. Most models talk about it but do not give me a framework to connect the "dots" with tools like for example pay-for-performance, knowledge-management, intra-firm communication, or planning and auditing.

Another problem for Kemp was the regular disconnect between the functional managers at the regional office and the business unit managers in the countries. He believed this lack of coherence created inefficiencies and potential vulnerability for the entire organization.

Over the years, Kemp had always been interested in the management literature. He met many of the top strategists in industry and academia at conventions and seminars. He particularly liked the idea of "managing managers," which to him was a key gap in the existing management literature. He thought leaders should build organizational capabilities and the internal discipline to help everyone in the organization to excel. He did not want to add complexity, a pitfall he believed many leaders fell into when restructuring organizations. He believed that strategy, and strategic thinking, while important, could only be as good as its implementation.

Kemp had always felt inspired by Alfred Sloan's restructuring success of General Motors in the 1920s and 1930s. When Sloan took over GM, he inherited an amalgamation of independent, entrepreneurial companies assembled by his predecessor, William Durant. Sloan saw that the strategies of the businesses could be made more coherent and that the entire organization could be more efficient by building systems to manage the managers. At the time, Sloan's approach was revolutionary.

Kemp pondered over the consultant's proposals and his own ideas and he wondered how to create a coherent strategy, which could be executed by the entire organization. He was determined to present his concept at the next executive committee meeting in two weeks' time but he had to decide where to focus (see Exhibit 8).

Exhibit 1   ING Global Business Lines and Shares

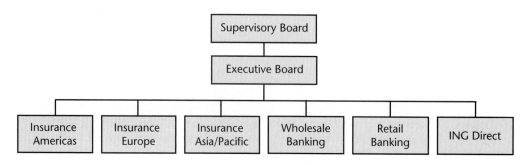

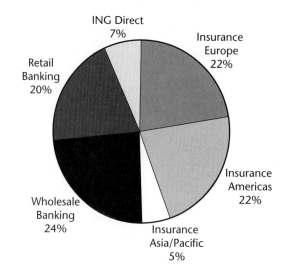

Source: ING Asia/Pacific

Exhibit 2   ING Asia/Pacific Insurance Product Offerings

Country	Term	Endowment	Whole Life	Health	Critical Illness	United Linked/ Universal Life	Variable Annuity	General Insurance	Group Insurance
Australia	✓	×	×	×	✓	✓	×	✓	✓
China-PALIC[1]	✓	✓	✓	✓	✓	✓	×	×	✓
China-ICLIC[2]	✓	✓	✓	✓	✓	✓	×	×	✓
Hong Kong	✓	✓	✓	✓	✓	✓	×	✓	✓
India	✓	✓	✓	×	✓	✓	×	×	✓
Japan	✓	✓	✓	✓	✓	×	✓	×	✓
ING Life Korea	✓	×	✓	✓	✓	✓	✓	×	✓
KB Life Korea	×	×	×	×	×	✓	×	×	✓
Malaysia	✓	✓	✓	✓	✓	✓	×	✓	✓
New Zealand	✓	×	×	✓	✓	✓	×	×	×
Taiwan	✓	✓	✓	✓	✓	✓	✓	✓	✓
Thailand	✓	✓	✓	✓	✓	×	×	×	✓
Indonesia	✓	✓	✓	✓	✓	✓	×	✓	✓
Singapore	×	×	×	✓	×	×	×	✓	×
The Philippines	✓	✓	✓	✓	×	×	×	×	✓

Notes:
Group insurance covers all types of products.
Education plans are considered as endowment plans.
Universal Life products are offered in Korea and China.
Hong Kong offers both universal life and unit linked products.
In Taiwan, General insurance only includes travel insurance products.
ING does not currently have insurance operations in Singapore, Indonesia or the Philippines.

Source: ING Asia/Pacific

[1] 50/50 joint venture operations in life insurance with Pacific Antai Life (PALIC) in Shanghai.
[2] 50/50 joint venture operations in life insurance with Beijing Capital Group in the northern city of Dalian. The new joint venture was known as ING Capital Life Insurance Company Ltd. (ICLIC).

Exhibit 3 Asset Management Product Offerings

Business Unit	Product Offerings
Australia	Australian equities and fixed income, Diversified (balanced) funds, International equities & fixed Income, Multi-manager (Optimix), Private equity, Global property securities and Global high dividend
China	Equity funds, Balanced funds and Bond funds
Hong Kong	Asian equities, Hong Kong equities & fixed income, Asian & Emerging Market debt, Proprietary equities and fixed income
India	Equity funds, Balanced funds and Bond funds
Japan	Japanese bonds and equities, International bonds and equities and Balanced funds
Korea	Domestic Korean bonds and equities, Offshore funds and Balanced funds
Malaysia	Proprietary domestic equities & fixed income, Unit-linked insurance investment products, Discretionary investment mandates, Corporate / residential mortgage loans and Domestic real estate
New Zealand	Domestic and International fixed income and equities
Philippines	Balanced funds, Advisory services, Peso fixed income, Domestic equities, Philippines USD bonds, Deposits, Securities and structured product offerings
Singapore	Offshore mutual funds, Singapore $ bond funds, ASEAN equity funds, Institutional discretionary mandates
Taiwan	Domestic Taiwanese equities, fixed income & balanced investments, Localized versions of ING global products, Discretionary account management and Offshore funds of various labels
Thailand	Mutual funds, Property funds, Real estate investment trusts, Private funds and Provident funds
Indonesia	ING Investment Management A/P does not have asset management business in Indonesia

Source: ING Asia Pacific

Exhibit 4 ING Asia/Pacific Financial Overview

Figures in Euro million	2002	2001	Change
Premium Income	7,798	6,497	20%
Annual Premium Equivalent	1,283	1,395	−8%
Underlying Profit before Tax	324	281	15%
Value of New Life Business	280	247	13%
Internal Rate of Return	15.4%	14.9%	3%
Assets under Management (€ billion)	37.3	25.6	46%

Source: ING Asia/Pacific

Exhibit 5　ING Asia/Pacific Organization Chart Prior to April 2003

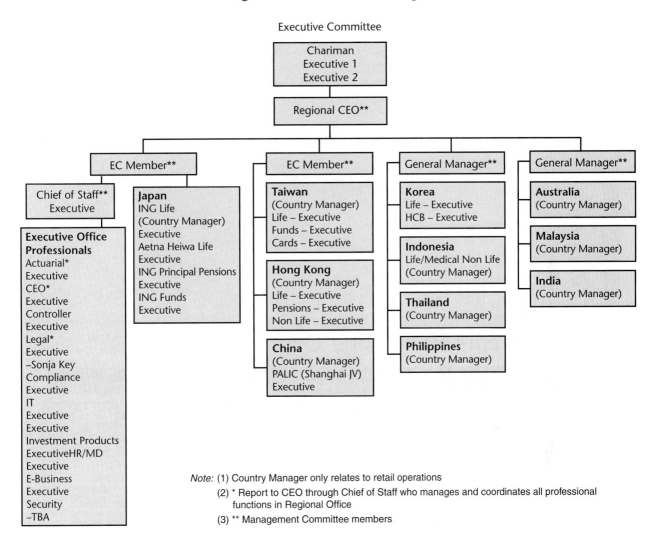

Executive Committee

Chariman
Executive 1
Executive 2

Regional CEO**

EC Member**

Chief of Staff**
Executive

**Executive Office
Professionals**
Actuarial*
Executive
CEO*
Executive
Controller
Executive
Legal*
Executive
–Sonja Key
Compliance
Executive
IT
Executive
Executive
Investment Products
ExecutiveHR/MD
Executive
E-Business
Executive
Security
–TBA

Japan
ING Life
(Country Manager)
Executive
Aetna Heiwa Life
Executive
ING Principal Pensions
Executive
ING Funds
Executive

EC Member**

Taiwan
(Country Manager)
Life – Executive
Funds – Executive
Cards – Executive

Hong Kong
(Country Manager)
Life – Executive
Pensions – Executive
Non Life – Executive

China
(Country Manager)
PALIC (Shanghai JV)
Executive

General Manager**

Korea
Life – Executive
HCB – Executive

Indonesia
Life/Medical Non Life
(Country Manager)

Thailand
(Country Manager)

Philippines
(Country Manager)

General Manager**

Australia
(Country Manager)

Malaysia
(Country Manager)

India
(Country Manager)

Note: (1) Country Manager only relates to retail operations
(2) * Report to CEO through Chief of Staff who manages and coordinates all professional
functions in Regional Office
(3) ** Management Committee members

Source: ING Asia/Pacific

Exhibit 6   Jacques Kemp's Key Issues

Sounds familiar.....?

⇨ Line and functions should be better aligned...

⇨ We should set clear objectives...

⇨ We should pay for performance...

⇨ We need a better operating/business model to execute...

Question: HOW??

Source: ING Asia/Pacific

Exhibit 7   The Consulting Proposals

The Problem:
Consultants Have Their Own Ideas

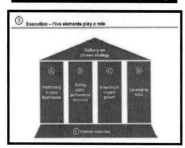

• Focus on business portfolio management	• Branding is the driving force for all processes	• BCG: 6 functional categories, in which capabilities should be built
• Human resources seen as fundamental		
Issue:	**Issue:**	**Issue:**
Vital functions such as marketing and operations are missing!	*Branding should be considered in most processes, but not as the driver of everything!*	*Reputation management (including Compliance) is still missing!*

Exhibit 8   The Problem

How to apply the Theory while faced with more and more Issues?

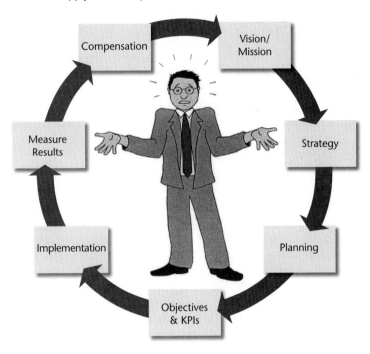

Source: ING Asia/Pacific

Case 32

Victoria Heavy Equipment Limited

Brian Walters sat back in the seat of his Lear jet as it broke through the clouds en route from Squamish, a small town near Vancouver, British Columbia, to Sacramento, California. As chairman of the board, majority shareholder, and chief executive officer, the 51-year-old Walters had run Victoria Heavy Equipment Limited as a closely held company for years. During this time it had become the second-largest producer of mobile cranes in the world, with 2007 sales of $150 million and exports to more than 30 countries. But in early 2008 the problem of succession was in his thoughts. His son and daughter were not ready to run the organization, and he personally wanted to devote more time to other interests. He wondered about the kind of person he should hire to become president. There was also a nagging thought that there might be other problems with Victoria that would have to be worked out before he eased out of his present role.

COMPANY HISTORY

Victoria Heavy Equipment Limited (Victoria) was established in 1917 in Victoria, British Columbia, to produce horse-drawn log skidders for the forest industry. The young firm showed a flair for product innovation, pioneering the development of motorized skidders and later, after diversifying into the crane business, producing the country's first commercially successful hydraulic crane controls. In spite of these innovations, the company was experiencing severe financial difficulties in 1970 when it was purchased by Brian Walters Sr., the father of the current chairman. By installing tight financial controls and paying close attention to productivity, Walters was able to turn the company around, and in 1977 he decided that Victoria would focus exclusively on cranes, and go after the international market.

Paul W. Beamish and Thomas A. Poynter wrote this case solely to provide material for class discussion. The authors do not intend to illustrate either effective or ineffective handling of a managerial situation. The authors may have disguised certain names and other identifying information to protect confidentiality.

At the time of Brian Walters Sr.'s retirement in 1990, it was clear that the decision to concentrate on the crane business had been a good one. The company's sales and profits were growing, and Victoria cranes were beginning to do well in export markets. Walters Sr. was succeeded as president by his brother James, who began to exercise very close personal control over the company's operations. However, as Victoria continued to grow in size and complexity, the load on James became so great that his health began to fail. The solution was to appoint an assistant general manager, John Rivers, through whom tight supervision could be maintained while James Walters' workload was eased. This move was to no avail, however. James Walters suffered a heart attack in 1992 and Rivers became general manager. At the same time, the young Brian Walters, the current chairman and chief executive officer, became head of the U.S. operation.

When Brian Walters took responsibility for Victoria's U.S. business, the firm's American distributor was selling 30 to 40 cranes per year. Walters thought the company should be selling at least 150. Even worse, the orders that the American firm did get tended to come in large quantities, as many as 50 cranes in a single order. This played havoc with Victoria's production scheduling. Walters commented, "We would rather have 10 orders of 10 cranes each than a single order for 100." In 1997, when the U.S. distributor's agreement expired, he offered the company a five-year renewal if it would guarantee sales of 150 units per year. When the firm refused, Walters bought it, and in the first month fired 13 of the 15 employees and cancelled most existing dealerships. He then set to work to rebuild, only accepting orders for 10 cranes or less. His hope was to gain a foothold and a solid reputation in the U.S. market before the big U.S. firms noticed him.

This strategy quickly showed results, and in 1998 Walters came back to Canada. As Rivers was still general manager, there was not enough to occupy him fully, and he began travelling three or four months a year. While he was still very much a part of the company, it was not a full-time involvement.

VICTORIA IN THE EARLY 2000s

Victoria entered the early 2000s with sales of approximately $75 million and by 2007, partly as a result of opening the new plant in California, had succeeded in doubling this figure. Profits reached their highest level ever in 2005, but declined somewhat over the next two years as costs rose and the rate of sales growth slowed. Financial statements are presented in Exhibits 1 and 2. The following sections describe the company and its environment in the early 2000s.

Product Line

The bulk of Victoria's crane sales in the late 1990s and early 2000s came from a single product line, the LTM 1000, which was produced both in its Squamish facility (the firm had moved from Victoria to Squamish in the early 1920s) and its smaller plant in California, built in 2001. The LTM 1000 line consisted of mobile cranes of five basic sizes, averaging $750,000 in price. Numerous options were available for these cranes, which could provide uncompromised on-site performance, precision lifting capabilities, fast highway travel, and effortless city driving. Because of the numerous choices available, Victoria preferred not to build them to stock. The company guaranteed 60-day delivery and "tailor-made" cranes to customer specifications. This required a large inventory of both parts and raw material.

Walters had used a great deal of ingenuity to keep Victoria in a competitive position. For example, in 2004, he learned that a company trying to move unusually long and heavy logs from a new tract of redwood trees in British Columbia was having serious problems with its existing cranes. A crane with a larger than average height and lifting capacity was required. Up to this point, for technical reasons, it had not been possible to produce a crane with the required specifications. However, Walters vowed that Victoria would develop such a crane, and six months later it had succeeded.

Although the LTM 1000 series provided almost all of Victoria's crane sales, a new crane had been introduced in 2006 after considerable expenditure on design, development and manufacture. The $975,000 A-100 had a 70-tonne capacity and could lift loads to heights of 61 metres, a combination previously unheard of in the industry. Through the use of smooth hydraulics even the heaviest loads could be picked up without jolts. In spite of these features, and an optional ram-operated tilt-back cab designed to alleviate the stiff necks which operators commonly developed from watching high loads, sales of the A-100 were disappointing. As a result, several of the six machines built were leased to customers at unattractive rates. The A-100 had, however, proven to be a very effective crowd attraction device at equipment shows.

Markets

There were two important segments in the crane market—custom-built cranes and standard cranes—and although the world mobile crane market was judged to be $945 million in 2007, no estimates were available as to the size of each segment. Victoria competed primarily in the custom segment, in the medium- and heavy-capacity end of the market. In the medium-capacity custom crane class Victoria's prices were approximately 75 per cent of those of its two main competitors. The gap closed as the cranes became heavier, with Victoria holding a 15 per cent advantage over Washington Cranes in the heavy custom crane business. In heavy standard cranes Victoria did not have a price advantage.

Victoria's two most important markets were Canada and the United States. The U.S. market was approximately $360 million in 2007, and Victoria's share was about 15 per cent. Victoria's Sacramento plant, serving both the U.S. market and export sales involving U.S. aid and financing, produced 60 to 70 cranes per year. The Canadian market was much smaller, about $66 million in 2007, but Victoria was the dominant firm in the country, with a 60 per cent share. The Squamish plant, producing 130 to 150 cranes per year, supplied both the Canadian market and all export sales not covered by the U.S. plant. There had been very little real growth in the world market since 2002.

The primary consumers in the mobile crane industry were contractors. Because the amount of equipment downtime could make the difference between showing a profit or loss on a contract, contractors were very sensitive to machine dependability, as well as parts and service availability. Price was important, but it was not everything. Independent surveys suggested that Washington Crane, Victoria's most significant competitor, offered somewhat superior service and reliability, and if Victoria attempted to sell similar equipment at prices comparable to Washington's, it would fail. As a result, Victoria tried to reduce its costs through extensive backward integration, manufacturing 85 per cent of its crane components in-house, the highest percentage in the industry. This drive to reduce costs was somewhat offset, however, by the fact that much of the equipment in the Squamish plant was very old. In recent years, some of the slower and less versatile machinery had been replaced, but by 2007 only 15 per cent of the machinery in the plant was new, efficient, numerically controlled equipment.

Victoria divided the world into eight marketing regions. The firm carried out little conventional advertising, but did participate frequently at equipment trade shows. One of the company's most effective selling tools was its ability to fly in prospective customers from all over the world in Walters' executive jet. Victoria believed that the combination of its integrated plant, worker loyalty, and the single-product concentration evident in their Canadian plant produced a convinced customer. There were over 14 such visits to the British Columbia plant in 2007, including delegations from China, Korea, France and Turkey.

Competition

As the world's second-largest producer of cranes, Victoria faced competition from five major firms, all of whom were much larger and more diversified. The industry leader was the Washington Crane Company with 2007 sales of $600 million and a world market share of 50 per cent. Washington had become a name synonymous around the world with heavy-duty equipment and had been able to maintain a sales growth-rate of over 15 per cent per annum for the past five years. It manufactured in the United States, Mexico and Australia. Key to its operations were 100 strong dealers worldwide with over 200 outlets. Washington had almost 30 per cent of Canada's crane market.

Next in size after Victoria was Texas Star, another large manufacturer whose cranes were generally smaller than Victoria's and sold through the company's extensive worldwide equipment dealerships. The next two largest competitors were both very large U.S. multinational producers whose crane lines formed a small part of their overall business. With the exception of Washington, industry observers suggested that crane sales for these latter firms had been stable (at best) for quite some time. The exception was the Japanese crane producer Toshio which had been aggressively pursuing sales worldwide and had entered the North American market recently. Sato, another Japanese firm, had started in the North American market as well. Walters commented:

> My father laid the groundwork for the success that this company has enjoyed, but it is clear that we have some major challenges ahead of us. Washington is four times our size and I know that we are at the top of their hit list. Our Japanese competitors, are also going to be tough. The key to our success is to remain flexible— we must not develop the same kind of organization as the big U.S. firms.

Organization

In 2001, a number of accumulating problems had ended Brian Walters' semi-retirement and brought him back into the firm full time. Although sales were growing, Walters saw that work was piling up and things were not getting done. He believed that new cranes needed to be developed, and he wanted a profit-sharing plan put in place. One of his most serious concerns was the development of middle managers, given a perceived lack of depth. The root cause of these problems, Walters believed, was that the firm was overly centralized. Most of the functional managers reported to Rivers, and Rivers made most of the decisions. Walters concluded that action was necessary: "If we want to grow further we have to change."

Between 2001 and 2004 Walters reorganized the firm by setting up separate operating companies and a corporate staff group. In several cases, senior operating executives were placed in staff/advisory positions, while in others, executives held positions in both operating and staff groups. Exhibit 3 illustrates Victoria's organizational chart as of 2005.

By early 2006 Walters was beginning to wonder "if I had made a very bad decision." The staff groups weren't working. Rivers had been unable to accept the redistribution of power and had resigned. There was "civil war in the company." Politics and factional disputes were the rule rather than the exception. Line managers were upset by the intervention of the staff VPs of employee relations, manufacturing, and marketing. Staff personnel, on the other hand, were upset by "poor" line decisions.

As a result, the marketing and manufacturing staff functions were eradicated with the late-2007 organizational restructuring illustrated in Exhibit 4. The services previously supplied by the staff groups were duplicated to varying extent inside each division.

In place of most of the staff groups, an executive committee was established in 2006. Membership included the president and head of all staff groups and presidents (general managers) of the four divisions. Meeting monthly, the executive committee was intended to evaluate the performance of the firm's profit and cost problems, handle mutual problems such as transfer prices, and allocate capital expenditures among the four operating divisions. Subcommittees handled subjects such as research and development (R&D) and new products.

The new organization contained seven major centres for performance measurement purposes. The cost centres were:

1. Engineering; R&D (reporting to Victco Ltd.)
2. International Marketing (Victoria Marketing Ltd.)
3. Corporate staff.

The major profit centres were:

4. CraneCorp. Inc. (U.S. production and sales)
5. Victco Ltd. (supplying Victoria with components)
6. Craneco (Canadian production and marketing)
7. Victoria-owned Canadian sales outlets (reporting to Victoria Marketing Ltd.)

The major profit centres had considerable autonomy in their day-to-day operations and were motivated to behave as if their division was a separate, independent firm.

By mid-2007, Brian Walters had moved out of his position as president, and Michael Carter, a long-time employee close to retirement, was asked to take the position of president until a new one could be found.

Walters saw his role changing.

> If I was anything, I was a bit of an entrepreneur. My job was to supply that thrust, but to let people develop on their own accord. I was not concerned about things not working, but I was concerned when nothing was being done about it.

In the new organization Walters did not sit on the executive committee. However, as chairman of the board and chief executive officer, the committee's recommendations came to him and ". . . they constantly tried me on." His intention was to monitor the firm's major activities rather than to set them. He did have to sit on the product development subcommittee, however, when "things were not working . . . there was conflict . . . the engineering group (engineering, R&D) had designed a whole new crane and nobody, including me, knew about it." Mr. McCarthy, the VP of engineering and R&D, called only five to six committee meetings. The crane his group developed was not to Walters' liking. (There had been a high turnover rate in this group, with four VPs leaving since 2005.) Recognizing these problems, Walters brought in consultants to tackle the problems of the management information system and the definition of staff/line responsibilities.

In spite of these moves, dissatisfaction still existed within the company in 2008. The new organization had resulted in considerable dissension. Some conflict centred on the establishment of appropriately challenging budgets for each operating firm and even more conflict had erupted over transfer pricing and allocation of capital budgets. In 2007-08, even though requested budgets were cut equally, lack of central control over spending resulted in over expenditures by several of the profit and cost centres.

The views of staff and the operating companies' presidents varied considerably when they discussed Victoria's organizational evolution and the operation of the present structure. Diane Walters, the president of Victoria International Marketing, liked the autonomous system because it helped to identify the true performance of sections of the company. "We had separate little buckets and could easily identify results." Furthermore, she felt that there was no loss of efficiency (due to the duplication of certain staff functions within the divisions) since there was little duplication of systems between groups, and each group acted as a check and balance on the other groups so that "manufacturing won't make what marketing won't sell." Comments from other executives were as follows:

The divisionalized system allowed me to get closer to my staff because we were a separate group.

We ended up with sales and marketing expertise that was much better than if we had stayed under manufacturing.

If you (run the firm) with a manufacturing-oriented organization, you could forget what people want.

In a divisionalized system there was bound to be conflict between divisions, but that was not necessarily unhealthy.

Some executives saw the decentralized, semi-autonomous operating company structure as a means of giving each person the opportunity to grow and develop without the hindrance of other functional executives. Most, if not all, of the operating company presidents and staff VPs were aware that decentralization brought benefits, especially in terms of the autonomy it gave them to modify existing practices. One senior executive even saw the present structure as an indicator of their basic competitive stance, "Either we centralize the structure and retract, or we stay as we are and fight with the big guys." With minimal direction from Brian Walters, presidents were able to build up their staff, establish priorities and programs, and essentially, were only held responsible for the bottom line.

Other executives believed that Victoria's structure was inappropriate. As one put it, "The semi-independence of the operating companies and the lack of a real leader for the firm has resulted in poor co-ordination of problem solving and difficulty in allocating responsibility." As an example, he noted how engineering's response to manufacturing was often slow and poorly communicated. Even worse, the executive noted, was how the priorities of different units were not synchronized. "When you manufacture just one product line all your activities are inter-related. So when one group puts new products first on a priority list, while another is still working out bugs in the existing product, conflict and inefficiencies have to develop."

The opposing group argued that the present organization was more appropriate to a larger, faster growing and more complex company. As one senior executive put it, "We're too small to be as decentralized as we are now. All of this was done to accommodate the Walters' kids anyway, and it's now going to detract from profitability and growth." Another executive stated that rather than being a president of an operating company he would prefer to be a general manager at the head of a functional group, reporting to a group head. "If we had the right Victoria Heavy Equipment president," he said, "we wouldn't need all these divisional presidents." Another continued,

> Right now the players (divisional presidents and staff VPs) run the company. Brian Walters gives us a shot of adrenaline four or six times a year, but doesn't provide any active leadership. When Brian leaves, things stop. Instead, Brian now wants to monitor the game plan rather than set it up for others to run. As we still only have an interim president (Carter), it is the marketplace that leads us, not any strategic plan or goal.

THE NEW PRESIDENT

Individual views about the appropriate characteristics of a new president were determined by what each executive thought was wrong with Victoria. Everyone realized that the new president would have to accommodate Brian Walters' presence and role in the firm and the existence of his two children in the organization. They all generally saw Brian as wanting to supply ideas and major strategies, but little else.

All, but one of Victoria's executives agreed that the new president should not get involved in day-to-day activities or in major decision making. Instead, he should "arbitrate" among the line general managers (subsidiary presidents) and staff VPs and become more of a "bureaucrat-cum-diplomat" than an aggressive leader. As another put it, "The company will drive itself; only once in a while he'll steer a little."

THE 2008 SITUATION

Due to the proliferation of subprime mortgages in the U.S. and the subsequent decline in real estate and construction, industry analysts predicted a decline of 10 per cent in world crane sales, which totalled 1,200 units in 2007, and as much as a 30 per cent decrease in the North American market in 2008. Victoria's sales and production levels were down. Seventy-five shop floor employees had been laid off at Squamish, bringing total employment there to 850, and similar cuts were expected in Sacramento. Worker morale was suffering as a result, and the profit sharing plan, which had been introduced in early 2007 at Walters' initiative, was not helping matters. In spite of the optimism conveyed to workers when the plan was initiated, management had announced in October that no bonus would be paid for the year. Aggravating the problem was the workforce's observation that while certain groups met their budget, others did not, and hence all were penalized. This problem arose because each bonus was based on overall as well as divisional profits.

Many of the shop-floor workers and the supervisory staff were also disgruntled with the additions to the central and divisional staff groups, which had continued even while the workforce was being reduced. They felt that the paperwork these staff functions created was time-consuming and of little benefit. They noted, for example, that there were four or five times as many people in production control in 2008 as there were in 2002 for the same volume of production. In addition, they pointed out that despite all sorts of efforts on the part of a computer-assisted production control group, inventory levels were still too high.

Brian Walters commented on the 2008 situation and his view of the company's future:

> What we are seeing in 2008 is a temporary decline in the market. This does not pose a serious problem for us, and certainly does not impact on my longer term goals for this company, which are to achieve a 25 per cent share of the world market by 2012, and reach sales of $375 million by 2021. We can reach these goals as long as we don't turn into one of these bureaucratic, grey-suited companies that are so common in North America. There are three keys for success in this business—a quality product, professional people and the motivation for Victoria to be the standard of excellence in our business. This means that almost everything depends on the competence and motivation of our people. We will grow by being more entrepreneurial, more dedicated, and more flexible than our competitors. With our single product line we are also more focused than our competitors. They manage only by the numbers—there is no room in those companies for an emotional plea, they won't look at sustaining losses to get into a new area, they'll turn the key on a loser . . . we look at the longer term picture.

"The hazard for Victoria," Walters said as he looked out of his window toward the Sacramento airstrip, "is that we could develop the same kind of bureaucratic, quantitatively oriented, grey-suited managers that slow down the large U.S. competitors. But that," he said, turning to his audience, "is something I'm going to watch like a hawk. We need the right people."

Exhibit 1   Victoria Balance Sheet For The Years 2003–2007 ($000s)

	2003	2004	2005	2006	2007
ASSETS					
Current Assets					
Accounts receivable	$12,492	$11,940	$14,664	$15,768	$16,426
Allowance for doubtful accounts	(439)	(465)	(423)	(445)	(474)
Inventories	31,729	36,637	37,047	38,439	40,567
Prepaid expenses	178	156	234	159	193
Total current assets	43,960	48,268	51,522	53,921	56,712
Advances to shareholders	1,950	1,950	1,950	1,950	1,950
Fixed assets: property plant and equipment	10,260	10,470	10,312	11,029	11,083
Total assets	$56,170	$60,688	$63,784	$66,900	$69,745
LIABILITIES AND SHAREHOLDERS' EQUITY					
Current Liabilities					
Notes payable to bank	$11,599	$12,328	$13,887	$15,241	$16,998
Accounts payable	14,568	17,029	15,814	15,697	16,479
Accrued expenses	1,611	1,678	2,613	2,251	1,732
Deferred income tax	628	600	594	612	517
Income tax payable	817	1,038	918	780	774
Current portion of long-term debt	1,368	1,336	1,300	1,332	1,354
Total current liabilities	$30,591	$34,009	$35,126	$35,913	$37,854
Long-term debt	9,426	9,165	9,030	9,007	9,171
Total liabilities	40,017	43,174	44,156	44,920	47,025
SHAREHOLDERS' EQUITY					
Common shares	300	435	442	585	652
Retained earnings	15,853	17,079	19,186	21,395	22,068
Total shareholders' equity	16,153	17,514	19,628	21,980	22,720
Total liabilities and shareholders' equity	$56,170	$60,688	$63,784	$66,900	$69,745

Exhibit 2   Victoria Income Statement For The Years 2003–2007 ($000s)

	2003	2004	2005	2006	2007
Revenue					
Net sales	$95,079	$116,566	$129,519	$142,329	$151,414
Costs and Expenses					
Cost of sales	73,857	89,755	95,994	107,727	113,712
Selling expense	11,205	13,851	16,402	17,155	19,656
Administrative expense	4,026	5,800	8,235	8,692	10,557
Engineering expense	2,013	2,533	2,748	2,923	3,163
Gross income	3,978	4,627	6,140	5,832	4,326
Income taxes	1,621	1,921	2,445	2,257	1,881
Net income	$ 2,357	$ 2,706	$ 3,695	$ 3,575	$ 2,445

Exhibit 3   Victoria Organizational Structure, 2001–05

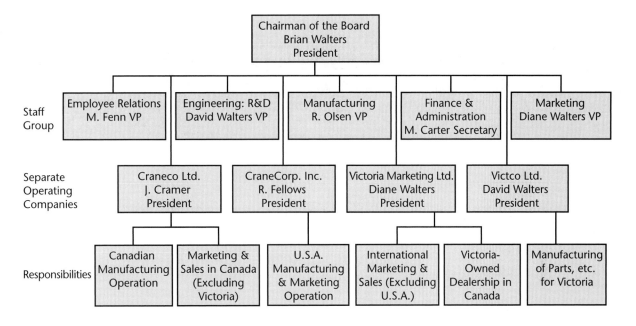

Exhibit 4   Victoria Organizational Structure, Late 2007

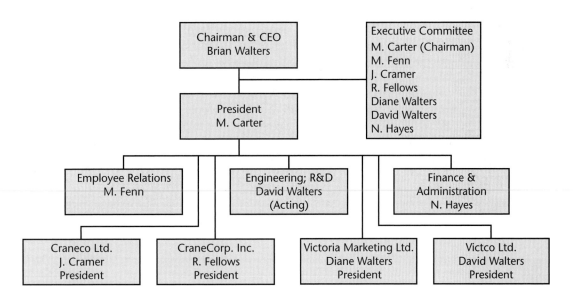

Case 33

Bombardier Transportation and the Adtranz Acquisition

On January 10, 2001, it had been one month only since Pierre Lortie was appointed president and chief operating officer of St. Bruno, Quebec-based Bombardier Transportation (BT).[1] BT was one of three major operating groups of Montreal, Canada-based Bombardier Inc. (BBD) and, with 2000 revenues amounting to Cdn$3.45 billion, it was one of the world's largest manufacturers of passenger rail cars. In an effort to expand BT's presence in the global rail equipment industry, executives at BBD had recently completed a successful negotiation for the acquisition of Adtranz from DaimlerChrysler for US$725 million. At approximately twice the size of BT, Adtranz (headquartered in Berlin, Germany) would not only expand BT's revenues and geographic scope but would significantly increase its competencies in propulsion systems and train controls and would complete its product portfolio. However, before the deal could close, BT required, among others, the regulatory approval of the European Commission (EC). Lortie was well aware that the EC process could be long and protracted.

Although Lortie had not been directly involved in the acquisition decision or negotiations, he was a supporter of the merger efforts. As he assumed his new responsibilities, Lortie began a thorough review of the work accomplished and the planning efforts undertaken to ensure an efficient integration of the two entities. As part of this process, he undertook a series of one-to-one meetings with members of his senior management team. The meetings were designed to measure the strengths and weaknesses of his key managers, but also to discuss the strategic and operational priorities.

Richard Ivey School of Business
The University of Western Ontario

David Barrett prepared this case under the supervision of Professor Allen Morrison solely to provide material for class discussion. The authors do not intend to illustrate either effective or ineffective handling of a managerial situation. The authors may have disguised certain names and other identifying information to protect confidentiality.

[1]St. Bruno was located on the south shore of the St. Lawrence River, in the suburbs of Montreal.

BT was structured into five geographically-based operating units—North America, Atlantic Europe, Continental Europe, Mexico and China—and one market/functional unit, Total Transit Systems—which focused on turnkey projects. In contrast, Adtranz was organized around product segments (i.e. high speed trains, cars, subway trams) and functions (i.e. bogies, drives, car bodies) making its structure and allocation of responsibilities quite foreign to Bombardier. Although each business complemented the other nicely and constituted a good strategic fit, the organizational structures were incompatible. Even though, BT's management team in Europe had not been involved in the discussions and reviews with Adtranz that had preceded and immediately followed the deal, they were keenly aware of the organizational issues and eager to establish their position as soon as the nod could be given to proceed with the takeover.

On January 10, 2001, Lortie had just finished his first in-depth meeting with Rick Dobbelaere, vice-president of operations of Bombardier Transportation, Atlantic Europe. Dobbelaere had come prepared with questions about how BT and the senior management team would set priorities during the interim period while awaiting EC approval. He presented these to Lortie in question form:

> Do we sit and await approval from the EC before taking steps towards the potential integration of Adtranz? Should we focus our planning on ways to improve the product quality and reliability of Adtranz equipment with existing customers? Should we start to institute personnel changes within BT in anticipation of the merger, and if so, at what pace? Do we focus on top-line revenue growth or start to immediately focus on bottom-line cost cutting?

Dobbelaere was highly respected, not only within the Atlantic Europe division but throughout Bombardier, and Lortie was aware that his concerns and questions were shared by others, particularly in Continental Europe.[2] But Lortie realized that he faced additional issues, including concerns over BT's ongoing operating performance. As Bombardier expected EC approval of the acquisition within a matter of weeks, Lortie and his team had little time to waste.

BOMBARDIER COMPANY HISTORY

The Early Years

In 1921, at the age of 19, Joseph-Armand Bombardier opened a garage in Valcourt, Quebec, where he earned his living as a mechanic. Early in his life he looked for a solution to the problem of traveling the snow-covered roads near his village, which kept many people isolated during the long winter months. Over a 10-year period, Bombardier used his garage to develop multiple prototypes of a vehicle that would make winter travel easier. In 1936, he submitted his B7 prototype, the precursor to today's snowmobile, for patent approval. This seven-seat passenger model sported a revolutionary rear-wheel drive and suspension system, both major innovations at that time.

After receiving an initial 20 orders, Bombardier assembled a work crew of friends and family to manufacture the B7s. Customers included country doctors, veterinarians, telephone companies and foresters. By 1940, Bombardier had built a modern factory in his village that had an annual capacity of 200 units. In 1942, Bombardier incorporated his business as L'Auto-Neige Bombardier Limitee (ANB). Shortly thereafter

---

[2]BT Continental Europe was based in Berlin and included six manufacturing facilities in Germany and one each in Austria and the Czech Republic.

the company began to receive orders from the Canadian government for specialized all-track vehicles for use by the armed forces efforts during the Second World War. Between 1942 and 1946, ANB produced over 1,900 tracked vehicles for the Canadian armed forces. Although not a profitable venture, the war-time manufacturing experience allowed Bombardier to refine his manufacturing process and develop competence in government relations.

The 1950s saw technological advances in lighter engines, improved tracking and high-performance synthetic rubber. In 1959, Bombardier achieved his lifelong dream when ANB introduced a one-passenger snowmobile. At an original price of Cdn$900, the Ski-Doo sported five-foot wooden skis, a coil spring suspension system and could travel at speeds of up to 25 miles per hour (mph). Sales increased from 225 units in 1959 to 2,500 units in 1962 and 8,000 units in 1964. Joseph-Armand Bombardier died in 1964, leaving a Cdn$10 million company to his son, Germain.

In 1966, Germain Bombardier passed on the presidency to his 27-year-old brother-in-law, Laurent Beaudoin, and in 1967, the company name was changed to Bombardier Limited. In 1969, the company went public with the intention of utilizing the funds to vertically integrate and increase its manufacturing capability. BBD grew as the market for snowmobiles rapidly expanded in the late 1960s and early 1970s. The North American snowmobile market grew from 60,000 units to 495,000 units in the period between 1966 and 1972, and BBD captured one-third of this market. Between 1966 and 1972, BBD's sales soared from Cdn$20 million to Cdn$180 million while profits rose from Cdn$2 million to Cdn$12 million. Under Beaudoin's leadership, the company pushed into the lucrative U.S. market, unveiled new products and utilized aggressive marketing initiatives to drive the business. In 1970, the company completed the acquisition of Austrian-based Lohnerwerke GmbH. Lohnerwerke's subsidiary, Rotax, was a key supplier of engines for Bombardier Ski-Doo snowmobiles and also a tramway manufacturer. This provided BBD with its first entry, albeit involuntarily, into the rail business. The energy crisis of the mid-1970s put the brakes on the snowmobile industry, and when the dust settled, the largest of the six remaining manufacturers was BBD.

Bombardier Begins to Diversify

Laurent Beaudoin, the chief executive of Bombardier, realized that in order to reduce cyclical risks and ensure its long-term survival, the company needed to diversify into other products beyond snowmobiles. To bolster sagging snowmobile sales, Beaudoin began to seek out opportunities for BBD within a more broadly defined transportation industry. In the late 1960s and early 1970s, BBD made several strategic acquisitions.

Transportation

In 1974, snowmobiles represented 90 per cent of BBD revenues. By securing a Cdn$118 million contract (US$99.14 million) with the city of Montreal to supply the local transit authority with 423 subway cars, BBD had made its first major move to diversify its revenues away from its predominant snowmobile business. Using rubber-wheeled cars licensed from the supplier to the Paris subway system, BBD's work won positive reviews from Montreal commuters. Further contracts followed, including supplying 36 self-propelled commuter rail cars to Chicago in 1977, 21 locomotives and 50 rail cars to Via Rail Canada in 1978, 117 commuter cars to New Jersey Transit Corporation in 1980, 180 subway cars to Mexico City in 1982, and 825 subway cars to the City of New York, also in 1982.

The mid-1980s was a turbulent time in the rail transportation industry, and BT looked to capitalize on industry uncertainty by purchasing companies at low prices and growing its market share through these acquisitions. Pullman Technology was acquired in 1987, Transit America in 1988, and controlling interests in rail equipment companies in France and Belgium in 1988. In the early 1990s, BT also acquired Concarril (Mexico's top rail manufacturer) as well as UTDC in Canada. These acquisitions and investments established BT as one of the leading supplier of rail cars and cemented its international reputation.

Aerospace

In 1973, BBD commenced diversification into the aerospace business with the acquisition of a controlling interest in Heroux Limited of Longueuil, Quebec. Heroux designed, manufactured and repaired aeronautical and industrial components at its two Canadian plants. In 1986, following an international bidding contest, BBD acquired struggling Canadair from the Canadian government at a total cash and share price of Cdn$293 million. By applying aggressive marketing tactics, cost-cutting measures and tight controls, BBD was quickly able to turn operations around. Subsequent acquisitions of Short Brother PLC (an aircraft producer in Northern Ireland) in 1990, Learjet Corporation in 1990 and a controlling stake in de Havilland in 1992 and the remaining interest in 1997 firmly entrenched BBD in the civil aircraft industry. During the 1990s, BBD introduced a series of new planes including the Lear 60, the Challenger 600-3A, the Challenger 604 and the Lear 45. BBD delivered its first Canadair Regional Jet in 1992 and its first Global Express business jet in 1999, the CRJ 700 (75 seat jet) in 2001.

Corporate Balance

By the early 1990s, BBD had diversified to the point where snowmobile sales represented less than 15 per cent of the company's revenues. BBD still controlled 50 per cent of the Canadian market and 25 per cent of the U.S. market for snowmobiles, but BBD had clearly established itself as a diversified company. By 1992, sales had increased to US$3.43 billion and profits to US$104 million. While, in many cases, the companies acquired by Bombardier were in poor shape, observers noted that the majority of Beaudoin's deals and acquisitions had been turned around and were making money.

Different operating groups at BBD took centre stage at different times during the 1990s (see Exhibit 1). In 1994, the recreational products group seemed to surge forward, fuelled by increased snowmobile sales and sales of Sea-Doo watercraft, first introduced in 1968. Profits from this group represented 37 per cent of the company's profits and made the recreational products group central to the company's success. The mid-1990s saw a boom in the aerospace group as both regional and business jet sales took off with the expanding economy. Many observers credited Bombardier with creating an entirely new commuter jet segment as the result of product innovation. Aerospace group sales grew from 1996 levels of US$3.16 billion to 2000 levels of US$7.79 billion. In 2000, the aerospace group represented 66 per cent of the company's revenues and 85 per cent of its profits.

BT continued to grow during this period as well. BT was awarded a prestigious contract to produce specialized rail cars for the huge Eurotunnel engineering project. In early 1995, Waggonfabrik Talbot KG of Germany was acquired for $130 million cash. In late 1997, BT acquired DWA Deutsche Waggonbau GmbH of Berlin for Cdn$518 million (approximately US$359.52 million) and thus doubled its train and subway car manufacturing capacity in Europe. In December of that year, BT secured a US$1.18 billion contract with Virgin Rail Group of Great Britain to supply 78 diesel/electric multiple units and rail cars. In November 1999, the company entered into a joint venture to construct a manufacturing facility in China and to subsequently build 300 inter-city mass transit railcars for the Chinese Ministry of Railways (see Exhibit 2).

Bombardier Growth Philosophy

BBD sought acquisition opportunities that allowed it to add value to the business through the application of its existing competencies. Acquisitions were typically not viewed solely as financial plays but as a way for BBD to complement or strengthen its existing businesses. BBD prided itself on thoroughly evaluating target companies so that pay-back was not reliant on the divestiture of some aspect of the acquired business. In negotiations, BBD had also shown that it was not afraid to walk away from a deal if it meant overpaying for a business. But once a deal was completed, BBD had a reputation for being patient in the integration of the acquired company.

In addition to a strong track record of integrating acquisitions, BBD had strengths in product costing and tendering. It also had extensive experience in product assembly. Whether aircraft, recreational products or rail cars, most products made by BBD were assembled as opposed to manufactured. Utilizing external suppliers and adopting just-in-time delivery methods resulted in substantially reduced inventory levels, throughput time and assets. BBD sought ways to control product technology and design, assembly and distribution while outsourcing other non-core functions.

When taking over a business, BBD tried to eliminate waste and turn around underperforming assets by applying tried and tested management approaches over time as opposed to rushing to replace existing methods. This approach to acquisitions had garnered strong employee support over the years as workers realized that BBD would invest in new products and thus protect jobs. When BBD entered the aerospace industry through acquisitions, it did not replace existing staff. Instead, it used personnel from BT to teach successful approaches and manufacturing methods developed elsewhere in the organization. Transfers were not all one way; aerospace also shared its best practices in engineering management. With a commitment to excellence in assembly, inventory and management control, the aerospace group and BT were both able to make significant gains in productivity and product quality.

Despite the similarities in operating strategy, BBD's businesses differed in important ways. Bombardier's rail business was counter-cyclical versus other businesses in the company. An event, such as an energy crisis, would affect the rail industry differently than recreation or aerospace. Also, technology and product development were somewhat different across the businesses. In recreational and aerospace products, a Ski-Doo or business jet was developed for the market in general while in rail, each customer had unique requirements and demanded tailor-made products. Generic rail cars simply did not exist. Customer demand varied according to a wide range of factors, including car size, weight, number of doors, propulsion system and so on. Other variables included the materials being used (steel versus aluminum), the type of car being produced (tramway, subway, inter city or high-speed rail) and the infrastructure interface (track width).

BT was well regarded for its competencies in assembling rail cars, but it had no in-house expertise in propulsion systems, locomotives and switching and communications gear. Mark Cooper, vice-president of supply management of the inter-city trains for Adtranz, commented on Bombardier's reputation:

> Overall, Bombardier had a good level of credibility in the market place, despite being the smallest of the four rail manufacturers and rail service providers. It was seen to be one of the most effective in terms of its ability to deliver contracts and to manage and govern itself.

THE GLOBAL RAIL TRANSPORTATION INDUSTRY

In 2001, the railway transportation industry could be divided into six distinct segments: services, propulsion and controls, total transit systems, rail control solutions, rolling stock and fixed installations. Bombardier was absent from the last segment which it considered as non-strategic and quite distinct in nature from the others.

1. Services included the planning and implementation of high quality production and maintenance programs for both new and existing systems. Services also included the development of long-term process improvements to both systems operation and rolling stock maintenance.

2. Propulsion and Controls provided the diesel and electric motors, traction drives and control systems for trains.

3. Total Transit Systems provided a process through which manufacturers developed and supplied complete transportation systems and services. Working in partnership with local civil contractors and suppliers, manufacturers designed, integrated, installed and delivered a broad range of technologies—from large-scale urban transit systems to airport people-movers.

4. Rail Control Solutions were required to operate safe and efficient railways. Customers needed effective and "fail-safe" rail control and signaling equipment and systems.

5. Rolling Stock included subway cars, locomotives, inter-city/regional trains, high speed trains, tram cars and light rail.

6. Fixed Installations referred to the building of rail infrastructure.

Public Policy and the Role of Governments in Regulating the Industry

The role of transportation and, with it, the attitudes and values of the public and government differed considerably from country to country and from continent to continent. Differences in public policy affected travel behaviors in a major way. While the cost of raw fuel amongst developed nations varied only marginally, fuel taxation levels differed by up to 800 per cent. As a result, public policy decisions affected not only the demand for fuel but also the demand for public transportation as an alternative to the automobile. Because of lower gasoline taxes and the promotion of automobile travel in the United States, public transport ridership was three to nine times lower there than in European countries.

Most industry analysts believed that European policies promoting reductions in congestion, pollution abatement, urban development, traffic safety and energy conservation would continue and that support for public transportation systems would continue for the foreseeable future. The question was whether the United States would embrace European norms as congestion increased in that country. The combination of greater geographic distances, car-friendly culture, efficient and large air travel system and aversion to government subsidies convinced many that U.S. rail policy would take a great many years to significantly change in a direction that supported an increase in rail transportation usage and investment.

Government regulations significantly affected industry structure in one other important way. Because U.S. passenger trains frequently shared tracks with freight trains, the government mandated that U.S. passenger rail cars be reinforced and strengthened in order to sustain collisions without collapsing with the ensuring high casualties that would result. As a result, U.S. trains were substantially heavier than European trains and were uncompetitive and poorly adapted to markets outside North America. European Union standards were widely embraced by governments and customers throughout the world, particularly in emerging economies such as China and India.

Infrastructure Model

A common perception in both Europe and the United States was that the rail industry, as a whole, was best designed to operate as a monopoly. High sunk costs, low marginal costs and demands for managerial co-ordination perpetuated this opinion. However, the emerging approach in the European Union (EU) was to separate the high-speed train industry and subject its component parts to competition. Although the potential technical, economic and social gains associated with this approach were perceived as exceptional, the process was often complicated by different national visions of how the industry should be divided between public and private ownership. Most countries opted to retain state ownership of infrastructure with the creation of a state agency to manage it. However, rolling stock companies were slowly becoming privatized. In 1998, the United Kingdom became the first country in the EU to totally privatize its rail system, including both infrastructure and rolling stock (see Exhibit 3).

The U.K. model of privately owned infrastructure and rolling stock had its troubles. The government was forced to operate the infrastructure element of the system when Railtrack, the private company it selected to manage the vast U.K. rail infrastructure (nearly 23,000 miles of track and 2,500 stations), went bankrupt in October 2001. Also, some in the United Kingdom worried about safety risks associated with spreading accountability across multiple for-profit companies. Conversely, the French model of public-owned, train operator had been a tremendous success. As one industry observer remarked,

> France was operating state-of-the-art 300 km/h trains on a new network of rail lines dedicated to fast passenger service, and making money doing it. Britain was operating 1960s technology, 200 km/h trains on the nation's undependable and failing 19th century freight/passenger network, and losing money.[3]

Despite the success of the publicly operated French system, the EU was not designed to promote monopolistic, country-centred railroad companies. As a result, the U.K. model of privatized rolling stock and state-operated infrastructure more closely fit the cultural and social paradigm emerging in the EU and was thus being adopted cautiously and to differing degrees throughout the EU. During the latter half of the 1990s, public sector funding gradually shifted from supporting nationally subsidized rail systems to include more significant involvement from local municipal governments and the private sector. The belief was that by shifting to private ownership of rolling stock, the railway industry would eventually emulate the automobile or air transport models. Airlines worked with governments to secure terminals and immediate air space and runways, while operating and maintaining their own or leased airplanes. In effect, the airlines rented the infrastructure. Many believed that rail companies should operate in a similar fashion.

---

[3]Andersen, Svein and Eliassen, Kjell (2001), *Making Policy in Europe*, London, Sage, p. 72.

High-Speed Trains

By the early 2000s, the European Commission continued to rank the development of a European-wide high-speed train infrastructure as its highest investment priority in transportation infrastructure. The Community of European Railways (COER), a continent-wide association of railway companies, asserted that high-speed rail services were especially appropriate for the 200 kilometre to 300 kilometre distances between heavily populated urban centres. Most of Europe fit this profile with mobility increasing as the prospects of a single European market progressed. But for Europe to fully benefit from the one market model, decisions in infrastructure policy required a European, and not a nationalistic, approach. However, many predicted that the tendency for governments to protect national producers would be detrimental to the continent-wide objectives for many years to come.

Customers

The privatization of many national railways had changed the financing arrangements and customer base within the European rail car industry. In the past, manufacturers like BT sold directly to government operated railroads. However, with the privatization of rolling stock operations increasing in Europe, leasing arrangements were now available to operators. In the United Kingdom, equipment manufacturers sold to one of three large rail equipment leasing companies (ROSCO) owned by one of three large British banks (Bank of Scotland, HSBC or Abbey National Bank) which then leased the new rolling stock to the train operators. This lease-versus-purchase option reduced up-front costs for rolling stock operators and significantly decreased their overall capital requirements. It also put a premium on standardized trains—necessary to protect residual values. This, in turn, significantly reduced the incentives to purchase rolling stock from within a rail operators' home country.

In countries with private rail operators, revenues were generated through ticket sales and government subsidies while expenses were incurred through infrastructure franchise fees, day-to-day train maintenance, fuel and labor costs and leasing expenses. Since leasing costs on old, existing stock were much cheaper than on new equipment, operators preferred to delay purchases for as long as possible. When equipment was ordered, rail operators would sometimes seek additional delays by complaining that delivered equipment suffered from low reliability, which prevented it from meeting defined service standards the operators had committed to achieve in order to gain the concession from the government to operate the train service. This, in turn, caused manufacturers to incur late delivery charges and inventory costs as rail cars piled up in shipping yards awaiting minor repairs or adjustments. Many observers believed that these dysfunctional practices would be repeated in other European nations as they evolved to private operating models.

DAIMLERCHRYSLER AND ADTRANZ HISTORY

Although the roots of Chrysler go back to 1920 in the United States, the history of Daimler-Benz dates to the 1880s in Germany and to the efforts of two inventive engineers—Gottlieb Daimler and Carl Benz. After a series of initiatives, Daimler-Benz was officially incorporated in 1926 and began producing cars under the Mercedes Benz brand.

By the 1980s, competition in the global automobile market had increased dramatically, and Daimler-Benz was looking to diversify its business. Between February 1985 and February 1986, the company acquired three conglomerates[4] for a combined US$1.11 billion. The cash expenditures of these 1985/86 acquisitions put a strain on its balance sheet, and by mid-1993, Daimler-Benz reported its first loss since the Second World War. In 1994, operations recovered somewhat with the company showing US$750 million in profits. But in 1995, the company's fortunes sagged again as it reported a loss of US$4 billion—the largest in German industrial history.

In 1995, Daimler-Benz's chief executive officer (CEO), Edvard Reuter, was forced to resign and was replaced by the aerospace division head, Jurgen Schrempp. One of Schrempp's first moves as CEO was the acquisition of 50 per cent of the rail division of Swedish-Swiss ABB Asea Brown Boveri Ltd. in exchange for US$900 million cash from Daimler-Benz. This joint venture formed the new ABB Daimler-Benz Transportation (Adtranz). Adtranz would become the largest rail service provider in the world with annual sales of US$4.5 billion.

By the mid-1990s, Robert Eaton had assumed the position of CEO at Chrysler at a time when the economic conditions in the automobile industry included an excess manufacturing capacity and an Asian economic crisis. Industry analysts were projecting an annualized global overcapacity of 18.2 million vehicles by the early 2000s. It came as no surprise that both Eaton and Schrempp were seeking partners due to the inevitable consolidation within the industry.

DaimlerChrysler AG was formed in November of 1998 when Daimler-Benz and Chrysler merged in a US$37 billion deal. In 1998, the newly formed company had revenues of US$130 billion, factories in 34 countries and sales of 4.4 million vehicles making it the fifth largest automobile manufacturer in the world. In 1999, DaimlerChrysler acquired the remaining 50 per cent of Adtranz from ABB for US$472 million.

ADTRANZ

Although the name Adtranz dates back only as far as 1995, the multiple production facilities that comprised the company date back to the 19th century. By the time of the DaimlerChrysler merger, the rail business in Europe had narrowed to four primary players: Alstom (France), Siemens (Germany), Adtranz and Bombardier. Unlike Altsom and Siemens, which had strong single country affiliations, Adtranz facilities and staff were a collection of multiple companies in multiple countries across the continent. Many of these companies also had a history of unstable ownership. For example, since 1989, the Adtranz facility in Derby, England, had experienced the following ownership changes: 100 per cent British Rail Engineering, then 40 per cent ABB, 40 per cent Trafalgar Rail and 20 per cent employee ownership, then 100 per cent ABB, then 50 per cent Daimler Chrysler and 50 per cent ABB and finally 100 per cent DaimlerChrysler. Each new ownership group brought its own philosophies to manufacturing, sales, contract tendering, personnel, etc. Mark Cooper commented on the cultural challenges in Adtranz:

> I don't think that Adtranz has had enough time to fully develop its own culture. Every two years there seems to have been a change of ownership, a change in structure, a change in values, and a change in processes. So under those circumstances you don't get a good sense of who you are.

---

[4]Daimler owned 50 per cent of Motoren-und Turbinen-Union (a manufacturer of aircraft engines and diesel motors for tanks and ships) and bought the remaining 50 per cent for $160 million. Daimler purchased 65.6 per cent of Dornier (a privately held manufacturer of spacecraft systems, commuter planes and medical equipment) for $130 million. Daimler additionally purchased control of AEG (a high-technology manufacturer of electronic equipment, such as turbines, robotics, data processing and household products) for $820 million.

In the late 1990s, Adtranz represented less than three per cent of DaimlerChrysler's revenues. Revenues of US$3.3 billion were recorded at Adtranz in 1999, and in 2000, after years of continual losses, Adtranz reported its first year of break-even results. Although Adtranz revenues were up over 15 per cent in 2000, the annual revenue growth over the previous four years averaged only 4.5 per cent. Given the complexity of the business and its peripheral role in DaimlerChrysler's overall strategy, many observers believed DaimlerChrysler would eventually divest its rail business.

Production Challenges

Although DaimlerChrysler's assembly process and knock-down capabilities had been introduced, Adtranz's reputation for producing high quality products was poor. In particular, Adtranz was having quality, reliability and certification problems with its core Electrostar and Turbostar model trains designed for the U.K. market (see Exhibit 4). In 2000, the Electrostar model had only eight trains in service as customers were refusing to accept this train. Reliability was achieved under the terms of the contract.[5] The Turbostar had 279 trains in service, but only 86.5 per cent were available for operation. Reliability was also not achieved under the terms of the contract. Deciphering the causes of these reliability problems was a challenge for BT managers. Neil Harvey, director of public affairs at BT, provided one common interpretation:

> In terms of the reputation of Adtranz's products and its overall reputation as a company, many believed there was a certain amount of mismanagement. In particular, some felt that too many contracts were being bought, and there was often very poor follow-through on products, production and subsequent support.

In addition, Adtranz's customer support function and its initial contract bidding processes were viewed by some as inadequate. Many at BBD believed that Bombardier's structured governance system, manufacturing controls and proven bidding systems would be excellent complements to Adtranz.

A STRATEGIC ACQUISITION FOR BOMBARDIER

Despite awareness that certain management practices needed adjustment, BBD viewed the acquisition of Adtranz as a smart strategic move for several reasons. Europe is the nexus of technological advances in the industry. Asia and South America primarily utilized European engineering concepts and had a history of failing to develop new technologies on their own. North American trains were too heavy and, hence, more expensive and costly to operate compared to the refinements in other world markets and therefore not competitive. Also, the green movement and strong government support signaled long-term growth in the demand for rail transportation in Europe.

Not only did BBD find the European rail market attractive, but it was increasingly interested in balancing the revenue streams produced by its various groups. Strengthening the company's rail business was viewed as an important move to counter-balance Bombardier's growing, but cyclical, aerospace group. Dr. Yvan Allaire, executive

---

[5]Reliability is measured as the total distance travelled by the rail car between breakdowns. The total performance of all rail cars is then averaged together to get the mean reliability number as a factor of distance travelled by each train model. This is then measured in subsequent periods to evaluate performance and reliability levels going forward.

vice-president at BBD, explained this strategic perspective: "Bombardier's value for shareholders is as a premium diversified company, not as an aerospace company."

Although margins were often lower in rail, (in 2000, margins for the aerospace group were 11 per cent—more than twice that of the transportation group) the industry benefited from the traditional business practice of advance and progress payments from customers. These payments translated to a low level of net utilized assets and very positive cash flow, contingent on a growing backlog of orders. These cash flows provided BBD with capital that was utilized throughout the company. Allaire explained this possibility:

> Transportation is a huge cash generator. While the margins are low, cash is large in this business. In fact, we have traditionally financed a large part of the investment in the aerospace sector from cash coming from transportation. A lot of people don't understand this.

Although low-margin businesses traditionally had profit levels driven by cost control, in the rail transportation industry, variability and project management performance were additional key drivers. For example, penalty charges for late delivery of each car generally amounted to 10 per cent of the value of such car. In comparison, period costs in sales, general and administration (SG&A) accounted for six per cent of expenses. Preliminary investigation by BT managers indicated that repair and late delivery charges amounted to nearly 20 per cent of Adtranz's expenses. By applying BT's production and cost control systems, it was thought that acquiring Adtranz would provide substantial upside potential to raise profits.

Finally, BT had a strong reputation for its expertise in subway, trams and light rail cars. Adtranz had expertise in propulsion systems, high-speed and inter-city cars and signaling systems. While the acquisition would clearly strengthen Bombardier's global reach, it would also bring needed technology and product expertise to the electrical locomotive, high-speed train, propulsion, and train control/communications. Closing this gap was becoming an imperative in Europe. For instance, in 2000, Bombardier was precluded to bid on the largest order ever awarded in the United Kingdom because Siemens, Alstom and Adtranz had refused to sell the propulsion system to them. In addition, Adtranz—at over twice the size of BT—would add $2.7 billion in backlog to maintenance and services while providing more service facilities for customers in the European marketplace.

THE ACQUISITION

Financial analysts had anticipated that DaimlerChrysler would seek a sales price of 25 per cent to 30 per cent of 1999 revenues of US$3.3 billion. However, ongoing problems in DaimlerChrysler's automobile business may have hastened their unloading of the non-core asset. Although Alstom and Siemens were BBD's main competitors in the rail industry, neither competed to acquire Adtranz in part because of the beliefs that the European Commission would probably not approve of the merger due to their current strong positions in several market segments.

On August 4, 2000, BBD announced its intention to buy Adtranz for US$715 million. In its negotiations with DaimlerChrysler, BBD agreed to pay the purchase price in two installments of cash—one at closing and one six months later. Under the deal, Bombardier also agreed to the assumption of certain debt. For the deal to proceed, regulatory approval was notably required in both the EU and the United States. Given the complimentary operations of both companies in the United States (mechanical versus propulsion), U.S. approval was never a significant issue. However, matters were different in Europe where it was initially estimated that the approval process would take between four and six months.

In negotiating the deal, DaimlerChrysler insisted on a limited due diligence process. In response, it was determined that any disagreement between the asset valuation done by BBD and the value given by DaimlerChrysler would lead to adjustments in a manner agreed upon; however, if adjustments exceeded a given amount, BBD could claim that there had been a material adverse change. This disagreement would then be submitted to an independent arbitrator for adjustment. Allaire commented on the limited due diligence process:

> It was certainly the first time that Bombardier agreed to go into an acquisition without first doing full due diligence. DaimlerChrysler basically said, "Look, have your people do an initial review and don't worry about the rest—we'll give you an equity guarantee. Adjustments will have to be made to the price if the provisions already taken in our books are not sufficient.

DaimlerChrysler had good reasons for wanting to limit the due diligence process. A new management team had just been put in place and was supposedly making progress streamlining Adtranz's operations. It was a natural concern that the management team would be seriously demoralized if Bombardier was invited in, only to later walk away from the transaction. And, secondly, Adtranz had serious worries about opening their books to a direct competitor. For Bombardier to come in and examine their pricing, cost structure, contracts and so on would have been off-limits under EU competition rules governing mergers and acquisitions.

NEGOTIATIONS WITH THE EUROPEAN COMMISSION

With the negotiations complete, BBD then applied to the EC for regulatory approval. Since 1990, the system for monitoring merger transactions in Europe has been governed by the Merger Regulation Committee of the European Commission. The Merger Regulation Committee eliminated the need for companies to seek approval for certain large-scale mergers in all European countries separately and ensured that all such merger requests received equal treatment. The control of mergers and acquisitions was one of the pillars of the EU's competition policy. When companies combined through a merger, acquisition, or creation of a joint venture, this generally had a positive impact on markets: firms became more efficient, competition intensified and the final consumer benefited from higher quality goods at lower prices. However, mergers that created or strengthened a dominant market position were prohibited in order to prevent abuses. A firm was in a dominant position when it was able to act on the market without having to account for the reactions of its competitors, suppliers or customers. A firm in a dominant position could, for example, increase its prices above those of its competitors without fearing any significant loss of sales.

In order to merge competing companies in Europe, the approval of the EC's merger task force was required. A review was comprised of two phases. Phase 1 involved a preliminary review, although full approval could be granted at this stage. Should Phase 1 identify potential competitive issues or conflicts associated with the proposed merger, a deeper investigation proceeded to Phase 2. This second phase could take months or years to complete as the depth and breadth of the investigation increased.

While many mergers were ultimately approved by the EC merger task force, this was in no way guaranteed. During the prior year, Alcan's proposed purchase of Pechiney was turned down by the task force. And GE's proposed acquisition of Honeywell was facing growing opposition. With this track record, some feared that the EC might have a bias against North American companies buying European businesses.

BBD utilized a negotiation strategy that it hoped would prove successful in gaining regulatory approval. It identified potentially contentious issues in advance and developed tactics to minimize disagreement. In order to comply with the likely EC demands, BBD volunteered to divest non-strategic transportation assets in Germany and, to extend for several years a series of supply contracts with smaller companies based in Austria and Germany. BBD was the main customer for these small suppliers and, with the acquisition of Adtranz, technologies previously purchased from these companies could now be manufactured within the newly assembled Bombardier/Adtranz. The few years of continued sales to BBD allowed these small companies to transition into new industries or to find new customers.

On a separate matter, BBD realized that the market share of the combined companies might be an issue for certain product segments in certain countries and so tried to shape the focus of the merger task force to the European market in total and not to any specific country. Primary geographical areas of concern were Germany, Austria and the United Kingdom. The German market was a key area with annual sales over US$1.8 billion; in Germany, Bombardier/Adtranz would have had a 50 per cent share. Concessions were made to ensure that a third competitor (Stadler) was allowed to strengthen its position in the German regional train market. Allaire, who led the negotiating team at the EC, commented on the efforts to win regulatory approval.

> You always have to make concessions—that's part of the deal over there. You don't get through the EC review process without some concessions unless you are buying something totally unrelated. But if there is any relatedness, the acquiring party must come up with concessions that will make the transaction acceptable.

For BBD, the preliminary result of the negotiation was not a Phase 1 approval, but a shortened Phase 2 process because issues were identified in Phase 1 and solutions were already designed. BBD believed, in March 2001, that Phase 2 would conclude within a month or so of further negotiations. While BBD was pleased with the results of its efforts to this point, the company had no firm guarantees that the transaction would be approved, or if approved, under what final conditions and timelines.

PIERRE LORTIE

A graduate of Université Laval (Canada) and Université de Louvain (Belgium), Pierre Lortie was both an engineer and an economist by training. He also received an MBA with honors from the University of Chicago. Prior to taking over BT, Lortie had been president and chief operating officer of Bombardier Capital (2000–2001). He had also been president and chief operating officer of Bombardier International (1998–2000), president of Bombardier Aerospace, Regional Aircraft (1993–1998), and president of Bombardier Capital Group (1990–1993). Before joining Bombardier in 1990, Lortie had been chairman, chief executive officer and president of Provigo Inc.—a major, Quebec-based retailer (1985–1989)—and president and chief executive officer of the Montreal Stock Exchange (1981–1985).

Over the years, Lortie had developed a reputation within BBD as a turnaround expert. His movements throughout BBD corresponded with the transformation of under-performing businesses into market leaders within a few years of his taking the helm. His philosophy included a combination of approaches: strong and decisive leadership, hands-on management, good relationships with existing personnel and the development of pride within those on the team. He also believed in the importance of rapidly achieving small, visible wins in order to build the support necessary to make subsequent larger changes. Lortie summarized his approach:

> You have to figure out the business model and focus everything on the key factors. You also have to work with the people … making sure they are focusing on what has to be done … helping them, coaching them and removing roadblocks. You should never forget that people like successes and being on the winning team.

Lortie recognized that his style and methods of change management were in some ways different than approaches taken by others in turnaround situations. Although aware of the need to streamline costs, he did not follow the traditional approach of implementing massive, short-term, cost-cutting tactics as an initial step in the turnaround plan. Instead, he focused first on creating a healthy operating environment through the implementation of reporting and governance systems aimed at monitoring key metrics and assessing current and potential success. His main objective was to ensure a balance between cost reduction or restructuring initiatives and revenue growth. He strongly held the view that balance was necessary because halting growth would hurt the market performance of a company far more than would a failure to rapidly reduce costs.

In promoting change, he not only engaged and empowered people at all levels, he also sought to create the trust and credibility necessary for a leader to implement further, more difficult changes that may be required based on assessment of the metrics. Lortie commented on the rationale behind his move to BT:

> My job at Bombardier has been to turn around operations that were not doing well. This is what I did at Bombardier Capital and Regional Aircraft. When Bob Brown (CEO of BBD) asked me to take over the job at transportation, he was concerned that there were difficulties in the current transportation group and high expectations involving the Adtranz merger. He felt that the magnitude of the task of stitching together the two organizations and rapidly delivering acceptable performance required someone who had a track record. There was some concern that I had not been at Bombardier Capital long enough to complete the restructuring process I had set in motion. But Adtranz was going to be Bombardier's biggest acquisition ever and getting it right seemed to be more important than keeping me at Capital.

Determining a Course of Action

While Lortie was a veteran of Bombardier and had participated in the strategic plan and budget reviews of the group over the years, he admitted knowing relatively little about Bombardier Transportation operations, per se. But he was convinced that the process for building and operating trains was not dissimilar to commercial aircraft. Many of the key success factors were thought to be the same. Beyond this core belief, Lortie faced an overwhelming number of decisions. He summarized the long list.

> What was the best way for us to leverage the potentially increased size of Bombardier Transportation? Should we take a top line approach to results or a bottom line approach? How can we tailor the integration to balance revenue and cost initiatives? How do we reconcile the fundamentally incompatible organizational structures, particularly in Europe? How do we go about designing the "best" organizational structure under the circumstances? How should we proceed to approve

new bids (those arising in the first few weeks and longer term) and ensure they are profit-making propositions? How should we develop and instill a project management culture in an organization that has no such tradition (or lost it)? How do we get management focused on the operations, on "getting it right," avoid finger pointing at former Adtranz management, create a climate conducive to teamwork while conducting a thorough due diligence of all Adtranz contracts and operations? How and when should Bombardier integrate its manufacturing philosophies into the existing Adtranz operations? What should Bombardier do to minimize tensions and maximize teamwork with personnel changes imminently on the horizon? How should those personnel changes be made? Who, in the management ranks of Adtranz and BT, should I keep and who should I replace and how should I go about the process of making these decisions? Should the headquarters of the merged companies be located in St. Bruno, Quebec, Berlin or a more neutral city like Brussels, Paris or London? And finally, what kind of style should I use in leading the organization forward? How directive should I be versus participative in making decisions?

The Richard Ivey School of Business gratefully acknowledges the generous support of The J. Armand Bombardier Foundation in the development of these learning materials.

Exhibit 1   Bombardier Revenue and Profit History, 1992 to 2001 (Cdn$ million)

Fiscal Year*	Overall	Transportation	Aerospace	Recreational Products	Capital	Other
2001e	16,101	3,043	10,562	1,687	1,033	(224)
2000	13,619	3,446	8,126	1,473	739	(165)
1999	11,500	2,966	6,444	1,628	571	(109)
1998	8,509	1,679	4,621	1,633	245	332
1997	7,976	1,597	4,011	1,866	162	341
1996	7,123	1,575	3,309	1,641	140	459
1995	5,943	1,310	2,981	1,111	112	430
1994	4,769	1,312	2,243	791	97	323
1993	4,448	1,238	2,228	556	58	367
1992	3,059	726	1,519	391	56	366

Profits Before Taxes—Segmented by Division

Fiscal Year*	Overall	Transportation	Aerospace	Recreational Products	Capital	Other
2001e	1,428	121	1,237	86	(15)	—
2000	1,124	174	904	18	28	—
1999	827	148	682	(46)	43	—
1998	627	85	462	1	64	16
1997	606	63	270	212	47	14
1996	461	100	150	174	42	(6)
1995	346	66	141	117	22	(1)
1994	207	(24)	137	76	14	4
1993	151	(73)	181	29	7	7
1992	121	4	137	(9)	(12)	2

Exhibit 1 (continued) Revenue—Segmented by Region

Fiscal Year*	Overall	Canada	Europe	United States	Asia	Other
2001e	16,101	1,241	4,757	8,592	471	1,040
2000	13,619	1,013	4,362	7,139	327	779
1999	11,500	900	4,049	5,497	259	796
1998	8,509	962	2,260	3,964	760	563
1997	7,976	949	2,342	3,712	605	367
1996	7,123	4,504	1,779	841	—	—
1995	5,943	3,619	1,536	789	—	—
1994	4,769	2,696	1,431	642	—	—
1993	4,448	2,335	1,675	438	—	—
1992	3,059	1,331	1,373	355	—	—

e - estimate

* fiscal year end January 31. As a result, 2001 data essentially covers results from 2000.

Source: Company files.

Exhibit 2 Overview of Bombardier Businesses in 2000

	Businesses	Leadership Position
Bombardier Inc.	**Recreational Products group** Snowmobiles (Ski-Doo) Personal watercraft (Sea-Doo) Small engines (Rotax) All-Terrain vehicles Neighbourhood electric vehicles (NEV) Sport Boats	No. 2 globally No. 1 globally No. 1 in ultra light aircraft engines Launching No. 1 globally
	Transportation Group Mass transit and systems	No. 1 in North America, No. 4 in Europe
	Aerospace Group Business jets (Challenger, Global Express, Learjet 31A, 45, 60) Commercial aircraft (Canadair Regional Jet, Dash 8) Amphibious Aircraft (CL415)	No. 2 globally No. 1 in 29-50 seat globally No. 1 globally
	Capital Group Dealer inventory financing Commercial industrial financing Railcar leases Manufactured housing mortages Targeted consumer financing	Strong positions in niche markets

Adapted from McKinsey Quarterly, 1997, Volume 2.

Exhibit 3   Growing Privatization of the European Union Rail Industry

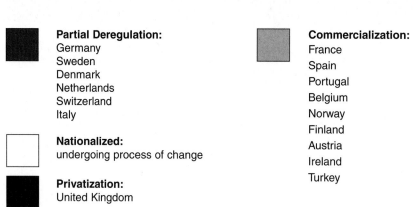

Partial Deregulation:
Germany
Sweden
Denmark
Netherlands
Switzerland
Italy

Nationalized:
undergoing process of change

Privatization:
United Kingdom

Commercialization:
France
Spain
Portugal
Belgium
Norway
Finland
Austria
Ireland
Turkey

Source: Company files.

Exhibit 4   Bombardier's Electrostar

Source: Company files.

Case 34

Leading Change at SJHC and LHSC: Burr Under the Saddle or a Grain of Sand in the Oyster

In April 1996, the Progressive Conservative government of Ontario, under the leadership of Premier Mike Harris, established the Health Services Restructuring Commission (HSRC). The HSRC was made up of representatives from industry, health organizations and government agencies. The HSRC reviewed all provincial health services, including hospitals, community care, home care and long-term care support services. The mandate of the HSRC was two-fold: first, to make decisions on restructuring public hospitals in Ontario; and second, to make recommendations to the Minister of Health and Long-term Care on reinvestments in, and restructuring of, other parts of the health system and other changes required to support restructuring generally, and the creation of a genuine health services system in the province.

In short, the HSRC attempted to recommend changes that responded to the needs of Ontario's communities in a cost-effective manner. Decisions about health system restructuring and reform were long overdue. Observers felt that the Ontario health care system needed to be restructured in order to do more—and better—with less. Moreover, given the changing demographics and the financial realities, changes could no longer be delayed. Establishing the HSRC signaled the seriousness of the need for change.

In 1995, the Thames Valley District Health Council formed the London Acute Care Teaching Hospitals' Restructuring Committee (LACTHRC) to make recommendations on the organization and coordination of care in London's acute care teaching hospitals. The philosophy of the leadership at the London hospitals was "if we don't change, someone else will force us to change." For an overview of the vision for London hospitals (see Exhibit 1).

Ken Mark prepared this case under the supervision of Professor Gerard Seijts solely to provide material for class discussion. The authors do not intend to illustrate either effective or ineffective handling of a managerial situation. The authors may have disguised certain names and other identifying information to protect confidentiality.

The financial report of this committee, issued in 1996, made recommendations to reconfigure hospital-based programs and services in London and to strengthen linkages with the community. For a summary of the final report of LACTHRC (see Exhibit 2).

The HSRC used the report by LACTHRC (as well as several other reports) as a starting point for its analysis of the needed health services reform in London. The HSRC invited individuals and organizations to provide input. In July 1996, the lead commissioner, along with the accompanying commissioner and senior staff, met with board members, administrators, local politicians, physicians and other health care providers to obtain more information and to clarify issues relating to London's restructuring plans.

In January 1997, the HSRC released a report containing recommended options for clinical activities, including, but not limited to, adult acute care; pediatric acute care; long-term care; adult acute mental health and chronic mental health. Recommendations in the areas of governance, reinvestment and manpower adjustment were also made; cost-savings and capital estimates were provided as well. The HSRC believed that the recommendations issued for the London area would begin a process of coherent, constructive change, renovations, and modernization that would strengthen the local health system. Key outcomes envisioned included better quality of care; management and administrative efficiency; broader health system integration; affordability of services and accessibility to health services in the community. For a description of the HSRC report (see Exhibit 3).

The HSRC directed St. Joseph's Health Care (SJHC, also St. Joe's) to plan a low-risk pregnancy program for approximately 1,500 births. (A pregnancy is categorized as low-risk when the attending physician expects the woman will have a vaginal delivery, and there is no reason to anticipate any of the following: other medical complications, a Caesarean section, premature delivery, or an induced birth.) All other services with respect to perinatal health would be transferred to the London Health Sciences Centre (LHSC), created when University Hospital and Victoria Hospital were integrated.

In 1998, a vision for the low-risk birth program was created. Members of the Department of Family Medicine and Department of Midwifery were to run the unit. Between 1998 and 2001, transition planning had begun. The original vision, however, was abandoned for several reasons. The Department of Obstetrics indicated that it was no longer able to provide support because several of the obstetricians who had initially supported this plan had either left London or stopped providing obstetrics services. The Department of Anesthesiology and Department of Paediatrics, which were also only marginally supportive, were also hit by human resource shortages. Without the full support from members at the above departments, the members of the Department of Family Medicine and the Department of Midwifery were uncomfortable continuing with the original vision. A clinical panel, under the leadership of Sandra Letton and Margaret Nish, concluded that based on clinical implications, potential risks, sustainability and academic impact, the low-risk birth program should be transferred to LHSC together with the Perinatal Program.

THE TRANSFER OF PERINATAL SERVICES

The transfer of Perinatal Services at SJHC to the Women's and Children's Services at LHSC included the relocation of clinical programs (e.g. the Neonatal Intensive Care Unit or NICU, and High-Risk Obstetrics / Gynecology), staff and physicians. More than 500 staff and about 40 physicians, trainees and researchers were involved. The new LHSC facility would house capacity for 6,000 births, 42 neonatal intensive care beds, 70 antenatal and postpartum beds, gynecology, ambulatory and inpatient services, reproductive endocrinology and other related support services.

SJHC's perinatal program had been among the hospital's premier programs and was recognized as a world-class tertiary perinatal program for more than 30 years. The hospital's comprehensive care for newborns included providing care of very sick infants and extremely premature babies, born as early as 23 weeks' gestation (full term is 40 weeks.). SJHC also did a full range of surgical procedures, with the exception of cardiac surgery. Because of the ancillary services that the program touched on, including radiology, ultrasound, dietary services, anesthesia, pediatrics and so forth, the perinatal transfer was a major project.

The move to LHSC, where the program would be one of many premier services, was a source of much concern to key stakeholders, leading scientists and specialists with potential negative impact on recruitment, retention and staff morale. For example, in January 2003, Insights Inc., a London-based market research and analysis organization, collected data from women who were recent and expectant patients of London's maternal care units; both telephone surveys and focus groups were used in the data-gathering process. The general perception was that LHSC and SJHC were good hospitals; both were seen as being able to handle "almost anything." But SJHC had been designated to handle the extremely complicated pregnancies and births by virtue of the neonatal intensive care unit and the specialists that were located there. Responses also indicated that, in the absence of any details, concerns about the one-site plan related to suspicions regarding the motives for changing a maternal care system that seemed to be working well the way it was.

Dr. Henry Roukema, director of nurseries (SJHC, LHSC), was pleased with the proposed consolidation. In his words:

> We're very pleased with the announcement that there were plans to consolidate the perinatal program into one site. In some ways, this has been in the works for 20 or 30 years, with the goal to have high-risk obstetrics, and neonatal care take place at the same place as pediatric care.
>
> For us right now it's a challenge because a lot of the sub-specialties that we need are actually off-site, at LHSC, so there's a lot of traveling back and forth across the city, in particular for the specialists who are needed at different sites.

But he also urged a word of caution:

> There is a real opportunity to think about what it is that we really want, and then go ahead and do it. One of my concerns is what would happen if things go wrong. What if we find that a certain part of the care model doesn't really work? What if we don't have enough storage space? I am involved in a lot of the planning, which means that, in some sense, I can get some of the credit but . . . I can also get some of the blame. We're looking at as much relevant literature as we can, and then trying to figure out how to execute things. But it's not my specialty . . . designing neonatal intensive care facilities . . . so it's a bit of a stretch sometimes, and it ends up taking a lot of time and individual resources.
>
> There's a lot of little things . . . we are wondering . . . we could have missed this, and we could have missed that. For example, parts of the adult intensive care were just moved to the Victoria Hospital site. There were certain parts of the design that were missed; and a few things needed to be retro-fitted. And so . . . we're trying to anticipate as much as possible. I also think we need to have some adaptability within the current design in order to cope with the unanticipated.

THE CHANGE AGENTS

In 2005, building on the learning from Milestone I,[1] and the affected programs at both organizations, Sandra Letton, vice-president, acute and ambulatory care, SJHC, and Ellen Rosen, vice-president, women and children's clinical business unit, LHSC, recognized the value of doing readiness work as early as possible. They advocated for a new model of organizational development resourcing, to prepare leaders throughout all stages of the clinical restructuring: pre, during and post.

Lianne Collins and Rebecca Parkes were appointed as the "citywide change agents." Collins and Parkes had extensive backgrounds and experience working together in change management, leader development and executive coaching in both the public and private sectors, and primarily in healthcare.

Collins had a background as a registered nurse, and she had worked in mental health counseling and hospital education. Parkes had an undergraduate degree in psychology, a diploma in counseling as well as training and development experience in both private and public sector with leadership. Both were very much involved in relevant continuing education, including certification in change leadership and organizational development models and tools. They also pursued non-traditional methods of personal transformation and growth and their applications to leadership and organizational efficacy (including the Hoffman Process; Parkes was a Hoffman teacher).

From 1995 to 1999, Parkes and Collins had been involved, as external consultants, in the integration of non-clinical services at University Hospital, and when University Hospital and Victoria Hospital integrated, they had organized a similar integration at LHSC. The objectives of the integration were cost reduction, an increase in customer service and patient satisfaction, as well as enhancing service workers' job satisfaction through better utilization of their skills and potential. Collins continued her external consultant role in clinical environments until 2003, whereas Parkes returned to a citywide role in 2000 as part of the clinical restructuring (mandated by the provincial government in 1996) between SJHC and LHSC. Collins joined the citywide clinical restructuring team in 2003. The first phase of clinical restructuring, Milestone I, included the transfer of 28 clinical programs and services (e.g. Emergency, Critical Care and General Surgery) between LHSC and SJHC. Parkes and Collins were reassigned to the second phase of clinical restructuring involving Perinatal Services at SJHC and Women's and Children's Services at LHSC in the fall of 2005.

The actual transfer of Perinatal Services would not take place until 2008; for one thing, the new physical facilities had yet to be built. The main task of Parkes and Collins was to establish a readiness for change, in the years leading up to the actual transfer.

THE CHALLENGES

At the outset, Collins and Parkes knew the complexities of this change would be challenging: fiscal constraints (dollars were limited, and the process for accessing money from the government was time consuming and arduous); there were expanding care

---

[1] Milestone I was the largest transfer of hospital programs and services in London. The transfer was a result of the Health Services Restructuring Commission. The first program to transfer was Acute Mental Health. Other transfers included Emergency, Critical Care, General Surgery, Family Medicine, Medicine, Orthopaedic, Perioperative Care, and Cardiac Surgery and Cardiology. More than 2,500 staff and physicians were relocated.

requirements (patients and their families still expected safe, high quality care throughout the change process); there was a changing demographic in the provider population (a significant number of nurses had the opportunity to retire, and the recruitment and skilling-up of new nurses places an additional burden on the system); and there were established citywide agreements with the unions of both organizations that dictates how and when transferring of staff would occur. The staff of both organizations were anxious about the change and its impact on care delivery, the workplace and the quality of work life. There were also some real cultural differences of the two hospitals.

Some of the cultural differences were differences in governance, the size (LHSC was much larger), the leadership structure and existing management systems. People familiar with both SJHC and LHSC indicated that SJHC was smaller and therefore more close-knit; it was "relationship-oriented." LHSC was perceived to be more task-focused and siloed in its approach.

A critical cultural difference was rooted in faith-based beliefs. Collins and Parkes were aware that many physicians, leaders and staff for SJHC found the transfer especially challenging given the many embedded processes based on Catholic beliefs, while operations at LHSC would be on a secular basis. For example, longstanding processes for ethical decisions had been created at SJHC for early inductions for lethal fetal anomalies. Abortions were not performed at SJHC but would be performed at LHSC. A guiding principle at LHSC was that the decisions belonged to the family and the physicians. In its mission, vision and values statement, shown in Exhibit 4, SJHC explained how it served people:

> Inspired by the care, creativity and compassion of our founders—the Sisters of St. Joseph, the Women's Christian Association, and the London Psychiatric Hospital and St. Thomas Psychiatric Hospital, we serve with respect, excellence, and compassion.

The mission, vision and values of LHSC are shown in Exhibit 5.

Chris Glen, a full-time nurse at SJHC, and the union leader for the Ontario Nurses' Association, predicted that the change agents would need to work through the differences in religious beliefs. Nurses chose to be at SJHC. She explained that, "We don't see the sisters anymore, but there's still kind of that presence that they are here—their pictures are all over the walls."

So questions that needed to be addressed included: What will the decision-making process be at the integrated LHSC? Who should decide? How should the transition in decision-making processes be communicated? How would top decision makers manage conflict in opinions and values? How could they create a common language? For example, because of the nature of care in the birthing process, there was no room for confusion or variations in procedures and practices at the time of delivery.

Said Dr. Roukema:

> I think part of what we're really focusing on in order to ensure safety is to handle as many components of the consolidation as possible prior to the move. So . . . we kind of talked a little bit about the culture and about different ways of doing things in one unit as opposed to another. I hope we can get the policies and procedures, and even the interpretations of the policies and procedures, the same, prior to moving . . . then you're not trying to do too many things at the same time. I think there'll be enough risk in the changes of the model of care related to the move with just the unanticipated things.

A third cultural element was the leadership structure and philosophy. Both SJHC and LHSC had a tri-partite mission—patient care, teaching and research. The organizational charts are shown in Exhibit 6. The differences in structure and leadership boiled down to the following. At SJHC, shared leadership provided a structure and process for involving health care providers in decision making, problem solving and improvement activities. For example, with regard to the transfer, Dr. Roukema observed:

> I guess I'm in a fortunate position . . . that I'm actually fairly senior in the planning process . . . and so in terms of the planning for the Perinatal Program and for the neonatal intensive care, I actually have a lot of say in what should happen. On the other hand . . . we have a very multi-disciplinary team from the neonatal intensive care unit that's doing a lot of planning and suggesting things . . . So . . . I do have accountability to the team . . . there's probably about 20 different people there . . . .

In contrast, at LHSC, the management model and organizational structure was more layered—it was designed around business units and four leadership layers. The leadership scope and decision-making required consultation across many layers, and this approach was quite different from that at SJHC. Shared leadership did not always play out at SJHC; but individuals identified themselves with it.

A registered nurse at SJHC explained:

> We'll go to a meeting and someone will stand up and say they do a certain job at LHSC; and we'll just look at each other and say, "Another new face?" Like, there's just so many different levels . . . and we just go director, care coordinator, staff nurse . . . that's it. That's all we have over here. And over there . . . it's just very confusing, and even though we've met with them several times I am still not entirely clear about what goes on over there.

Chris Glen volunteered:

> We have a lot of shared leadership and staff involvement, and I don't sense that there's the same involvement at LHSC. A lot of what I've heard . . . as being a union leader in the monthly program transfer meetings . . . I would often hear things like, "Well we've made a decision . . . this is the way we're going to do it." And I would say, "Well at St. Joe's . . . you take it to the staff, everybody has some input into it and then some decisions are made." I sense is that the people do have a say; but from the transfers that I've seen and done, it doesn't always happen at LHSC.

Dr. Roukema echoed these sentiments:

> There are differences in the feel of the administration . . . LHSC as well. Sometimes the perception is as important as an actual difference in practice. If people really had the perception (accurate or not) that LHSC is very, very different, and they don't want to work at LHSC . . . they may choose not to move with the program.

At least one nurse from LHSC was not concerned about the cultural differences. In her words:

> I really don't see that it's going to be a big huge change. Nurses are nurses no matter where you go, and we seem to just manage and flock together and band together. I think just getting used to the new home, the new building, where everything is set up . . . I think we will manage. I think we will do a great job. For

those of us at LHSC it's a chance to do more high-risk nursing, and I think that's exciting . . . we do some now, but not to the degree that they do at SJHC. So I'm excited about the changes.

A nurse from SJHC shared those views:

I'm not really concerned about going to work there. I know that I will just drive to a different place. I don't think people realize that they've been talking about us moving to LHSC for a long, long time. I've been here for 21 years and I've been hearing about it for 21 years, and even the change for the date for this move has changed to I believe 2008 right now, or maybe 2009. It's almost a bit of a joke because we don't know when it's going to happen.

I'm not being forced to do anything . . . I know some people won't go; they probably will decide to stay and work at St. Joe's in some capacity, that's another option too. I'm certainly not thinking that way, because I want to stay with the NICU.

Demographics: An Aging Workforce

The staff at SJHC was getting older; a significant number of individuals could elect to retire when Perinatal Services would transfer to LHSC. The health care landscape in Ontario was faced with a competition for talented health care providers. There was a real concern among several of the hospital senior administrators that the standard of service could be compromised if a large number of staff would choose to retire; as many as 40 per cent of staff at SJHC would be eligible for retirement. Would there be enough nurses to staff the new unit? SJHC was on a nursing shortage already. What could the leadership at the two hospitals do to retain the best people? How to attract the best health care providers in the new unit, and thereby guaranteeing the highest quality of care for women who give birth, and continued excellence in research and teaching?

Collins and Parkes wanted to explore the role that a divided culture could play in the decision to continue employment or leave the integrated LHSC. Conflict in patient care teams—composed of SJHC and LHSC staff and physicians—could linger for many years.

Dr. Roukema indicated the physicians were also highly mobile. For example, he stated that:

There's a shortage of neonatologists across the country. If we move and they really don't like it at LHSC . . . there's the potential for people to leave; on the other hand, if we design it right there's the potential to really attract people too.

Potential for Conflict in Teams

There was no doubt that conflict could affect team effectiveness and the subsequent level of care that families and their children would receive. How would LHSC ensure public confidence in the services it provided? The Insights report cited earlier found that the respondents were equally split between positive and negative reactions to move all high-risk care to LHSC and maintain a low-risk pregnancy program at SJHC. Women who had given birth at SJHC were more likely to have negative feelings, based on a sense of loss for "their" maternity hospital. But responses also indicated that even those who felt positive about the plan had nagging concerns about the availability of care in a large unit with staff forced to merge. Women wanted to know that all of the front-line workers—physicians, staff and midwives—supported the changes involved. One woman responded:

> I don't want a nurse who was just transferred and took a pay cut taking care of my baby. I wouldn't want to be there the first year.

Was the ability to deliver safe patient care a legitimate concern? Should LHSC be worried about potential conflict in patient care teams? What can be done about the potential for conflict?

The LHSC perinatal staff expressed concerns about being overwhelmed by the large influx of SJHC staff. There was the usual concern about, "How will the transfer affect me?" For example, the Perinatal Services group at SJHC, and in particular its Neonatal Intensive Care Unit, had a reputation of "being the best of the best"—world-class and cutting-edge. Physicians and nurses at LHSC provided primary and secondary level care (e.g. birthing services). Providing these services, however, was not as complex as quaternary care (e.g. care for babies with unique life-threatening needs) that was provided at SJHC. Naturally, people at LHSC were anxious about new knowledge and skill requirements as well as concerns about learning curves for the physicians in less acute, less technical primary and secondary programs.

Some people at LHSC did not perceive themselves to be "the top of the heap." As a result, there were worries about their individual status in the new program. For example, a registered nurse in the birthing centre at LHSC explained concerns that she and her colleagues had:

> The biggest concern is the melding of the staff . . . it's not like one new staff member is coming in, it's going to be a whole group of individuals. There's always the concern of personalities and possible power struggles. SJHC has always been kind of looked at as the big fish and we're the little fish . . . there's always that concern.

Dr. Roukema explained that, from the perspective of the neonatal intensive care side, it was a rather unique situation:

> It's a little bit different for us because we're not really amalgamating with anyone, we're moving in. LHSC doesn't have a neonatal intensive care unit right now . . . . We have a model of care which is very interdisciplinary; we have physicians and there's nurse practitioners that work together in the NICU, and that's a model that's not as much in effect in LHSC. They do have nurse practitioners in their Perinatal Program, but not to the same extent that we do, where on any given day we will have two or three nurse practitioners working in the unit along with the pediatric residents and other residents from obstetrics or anesthesia, and the attending physicians as well, so they're always working together as part of the team. So for us it's not going to be so much of a change in culture, at least with respect to the amalgamation. We plan on taking the organizational model as we have it.

And Glen observed:

> Some of the nurses are close to retirement, and some of them are just not quite ready to move. They don't want to move, but . . . there's going to be no work left at St. Joe's for them, for what they currently do. Their concerns are, What's it's going to be like? Is it going to be the same? and Am I going to have a job? They're

going to be blended with another group of nurses who are already there. So their question is, Will we get along?

A lot of the nurses that are currently in this program have been working in this area 20 to 30 to 35 years. They chose to work at this facility, at St. Joe's; and they never wanted to move somewhere else . . . now they're being forced to move.

How should Collins and Parkes manage the human side of change? Physicians and staff were expected to work in teams. But the values espoused and cultures at SJHC and LHSC were quite distinct. What steps would need to be taken to enable a smooth and safe transition; to create respect and high-performing teams? The hospital administration was committed to the best care: clinical excellence and the consideration for individual preferences and emotional needs of the mother, baby and their family.

Without adequate support to enable the integration of care delivery practices and culture transformation, there would be increased liability to the hospital, and if physicians and staff were ill prepared for the transfer of programs, services and people, the desired outcomes were likely to be compromised. Glen explained:

If this doesn't go well, first of all, the patients will be compromised. You won't have nurses—if they're in turmoil . . . they're not going to be focused on their work. I would be concerned that they're not safely practicing nursing, so we need to make sure that they're prepared as much as they can for this transfer. So we try and think ahead . . . how are we going to get people there? And we try to give people as much information as we can. Don't hide anything from them, they need to know, and they need to hear it from their leaders.

Implications of Union Agreements

Parkes and Collins had to operate with the limitations and constraints of the internal organizational collective agreements with the various unions, as well as the citywide agreements with all unions designed to govern how and when staff would transfer between organizations. The citywide agreements were originally constructed and signed at a time when there was a surplus of staff and lay-offs were predicted. Although the healthcare environment has changed dramatically the agreements are binding until clinical restructuring is completed. The agreements dictate that staff who have elected to transfer can change their mind right up to the actual transfer date and they can bump back to their organization any time within one year following the transfer date. During the transfer year union members operate within the collective agreement of their original organization.

The implications of the citywide agreements to operational effectiveness and relationships across the teams are profound. It is difficult to finalize the planning for adequate staffing at both organizations when at any time one staff member reversing their decision (right up to the actual transfer date) has a domino affect on seniority lists, and the need to recruit (which often is a three to six month process). The potential gaps created in staffing magnify the already existing problems of staffing shortages and an inadequate casual pool of nurses

Staff who opt to "bump back" to SJHC within the first transfer year not only displaced a junior nurse at SJHC, but have left behind strained relationships and perceptions of being rejected within the LHSC team. The negative feelings generated at both sites are additional challenges that need to be managed and healed. Staff from the first phase of clinical restructuring bumped back into Perinatal Services and carried with them unhappy transfer experiences. Collins and Parkes had to work with the remnants and residue of these negative experiences as they began the readying work of the second phase of restructuring.

Even when staff choose to transfer there are impacts that need to be managed. The resultant unit now has an integrated seniority list from both organizations. A staff who was previously a senior member at one organization may now find themselves less senior within the integrated team. This change in seniority status had implications for selection of time off, vacation time, and promotions. Also during the year post transfer, nurses operated according to the rules of the collective agreement of their original organization which meant differences in pay, scheduling, benefits, etc. for nurses working side by side on the same shift. The disparity generated feelings and emotions on the team that interfered with team integration.

Complacency and Urgency for Change

The atmosphere at both SJHC and LHSC was very pressure-prompted, dealing with what was urgent and pressing, first. Parkes and Collins described complacency as an individual's inability to deal with the feelings of ambiguity and discomfort of a future that was relatively unknown and unpredictable.

The actual transfer of Perinatal Services to the new LHSC facilities would not take place until 2009. In the first phase of clinical restructuring, dates and timelines were postponed for very sound reasons (e.g. construction delays and facility readiness). As a result, feelings of skepticism and complacency were generated in leaders, physicians and staff. Although those attitudes may linger in both organizations, the actual leaders of the programs transferring as part of phase two, are experiencing a sense of urgency to consolidate the full continuum of services at one site because of the clinical implications to delays.

Many nurses had an attitude of ". . . yeah . . . yeah . . . we've waited this long . . . when the day comes please tell me . . . ." Glen explained:

> People don't believe it's going to happen because all of this was supposed to have been done in early 2000. I think everything was supposed to have moved by 2000, so each program is delayed by a couple of years. And, now, with regard to the Perinatal Program, we're hearing 2009. So every time nurses hear that, they say to themselves, "That is one year closer to retirement."

Comments from nurses at SJHC and LHSC included: "The move is still at least three years away. I don't worry about it now. It's just a waste of energy to get concerned about it at this time." Developing strategies to deal with both feelings of complacency and those of impatience and urgency proved to be a real challenge for Parkes and Collins given that the timelines were out of their control.

Context

Collins and Parkes were cognizant of particular "organizational realities." For example, they reported to the Human Resources and Organizational Development Directors at SJHC and LHSC. Neither Parkes nor Collins was part of the perinatal group; they had no formal authority over the medical staff. How would they, as citywide organization development consultants, engage the physicians, patient care teams and front-line leaders?

Observers described physicians using such terms as "entrepreneurs," "less rule–based," "the best of the best" and "not used to seeking approval." How would Collins and Parkes engage them?

Both hospitals had unions representing nurses, some allied health workers and support services. How would Collins and Parkes generate enthusiasm and cooperation from the union leadership?

Their task was to cultivate "leaders" who had the capabilities to obtain buy-in and cooperation from many self-directed and autonomous groups and interact with people with a broad range of feelings, perceptions and behaviors. To be successful, these leaders would need to actively attend to the human side of change and deal effectively with their own, and other people's feelings and emotional reactions while implementing the complex changes

HOW TO PROCEED

Parkes and Collins were selected to lead the transformational change project based on their experiences of designing and implementing systems-wide change in healthcare systems, as well as the practical experience and learnings acquired from earlier transfers.

Said Glen:

Each transfer has built upon the last one, and we've had facilitators that have helped us work through the challenges. When we first started moving . . . people were just basically moved. There were a lot of upset people. So what happened then was we started to do evaluations—we identified what went well, what didn't go well, and what we needed to learn from the transfers. That's really what we've done . . . and out of that came clinical action teams, where the nurses were involved in the decision-making process. For example, what will the care delivery model look like in the future? How are we going to get there? Some transfers go very well, and others don't. I think leaders need to understand that the transfer affects people's lives in so many different ways. I learned that nurses weren't very concerned about how they were going to nurse; they wanted to know where am I going to park my car, where's the washroom, where's the cafeteria and so forth. It's such a disruption in their day-to-day lives.

Parkes and Collins were well aware of what they could influence and what was outside of their control including:

- facilities readiness and timelines
- dollars available for clinical restructuring
- citywide union agreements
- launching of other organizational changes

The agents designed a strategy for the current transformation based on three pillars:

1. Leadership
2. Culture
3. Systems Integration and Alignment

Their task was not an easy one. If left unsupported and mismanaged the transfer could compromise clinical outcomes, recruitment and retention of talented providers (nursing, allied health and physicians) and escalate costs.

Exhibit 1   Vision for London Hospitals

"London Health Sciences Centre and St. Joseph's Health Care London continue to work together as we plan and build world class health care facilities and services. We have already led the way in integrating services and sharing resources. Our ongoing fundraising efforts have already brought in hundreds of millions of dollars from the public sector and our community. Now, with the onset of the largest construction project in London's history, we are poised to take bold new steps toward implementing our vision for London hospitals.

The vision for London hospitals is not about new buildings; it is about providing our physicians and staff with the tools they need to give patients the best possible care. Toward that end, much is changing. Emergency services will consolidate in expanded facilities at Victoria and University Campuses. A new tower will rise at the corner of Commissioners and Wellington roads and the tired facilities at South Street will finally close. St. Joseph's Hospital will become the focal point for ambulatory care and day surgery in the city. City-wide rehabilitation services have centralized at the redeveloped Parkwood Hospital.

The road ahead is challenging but full of promise. At the end of this journey, we will set a standard of health care excellence that will endure for generations to come."

Source: http://www.londonhospitals.ca/vision/vision.htm, June 13, 2006.

Exhibit 2   Summary of the London Acute Care Teaching Hospitals' Restructuring
Committee Report

The Final LACTHRC Report was released February 29, 1996 and outlined the Committee's work and analysis in the following major areas:

- Profile of the Thames Valley Health District, including socio-demographics, health status indicators and health service utilization
- Health Services framework in southwestern Ontario
- Review of acute care services in London
- Results of broad consultation and analysis of feedback
- Restructuring recommendations for the acute hospitals

Option Development and Analysis

As part of its decision-making process, LACTHRC used five criteria: quality of care, affordability, teaching and research, research and future service needs, partnership and coordination.

These criteria were applied to three models for the London acute care hospitals:

Model 1
- Consolidation of 32 services onto one or two sites
- Continuation of three tertiary / quaternary hospitals
- Differentiated roles based on recognized excellence

Model 2
- Two comprehensive adult tertiary care centres: Victoria Campus and University Campus
- St. Joseph's Grosvenor site to become child / maternal, family medicine, mental health and rehabilitation centre with onsite medicine and surgery to support these roles

Model 3
- Consolidation of most tertiary and quarternary care on two sites: University Campus and Victoria Campus
- New role for St. Joseph's on Grosvenor site to combine community hospital services with specialty services in a teaching environment
- Westminster Tower would be leased from LHSC to create the child / maternal continuum under St. Joseph's leadership on the site of a network of adult and children's services

Exhibit 2   (continued)

Key Recommendations

LACTHRC made five major restructuring recommendations, including a recommendation to adopt Model 3, as outlined above.

1. Link care through a directory system and common information systems
2. Enhance primary care services in east London with community health centres as a preferred model
3. Redesign emergency care by reducing the number of emergency departments from four to three and reducing deferrable emergency visits by 33 to 40 per cent
4. Restructure hospital patient care services using Model 3. The impact of this option is as follows:
   - South Street site would close
   - A new tower would be required on the Victoria campus to consolidate tertiary fetal / maternal program from St. Joseph's with pediatrics at Victoria
   - The role of the St. Joseph's Health Centre would change to community teaching with some tertiary
   - All major clinical programs would be consolidated, with two hospitals operating collaboratively at three sites (Perth, Commissioners, Grosvenor)
   - A capital investment of $188 million would be required
   - Operating annual savings of $79 million would be achieved
5.   Design the facilities to meet the newly recommended roles

---

Source: www.health.gov.on.ca/hsrc/london_ir_0297.doc, accessed June 13, 2006.

Exhibit 3   Health Services Restructuring Commission Report for London

---

On June 16, 1997, as part of a province wide initiative, the Health Services Restructuring Commission (HSRC) delivered its report for London, outlining the required changes to the hospitals in this city.

The HSRC wanted to ensure that the implementation of the restructuring directives achieves an optimal configuration of health services, fully integrated and linked, and will maintain and enhance the significant education and research activities in the local health system. Consequently, the HSRC concluded that a Joint Committee of the LHSC, SJHC, and the University of Western Ontario (UWO) should be established to manage and coordinate the implementation of restructuring. The Joint Committee also has representation from the Community Care Access Centre (CCAC) of London and Middlesex, London / St. Thomas Mental Health, Thames Valley District Council and City of London.

Highlights of the HSRC Report for London:
- Consolidating all inpatient services in newer facilities at two London Health Sciences Centre sites resulting in closure of the aging South Street site;
- Changing the role of St. Joseph's Health Centre's Grosvenor site to a focus on ambulatory care, low-risk obstetrics and day surgery;
- Rebuilding mental health services at the Parkwood site of St. Joseph's Health Centre, resulting in the closure of London and St. Thomas provincial psychiatric hospitals;
- Rebalancing the mental health system to better support the shift from inpatient to community-based mental health services;
- Strengthening the role of London as an academic health sciences centre;
- $190 million for capital reinvestment in hospitals (an increase of $40 million); and
- $2.3 million for long-term care, home care and transitional/sub-acute care services.

Source: www.londonhospitals.ca/restructuring/hsrc.htm, accessed June 13, 2006.

Exhibit 4   St. Josephs' Health Care Mission, Vision and Values

Our Mission, Vision and Values

Who We Are - St. Joseph's Health Care, London

St. Joseph's Health Centre, Parkwood Hospital and the London/St. Thomas Psychiatric Hospital have joined together to create a new health care organization to serve the residents of London and Southwestern Ontario, and the Veterans of Canada. We are owned by the St. Joseph's Health Care Society of the Roman Catholic Diocese of London, and governed by a volunteer board of directors representing the community. Our services are publicly funded.

We are a major teaching and research centre affiliated with the University of Western Ontario and Fanshawe College.

What We Do (Mission)

We help people to maintain and improve their health and work with them to minimize the effects of injury, disease and disability.

We do this by pursuing excellence in care, research, and education in a wide range of hospital, clinic, long term and community-based settings.

We work with our partners to create a better health care system.

What We'll Be (Vision)

A respected source of excellent health service guided by the people we serve... provided by people who care.

How We Serve (Values)

Inspired by the care, creativity and compassion of our founders – the Sisters of St. Joseph, the Women's Christian Association, and the London Psychiatric Hospital and St. Thomas Psychiatric Hospital – we serve with...

Respect	Excellence	Compassion
• Honour the people we serve • Appreciate the work of others • Welcome the contributions of all • Celebrate diversity • Be truthful, honest and open	• Give our best each day • Be creative and resourceful with our gifts, skills and talents • Build on our proud past • Work as a team to seek the new, undiscovered • Make a difference	• Be with others • Understand their needs, realities and hopes • Give from the heart • Sustain the spirit
Listen	Learn	Care

In the spirit of community, in the pursuit of health

Source: sjhc.london.on.ca/corp/about/mission.pdf, accessed June 13, 2006.

Exhibit 5   London Health Sciences Centre Mission Statement

LONDON HEALTH SCIENCES CENTRE MISSION STATEMENT
To Fulfill Our Mission, We Make The Following Commitments

To our Patients and their Families:
We will work with you to improve your health and provide compassionate and high quality care.

To Our Health Care Partners and Referring Physicians:
We will work with you, sharing expertise, information, and assistance, so that patients can be cared for in their own communities.

To Those Who Entrust Us With the Stewardship of Resources:
We will operate within our means.
We will use our resources responsibly and ethically to provide cost-effective services.
We will use external objective standards to measure our overall performance.

To the People of London and Middlesex:
We will, in partnership, facilitate the provision of quality health care services for all age groups.

Together we care, we learn, we discover
London Health Sciences Centre, a university teaching hospital, is committed to improving health. Building on our tradition of leadership and partnership, we champion patient-centred care, a spirit of inquiry and discovery, and a commitment to life-long learning.

To our researchers:
We will, with our research partners, promote leadership, encourage innovation, advance scientific knowledge and its dissemination, and seek solutions to health issues through the provision of facilities and resources.

To the People of Southwestern Ontario and Beyond:
We will offer quality health services for those conditions or circumstances requiring our specialized care.

To Our Students, Trainees, and Their Teachers:
We will, in collaboration with our educational partners, foster learning and development opportunities through expert teaching and optimal resources and facilities.

To Our Employees, Physicians, and Volunteers:
We will attract and retain the best people.
We will provide a safe and healthy environment that inspires teamwork, respect for the individual, collaboration, and professional development.

LONDON HEALTH SCIENCES CENTRE SHARED VALUES
In achieving our mission, we will be guided by the following shared values

Caring and Compassion
Our renewed commitment to a patient-centered philosophy will ensure that we always show a genuine concern for patients and their families.

Collaboration and Teamwork
Working in association with others, whom we commit to treat with consideration as equals, we will always put the needs of the communities and patients we serve above our own needs as individuals.

Integrity and Responsibility
By recognizing that we are stewards of a public trust, we will allocate resources and protect privileged information in an uncompromising manner.

Pride and Enthusiasm
By celebrating our achievements and outcomes, we will foster a strong sense of energy, excitement and ownership.

Innovation and Achievement
By supporting the discovery process, we will continue to bring forward new contemporary models of patient care. Our achievements will come as a result of persistence, team work and resolve.

Excellence and Professionalism
By striving for higher quality through learning, we will focus on achievement and contribution and will demonstrate behaviour which is worthy of emulation by others.

Source: lhsc.on.ca/mission, accessed June 13, 2006.

Exhibit 6 St. Joseph's Health Care and London Health Sciences Centre Organizational Charts

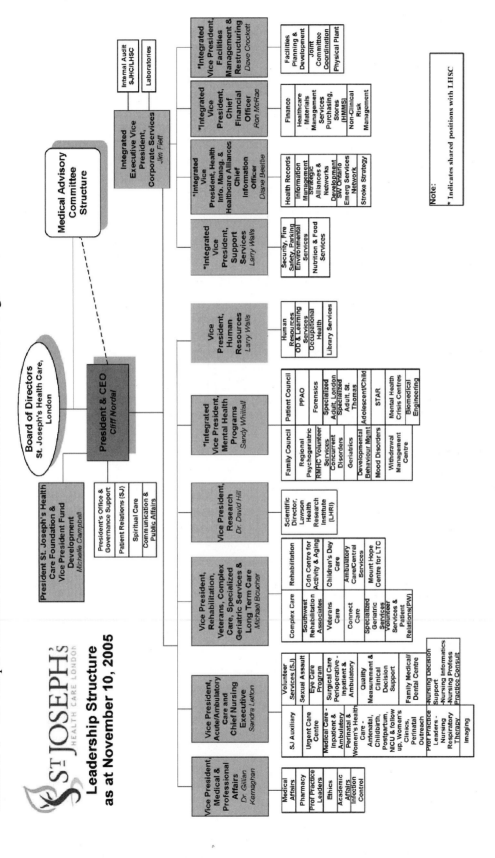

Exhibit 6   (continued)

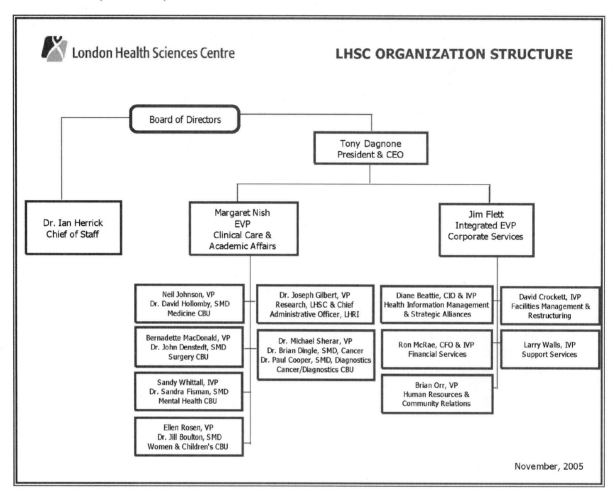

London Health Sciences Centre

LHSC ORGANIZATION STRUCTURE

Board of Directors

Tony Dagnone
President & CEO

Dr. Ian Herrick
Chief of Staff

Margaret Nish
EVP
Clinical Care &
Academic Affairs

Jim Flett
Integrated EVP
Corporate Services

Neil Johnson, VP
Dr. David Hollomby, SMD
Medicine CBU

Dr. Joseph Gilbert, VP
Research, LHSC & Chief
Administrative Officer, LHRI

Diane Beattie, CIO & IVP
Health Information Management
& Strategic Alliances

David Crockett, IVP
Facilities Management &
Restructuring

Bernadette MacDonald, VP
Dr. John Denstedt, SMD
Surgery CBU

Dr. Michael Sherar, VP
Dr. Brian Dingle, SMD, Cancer
Dr. Paul Cooper, SMD, Diagnostics
Cancer/Diagnostics CBU

Ron McRae, CFO & IVP
Financial Services

Larry Walls, IVP
Support Services

Sandy Whittall, IVP
Dr. Sandra Fisman, SMD
Mental Health CBU

Brian Orr, VP
Human Resources &
Community Relations

Ellen Rosen, VP
Dr. Jill Boulton, SMD
Women & Children's CBU

November, 2005

Source: Hospital files.

Gonchar Investment Bank

It was late April 2004, and Allan Grant, vice-president (VP) equity sales, sat staring at his computer screen in his downtown, Kiev, Ukraine, office. He had been working at Gonchar Investment Bank (Gonchar), a large Ukrainian investment bank, for almost two years. He had built numerous strong relationships with clients throughout the world while offering them access to the Ukrainian stock market. Gonchar had traditionally acted purely as an agent, buying and selling shares for clients without taking any ownership position itself. Last Wednesday, Managing Director Marko Kovol had asked for Grant's opinion with respect to adopting a policy that permitted Gonchar to make investments in Ukrainian stocks. While this policy could help clients gain access to the Ukrainian stock market and potentially provide a new source of revenue for the firm, it could also potentially be seen as a conflict of interest in which Gonchar was making money at the expense of its clients. Which option best suited both Grant and Gonchar? Grant had thought about this off and on for the last week, but his report was due at 6 p.m., a mere five hours away. It was time to make a decision.

ALLAN GRANT

Allan Grant, a 2001 MBA graduate, fell in love with the former CIS (Commonwealth of Independent States) in May 2000 while teaching in Moscow as a part of a student-run teaching project.[1] He returned in 2001 and was able to land an equity sales job in Kiev that, in 2002, led him to commence work with a newly formed investment bank, Gonchar. In April 2004, Grant was VP equity sales and loving his job. In fact, he strongly believed that there was tremendous opportunity to make money in Ukraine, as

Jonathan Royce prepared this case under the supervision of Professor Paul W. Beamish solely to provide material for class discussion. The authors do not intend to illustrate either effective or ineffective handling of a managerial situation. The authors may have disguised certain names and other identifying information to protect confidentiality.

Copyright © 2004, Ivey Management Services · · · · · · · · · · · · · · · · · · · Version: (A) 2005-03-23

Ivey

Richard Ivey School of Business
The University of Western Ontario

[1]www.leaderproject.com.

long as one was willing to absorb some risk, "after all, I have bet my life on it." From real estate to the financial market, as long as one could negotiate around the obstacles of modern Ukraine, it seemed success was at the door. However, such obstacles, in all their guises and sizes, made for interesting decisions.

GONCHAR INVESTMENT BANK

Gonchar was founded in 1999 when its senior partners planned to create a full-service brokerage with a corporate finance focus on privatization of formerly state-run companies. In April 2004, Gonchar had a strong institutional sales department as well as the beginnings of a corporate finance department. Over the previous five years, Gonchar had grown to 45 employees while maintaining profitability. Gonchar continued to grow through new hirings. This growth, plus the lack of a human resources department made it difficult to keep track of who was working at Gonchar at any given time. Further, its analyst department was in a separate building from the rest of the firm. Nonetheless, Gonchar's trading profits were more than US$2 million in 2003, resulting in an approximate 63 per cent return on equity (ROE). While only 12 people at Gonchar spoke English, all research was written in English, and all decisions were discussed in U.S. dollars. Gonchar's website detailed its recruiting requirements: "(I)ntroverted people need not apply." One needed to be opportunistic and persistent to make money in an economy like Ukraine's.

UKRAINE

Despite a long history of Ukrainian national identity, Ukraine had frequently felt the power of its neighbors for various periods of time, falling under the control of the Mongols, Lithuanians, Poles, Austrians and Russians. Although the previous attempt to create an independent Ukraine, in 1918, failed after only one year, in 2004, there was domestic optimism that Ukraine, which had declared independence from the Union of Soviet Socialist Republics (U.S.S.R) after a referendum on December 1, 1991, would remain independent into the future.

For investors, there were encouraging signs. In 2001, the International Monetary Fund (IMF) began granting generous loans to Ukraine, on the condition that Ukraine continued to make progress with its economic reforms. These reforms appeared to be showing results. In the first nine months of 2003, Ukraine's economy had grown at an annualized rate of 9.3 per cent, and its nominal gross domestic product (GDP) had reached US$49.4 billion. The annual GDP per capita in 2003 was US$4,437 on a purchasing power parity basis (PPP), having grown by 9.8 per cent per year since 2001, but this figure reflected a divided economy in which the vast majority of Ukrainians earned far less, while the business owners at the top made considerably more. While the Ukrainian currency, the Hryvna[2] (UAH), had only floated since early 2000, it had been stable at about 5.33 UAH:US$1 and at about 1.75 UAH:1 Russian ruble since the end of 2000. Inflation had varied from a high of 25.8 per cent in 2000, to a low of -0.6 per cent in 2002, but the Economist Intelligence Unit predicted it would stabilise around 7.2 per cent for the next several years. Official numbers showed a positive foreign direct investment (FDI) inflow of US$700 million in the first nine months of 2003, however, an accurate picture of the economy was difficult, due to the large black

---

[2]Pronounced "Greevna."

market and the extent to which industries that operated in Ukraine were based outside of Ukraine. Nonetheless, for speculative investors, there were reasons to watch Ukraine.

Ukrainian politics and business groups clouded the Ukrainian economic picture. While official policies seemed pro-business, they frequently benefited the politicians' business interests. For everyone else, actual implementation made life somewhat more complicated. The presidency remained very strong in the Ukrainian government, but there were strong movements afoot to shift the balance of power to the parliament. While it was likely that this change, which could strengthen democracy in Ukraine, would occur in 2004, there was no guarantee. The President, Leonid Kuchma, had made many changes in the previous several years, including the pro-U.S. move of sending troops to join the Polish stabilization force in Iraq, and reductions in corporate[3] and personal[4] taxes. However, Kuchma's regime was still widely regarded as undemocratic. Among its problems, in 2003, Ukraine was cited as one of the worst countries for journalists,[5] with 38 Ukrainian journalists having been murdered since 1991.[6] According to BBC News,[7] one journalist's murder, in 2001, was speculated to have been ordered by President Kuchma, who strongly denied the allegations. Economic and social reforms would likely have to wait until after the widely anticipated victory of the opposition in the October 2004 election.

As in Russia, Ukraine's largest businesses were run by a relatively small group of individuals, most of whom were state officials in the U.S.S.R who bought state-run businesses from the government in the early 1990s at a considerable discount of their estimated fair market values. These business groups were extremely wealthy and while many of their companies traded publicly on the Ukrainian stock markets, there was little in the way of law enforcement limiting their actions. As Sergei Boychuk, VP Corporate Finance at Gonchar, commented with only some facetiousness: "If you have the connections, you can do anything in this country."

KIEV

Kiev (population: 2.6 million) was founded as a trading post between the Vikings and the Byzantine Empire, as its two rivers allow access to the Baltic Sea and the Black Sea. Kiev has been considered the cradle of Slavic civilization; and its open, public spaces, considerable greenery, similarity to many Western capitals and extensive construction boom, will likely attract visitors who will explore the city's rich history in the future. Life in Kiev modeled the economy: very expensive accommodations and restaurants were being built, while ever-present farmers markets and old Ladas represented the life of many other Kiev residents. It is a city of contrasts.

UKRAINIAN FINANCIAL MARKET

Ukraine had several stock markets, including the small Ukrainian Stock Exchange, the over-the-counter (OTC) PFTS index and several other OTC markets. The PFTS was Ukraine's principle stock exchange, where most of Gonchar's stocks were traded.

---

[3] Reduced from 30 per cent to 25 per cent, effective January 1, 2004.
[4] A flat income tax of 13 per cent on personal income was implemented on January 1, 2004.
[5] www.reporterswithoutborders.com.
[6] Foreigners were generally immune from direct threats and violence, but some still ran into problems if they became involved in sensitive areas of Ukrainian politics or business.
[7] Tuesday, February 27, 2001.

The Ukrainian financial market structure resembled many others, and thus, the problems faced by its participants were not unique. However, in 2004, the overall risk profile of the Ukrainian stock market was much higher than that of many of its European neighbors, largely due to lower transparency. While many securities laws were in place, implementation was barely noticeable. Scandals involving Ukrainian companies seemed almost constant, with foreign investors frequently being hurt the most. Many investigations that progressed too close to a powerful figure simply ended without a conclusion. In fact, the private-run organization Transparency International ranked Ukraine as having "one of the highest levels of corruption in the world" and noted that Ukraine was "suspected of (harboring) large-scale money laundering." In this climate, investing frequently seemed more like gambling. "We spend a lot of time arguing about DCF models," commented Grant.

Corporate earnings were based on "Ukrainian accounting," which while supposedly in compliance with International Accounting Standards, in actuality showed little evidence of such adherence. It was difficult for Gonchar's analysts to decide how to determine the corporate discount rate,[8] although their best guess was 16 per cent. However, what evidence that had been compiled spoke to the reason why Gonchar could be successful. The Ukrainian Eurobond's yield[9] had fallen from 12.75 per cent in 2002 to 6.875 per cent on a new April 11, 2004 issue, while the average corporate bond spread[10] had fallen noticeably as well. This decrease in bond yield had led to a 49 per cent increase in the Ukrainian Eurobond price since April 2001. Despite this fluctuation, the PFTS index rose 169.6 per cent over the same period. These gains were likely the result of a combination of factors, including falling global interest rates and increasing demand from investors who were scouring the globe for better-than-average returns amidst stagnant mature markets, such as in Japan and the United States. These were the investors with whom Grant worked.

Gonchar's target market comprised Western institutional investors, and Grant's clients included some of the world's largest mutual fund companies and financial institutions. Within each of these institutions, there were emerging market funds that sought out the best investment opportunities in markets that were not large enough to have dedicated country funds.

Grant's workday started at 10 a.m. when he would send out market research and his comments thereon to clients. He spent 11 a.m. to 4 p.m. talking to portfolio managers who ran emerging market funds in London, England. Next, Grant spent a couple of hours reading research and keeping up with the day's news from his Bloomberg terminal and other sources. His day ended around 9 p.m. after three hours of conversations with clients in New York as their thoughts turned away from the American markets.

LIQUIDITY[11]

"There are not many liquid stocks here," commented Roman Melnyk, a chartered financial analyst (CFA), and Gonchar's head of research, a comment that was both a help and a hindrance to Grant. On more developed stock exchanges, even large orders could be

---

[8] A new website, www.istock.com.ua, recently created to compile public records of Ukrainian companies, thereby helping investors gather information, stated that it hoped to increase the transparency of Ukrainian publicly traded companies. Discount rates are the interest rate used to discount future cash flows—in theory discount rates take into account the return on risk-free government bonds plus a risk premium for the company. Thus, the higher the discount rate, the riskier the company, and vice versa.

[9] Bond yield is the annual compounded return investors will receive if they buy a bond and hold it until maturity.

[10] Corporate bond spread = corporate bond yield – comparable government bond yield.

[11] Liquidity refers to the amount of trading in a share or stock market. If there is a lot of trading, it trades, to use a trader term, "like water" so it is considered very liquid. The opposite holds too.

absorbed by the large, combined interest of small, retail investors and larger institutional buyers. However, due to the relatively small number of large, public Ukrainian companies and the small percentage of their shares that actually traded, for every buy order Grant received from an institution, he had to find a matching sell order, and vice versa. Due to the lack of liquidity, his clients had to deal with an equity salesperson like Grant because they had no way of finding a matching buyer or seller on their own. This situation plus relatively low competition meant that there was little downward pressure on the trading commissions Gonchar charged. However, Grant faced a perpetual conflict of interest in which he had one client buying from another, and he had to get both of them the best deal possible. While he had managed this conflict of interest without complaints, the possibility of Gonchar investing in Ukrainian stocks meant that he might have even more conflicts to balance.

TRADING ENVIRONMENT

Gonchar's trading desk had traditionally acted exclusively as an agent for its clients (principles). The agent/principle relationship is generally defined under North American and British law as follows: Agents act on behalf of a principle without taking ownership of any pertinent asset while legally obliged to act in the best interest of the principle. Grant had effectively built relationships through cold calls, warm leads and persistence. In exchange for Grant's work, Gonchar, like most investment banks, received a commission per share bought and/or sold. Grant received a fixed percentage of each dollar of commission. Thus, the more shares he bought or sold for clients, the more commission he received.

In 2003, Gonchar Investment Bank built a team of analysts, headed by Melnyk. The team of analysts began producing economic and company-specific reports for Gonchar's clients. Being an analyst in Ukraine was not easy. Aside from companies that did not act as if they were bound by any particular accounting rules, there were concerns about fraudulent behavior by management. While such concerns were certainly not unique to Ukraine, as the secretive off-balance sheet financing at Enron and excessive executive pay at Hollinger International showed, nonetheless, it frequently appeared to be more the rule than the exception. Perhaps the most famous scandal had involved Ukraine's largest tire manufacturing firm, Rosava. Rosava's management team had transferred the usable assets of the firm to an established joint venture (JV) based across the street from Rosava. This JV had a controlling block owned by an Irish company (Tapistron Ltd., majority shareholder unknown), thus leaving Rosava with no control over its previous useful assets. The outside shareholders, who held 24 per cent of Rosava, and the state, which owned the remaining 76 per cent, approved the transfer when they voted on a motion by management asking for "approval of contracts concluded by management," despite not knowing the nature of those contracts. These shareholders were left with an empty building and the firm's social assets,[12] including the responsibility for their operating costs. When Rosava shareholders sued, a court ruling upheld the transfer despite the fact that it was clearly against the law when the transfer had occurred. Although the Rosava scandal unfolded in 2000, and asset

---

[12]Social assets were a remnant of the U.S.S.R. in which state-owned factories were required to provide for the local community by building, managing and owning certain assets, including schools, hospitals, housing, etc. These legacy commitments remain for former state-owned corporations, but not for new corporations. While many Ukrainian companies have begun divesting these assets, the high operating costs remain a burden to some firms, while the opportunity to use these assets to divert funds poses a hazard to investors.

stripping was no longer a serious problem in 2004, it was only one example of many in which investors, including foreign investors and the government, although rarely government officials, were hurt by the lax implementation of Ukrainian laws.

On top of concerns about management ethics, conflicts of interest pervaded the Ukrainian political and corporate environment. It was of public record that government officials were permitted to own shares in, and sit on the boards of, public companies. One energy minister was to have commented that sitting on the board of a public oil company helped him understand the industry. While undoubtedly true, it is unlikely that it made for a fairer bidding process when government tenders were opened.

A NEW DIRECTION

Within this environment, Gonchar's analysts made their predictions as to the future movements of Ukrainian stocks with varying degrees of success. In August 2003, Gonchar's senior management decided that, as a part of its growth, Gonchar should open an asset management arm to invest in stocks for clients. Asset management firms take money from clients, pool the funds and then invest the funds on behalf of the clients. In exchange for managing the assets, North American asset management firms take a fee, usually around 1.5 per cent to two per cent of assets per year. Hedge funds, which used more complicated investing strategies than mutual funds, would take up to an extra 25 per cent of capital gains.

Reacting to the new decision to open an asset management arm, Melnyk and his team began creating a monthly model portfolio that was active, although not public, by March 2004. In fact, by mid-April, the team had made an official recommendation to a Russian portfolio manager, suggesting a move to diversify out of oil and into chemicals. From this move, an inevitable decision arose. If the analysts' predictions were good enough to recommend to clients, why should the firm not allow its traders to use the same information? Most investment banks allowed certain employees to invest corporate funds (or "trade or build a book" where the book is the trader's inventory of stock holdings or "positions"). In fact, many such companies borrowed funds to allow their employees to invest it in the stock market. After all, how would it look to clients if an investment bank did not invest its own funds based on analysts' research that it was offering to clients? Further, if an investment bank had employees who could make good recommendations to clients, why not profit from these recommendations with the firm's money? The decision as to who was allowed to trade for a firm varied, but certainly those with the best track record of making money in the stock market were almost always allocated the most money. While there was considerable debate about how American and European firms should use their own analysts' research, there was a general consensus that as long as the analysts' reports had been made public, the firm should be able to invest its own money in those stocks. While Grant commented favorably on how fast Gonchar's analysts were improving, he believed that they still had more to learn about stock markets, and he was not sure if Gonchar had the resources to handle the uncertainty in the Ukrainian stock market. Nonetheless, Grant noted, "There is no better company to be investing in Ukraine than us." Melnyk added, "When we consider the industries in Ukraine it is clear we should invest . . . . Many stocks are neglected but fundamentally good."

The price to earnings (P/E) ratios of most Ukrainian companies were comparable to North American companies, with ratios ranging from 1.5 to 169, with most in the mid-teens. However, these ratios were calculated based on Gonchar's estimates of earnings. Due to the riskiness of Ukrainian companies, these estimates were usually substantially discounted from anticipated actual results. Thus, as long as nothing unusual occurred at a company, actual earnings frequently beat estimates by a large percentage. Therefore, the P/E ratios of companies based on actual earnings were much lower than those based on estimated earnings, and there appeared to be many bargains in Ukraine. While the opportunity in Ukraine seemed apparent, Grant anticipated that profiting from it would be more difficult: "We have traders (to execute trades) available (but) . . . We are not certain who would run the portfolio."

It was not easy to find employees with brokerage experience willing to work in Ukraine. People with considerable experience would likely find it easier to make more money in developed global markets, such as Hong Kong and New York, where, despite more competition, there were large capital flows and many niches that could be exploited. Gonchar hired most of its employees out of school or without any financial experience and allowed them to learn on the job. Employees were hired at very low base salaries, sometimes starting at US$1,000 per month, which was very low by American standards. Employees were rewarded based on the revenue that they brought in to the firm. As Grant had realized, there was substantial opportunity in Ukraine to make as much money as the top American salesmen and traders. Nonetheless, this potential market did not make it easier to hire experienced financial professionals.

The fact that there was no one working at Gonchar with portfolio management experience concerned Grant. In general, analysts make long-term predictions about the price of a stock 12 months into the future by using financial models and by comparing companies to other publicly traded companies. Trading a book requires a time horizon that might contract to minutes as traders buy and sell shares whenever they think that they can make a profit. The holding period for shares may be less than a minute. In general, a trader does not want to hold shares for more than several days. Knowing this, Grant noted "brokerages do not require the same strategic knowledge as asset management. It is just matching trades rather than taking a position and managing it." Despite Gonchar's analysts writing regular research that was being sent to clients on a daily basis, and despite Grant and his colleagues having spent years watching the Ukrainian stock markets, there was no guarantee that Gonchar could profit from this knowledge.

For Grant, the debate was especially pertinent. He had built his relationships with clients as an equity salesman who worked solely as an agent. His office bore this out, as a whiteboard sat in the corner with a list of orders and indications he still had open. As he considered his report, he stared at the whiteboard and noted how many orders he had outstanding. From the buy order for 14.5 million shares of a major telecom from an American portfolio manager to the sell order for 75,000 shares of a Ukrainian oil company from a London-based pension fund, he faced a long list. Those two specific orders had been on the whiteboard for almost a week, "Ukraine is certainly a slow moving market," he thought to himself, not for the first time.

Unlike many firms where professional traders (or "pro traders") made decisions concerning buying and selling shares and thus had an inventory of shares to manage and potentially sell to its clients, Gonchar did not buy from or sell to any of its clients. In many ways, life would be a lot easier, and more profitable, for Grant if Gonchar started pro trading. Many of the orders that he was given had expired without him completing the trade; either another broker had been able to complete the trade, or the client had lost interest. If Grant could find buyers and sellers faster, he could complete many more trades. If Gonchar bought and sold shares, every time a client gave him an order, Grant could show the order to whoever managed Gonchar's portfolio. There was a chance that Gonchar would be able to buy shares from or sell shares to his clients on a regular basis, and his personal income could easily increase by 25 per cent. Also, clients would benefit, as they would be able to buy or sell positions in Ukrainian stocks more quickly.

While Gonchar's decision to avoid investing meant that it frequently took much longer for Grant to complete a trade with a client, in many ways, it also helped him. Grant's clients invested in Ukraine because of the chance to make money, but as he noted, "Clients do not know the real price (of Ukrainian stocks). This is my biggest problem.... Running a book would compound my problems." As clients did not really understand his market, they relied on him for advice, and they trusted him to keep their interests ahead of his own. "I always put my clients first," Grant explained. However, there were always potential conflicts. Grant commented that because of the lack of liquidity in Ukrainian stocks, "It is very easy (for unscrupulous participants) to manipulate stock prices."

As Grant stared at the PFTS screen on his computer, he looked at the market for a large Ukrainian telco's stock. The highest bid was $0.09. There were only 100 shares for offer at $0.12. The next offer was 200 shares at $0.13. Thus, it would be very easy to buy one million shares from a client at $0.10 (which appeared to be a fair price), then buy the 100 shares at $0.12, the 200 shares at $0.13 and then put in a bid at $0.13. On paper, it would then appear that the value of the shares had risen from $0.10 to $0.13. Since clients did not know the fair price of the stock, a dishonest broker could probably then convince another client that the fair price was now $0.13 and make $0.03 per share. It was this sort of trading with which Grant wanted no part, and only reminded him of how difficult it would be to value the shares that Gonchar bought. If someone asked how much a position was worth, what price should they use? Higher may look better, but it would not necessarily be more accurate.

Grant then contemplated how he would deal with his clients if Gonchar began investing in Ukrainian shares. How could he convince a client to buy shares from Gonchar? If Gonchar thought the shares were such a good buy for the client, why was Gonchar selling them? Likewise, if, in good faith, he recommended that the client sell a stock because it was too risky or that it was unlikely to rise in price any more, why would Gonchar want to buy it? It seemed that it would only make sense to buy from a client if Gonchar thought the price was going up and to sell to a client if Gonchar thought that the stock price was going to fall. Grant shook his head. That was not his job. He wanted to be seen as an honest broker, thus deserving of his clients' business, but this policy entailed helping the clients buy the stocks that were rising and sell those that were falling. How could he prevent this policy from damaging his relationship with his clients? And what would happen if the asset management division actually found a manager and began managing the money that a large client had promised to invest with Gonchar? It seemed that there could be many problems if the new division was not adequately separated from the rest of the firm.

COMPETITION

Despite the almost 190 investment banks and brokerages in Ukraine, Grant felt that there were only "a couple of players in brokerage services." In fact, he believed that he only faced competition from two other firms: Alpha Securities and Omega Securities. Grant believed that their equity salesmen were almost exclusively Ukrainian, although many of Alpha's employees had attended European or American universities. Gonchar was ranked number two in equity trading, accounting for 45 per cent of the OTC ADR[13] trades of Ukrainian companies, only a small percentage of their total trades.

---

[13]ADRs (American depository receipts) are securities of foreign companies that trade on a domestic exchange. Each ADR holds a certain number of that firm's stock. In this case, Ukrainian stocks trading on non-Ukrainian exchanges.

Alpha Capital (Alpha), like Gonchar, had commenced operations in 2000, and had offices in Kiev and Prague. Alpha had a total of 20 employees in these two offices, and its website declared that it made markets in all PTFS securities.[14] Omega Securities did not have a website and made no such claims. Nonetheless, if Gonchar's competition was running a book, it was possible that it might make considerable trading profits and be able to grow faster than Gonchar. Profits from trading might also allow Alpha to reduce the commissions it charged clients, thereby squeezing Gonchar's profits, and decreasing Grant's potential income.

Gonchar would not be able to take on large positions, as its capital base was small by international standards where hundreds of millions of dollars could be invested by large American investment banks in a single position. However, Gonchar had arranged short-term financing with a Ukrainian bank that would allow it to take positions in Ukrainian stocks. It was likely that Gonchar would be able to take on positions of up to US$4 million. If Gonchar had invested US$4 million in the PFTS index last year, it would have been worth more than US$8.8 million in March 2004. Further, traders, due to their expertise, are supposed to be able to make more money than the index returns, so Gonchar could have made substantially more. "No wonder pro trading seemed like a good idea," Grant reflected. However, the past does not dictate the future, and there was no certainty that the next year would be as profitable as 2003. In fact, the market could go down, and if Gonchar lost money, it was not certain from where the money to repay the loss would come.

Traditionally, Gonchar decision-making followed "no rule books, no protocol, no hierarchy of command. Decisions were made based on what made money . . . . We are narrowing down our focus which is great." With this in mind, Grant wanted to ensure that his position was well presented.

CONCLUSION

While it might be easiest for Gonchar to continue to trade for its clients exclusively as agents, Grant realized that there were definite advantages for his clients, his firm and even himself if Gonchar started to take on positions. However, as he stared at the order board sitting in the corner of his office, he realized that no matter what he recommended, he had to first consider what impact the decision would have on his relationship with his clients. What would he tell them? How would they view this? Given the importance of his clients' perception of him, Gonchar and the Ukrainian market, which option was best? At the same time, there was the question of whether Gonchar was ready to take on the risks of investing in the Ukrainian stock market. What changes were required for Gonchar to benefit from this new policy? It all made for a great deal to think about. It was already 2 p.m.

---

[14]A firm that makes markets is essentially stating that it is willing and able to buy and sell securities from clients.

Case 36

Phil Chan
(A)

Saturday, February 16, 2008. "We're getting there!" thought Phil Chan as the Air France flight took off from Paris on its way to Lagos, Nigeria. Phil Chan was the Vice-President Marketing of Basic Software, a middle-sized software producer. He was going to Lagos to close a business deal that Allen Lee, the owner of Basic Software, had been negotiating in the preceding weeks. Phil had left his home sixteen hours earlier and he looked forward to reaching his final destination.

Phil decided to review one more time the specifics of the deal, and the strategy that he would follow in the next day's meeting with his Nigerian partners. This was his first trip to Africa and he was somewhat uncertain about local business practices. Since he would be in Lagos for a short stay, he wanted everything to go smoothly.

THE DEAL

The deal required Basic Software to facilitate a financial transaction involving an international transfer of funds and would earn the company over $5 million, their 35 per cent share of the US$14.3 million deal. Allen Lee had been approached a month earlier by Tokunbo Jacobs with the business proposal (see Exhibit 1 for a copy of Mr. Jacobs' initial letter to Mr. Lee). Intrigued by the prospect, he entered into discussions with Mr. Jacobs. Mr. Lee was in the process of negotiating a sale in Bahrain on the Persian Gulf and thought that Africa could offer additional prospects for his company: "Business is all over the world for us. You have to adapt yourself to the fact that conditions are different in other countries from how they are here. This is just part of living in today's world."

In response to his inquiries, he received further details on the deal (see the two faxes in Exhibit 2 and Exhibit 3) and decided to send Phil Chan to Nigeria to complete the negotiations with the Nigerians.

THE NIGERIAN CONTEXT

Nigeria offered significant business opportunities (for a profile on Nigeria, see Exhibit 4). With 144 million people, Nigeria was the giant among Africa's 55 countries. Home to both Christians and Muslims, it possessed great assets. Nigeria's Gross National Product was the fifth largest on the African continent (in 2005 it amounted to US$73 billion). However on a per capita basis it was only about $650. The country was endowed with significant resources. For example, Nigeria was among the world's largest producers of peanuts and rubber. It also produced important quantities of cotton, cocoa, yams, cassava, sorghum, corn and rice.

Nigeria was a major producer and exporter of petroleum. Oil revenues were channeled towards the creation of an industrial base and the strengthening of the agricultural sector. Other important industries included mining (natural gas, coal) and processing (oil, palm, peanuts, cotton, petroleum).

PHIL'S POSITION

Phil Chan wondered how to approach the negotiations with the Nigerians and resolve a few issues which had not been addressed. He wanted the deal to go through without upsetting his partner. Phil had recently read a business publication which emphasized the need to be "skillful in the art of bargaining" when dealing with Nigerians (see Exhibit 5).

Phil and Allen had agreed on what should be obtained from the Nigerians. They believed that five per cent (i.e., $715,000) was more than sufficient to cover the contingencies associated with the completion of this deal. They wanted the contingency fund reduced from 10 per cent to five per cent and their share raised from 35 per cent to 40 per cent.

Phil's plan was to negotiate the financial commitments to be made by both sides prior to the release of funds in order to minimize Basic Software's exposure. To have a clear picture of the expenses to be incurred in the implementation of the deal and of the respective contributions expected from each side, he wanted to examine the pro-forma financial statements prepared by Mr. Tokunbo. His objective was to modify them to Basic Software's advantage.

In a phone conversation with Mr. Tokunbo, Phil had found that in order to do business with the Nigerian government and its agencies, it was necessary to be registered in the official list of pre-qualified suppliers. Various approvals and stamps were required in the registration process. The US$48,000 requested in the September 21st fax was for that purpose.

Phil also wanted to obtain a written commitment that all expenses and advances incurred by Basic Software would be reimbursed from the contingency fund including his travel and accommodation expenses that amounted to just over $6,000.

Phil brought with him all the documents requested by the Nigerian partners, including a power of attorney signed by Allen Lee which authorized him to conclude the deal on behalf of Basic Software.

As he closed the Nigerian file and put it back in his briefcase, Phil wondered how he should conduct the negotiations in order to achieve his objectives without jeopardizing the relationship.

Exhibit 1   Initial Letter Sent by Tokunbo Jacobs to Allen Lee

22nd January 2008

> Tokunbo Jacobs
> 32 Falkar Street, Lagos, Nigeria
> Tel. 234-1-874235, FAX 234-1-442157
> TELEX 37854 RT NG

Dear Mr. President,

I am Mr. Tokunbo Jacobs, a staff of Nigerian National Petroleum Corporation (NNPC) and a member of the "Tenders Committee" of same corporation. I got your contact address through a close relation who is the corporate affairs manager of Nigerian Export Promotions Council. The transaction which is detailed below is being presented to you based on mutual trust and confidentiality.

After due consultation with other members of the Tender Committee, I have been specifically mandated to arrange with you the remittance of US$14.3M. being an over estimated sum resulting from contract executed by an expatriate contractor. The original value of this contract was purposely over inflated by us (Tender Committee) with the sum of $14.3M. Now that the firm have received their supposed payments accordingly and the projects commissioned, I want you to nominate an account into which this money will be paid for division between us and you.

Sharing terms are: 35% to you as the owner of the account into which the money will be paid, 55% to the officials of the three parastatals. 10% is set aside for contingencies. The big bosses of the three parastatals involved in this transaction namely: Nigerian National Petroleum Corporation (NNPC) Federal Ministry of Finance (FMF) and Central Bank of Nigeria (CBN) are aware and behind the deal.

Meanwhile, you are required to indicate your interest through my <u>FAX LINE</u> or <u>TELEX</u> or by <u>personal call</u>. Please in your reply include your personal telephone, fax and telex numbers for easy communications.

You can be rest assured that within few weeks of my receipt of your positive reply this amount will be remitted into your nominated account.

May I demand with the highest respect for the code of business morality and secrecy that under no circumstance should you circumvent or share with any uninvolved person the contents of this letter and other vital documents that may arise in the course of this noble transaction until it is accomplished.

I look forward to your pragmatic conformity to this mutual proposition.

Yours faithfully,

TOKUNBO JACOBS

The text of the letter is original. The address, phone, FAX and TELEX numbers have been disguised.

Exhibit 2   February 2 Fax From Jacobs to Lee – 2 February 2008

FROM: TOKUNBO JACOBS

ATTENTION: ALLEN LEE

Thanks for your fax of 22nd January 2008 accepting to do this business with us. As you rightly mentioned there must be some responsibilities from your company to see this deal through. As a matter of fact you will be required to send to us some basic documents regarding your company to enable us process payment to your account.

These requirements are:

Two of your company's letter headed papers
Two of your company's proforma invoices
Bank particulars in which the said money will be transferred to:
the name of the bank, the account number, the telex number of the bank

On receipt of these above requirements the money will be remitted within twenty one working days.

Allen, I will suggest you visit us with the requirements to expedite this deal and to enable the officials involve in this transaction meet with you person to person for more confidence and to enable to meet who we are entrusting our money. Furthermore I want your personal home phone number for easy communications. Remember we will not hesitate to ask for your assistance financially if the need arises which will be duely deducted from the 10% set aside as contingencies during the process of this transaction. All request needed by you will be given proper attention.

Note: There is no risk whatsoever in this transaction putting into consideration our good home work and calibre of people involve in this deal.

Acknowledge receipt of this message through my fax number 442157.

Thanks and God bless.

TOKUNBO JACOBS

Exhibit 3   February 11 Fax From Jacobs to Lee

FAX: 11th FEBRUARY 2008

FROM: TOKUNBO JACOBS
<u>ATTENTION: ALLEN LEE</u>

Consequent to our telephone discussions, these are the required information. When you despatch those documents via DHL courier service, including your company's catalogues fax the air way bill number to me to enable me pick them up in earnest.

I want you to realize that there are some expenses which we cannot afford to ignore if this transaction <u>must</u> succeed highfreely. We will need US$48,000.00 in order to off-set these expenses. We therefore solicit you to assist us with the already set aside amount. As regards the account:

<u>Beneficiary:</u>   Larry Olunitgo
<u>Bank Name:</u>   National First Bank of Nigeria PLC
                          Broad Street, Branch Lagos
                          Nigeria

<u>Account Number:</u>   1554

Below is the format for the attorney:

The Governor of Central Bank of Nigeria
Tinubu Square Lagos

Dear Sir,
<u>Letter of Authority</u>

I wish to inform you that I Mr. Allen Lee, the president of Basic Software Company of Hong Kong hereby authorize barrister Eze Bakoto to sign on my behalf for the release of the sum of US$14.3 million U.S. dollars being payment for contract completed in 2004 for N.N.P.C. This is due to my present indisposed condition.

I look forward to your anticipated co-operation.

Yours faithfully,

Allen Lee (President).

N.B.:   The about format should be typed on your company's letter-headed paper and should be included with the courier documents.

Exhibit 4   Nigerian File

1963	The establishment of the Republic of Nigeria.
1966	Military coup. The Biafran war begins, lasting two years and causing several million deaths of which approximately two million were Biafran.
1983	Military coup. Benral Buhari overturns President Shagari.
1984	Demonetization operations; bank notes are no longer in circulation and are replaced by a new currency.
1985	State coup. General Ibrahim Babangida replaces General Buhari.
1986	End of the flat exchange rate. Seventy per cent devaluation of the Naira and currency fluctuations.
1990	Unsuccessful state coup against President Babangida. 42 military shot after aborted state coup of April 22nd, 1990.
1991	Riots provoked by Shiite fundamentalists cause two hundred deaths.
1993	Civilian elections held. Results annulled by Babangida, who then steps down and gives power to an interim government.
1994	General Abacha overthrows government. Widespread strikes against regime of Abacha, who arrests union leaders.
1995	Dissident writer Sara-Wiwa hanged. International pressure on Abacha builds.
1996	National Election Commision of Nigeria names five political parties allowed to participate in future elections.
1997	Commonwealth fails to make good on promise to expel Nigeria for human rights violations and not restoring democratic processes.
1998	Following the death of Abacha, successor General Abdulsalam Abubakar promises to end military rule and restore democratic processes within one year.
1999	Former President Obsanjo re-elected in Nigeria's first democratic election since the end of military rule.
2000	Several northern states adopt Islamic, or Sharia law. Clashes between Muslims and Christians break out.
2002	Nigerian government attempts to suppress EU report implicating it in fuelling violent clashes between ethnic and religious groups in the area that have killed thousands.
2003	Obsanjo re-elected in first legislative elections since 1999. Election marked by delays and accusations of ballot rigging.
2004	State of emergency declared after religious clashes result in the death of 200 Muslims.
2005	Lenders agree to write off $20 billion of Nigeria's $30 billion debt.
2006	Obsanjo denied the ability to stand for a third term as senate refuses to alter constitution.

Exhibit 5   Doing Business in Nigeria

Greetings: In Nigeria, greetings are highly valued among the different ethnic groups. Refusing to greet another is a sign of disrespect. Due to the diversity of customs, cultures, and dialects that exist among the different ethnic groups in Nigeria, English is widely used in exchanging greetings throughout the country. Visitors are advised and encouraged to greet while in Nigeria. "Hello" is the most popular greeting. More formal greetings, such as "Good Morning", "Good Afternoon", and "Good Evening" are also appropriate. Avoid the use of casual or colloquial greetings and phrases such as "Hi" or "What's happening?" In addition, visitors are also encouraged to be courteous and cheerful when exchanging greetings. Do not be arrogant. Nigerians treat visitors with respect and, in return, expect to be treated with respect. Personal space between members of the same sex is much closer than in North America. This may cause discomfort to those not accustomed to conversing at close quarters.

Visiting: Nigerians try very hard to please their guests. Although Nigerians are generally not too concerned with time, they know about the western habit of punctuality and expect their western friends to arrive at the appointed time. Most Nigerians prefer "African time" to western punctuality. Nigerians treat their guests with congenial respect and expect their guests to respond in the same manner. Nigerians possess a rich heritage and hope for a bright future as a modern African nation, and thus can be offended by the "superior" attitude of some visitors.

Tipping: A dash (from the Portuguese word das, meaning "give") is a common Nigerian form of compensation in money, goods, or favours for services rendered. With the exception of services performed by waiters or bellhops, a "dash" is normally paid before the service is given. If the service offered is not desired, a firm refusal is usually necessary. The government is officially committed to discouraging certain kinds of "dash" that resemble bribery, such as payments for help in clearing customs, getting visas, or obtaining preferential treatment from government officials. But the custom is widespread and one has to be skillful in the art of "bargaining".

Personal Appearance: Dress varies according to the area and the culture. In the Muslim north, dress is very conservative for both men and women. Dress is more casual in the non-Muslim east and west. Shorts are not considered appropriate attire for Nigerian adults. For men, a shirt and tie are appropriate for formal and most other semi-formal occasions. Visitors will be most comfortable in cotton clothing—polyester is too warm. Traditional Nigerian men's dress is loose and comfortable. Although women in the cities and young girls often wear western dress, most women wear traditional long wraparound skirts, short-sleeved tops and head scarves. The fabric is renowned for its color and patterns.

Gestures: Nigeria is a multicultural nation and gestures differ from one ethnic group to another. Generally, pushing the palm of the hand forward with the fingers spread is a vulgar gesture and should be avoided. One should not point the sole of the foot at a person. Using the left hand in eating (unless left-handed) or in receiving something from someone has a bad connotation. The Yorubas (a large major ethnic group), in addition to the Ibibios and Igbos (two smaller, although major ethnic groups) will wink if they want their children to leave the room.

General Attitudes: Individual Nigerians are proud of the unique cultural heritage of their particular ethnic group. There is some ethnic tension, but continuing efforts are gradually unifying the nation. The Nigerians are striving to create a modern industrial society that is uniquely "African", and not "western". Because of negative connotations attached to the word "tribe", Nigerians avoid its use and "ethnic group" is often used in its place. Life in Nigeria moves at a relaxed pace with the exception of Lagos which can be very frenzied. People are generally not as time-conscious as in the west.

Language: English is the official language in Nigeria. However, because of the Nigerian mother tongue influence, spoken English may be difficult to understand. Pidgin English (broken English) is widely spoken by uneducated Nigerians, although even educated people widely use Pidgin English as a medium of informal conversation among themselves. Each of the over *250* ethnic groups also has its own distinct language. Hausa, Yoruba, and Ibo are widely spoken. Educated Nigerians usually are fluent in several languages.

(continued)

Exhibit 5   (continued)

Religion: In very general terms, Nigeria can be said to be divided between the Muslim North (47%) and the Christian South (34%), with a strong minority of traditional religions throughout the country (18%). However, it is important to note that both the Christians and the Muslims have strong missionary movements all over the whole country making the division of faiths into particular regions not exactly accurate. In addition, Nigerians may claim membership in a particular religion but may also incorporate traditional worship practices and beliefs into their daily life.

Family: Although the technical details of family structure vary from culture to culture, Nigerian families are generally male-dominated. The practice of polygamy is common throughout the country. The protected status of Muslim women in Nigeria is similar to other Muslim countries; however, most other Nigerian women enjoy a great degree of freedom by influencing family decisions and engaging in open trade at the market place, where the money they make is their own. Large families traditionally help share the workload at home. Nigerians pay deep respect to their elders. Children are trained to be quiet, respectful, and unassertive in their relations with adults. Marriage customs vary, but the payment of bridal wealth (money, property, or service traditionally given to the family of the bride by the husband) is common throughout the country.

Social and Economic Levels: Nigerians have the third highest average income in sub-Sahara Africa, but are still very poor by western standards. The average home consists of 1.4 rooms and more than three people per room. About 30% of the people live in absolute poverty. Nigeria once had the ninth lowest crime rate in the world, but without current statistics, it is difficult to determine the country's rank today.

Business Schedules: Most businesses are open from 8:00 AM to 12:30 PM, and then reopen from 2:00 to 4:30 PM. Government offices are open from 7:30 AM to 3:30 PM Monday through Friday. Many establishments and shops are also open on Saturdays with shorter hours. Every fourth Saturday is "Sanitation Day" (where no one is allowed on the street before 10:00 AM) and shops normally are not ready to receive business before noon. Sunday is the normal day of rest. Business appointments must be made in advance. Due to the poor telephone communication, business is often discussed on a person-to-person basis rather than via the telephone. Westerners are expected to be prompt, even though they may have to wait for some time after arriving.

Source: Canadian High Commission, Lagos

Case 37

GE Energy Management Initiative (A)

In August 1992, Raj Bhatt, business development manager for GE Canada, met with executives from GE Supply, a U.S.-based distribution arm of GE. The purpose of the meeting was to discuss new business opportunities in Energy Efficiency, an industry that focused on the reduction of energy usage through the installation of energy-efficient technologies. Bhatt had recently gained pre-qualification for GE Canada to bid in a $1 billion program to install energy-efficient technologies in all Federal Government buildings. He was confident that GE's expertise in lighting, motors, appliances and financing was sufficient to win at least some of the contracts. Furthermore, he saw the program as a stepping stone to building a new GE business to service the Energy Efficiency needs of a range of clients.

The GE Supply executives informed Bhatt that they had already established a position in the U.S. Energy Efficiency industry, through a joint venture with a new Energy Service Company (ESCo), and had retained the services of a full-time consultant to develop the business. They were interested in the Federal Buildings program that Bhatt had been working on, but felt that it would be more efficiently run as a division of GE Supply, rather than as a locally managed Canadian venture. The meeting posed a dilemma for Bhatt. He was encouraged by the level of interest that already existed for Energy Efficiency within GE, but at the same time held certain misgivings about folding the Federal Buildings program into GE Supply's nascent business. Specifically, he was concerned that a lot of interesting Energy Efficiency opportunities existed in Canada, which a U.S.-focused business would not be in a position to exploit. Bhatt left the meeting uncertain how to proceed.

GENERAL ELECTRIC (GE)

GE, with $60 billion dollars in revenues in 1991, was among the top ten industrial corporations in the world. From the early days of Thomas Edison, it had grown to be a diversified 54-business corporation by the early eighties. With 400,000 employees

and a very strong corporate planning division, it exemplified the traditional strategic planning oriented corporation of the 1970s.

In 1980, Jack Welch, the incoming CEO, made a series of sweeping changes. The corporate planning department was eliminated, layers of management were eliminated and the concepts of empowerment and customer focus became the new drivers behind GE's activities. GE's many businesses were restructured into 13 autonomous groups (GE Aerospace, Aircraft Engines, Appliances, Communications and Services, Electrical Distribution and Control, Financial Services, Industrial and Power Systems, Lighting, Medical Systems, Motors, Plastics, Transportation Systems and NBC) which were further subdivided into a number of operating divisions. In the course of a series of divestments, acquisitions and amalgamations, Welch declared that a major criterion for holding on to a business was that it was number one or number two worldwide in its chosen industry.

Each business group worked from a U.S. head office and was charged with global responsibility for its operations. This move, which by-passed the traditional country organizations, was intended to give priority to the global demands of the businesses, rather than to national interests. International operations, which accounted for about 25 per cent of GE's revenues, were structured under a vice chairman, international, but the reality under a so-called direct-connect model was that the operating authority in each country was held by the relevant global business unit. Typically, this meant that general management roles in country operations were eliminated and that business leaders or functional managers of specific businesses reported to their headquarters in the U.S., rather than through their country organization. For example, the marketing manager of GE Lighting's Canadian operations reported directly to the GE Lighting group headquarters marketing manager in Cleveland, Ohio.

GE Canada

The shift to global management had a major impact on GE's Canadian business. In the 1970s, GE Canada operated as a "miniature replica" of its parent company; most businesses and all functions were represented in Canada, and typically a full line of products was made, primarily for the Canadian market but with some exporting possibilities. The Canadian CEO was fully responsible for the profitability of the Canadian operating divisions. This changed dramatically under direct-connect structure implemented in the late 1980s.

In 1992, Matthew Meyer, CEO of GE Canada, had a vastly different role from his predecessors. With all operations reporting straight to their U.S. divisional bosses, Meyer was directly responsible only for the activities of a very small number of employees. He had vice-presidents in finance, environmental affairs, legal, human resources and government affairs. These managers were responsible for all the uniquely Canadian issues that cropped up, such as new legislation, tax accounting, government grants and so on. In addition, there was a small business development group, consisting of three managers. Traditionally, this group had been involved in feasibility studies and new market development for the business units in Canada. Following the shift to a 'direct-connect' structure, the role had become primarily one of looking for opportunities to leverage the strengths of Canadian activities on a global basis. They were also concerned with identifying new business opportunities in Canada. Bhatt, one of the business development managers, explained:

> Canada is a relatively small marketplace. Consequently, most U.S.-based business leaders have a limited awareness of the opportunities here because they have either a U.S. or a global focus. The role of business development is to attempt to identify investment or market opportunities here that they might find valuable.

There was some discussion among business development managers over the extent to which they should actively 'sell' business opportunities to the GE businesses. Some felt that a proactive strategy of promoting Canadian opportunities was appropriate; others preferred to investigate only those cases where business development's involvement had been solicited. The recent decision to promote the vice-president of business development, but not replace him, added further to the uncertainty over the group's role.

Raj Bhatt

Bhatt was only 29. He had worked at GE for just one year, following a successful period at Northern Telecom and an MBA at the University of Western Ontario.

> Business development is quite a challenging experience. There are lots of good opportunities in Canada, but it is sometimes difficult to achieve the level of interest and buy-in necessary to attract the appropriate attention. The Oakville lighting plant, a global manufacturing mandate, is a planned $144 million investment and is certainly our biggest success so far, but there have been a lot of ideas that failed to materialize.

The business development manager typically held that post for only two years, after which he or she was expected to take a line position in one of the businesses. Bhatt had been given a number of attractive options, but had turned them down because he was afraid that his involvement was critical to a number of projects. Specifically, he was concerned that the Energy Efficiency business opportunity he had championed up to now would die because no one else had the knowledge of, or the enthusiasm for, that particular opportunity.

ENERGY EFFICIENCY

Energy Efficiency covered the multitude of ways that energy usage could be optimized, including conservation, use of efficient appliances and off peak usage. Energy Efficiency was originally conceived in the early 1970s as a response to rising oil prices. It recently saw a resurgence due to the environmental movement and the increasing need for cost competitiveness in the late eighties. Although strongly motivated by public opinion and government pressure, Energy Efficiency initiatives were usually sponsored by the energy supply utilities. They recognized that they could more effectively keep their investment down by reducing demand than by building expensive new power stations. There were also obvious benefits to consumers (in reduced costs) and to the environment.

The growth in utility-sponsored programs for Energy Efficiency was responsible for the formation of many Energy Service Companies (ESCos). These companies aimed to meet the demands and needs of their customers by utilizing these programs. Under the most common arrangement (called a performance contract), the ESCo would install energy efficient technologies at no upfront cost to the client. The costs would be recouped from the savings realized. Such an arrangement could be very lucrative, but the ESCo bore all the risk in the event that the promised savings never materialized.

The ESCo Industry in Canada

The Canadian ESCo industry was among the most advanced in the world. Both Federal and Provincial governments had active energy-management programs to promote 'green' issues, and had targeted Energy Efficiency as a critical industry. Ontario Hydro and

Quebec Hydro had budgets for Energy Efficiency of $800 million and $300 million respectively, in comparison to the Cdn$1.5 billion budget for all U.S. utilities combined.

As a result of the utilities' involvement, the Canadian ESCo industry was growing very rapidly; 1989 revenues of $20 million had grown to $100 million by 1992, and one estimate put the total market potential in the billions of dollars. Three major segments could be identified, each accounting for approximately one third of the total volume. They were Commercial, which consisted primarily of office buildings, hospitals and other public buildings; Industrial, which consisted of factories and production plants; and Residential, which consisted of single-family dwellings. So far the commercial sector had been the most rewarding to ESCos, largely due to the similarities between (for example) one hospital and another. Industrial also had potential, but required knowledge of the specific process technology used in each case.

Over the past decade, the ESCo industry in Canada had experienced mixed fortunes, as companies struggled to understand the dynamics of the market. Lack of technical and risk management experience, flawed contracts, lack of financial strength and energy price collapses had all led to very low levels of profitability among major players. The recent upsurge of interest in Energy Efficiency, however, had pushed the industry onto a more steady footing. Furthermore, a shake-out had occurred, leaving between five and 10 serious competitors in Canada.

ESCo Strategies

ESCos saw themselves as undertaking three useful functions with commercial and industrial customers. First, they could undertake energy audits of client sites and advise what forms of energy management were most appropriate. Second, they could engineer and provide access to a wide range of energy-efficient technologies that would normally be hard to get hold of. Third, they could install new energy-efficient equipment, under a performance contract or similar. In the Canadian industry, there were several hundred consulting engineers that participated in energy audits, but only seven "full-service" ESCos that undertook all three functions.

Of the three functions, programs such as performance contracting offered the greatest potential return to ESCos, but also the highest degree of risk. Following an installation, it took between five and ten years before the financial benefits were realized. ESCos were paid at the time of installation by their financing partners, who recovered their costs over the lifetime of the project, but in the event that the project was badly estimated, the shortfall in revenue would have to be made up by the ESCo. Access to capital at a reasonable cost was thus critical. Some ESCos had parent companies with deep pockets. The audit and supply functions, while less lucrative, were important elements of the ESCo's business because they established legitimacy in the eyes of the customer. Many commercial clients were extremely skeptical of the estimated energy savings provided by ESCos, but if they agreed to an energy audit, there was a greater likelihood they could be sold on the merits of an installation. The credibility of the guarantee provided by the ESCo was thus of great importance.

THE GE ENERGY MANAGEMENT INITIATIVE

The Initial Opportunity

As GE Business Development Manager, Raj Bhatt received a communication from the Federal Government inviting ESCos to seek to be prequalified for the implementation of performance contracts in 50,000 federal buildings in Canada. The program had a potential total value of $1 billion, which was to be split into a number of smaller contracts. Bhatt was struck by the potential fit between GE's areas of expertise and the requirements of the program. ESCos had to be able to provide energy-efficient lighting, motors and controls and provide financing for the project; GE was a leading supplier of many of the required products and had a large financing division. Unlike rival firms that would have to form consortia between electrical and financing companies, GE could do many things in-house.

Bhatt submitted a proposal for the Federal Buildings program and, along with a number of other consortia, achieved 'prequalification', meaning the right to bid on subsequent contracts that fell under the Federal Buildings umbrella. This success underlines the magnitude of the opportunity that GE was facing in the ESCo industry. Rather than limiting GE's involvement to the one-off federal Buildings program, Bhatt thought there was potential for an ongoing GE business to meet the expected surge in demand for energy management services. He began to think through the best way of proceeding.

The GE Canada Executive Meeting

Bhatt's first move was to meet with the GE Canada executive group and get their reaction to his idea for an Energy Management Business. Attending were Matthew Meyer, chairman & CEO, Mike Kozinsky, vice-president of finance; and Scott Larwood, vice-president of government relations. Larwood had already been heavily involved in the Federal Buildings program and was in favour of Bhatt's proposal.

Bhatt:	GE Canada is very well-positioned to start an Energy Management business. We have a broader range of relevant products and services than any other ESCo, and the Ontario and Quebec Hydro programs are among the most advanced in the world.
Kozinsky: (Finance)	But this is a systems business. We have never been very good at systems implementation.
Bhatt:	I realize that we may have to find partners. We are working with a small ESCo on the Federal Buildings project which will do all the installation work. We can identify suitable future partners as things progress.
Kozinsky:	But what is our experience in being a prime contractor? This seems to be very different from any business we have been involved with before.
Larwood: (Government Relations)	That's not quite true. The Apparatus Technical Service (ATS) business in Power Systems manages service contracts, and there is a lot of project experience in the States.
Meyer: (CEO)	But there seems to be a considerable risk here. What happens if we pull down a load of asbestos when we're changing a lighting system? GE is an obvious target for legal action.
Kozinsky:	And you stated earlier that there is some downside financial risk if the performance contract does not yield the expected savings.
Bhatt:	True, but the estimates are conservative. The overall financial projections are very promising, and involve very little upfront cost. Apart from the salaries of three or four employees, most costs are on a contract-by-contract basis.

Meyer: Have you given any thought as to how this business would fit into the GE structure?

Bhatt: One of the strengths of GE Canada is that it already taps into all the different businesses. I would like to see the Energy Management business based in Canada, and drawing from the other GE businesses as required.

Bhatt received a lot of questioning and cautioning on various aspects of the proposal, but there was consensus at the end that the project was worth pursuing. Meyer recommended that Bhatt investigate the level of interest in the U.S. businesses and at the corporate level before any formal proposal was put together.

The GE Supply Opportunity

In discussion with U.S. colleagues, Bhatt discovered that three U.S. divisions were attempting to establish their own ESCo-like initiatives. Two of them were at about the same stage of development as Bhatt. The third, GE Supply, which was a division of the GE Industrial and Power Systems Group, was more advanced. They had been working with an ESCo for a number of months, and had retained a well-connected consultant to advise them. Up to now, the ESCo had assumed all the risk, with GE providing their name, their products and some servicing expertise, but the division was planning to create a joint venture with the ESCo in the near future.

On hearing about the GE Supply initiative, Bhatt went to Connecticut to visit the GE Supply executives to discuss their respective plans. Present at the meeting were Bhatt, Doug Taylor, CEO of GE Supply, and Fred Allen, manager of the Energy Management business.

Taylor:
(CEO) Last week we signed a formal alliance agreement with Wetherwell Inc. to run for 18 months. We are now actively looking for contracts.

Allen: But the U.S. market requires some education. How is the market in Canada?

Bhatt: There is a very promising opportunity that we are working on right now. Basically, the Federal Government is looking for bidders on a $1 billion program, and we have already gained prequalification.

Allen: That beats anything we've got down here. I think there could be some real opportunities for us to work together. We have gained quite a lot of experience over the past 12 months, and combined with your market, we could have a winning combination.

Bhatt: I am certainly interested in exploring opportunities. How do you see a Canadian Energy Management business fitting with your business?

Taylor: We could manage the Canadian business out of our office here.

Bhatt: That causes me some concern. The business relies on close coordination with utilities and government bodies, and a strong local presence would definitely be necessary. I must admit, we considered that management of at least part of the business should be in Canada. The opportunities in Canada are unmatched.

Taylor: Well, there is some strength to your argument, but I don't see why this business should not fit the normal model.

Case 38

MapQuest

On October 1, 1999, Chief Executive Officer (CEO) Mike Mulligan's team at MapQuest closed the third quarter books. Revenue was strong and the company's cash position was good. During the past year, Mulligan had led the firm through a successful initial public offering (IPO) and record growth. However, Mulligan questioned being able to sustain the growth rate and the market value of the firm, which many called irrational. He wondered how he could take advantage of the stock price and continue to sustain growth (see Exhibits 1 and 2) and value going forward. Mulligan planned to lay out a course of action for the board later that month.

INDUSTRY BACKGROUND

Growth of the Internet

The Internet had become an increasingly significant global medium for distributing and collecting information, conducting commerce and communicating. Internet growth was being fuelled by increased use of personal computers, improvements in network infrastructure, more readily available and lower cost Internet access, an increased acceptance of conducting transactions online and the proliferation of compelling available content.

MapQuest and many of its competitors had been in the mapping, printing and location information businesses for years and were now faced with the prospects of this dynamic digital business environment. Many of the existing offline companies and many start ups that were focused on the space, some very well funded with growth capital, saw the opportunity to leverage their offline assets online.

Richard Ivey School of Business
The University of Western Ontario

Kevin K. Boeh prepared this case under the supervision of Professor Paul W. Beamish solely to provide material for class discussion. The authors do not intend to illustrate either effective or ineffective handling of a managerial situation. The authors may have disguised certain names and other identifying information to protect confidentiality.

Convergence of Traditional and Digital Mapping

Geospatial information had traditionally been provided through reference materials including atlases, maps, travel guides, telephone directories and textbooks. According to the International Map Trade Association, the annual market for such publications in the United States alone would exceed $1.6 billion. Advances in technology allowed companies to put their geospatial information into computer applications and to place their databases onto CD-ROMs and the Internet. MapQuest had followed just such a path and was using its extensive databases of geographically relevant information to provide online services.

Online Destination Information for Business and Consumers

Businesses had traditionally communicated their existence and location to customers using print media including newspapers and the Yellow Pages, which targeted only a narrow geographic audience and had limited ability to provide updated information. MapQuest gave businesses the opportunity to provide customized driving directions and real-time physical location information. As well, MapQuest provided businesses with an additional set of information and tools that online sites used to enrich and differentiate their own offerings. Very few of these companies had the personnel or technical resources to cost effectively develop the services in-house that MapQuest provided to them.

Consumers and travellers had traditionally located businesses and other points of interest using maps and telephone inquiries, among other methods. As the Internet was growing, consumers were increasingly turning to the Internet for such information.

Geographically Targeted Online Advertising

Forrester Research estimated that online advertising of approximately $1.0 billion in 1998 would grow to over $8.1 billion over the next four years. While online advertising was growing, it was primarily national or international advertising. That is, the products and services offered were not location-specific, yet most actual consumer expenditure was indeed local. While figures varied, it was estimated that as much as 80 per cent of a consumer's expenditure, net of housing, occurred within five miles of the primary residence. As well, of the offline advertising market, nearly 80 per cent of the total expenditure was for local businesses, using location-specific advertising media. The opportunity to allow online advertising to be location-specific had yet to be realized.

COMPANY BACKGROUND
History and Transformation

R.R. Donnelley & Sons, a media and printing company, founded MapQuest, originally called GeoSystems Global Corporation, in Lancaster, Pennsylvania, in the late 1960s as a cartographic services division responsible for creating free road maps for gas station customers. In the 1970s, MapQuest became a leading supplier of custom maps to reference, travel, textbook and directory publishers. The company grew in the mapping industry as a high-quality custom mapmaker and expanded its client base to include American Express, Bertelsmann, Langenscheidt, Reader's Digest, Houghton Mifflin, Reed Elsevier, The National Geographic Society, and World Book.

In 1991, R.R. Donnelley combined its mapping expertise with technology to pioneer electronic publishing software for interactive mapping applications. MapQuest developed electronic applications for call centres, kiosks, client-server environments and wireless devices, as well as packaged software applications for travel, directory, reference and street mapping. In 1994, MapQuest created travel titles for the first handheld devices brought to market by Apple Computer. MapQuest produced travel titles that allowed Fodor's, TimeOut and Michelin to bring top international city guides, tour information and directory mapping to consumers. In this same year, MapQuest was split into a separate entity from its corporate parent, R.R. Donnelly and Sons, to management and certain investors, including R.R. Donnelley.

In 1996, MapQuest launched the first consumer-focused interactive mapping site on the Web. The company began to offer business solutions to map-enable other Web-sites. This innovative business model captured the attention of the Internet consumer and the business market.

In April 1997, The National Geographic Society entered into a cartographic product development, publishing, marketing and distribution agreement with the firm. The agreement was for five years, ending in May 2002. National Geographic took a seat on the board and received warrants to purchase 954,147 shares at $1.04 per share.

In July of 1997, outside venture investors, including Highland Capital, Weston Presidio Capital and Trident Capital, invested in the firm, taking 3.4 million shares for $12 million. In November of that year, insiders, including the chief financial officer and senior vice-president also purchased stock, largely funded using interest-bearing notes from the firm.

In May 1998, R.R. Donnelley & Sons and 77 Capital Corporation, two of the original investors from the spin-off, sold their equity positions to Highland Capital, Weston Presidio Capital and Trident Capital for an additional $7 million. In June of this same year, Chief Executive Officer Barry Glick took a voluntary termination of employment as, whereby MapQuest agreed to pay Glick $43 thousand representing separation and salary. In August, Michael Mulligan was hired from American Express Travel as CEO and chairman of the board. At American Express, Mulligan had been responsible for Corporate Services Interactive, an American Express Travel offering. Prior to American Express, Mulligan was the chief operating officer (COO) of OAG, the Official Airlines Guide, and was thus a very fitting candidate to lead the company.

The Initial Public Offering

In late 1998, the board of directors selected underwriters to lead an initial public offering. The company officially changed its name to MapQuest.com, established its corporate headquarters in New York City, along with its development facilities in Mountville, Pennsylvania, and Denver, Colorado. The investment banks drafted the IPO prospectus in January 1999, and filed an initial registration statement (S-1) on February 19 to sell up to $50 million of stock. On April 12, an amended S-1 was refiled with an offer to sell 4.6 million shares in the range of $10 to $12 per share with an over-allotment option to the underwriters to increase the number of shares by up to 15 per cent (see Exhibit 3).

The IPO roadshow was held during the last two weeks of April, continuing into the first few days of May. On May 3, 1999, the pricing range was increased to $12 to $14 per share to allow flexibility of pricing to meet the hot market demand. The shares were priced after the close of Nasdaq trading on May 3 at $15 per share, and began trading on Tuesday, May 4. Shares debuted late in the morning at $28 per share, an 87 per cent gain from the pricing to IPO buyers. The stock price made the market capitalization of the firm approach $1 billion in its first day of trading.

MAPQUEST—THE BUSINESS

The Solution

MapQuest was a leading online provider of mapping and destination information for businesses and consumers. MapQuest's online products and services enabled businesses to:

- Provide customized maps, destination information and driving directions to potential customers;
- Expand the service offerings of their websites to attract and retain users;
- Use outside sources to meet their map-generating and destination information needs, thereby avoiding a significant portion of the expenses normally associated with establishing and maintaining a map-generating personnel and technology organization; and
- Provide potential customers with information regarding which of a business's multiple locations was closest to the potential customer.

MapQuest's online products and services enabled consumers to:

- Receive maps and destination information on a real-time basis based on specific location parameters provided by the customer;
- Generate detailed, door-to-door driving directions at any time; and
- Create and retrieve customized maps based on the consumer's preferences.

MapQuest was also a leading provider of traditional and digital mapping products and services to the educational, reference, directory, travel and governmental markets in the United States. In addition, companies that incorporated call centres, CD-ROMs or driving direction kiosks into their information delivery strategy required non-Internet customized mapping solutions. MapQuest had adapted its map-generating software to promote the rapid development of mapping applications in these environments.

MapQuest Strategy

MapQuest's objective was to be the leading online provider of destination solutions for businesses and consumers. Key elements of MapQuest's strategy, as put forth in the IPO prospectus, included their intention to:

- *Build Brand Awareness*: In addition to branding on its website, MapQuest co-branded its products and services on each of its business customer's websites. MapQuest intended to expand its use of advertising, public relations and other marketing programs designed to promote its global brand and build loyalty among its customers. In the future, MapQuest planned to expand both its online and offline marketing programs.
- *Expand and Enhance the MapQuest Service*: The company planned to continue to broaden and deepen its services by providing comprehensive, cost-effective, accurate and easily accessible information and value-added tools and features. The company was developing product and service enhancements aimed at its business customers, including enhancing their opportunity to offer geographically targeted advertising programs on their websites. MapQuest's planned enhancements to its consumer service included introducing greater personalization features to mapquest.com.
- *Grow Sales Channels Aggressively*: The company hoped to build its sales capabilities in order to broaden penetration of its products and services and increase

revenue. The company planned to build its direct field sales force to target United States and international markets, and it sought to develop strategic relationships in the value-added-reseller channels. The company also intended to build its own advertising sales force in order to augment the current third-party representative sales force it had engaged to sell advertisements on mapquest.com.

- *Develop Additional Advertising Opportunities*: The company intended to increase and expand its advertising revenue opportunities by offering new methods of targeted advertising based on a consumer's geographic information. The company planned to use consumer-provided information to provide advertisers the ability to base their advertising and promotions on a consumer's geographic information.

- *Use Existing Integrated Geographic Data as a Platform*: The company wanted to develop new products and services by effectively employing the comprehensive integrated geographic databases it had been developing since 1967. The company had utilized proprietary editing software tools to create its geographic data from multiple content providers in a variety of data formats.

- *Pursue International Opportunities*: The company believed that significant opportunities existed to expand MapQuest's products and services internationally. As of December 1998, approximately 10.8 per cent of the maps that MapQuest generated from its own website represented international locations. The company intended to expand its international marketing efforts to gain access to additional business customers seeking to improve the service offerings of their websites and consumers seeking online map-related information.

MapQuest Products and Services—Internet and Traditional

Internet—Business Products/Services

Connect	Enabled businesses to display requested maps based on any combination of city, state, street address and ZIP code.
InterConnect	Enhanced MapQuest Connect. Enabled consumers who visited a business's website to find the closest location to a user's location.
Locator	Enhanced MapQuest InterConnect. Enabled more advanced searching by integrating MapQuest with specific geographic search parameters contained in its business customer's database, such as "find closest gas station with a car wash."
TripConnect	Enabled businesses to provide consumers with door-to-door driving instructions, including a route-highlighted map, trip mileage and estimated driving time.
Enterprise Service	Provided mapping and routing capability designed primarily for high-volume websites. Enabled business customers to integrate generated map pages into their websites.
Enterprise Server	Non-hosted. Provided mapping and routing capability designed primarily for high-volume websites. Enabled business customers to integrate generated map pages into their websites.
Server for NT	Non-hosted. Provided mapping and routing capability designed primarily for low-volume websites. Enabled business customers to customize their own mapping solutions.

Internet—Consumer Products/Services

The mapquest.com website offered several menu options for consumers:

- Maps—enabled map generation either based on detailed supplied information or a more general location request;
- Driving Directions—provided the most direct route from a point of origin to a destination using a variety of options and formats, including door-to-door, city-to-city, overview map with text, text only or turn-by-turn;
- Travel Guide—provided access to lodging, dining, city and weather information for most consumer-requested destinations, all of which could be tailored by the consumer to fit his or her particular information needs;
- Buy A Map—provided access to the MapStore to buy United States and international maps, road atlases, travel guides and other map and travel-related products; and
- Membership—by becoming a member, the consumer could save generated maps, place personalized icons on generated maps that could be stored for future use, receive advance notice of new MapQuest features and enhancements and become eligible for promotional offers.

Digital Mapping (Traditional) Products/Services (DMS)

MapQuest published or provided the relevant geographic data for printed road maps, atlases, travel guides, hotel and telephone directories, maps used in textbooks and reference books, and CD-ROMs. In addition, MapQuest's products and services included software applications incorporating customized mapping solutions for publishers and producers of CD-ROMs. MapQuest also provided extensive cartography, geographic database development, comprehensive map data maintenance, advanced mapping technology and consultation services to a wide variety of customers on a fee-for-service basis. MapQuest's traditional and digital mapping customers included National Geographic, Galileo International, Ryder, Exxon, Best Western and the Alamo and National Car Rental (Republic).

Future Product and Service Directions

The technology team had integrated MapQuest services, including driving directions, into the Palm Pilot 7, the first full-time Internet-connected handheld, using an advertising-based business model. The firm planned and budgeted for a nationwide rollout later in the year. The firm also considered opportunities for products and services to be supplied to and bundled with competing Internet appliances, including the latest cell phones with LCD screens. Finally, the team foresaw the integration of its products and services into the digital mapping capabilities and GPS in autos and other forms of transportation.

Sales and Marketing

MapQuest sold its Internet business products and services in the United States through a sales organization of 17 employees as of January 31, 1999. This sales organization consisted of 12 direct field salespeople based throughout the United States and five telemarketers located at MapQuest's Denver office. In addition, MapQuest sold its Internet products and services through indirect sales channels, including value-added resellers such as Moore Data and SABRE BTS.

Sales of advertisements on mapquest.com were generated by third-party advertising sales representatives and, to a lesser extent, by MapQuest's internal advertising sales force, which consisted of two persons as of January 31, 1999.

MapQuest sold its traditional and digital mapping products through a direct sales force of 11 field salespersons and telemarketers. MapQuest marketed its products and services online by placing advertisements on third-party websites. In addition, MapQuest advertised through traditional offline media and utilized public relations campaigns, trade shows and ongoing customer communications programs.

MapQuest Customers

MapQuest had licensed its products and services to over 380 business customers. No one customer accounted for over 10 per cent of MapQuest's overall revenues (see Exhibit 4).

MapQuest Suppliers—Geographic Data

MapQuest licensed a significant portion of its primary geographic data from a limited number of sources through non-exclusive, short-term contractual arrangements. MapQuest relied on U.S. street level data drawn from the U.S. government and through agreements with NavTech and Geographic Data Technologies (GDT). Data covering Canada were supplied by Desktop Mapping Technologies Inc. MapQuest obtained Western European street and major road data from TeleAtlas, NavTech and AND Mapping NV. Major road data for the rest of the world was obtained from AND Mapping NV. MapQuest relied on these sources of third-party data, and if any were to change, MapQuest would have needed to substitute alternative sources of data or attempt to develop substitute sources of data internally.

MapQuest's own proprietary data assets also supported its online and traditional and digital mapping products and services. MapQuest had spent approximately six years developing a U.S. major road database. MapQuest also maintained a graphical image database that contained over 190,000 archived files to serve as an internal reference library. In addition, MapQuest had developed a suite of international city map data that included over 300 metropolitan maps and over 500 downtown maps of most major international tourist and business destinations.

THE CAPITAL MARKETS

The capital markets for Internet and technology companies were doing well (see Exhibit 5), and had experienced one of the greatest run-ups in history (see Exhibit 6).

Initial Public Offerings and Venture Capital

The number of venture-backed companies was increasing as well, which made Mulligan feel that more potential customers would get funded, but might also allow more competitors to emerge (see Exhibit 7).

As more and more companies were funded in the private markets and had the capital to fuel growth, more companies drove quickly to the public markets and created a heated market for initial public offerings (see Exhibit 8).

Mergers and Acquisitions

The mergers and acquisitions market had picked up tremendously as new capital flowed into the hands of IPO- and venture-backed companies. Inflated stock valuations were driving many companies to use their own stock as acquisition consideration. These factors helped drive the market for the acquisition of venture-backed companies (see

Exhibit 9). However, there was fear that the Financial Accounting Standards Board (FASB) in the United States would rule to make the use of pooling-of-interests more difficult in a merger, if not impossible altogether. Such a move would require acquirers to use the purchase accounting method, likely slowing acquisition activity, since acquirers would have to immediately take a full write-off of goodwill rather than write it off over an extended period.

THE COMPETITIVE LANDSCAPE

The market itself was still shaping, and new players, new technologies and new offerings were rapidly emerging. Stock analysts and venture capitalists frequently spoke of "eyeballs" (Internet traffic), stickiness (how long users used a site), and wallet-share (how much of a consumer's total expenditure could be influenced) when touting the merits of a particular business model or offering (see Exhibits 10 and 11).

Data and Map Data Vendors

There were two sources of data used in the industry. First, there were numerous data vendors that sold demographic and business information such as white pages listings, business listings, demographic and address data. Players included:

- InfoSpace—(Nasdaq: INSP) A data and content provider to sites and online information providers, the company was also very focused on its consumer site. InfoSpace relied heavily on InfoUSA as a data source.
- InfoUSA—(Nasdaq: IUSA) A long-time data directory and demographic information provider. InfoUSA was a source of primary data to most white pages and directory publishers in the United States. The company's online site offering such information had little traffic.

A second group of data providers included mapping specialized data vendors. These vendors collected and created specific mapping information from primary sources, including governments and survey data, as well as from secondary sources. While there was some competition, these companies tended to offer coverage of specific locations or types of data. Major players included:

- Nav-Tech—(Private) Founded in 1985, based in Chicago, the company offered digital mapping data and technologies, including GPS systems.
- GDT—(Private) Founded in 1980, the company was a major supplier of data to both Vicinity and MapQuest, the first use of its data on the web.
- TeleAtlas—(Private) Founded in 1984, the company had broad data coverage of Europe.

See Exhibit 12.

Map Enablers

These companies offered products and services that enabled businesses and portals to offer richer, better content and services on their own sites. Since growth capital was plentiful among their customers (e.g. the Portals), revenue growth was rapid. Key players included:

- Zip2—(Owned by Alta Vista, owned by CMGI, Nasdaq: CMGI) A pioneer in local content and city guides, the firm sold in February 1999 for $347 million to Alta Vista.

- MapInfo—(Nasdaq: MAPS) A software provider focused on location enabling services for businesses.
- Vicinity—(Private, owned partly by CMGI, Nasdaq: CMGI) An information services provider to businesses, it also owned MapBlast, the consumer-focused mapping site. CMGI, the part owner, was a holding company that invested in pre-IPO companies.
- Etak—(Owned by Sony) Sony had purchased Etak from NewsCorp. Etak was a provider of mapping software and technologies.
- ESRI—(Private) Primarily a software provider for GIS applications for locating telecom and pipeline infrastructure, as well as consumer application software.

"Local" Portals

The Internet mega-portals had realized the "local" opportunity and had each begun to offer localized content. These large players had abundant capital and were eagerly spending to gain market share. Major local offerings included:

- AOL Digital Cities—(NYSE: AOL) AOL was the world's largest Internet service provider with a portal specifically for its subscribers.
- Microsoft Sidewalk—(Nasdaq: MSFT) Microsoft offered a competing set of local sites. In July of 1999, it sold its Sidewalk business to TicketMaster CitySearch in a deal that included providing local information and content back to Microsoft under the Sidewalk brand.
- CitySearch (TicketMaster)—(Nasdaq: TMCS) A comprehensive set of city/local guides and information, including local event ticket sales, from the world's largest event ticketing company.
- Yahoo Local—(Nasdaq: YHOO) A set of localized sub-sites tailed to specific cities.
- Alta Vista—(owned by CMGI, Nasdaq: CMGI) Purchased in August 1999 from Compaq, the firm announced its plans for an IPO. Alta Vista owned Zip2.

Competition—MapQuest Business Offering

Of the approximately 764 websites that were currently map-enabled, MapQuest had roughly a 50 per cent market share (see Exhibit 13). The largest historical competitors were Vicinity and Zip2, but MapQuest was taking share and was by far the largest provider in the market. MapQuest also faced potential competition from "one-stop shop" content suppliers such as InfoSpace, which offered a wide range of services and had broad distribution for many of its products but with no current focus on a competing product or service offering.

Competition—MapQuest Consumer Offering

MapQuest was the leading travel/mapping site on the Internet (see Exhibit 14). Traffic data showed MapQuest gaining share against competitors even while little was spent on marketing and promotion. After the IPO, the launch of a $2 million promotional campaign accelerated share gains.

Competition—MapQuest Digital Mapping (Traditional)

The company faced a wide range of competitors including Rand McNally, Langenscheidt (American Map), Universal, Magellan, ESRI and DeLorme. However, MapQuest management had planned to shift focus away from the DMS business to the high growth, higher margin Internet mapping opportunity.

THE MEETING OF THE BOARD

Mulligan and his executive team planned to present strategic alternatives to the board of directors. Recently, MapQuest stock traded around $12 per share. This price was below the IPO price of $15, while the Nasdaq index was up about 10 per cent during the same period. Still, the $12 price made the firm worth around $400 million in market cap. However, other "pure-play" software and content providers were trading at higher multiples. Mulligan wondered whether the traditional DMS business was anchoring the firm value. Investors were hungry for Internet businesses. Or, given that the market valued revenue, how could he grow the revenue streams? If nothing else, Mulligan wondered whether to believe pundits in the market suggesting an overall market bubble. If this *was* a bubble, Mulligan wondered what he could do to take advantage of it.

Exhibit 1 MapQuest—Income Statement and Projections (all amounts in millions, except per share amounts)

	1996	1997	1998	1999e	2000e	2001e	2002e
Revenue							
Internet Business	$7.0	$4.8	$6.5	$12.8	$20.6	$42.6	$63.3
Internet Consumer	0.1	1.3	1.4	6.4	13.9	26.4	44.4
Traditional DMS	12.4	15.4	16.8	14.7	20.0	24.0	28.0
TOTAL	19.6	21.4	24.7	33.9	54.5	93.0	135.7
Cost of Revenue							
Internet	4.3	4.5	4.8	9.7	13.2	18.5	24.4
Traditional DMS	8.0	10.8	12.8	11.4	14.7	17.6	21.0
TOTAL	12.3	15.3	17.6	21.1	27.9	36.1	45.4
Gross Profit	7.3	6.1	7.1	12.8	26.6	56.9	90.3
Sales & Marketing	4.5	7.3	5.2	19.0	25.1	30.0	40.0
General & Admin	1.9	1.8	2.3	4.8	6.4	8.0	11.5
Product Development	2.6	5.0	3.0	5.6	7.5	11.0	15.0
TOTAL OPEX	9.0	14.1	10.5	29.4	39.0	49.0	66.5
Operating Income	(1.7)	(8.0)	(3.5)	(16.6)	(12.4)	7.9	23.8
Interest Income (Expense)	0.2	0.1	0.1	1.6	1.0	—	—
Other Income (Expense)	0.2	0.3	0.2	0.3	0.4	—	—
Pretax Income	(1.3)	(7.6)	(3.2)	(14.7)	(11.1)	7.9	23.8
Tax Expense	0.0	0.0	0.0	0.0	0.0	0.0	0.0
EPS			$(0.12)	$(0.47)	$(0.33)	$0.21	$0.66
Total Shares Outstanding			27.6	31.4	33.8	36.9	36.2

Note: e = estimates

Exhibit 2   MapQuest—Balance Sheet (all amounts in thousands, except share counts)

	Dec. 31, 1998	Sep. 31, 1999
Assets		
Current assets		
Cash and cash equivalents	$ 564	$29,685
Short term investments	—	17,940
Accounts receivable, net of allowances	6,647	9,840
Accounts receivable - affiliates	128	707
Inventories	1,365	1,126
Contracts works in progress	147	231
Prepaid expenses and other current assets	482	1,684
Total current assets	9,333	61,213
Property and equipment, net of accumulated depreciation	1,844	4,488
(1998 – $3,433; 1999 – $4,455)		
Goodwill, net	178	155
Other assets	95	825
Total assets	**$11,450**	**$66,681**
Liabilities and stockholders' equity (deficit)		
Current liabilities		
Accounts payable	$ 1,715	$ 2,719
Current portion of note payable	48	5
Accrued personnel costs	562	1,231
Advance billings on contracts	498	686
Deferred revenue	1,208	2,434
Other accrued liabilities	1,001	2,411
Total current liabilities	5,032	9,486
Stockholders' equity (deficit)		
Convertible Preferred Stock, Ser. A, B and C	26,477	—
Notes receivable from issuance of preferred stock	(291)	—
Preferred stock, $01 par; 5 million authorized	—	—
Common stock, $.001 par; 100 million authorized; 336,038 o/s in 1998; 33,572,562 o/s in 1999		
Notes receivable for common stock	—	—
Additional paid in capital	140	88,246
Retained deficit	(19,908)	(30,861)
Total stockholders' equity (deficit)	(19,768)	57,195
Total liabilities and SE (deficit)	**$11,450**	**$66,681**

Exhibit 3   Closing Stock Prices—Weekly

Date	Nasdaq Index	MQST
7-May-99	2,503.62	$22.19
14-May-99	2,527.86	21.38
21-May-99	2,520.14	17.56
28-May-99	2,470.52	16.75
4-Jun-99	2,478.34	16.38
11-Jun-99	2,447.88	15.69
18-Jun-99	2,563.44	15.00
25-Jun-99	2,552.65	15.69
2-Jul-99	2,741.02	18.13
9-Jul-99	2,793.07	19.63
16-Jul-99	2,864.48	20.13
23-Jul-99	2,692.40	17.00
30-Jul-99	2,638.49	14.94
6-Aug-99	2,547.97	10.13
13-Aug-99	2,637.81	10.31
20-Aug-99	2,648.33	13.94
27-Aug-99	2,758.90	12.38
3-Sep-99	2,843.11	12.00
10-Sep-99	2,887.06	12.88
17-Sep-99	2,869.62	13.50
24-Sep-99	2,740.41	12.50
30-Sep-99	2,746.16	$11.88

Exhibit 4   MapQuest Customers

Content Providers:
- Excite
- Infoseek
- Lycos
- TicketMaster Citysearch
- Yahoo!

Media:
- LA Times
- National Geographic

Real Estate:
- Cendant
- Moore Data

Other:
- Citgo
- Exxon

Telecoms/Directories:
- Ameritech
- APIL (Don Tech)
- GTE
- Pacific Bell
- Southwestern Bell
- US West

Publishers/Ad Agencies:
- Classical Atlas
- DDB Needham
- Harte Hanks
- McGraw-Hill
- Modem Media-Poppe Tyson
- RR Donnelley

Travel/Entertainment:
- American Auto Assoc
- American Express
- Avis
- Best Western
- Budget
- Galileo International
- Hertz
- Republic Industries
- Ryder
- Sabre Group (Travelocity)

Retail/Services:
- Blockbuster
- Border's
- Home Depot
- Kinko's
- Sears

Exhibit 5   Market Valuations and Statistics

Company	Ticker	Stock Price (Sep 3, 1999)	Shares O/S	Market Cap (M)	Trailing Quarter Rev (M)	Enterprise Value (EV) (M)	Unique Visitors Jul-03
About	BOUT	$39.50	12.1	$ 478	$ 3.7	$ 416.5	8.3
America Online	AOL	97.06	1,207.0	117,151	1,377.0	113,927.4	42.2
Ask Jeeves	ASKJ	33.75	24.9	840	2.7	777.1	4.2
CNET	CNET	41.50	80.1	3,324	25.6	3,083.0	8.2
EarthWeb	EWBX	35.88	9.1	327	7.2	293.9	0.6
Excite@Home	ATHM	40.94	361.0	14,779	100.4	14,654.0	16.4
Go2Net	GNET	66.81	41.1	2,746	5.7	2,475.1	11.2
GoTo	GOTO	37.56	35.8	1,345	3.6	1,217.8	7.3
Infoseek	SEEK	31.00	62.0	1,922	36.1	1,838.6	21.1
LookSmart	LOOK	27.50	84.1	2,313	10.5	2,214.4	10.1
Lycos	LCOS	44.75	89.4	4,001	45.1	3,850.2	30.2
MapQuest	**MQST**	**12.00**	**33.0**	**396**	**7.4**	**366.3**	**5.4**
The Globe	TGLO	10.63	24.4	259	4.1	187.1	3.7
Ticketmaster CitySearch	TMCS	25.63	72.9	1,868	25.5	1,779.6	4.0
VerticalNet	VERT	33.94	16.8	570	3.6	540.2	n/a
Xoom	XMCX	37.63	16.8	632	6.5	421.4	8.7
Yahoo!	YHOO	155.00	300.0	46,500	128.6	45,707.0	38.9
ZDNet	ZDZ	15.69	80.9	$ 1,269	$ 22.9	$ 1,268.9	8.0

Exhibit 6   NASDAQ Index, September 1994 to September 1999

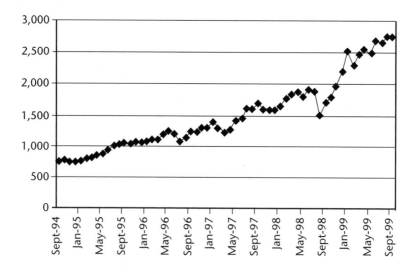

Exhibit 7   Venture Capital Funding, United States

Year	Deals	US$ Total (Millions)
1994	1,207	$ 4,143.9
1995	1,870	7,630.8
1996	2,609	11,506.8
1997	3,181	12,772.3
1998	3,691	$21,244.3

Source: NVCA

Exhibit 8   Initial Public Offering Markets, United States

Period	Number of IPO's	Avg. Offer Amount US$ (Million)	Avg Valuation US$ (Million)
YTD 1999	180	$72.4	$435.6
1998	78	49.2	229.1
1997	138	35.9	164.3
1996	280	43.6	209.3
1995	204	$40.6	$163.0

Source: NVCA, as of October 1, 1999.

Exhibit 9   Mergers of Venture-Backed Companies, United States

Period	Total # of Companies	Total US$ (Billions)	Avg Price US$ (Millions)
1999 (1st half)	91	$7.2	$119.9
1998	195	8.4	72.8
1997	161	7.6	66.4
1996	103	5.4	82.4
1995	99	3.7	65.6
1994	104	$3.2	$ 49.5

Exhibit 10 Internet Traffic Statistics—September, 1999

Company	Reach % (Home & Work)	Avg Daily Unique Pages Per Visitor (Home & Work) (millions)	Unique Visitors (Home & Work) (millions)	Home/Work	Home	Work
City Search-TicketMaster Online	7.8	12.5	3,112	9.7	9.1	9.9
MapQuest	**4.8**	**8.9**	**3,062**	**10.9**	**9.2**	**10.1**
Expedia	1.9	9.8	4,140	11.0	10.1	9.9
Travelocity	5.5	16.5	3,498	16.2	14.2	15.2
CheapTickets.com	1.6	7.3	1,002	9.5	9.6	8.7
Delta-Air.com	1.9	6.3	1,219	9.7	8.1	10.4
LowestFare.com	2.2	4.7	1,382	3.6	3.2	3.6
MapBlast.com	1.1	10.9	707	n/a	n/a	n/a
MapsOnUs.com	1.3	2.0	831	0.9	0.9	0.8
PreviewTravel	4.5	11.4	2,826	11.7	10.5	10.3
TicketMaster	4.0	13.1	2,514	9.1	9.2	8.0
Trip.com On Line	1.6	5.5	1,015	9.9	7.4	10.3
USAirways	1.5	7.4	961	7.1	6.1	6.4
1travel.com	0.7	8.5	287	8.2	7.2	9.7
AA.com	2.3	6.7	1,442	11.6	8.5	12.6
Travelscape	1.0	6.7	481	7.2	8.0	4.4
Tickets.com	0.5	7.5	311	6.7	6.9	n/a
UAL.com	2.1	5.6	1,317	11.5	9.7	9.9
NWA.com	1.9	7.0	1,175	6.2	5.8	5.3
Domain Category						
Travel/Tourism	31.3	21.2	19,857	22.7	17.2	22.5
Airline Sites	9.7	12.8	6,170	16.2	12.7	15.2
Shopping	66.1	72.2	41,869	70.2	55.7	56.5

Exhibit 11 MapQuest—Recent News

Mapquest.com Licenses Routing Software To Onstar Communications
NEW YORK, N.Y. (Dow Jones)—Sept 22, 1999 MapQuest formed an alliance with OnStar Communications, an in-vehicle safety, security and information service used in GM vehicles.

Nokia Selects MapQuest.com to Provide Driving Directions to Nokia's New Media Phones; MapQuest.com Expands Its Wireless Reach With Addition
NEW YORK—(BUSINESS WIRE)—Sept. 22, 1999—MapQuest announced an agreement with Nokia (NYSE:NOK) to provide MapQuest.com driving directions and travel information.

AOL's Digital City, Inc. Expands Relationship With OnHealth Network Company
SEATTLE, Sept. 21 /PRNewswire/—OnHealth Network Company (Nasdaq: ONHN), a leading online health and wellness destination, today announced the expansion of its strategic relationship with AOL's Digital City, Inc.

Getting Local Online Knight Ridder draws from its newspapers to build a national network of local portal sites
Network World Fusion , 20 September 1999, From job portals to music portals to personal portals, it's hard to keep track. Here's another growing category to add to the list: local portals.

infoUSA.com Announces 5 New Partners for Free Internet White and Yellow Page Services
SILICON VALLEY—(BUSINESS WIRE)-Sept. 20, 1999—The leading provider of proprietary business and consumer databases and Internet white and yellow page directory services...

MapQuest.com Teams With Adace to Provide Small Businesses With Geographically Targeted Advertising
NEW YORK-(BUSINESS WIRE)-Sept. 14, 1999. MapQuest strengthens position as leader in Geo-targeted web advertising by announcing a partnership with AdAce, a nationwide ad firm.

MapQuest Selects SpeechWorks Tech For Phone Svc >MQST
NEW YORK (Dow Jones)—Sept 13, 1999—MapQuest selected SpeechWorks International Inc., to develop speech recognition technology for a MapQuest service that will provide driving directions over the telephone.

SPRINT PCS, MAPQUEST PARTNER ON DRIVING DIRECTIONS
NEW YORK--Sept 13, 1999—MapQuest announced a new partnership with Sprint PCS to provide driving directions to Sprint PCS Wireless Web phone users.

MapQuest.com Seeks Agency Partner
NEW YORK—Aug 30, 1999—MapQuest is looking for a medium to large-size agency to handle its estimated $10 million to $15 million account.

MapQuest.com Selected to Provide Enhanced Mapping Technology for Sabre Inc., Including the Travelocity.com Web Site
NEW YORK—(BUSINESS WIRE)—August 23, 1999—Sabre Inc., Including Travelocity.com, Upgrades Agreement With MapQuest.

MapQuest.com Partners With Metro Networks, Adding Real-Time Traffic to MapQuest.com and Its Partner Sites
NEW YORK—(BUSINESS WIRE)—August 18, 1999 MapQuest.com Now Offers Exclusive Package of State-of-the-Art Digital Traffic Information, Maps and Driving Directions.

Exhibit 12   Geospatial Data and Mapping—Industry Structure

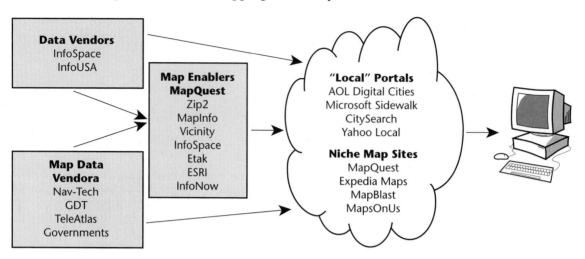

Exhibit 13   Market Share of 764 Map-Enabled Websites

MapQuest	49%
Zip2	21%
Vicinity	11%
ESRI	10%
InfoNow	4%
MapInfo	3%
Etak	1%
InfoSpace	1%

Source: MediaMetrix

Exhibit 14   Market Share of Site Page Traffic

MapQuest	64%
Expedia Maps	18%
MapBlast	12%
MapsOnUs	3%
All others	3%

Source: MediaMetrix